P9-DMW-991

FEB 27 '78

PUBLICATIONS OF RUSSELL SAGE FOUNDATION

MARION R. FREMONT-SMITH

FOUNDATIONS
and
GOVERNMENT

STATE AND FEDERAL LAW AND SUPERVISION

RUSSELL SAGE FOUNDATION

New York, 1965

Contents

Preface

In this book I have attempted to bring together the many facets of the law which affect the creation and operation of philanthropic foundations and to describe the methods by which the agencies of state and federal government assure the observance of these laws. In brief, this is a legal study of foundations. It is designed to serve as a starting point for attorneys desirous of finding references for this branch of the law. It has as a second purpose the presentation of material that will provide a basis for constructive evaluation of the methods by which government supervises foundations. Because this latter purpose is of concern to many who are not attorneys, I have included certain explanations of legal doctrines which may appear elementary to the professional. It is my hope that this book will thereby provide an incentive for all who search for better methods of cooperative action by foundations and government to further their common goal of public service.

I wish to thank Dr. F. Emerson Andrews, president of The Foundation Library Center, for encouraging me to undertake this study and for his generous assistance throughout. Support for this work was provided by Russell Sage Foundation as part of its continuing program of studies in philanthropy.

It has been a privilege to be associated with Dr. Orville G. Brim, Jr., president of Russell Sage Foundation, and his predecessor, Dr. Donald Young. I owe a special debt to Edward J. McCormack, Jr., former attorney general of the Commonwealth of Massachusetts, for affording me the opportunity to learn at firsthand the practical aspects of enforcement of the law of charity.

The Harvard Law School generously made its extensive facilities available for research on this project. Earl C. Borgeson, librarian, and Philip A. Putnam and George A. Strait, assistant librarians, were particularly helpful.

In the preparation of this study I have been accorded the gracious cooperation of many officials of the federal government, the attorneys general of almost all of the states, and their assistants and staff members. Their interest and concern with improving the administration of philanthropy deserves wide recognition. The National Association of Attorneys General, the National Conference of Commissioners on Uniform State Laws, the American Bar Association Committee on Charitable Trusts, and the Council on Foundations, Inc., have all provided expert assistance for which I am extremely grateful.

The comments and criticisms of Professors Austin W. Scott and Albert M. Sacks of Harvard Law School and Professor John G. Simon of Yale Law School have been invaluable. I am also indebted to Paul Sargent, former assistant attorney general and director of public charities in Massachusetts.

I have been privileged to have the assistance of Mrs. Sieglinde Martin, who gathered material for the tables and typed the entire manuscript. I would also like to acknowledge the help of Michael Magruder, particularly his checking of citations. My severest, yet most encouraging critics have been my husband and children. To them go my deepest thanks.

M.R.F-S.

Cambridge, Mass.
June, 1965

CHAPTER I

Foundations
In Historical Perspective

THE ADJECTIVES PHILANTHROPIC, eleemosynary, charitable, and benevolent are commonly used to describe certain activities which have
as their aim the improving or uplifting of mankind. The concept of
charity existed in early cultures and has formed an important part of
the entire Judeo-Christian tradition.

Organizations to carry out the concepts of charity are to be found
in early Egyptian, Greek, and Roman records. The Ptolemies endowed
a library in Alexandria; Plato bequeathed funds to support his Academy after his death; and in the early centuries A.D. in Rome, private
associations for relief of the poor, educational institutions, hospitals,
foundling asylums, and old people's homes were established. In the
Middle Ages, the Church became the chief dispenser of charity, and
its role in the field of philanthropy has continued to be a dominant
one. During the Reformation in England, the guilds and companies
replaced the Church as the administrators of many charitable gifts. A
wave of philanthropy arose among the new middle classes leading to
the establishment of permanent funds, usually trusts, for certain specific charitable objects administered by private individuals or corporations. Philanthropic societies and associations also developed and
multiplied following the industrial revolution.

The twentieth century has witnessed the rapid growth of government spending in fields that were previously the province of independent charity. In the United States this development began in the 1930's
and was signified primarily by the enactment of social security legisla-

11

tion. In 1950 it was estimated that government expenditure was about nine times that of voluntary giving for purposes which a generation or two ago would have been deemed to lie wholly within the field of private charity.[1] The ratio today is not known, but it is certainly as great if not greater.

The rise in government spending has not been accompanied by a decline in nongovernmental charitable activities. On the contrary, the field of private philanthropy has been constantly increasing, fostered chiefly by governmental action in the form of exemption from taxation. One aspect of this increased activity has been a large growth in the number of philanthropic entities known as foundations. It is the purpose of this study to describe the relationship of government, through its legislative, judicial, and administrative organization, to this form of philanthropic institution. In short, this is a study of foundations as legal instrumentalities.

A foundation has been defined by Andrews as "a nongovernmental, nonprofit organization having a principal fund of its own, managed by its own trustees or directors, and established to maintain or aid social, educational, charitable, religious, or other activities serving the common welfare."[2] The foundation therefore engages in a distinctive form of charitable activity that is part of a much larger group of organized philanthropic endeavors. The classification of the latter is helpful for an understanding of the particular nature of foundation activity. Karst makes the following groupings of organized philanthropy in the United States today:

(1) large endowed funds, which make grants for education, research, etc., such as the Ford and Rockefeller Foundations, the various Carnegie endowments, and the Twentieth Century Fund; (2) smaller foundations which are primarily instruments for channeling the annual giving of their founders, during their lives, and of their families thereafter—sometimes called "family foundations"; (3) operating charities such as hospitals, youth centers, settlement houses, schools, museums, the Red Cross—frequently dependent on public contributions for their support; (4) fund-raising organizations which solicit public contributions and then make distributions to worthy causes, such as the cancer, polio, and heart funds; (5) community trusts, which are organizations formed to give centralized administration to separate charitable funds—a form of

---

[1] Andrews, F. Emerson, *Philanthropic Giving*. Russell Sage Foundation, New York, 1950, p. 43.

[2] Andrews, F. Emerson, in the introduction to *The Foundation Directory, Edition 2*. Edited by Ann D. Walton and Marianna O. Lewis. Russell Sage Foundation, New York, 1964, p. 9.

pooling for investment and management purposes; (6) company foundations (other than those formed for purely commercial purposes); and (7) small funds formed for particular purposes (such as scholarship funds which are separately administered).[1]

Andrews' definition of foundations would include categories 1, 2, 5, 6, and 7, although much of the literature regarding foundations excludes the last category.

The phrase "public charities" is sometimes used by the courts to describe these various philanthropic entities. The term applies to all instrumentalities organized to contribute private wealth for the benefit of an indeterminate number of persons for certain legally recognized purposes which may be broadly described as of "public benefit."

The word "public" in the term "public charity" has often led to misconceptions as to the status of charitable activities in a free society. Charities are public in the sense that they are devoted to benefiting the public at large. There can be no such thing as a private charity in law, since a trust or corporation devoted to benefiting one or a few named individuals, even if its stated purpose is to ease their suffering or to improve their mind (or any clearly "charitable" purpose), is not considered under law to be a charity.[2]

There is no clear-cut body of American law which can be called "the law of (public) charities." Relevant law is to be found primarily in the law of trusts, but it is also contained in the laws relating to corporations, the laws of taxation, the law of decedents' estates, and the entire field of property law. It was under the law of uses, the forerunner of the present law of trusts, however, that the legal concept of charity originated, and a study of governmental relations to foundations must start with this branch of the law.

Theoretically, the acquisition of legal status as a charity is not necessary in order to perform philanthropic works. However, organized charity has grown and developed because society has granted to those institutions meeting certain requirements benefits not accorded to private enterprises. The best known of these benefits is, of course, exemption from taxation; but equally important from a historical

---

[1] Karst, Kenneth L., "The Efficiency of the Charitable Dollar: An Unfulfilled State Responsibility," *Harvard Law Review*, vol. 73, 1960, p. 433. Copyright © 1960 by the Harvard Law Review Association.

[2] "The terms 'public charity' and 'private charity' are sometimes used. . . . For the purposes of the law of charitable trusts it is believed confusing to use these two phrases. . . . The words 'charitable' and 'public' are synonymous." Bogert, George G., and George T. Bogert, *The Law of Trusts and Trustees*. 2d ed. West Publishing Co., St. Paul, 1964, sec. 362.

standpoint is the relaxation of certain rules of law applicable to private property. Thus, charitable entities are granted existence in perpetuity, the right to accumulate income, and the privilege of having their initial purposes revised if they become obsolete. The legal requirements for classification under law as a charity have developed through the centuries, and are still in flux.

Evolution of Foundations in Early Society

The emergence of foundations as legal entities was closely tied to religious philosophy and the development of the concepts of wills, testamentary dispositions, and corporate entities. Even before the right to make wills and testaments developed, the practice of leaving property in perpetuity to other than paternal heirs was encouraged for religious purposes in both Egypt and Chaldea.[1] The Greeks first developed a concept of a "living legal heir" to whom property could be given in perpetuity during a person's life with the consent of his natural heirs. In the first century B.C. the Roman law modified this concept to declare that associations were at one and the same time "sentient reasonable beings" and "immutable undying persons," and by the first century A.D. they were permitted to receive bequests.[2]

From A.D. 96 to A.D. 180, these associations, or foundations as they were called, were greatly encouraged throughout the Roman Empire. Cities and towns were accorded the right to accept funds by bequest, and gradually the motive behind these donations shifted from honoring the gods to helping the underprivileged. The funds of these foundations were confiscated during the reigns of the 30 "barracks emperors" from A.D. 192 to A.D. 324. It was Constantine who recognized the need for the State to assist the causes formerly aided by the foundations. By edict he reiterated the legal rights of the Christian Church as an association whose property could be neither alienated by any individual nor used within the Church for purposes other than those designated by the donor. Thereafter, the Church was utilized as the medium for the distribution of all public funds for the underprivileged, and all individuals were encouraged by the State to make donations to the Church for charitable purposes.[3] These gifts, called *piae causae,*

---

[1] Hollis, Ernest V., "Evolution of the Philanthropic Foundation," *Educational Record,* vol. 20, 1939, pp. 575, 578 ff.

[2] *Ibid.,* p. 576.

[3] Duff, P. W., "The Charitable Foundations of Byzantium," *Cambridge Legal Essays,* W. Heffer and Sons, Cambridge, England, 1926, pp. 83, 84.

were administered by the bishop of the church where the donor was domiciled. As large amounts of wealth were amassed by the local churches, abuses in the management and disbursement of funds became increasingly prevalent.

An attempt was made to rectify the situation at the time of the revision of the Roman Law in 550 and the enactment of the *Corpus Juris Civilis* (the Code, Digest, and Statutes of Justinian). Their aim was to place the church foundations on legal bases more appropriate to the changing society of the times. Ecclesiastical foundations were declared legal persons of an ecclesiastical nature whose personality derived from the Church but who had a legal capacity of their own.[1] A comprehensive list of safeguards was enacted to protect the foundations and keep them socially useful. The bishops were given appointive and supervisory power over administration of the funds, and were directed to keep "a watchful eye over them to remove those who were negligent and in such case to appoint other trustees who had the true fear of God."[2] The bishops, in turn, were responsible to their superiors, and the actions of the entire hierarchy were reviewable by the citizens, who were empowered to make a judicial complaint if a testator's intention was not fulfilled.[3] Provision was made for the selection of a similar cause if the original purpose of a gift should lose its social utility,[4] and rules were laid down concerning the investment and management of funds, including the leasing and mortgaging of property. A gift was to revert to a donor or his heirs if not made effective within a certain period, and the Church was prohibited from permanently alienating any property given it.

The managers were also accorded the right to act as guardians, or to appoint and supervise guardians, for all legally incompetent persons under their care. These prerogatives gave great power to the Church throughout the entire period of the Middle Ages.[5]

The Islamic Foundations

In the seventh century Mohammed recommended the establishment of what is the Islamic equivalent of the charitable foundation or

---

[1] Hollis, Ernest V., *op. cit.*, p. 579.
[2] Comment, "Supervision of Charitable Trusts," *University of Chicago Law Review*, vol. 21, 1953, p. 139.
[3] *Ibid.*
[4] Hollis, Ernest V., *op. cit.*, p. 580.
[5] *Ibid.*, p. 581.

trust.[1] The *vaqf,* as this institution is called, has received little attention in the West; it apparently developed independently of Roman and Anglo-Saxon equivalents, but the similarities between the two are striking. A *vaqf* may be established for any purpose recognized as laudable by Islam and the religion of the founder. It is characterized by perpetuity, but accumulation of income is forbidden. The founder may appoint himself the first *mutawali,* or trustee, and assign to himself a remuneration, commonly 10 per cent of income, which cannot be above that which he appoints for subsequent trustees.

The three recognized categories of usages are a man's duty to his own family, the maintenance of God's worship according to the tenets of Islam, and charities in the English sense, including works of public utility. The first usage is, of course, contrary to the western concept of a charitable trust and reflects the influence of Mohammedan philosophy and culture.

The primary difference between the *vaqf* and the charitable trust or foundation, however, is that the *vaqf* has remained under religious sanction; no secular law relating to its position in society similar to that in the West has developed. The number of *vaqfs* in existence today is reported to be considerable in the Mohammedan countries of the Middle East, and some are said to have great wealth.[2]

Foundations in England

Roman concepts of foundations were carried to England and can be found in the laws which developed there, although they received the distinctive imprint of the Anglo-Saxon legal system which developed during the period of the Reformation. The Saxon kings followed the Roman practice and gave to the local bishops the duty of supervision of charitable gifts as well as the religious institutions which administered them.

The word "corporation" came into use in Saxon times to describe religious institutions and monastic orders as well as religious persons. The parson of a parish or an order of friars was regarded as a corporation by prescription and was therefore a separate legal entity which

---

[1] Andrews, F. Emerson, "On the Nature of the Vaqf," *Foundation News,* vol. 5, September, 1964, pp. 8–9.

[2] Further information on the legal aspects of the *vaqf* is to be found in Vesey-Fitzgerald, Seymour, *Muhammadan Law,* Oxford University Press, London, 1931; see also Gibb, H.A.R., and Harold Bowen, *Islamic Society and the West,* Oxford University Press, London, 1950, vol. 1, pts. 1 and 2.

could exist in perpetuity. Present-day corporate concepts have their roots in these early views.

A system of ecclesiastical courts developed in England following the Norman Conquest (1066). Starting from their special jurisdiction in respect to pious causes, these courts gradually developed general jurisdiction over all testamentary matters. During this period, under the protection of the ecclesiastic courts, charitable gifts acquired three distinct characteristics that still survive: (1) the privilege of indefinite existence; (2) the privilege of validity even if the gift is in general terms, so long as its objective is exclusively charitable; (3) the privilege of obtaining fresh objects if those laid down by the founder become incapable of execution, known today as the doctrine of *cy pres*.

The power of the Church and the ecclesiastical courts was challenged after 1066 in a struggle that lasted four hundred years. Although the conflict was political and economic, its repercussions in the law resulted in the eventual extinction of the jurisdiction of the ecclesiastical courts and in the curtailment of the charity holdings of the Church. Henry II (1154–1189) decreed that the bishops and abbots held their possessions "of the king and were answerable to the king's justice." Thus the Crown was recognized in law as guardian of the revenues of all vacant bishoprics and patron of all charity funds. The church corporations held land by a form of tenure called *frankalmoign* under which they rendered no service to any superior lord. By the time of Henry VIII these holdings amounted to an estimated one-third to as much as one-half of the entire wealth of England.[1]

In an attempt to curtail this general power of the Church, statutes were enacted, starting with Magna Charta (1215)[2] that limited gifts of land to charitable corporations. These statutes were called acts of Mortmain, since their purpose was to prevent land from coming to a "dead hand." Section 32 of Magna Charta forbade freemen to alienate "so much of his land as will render the residue insufficient to secure the service due to his Lord."[3] Section 36 forbade a "dodge" whereby after tenants gave land to a religious house and thereby discharged it from service, it was deeded back to themselves. The Statute de Viris Religioses of 1279[4] attempted a general prohibition against the holding of

---

[1] Orton, William A., "Endowments and Foundations," in the *Encyclopaedia of the Social Sciences,* The Macmillan Co., New York, vol. 5, 1931, p. 531.

[2] As issued in 9 Henry III (1225).

[3] Tyssen, Amherst D., *The Law of Charitable Bequests.* Sweet and Maxwell, London, 1888, p. 2.

[4] Stat. 7 Edward I (1279).

land in mortmain and removed the right of the overlord to grant licenses for such alienation. It should be noted that these statutes did not prevent the transfer; they denied the right of the corporation to hold the land if it was claimed by the overlord of the donor. If the overlord did not exercise this right within one year, his overlord might take it within the next half year, and so on, the ultimate right devolving to the crown.

Development of Trusts

Conveyances to religious corporations were not the sole method of making charitable gifts; during this same period (following the Norman invasion) a new form of conveyance known as the use developed. The origin of this method of conveyance, which was the precursor of the modern trust, is not clear. Maitland suggests that it first appeared in the thirteenth century when lands were conveyed to individuals who agreed to hold them for the use of the Franciscan friars, whose order did not allow the holding of property, either individually or communally.[1]

At this time uses were not recognized by the courts and therefore were not enforceable, so that the practice was not felt to violate the vows of poverty. Following the enactment of the early mortmain statutes, the device of conveyances to an individual for the use of a religious corporation became common. In fact, it was so common that in 1391 Parliament enacted a new mortmain statute which specifically prohibited the practice of granting the use of lands to religious corporations. Scott notes that "the *cestui que use* (or beneficiary) in these cases had no enforceable interest in the property conveyed, but the danger that the feoffee would carry out his moral obligation was so great, and the result of his doing so was regarded as so subversive of public policy, that Parliament felt compelled to interpose."[2]

The period from 1200 to 1400 has been characterized as the first in the development of uses and trusts.[3] The second historical period in the development of uses, and thus of charitable trusts, began early in the fifteenth century when the Courts of Chancery in England began to enforce the conveyance to uses.

---

[1] Maitland, Frederic William, *Equity*. 2d ed. The University Press, Cambridge, England, 1936, p. 25.

[2] Scott, Austin W., *The Law of Trusts*. 2d ed. Little, Brown and Co., Boston, 1956, sec. 1.3.

[3] *Ibid.*, sec. 1.2.

Scott has said that the present-day trust would never have developed had it not been for the more or less accidental circumstance that in England in the fifteenth century, and for four hundred years afterward, there were separate courts of law and equity.[1] The powers of the courts which are called equitable[2] were first exercised by the Common Law Courts.[3] In the early fourteenth century, however, these courts became more rigid and their equity powers disappeared. When injustices arose from the application of the strict rules of law by the Common Law Courts, resort was taken to Parliament or the King's Council for relief.[4] Gradually, these petitions were referred to the Chancellor, who was usually an ecclesiastic, and in time, the Court of Chancery began to exercise equity jurisdiction, becoming an established court

---

[1] *Ibid.*, sec. 1.

[2] "Equity" is used in law to describe a system of jurisdiction as well as the principles and standards of that system. The standards are based on the concepts of justice and fairness, and their development in the English legal system sprang from the "old idea that when ordinary justice fails there is a reserve of extra-ordinary justice which the king can exercise. . . . In civil cases men made their way to the king's Chancellor begging him in piteous terms to intervene 'for the love of God and in the way of charity.' It is not of any defect in the material law that they complain; but somehow or other they cannot get justice." (Maitland, Frederic William, *Collected Papers*. Edited by H. A. L. Fisher, The University Press, Cambridge, England, 1911, vol. 3, pp. 334–335.) Today in the United States there are no longer separate courts of equity; but certain forms of remedies, which developed in the Courts of Chancery, are referred to as "equitable" and are interpreted and enforced according to the doctrines of equity based on precedents which originally developed in those courts. Equity jurisdiction provides such remedies as rescinding contracts, canceling or reforming instruments, requiring performance of contracts, remedying misrepresentation, concealment, or mistake, preventing illegal actions by means of injunction, and, in the field of trust law, defining rights of parties and the means of enforcing them.

[3] The term "common law" has several slightly different meanings: (a) It is used here to describe the system of law based on precedents which developed in England after the Norman Conquest in the eleventh century, and was followed by the royal courts. (b) In its broadest sense, "common law" is used as a designation for the Anglo-American legal tradition which prevails in most English-speaking countries. This tradition is often contrasted with the "Civil Law" tradition which derives from the Roman law and prevails today in the countries of continental Europe. (c) After the emergence of the Court of Chancery in fourteenth century England, the phrase "common law" was used to distinguish the body of rules administered by the royal courts of law from the rules of equity administered by Chancery. (d) "Common law" is often used to refer to all judge-made rules built on precedents, as distinguished from legislative enactments and the decisions in which these enactments are interpreted. (e) On some occasions the phrase is used to signify the entire body of English rules that was transplanted to the American colonies and was in force in 1776 when the colonies claimed their independence. Houghteling, James L., and George G. Pierce, *The Legal Environment of Business*. Harcourt, Brace and World, New York, 1963, p. 58.

[4] Holdsworth, H. V., "The Early History of Equity," *Michigan Law Review*, vol. 13, 1915, p. 293.

of the realm by 1422. This Court based its decisions on ethical principles, not legal precedents. Its procedure was more flexible than that of the common law courts; and its freedom from fixed forms of action and its power to enforce a defendant's duties, not merely to uphold a plaintiff's rights, made it particularly suited to assuming jurisdiction over uses.

By the mid-fifteenth century, the Chancellors were interfering to enforce on the trustee his duties and to protect the interest of the beneficiaries. Uses were assignable and descendable. They were employed not only to avoid the restrictions on ecclesiastic corporations, but also to circumvent creditors, to defeat certain claims of the feudal lords, and to prevent the confiscation of property, a consequence of conviction for high treason. In time, Parliament acted to prevent most of these evasions, and the primary purpose for employment of the use soon came to be to secure the effect of the devising of land.[1]

The English feudal laws did not permit testamentary disposition of land; they required that land descend according to the laws of primogeniture. The great landowners, however, wanting to make broader testamentary dispositions, employed the use to circumvent the legal restriction through the device of enfeoffing to the use of such persons as a man might designate by will. It has been said that at the time of the reign of Henry V (1413–1422), the greater part of the land in England was held in use.[2] It was, of course, during this period that the system of feudal tenure was disintegrating. Its demise was hastened by the confusion with respect to title resulting from the widespread employment of the use.

An attempt to stem the tide and correct the abuses and obscurities arising from uncontrolled employment of uses was made by Henry VIII through the passage of the Statute of Uses in 1535.[3] It is of great importance that this act did not outlaw the use entirely, but merely declared that the legal title as well as the beneficial interest passed to the *cestui que use* (or the person who had the use, as he was called). The intent was that the use should no longer be merely an equitable interest protected by Chancery, but should be an ordinary legal interest subject to the jurisdiction of the law courts. The act, therefore, removed the possibility of devising land, a result highly dissatisfactory

---

[1] Maitland, Frederic William, "Trust and Corporation" in *Collected Papers, op. cit.,* p. 335.
[2] Scott, Austin W., *op. cit.,* sec. 1.3.
[3] Stat. 27 Henry VIII, c. 10 (1535).

to the majority of landowners in Parliament. It was rectified five years later by the passage of the Statute of Wills,[1] which authorized devises of certain important categories of land but expressly excepted devises to bodies politic or corporate.

The Statute of Uses was of great importance in the development of English law, particularly the law of conveyancing. It cleared away the obscurities of titles which had arisen during the previous centuries; and, by forcing the enactment of the Statute of Wills, it eased the transition period that marked the end of feudalism. It did not, however, mean the extinguishment of the use or trust as a device for the disposition of property. Both the common law judges and the Chancellors acted to continue the possibility of creating beneficial interests separate from legal title. The Statute of Uses was strictly construed. Active, as opposed to passive, trusts, where the trustees had duties to perform beyond merely holding title, continued to be recognized in equity, as were trusts for a period of years and a use which was placed upon a prior use. Thus, the main lines of development of the modern law of trusts were clearly laid out, and the groundwork prepared for the development of the modern law of charitable trusts.

Restrictions on Charitable Gifts in England

The period which marked the development of the trust was coterminous with the period of struggle between the King and the Church; it was also characterized by an increasing interest in secular charitable activities.[2] As early as 1391, the mortmain statute, which prohibited the practice of granting the use of land to religious corporations, contained a restriction on the holding of land without license of the Crown by all civil corporations and municipalities.[3] Such a restriction was included because the effect of granting lands to guilds, fraternities, and municipal corporations "had come to be regarded as equally detrimental to the rights of the overlord."[4]

The years 1300 to 1500 saw the creation of the great nonmonastic charitable associations such as the Oxford and Cambridge colleges for the promotion of education[5] and the establishment of hospitals for the

---

[1] Stat. 32 Henry VIII, c. 1 (1540).
[2] For a detailed, scholarly study of this subject, see Jordan, W. K., *Philanthropy in England, 1480–1660*, Russell Sage Foundation, New York, 1959.
[3] Stat. 15 Richard II, c. 5 (1391).
[4] Keeton, George W., *The Modern Law of Charities*. Sir Isaac Pitman and Sons, London, 1962, p. 171.
[5] Davis, John P., *Corporations*. Capricorn, New York, 1961, chap. 7.

maintenance of the sick, indigent, or infirm. Many charitable gifts were administered by the guilds. Charitable uses and trusts, constituted for the administration of charitable gifts, appeared with increasing frequency from the reign of Henry VI (1422–1460) onward.

The Courts of Chancery assumed jurisdiction over these charitable gifts, but in so doing they preserved the privileges that had been conferred by the ecclesiastical courts in Norman times, thereby offering the encouragement of the state to charitable benefactions.[1]

Records of the Court of Chancery for this period are meager, but it is clear that the Chancellor was issuing subpoenas for the enforcement of charitable uses from the early part of the fifteenth century. Suits were usually brought by inhabitants of a town or parish in behalf of themselves and the other inhabitants or parishioners. In some cases they were in the name of the poor of a town or parish, and in a few cases they were brought by the Attorney General.[2] Relief was granted by means of orders of the court compelling trustees to restore funds taken improperly, or by injunctions forbidding trustees to commit acts not authorized by the terms of the agreement to uses.

By the middle of the fourteenth century many of the monastic institutions which had been the chief dispensers of charity were beginning to decay.

> This long and inexorable process of the deterioration of monasticism was far advanced well before the advent of the Reformation. This was true throughout western Europe, but perhaps most dramatically so in England where, almost a generation prior to the Dissolution, the fabric was in decay, contributions were drying up, and many foundations were so reduced in numbers that the spiritual offices required by the rule could not be maintained.[3]

The formal dissolution of the monasteries which occurred from 1541 to 1560 added to a growing situation of poverty in fifteenth- and sixteenth-century England, which was caused primarily by economic upheavals, the growth of towns, changes in agricultural methods, and the extension of commerce. In 1414 an important statute was passed[4] which attempted to correct and repair the decay and disappearance of a large number of endowed foundations for relief of the poor. The ecclesiastical authorities were ordered to inquire into the manner of

---

[1] Keeton, George W., *op. cit.*, p. 3.
[2] Scott, Austin W., *op. cit.*, sec. 348.2; and Jordan, W. K., *op. cit.*, p. 119.
[3] Jordan, W. K., *op. cit.*, p. 58.
[4] Stat. 2 Henry V, c. 3 (1414).

founding of such institutions and to make reparations. Jordan observes, "There is, however, little evidence that the statute was given full effect or that the calamitous decay of medieval charitable institutions, already far advanced, was significantly retarded."[1]

Restraints were imposed on the creation of trusts for religious purposes during the reign of Henry VIII by the passage in 1531–1532 of a statute[2] that reiterated the mortmain doctrine denying corporations the right to hold land without license and prohibited the creation of trusts for religious uses of more than twenty years.

> From this day forward, indeed, the whole weight of law as well as of policy was exerted to mould the charities of England to secular ends and to assist donors in creating the great charitable institutions which were so profoundly to alter the structure of the English society.[3]

The far-reaching social changes of the sixteenth century had a profound and direct impact on the law of charities.

> The Reformation and the social and economic upheavals of the century . . . had important consequences not only for the relation between charitable trusts and public welfare services, but also for the law of charity. Unemployment and vagrancy were prevalent, the Guild system of apprenticeship was breaking down and the welfare and educational services, provided by the Church before the Reformation, were interrupted. Something had to be found to take their place. The refounding of grammar schools under new deeds, the Elizabethan Poor Law and the Statute of Charitable Uses of 1601 "to redress the Misemployment of Lands Goods and Stocks of Money heretofore given to Charitable Uses" was the answer. . . . This statute was passed at practically the same time as the Statute for Relief of the Poor and formed part of a concerted plan for dealing with the economic and social problems of the day.[4]

The Elizabethan Contributions

The Statute of Charitable Uses, enacted in 1601,[5] has been described as "the starting point of the modern law of charities."[6] There

---

[1] Jordan, W. K., *op. cit.,* pp. 114–115.

[2] Stat. 23 Henry VIII, c. 10 (1532).

[3] Jordan, W. K., *op. cit.,* p. 115.

[4] Committee on the Law and Practice relating to Charitable Trusts, *Report.* Cmd., 8710. H. M. Stationery Office, London, 1952, p. 18. This report, prepared under the chairmanship of Lord Nathan, and commonly referred to as the "Nathan Report," contained the results of a study made by a parliamentary committee of charitable trusts in England and its recommendations for new legislation. See p. 30 of this chapter for details.

[5] Stat. 43 Elizabeth I, c. 4 (1601).

[6] Keeton, George W., *op. cit.,* p. 10.

can be no doubt that it profoundly influenced development of the concept of charitable purposes in England and the United States, and that it stimulated the rapid growth of charitable trusts in England immediately following its enactment.

The purpose of the statute was to create a code for the encouragement and organization of private almsgiving. Accordingly, there were two specific objects: the first was to provide a method for correcting the abuses in the administration of charitable gifts which had been multiplying in the previous period. The second was to encourage further gifts to charity "by listing a great variety of specific charitable purposes, and thus removing the uncertainties that had arisen with the Reformation."[1] The preamble enumerated the purposes for which charitable gifts had heretofore been made. Henry Allen Moe[2] has pointed out the similarity between the language of the preamble and the fourteenth-century poem *The Vision of Piers the Plowman* of William Langland, wherein anxious (and rich) merchants are counseled by Truth to obtain remission of sins and a happy death by using their fortunes:

> And therewith repair hospitals,
> help sick people,
> mend bad roads,
> build up bridges that had been broken down,
> help maidens to marry or to make them nuns,
> find food for prisoners and poor people,
> put scholars to school or to some other craft,
> help religious orders, and
> ameliorate rents or taxes.[3]

Historians feel that this similarity reflects the fact that the definitions of charitable purposes that were well established by 1601 were those known in the fourteenth century, whether or not there was a direct borrowing from the poem,[4] and support for this view is to be found in the reports of cases on charitable trusts in Chancery during the fifteenth century.[5]

A major omission in the Statute of 1601 that reflected the temper

---

[1] Committee on the Law and Practice relating to Charitable Trusts, *op. cit.,* p. 18.

[2] Henry Allen Moe in a statement to the Select (Cox) Committee to Investigate Tax-Exempt Foundations, quoted in Jordon, W. K., *op. cit.,* p. 112.

[3] Langland, William, *The Vision of Piers the Plowman.* Translated into modern English by W. W. Skeat. Chatto and Windus, London, 1931, p. 114.

[4] Keeton, George W., *op. cit.,* p. 4.

[5] Scott, Austin W., *op. cit.,* sec. 1.

of the times was that of gifts for religion other than the repair of churches. The mention of education is also scanty, leading to the conclusion that the statute was not an attempt at a definition of charity, but an enumeration of some of the charitable purposes that had become the subject of benefactions. There is no evidence that the court in the seventeenth century treated the list as comprehensive, and only in later centuries did the device of regarding the preamble to the statute as a definition of charitable purposes occur. The importance of the "definition" lay not in the exact list, but in the fact that it implied the necessity of some form of public benefit.[1]

The body of the statute provided for the appointment of ad hoc commissioners to inquire into allegations of negligence, maladministration, and diversion of charitable funds by reason of which property was not being employed according to the intent of the donors. The commissioners were to be appointed by the Chancellor, and were to include the bishop and chancellor of the diocese and other persons of good and sound behavior. They were given the power to "enquire by oath of twelve lawful men" as well as by other means. They could, accordingly, impanel juries, summon and hear witnesses, and make reviews of the current status of all known charitable funds in a given region. They were empowered to make decrees that would be valid until undone or altered by the Chancellor. Persons aggrieved by these decrees were given a right of appeal to the Chancellor, who might make such degrees as "should be thought to stand in equity and good conscience according to the true intent and meaning of the donors and founders."[2]

At first the commissions were created at frequent intervals. During the first year of the act, 45 commissions were established, and before 1700 more than 1,000 investigations were made; but during the eighteenth century they were rarely formed, and by 1803 the practice had died out.[3] Nevertheless, the main object of the statute was accomplished. The growth of charitable trusts in the period immediately following enactment of the statute has been described as "a torrent." Jordan states,

> The consequence [of the work of the commissioners] was that charitable funds were on the whole administered with quite astonishing probity

---

[1] Committee on the Law and Practice relating to Charitable Trusts, *op. cit.*, p. 18.

[2] Scott, Austin W., *op. cit.*, sec. 348.2.

[3] Committee on the Law and Practice relating to Charitable Trusts, *op. cit.*, p. 18.

and skill and that a tradition of the highest fidelity in the discharge of duty was quickly established. This fact in itself lent powerful encouragement to substantial men considering benefactions and accounts in no small part for the huge sums vested in charitable trusts during the last two generations of our period.[1]

Two other statutes of the Elizabethan era contributed to the reframing and molding of the law of charities to the purposes of the state. In 1572 an act was passed to assist benefactors who wished to found hospitals and almshouses; it provided that a gift in a will should be "good and available in law despite the misnaming, misreciting or not true naming or reciting" of the intended foundation.[2] In 1597 an "Act for erecting of hospitals or abiding and working houses for the poor" gave power to donors to give or bequeath lands in fee simple by simply enrolling a deed in Chancery without having to secure a special royal license or act of Parliament to achieve incorporation, so long as the yearly value of the endowment was at least £ 10.[3] The Preamble to this statute includes a list of charitable purposes identical with that in the Statute of Charitable Uses of 1601.

The enactment of these statutes has been described as part of a concerted plan for dealing with the economic and social problems of the day. The philosophy behind the legislation was thought to be that of a partnership between private charity and the State "in which the state filled in gaps left by charity rather than charity filling in gaps left by the state; and this has continued down to the changed situation of our own day."[4]

In the two centuries following the enactment of the Statute of Charitable Uses of 1601 the number of charities being founded rapidly increased. The Statute of Charitable Uses was interpreted by the courts as rendering valid in equity devises in trust or otherwise to charitable corporations, a practice which had previously been prohibited by the Statute of Wills.[5] Then in 1695–1696 the Statute of Mortmain empowered the Crown to grant licenses to schools, colleges, and other bodies politic or incorporated for "other good and public uses," permitting

---

[1] Jordan, W. K., *op. cit.*, p. 117.
[2] Stat. 14 Elizabeth I, c. 11 (1572).
[3] Stat. 39 Elizabeth I, c. 5 (1597).
[4] Committee on the Law and Practice relating to Charitable Trusts, *op. cit.*, p. 8. Keeton adds, "It may be remarked, however, that since the Statute of 1601 the state has increasingly assumed responsibility for some of the purposes mentioned in the statute." *Op. cit.*, p. 11.
[5] Scott, Austin W., *op. cit.*, sec. 362.2.

them to hold land free from liability of forfeiture to either the Crown
or the mesne lord.[1]

Enforcement Procedures

With the decline of the use of the commissions provided for in the
Statute of Charitable Uses, it fell to the Attorney General, representing the Crown as *parens patriae* with a prerogative right, to protect all
charitable trusts. Procedure during this period was slow and costly,
and rarely were abuses called to the attention of the Attorney General
or the courts.[2] Individuals were unwilling to apprise the Attorney General of malpractices because they were liable to pay the costs if he instituted proceedings and was defeated.

A limited improvement was undertaken with the enactment of Gilbert's Act in 1786, which required that returns of trusts for the benefit
of the poor be made to the clerk of Parliament by the ministers or
church wardens of the parish where the trust was to operate under pain
of penalty.[3] Some returns were made, but the act was not complied
with in any great degree. A similar fate befell the Charitable Donations Registration Act of 1812[4] which provided that all charitable
trusts should be registered with the clerk of the peace of the county,
city, or town wherein the beneficiaries were situated. "This act, however, was very generally ignored. . . ."[5]

Another act of 1812 also attempted to simplify the procedure for
redress against maladministration by way of information initiated by
the Attorney General.[6] The act was limited to actions against trustees
at the suit of beneficiaries, and did not provide a notable improvement
over the existing method.

The most important development in the nineteenth century was the
creation by Parliament in 1819 of a Charities Commission, known
originally as the Brougham Commission, to investigate and record all
charitable trusts in England and Wales. The impetus for this move
came from the efforts of Lord Brougham and his associates to improve
public education, and from the findings of his Committee of Inquiry

---

[1] Stat. 7 & 8 William III, c. 37 (1695–1696). Keeton, George W., *op. cit.,* p.
171.
[2] Committee on the Law and Practice relating to Charitable Trusts, *op. cit.,*
p. 19.
[3] Return of Charitable Donations Act, Stat. 26 George III, c. 58 (1786).
[4] Stat. 52 George III, c. 102 (1812).
[5] Keeton, George W., *op. cit.,* p. 13.
[6] Charities Procedure Act, Stat. 52 George III, c. 101 (1812).

on the Education of the Lower Orders, which had been created in 1816, that many trusts for educational purposes were being badly misused or neglected. By the act of 1819,[1] the Commissioners were authorized to give evidence to the Attorney General, who would commence proceedings for correction of abuses. Charitable trustees were given the power to apply to court for amendment of their statutes or regulations in places where they gave insufficient powers. The Brougham Commission and its successors conducted their inquiries for nineteen years, and the 60 volumes of their reports revealed many cases of malversation of charitable funds.

Brougham's initial bill providing for the creation of the Charities Commission had met with some opposition in Parliament, and the government succeeded in removing from the scope of the Commission's inquiry the universities and principal public schools. Even with the exclusion, however, much valuable work was accomplished. The level of administration of charitable trusts improved,[2] and the information in the reports persuaded Parliament of the need for some regular form of supervision.

In 1835 a Select Committee was constituted to examine the reports of the Commission and make recommendations for further legislation. At this time the Commission had completed its work in only 28 counties. The Committee made two major recommendations: (1) the establishment of administrative control over charitable trusts by an independent body, without, however, removing the final jurisdiction of the courts; (2) the institution of legal changes to permit the broadening of charitable trusts that were too narrow in operation and, in some instances, the transfer of funds to objects more socially appropriate.[3] This second recommendation was in effect a request for extension of the *cy pres* doctrine, which had been narrowly employed by the courts.

The "stubborn, influential, and strongly entrenched resistance of some of the most important charities to any form of control"[4] resulted in the failure of Parliament to enact any corrective legislation for eighteen years, although 13 bills were introduced during those years.

The Charitable Trusts Act finally became law in 1853.[5] It provided

---

[1] Stat. 59 George III, c. 91 (1819).
[2] Keeton, George W., *op. cit.*, p. 15; and Committee on the Law and Practice relating to Charitable Trusts, *op. cit.*, p. 19.
[3] Keeton, George W., *op. cit.*, p. 17.
[4] *Ibid.*, p. 18.
[5] Stat. 16 & 17 Victoria, c. 137 (1853).

for the creation of a permanent Board of Charity Commissioners, which was given authority to examine into all charities in England and Wales, as to their objects and management and the value of their property, and to require all trustees to furnish accounts and statements.[1] The Commissioners were not subordinate to any government department. Two were normally full-time professional and salaried appointments, and the third was usually a member of Parliament who answered parliamentary questions and introduced bills for the Commissioners. The act also provided for the creation of two new institutions, the Office of Trustee of Charitable Lands and the Office of Trustee of Charitable Funds. In the latter, title to charitable funds could be vested without cost to the trustees, thereby obviating the problems and expense arising from a change in trustees.

In 1860 the powers of the Commissioners were broadened to allow them to make such effectual orders as were then made by a judge of the Court of Chancery for the establishment of a scheme for the administration of any charity with an annual income of less than £50.[2] The exercise of these quasi-judicial powers was subject to review on appeal by the Court of Chancery, which interpreted them narrowly to apply only to the machinery for carrying out a testator's intent, not to reformation of the originally stated charitable purpose. For example in *In re Weir Hospital*,[3] the court rejected a scheme which the Commissioners had approved for the joint administration of the funds of two inadequately endowed medical colleges in London. In 1899 the jurisdiction of the Board of Charity Commissioners over educational endowments was transferred to the Board of Education.[4]

The Board functioned under the powers of the acts of 1853 and 1860 for a century. The Commissioners exercised few active supervisory powers over trustees and functioned chiefly to receive complaints on abuses of administration, correcting them where possible under their own powers and referring others to the Attorney General for action. The requirement for filing accounts was largely ignored.

The mortmain provisions were changed during this period, primarily by the Mortmain and Charitable Uses Acts of 1888 and 1891 which repealed most of the earlier legislation.[5] The act of 1888 pro-

---

[1] Scott, Austin W., *op. cit.*, sec. 391.
[2] Charitable Trusts Act, Stat. 23 & 24 Victoria, c. 136 (1860).
[3] *In re Weir Hospital* [1910] 2 Ch. 124.
[4] Board of Education Act, Stat. 62 & 63 Victoria, c. 33 (1899).
[5] Stat. 51 & 52 Victoria, c. 42 (1888); and Stat. 54 & 55 Victoria, c. 73 (1891).

hibited acquisition of land by a corporation through mortmain except under license from the Crown or under statute; trusts of land for charitable uses were required to be made by deed to take effect at once, and had to be made at least twelve months before the death of the donor. The act of 1891 permitted devises of land in trust to a charitable corporation provided the land was sold within one year from the testator's death, unless the court or the Charity Commissioners had extended the period or had authorized retention when the land was to be used for the charity's purposes.

The Nathan Committee and the Charities Act of 1960

In 1950 Parliament established a Committee on the Law and Practice relating to Charitable Trusts. Its Report, commonly called the Nathan Report, was presented by the Prime Minister to Parliament in December, 1952.[1] It contained an excellent summary of the history of charity law and the activities of the Commissioners. The Nathan Committee made extensive recommendations for legislative change, the great bulk of which were incorporated in an act of 1960 entitled "An Act to replace with new provisions the Charitable Trust Acts, 1853 to 1939, and other enactments relating to charities or with respect to gifts to charities and for purposes connected therewith."[2]

This act repealed most of the prior legislation on charities, abolished certain technicalities with regard to transfers of property, repealed all previous mortmain legislation, and extended the doctrine of cy pres. It provided for a new administrative system that enlarged the supervisory powers of the Charity Commissioners and created a new relationship between them and the Parliament that was designed to facilitate the introduction of new legislation. It also required the registration of all charities in England. Registration is now under way, and when it is completed, a better picture of the number and size of charitable trusts in England will be available.

The Nathan Committee Report estimated that there were some 110,000 charitable trusts known to the Commissioners. Of these, 30,000 were for educational purposes. No statistics on the purposes of the remaining 80,000 were available; based on the figures of the Charities Commission of 1876, however, more than one-half were

---

[1] Committee on the Law and Practice relating to Charitable Trusts, op. cit.
[2] Stat. 8 & 9 Elizabeth II, c. 58 (1960).

thought to be for the aid of the poor, often of a specific geographical area.[1]

Developments in Substantive Law

The description of the law of charities in England since the enactment of the Statute of Charitable Uses has centered chiefly on legislative enactments. The legal doctrines that shaped and defined the nature of charitable trusts and corporations had been laid down and accepted prior to the passage of that act. The right to existence in perpetuity; the doctrine that a charitable trust will not fail for want of a trustee, because of uncertainty as to the precise object or the mode of its application, or as the result of an imperfect trust provision; the legal meaning of charity; and the *cy pres* doctrine all became part of the established law in the early days of the Court of Chancery, much of it being adopted from doctrines developed in the ecclesiastical courts.

After the sixteenth century the Chancery Court became more and more similar to the Common Law Courts. The rule developed that "equity follows the law," and decisions came to be based on precedent. In the 1870's the entire English legal system was reformed. The old distinctions between Common Law Courts and Equity Courts were abolished, and all courts received the right, where necessary, to use both kinds of law.

In a legal system that is based on precedent and "judge-made law," as is the Anglo-American, it is inevitable and desirable that certain concepts be modified over a period of time as the cases on a specific subject multiply. In the field of charity law in England, the development was toward a narrowing and restriction of some of the early concepts, particularly the definition of charity and the doctrine of *cy pres*.

It was noted earlier that the doctrine of *cy pres* originated with the Romans and was subsequently adopted by the English ecclesiastical courts. The term itself is Norman-French and means either "near this" (*ici près*) or "as near as possible" (*aussi-près*) to the declared object. A recent study suggests that the doctrine originally was given a liberal interpretation in accord with the first definition, but that through the years it came to have the second meaning.[2]

---

[1] Committee on the Law and Practice relating to Charitable Trusts, *op. cit.*, p. 27. See Owen, David, *English Philanthropy 1660–1960,* Belknap Press of Harvard University Press, Cambridge, Mass., 1964, pt. 4, for a description of modern foundations in England, the work of the Nathan Committee, and the legislative history of the Charities Act of 1960.

[2] Sheridan, L. A., and V. T. Delany, *The Cy Pres Doctrine.* Sweet and Maxwell, London, 1959, p. 2.

As developed by the English courts, the doctrine of *cy pres* was used where a clear charitable intention was expressed, but the mode or purpose specified by the donor was or became impossible to carry out. During the nineteenth century the courts refused to apply the doctrine unless clear impossibility was shown. This requirement was relaxed for educational trusts by the Endowed Schools Act of 1869,[1] which empowered an independent commission (and later the Charity Commissioners), subject to court review, to adopt new schemes in such manner as might render educational endowments most conducive to the advancement of the education of boys and girls. These powers were transferred in 1899 to the Board of Education, and they are now vested in the Ministry of Education.

An even broader power was granted to the Secretary of State to frame schemes for the government and management of educational endowments in Scotland.[2] However, the power of the Charity Commissioners to frame schemes for other than educational trusts, initially authorized by the Charitable Trusts Act of 1860, was very narrowly interpreted by the courts, and the requirements of impossibility or impracticality were strictly construed.[3] Requests for extension of the doctrine are to be found in legal literature, particularly in the Reports of the Charity Commissioners from 1857 to 1894, but Parliament took no action until 1960.

There were also certain situations where it was held that the Crown, not the courts, had the power to make dispositions *cy pres*. This right, called the prerogative power, was based on the supervisory power of the Crown, as *parens patriae,* over all charities. It was thought to have originated from the sovereign's power to ensure justice to all his subjects. In time it came to be administered by the Lord Chamberlain acting in his administrative capacity.[4] The prerogative *cy pres* power was applied in three types of cases: (1) where there was a gift directly "to charity" with no further specific purpose; (2) where there was an outright gift for a specified object of charity involving a charitable institution which failed by reason of its not existing at the death of the testator, or which subsequently ceased to operate, and a general intention in favor of charity was evidenced; and (3) where the object

[1] Stat. 32 & 33 Victoria, c. 56 (1869).
[2] Stat. 45 & 46 Victoria, c. 59 (1882), now Stat. 9 & 10 George VI, c. 72, secs. 115 to 134 (1946).
[3] See Keeton, George W., *op. cit.,* chaps. 9, 10.
[4] Sheridan, L. A., and V. T. Delany, *op. cit.,* p. 65.

of the gift was illegal or was void as contrary to public policy (usually a gift for a forbidden religion). The property subject to the power of prerogative *cy pres* was held by the court pending a direction "by the sign manual" of the King, made at the suggestion of the Attorney General.[1] The doctrine of prerogative *cy pres,* though still in existence in England today, has been narrowed in its application and is only rarely cited as the basis of court action.[2]

The Nathan Committee devoted considerable attention to the question of extending the application of the *cy pres* doctrine and made recommendations which were embodied in The Charities Act of 1960. The act now authorizes the *cy pres* application of charitable funds under the following circumstances:

(a) Where the original purposes, in whole or in part,—
    (i) have been as far as may be fulfilled; or
    (ii) cannot be carried out, or not according to the directions given and to the spirit of the gift; or
(b) Where the original purposes provide a use for part only of the property available by virtue of the gift; or
(c) Where the property available by virtue of the gift and other property applicable for similar purposes can be more effectively used in conjunction, and to that end can suitably, regard being had to the spirit of the gift, be made applicable to common purposes; or
(d) Where the original purposes were laid down by reference to an area which then was but has since ceased to be a unit for some other purpose, or by reference to a class of persons or to an area which has for any reason since ceased to be suitable, regard being had to the spirit of the gift, or to be practical in administering the gift; or
(e) Where the original purposes, in whole or in part, have, since they were laid down,—
    (i) been adequately provided for by other means; or
    (ii) ceased, as being useless or harmful to the community or for other reasons, to be in law charitable; or
    (iii) ceased in any other way to provide a suitable and effective method of using the property available by virtue of the gift, regard being had to the spirit of the gift.[3]

Subsection 2 contains a proviso, however, that the case law on *cy pres* remains in effect in all instances where the enumeration in the 1960 act merely restates prior law. According to Keeton, the principal ex-

---

[1] Tyssen, Amherst D., *op. cit.,* pp. 211–214; see also Bogert, George G., and George T. Bogert, *op. cit.,* sec. 432; Scott, Austin W., *op. cit.,* sec. 399.
[2] Sheridan, L. A., and V. T. Delany, *op. cit.,* p. 65.
[3] Stat. 8 & 9 Elizabeth II, c. 58 (1960), sec. 13(1).

tensions of the *cy pres* doctrine are to be found in paragraphs (c) (d) and (e) (iii) quoted above.[1]

A restatement of the legal definition of charitable purposes, also recommended by the Nathan Committee, was not incorporated in the Charities Act of 1960. The act repealed the preamble to the Statute of Elizabeth of 1601 which was still in force, but included no attempt to define what a charity is in terms of its purposes.

> This, as before, has been left to the courts, whose intervention in this field is probably the worst exhibition of the operation of the technique of judicial precedent which can be found in the law reports. Whether the new Act will inspire the Judiciary to introduce a little coherence into this branch of the law remains to be seen. In deciding what is, and what is not a charity, the courts are really making decisions upon questions of public policy which, in an age of rapid social change, are of steadily increasing importance. It is, therefore, inevitable that decisions upon what is, and what is not a charity should be frequent, and should provoke criticism.[2]

Corporate Charities in England

The earliest forerunners of the modern business corporation were the ecclesiastic and charitable organizations, and the municipalities, guilds, and universities of early England. Since the Reformation, the trust has been the predominant form of organization for charitable activities, and remains so today. Part of the explanation lies in the nature of the development of the corporation in England. Although these early charitable organizations had some attributes in common with the present-day corporation, not until the middle of the sixteenth century did the important attributes of modern corporations begin to develop. The first large business corporations in England were the foreign trading companies formed during the period of exploration and colonization of the sixteenth and seventeenth centuries. Created by royal charter or special act of Parliament, they were granted the privilege of exploring and trading with certain lands across the seas. The East India Company, chartered in 1600, and The Hudson Bay Company, chartered in 1670, are examples.

In the eighteenth century the privileges of incorporation, usually with monopoly rights, were granted by special acts of Parliament to certain groups to protect or promote the use of improved processes or

---

[1] Keeton, George W., *op. cit.*, p. 165.
[2] *Ibid.*, p. vi.

inventions or to encourage the development of the natural resources of localities.[1] Stock companies became a popular form of organization for business enterprises, and with them came the concept of transferable shares of stock.

The rapid rise in economic activity during the nineteenth century caused a demand for enactment of legislation permitting the formation of companies offering limited liability to their shareholders. Starting in 1855, Parliament passed a series of acts which permitted general incorporation for certain purposes. Thus, there was a transition from the concept of specific government sanction and the grant of a privilege to incorporate for purposes of community benefit to the concept of a wide grant of power to individuals freely to form associations for their private benefit. This change paralleled the growth of individualism as a political concept and the decline in the powers of the sovereign.

The business motive completely overshadowed the place of charitable enterprises in this development. The Companies Act of 1867 did permit incorporation for nonpecuniary ends; but since the state was the source of power to create corporations whereas the creator of a charitable trust was afforded great freedom, the trust form continued to be preferred. Moreover, incorporation did not have the advantage of relieving managers of charitable funds of the supervision of the Charity Commissioners or the courts.[2]

Unlike the law of charities as it developed in the United States, the English law did not make distinctions as to the nature of ownership of property between the corporation and the trust. Tyssen, discussing the nature of a devise to a charitable corporation, describes a situation wherein land was devised to a corporation without any expression of trust, "but as the corporation existed solely for charitable purposes, this was held equivalent to a devise upon a charitable trust."[3]

The Charities Act of 1960 contains the following definitions:

"charity" means any institution, corporate or not, which is established for charitable purposes and is subject to the control of the High Court in the exercise of the court's jurisdiction with respect to charities. . . .

---

[1] Davis, John P., *op. cit.*, p. 260.
[2] Freund, Ernst, "Legal Aspects of Philanthropy," in Faris, Ellsworth, Ferris Laune, and Arthur J. Todd, editors, *Intelligent Philanthropy.* University of Chicago Press, Chicago, 1930, pp. 156, 175.
[3] *Incorporate Society* v. *Richards,* 1 Dr. War. 258, cited in Tyssen, Amherst D., *op. cit.*, p. 10.

"charity trustees" means the persons having the general control and management of the administration of a charity.

"trusts," in relation to a charity, means the provisions establishing it as a charity and regulating its purposes and administration, whether those provisions take effect by way of trust or not, and in relation to other institutions, has a corresponding meaning.[1]

Therefore, it can be said that there is "a law of charities" in England. Historical accident has led to a different situation in this country, however.

Charitable Trusts in the United States

In colonial America, an atmosphere favorable to the creation of charitable trusts and institutions was fostered by the encouragement of philanthropic activities under English law, the teaching of charity by the churches, and the needs of the settlers.

The colonists did not debate the question of public versus private responsibility. . . . Public and private philanthropy were so completely intertwined as to become almost indistinguishable. The law itself reflected a pragmatic approach to the solving of social problems through philanthropy. Colonial assemblies went out of their way to remove obstacles in the way of charities. The courts, valuing social betterment above legal technicalities, asserted a permissive charity doctrine that supported donors' benevolent intentions, even when the formulation of their plans was clearly imperfect.[2]

Following the Revolution, there was a rise in nationalistic sentiment and an antagonism to all things British. The effect on the law of the new country was the adoption in state constitutions or statutes of provisions that were aimed at retaining the framework of English jurisprudence "cleansed of what they considered to be its most undesirable elements," particularly all vestiges of royal power and prerogative.[3] These enactments generally provided for the adoption of all English statutes made in aid of or to supply defects of the common law enacted prior to 1607 (the time of the first settlement in Virginia), and not inconsistent with the philosophy of the new democracy.

The applicability of these provisions to charitable trusts was not questioned in the majority of states, which consistently upheld their validity, although the doctrine of prerogative *cy pres* was rejected. As

---

[1] Stat. 8 & 9 Elizabeth II, c. 58 (1960), sec. 45(1).
[2] Miller, Howard S., *The Legal Foundations of American Philanthropy, 1776–1844.* State Historical Society of Wisconsin, Madison, 1961, p. xi.
[3] *Ibid.*

new states entered the union, they followed the lead of the early states, primarily Massachusetts, whose constitution had provided for adoption of the common law and English statutes,[1] or Connecticut, which had enacted legislation in 1702 specifically upholding charitable trusts.[2]

Charitable trusts were exempted from local taxation and the courts adopted an attitude of liberality to the legal meaning of charity. Incorporation by special act of the legislature was the usual method of establishing schools, hospitals, religious groups, and other operating charitable institutions. Fear of the rise in power of the Church led to passage of restrictions on the holding of property by charitable, particularly religious, corporations, and in some states the legislature was on occasion reluctant to grant charters to these groups.[3] A policy of encouraging charity predominated, however, and as incorporation for business purposes increased, so did incorporation for charitable ventures of all types.

The development of charitable uses did not parallel that of England, however, for eight states rejected the doctrine of charitable trusts. In these states, the only method of devoting money to charitable purposes was through gifts either to established charitable corporations or to trustees who were directed to form a corporation within the period of the Rule Against Perpetuities.[4]

The first difficulty occurred in Virginia, where all English statutes and acts of Parliament were specifically repealed in 1792. The problem arose from an erroneous determination by the Supreme Court of the United States that the law of charitable trusts had its origins in, and was based upon, the Statute of Charitable Uses of 1601, and that with the repeal of that statute by Virginia in 1792, any trust without beneficiaries who were definitely named was invalid. This opinion, delivered by Chief Justice Marshall in the case of *Trustees of Philadelphia Baptist Association* v. *Hart's Executors*,[5] was based on false and incomplete historical evidence and on the dicta in certain English cases that led to the impression that charitable trusts for indefinite

---

[1] Mass. Constitution, ch. 6, sec. 6 (1780).
[2] Conn. Gen. Stat. Rev., secs. 45–79 and 47–2 (1958).
[3] Miller, Howard S., *op. cit.*, p. 19.
[4] For a detailed discussion of this history, see Blackwell, Thomas E., "The Charitable Corporation and the Charitable Trust," *Washington University Law Quarterly*, vol. 24, December, 1938, pp. 1–45; and Fisch, Edith L., *The Cy Près Doctrine in the United States*, Matthew Bender and Co., New York, 1950.
[5] 4 Wheat. 1, 4 L. Ed. 499 (U.S. 1819).

beneficiaries did not exist in England prior to the enactment of the Statute of Elizabeth.

The *Hart* case was followed in Virginia, Maryland, the District of Columbia, and West Virginia for nearly one hundred years; and it influenced the development of charitable trusts in New York, Michigan, Wisconsin, and Minnesota. It had this effect despite the fact that twenty-five years later the Supreme Court reversed itself, holding that charitable trusts should be afforded recognition in the United States regardless of statutes abolishing English law.[1]

In the interval between the decision in the *Hart* case and that of *Vidal* v. *Girard's Executors*,[2] the Supreme Court ruling had aroused great interest, both in the United States and England, and stimulated further research into the early history of equity jurisdiction. The result was the definite establishment of the fact that charitable trusts had been recognized by the English courts prior to 1601. In the *Vidal* case, the Supreme Court was asked to determine the validity of a charitable trust created in the will of Stephen Girard for the establishment of a school or college for orphan children in Philadelphia. The decision would be based on the law of Pennsylvania, where the Statute of Elizabeth had been previously declared to be of no force. The Court declared that the lack of effect of the Statute of Elizabeth in Pennsylvania was immaterial, since equity had inherent jurisdiction independent of the Statute of Elizabeth or of the prerogative power to sustain, because of their charitable purposes, trusts which would otherwise be invalid. "Few cases ever more keenly interested the general public or brought it more closely in contact with the court."[3] However, the interest was not sufficient to persuade either the courts or the legislatures in Virginia, Maryland, the District of Columbia, or West Virginia, which persisted in holding to the rule of the *Hart* case.

In New York charitable trusts were declared invalid because of judicial interpretation of the codification of the law of trusts made there originally in 1789. This first code contained no English statutes, thereby repealing by implication the Statute of Elizabeth.[4] A second

---

[1] *Vidal* v. *Girard's Executors*, 2 Howard 127, 11 L. Ed. 205 (U.S. 1844).
[2] *Ibid.*
[3] Warren, Charles, *The Supreme Court in United States History*, Little, Brown and Co., Boston, 1926, vol. 2, p. 398, quoted in Miller, Howard S., *op. cit.*, p. 38, who added that this interest in the case was due more to the fame of counsel than to the points of law at stake. These noted counsel were Daniel Webster for the heirs of Stephen Girard, and Horace Binney representing the city of Philadelphia.
[4] Jones and Varrick Laws of New York, 1789.

codification of the laws enacted in 1829 abolished all uses and trusts of land except those specifically authorized or modified therein. It contained no mention of charitable trusts, leaving the state with no clear policy as to their validity.[1] The Court of Chancery held in 1844 that the act of 1829 implied no ban on charitable trusts.[2] The decision was severely criticized six years later, however, by the New York Supreme Court, which held that no trusts could be recognized unless specifically authorized by statute.[3] In 1853 in the case of *Williams* v. *Williams*[4] a charitable trust of personal property was upheld on the grounds that jurisdiction over charities existed independently of statute, but this case was not followed. Zollmann described it as "the last ray of light preceding a total eclipse."[5]

The attitude of the New York courts for the next fifty years was summarized in a decision of 1866[6] which stated that the intention of the legislature to abolish all charitable trusts was evidenced by the repeal of the Statute of Elizabeth and the omission of charitable purposes from the revision of 1829. In the opinion of the court, it was better policy to limit charitable gifts to those charitable corporations that were regulated by statute than to allow "every private citizen the right to create a perpetuity for such purposes as to him seem good, and to endow it with more than corporate powers and more than corporate immunity."[7]

In 1891 the failure of a legacy of almost $4 million left by Governor Tilden to found a free library in New York City[8] led to a public reaction against the ban on charitable trusts that culminated in the passage of the "Tilden Act" in 1893.[9] This act declared that charitable trusts should thereafter be valid. Subsequent amendments restored to New York the entire doctrine of charitable trusts, which received thereafter favorable construction in the courts.[10] However, the New York code of 1828 had been copied in Michigan, Wisconsin, and Minnesota, and not until the early years of the twentieth century did the

---

[1] Rev. Stat. of New York, 1829, p. 727.
[2] *Shotwell* v. *Mott,* 2 Sandf., Ch. 46 (N.Y. 1844).
[3] *Yates* v. *Yates,* 9 Barb. 324 (1850).
[4] 8 N.Y. (4 Seld.) 525 (1853).
[5] Zollmann, Carl F. G., *American Law of Charities.* The Bruce Publishing Co., Milwaukee, 1924, p. 31.
[6] *Bascom* v. *Albertson,* 34 N.Y. 584 (1866).
[7] *Ibid.,* p. 615; Scott, Austin W., *op. cit.,* sec. 348.3.
[8] *Tilden* v. *Green,* 130 N.Y. 29, 28 N.E. 880 (1891).
[9] Acts of 1893, ch. 701, now N.Y. Real Prop. Law, sec. 113, N.Y. Pers. Prop. Law, sec. 12.
[10] Zollmann, Carl F. G., *op. cit.,* p. 35.

validity of charitable trusts come to be generally recognized in those states.

Today charitable trusts are upheld in all the states, either by court decision or legislative enactment, but these early decisions affected the entire development of the law of charities in the country, particularly the legal status of property held by charitable corporations and the acceptance of the *cy pres* doctrine.

Charitable Corporations in the United States

The influence of the New York and Virginia attitude toward charitable trusts and the development of the business corporation to a position of predominant importance in American business law combined to make inevitable the greater use of the corporate form in the United States than in England for all types of charitable activities.

Development of the corporation in America paralleled that in England, but with the growth of the continent and the expansion of the American economy, the American corporation soon overtook its English predecessor. In the colonies corporate rights were conferred by the issue of "letters patent" or charters from either the Crown or the Royal Governors acting for the Crown. The power was also delegated in some instances to the colonial assemblies.

The most numerous group of private corporations in the colonies were those for religious worship. Charitable and educational institutions usually were chartered under religious auspices, although some were the result of private bequests. One of the earliest corporate charters was granted by act of the Massachusetts General Court in 1756 to "The Feoffees of the Grammar School of the Town of Ipswich to administer a private bequest in the interest of public education there." Similar acts can be found in the records of the assemblies of Virginia, New Jersey, and Connecticut.[1] General acts for incorporation for charitable purposes preceded those for business purposes in some instances. For example, New York passed a general incorporation act for religious purposes in 1784, and adopted the first act permitting general incorporation for business purposes in the United States in 1811.[2]

By 1850 general corporation laws were common throughout the

---

[1] Davis, J. S., *Essays in the Earlier History of American Corporations.* Harvard University Press, Cambridge, Mass., 1917, vol. 1, p. 75.
[2] N.Y. Laws, Acts of 1811, ch. 67.

United States, and in the latter half of the nineteenth century, statutory restrictions on the size and activity of corporations were gradually removed. Incorporation by special act died out, so that by 1900 all but four states had adopted constitutional amendments prohibiting incorporation for business purposes by special acts.[1] Where special acts for business corporations are permitted today, they are limited in application to special forms of corporations, and are only rarely used. Incorporation for charitable purposes by special act of the legislature persisted in some jurisdictions until the start of the twentieth century.

Charitable corporations were considered to be quite different from business corporations. The commentators, following the English cases, described charitable corporations as those founded for the administration of charitable trusts.

> A charitable corporation is merely a trustee or agent selected by the donor of the charity for the purpose of administering funds given for charitable purposes, and the beneficiaries are frequently the public, or parties outside of the corporation. The principles of law applicable to charitable corporations differ, on this account, from those which apply to ordinary business corporations.[2]

However, in those states which refused to uphold the validity of charitable trusts, it was necessary to devise a different theory concerning the nature of ownership of property by a charitable corporation. Some courts, desirous of upholding charitable gifts, went out of their way to state that a gift to a charitable corporation created no trust but was an absolute gift to the corporation to be used for the purposes for which it was chartered.

Problems arose, however, when a testator bequeathed property to a charitable corporation to be used for only one of its stated corporate purposes, or when he provided that the property should be held in perpetuity and only the income expended. To hold that gifts of this nature were trusts would be to defeat the gift. On the other hand, if the gift were declared absolute, the restrictions could not be enforced, since an absolute owner of property cannot be restricted in its use. Some cases, accordingly, held that no trust was created and that the restrictions were only precatory. Others held that while no true or

---

[1] Chayes, Abram, in the "Introduction" to Davis, John P., *op. cit.*, pp. xi–xii.

[2] Morawetz, Victor, *A Treatise on the Law of Private Corporations*. Little, Brown and Co., Boston, 1886, sec. 4.

technical trust was created, the question of enforcement did not depend on this, and the court would enforce the restriction. This is now the accepted view in most states.[1]

There is still no unanimity among the states as to the description of this type of ownership. The cases are almost evenly divided between those which describe the relationship as a trust and those which do not.[2] In the first edition of the *Restatement of the Law of Trusts*,[3] an introductory note to Chapter II on charitable trusts states: "When property is given to a charitable corporation a charitable trust is not created." This note was not included in the second edition of the *Restatement* published in 1959, and in its stead the following comment was inserted:

> When property is given to a charitable corporation particularly when restrictions are imposed by the donor, it is sometimes held by the courts that a charitable trust is created and that the corporation is a trustee. It is sometimes held, however, that a charitable trust is not created. This is a mere matter of terminology. The important question is whether and to what extent the principles and rules applicable to charitable trusts are applicable to charitable corporations.[4]

Unfortunately, the matter has not always been treated as one of terminology alone. On some occasions the language of decisions from states that did not recognize charitable trusts has been used as authority in states that have always considered them valid.

Distinctions have been made between charitable trusts and charitable corporations on the basis of their form of organization alone. The courts have been unable or unwilling to apply the body of trust law to corporations, and influenced by the similarities of charitable corporations to business corporations, they have drawn analogies from business corporation law to the duties of directors of charitable corporations. Karst has commented on this situation as follows:

> A distinction which gives such great weight to organizational form rather than operational need carries a substantial burden of justification,

---

[1] *St. Joseph's Hospital* v. *Bennett,* 281 N.Y. 115, 22 N.E. 2d 305, reversing 256 App. Div. 120, 8 N.Y.S. 2d 922 (1939); Zollmann, Carl F. G., *op. cit.,* p. 326; Scott, Austin W., *op. cit.,* sec. 348.1.

[2] See Scott, Austin W., *op. cit.,* sec. 348.1, for citations.

[3] The *Restatements of Law* series, published by the American Law Institute, St. Paul, represents attempts by legal scholars and practitioners to summarize and unify American judicial thought in specific fields. A *Restatement of the Law of Trusts* first appeared in 1935, and a second edition was published in 1959. Unless otherwise noted, references in the text are to the second edition.

[4] *Restatement of the Law of Trusts (Second)*, *op. cit.,* sec. 348, comment f. Copyright 1959. Reprinted with the permission of the American Law Institute.

and as yet that burden has not been met. It may be sound to hold that the manager of a small scholarship fund may not delegate [a general principle of trust law], but that more latitude will be given the manager of a large foundation in the business of sponsoring project research. But there is no good reason for making different rules for the managers of two large foundations simply because one is a corporation and the other a trust. The law should recognize that the charitable trust and the charitable corporation have more in common with each other than each has with its private counterpart. The important differences among charities relate not to their form but to their function. In the area of fiduciary duties, a law of charities is needed.[1]

This aspect of the development of the law relating to charitable enterprises in the United States is particularly important to a study of foundations, since incorporation is today the prevalent legal framework for foundations of all sizes.[2] It has been estimated that three-fourths of all foundations have been created as corporations;[3] and of the 13 largest in the United States today, each with assets of more than $100 million, 10 were created as corporations, and only 3 as trusts.[4]

Foundations Today

Although many of the trusts created in the United States and in England from the time of Elizabeth fall within the definition of foundations used in this study, the term is popularly applied to those organizations created in the United States in the past sixty years which have substantial capital assets and purposes characterized by a wide freedom of action.[5] Foundations of this type first took deep root in the United States at the start of the twentieth century.

Foundations, of course, come only from surplus wealth, and therefore one cannot expect to find many examples in the early history of the United States. Some that we do find are of importance. Benjamin Franklin's two bequests of one thousand pounds each to the cities of Boston and Philadelphia, have had an eventful history. In 1803 came the first

---

[1] Karst, Kenneth L., "The Efficiency of the Charitable Dollar: An Unfulfilled State Responsibility," *Harvard Law Review,* vol. 73, 1960, p. 436. Copyright © 1960 by the Harvard Law Review Association.

[2] Andrews F. Emerson, *Philanthropic Foundations.* Russell Sage Foundation, New York, 1956, p. 48.

[3] *American Foundations and Their Fields.* 7th ed. Compiled by Wilmer Shields Rich, American Foundations Information Service, New York, 1955, pp. xvii, xviii.

[4] *The Foundation Directory, Edition 2, op. cit.,* p. 18.

[5] Andrews, F. Emerson, *Legal Instruments of Foundations.* Russell Sage Foundation, New York, 1958, p. 12.

social service endowment, the White-Williams Foundation being established in the interest of the "unhappy females who were desirous of returning to a life of rectitude." The next mile-post was set not by an American, but by an Englishman, James Smithson, who in 1846 bequeathed $508,000 to an American foundation, the Smithsonian Institution, "for the increase and diffusion of knowledge among men." The Peabody Fund of more than $2,000,000, created in 1867 and closed in 1914 [is another example].[1]

Statistics and historical data as to the rise in the number of foundations are incomplete. However, directories of known foundations, which were published from time to time, beginning in 1915, give some indication of their development, particularly of the larger ones. Moreover, since 1950, the returns to the Internal Revenue Service from tax-exempt organizations have been available to the public, and three directories of foundations published since then also add to the accuracy of the picture of foundation growth. Of greatest importance has been the establishment of The Foundation Library Center, an independent agency charged with the tasks of gathering comprehensive information about foundations, stimulating adequate reporting where such does not yet exist, and making its collections freely and generally available. The Center published its first *Directory* in 1960, and *Edition 2* in 1964. The introductory materials for both volumes, prepared by F. Emerson Andrews, director of The Foundation Library Center, contain detailed analyses of statistics relating to the foundations listed therein.[2]

These studies indicate that, numerically, the major growth in foundations occurred from 1940 to 1960. "For the United States as a whole, and counting only foundations meeting the size qualifications of *The Foundation Directory*, 88 per cent have been set up since 1940. If 'foundations' of all sizes were included, the recency factor would be further accented."[3]

Edition 2 lists 6,007 foundations with total assets of $14.5 billion. In addition, the 9,000 known foundations too small for inclusion in

---

[1] Keppel, Frederick P., *The Foundation*. The Macmillan Co., New York, 1930, p. 17.
[2] The only qualification necessary in applying the data prepared by Mr. Andrews is that rigid size qualifications were applied in the compilation. Edition 1 contained all known foundations that either possessed assets of $50,000 or made grants of at least $10,000 in the latest year of record. In Edition 2, the size definition was increased so that foundations with assets below $100,000 were excluded unless they made grants of $10,000 or more in the year of record.
[3] *The Foundation Directory, Edition 2, op. cit.*, p. 16.

the *Directory* hold assets estimated at $125 million, with the average holding estimated at $13,660.[1] Ninety per cent of the assets of the 6,007 foundations in the *Directory* are held by 1,023 foundations; and 76 per cent of the assets, by 176 foundations, each of which holds $10 million or more.[2]

The Treasury Department conducted a study of foundations in 1964 that complements this information compiled by the Foundation Library Center office in Washington.[3] It relies on the same definition of foundations as was used for *The Foundation Directory,* but the survey covered foundations of all sizes. The data obtained from Form 990–A and from a questionnaire sent to 1,300 foundations were extrapolated to provide estimates for 15,000 foundations, the total number estimated to meet The Foundation Library Center's definition.

The Treasury survey indicated that at the end of 1962 the book or ledger value of foundation assets was $11.6 billion and the net worth was $10.9 billion. In terms of market values, the figures were $16.3 billion for total assets, and $15.5 billion for net worth.[4] The estimates of the number of foundations of each size in terms of assets were similar in almost all cases to those compiled by the Foundation Library Center.

Andrews describes the changes in the growth of foundations during each decade since 1900.[5] Before 1900 less than 0.5 per cent of the foundations listed in the *Directory* were organized. During the first decade of the twentieth century, the rate of growth was under two per year, but these included two foundations which are presently worth $25 million or more. Between 1910 and 1919, the rate increased to more than seven per year for a total of 76, including three of great size: The Rockefeller Foundation, the Carnegie Corporation of New York, and the Commonwealth Fund. It was also during this decade that community foundations began to be organized.

In the 1920's, the rate again more than doubled, reaching some 17 per year, a total of 12 of which were in the large asset size. Although the depression period of the 1930's was a time when some foundations perished and others lost substantial assets, the rate of creation again

---

[1] *Ibid.,* p. 18.
[2] *Ibid.,* p. 19.
[3] See p. 374 for a description of the sample.
[4] U.S. Congress, Senate, Committee on Finance, *Treasury Department Report on Private Foundations* (Committee Print). 89th Congress, 1st Session, Government Printing Office, Washington, February 2, 1965, p. 82.
[5] *The Foundation Directory, Edition 2, op. cit.,* pp. 15–16.

almost doubled to nearly 30 a year; 8 per cent of the foundations listed in the *Directory, Edition 2,* were established in this period. Among them were 13 that now have assets of more than $25 million. "In fact, over 40 per cent of the assets of all American foundations is in the present possession of the foundations established in the depression decade. The extremity of this peak is due to The Ford Foundation, but even if it were excluded, the record would remain noteworthy."[1]

A major change in the structure of income and corporation taxes following the end of World War II led, in part, to what Andrews describes as "a new wave of foundations" sweeping over the country. In the 1940's six times the number of foundations created in the previous decade came into existence, almost ten times the record of the 1920's. This wave mounted still higher in the 1950's. More than half of the foundations in the *Directory* for which date of establishment is indicated were created in the decade 1950–1959, but of these only five have assets of $25 million or more, and 89 per cent are in the category of less than $1 million.[2]

In addition to the numerical increase in foundations since World War II, there has been a change in the types of foundations being created. Andrews describes the new types as follows:

> Many of these were family foundations, set up by living individuals, with both contributions and direction related closely to the family group. Another large segment were company-sponsored foundations, set up by business corporations to receive substantial contributions in years of good profits—or especially high taxes—and to disburse these funds, through good years and bad, in the customary patterns of corporation giving. Both family and company-sponsored foundations differed in one significant respect from the older, traditional type; they usually had no large initial corpus, but carried on their often substantial programs with moneys received currently. They may and sometimes do accumulate corpus, but typically they are "conduit" foundations rather than the fixed endowment type.[3]

Family foundations represent 59 per cent of all those listed in *Edition 2* of the *Directory*. The 3,520 foundations in this category also include some miscellaneous foundations on which some information is lacking or inadequate. They hold $2.3 billion or 16 per cent of tabulated assets.[4] Andrews points out that many of the large general

---

[1] *Ibid.,* p. 15.
[2] *Ibid.,* p. 13, Table 2.
[3] *Ibid.,* p. 15.
[4] *Ibid.,* p. 33.

research foundations of today began as family funds oriented to the personal charity of the donors.[1] The second new type of foundation, the company-sponsored fund, represents more than 28 per cent of all foundations.[2]

The 1964 Treasury Department survey did not discuss family foundations as such. However, it did attempt to estimate the number of foundations of varying sizes in which donors and related persons take some voice in investment policy, including the determination of sums to be applied for charitable purposes. Of an estimated total of 14,850 foundations, in 10,990, or slightly over two-thirds, donor-related influence was thought to be 50 per cent or more.[3] In terms of assets, it was found that slightly more assets are held by foundations with less than 20 per cent donor influence than by foundations with 50 per cent or more influence, but this was felt to result from the presence of several very large foundations such as The Ford Foundation in the former category.[4]

There is another type of foundation which must be described separately; that is the community trust. This type is usually concerned with problems of social welfare but acts under community control in a sense seldom found in the usual philanthropic foundation. These trusts have been created to administer a number of separate, named funds, usually designated for specific purposes, as well as composite or combined funds for handling smaller sums. The principal is usually managed by the trust department of a qualified local bank and trust company, and funds are distributed by a committee of citizens selected for their representative character and knowledge of charitable affairs. Some do operate under corporate charters, but the administration does not thereby differ. The first community trust, The Cleveland Foundation, was created in 1914, and both the number and assets of this type of foundation have risen steadily since that time. An important provision in these trusts is the reservation to the distribution committee of a form of *cy pres* power to transfer to other purposes any funds which can no longer be effectively used for the purposes originally designated.

The Council on Foundations, with headquarters in New York,

---

[1] *Ibid.,* p. 34.
[2] *Ibid.,* pp. 29–31.
[3] See pp. 377 ff. for further information on this aspect of the Treasury survey.
[4] U.S. Congress, Senate, Committee on Finance, *Treasury Department Report on Private Foundations, op. cit.,* p. 84.

serves as a clearinghouse for information from these trusts as well as for foundations whose field of interest is community affairs; it has made contributions to the entire field of foundation activity through its publication of information of interest to its members and of statistics as to the status of this type of foundation. Its report for 1963 listed 186 community foundations with assets of $480 million.[1] *The Foundation Directory, Edition 2,* lists 102 community foundations that hold active capital of $425 million—3 per cent of the assets of all foundations listed.[2]

Foundations and the American Economy

In the 1964 survey of foundations conducted by the Treasury Department an attempt was made to describe the rate of growth of foundations in comparison to that of the total economy. Although admitting that the evidence was meager, the Report made two conclusions: (1) there was some growth of foundations in relation to the economy in the 1930's and 1940's which could be associated with changes in the estate and income taxes during that period; (2) since 1950, the total wealth of foundations has grown faster than the rest of the economy, but this faster growth can probably be attributed to the fact that the principal assets of foundations, namely corporate stocks, were increasing in price faster than other assets.[3]

Statistics on the income of foundations in 1962 were also analyzed to obtain information on growth rate. It was estimated that approximately 2 per cent of the net worth of foundations as of the beginning of 1962 was set aside from current operations and contributions for growth purposes. To this was added an estimate of anticipated appreciation in total assets of 3 per cent, indicating a rate of growth for existing foundations of about 5 per cent a year.[4]

> This is itself in line with the common expectation of the growth of the gross national product, and if all foundations taken together grew at this rate, they would simply maintain their present relative importance compared to other wealthholders. . .[5]

---

[1] *Community Foundations in the United States and Canada, 1914–1961.* 2d ed. Prepared by Wilmer Shields Rich. Council on Foundations, Inc., New York, 1961. *Supplement, 1963, Status.*

[2] *The Foundation Directory, Edition 2, op. cit.,* p. 29.

[3] U.S. Congress, Senate, Committee on Finance, *Treasury Department Report on Private Foundations, op. cit.,* p. 76.

[4] *Ibid.,* pp. 80–81.

[5] *Ibid.,* p. 81.

The Report noted, however, that this total growth rate would be increased if foundations were created at a rate equivalent to that of 1962. It then added: "It is not here proposed that foundations in the aggregate should grow at exactly the same rate as the private sector. This analysis only goes to throwing some light on the rate of growth that does exist."[1]

Andrews has made the following observation on the place of foundations in the American scene.

> Although the increase in foundation assets has been notable, the resources of American foundations are not relatively large in the American economy, and may be shrinking. For example, in 1913 the federal government's total expenditures for education amounted to $5 million. Carnegie Corporation of New York in that year spent $5.6 million, so that if it had devoted all its funds to the field of education, it could have more than equaled the federal government total. In 1959 federal programs for education cost $2,413 million; in that year Carnegie Corporation's total expenditures amounted to $8.7 million. It would take more than 275 years of Carnegie expenditures at the 1959 rate—or 275 foundations of Carnegie's size—to match federal government expenditure that year in just this one area.
>
> Similarly, in 1915 the total receipts of the United States government amounted to $698 million. In that year the assets of The Rockefeller Foundation were $107 million, a little more than one seventh of federal receipts. In 1962 federal tax receipts amounted to about $97 billion. In that year the estimated total assets, not of one foundation but of all 15,000 foundations together, were about $14.5 billion, one seventh the federal receipts for the single year.[2]

Foundations in a Pluralistic Society

Philanthropy in the United States has been claimed by one writer to be "our freest enterprise,"[3] and this phrase does emphasize what the dominant policy of both the federal government and the individual states toward charitable activities has been since colonial times. With the exception of the restrictive legislation regarding charitable trusts which has been described, the enactment of legislation in a few states designed to protect heirs against complete or unreasoned disinheritance in favor of charity and minor restrictions on the holdings of charitable corporations, the great body of legislation and court decisions has been directed toward the removal of restrictions on charita-

---

[1] *Ibid.*

[2] *The Foundation Directory, Edition 2, op. cit.,* pp. 19–20.

[3] Jenkins, Edward C., *Philanthropy in America.* Association Press, New York, 1950, p. 5.

ble funds and toward the grant of almost complete freedom of action to the managers and directors of these funds.

The power to ensure proper application of charitable funds rests with the attorney general in 45 states, but before World War II it was rarely invoked. No measures comparable to those in England establishing the Brougham Commission or the Board of Charity Commissioners have ever been enacted by the federal government, and it is only in recent years that supervisory legislation has appeared in the states or that the Internal Revenue Service has made any attempts to police the exemption provisions of the tax laws.

The tendency of the courts in the majority of the states has been to give a broad interpretation to the legal meaning of charity and to uphold, wherever possible, the intent of a donor.[1] The *cy pres* doctrine has also been liberally interpreted, although there was a period when it was rejected in some states, because an erroneous interpretation of English cases led to the assumption that the power stemmed only from royal prerogative and not from the inherent equity jurisdiction of the courts. Today it is applied in almost all the states[2] to charitable trusts and corporations alike, and with few exceptions the scope of its application has been broader than that given by the English courts. An exemption from taxes for charitable enterprises has been included in all major federal tax legislation since the first such enactments and has been equally present in state law.

A further measure of the freedom accorded to foundation activity can be seen from the almost total lack of congressional interest in foundation activity before 1940.[3] The inclusion of provisions granting tax exemption to charitable enterprises and charitable donations was rarely questioned during congressional debate on tax bills throughout that entire period.

There was one brief period, from 1910 to 1916, when the question of foundation activity was debated in the Congress and did receive considerable public notice. The initial focus was on the attempt to secure a federal charter of incorporation for The Rockefeller Foundation. The bill was debated in the Congress during three successive sessions, and became the center of public controversy. It was branded

---

[1] See Chapter II.
[2] See Appendix A, Tables 1 and 2.
[3] See Lankford, John, *Congress and the Foundations in the Twentieth Century,* Wisconsin State University, River Falls, Wis., 1964, for an excellent summary of this period.

as an indefinite scheme for perpetuating vast wealth in the name of a man whose corporate holdings were at that very moment under attack by the federal government as illegal monopolies.[1]

The Rockefeller interests finally abandoned attempts to secure incorporation by Congress and instead obtained with no trouble a charter from New York state in April of 1913.[2]

Two years later a series of public hearings on foundation activity were commenced by a Commission on Industrial Relations, created by an Act of Congress of August 23, 1912, and composed of representatives of labor, employers of labor, and members of the Congress, all appointed by the President with the advice of the Senate. The Final Report of the Walsh Commission, as it was called, published in 1916,[3] charged that the concentration of wealth in the large foundations, such as the Carnegie and Rockefeller, was being used by industrial magnates to gain control of the universities and, thereby, the social and educational side of American life. The majority of the Commission recommended enactment of legislation requiring federal charters for the incorporation of all nonprofit organizations with more than one function and funds of more than $1 million, limitation on the size, income, and life of the foundations, and the creation of rigid supervisory procedures.[4]

Various reasons for this attack have been propounded. Kiger ascribed it to the suspicion aroused by the proposal of The Rockefeller Foundation to investigate industrial relations and the fear that the study would be merely a whitewash of big business in its controversies with labor.[5] Keppel pointed out that the investigation followed closely a basic change in foundation policies and their departure from activities such as library building, farm demonstrations, and scientific research into the more controversial fields of education in general and social studies in particular.[6] Keele added to these theories the observation that the period was one in which industrial unrest, combined with the awakening of social consciousness, culminated in a series of

---

[1] Fosdick, Raymond B., *The Story of The Rockefeller Foundation.* Harper and Bros., New York, 1952, pp. 18–19.

[2] Laws of N.Y., 1913, ch. 488.

[3] U.S. Congress, Senate, Commission on Industrial Relations, *Industrial Relations: Final Report and Testimony* submitted to Congress. 64th Congress, 1st Session, Senate Document 415. Government Printing Office, Washington, 1916.

[4] *Ibid.*, p. 85.

[5] Kiger, Joseph C., *Operating Principles of the Larger Foundations.* Russell Sage Foundation, New York, 1954, pp. 85–86.

[6] Keppel, Frederick P., *op. cit.*, p. 26.

enactments which he characterized as "social legislation." It was also the period of trust-busting and union battles. Feeling against monopolies and the accumulation of vast wealth symbolized by the names of Carnegie and Rockefeller was high. It was therefore natural that liberals would denounce foundations as the instruments of this wealth and its corporate structure.[1]

In terms of a survey of government relations to foundations, however, this brief period must be regarded as one apart from the central theme of the American attitude toward philanthropy, and in particular toward foundations. No action was taken by Congress on the Walsh Commission's recommendations. Suspicion of large foundations did continue to appear from time to time,[2] but no major change in the approach of the Congress or the state governments toward foundations was apparent until after World War II.

The rapid growth in the number and size of foundations since 1940 has created a renewed interest in foundation activities. In the brief period since World War II there have been three congressional investigations of foundations, a revision of the tax laws relating to charity, a major study of foundations by the Treasury Department, and the institution of new administrative rulings and procedures by the Internal Revenue Service. Further amendments to the Internal Revenue Code will be considered by the Congress in 1965 and 1966. Ten states have enacted legislation establishing mandatory reporting provisions for foundations, a Uniform Supervision of Charitable Trustees Act has been promulgated, and legislation regulating solicitation of charitable funds is being enacted in many states. Both the American Bar Association and the National Association of Attorneys General have created committees on charitable trusts.

The foundations themselves have played a major part in the reassessment of their position and role in American society. The trend toward voluntary public reporting of foundation activities, long advocated by a few of the larger foundations, has accelerated. The establishment of The Foundation Library Center and the publication of its *Directory* and *Bulletin,* sponsored and financed by voluntary efforts

---

[1] Keele, Harold M., "Government's Attitude Toward Foundations," *Michigan State Bar Journal,* vol. 33, October, 1954, pp. 9, 18.

[2] Lindeman, Eduard C., *Wealth and Culture:* A Study of One Hundred Foundations and Community Trusts and Their Operations During the Decade 1921–1930. Harcourt, Brace and Co., New York, 1936; Orton, William A., *op. cit.,* p. 534.

of the foundations, are tangible reflections of their sense of responsibility to the public. It has best been summarized by Andrews:

A foundation, when it seeks and acquires tax-exempt status, enters upon certain privileges, of which tax exemption is the most tangible. In return for such solid benefits, and in view of the fact that the ultimate beneficiary is society itself, however particularly the gift may have been directed, it seems wholly proper that the foundation should account for its stewardship. Availability of the social asset, and its amount, should be known. Operations of the exempt organization should be fully disclosed, and, if it is of substantial size, regularly and fully reported. Such disclosure may be all that is necessary in the public interest. But unless wide voluntary cooperation is secured for this degree of accountability, controls may be imposed by government that will limit, and may destroy, the very freedom which has made foundations so significant a factor in pioneering research and social progress.[1]

The focus of the new interest, therefore, is primarily on devising means to assure public accountability of foundation activity without sacrificing a basic freedom of action.

It is not a problem peculiar to foundations alone. The prospect of any government action in a free society raises the same issue. But charitable institutions are special entities with characteristics which require special treatment. They have been described by one legal authority as "an anomalous dichotomy: [a] manifestation of quasi-socialism on the one hand, and of the most extreme incidents of a regime of private property on the other."[2]

Perhaps Sacks presented the question most succinctly when he characterized it as a search for the ideal methods for maintaining "the delicate balance of public ends and private means that is embodied in the charitable foundation."[3]

The future of foundations in American society depends on the outcome of this search.

---

[1] *The Foundation Directory, Edition 2, op. cit.*, pp. 45–46.
[2] Simes, Lewis M., *Public Policy and the Dead Hand.* University of Michigan Press, Ann Arbor, 1955, p. 111.
[3] Sacks, Albert M., "Use and Misuse of the Private Foundation," *Proceedings* of the New York University Fifth Biennial Conference on Charitable Foundations, Edited by Henry Sellin. Matthew Bender and Co., New York, 1961, p. 217.

CHAPTER II

The Law of
Charitable Dispositions

THE FUNCTIONS that a foundation may perform are enumerated in the statement of purposes in its charter or deed of trust. They are governed by a body of laws which is often referred to as the law of charitable dispositions. In all but two states, this law is to be found not in statutes, but in the case law.[1]

At one time in England charitable dispositions had to conform to strict standards of public policy dictated by the Crown. Today, however, particularly in the United States, the law governing charitable purposes gives wide latitude to a donor to choose the objects of his beneficence. The philosophy underlying this attitude has been described as an outgrowth of the basic political philosophy of the American colonies, which viewed the function of government as that of preserving liberties, not of imposing burdens. "High on the list of liberties was the right of every owner to control his property unaffected by governmental intrusion."[2] Although this absolute view of property rights has been modified considerably since the seventeenth century, the position of supremacy of the settlor of a charitable trust has remained. It is justified today, not on the basis of the natural rights of an

---

[1] Ga. Code Ann., sec. 108203; Pa. Estates Act of 1947 (Pa. Stat., tit. 20, sec. 301.1) uses language of the *Restatement of the Law of Trusts (Second)*, American Law Institute, St. Paul, 1959, sec. 368.

[2] Clark, Elias, "Charitable Trusts, the Fourteenth Amendment and the Will of Stephen Girard," *Yale Law Journal*, vol. 66, 1957, pp. 979, 995. See also Miller, Howard S., *The Legal Foundations of American Philanthropy, 1776–1844*, State Historical Society of Wisconsin, Madison, 1961, p. xi.

owner of property, but because of the benefits which have been conferred on society by the practice of philanthropy.[1]

Definitions of "Charity"

The extent of the freedom given to donors to choose charitable
purposes is most clearly seen in attempts to frame a definition of those
charitable purposes that the law recognizes as valid. The starting point
in the case law for such a definition is usually the Preamble to the
Statute of Charitable Uses of 1601.[2] The statute itself contained a
procedure for remedying abuses which had arisen in the administration of charitable funds by private individuals. The preamble contained an enumeration of the charitable purposes for which property
had been given and which were to be henceforth protected by the
State:

> . . . some for relief of aged, impotent and poor people, some for main
> tenance of sick and maimed soldiers and mariners, schools of learning,
> free schools, and scholars in universities, some for repair of bridges,
> ports, havens, causeways, churches, seabanks and highways, some for
> education and preferment of orphans, some for or towards relief, stock
> or maintenance for houses of correction, some for marriages of poor
> maids, some for supportation, aid and help of young tradesmen, handi
> craftsmen and persons decayed, and others for relief or redemption of
> prisoners or captives, and for aid or ease of any poor inhabitants con
> cerning payments of fifteens, setting out of soldiers and other taxes.[3]

Some early cases state that a purpose is not valid if not specifically
referred to in this statute,[4] but since the early eighteenth century,
courts in both England and the United States have generally regarded
the enumeration as descriptive or illustrative. The prevailing rule of
construction today is that in determining what purposes are charitable,
the courts are to be guided not by the letter of the Elizabethan statute,
but by its manifest spirit and reason; and they are to consider not what
uses are within its words, but what uses are embraced by its meaning
and purpose.[5]

From time to time, judges have attempted to frame definitions of
charity and charitable purposes. The problems inherent in such a task

---

[1] Clark, Elias, *op. cit.*, p. 996.
[2] Stat. 43 Elizabeth I, c. 4 (1601).
[3] Stat. 43 Elizabeth I, c. 4 (1601).
[4] *Sanderson* v. *White*, 18 Pick. 328, 333 (Mass. 1836).
[5] *Drury* v. *Inhabitants of Natick*, 10 Allen 169, 177 (Mass. 1865).

are illustrated in Lord Macnaghten's opinion in the leading English case of *Commissioners for Special Purposes of Income Tax* v. *Pemsel.*

> No doubt the popular meaning of the words "charity" and "charitable" does not coincide with their legal meaning; and no doubt it is easy enough to collect from the books a few decisions which seem to push the doctrine of the Court to the extreme, and to present a contrast between the two meanings in an aspect almost ludicrous. But still it is difficult to fix the point of divergence, and no one as yet has succeeded in defining the popular meaning of the word "charity". . . . How far then, it may be asked, does the popular meaning of the word "charity" correspond with its legal meaning? "Charity" in its legal sense comprises four principal divisions: trusts for the relief of poverty; trusts for the advancement of education; trusts for the advancement of religion; and trusts for other purposes beneficial to the community, not falling under any of the preceding heads. The trusts last referred to are not the less charitable in the eye of the law, because incidentally they benefit the rich as well as the poor, as indeed every charity that deserves the name must do either directly or indirectly.[1]

One of the most widely quoted definitions of a charitable trust from the United States cases is that of Chief Justice Gray in *Jackson* v. *Phillips.*

> A charity, in the legal sense, may be more fully defined as a gift, to be applied consistently with existing laws, for the benefit of an indefinite number of persons, either by bringing their minds or hearts under the influence of education or religion, by relieving their bodies from disease, suffering or constraint, by assisting them to establish themselves in life, or by erecting or maintaining public buildings or works or otherwise lessening the burdens of government.[2]

The *Restatement of the Law of Trusts* declares that a charitable trust is one devoted to charitable purposes, and then amplifies: "A purpose is charitable if its accomplishment is of such social interest to the community as to justify permitting property to be devoted to the purpose in perpetuity."[3] It then enumerates five broad sectors of activity similar to those in Justice Gray's definition, but concludes: "There is no fixed standard to determine which purposes are of such social interest to the community as to justify treating them as charitable; the interests of the community vary with time and place."[4]

---

[1] [1891] A. C. 531, 583.
[2] 14 Allen 539, 556 (Mass. 1867).
[3] *Restatement of the Law of Trusts (Second), op. cit.,* sec. 368, comment b.
[4] *Ibid.* See also Scott, Austin W., *The Law of Trusts,* 2d ed., Little, Brown and Co., Boston, 1956, sec. 368.

The problem of definition has received more attention in England than in the United States because the English courts have tended toward a strict construction of the uses listed in the Preamble to the Statute of Elizabeth.[1] In the Nathan Report of 1952, the Committee acknowledged that a rewording of the definition of charity was needed to permit greater flexibility in interpretation. It recommended repeal of the existing definition of charity by reference to the Preamble to the Statute of Charitable Uses and the enactment of a new definition, "based on Lord Macnaghten's classification, but preserving the case law as it stands."[2] Keeton commented on this recommendation as follows: "It is difficult to see what would be gained by this. The 'Macnaghten definition' is not a definition but a classification, and few statutory enactments have been followed as faithfully by the courts as these observations have been."[3] When the 1960 Charities Bill was presented to Parliament, the recommendation of the Nathan Committee was extensively discussed, but no new definition was adopted; however, the Preamble to the Statute of 1601 was repealed.[4]

Scott has said, "The truth of the matter is that it is impossible to frame a perfect definition of charitable purposes. There is no fixed standard to determine what purposes are charitable."[5] Nevertheless, Clark's description does indicate the attitude of the American courts toward charitable uses:

> The courts have found no way to make an effective classification [of valid charitable purposes]. Purposes worthy of community support are as diffuse as the winds. They vary with time. . . . Because of this constant flux, attempts to formalize the community benefit into abstract rules inevitably degenerate into a listing of ad hoc responses to particular situations. The courts have clearly perceived these dangers and have adjusted to them by accepting as charitable those trusts which benefit a group larger than the settlor's immediate family and friends

---

[1] Keeton, George W., *The Modern Law of Charities.* Sir Isaac Pitman and Sons, London, 1962, pp. 38–44.

[2] Committee on the Law and Practice relating to Charitable Trusts, *Report.* Cmd. 8710. H.M. Stationery Office, London, 1952, p. 36.

[3] Keeton, George W., *op. cit.,* p. 39.

[4] Charities Act 1960, Stat. 8 & 9 Elizabeth II, c. 58 (1960), sec. 45. See also Clark, Elias, "The Limitation on Political Activities: A Discordant Note in the Law of Charities," *Virginia Law Review,* vol., 46, 1960, pp. 439, 442. English cases have consistently withheld charitable status for purposes which seem to be clearly acceptable under American law. Clark cites several examples, among them *Gilmour* v. *Coats* [1949] A.C. 426 (Roman Catholic contemplative community held not charitable). For a discussion of the English meaning of charity see Keeton, George W., *op. cit.,* chap. 2.

[5] Scott, Austin W., *op. cit.,* sec. 368.

and which are not affirmatively absurd, obscene, illegal, excessively selfish or specifically offensive to some considerable segment of the population."[1]

Public Policy Considerations

The grant by government of a wide latitude to donors to choose the purposes of their beneficence does not extend, of course, to purposes that are illegal or will involve illegal acts. A purpose may be illegal because its performance requires or tends to encourage conduct that is a criminal offense. In some instances, the courts have used a standard of public policy which extends beyond whether or not the conduct is proscribed by a criminal statute; thus, early cases refused recognition to trusts which were formed to teach atheism.

The standard of public policy is, of course, constantly changing. Today it is manifest in certain cases wherein the courts have been asked to modify trusts that require discrimination on account of race, color, or creed. The most common of these relate to scholarship funds that either limit the class of recipients to a group or require the exclusion of a group. Some courts have permitted a deviation and the striking out of the discriminatory provision.[2]

The courts have also been asked to apply to charitable trusts the provisions of the Fourteenth Amendment of the United States Constitution, which prohibits state action that is discriminatory. The Supreme Court in 1957 held that the Fourteenth Amendment did prohibit the city of Philadelphia from acting as trustee of a trust to establish and operate a school for poor white, male orphans.[3] The Pennsylvania court then removed the city officials and appointed individual trustees. The action was upheld by the Supreme Court of Pennsylvania, and the United States Supreme Court refused to hear further appeal.[4] Some would argue that the state's interest in a charitable trust

---

[1] Clark, Elias, "Charitable Trusts . . . ," *op. cit.*, pp. 997–998. See also Clark, Elias, "The Limitation on Political Activities," *op. cit.*, p. 443.

[2] For example, in *Howard Savings Institution of Newark* v. *Peep et al.*, 34 N.J. 494, 170 A.2d 39 (1961) affirming *Howard Savings Institution* v. *Trustees of Amherst College*, 61 N.J. Super. 119, 160 A.2d 177 (1960), the court applied the *cy pres* doctrine and permitted the exclusion of a restriction to Protestant, gentile boys of a scholarship loan fund bequeathed to Amherst. The college had refused to accept the gift with the restriction, stating that it was contrary to its charter.

[3] *Pennsylvania* v. *Board of Directors of City Trusts,* 353 U.S. 230, 989; 77 S. Ct. 806, 1281; 1 L. Ed. 2d 792, 1146 (1957).

[4] *In re Girard College Trusteeship,* 391 Pa. 434, 138 A.2d 844 (1958), certiorari denied and appeal dismissed. 357 U.S. 570 (1958).

is so great as to make any discriminatory action by trustees the equivalent of state action and therefore within the constitutional limitation. If such a view is upheld, it will, of course, represent a new and far-reaching limitation on a settlor's power to dispose of property.[1]

Motives of Donors

The motive of the donor of a charitable trust is not usually a factor which the courts will consider in determining the validity of a charitable purpose. The effect of the gift is the controlling feature, not what the donor intended it to accomplish. A request that a marker be placed on a building indicating the name of the donor, a stipulation that a foundation's title always have the donor's name in it,[2] or any other direction concerning administration which is aimed at keeping the name of the settlor for posterity does not in any way detract from the gift's validity.[3]

> The settlor may have founded the trust solely to satisfy his family pride, for self-glorification, in order to emulate and rival a neighbor's bounty, to improve living conditions in his home city and thus strengthen his own business interests, or for other reasons unconnected with social advancement in the region in question. The court should not be interested in these incidental psychic or even material advantages to the settlor or his family. The court should, and generally does, direct its attention merely to the question whether the net result of the trust in operation will be to advance the religious, educational, eleemosynary, governmental, or other charitable interests of the community and thus to produce the social advancement required for the charitable trust.[4]

However, if the result of the undertaking is such that private profit will inure to the donor, it is not charitable. This question is of greater importance in tax cases where the Internal Revenue Code specifically prohibits private inurement. It can be of importance in the case of bequests or of trusts for the permanent benefit of an enterprise such as a school,[5] which, if declared to be for private profit, will result in failure of the trust or gift.

---

[1] For an excellent discussion of this question, see Clark, Elias, "Charitable Trusts . . . ," *op. cit.*, p. 979.

[2] *Taylor* v. *Columbian University*, 226 U.S. 126, 33 Sup. Ct. 73, 57 L. Ed. 152 (App. D.C. 1912).

[3] *Massachusetts Institute of Technology* v. *Attorney General*, 235 Mass. 288, 126 N.E. 521 (1920).

[4] Bogert, George G., and George T. Bogert, *The Law of Trusts and Trustees.* 2d ed. West Publishing Co., St. Paul, 1964, sec. 364.

[5] *Stratton* v. *Physio-Medical College*, 149 Mass. 505, 21 N.E. 874 (1889).

Imperfect Trust Provisions

Ordinarily a gift to charity never fails for uncertainty. If the gift is "for charity," whether in trust or not, the court will direct a scheme for the disposition of the property. If the gift is "to such charitable purposes as X shall select," and X fails to select, the court will either appoint a new trustee to make the selection or approve a scheme for the administration of the trust.[1]

The courts have not been as consistent in their treatment of cases where the gift has involved a choice between charitable and noncharitable objects. The situation in these cases is complicated by the fact that certain purposes, if not declared charitable, are not proper subjects for trusts that may exist in perpetuity. Usually this is because they are considered too indefinite, so that they do not meet the requirement that there be a beneficiary capable of enforcing every private trust. A requisite for determination of these cases, therefore, is a definition of charitable purposes; yet no such definition exists. The struggles of the judges to find a way out of this dilemma are evident, whether their results are approved or criticized.

An English case exemplifies the difficulties: "What 'charitable' is, I should be sorry to have to define with precision, but what does not come under 'charitable' I think is usually fairly plain."[2] So saying, Lord Haldane, in the House of Lords, attempted to explain a decision that a trust "for such patriotic purposes or objects and such charitable institution or institutions or charitable object or objects in the British Empire" as the trustees in their discretion should select failed for uncertainty.

This case is only one in the long line in which the courts, particularly in England but to some extent in the United States, have refused to uphold trusts where a donor has coupled a valid charitable purpose with other purposes that, in the opinion of the court, are wider and less definite than charitable. The most common cases have involved a linking with the word "charitable" of such commonly accepted synonyms as "benevolent," "public," "deserving," "philanthropic," and "patriotic." The courts have held in these cases that, in law, these words are not synonyms, and although the purpose is broad enough

---

[1] Scott, Austin W., *op. cit.,* secs. 396 to 397.4; and *Kirwin* v. *Attorney General,* 275 Mass. 34, 175 N.E. 164 (1931).
[2] *Attorney General* v. *National Provincial Bank* [1924] A.C. 262.

to include "charity," it does not limit the gift to charitable purposes in the legal sense.

The leading British case which recited this point of view involved a gift in trust to the Bishop of Durham "to dispose of the ultimate residue to such objects of benevolence and liberality as the Bishop of Durham shall most approve of." Even though the Bishop agreed to hold the property only for valid charitable purposes, the court held that the gift failed and the property reverted to testatrix' heirs.[1] This case was followed for the next century and a half and was reaffirmed as recently as 1944 by the House of Lords in a case involving the validity of a trust for the benefit of "such charitable institution or institutions or other charitable or benevolent object, or objects in England, as the executrix in her absolute discretion should select."[2] An attempt has now been made to reverse this trend in England through legislation, although the legislation itself has been criticized as not going far enough.[3]

In the United States some cases have followed the strict English rule,[4] but in a large and increasing number of cases the courts have held that dispositions of this type were for charitable purposes and have upheld the trusts.[5] The wisdom of this liberal attitude is self-evident. It has been given further support in this country by the large number of statutes relating to charitable dispositions that use the word "benevolent," and by the court interpretations holding that the two words "charitable" and "benevolent" are synonymous.

Where a gift is for specific named purposes, some of which are charitable and others of which are clearly not, if the noncharitable purposes are also recognized in law and the trust does not involve a violation of the Rule Against Perpetuities, the trust will not ordinarily fail; if necessary, the court will order a division of the gift. If, however, the noncharitable purposes are not recognized in law as the proper subject of a trust, or if the trust would involve a violation of the Rule Against Perpetuities, the courts have divided as to the proper disposition of the property. In some cases an apportionment has been made among the charitable and noncharitable purposes; those which were

---

[1] *Morice* v. *Bishop of Durham,* 9 Ves. 399 (1804), 10 Ves. 522 (1805).

[2] *Chichester Diocesan Fund* v. *Simpson,* [1944] A.C. 341, affirming *In re Diploch* [1941], Ch. 253, which reversed [1940] Ch. 988.

[3] See Keeton, George W., *op. cit.,* chap. 8, for a full discussion of the English cases and statutes.

[4] *In re Hayward's Estate,* 65 Ariz. 228, 178 P.2d 547 (1947) (trust for the benefit of any purposes deemed by trustees beneficial to town failed).

[5] Scott, Austin W., *op. cit.,* sec. 398.1, for citations.

valid were upheld, and the rest were declared to revert to the testator's heirs. In other cases the court directed that all of the property be applied to charitable purposes with the exception of a maximum amount which could conceivably be required for the invalid purpose, ruling that the trust failed as to that amount. In some cases the entire disposition has been upheld as charitable; while in others the entire gift has failed. The deciding factor in each of these situations has usually been the nature of the disposition and the willingness of the court to apply liberal rules of construction.[1]

Charitable Corporations

These definitions and descriptions of charitable purposes have referred almost exclusively to charitable trusts. For charitable corporations, the legal limitations as to purpose are initially to be found in the statutes authorizing creation of the corporation. These statutes vary from state to state. Some states have separate statutes for different types of charitable organizations, such as religious societies, educational institutions, or charitable foundations. Thus, in some jurisdictions there may be two or more statutes under which a foundation may be created.[2] In still others, provision for incorporating all types of charitable organizations are included in a statute providing for incorporation of not-for-profit organizations.[3] Under the latter statutes, the same procedure may be followed to incorporate a social club, a golf club, a political organization, or a foundation.

Rarely is there a statutory definition of the purposes that are listed in these corporation laws.[4] The test for determining if a corporation is

---

[1] *Ibid.,* sec. 398.2.

[2] See, for example, Cal. Corp. Code, secs. 9000ff. (Gen. Nonprofit Corp. Law) and secs. 10200ff. (Corps. for Charitable or Eleemosynary Purposes); Mich. Stat. Ann., secs. 21.118 ff. (Nonprofit Corps.) and secs. 21.164 ff. (Foundations).

[3] As in Conn. Gen. Stat. Rev., secs. 33–419ff. (Nonstock Corp. Act); Del. Code Ann., tit. 8, secs. 101 ff.; and Iowa Code Ann., secs. 504.1 ff. (Corps. not for pecuniary profit).

[4] The Louisiana law states merely that a nonprofit corporation is "a corporation organized for purposes not having pecuniary profit or gain to its shareholders or members and not paying dividends" (La. Rev. Stat., sec. 12:101). The Wisconsin Nonstock Corporation Law (Wis. Stat., sec. 181.03) states, "Corporations may be organized under this chapter for any lawful purpose whatever except banking insurance, and building or operating public railroads. . . ." The Texas act (Tex. Rev. Civ. Stat., art. 1396–2.01) states, ". . . nonprofit corporations may be organized under this Act for any lawful purpose . . . which may include . . . charitable, benevolent, religious, eleemosynary, patriotic, civic, missionary, educational, scientific, social, fraternal . . . ," etc.

"charitable" in the legal sense of the word is made by the courts by reference to the law of charitable dispositions discussed above.[1]

In some states, incorporation is possible by means of special acts of the legislature as well as under general corporation laws. Throughout most of the nineteenth century, this was the only method of incorporation; but with the enactment of general statutes prescribing administrative methods for incorporation, it fell into disuse and has actually been prohibited by the constitutions of many states. Where a state legislature retains the power to create corporations by special act, of course, its authority is broad enough to enlarge the class of charitable purposes. Once a corporation is created by means of a special act, its existence, powers, capacities, and mode of exercising them will be dependent on the law creating the corporation, not on the general body of law relating to charitable corporations of the state unless the special act is silent as to the matter.[2]

The power of the legislature is not absolute, however. Once a charitable corporation is formed, no legislature may change its initial purpose or control the method of administration designated in its charter. This is because Article I, Section 10 of the United States Constitution prohibits a state from passing any law impairing the obligation of contract. The constitutional provision was first applied to corporations in the case of *Trustees of Dartmouth College* v. *Woodward*,[3] involving an attempt by the legislature of New Hampshire to alter the charter of a charitable corporation, Dartmouth College, which had been created by special act. The Supreme Court held that there was an implied contract on the part of the state with every benefactor who should give money to the corporation. An alteration of the charter without the consent of the trustees would be a violation of this contract and therefore an unconstitutional act.[4]

Today the statutes providing administrative methods for incorporation include clauses that reserve a power to amend charters granted thereunder. While these have minimized the effect of the *Dartmouth* case, they have been held to be applicable to changes in administra-

---

[1] "The test of a charitable gift or use and a charitable corporation are the same." *Matter of Rockefeller's Estate,* 165 N.Y.S. 154, 177 App. Div. 786 (1917), affirmed 223 N.Y. 563, 119 N.E. 1074 (1918).

[2] *Penobscot Boom Corp.* v. *Lamson,* 16 Me. 224 (1839).

[3] 4 Wheat. 518, 4 L.Ed. 629 (U.S. 1819).

[4] See Scott, Austin W., "Education and the Dead Hand," *Harvard Law Review,* vol. 34, 1920, p. 1, for a general discussion of the power of the legislature to authorize amendments to the charters of charitable corporations.

tion, but not to any "alteration that defeats or fundamentally changes the corporate purpose." Such a measure is unconstitutional, no matter what powers a legislature may attempt to reserve to itself at the time of creation.[1] However, if the governing body of the charitable corporation assents to an amendment, the legislation is not unconstitutional.[2]

In the absence of a specific legislative declaration, the method of creation and, therefore, the form of a charitable institution does not influence the courts in the determination of the validity of its purposes. Once the determination of validity has been made, the enforcement procedures, the application of the *cy pres* doctrine, and the eligibility for certain tax exemptions from both the state and federal governments are applicable to a corporation just as they are to a charitable trust. Thus, it is necessary to define carefully the purposes of a corporate foundation in terms of both the statute under which it will be organized and the law of charitable uses of the state where it is to be created.

Definitions in Federal Tax Laws

This entire problem of definition of charitable purposes in terms of property or corporation law has been subordinated in recent years by another facet of government restriction on charitable activities: that of the federal laws of taxation.

Tax privileges are granted by the United States government to those foundations that meet certain requirements as to function and operation. The requirements as to function were included in the first income tax law of 1894,[3] which allowed an exemption for any corporation or association organized exclusively for religious, education, or charitable purposes. Although this statute was declared unconstitutional by the United States Supreme Court in 1895,[4] subsequent enactments have all contained exemptions based on this wording. The Corporation Excise Act of 1909[5] contained the provision that the tax did not apply "to any corporation or association organized or operated exclusively for religious, educational, or charitable purposes, no part

---

[1] *Board of Regents of the University of Maryland* v. *Trustees of the Endowment Fund of the University of Maryland*, 206 Md. 559, 112 A.2d 678, certiorari denied, 350 U.S. 836 (1955).

[2] *Matter of Mt. Sinai Hospital*, 250 N.Y. 103, 164 N.E. 871 (1928).

[3] 28 Stat. 556 (1894).

[4] *Pollock* v. *Farmers' Loan & Trust Co.*, 158 U.S. 601 (1895).

[5] 36 Stat. 11 (1909).

of the net income of which inures to the benefit of any private stock-holder or individual." The language of this exemption, with the addition of the word "scientific," was repeated in the Income Tax Act of 1913,[1] and again in 1916[2] and 1918.[3]

In 1917 the important corollary provision was enacted that permitted a taxpayer to deduct contributions to exempt organizations from his personal income tax.[4] In the Revenue Act of 1921, the word 'literary" and the phrase "or the prevention of cruelty to children or animals" were added to the descriptive phrase;[5] and in 1934 a qualification in regard to political activity first appeared as part of the statute,[6] although political activity had been regarded as grounds for denial of exemption by regulation and decisions prior to that time.[7]

Similar exemptions were included in the Estate and Gift Tax Laws of 1916[8] and 1926[9] and in the Excise Tax Law for admissions.[10]

Today these provisions are to be found in the Internal Revenue Code of 1954 in sections 501(c)3, 170(c), 642(c), 2055, 2106(a) (2), and 2522. These provisions currently exert the greatest governmental influence on the stated purposes for which foundations are being formed. In fact, the great majority of charitable foundations that have been established in this decade recite as their purpose the exact language of the provision of section 501(c)(3) of the Internal Revenue Code, which states that exemption from taxation shall be granted to:

> Corporations and any community chest, fund, or foundation, organized and operated exclusively for religious, charitable, scientific, testing for public safety, library or educational purposes, or for the prevention of cruelty to children or animals, no part of the net earnings of which inures to the benefit of any private shareholder or individual, no substantial part of the activities of which is carrying on propaganda, or otherwise attempting, to influence legislation, and which does not participate in, or intervene in (including the publishing or distributing of statements), any political campaign on behalf of any candidate for public office.

---

[1] 38 Stat. 172 (1913).
[2] 39 Stat. 756 (1916).
[3] 40 Stat. 1057 (1918).
[4] 40 Stat. 300, 330 (1917).
[5] 42 Stat. 227 (1921).
[6] 48 Stat. 680, 690, 700, 755, 760 (1934).
[7] Clark, Elias, "The Limitation on Political Activities . . . ," *op. cit.*, p. 445.
[8] 39 Stat. 777 (1916).
[9] 44 Stat. 69 (1926).
[10] 43 Stat. 320 (1924).

In an article entitled "How to Draft the Charter or Indenture of a Charity so as to Qualify for Federal Tax Exemption,"[1] prepared by three members of the Section on Taxation of the American Bar Association, the authors strongly recommend that purposes should "track the statute."

> There is often a desire to use special language that is more descriptive of the particular purposes for which the foundation is organized. The Regulations recite that the articles of organization may be as broad as, or more specific than, the purposes stated in Section 501(c)(3) of the Code. In no event may the purposes be *broader* than those specified in Section 501(c)(3). Reg. secs. 1. 501(c)(3)-1(b)(1) and (2). For this reason there is danger in using special language in the trust instrument. Where such language is used, care must be exercised, and patience may be required before the exemption is approved. The use of the simple language of the federal tax statute has obvious advantages. The Service prefers that the instrument adhere to simple purposes.[2]

This suggestion was strongly criticized on the grounds that laws and regulations change so that "what successfully 'tracks' today's statute, or eases the minds of our present Internal Revenue Service, may actually obstruct foundation operations in years to come . . ."[3] It was noted, however, that the broad all-inclusive language that results from "tracking the statute" does have the advantage of obviating possible conflicts between state and federal laws as to the validity of particular charitable purposes. The federal courts are not bound by state law in determining whether a particular charitable organization is eligible for tax exemption within the terms of the federal tax laws. The rule is based on the obvious need for uniformity in the administration of federal laws.[4]

---

[1] Eaton, Berrien C., Jr., and collaborators, in *Practical Lawyer,* vol. 8, October, 1962, p. 13; and vol. 8, November, 1962, p. 87.

[2] *Ibid.,* November, 1962, p. 90.

[3] Raffel, Burton, "Philanthropy and the Legal Mind: An Editorial," *Foundation News,* vol. 4, March, 1963, p. 6.

[4] An example of the attitude of the federal courts is to be found in the following language from the Federal Tax Court in the case of *Susan Young Egan* v. *Commissioner,* 17 B.T.A. 694, 702 (1929), reversed, 43 F.2d 881 (5th Cir. 1930). "The administration of this act must, in matters such as this, transcend any local law of statute or decision. . . . There would be hopeless confusion if deduction were allowed of a bequest because of the state of decedent's domicile recognized it as charitable in consonance with the Statute of Elizabeth, and denied a similar bequest of a decedent residing in a state holding a different view." See also Paul, Randolph E., *Federal Estate and Gift Taxation,* Little, Brown and Co., Boston, 1942, vol. 1, secs. 12.05 to 12.17; and Baker, Newman F., "Judicial Interpretation of Tax Exemption Statutes," *Texas Law Review,* vol. 7, 1929, p. 385.

Internal Revenue Service Regulations, promulgated from time to time to clarify provisions of the Code, have included attempts to define "charitable." The most recent regulations relating to exempt organizations, approved on June 22, 1959 (T.D. 6391), define "charitable" as follows:

> The term "charitable" is used in Sec. 501(c)(3) in its generally accepted legal sense and is, therefore, not to be construed as limited by the separate enumeration in Sec. 501(c)(3) of other tax-exempt purposes which may fall within the broad outlines of "charity" as developed by judicial decisions. Such term includes: relief of the poor and distressed or of the underprivileged; advancement of religion; advancement of education or science; erection or maintenance of public buildings, monuments or works; lessening of the burdens of government; and promotion of social welfare by organizations designed to accomplish any of the above purposes, or (i) to lessen neighborhood tensions; (ii) to eliminate prejudice and discrimination; (iii) to defend human and civil rights secured by law; or (iv) to combat community deterioration and juvenile delinquency.[1]

The influence of the Statute of Charitable Uses is again evident in this enumeration, but it is the federal courts that decide the individual cases on the basis of federal precedents, not the decisions of state courts as to validity under state law.

This does not mean that the federal courts make their determination in a vacuum. Some cases even suggest that the federal decision was made on the basis of state law.[2] In the majority of these instances, however, the court referred to state law for an interpretation of the meaning assignable to particular words or terms in a charter or trust indenture of a particular charity. Treasury Regulation 1.501(c) (3)–1(b) (5) states:

> The law of the State in which an organization is created shall be controlling in construing the terms of its articles (i.e. charter, trust instrument). However, any organization which contends that such terms have under State law a different meaning from their generally accepted meaning must establish such special meaning by clear and convincing reference to relevant court decisions, opinions of the State attorney-general, or other evidence of applicable State law.

---

[1] Treas. Reg. 1.501(c)(3)–1(d)(2) (1959). Definitions of "educational" and "scientific" are contained in Treas. Reg. 1.501(c)(3)–1(d)(3) (1959) and 1.501(c)(3)–1(d)(5) (1959).

[2] *Gallagher* v. *Smith*, 223 F.2d 218 (3d Cir. 1955); *Schoellkopf* v. *U.S.*, 124 F.2d 982 (2d Cir. 1942).

When a settlor decides to create a foundation, his first consideration is usually the likelihood of obtaining a federal tax exemption. It is extremely unlikely that the purposes of the foundation will be questioned by a state official at the time of creation,[1] and if they are challenged, the policy of the state courts is to uphold, wherever possible, the intent of the donor. Interpretation of tax law is a different matter. The general rule of construction is that exemption provisions of tax laws are to be strictly construed in favor of the government, although the rule is not always applied to cases involving charitable organizations.[2] However, only a minority of cases reach the courts. The average donor is not interested in the extended, expensive litigation which a resort to the federal courts entails. His aim is to obtain exemption from the Internal Revenue Service as easily as possible. This means meeting the standards and tests laid down by Treasury officials who are trained to consider all requests for exemptions as suspect. Their orientation is toward producing revenue for the federal government. To them, every tax exemption granted means loss of revenue. They have not been grounded in the concepts which underlie the law of charity.

It follows that there are certain categories of charitable purposes which invariably cause difficulty. A large number of these in recent years have involved charitable foundations which benefit employees of a company that is owned or controlled by the donor. Thus, a trust where the principal purpose was determined by the court to be the payment of pensions to employees of the donor was denied exemption,[3] as was a trust to erect homes for employees,[4] although exemption was allowed to a foundation which was created to assist employees and their families in case of illness, misfortune, temporary unemployment, or death.[5]

A second area of conflict has involved educational or scientific research foundations which do work on contract for private industry. In fact, regulations[6] relating to scientific purposes were promulgated a full year after the regulations of 1960, because of a need for extended discussion and revision of the original Treasury proposals. They still contain no definition of the term "scientific," although they discuss in

---

[1] See Chapter IV.
[2] *Helvering* v. *Bliss,* 293 U.S. 144, 151, 55 Sup. Ct. 17 (1934).
[3] *Duffy* v. *Birmingham,* 190 F.2d 738 (8th Cir. 1951).
[4] *Harvey* v. *Campbell,* 107 F. Supp. 757 (D.C.N.D. Tex. 1952).
[5] *Moss Tie Co.,* 18 T.C. 188 (May 7, 1952), appeal dismissed per curiam 201 F.3d 5–12 (8th Cir. 1953).
[6] Treas. Reg. 1.501(c)(3)–1(d) (5) added by T.D. 6525, Jan. 10, 1961.

detail the question of "scientific research" and contain a "public interest" test for determining eligibility for exemption.[1]

The question of the donor's motive may be raised in the determination of tax exemption, but it is not the subjective motive that is questioned. The subjective motive of many charitable donations is the avoidance of taxes, and the tax laws are actually written so as to bring this motive to the fore for many donors. The tax laws direct the administrators to look to the actual results of a disposition and if they find either lack of public benefit or private profit to the donor, to deny the exemption.[2] Thus, if the purpose is merely to further a special interest of the donor, exemption is usually denied. For example, a foundation whose purpose was to make known and explain to the world the meaning of the donor's writings was denied exemption,[3] as was a "church" which was organized to be a vehicle to finance a personal feud of the donor.[4]

If the private benefit is incidental to a clearly public purpose, however, exemption is usually allowed. Thus, exemption was granted to a general charitable foundation established by Bob Hope and his wife to which they conveyed all the rights to their life story, which when it was subsequently sold and published, gave the Hopes the benefit of publicity. The court held that the publicity was neither the dominating motive nor the primary purpose of the foundation.[5] At the opposite extreme was the case of a foundation created by Horace Heidt to assist young people in the entertainment world and also to make expenditures for education, medicine, and public health. The foundation was denied exemption because it publicized the founder's shows and reduced his personal expenses by assisting only the young artists who were his employees. Here, the factors of motive plus a personal benefit to the founder combined to create a situation which the court held was beyond the provision of the tax laws.[6]

It should be noted, however, that tax law differs most markedly from substantive property law in its denial of exemption to organizations whose purpose is to change existing laws. However, it is not the

---

[1] Treas. Reg. 1.501 (c) (3)–1(d)(5)(iii).
[2] Int. Rev. Code of 1954, sec. 501 (c(3).
[3] Rev. Rule 55–231, 1955–1 Cum. Bull. 72.
[4] *Puritan Church,* 10 T.C.M. 485 (1951), affirmed 209 F.2d 306 (C.A. D.C. 1953), certiorari denied 347 U.S. 975, 98 L.Ed. 1115 (1953).
[5] *Bob & Dolores Hope Foundation,* 61–1 U.S.T.C. paragraph 9437 (D.C.S.D. Cal. 1961).
[6] *Horace Heidt Foundation* v. *U.S.,* 170 F. Supp. 634 (Ct. Cl. 1959).

Treasury but the Congress itself that has demarcated the difference by specifically denying exempt status to any organization that devotes a substantial part of its activities to "carrying on propaganda, or otherwise attempting, to influence legislation."[1]

Definitions in State Tax Laws

A parallel situation exists in connection with the exemption of charitable enterprises from inheritance, estate, income, and property taxes imposed by the various states. Decisions as to imposition of tax are made by the state courts by reference to the statute granting exemption. There is little uniformity in these taxation statutes.

Exemption from taxes on real property is usually granted only to property actually occupied and in use for the charitable purpose of the organization, and exemption is rarely allowed for income-producing property even if the income is applied to the charitable purpose. Often the exemption is not available to a foreign corporation without a showing that a substantial portion of its activities is carried on within the state. In some jurisdictions a further distinction is made between property owned by a charitable corporation, which is granted exemption, and property owned by a trust, which may not be.[2]

The wording used in the statutes to describe the "purposes" of institutions eligible for tax exemption also varies from state to state. Usually it takes the form of a statement like that of the New York statute, which exempts the property of corporations or associations organized for any of 22 different specific charitable purposes.[3] The Pennsylvania statute exempts institutions of purely public charity.[4]

It is, of course, possible to have a determination that property of a particular institution is not eligible for tax exemption, even though there may be a court determination, based on other issues, that the institution is a valid charity. A classic case of this nature involved the Boston Symphony Orchestra. The Massachusetts court held that the orchestra was subject to a property tax on its hall, since it charged admission and permitted certain renewable season ticket privileges. This decision was criticized by Scott on the grounds that the fact that admission is charged is not sufficient to deny status as charitable to an

---

[1] Int. Rev. Code of 1954, sec. 501(c)(3); Treas. Reg., sec. 1.501(c)(3)–1(c); see also Clark, Elias, "The Limitation on Political Activities . . . ," *op. cit.*

[2] For example, see Mass. Gen. Laws Ann., ch. 59, sec. 5, and N.Y. Real Prop. Tax Law, secs. 402, 438.

[3] N.Y. Real Prop. Tax Law, sec. 402.

[4] Pa. Stat. Ann., tit. 72, sec. 3244.

organization.[1] In 1961 the Massachusetts court determined that the orchestra was not subject to tort liability on the basis of the fact that it was a valid charitable organization.[2]

The state courts are more frequently liberal in cases involving the validity of a charity than in cases interpreting tax laws.[3] The provision in the Ohio property tax law grants exemption only if the property is used for the charitable purpose. In *Wehrle Foundation* v. *Evatt et al.,*[4] the Ohio court ruled that property used as offices by a foundation which was engaged solely in making grants to other charitable organizations was not property used for charitable purposes within the meaning of the statute.

The matter of exemption from state inheritance, gift, and income taxes is of greater immediate importance to the majority of foundations. Here again there is wide variation in the statutory language in the various states. At one time it was the general rule that deductions would be permitted only for transfers to institutions and corporations located in the state granting the deductions and that all exempt trusts must be limited to use within the state. Often these restrictions were not based on express statutory language, but were the result of court determinations that exemption statutes should be strictly construed and that the state should not be presumed to authorize exemption for purposes having little or no relation to the welfare of its inhabitants.[5] Today, however, the majority of states have provisions permitting exemption for legacies to nonresident charities if there would be no tax under the laws of the state where the foreign charity is located or if that state has provisions granting reciprocity for exemptions of this type. Variations are so great, however, that the provisions of each jurisdiction must be carefully scrutinized.[6]

The existence of these conflicting decisions and policies is inevitable in our system of government. It is accentuated in the United States by the federal system of government, but it is equally evident

---

[1] *Boston Symphony Orchestra, Inc.* v. *Board of Assessors,* 294 Mass. 248, 1 N.E.2d 6 (1936).

[2] *Boxer* v. *Boston Symphony Orchestra, Inc.,* 339 Mass. 369, 159 N.E.2d 336 (1959); and 342 Mass. 537, 174 N.E.2d 363 (1961).

[3] *Rivers Oaks Garden Club* v. *City of Houston,* ____ Tex. ____, 370 S.W.2d 851 (1963); but see *Samarkand of Santa Barbara* v. *County of Santa Barbara,* 31 Cal. Rept. 151 (1963).

[4] 141 Ohio St. 467, 49 N.E.2d 52 (1943).

[5] Bogert, George G., and George T. Bogert, *op. cit.,* sec. 290b.

[6] See *Inheritance Estate and Gift Tax Reporter, State,* 7th ed., Commerce Clearing House, Chicago, 1960, vol. 4, p. 81,029, paragraph 12,020; pp. 80,078 to 80,079, paragraph 1310D-A, for provisions in all states.

in England.[1] Liberality of construction and flexibility of definition have kept the conflicts to a minimum, however, and have created safeguards against rigidity. There is no question, however, that greater communication among the state and federal officials in the legislative, administrative, and judicial branches who deal with the questions of charitable purposes would be of substantial value, not only for reconciling technical or minor questions, but for broadening the viewpoint of all concerned. The aim of such interchange should be, as one writer has stated, to keep "statutes, judicial decisions and administrative rulings in realistic as well as theoretical mesh with the developments of the day, so as to minimize the possibility of abuse or distortion, and to preserve the field in which philanthropic enterprises continue to perform socially valuable services in a pluralistic society."[2]

The Obsolete Purpose

A consideration of the purposes recognized as valid for creating a perpetual charity raises the question of the means by which the law assures that these perpetuities will continue to be of public benefit in a changing society.

The currently popular practice of adopting the broad language of the federal tax exemption statute to describe a foundation's purposes, although it is unimaginative,[3] does have the advantage of assuring that initial purposes will not become obsolete in future years. This is of great importance in view of the rise in the number of foundations created in the past twenty years.

The problem of obsolescence has been further minimized by a provision of the Treasury Regulations which requires as a condition for exemption that upon dissolution or termination a foundation's assets must be distributed for one or more exempt purposes or turned over to a federal, state, or local government for public purposes.[4] This requirement may be satisfied either by an express provision in the articles of incorporation or trust indenture or by establishing that under the state law the assets must be so distributed. In short, the Internal Revenue Service requires that there be at least a limited application of the concepts of the *cy pres* doctrine available for each foundation granted exemption.

---

[1] Keeton, George W., *op. cit., passim.*
[2] Chambers, M. M., *Charters of Philanthropies.* Carnegie Foundation for the Advancement of Teaching, New York, 1948, p. 4.
[3] Raffel, Burton, *op. cit.,* p. 6.
[4] Treas. Reg., sec. 1.501(c)(3)–1(b)(4).

There can be no question of the wisdom of such a policy. The law records are replete with examples of charitable trusts whose purposes or manner of operation have become outmoded. In England, where the application of the doctrine of *cy pres* has been narrowly limited by the courts, the examples of obsolete charities or obsolete restrictions that have been carried out for decades are numerous.[1] In the United States, although the *cy pres* doctrine has been applied with greater liberality, there are still many instances of the "dead hand" ruling long after the utility of the original plan has become outdated.[2] Of the 6,007 foundations listed in *The Foundation Directory, Edition 2,* 479 are classified as "special purpose," meaning that these funds are devoted to closely detailed charitable purposes. It can also be assumed from past experience that some of the 9,000 foundations too small for inclusion in the *Directory* are also in this special purpose category. The problem of obsolescence, and more particularly of inefficiency, is even greater in the case of these small endowments.

The *cy pres* doctrine is now generally accepted as part of the common law of the majority of the states.[3] Thirteen have statutes embodying the doctrine and applying it to charitable trusts. A Model Act Concerning the Administration of Charitable Trusts, Devises, and Bequests, containing *cy pres* provisions, was recommended by the Commissioners on Uniform State Laws in 1944. It has been enacted in Maryland, Vermont, and, with some modification, in Alabama.

In the absence of statute, the doctrine of *cy pres* is generally applicable only after three conditions have been met: (1) A valid charitable trust or a corporation that can be considered a valid charity must exist. (2) It must be impossible or impractical to carry out the donor's original intention. (3) The donor must have had a general charitable intention as well as the intention to benefit the particular charitable object he designated.[4]

To invoke the doctrine of *cy pres,* the trustees or the attorney gen-

---

[1] See Committee on the Law and Practice relating to Charitable Trusts, *op. cit.,* pp. 70–92, for a full discussion. The Charities Act of 1960 represents an attempt to remedy the situation. See pp. 33–34 for a discussion of its provisions.

[2] For examples see Simes, Lewis M., *Public Policy and the Dead Hand,* University of Michigan Press, Ann Arbor, 1955, pp. 125–131.

[3] See Table 1, Appendix A, for a complete list.

[4] Fisch, Edith L., *The Cy Près Doctrine in the United States,* Matthew Bender and Co., New York, 1950, pp. 128–201; *Restatement of the Law of Trusts (Second),* *op. cit.,* sec. 399; Scott, Austin W., *The Law of Trusts, op. cit.,* secs. 399, 399.4.

eral applies to the court for its permission or direction to deviate from the terms of the trust and to frame a scheme for the application of the property. The trustees or the attorney general often suggest a plan that the court may adopt. In complicated situations the court may appoint a master who will hear all interested parties and submit a proposal to the court. The attorney general is a necessary party to these proceedings.

The case of *Jackson* v. *Phillips*,[1] in which the court recited what is now considered a classic definition of valid charitable purposes, was brought by trustees seeking instructions as to the validity of a bequest in trust to create by various means "a public sentiment that will put an end to Negro slavery in this country." An additional sum was also left in trust to assist fugitive slaves. The testator died in 1861, and in 1865 the Thirteenth Amendment to the Constitution was adopted. The testator's heirs claimed that the trust failed, but the court held that the doctrine of *cy pres* was applicable. "Neither the immediate purpose of the testator—the moral education of the people; nor his ultimate object—to better the conditions of the African race in this country, has been fully accomplished by the abolition of slavery." The case was referred to a master, whose report was approved with minor changes by the Massachusetts Supreme Judicial Court. The trustees were directed to hold in trust the money left to create a public sentiment that would put an end to slavery and pay over in their discretion such sums, at such times, as they thought fit to the treasurer of the New England Branch of the Freedmen's Bureau, to be expended to aid former slaves in the states in which slavery had been abolished by the Emancipation Proclamation or the Thirteenth Amendment. The money left to assist fugitive slaves was to be applied to the use of necessitous persons of African descent in the city of Boston and its vicinity, preference to be given to those who had escaped from slavery.

Criticism of the application of the *cy pres* doctrine in the United States today has centered on each of the three conditions listed above. Some critics believe that the requirement of a showing of general charitable intent should be eliminated.[2] They suggest that any gift for a charitable purpose should be, by implication, "for charity," and the

---

[1] 14 Allen 539 (Mass. 1867). See p. 56.

[2] Simes, Lewis M., *op. cit.*, p. 139; Karst, Kenneth L., "The Efficiency of the Charitable Dollar: An Unfulfilled State Responsibility," *Harvard Law Review*, vol. 73, 1960, p. 433. Bogert, George G., and George T. Bogert, *op. cit.*, sec. 436.

only way to avoid this implication should be for a donor to affix a condition or limitation to the gift specifically calling for termination of the trust on failure to carry out the specific purpose. Furthermore, they propose, such a condition or limitation should be void unless limited to take effect within a fixed period of time such as thirty or thirty-five years or within the time prescribed in the Rule Against Perpetuities.

It is true that some of the recent cases have assumed a general charitable intent from the existence of the gift in question, particularly if it was in the residue of a testator's estate. The Massachusetts Supreme Judicial Court in a recent decision permitted the *cy pres* application of a gift of a testatrix's "homestead" and funds to establish a home for aged women in the town where she resided with a requirement that only women over sixty-five who did not smoke or drink be admitted. The bequest was not contained in the residuary clause. The court said:

> We accordingly attach no particular significance to the fact that the testatrix included a general residuary clause, naming as residuary legatees her closest relatives. The use of a residuary clause does not per se manifest a desire to benefit the residuary legatees if the trust cannot be executed in the precise manner described in the will. Per contra, the absence of a gift over provision if the trust should fail does carry significance as indicating a general charitable intent.[1]

Moreover, the court did not consider either the request to restrict admissions or a further direction that the home be named for the testatrix to be evidence of lack of general intent.

An example of a gift which failed because the court refused to find a general charitable intent was a recent Connecticut case where the court held that two charitable funds established in 1936 for the distribution of interest-free loans and food to needy Jews of Charrish, Poland, failed since the later extermination of the Jewish population in 1942 made it impossible to effectuate the trusts.[2]

Major criticism has also been directed against the second requirement—that it must be impossible or impracticable to carry out the donor's purposes. The model act recommended by the Commissioners

---

[1] *Caroline S. Rogers et al.* v. *Attorney General et al.* 347 Mass. 126, 196 N.E.2d 855 (1964).

[2] *Conn. Bank & Trust Co., Trustee* v. *Coles, Attorney General,* 150 Conn. 569, 192 A.2d 202 (1963).

on Uniform State Laws and adopted in Maryland[1] and Vermont[2] permits administration *cy pres* if the trust is or becomes "illegal or impossible or impracticable of fulfillment." Similar legislation is found in the statutes in Louisiana,[3] Wisconsin,[4] New York,[5] and Pennsylvania.[6]

In Alabama the statute refers only to impracticability,[7] in Virginia, only to impossibility.[8] In Georgia, the stationary standard is that the trust is "incapable for some reason of execution in the exact manner"[9] designated by the donor. The West Virginia statute is applicable to a trust that does not admit of specific performance or literal execution;[10] and the Rhode Island wording is "purposes which cannot be literally carried into effect."[11]

Proponents of change feel that it should be sufficient to show that it is inexpedient or not in the public interest to carry out the stated purposes. This is the approach of the English law today. Only two states, Minnesota[12] and South Dakota,[13] however, have enacted statutes which include the word "inexpedient." Furthermore, the Minnesota statute requires the consent of the trustees and the donor if living and mentally competent, and the South Dakota statute requires consent of the donor.

The director of the Register of Charitable Trusts in the Office of the Attorney General in New Hampshire introduced legislation in that state in 1963 which provided:

> If property is or has been given in trust to be applied to a charitable purpose, and said purpose or its application is or becomes impossible or impracticable or illegal or obsolete or inexpedient or ineffective or prejudicial to the public interest to carry out, the trust will not fail but the court, upon petition by the trustee or trustees or the director of charitable trusts, will direct the application of the property to some charitable purpose which is useful to the community.[14]

---

[1] Md. Ann. Code, art. 16, sec. 295.
[2] Vt. Stat. Ann., tit. 14, sec. 2328.
[3] La. Rev. Stat., secs. 9:2331 to 9:2337.
[4] Wis. Stat., sec. 231.11(7)(d).
[5] N.Y. Pers. Prop. Law, sec. 12(2); and N.Y. Real Prop. Law, sec. 113(2).
[6] Pa. Stat. Ann., tit. 20, sec. 301.10.
[7] Ala. Code, tit. 47, sec. 145.
[8] Va. Code Ann., sec. 55–31.
[9] Ga. Code Ann., secs. 108–202, 113–815.
[10] W. Va. Code Ann., sec. 3502.
[11] R.I. Gen. Laws Ann., sec. 18–4–1.
[12] Minn. Stat. Ann., sec. 501.12, subdiv. 12.
[13] S.D. Code, sec. 59.0603.
[14] State of New Hampshire, Senate Bill No. 27 (1963).

The bill was passed by the Senate, but was referred by the House to the Judicial Council for an opinion. The wording of this bill is broader than that of any other that has appeared in this country.

In jurisdictions where the exeicse of the *cy pres* doctrine is considered part of the common law equity powers of the court, the early decisions refused to permit changes on the grounds of impracticability. A leading case was *President and Fellows of Harvard College* v. *Attorney General*,[1] where a testator left a large sum of money to Harvard College for the purpose of founding an engineering school. The College requested permission of the court to apply part of the funds for expansion of the admittedly superior engineering school at Massachusetts Institute of Technology and for the use of the liberal arts facilities of Harvard by M.I.T. students. The court agreed that the plan provided for a more effective use of testator's gift, but since there was no fundamental reason why his plan could not be carried out, the petition was denied.

This attitude is still to be found in many decisions. Karst voiced criticism of a similar holding in a more recent Colorado case.[2]

> Presumably such decisions are rested on the notion that we must preserve the testator's scheme in order to encourage more testators to give for charity. That may be, and there are other good reasons for respecting a man's disposition of his property. But decisions such as *Moore* assume that a testator such as George Clayton would be fool enough to insist on a rigid adherence to his original plan long after it had ceased to make sense. Such an assumption does no respect to the founders of charities.[3]

Another aspect of the question of impracticability is the problem raised by funds too small to be operated efficiently. At the extreme are trusts for the benefit of inhabitants of small towns, the income of which is barely sufficient to cover the cost of preparing the trustee's accounts for court filing. Several trusts of this nature are on record in Massachusetts. Pennsylvania recognized this problem in 1933 and, by statute, permits a court having jurisdiction over two or more char-

---

[1] 228 Mass. 396, 117 N.E. 903 (1917).

[2] *Moore* v. *City and County of Denver,* 133 Colo. 190, 292 P.2d 986 (1956). See also *Hinkley Home Corp.* v. *Bracken,* 21 Conn. Supp. 222, 152 A.2d 325 (Super. Ct. 1959).

[3] Karst, Kenneth L., "The Efficiency of the Charitable Dollar: An Unfulfilled State Responsibility," *Harvard Law Review,* vol. 73, 1960, p. 471. Copyright © 1960 by the Harvard Law Review Association.

itable trusts with substantially the same purposes to combine them if it is found that they can be thereby "more effectively administered."[1]

New Hampshire, in 1955, enacted legislation empowering a judge of probate to appoint a public trustee to administer such small charitable trusts as the court may assign to him where it is found that the difficulties or expense involved in each trust would tend to defeat its purpose, provided the trustee consents. The public trustee is authorized to establish common trust funds in which he may combine the trusts under his care, if the instrument contained no explicit prohibition.[2] This legislation is similar to provisions in the English law. The recent enactment of statutes in nearly every state permitting investment by trustees through common trust funds[3] will make it possible for trustees voluntarily to combine funds for investment. In the majority of states, however, compulsory pooling will depend on court interpretation of its *cy pres* doctrine or its willingness to expand the doctrine of "deviation." This latter doctrine, applicable to all trusts, grants to an equity court the power to permit deviations from the terms of a trust if compliance appears to be impossible or illegal. It is generally limited to administration provisions, however, and does not extend to alterations of purpose.[4]

The third condition for application *cy pres* is that the property be applied to purposes as near as possible to those of the initial gift.[5] Some writers have advocated that the standard be broadened to permit an application that observes the spirit of the donor's intention. Such a procedure was followed in an Ohio case in 1955 where permission was granted to use the income from three trusts established for the purchase of art objects for the Cleveland Museum of Art to help build an addition to the building.[6] Similarly in a New Jersey case in 1949, funds left by a testator to be used to publish his scientific works, which turned out to have no scientific value whatever, were given by the court to Princeton University to hold and apply the income to support research in the philosophy department.[7]

---

[1] Pa. Stat. Ann., tit. 20, sec. 301.9.

[2] N.H. Rev. Stat. Ann. secs. 564:2-a to 564:2-c.

[3] See pp. 277–278.

[4] See p. 102.

[5] The closely related question of where the authority for framing schemes should be placed will be discussed as part of the entire problem of supervision of charitable foundations.

[6] *Cleveland Museum of Art* v. *O'Neill*, 72 Ohio L. Abs. 11, 129 N.E.2d 669 (C.P. 1955).

[7] *Wilbur* v. *Owens*, 2 N.J. 167, 65 A.2d 843 (1949), affirming *Wilbur* v. *Asbury Park National Bank & Trust Co.*, 142 N.J. Eq. 99, 59 A.2d 570 (Ch. 1948). See also Karst, Kenneth L., *op. cit.*, p. 470.

The lack of uniformity in the approach of the courts to questions of *cy pres* strengthens the argument for legislation establishing broader provisions for its application. For example, in jurisdictions that have rejected the *cy pres* doctrine, it is possible to find cases where the courts have permitted changes in the plan of the donor under the doctrine of deviation; these would be considered *cy pres* actions in jurisdictions that accept the doctrine. In the recent case of *Bell* v. *Shannon*,[1] the court permitted two trusts created by a husband and wife for the purpose of constructing and maintaining a charitable hospital to be administered jointly, and approved a request by the trustees that the funds be used to build a charity wing to an existing hospital. The court stated that this action did not constitute a prohibited application of the *cy pres* doctrine, which had been rejected many times by the courts of Tennessee; yet it discussed the general charitable intent of the donors, the fact that the funds were insufficient to build a hospital according to the original plan, and the similarity of the proposed scheme to that in the wills.

Most of the cases dealing with the *cy pres* doctrine have arisen in connection with trusts, although some have related to funds held in trust by charitable corporations. There are two cases which have been cited as holding that upon dissolution of a charitable corporation, any remaining assets are to be distributed among the members of the corporation.[2] The purpose of the corporation in each case was to promote temperance, and the organizations were not purely charitable but had certain characteristics of fraternal-benevolent societies. In the *McAlhany* case, the question before the court was whether the property should revert to the grantors or to the members. The court characterized the corporation as a benevolent and social group, not a charitable one, and held that the assets should be distributed to the members, not revert to the donors. The Alabama case cited *McAlhany* and followed its result.

Aside from the fact that it is doubtful that either of these corporations could be considered "charitable" in the legal sense, the question raised in both cases was the determination of the rights of grantors versus members to corporate property on dissolution. It has been stated that at early common law, upon the dissolution of a corporation, the realty reverted to the grantor, and the personalty reverted to the Crown. The American cases rejected this view in relation to business

---

[1] 212 Tenn. 28, 367 S.W.2d 761 (1963).
[2] *McAlhany* v. *Murray et al.*, 89 S.C. 440, 71 S.E. 1025 (1911); *Mobile Temperance Hall Association* v. *Holmes*, 189 Ala. 271, 65 S. 1020 (1914).

corporations,[1] but a few followed it in regard to nonprofit corporations.[2] The question became the subject of a "scholarly controversy" when Gray in the third edition of *The Rule Against Perpetuities* stated that the so-called common law doctrine rested on a dictum in a fifteenth-century case, was contrary to English law, and was "probably among those decantata which when carefully examined will be found not only 'obsolete and odious' but in fact to have never been law at all."[3] The *McAlhany* case, therefore, represented a return to what was characterized as the "modern" view which rejected the rights of a donor, but in that instance the court favored them only over members.

Most recent cases have tended to follow an early Pennsylvania decision which held that property of a charitable corporation is to be distributed on dissolution to another charitable corporation for similar purposes.[4] In *In re Los Angeles County Pioneer Society,*[5] the court said specifically that transfer of the assets of a charitable corporation to another similar organization was not a confiscation of members' property in contravention of the Fourteenth Amendment of the United States Constitution, since the members at no time had a right to receive the property. The court also rejected, in that case, the right of grantors or their heirs to receive the property.

In 23 states the subject is now covered by specific legislation[6] requiring distribution *cy pres;* and most of these statutes do not require a showing of general charitable intention, although they permit recognition of a right of reversion if it is expressly stated.[7] Scott has suggested that it would be well to limit the right of reversion to the duration of the period of the Rule Against Perpetuities. The suggestion would certainly obviate the technical difficulties that arise when dissolution occurs many years after the death of the original donor.[8]

---

[1] Note "The Charitable Corporation," *Harvard Law Review,* vol. 35, 1921, p. 85; Ballantine points out that whether there is any real authority for this doctrine of reversion in the case of business corporations is very doubtful, but he notes that it has been applied in some American cases dealing with nonstock corporations. Ballantine, Henry Winthrop, *The Law of Corporations,* Callaghan and Co., Chicago, 1946, sec. 314.

[2] See *Mott* v. *Danville Seminary,* 129 Ill. 403, 21 N.E. 927 (1889).

[3] Gray, John Chipman, *The Rule Against Perpetuities.* 4th ed. Little, Brown and Co., Boston, 1942, sec. 51.

[4] *In re Centennial and Memorial Association,* 235 Pa. 206, 83 Atl. 683 (1912).

[5] 40 Cal.2d 852, 257 P.2d 1 (1953).

[6] See Table 2, Appendix A.

[7] *McDonough County Orphanage et al.* v. *Burnhart et al.,* 5 Ill. 2d 230, 125 N.E.2d 625 (1955).

[8] Cases which have upheld a revisionary right include: *Industrial National*

In those states where there is no specific legislation or court decisions requiring application of the funds *cy pres,* the situation may be complicated by the statutory provision for dissolution of corporations. If the corporation was organized under a business corporation law, the dissolution provisions are clearly inapplicable. General statutes for nonprofit corporations often provide for distribution of property among the members; this is the usual situation for fraternal organizations or clubs, but should not be presumed to apply to charities. The lack of such a statement in the corporation laws is misleading. However, the requirement of the Treasury Regulations[1] should serve to dispose of any questions in regard to corporations formed since its promulgation. This entire question of corporate dissolution is one which needs clarifying legislation in those states where the acts are silent as to corporations organized for charitable purposes.

Clearly the social utility of foundations can be preserved only by assuring that they may adjust to the ever-changing society they are designed to serve. The Anglo-American law reflects a policy decision that it is better not to limit the initial choice of a donor, but to permit adjustment when his chosen purposes become outmoded. The need for a liberal and broad application of the *cy pres* doctrine is evident so long as the law continues to follow this policy of granting freedom to the donors of charitable dispositions.

Bank v. *Drysdale,* 83 R.I. 172, 114 A.2d 191 (1955), affirmed 84 R.I. 385, 125 A.2d 87 (1956); *Townsend* v. *Charles Schalkenbach Home for Boys, Inc.,* 33 Wash.2d 255, 205 P.2d 345 (1949).

[1] Treas. Reg. sec. 1. 501(c)(3)–1(b)(4).

CHAPTER III

Foundations as Trusts

FOUNDATIONS ARE USUALLY CREATED in one of two distinct legal forms: trusts or corporations. Voluntary associations for charitable purposes are also recognized in law, but this form is rarely employed. The historical roots of the laws relating to charities are to be found in the law of trusts as it developed in the Courts of Chancery in England. This is a well-defined body of law, of which the law of charitable trusts forms a part.

A trust is a device for making dispositions of property whereby the legal title and the duties of management are given to a trustee who is charged with managing the property and applying it for the benefit of named beneficiaries. The right to enjoyment or the beneficial interest in the property belongs to the beneficiaries, who can enforce their rights against the trustees and the donor through appropriate court action.[1]

The *Restatement of the Law of Trusts* (*Second*) defines a charitable trust as follows:

> A charitable trust is a fiduciary relationship with respect to property arising as a result of a manifestation of an intention to create it and subjecting the person by whom the property is held to equitable duties to deal with the property for a charitable purpose.[2]

---

[1] Trusts are peculiar to Anglo-American law; although there are analogous institutions in other legal systems, none is as flexible. Maitland has said: "If we were asked what is the greatest and most distinctive achievement performed by Englishmen in the field of jurisprudence I cannot think that we should have any better answer to give than this, namely, the development from century to century of the trust idea." Maitland, Frederic W., *Equity*. 2d ed. University Press, Cambridge, England, 1936, p. 23.

[2] *Restatement of the Law of Trusts* (*Second*). American Law Institute, St.

Although technical, this definition does indicate the specific elements required by law for the creation of a charitable trust and the nature of the legal duties of the trustee which the law will enforce.

Requisites for the Creation of Charitable Trusts

There are three requirements for creating a charitable trust: (1) property that is to become the subject matter of the trust; (2) evidence of an intention to create the trust; (3) devotion to a purpose that the courts of the state where the trust is created will recognize as charitable.

The evidence required to establish an intent to create a charitable trust is usually a written declaration or deed, called the trust instrument or trust indenture. A written instrument may be required by law if the subject matter of the property is land and if the state where the land is situated has enacted a statute called the Statute of Frauds requiring that all transfers of land be in writing. Aside from this, there is no need for a written instrument, just as there is no need for consideration. An individual may create a charitable trust by declaring orally that he holds certain specific property as trustee for the benefit of some specific charitable purpose. This is rarely done, however, since the problem of proof is often difficult, particularly in connection with tax questions; and a donor will usually desire to specify provisions for its implementation.

Inter vivos trusts created during the lifetime of a donor may be formed without recourse to any court or state authority. In some states a donor may have the instrument recorded in a local court, although this again is rarely done.

Charitable trusts are often created by will, in which case they will not come into existence until sometime after the death of the donor. The document evidencing the creation of these trusts must conform to the requirements established for all testamentary dispositions in the state in which the will is executed. The trust will later be established under the supervision of the court of the state where the testator was domiciled at his death. This court will then oversee the disposition of the testator's entire estate and will usually retain power over the trust for its duration.

Provisions for Court Supervision

In many states a duty is placed on testamentary trustees to present accounts to the overseeing court at regular intervals for allowance.[1] For example, in Ohio a fiduciary is required to file at least once in each two years an account that includes itemized statements of receipts, disbursements, distributions, assets, and investments.[2] In Michigan he must file such a report at least once a year.[3] In other states trustees may in their discretion present accounts for allowance, but they are not required to do so until they resign or are removed, or the trust is ready for termination. Only four states have no provision regarding accounts of trustees. The Uniform Trustees' Accounting Act,[4] which has been enacted in Kansas,[5] Nevada,[6] and New Mexico,[7] provides that testamentary and nontestamentary trustees file accounts annually with the probate court. These accounts must show: the period covered by the account; the names and addresses of the beneficiaries; the trust principal at the beginning and end of the accounting period and how it is invested; the income on hand at the beginning of the period, income received, income on hand at end of the period and how it is invested; proof of no self-dealing; a statement of unpaid claims; a brief summary of the account; and such other facts as the court may require. The act specifically states that it applies to charitable trusts.

Restrictions on Amount of Charitable Bequests

The common law placed no restrictions on the amount of property which a testator could dispose of by will for charitable purposes. In England and in some of the states, however, statutes have been enacted which place certain restrictions on the power to make charitable dispositions, whether they are to be in trust or not. The early statutes, particularly in England, were designed to prevent property from being kept out of commerce in perpetuity. The restrictions in the United

---

[1] See Table 1 of Appendix A for list of these statutes by states.
[2] Ohio Rev. Code, sec. 2109.30.
[3] Mich. Stat. Ann., sec. 27.3178 (289).
[4] Uniform Trustees' Accounting Act, *Uniform Laws Annotated*. Edward Thompson Co., Brooklyn, N.Y., 1957, vol. 9C, p. 273.
[5] Kan. Gen. Stat. Ann., secs. 59–301, 59–1601 to 59–1611, 59–2253 to 59–2256.
[6] Nev. Rev. Stat., secs. 165.010 to 165.250.
[7] N.M. Stat. Ann., secs. 33–2–1 to 33–2–24.

States have been primarily directed toward preventing a testator from disinheriting his family by so-called death bed provisions. This legislation is of two types. In some states a gift to charity in a will executed within a certain time before the testator's death, such as thirty days or six months, is invalid.[1] Some of these statutes apply only if the testator leaves near relatives, such as a spouse or a child or descendants of a child.[2] The second type of restrictive statute places a limit on the proportion of an estate which a testator can leave to charity if he is survived by certain near relatives.[3]

It should be noted that statutes combining both types of restriction are in force in certain states,[4] and in Montana the restriction regarding the time of creation of the will applies to gifts of more than one-third of an estate.[5]

Requirement of Indefiniteness of Beneficiaries

The *Restatement* definition of a charitable trust does not include the word "beneficiary," and therein lies an important distinction between a charitable trust and a private trust. For a private trust to be valid, there must be a named or ascertainable beneficiary who is capable of providing a continuing scrutiny of the activities of the trustee and who is able to call abuses to the attention of the court for correction. The beneficiaries of a charitable trust, on the other hand, are in the broadest sense the public at large. There can be no single individuals comparable to the beneficiaries of a private trust, or there is no valid charity.

The individuals who receive benefits from a foundation, whether they be recipients of scholarship grants, money, food, clothing, or any other direct assistance, are merely the "conduits of the social benefits to the public and are not in reality the beneficiaries of the trust."[6]

---

[1] Cal. Prob. Code, sec. 40–43 (thirty days); D.C. Code, sec. 12–202; Fla. Stat. Ann., sec. 731.19 (six months); Ga. Code Ann., sec. 113–107 (ninety days); Idaho Code Ann., sec. 14–326 (thirty days); Mont. Rev. Code Ann., sec. 91–142 (thirty days as to more than one-third); Ohio Rev. Code, sec. 2107.06 (one year); Pa. Stat. Ann., tit. 10, sec. 17; tit. 20, sec. 180.7 (thirty days).

[2] Miss. Constitution, art. 14, sec. 270.

[3] Cal. Prob. Code, secs. 40 to 43, *In re Moore's Estate,* 31 Cal. Rept. 757; (1963); Ga. Code Ann., sec. 113–107; Idaho Code Ann., sec. 14–326; Iowa Code, sec. 633.3; Miss. Constitution, art. 14, sec. 270; N.Y. Deced. Est. Law, sec. 17.

[4] California, Georgia, Idaho, Mississippi.

[5] Restrictions on the property that charitable corporations may hold are discussed on pp. 123 ff.

[6] Bogert, George G., and George T. Bogert, *The Law of Trusts and Trustees.* 2d ed. West Publishing Co., St. Paul, 1964, sec. 362.

This does not mean that at certain times and in certain circumstances there cannot be individuals who would have a right similar to that of the beneficiaries of a private trust to sue for enforcement. For example, charitable trusts for the benefit of the minister of a particular church have been upheld on the ground that, although the direct beneficiary for a certain finite time is a specific ascertained individual, the underlying and main purpose of the trust is to promote religion, and the total number of beneficiaries over a long period of time is not ascertainable.[1] This same reasoning has been applied to uphold trusts the income of which is to be used for: a prize or an award,[2] research or scholarship grants to individuals meeting certain requirements,[3] prizes to winners of competitions, or awards to a specified number of individuals to be picked each year by the trustee.[4] In addition, a donor may direct that certain individuals shall be preferred as beneficiaries, so long as the primary purpose can be considered of public benefit. For example, a trust for the poor with instructions that it be applied first to the donor's poor relatives was upheld in *Bullard* v. *Chandler*,[5] but a trust solely for the descendants of a donor who may be in need is not usually considered a valid charitable gift.[6]

As with the determination of charitable purposes, judicial interpretation of the requirement of indefiniteness has varied considerably. Whereas the English courts tend to exclude trusts to aid special groups not open to the general public, the United States courts have usually considered these trusts to be valid. For example, an English trust for the benefit of workers in a factory employing 110,000 was held to be invalid as benefiting too narrow a class,[7] but trusts for even smaller groups of employees have been upheld in the United States.[8] The rulings of the Commissioner of Internal Revenue on trusts of this type are generally stricter than the court decisions on validity; but the denial of exemption has usually been based on the fact that there would be inurement to the donor, not that the class was too definite.[9]

---

[1] *Curtis* v. *First Church in Charlestown*, 285 Mass. 73, 188 N.E. 631 (1934); Scott, Austin W., *The Law of Trusts*, 2d ed., Little, Brown and Co., Boston, 1956, sec. 375.1.

[2] *Powell's Estate*, 71 D. & C. 51 (Pa. 1950).

[3] *Hoyt* v. *Bliss*, 93 Conn. 344, 105 Atl. 699 (1919).

[4] *Sherman* v. *Shaw*, 243 Mass. 257, 137 N.E. 374 (1922).

[5] 149 Mass. 532, 21 N.E. 951 (1889).

[6] *Kent* v. *Dunham*, 142 Mass. 216, 7 N.E. 730 (1886); see also Scott, Austin W., *op. cit.*, sec. 375.3.

[7] *Oppenheim* v. *Tobacco Securities Trust Co.* [1951] A.C. 297.

[8] *In re Fanelli's Estate*, 207 Misc. 719, 140 N.Y.S.2d 334 (1955); *In re Scholler's Estate*, 403 Pa. 97, 169A.2d 554 (1961).

[9] See pp. 67 ff.

In many of these cases the individuals eligible to receive the benefit at a particular moment may have a right to sue to secure enforcement of the trust, even though it is sometimes stated that the attorney general alone has the power to maintain suits for enforcement of charitable trusts. Members of the public at large have been barred from court action to enforce charitable trusts on two grounds: that the unlimited grant of this power would be impractical, causing a constant threat of expensive, harassing litigation; and that the attorney general can adequately represent this public interest. If suit is brought by an individual who can show a specific beneficial interest, such as the temporary holder of an endowed professorship, most courts will require that the attorney general also be a party to the suit to represent the broader public interest presumed to exist in the case of every charitable trust.

The terms of some charitable trusts require the trustees to manage the capital fund and pay over income to a charitable corporation or association for its general purposes or for a specific limited purpose. In these cases the beneficiary of the first trust is a definite, identifiable legal entity. However, the trust is valid as a charity, since the ultimate benefit will be to the community at large.

In general, the rule is that the class of beneficiaries must be so broad that a court can conclude that there is indirect benefit to the community from direct aid to the particular class in question, considered both over a period of years and for any given moment of time.

Duration and the Restrictions on Remoteness of Vesting

A further distinction between a private trust and a charitable trust exists in terms of the duration of the trust. Private trusts are generally subject to the so-called Rule Against Perpetuities. The classic statement of the rule, given by Professor Gray, is that "No interest is good unless it must vest, if at all, not later than twenty-one years after some life in being at the creation of the interest."[1] The purpose behind the rule is to prevent the withdrawal of property from commerce. The public interest in encouraging charitable dispositions has led to their exclusion from the provisions of this Rule in all states by either case law or statute.[2]

---

[1] Gray, John Chipman, *The Rule Against Perpetuities.* 4th ed., Little, Brown and Co., Boston, 1942, sec. 201.

[2] "The cases so holding are so numerous that it is unnecessary to cite them; indeed, most charitable trusts are of indefinite duration." Scott, Austin W., *op. cit.,* sec. 365, n. 1, which also includes a partial list of citations; *Restatement of the Law of Trusts (Second), op. cit.,* sec. 365.

The Rule Against Perpetuities is applicable to noncharitable dispositions where there is a contingent gift over to charity on the happening of some future event. If the gift to charity will not vest within the period of the Rule, it fails. It also fails if there is an attempt to create a charitable trust to last for a period longer than the Rule with a gift to individuals at the end of the period. A gift over from one charity to another, however, is valid regardless of the time at which it may occur.

In addition to restrictions on the duration of trusts that arise from the operation of the Rule Against Perpetuities, there are statutes in a number of states that prohibit the suspension of absolute ownership or limit the power of alienation to a certain period of time. The time given in these statutes is usually measured in the same terms as the Rule Against Perpetuities, but the statutes operate to prevent restrictions on the disposition of property by an owner; they do not act on the question of whether an interest will vest within the given period. The most noteworthy example appears in section 42 of the New York Real Property Law. As with the Rule Against Perpetuities, however, charitable trusts are generally exempt from these restrictions.

It is not, of course, essential to the validity of a charitable trust that it exist for an indefinite term. Some American foundations, such as the Rosenwald, were created with the express purpose of distributing all of their capital funds within a finite period. Some writers have advocated that there be a limit on the existence of charitable trusts on grounds of public policy.[1] The law, however, takes no position as to the desirability of existence in perpetuity as opposed to limitation on existence, and permits both without distinction.

Termination

It is the intent of the settlor that determines the duration of charitable trusts, and a court will not usually order termination where such action could be considered to be against the intent of the settlor. Thus in cases where there has been a gift to trustees to hold property and pay the income to a charitable corporation, the courts have refused to turn over the trust to the corporation to manage.[2]

An interesting example of this rule involved a trust created in the will of Benjamin Franklin. Franklin directed that the fund was to

---

[1] See Hobhouse, Arthur, *The Dead Hand,* Chatto and Windus, London, 1880; Kenny, Courtney Stanhope, *Property Given for Charitable or Other Public Uses,* Reeves and Turner, London, 1880; Rosenwald, Julius, "Principles of Public Giving," *Atlantic Monthly,* vol. 143, 1929, p. 599.

[2] *Winthrop* v. *Attorney General,* 128 Mass. 258 (1880).

accumulate for two one-hundred-year periods, during which time loans were to be made to young artificers on certain specified conditions, and after which time the principal and accrued income were to be paid to the Commonwealth of Massachusetts and city of Boston. At the turn of the century, it became impossible to make loans under the terms of the will, and the funds were invested. In 1959 the state legislature and the city both agreed to turn their interest in the gift over to the Franklin Foundation, which had been created to manage the distribution under the trust after the first one hundred years. The Foundation then brought suit as the sole beneficiary to have the trust terminated, but the court refused, holding that the testator's purpose was not merely to aid citizens but to accumulate funds for the commonwealth and the city for the one-hundred-year period.[1]

The rule as to termination is applied in cases of partial termination. However, if the reason for duration of the trust is no longer valid, the court may permit termination. An example of this type of situation occurred in the case of *State Historical Society* v. *Foster,*[2] where a testator left property in trust to pay an annuity to his son and, if he should marry, to his wife, with a gift over to a charitable corporation on his death without issue. The son died without issue leaving a wife, and the court permitted the corporation to compel the trustees to convey the trust estate to it subject to a duty to pay the annuity to the son's widow.[3]

A charitable trust may be created with a provision that on the happening of a certain event the trust will terminate and the funds will revert to the donor or his heirs. Such a condition or limitation must be clearly stated; it will not be implied. There will be no reversion merely for breach of trust unless that condition is explicitly stated. Furthermore, such limitations are strictly construed by the courts and may even be disregarded if, under all the circumstances, it would be inequitable to abide by the condition.[4] The Rule Against Perpetuities is not applicable to gifts subject to conditions or limitations where the property is to revert to the donor or his heirs.

---

[1] *Franklin Foundation* v. *Attorney General,* 340 Mass. 197, 163 N.E.2d 662 (1960). Following a suggestion made by the court in this case, the Foundation in 1962 successfully brought suit for application of the *cy pres* doctrine to the loan provision, so that loans may now be made to needy medical students and others studying in technical or scientific schools.

[2] 172 Wis. 155, 177 N.W. 16 (1920).

[3] See also *Armstrong Estate,* 29 D. & C.2d 220 (Pa. 1963).

[4] Scott, Austin W., *op. cit.,* secs. 401 to 401.4.

Accumulation of Income

Just as the Rule Against Perpetuities is an expression of public policy, so is the rule that income from property in trust may not be allowed to accumulate for a period longer than that of the Rule Against Perpetuities. This is the general rule in regard to private trusts in both England and in most of the states. In regard to charitable trusts, however, English and American rules are somewhat different. In England directions to accumulate income of a charitable trust for a period are invalid, no matter what the purpose, and the court may direct immediate application of income to the beneficiary.[1] In the United States, on the other hand, where the courts have been more disposed to upholding a donor's wishes, the rule has developed that provisions for accumulation of income will be upheld if they are not to continue for an unreasonably long time.[2] The fact that the period may be longer than the period of the Rule Against Perpetuities is not fatal. Thus in a recent case the federal Circuit Court of Appeals upheld the validity of a trust that was to accumulate for five hundred years after which the principal and accumulated income were to be paid to the state of Pennsylvania for the purpose of concentrating the wealth of the world in a single governmental unit. The court stated that the provision for accumulation, while not invalidating the entire trust, was to be given effect only so far as public policy permitted.[3] In those states where statutes prohibit accumulation in prviate trusts for certain periods, exceptions are made for charitable dispositions.[4]

The Fiduciary Relationship

In thc *Restatement* definition of a charitable trust, the word "fiduciary" is used to characterize the relationship that arises when a charitable trust is created. The expression "fiduciary relationship" applies in law to those situations where one individual is under a positive duty

---

[1] *Wharton* v. *Masterman* [1895] A.C. 186. Today in England a provision for accumulation often will not cause an otherwise valid charitable trust to fail, but the court, on application by the attorney general, may compel the trustees to make immediate application of the trust property in spite of a provision made by a donor postponing such application and providing for accumulation of the income in the meantime. Scott, Austin W., *op. cit.*, sec. 401.9.

[2] *Restatement of the Law of Trusts (Second)*, *op. cit.*, sec. 442.

[3] *Holdeen* v. *Ratterree*, 292 F.2d 338 (2d Cir. 1961) reversing 190 F. Supp. 752 (N.D.N.Y. 1960).

[4] N.Y. Pers. Prop. Law, sec. 16; and N.Y. Real Prop. Law, sec. 16-a, inserted by Laws 1961, ch. 866; Pa. Stat. Ann., tit. 20, sec. 301.6; Note "Accumulations in Charitable Trusts," *Harvard Law Review*, vol. 41, 1927, p. 514.

to act for the benefit of another party to the relation as to matters within the scope of the relation.[1] It is, in essence, a duty of loyalty, and has as its corollary the rule that the fiduciary may not profit at the expense of the other party. Dealings between partners, attorneys and clients, agents and principals, corporation directors and stockholders are all examples of fiduciary relations, although the relationship is found in a peculiarly intense degree in a trust. The popular nonlegal meaning of the word "trust" is, in fact, almost synonymous with the concept of fiduciary relations.

The characterization of a trustee as a fiduciary is crucial to an understanding of his duties, and underlies the determination of all of his powers. The moment a trust is created, certain duties are imposed upon the trustee. These duties have two sources: the terms of the trust instrument or indenture (conferred by the donor) and certain well-established rules of law that apply to all trustees.

The settlor of a charitable trust may eliminate or limit the application of certain of these rules of law. The courts, however, interpret such provisions strictly and do not infer them from unclear language. Furthermore, a donor may not impose duties on a trustee that will be impossible to accomplish or will require him to perform acts that are illegal or inconsistent with public policy. The trust instrument cannot relieve a trustee from responsibility for performing any of these acts, and the trustee commits a breach of trust if he complies with the instrument. For example, a provision in a trust instrument relieving a trustee from all duty to account to the courts has been declared inconsistant with public policy, and in some states it may be illegal.[2]

Deviation from the Terms of a Trust

The equity courts do have power to permit deviations from the terms of a trust if compliance appears to be impossible or illegal, or if, owing to circumstances not known to the settlor and not anticipated by him, compliance will defeat or substantially impair the accomplishment of the purposes of the trust.[3] The most common types of devia-

---

[1] *Restatement of the Law of Trusts (Second)*, *op. cit.*, sec. 170, comment b; Scott, Austin W., "The Fiduciary Principle," *California Law Review*, vol. 37, 1949, p. 539.
[2] Scott, Austin W., *The Law of Trusts, op. cit.*, sec. 172; Bogert, George G. and George T. Bogert, *op. cit.*, sec. 973; *Restatement of the Law of Trusts (Second)*, *op. cit.*, secs. 165, 166, 187.
[3] *Restatement of the Law of Trusts (Second)*, *op. cit.*, sec. 381.

tions permitted have related to sales of real estate which were part of the original trust property and to changes in investment procedure.[1]

A recent case of importance to foundation trustees involved the denial of a request by the Trustees of the Duke Endowment for authority to make investments not permitted by the terms of the trust indenture. The Supreme Court of North Carolina, while not denying the power of the court to permit deviations under certain circumstances, held that that power was confined to cases of emergency or where necessary to preserve the trust estate, but that a mere showing of change of economic conditions was not a sufficient basis to permit a deviation.[2]

The importance of this case lies primarily in the fact that one of the motives of the trustees in bringing the suit, although not explicitly stated in the petition, was a fear that the foundation's ownership of the controlling stock of the Duke Power Company, which was necessitated by the investment provisions in the trust indenture, might result in a ruling by the Internal Revenue Service that the foundation's income from the company was unrelated business income and therefore subject to tax.

In the previous year (1962), the Ohio Supreme Court refused, on a similar basis, to permit a deviation from the terms of a testamentary trust which required that all investments of capital be in interest-bearing securities issued by the United States or any state or by a governmental subdivision of the state of Ohio. The court held that general inflationary factors and changing economic conditions over a twenty-year period did not constitute grounds for permitting deviation, regardless of the fact that the purpose of the trust was to create a fund sufficient to build a hospital. The attorney general of Ohio, a party to this case, had taken the position that the court should not grant the trustee's request.[3]

This power of the courts to permit deviations should not be confused with the *cy pres* power. The latter is applicable when the pur-

---

[1] *American Academy of Arts and Sciences* v. *President and Fellows of Harvard University*, 12 Gray 582 (Mass. 1832); N.Y. Real Prop. Law, sec. 113(4) permits the Supreme Court to authorize the sale or mortgage of real property held for charitable purposes where such action will be in furtherance of the charitable objectives. Similar statutes are in force in Kentucky (Rev. Stat., sec. 273.140), Michigan (Stat. Ann., sec. 26.1211), New Jersey (Rev. Stat., secs., 15:14–7, 16:1–22), and Pennsylvania (Stat. Ann., tit. 20, sec. 2254).

[2] *Cocke* v. *Duke University*, 260 N.C. 1, 131 S.E.2d 909 (1963).

[3] *Toledo Trust Co., Trustee* v. *Toledo Hospital; McElroy, Attorney General, Appellee*, 174 Ohio St. 124, 187 N.E.2d 36 (1962). See also *Bank of Delaware* v. *Allmond* _____ Del. ch. _____, 183 A.2d 188 (1962).

poses are no longer capable of being accomplished. The power to permit deviations does not usually extend to the purposes of the trust, but is confined to matters relating solely to administration.

Exculpatory Clauses

One of the most common provisions found in trust instruments to-day is the so-called exculpatory clause, designed to relieve a trustee from liability for certain kinds of breaches of trust. Provisions of this nature are strictly construed by the courts. In addition, no clause in a trust instrument is effective to relieve a trustee from liability for a breach of trust that is committed in bad faith, intentionally, with reckless indifference to the interests of the beneficiary, or for a breach of trust from which the trustee personally profits.[1] New York has gone further and by statute has declared that an attempted grant to an executor or trustee of a testamentary trust of exoneration of his fiduciary liability for failure to execute reasonable care, diligence, and prudence shall be deemed contrary to public policy and void.[2] This statute was applied in the case of *In re Schechter's Estate*,[3] where a clause in a trust for religious purposes stating that the trustee should be neither responsible for any loss or injuring to the property nor accountable for its distribution was declared void as against public policy.[4] However, the presence of an exculpatory clause does relieve a trustee from the strict personal liability often associated with the office of trustee, and under certain circumstances may make the position more like that of a corporate director.[5]

Duties of Trustees

The rules of law imposing specific duties on trustees are to be found in the statutes and cases of all the states. They are not only important in determining the nature of a charitable trust; they contain the limits on the enforcement powers of the state against the trustees of charitable trusts. Some of them can be characterized as technical rules, while others are basic to the concept of trust and fiduciary rela-

---

[1] *Restatement of the Law of Trusts (Second)*, *op. cit.*, sec. 222; Scott, Austin W., *The Law of Trusts*, *op. cit.*, secs. 222 to 222.3.

[2] N.Y. Deced. Est. Law, sec. 125.

[3] 35 Misc.2d 371, 229 N.Y.S.2d 702 (1962).

[4] Scott, Austin W., *The Law of Trusts*, *op. cit.*, sec. 222; Bogert, George G., and George T. Bogert, *op. cit.*, 1960, sec. 542.

[5] See Chapter IV.

tions. Those duties which are basic to the trust relationship may be classified as follows.

1. *The duty of loyalty.*[1] This is the duty that restates the fiduciary relationship. The classic restatement of this requirement of individual loyalty was expressed by Judge Cardozo:

> Many forms of conduct permissible in a workaday world for those acting at arm's length are forbidden by those bound by fiduciary ties. A trustee is held to something stricter than the morals of the market place. Not honesty alone, but the punctilio of an honor the most sensitive, is then the standard of behavior. As to this there has developed a tradition that is unbending and inveterate. Uncompromising rigidity has been the attitude of courts of equity when petitioned to undermine the rule of undivided loyalty by the "disintegrating erosion" of particular exceptions. Only thus has the level of conduct for fiduciaries been kept at a level higher than that trodden by the crowd.[2]

A trustee's interest must always yield to that of the beneficiary. The fact that a trustee acted in good faith in a transaction where there was a question of self-dealing or self-interest is not an adequate defense to a charge of violation of the duty of loyalty; neither is ignorance or innocence. It is immaterial whether the beneficiary is damaged. A trustee will be liable to the trust estate for any loss from an investment involving self-dealing. Any benefit or profit which he may obtain belongs to the trust estate, regardless of whether the transaction involved a loss. The rule extends to the trustee's spouse and relatives as well as to trust companies or banks acting as trustees. The only conditions under which relief from this strict rule can be obtained, other than under a specific provision in the terms of the trust, are those where the trustee deals directly with the beneficiary, or where he makes full disclosure to him, takes no advantage of his position, obtains his consent, and where the transaction is in all respects fair and reasonable. Of course, in the case of a trust for charitable purposes, there are no beneficiaries capable of giving this consent.

> It might be more accurate to say that when a trustee is guilty of self-dealing which has not been ratified by the beneficiary (and in the case of a charity, there is no one to ratify), he is an insurer for losses incurred by the trust, and he is accountable for any gains which he receives.[3]

---

[1] *The Restatement of the Law of Trusts (Second)*, op. cit., sec. 170, and Scott, Austin W., *The Law of Trusts*, op. cit., secs. 170 to 170.25, deal in great detail with the many aspects of this question.

[2] *Meinhard v. Salmon*, 249 N.Y. 458, 469, 164 N.E. 545, 547 (1928).

[3] Karst, Kenneth L., "The Efficiency of the Charitable Dollar: An Unfulfilled State Responsibility," *Harvard Law Review*, vol. 73, 1960, pp. 443, 439. Copyright © 1960 by the Harvard Law Review Association.

A number of state statutes expressly prohibit self-dealing by fiduciaries.[1] For example, the California Civil Code states, "A trustee may not use or deal with the trust property for his own profit, or for any other purpose unconnected with the trust, in any manner."[2] The Ohio statute provides that court approval of a transaction involving self-dealing is necessary even if the terms of trust allow self-dealing.[3] The Uniform Trusts Act, adopted in several states, provides that "No trustee shall directly or indirectly buy or sell any property for the trust from or to itself or an affiliate; or from or to a director, officer, or employee of such trustee or of an affiliate; or from or to a relative, employer, partner, or other business associate."[4]

By the terms of the trust, a donor may relieve a trustee from the stringent effects of this duty of loyalty, and may permit a trustee to deal with the property on his own account unless this is expressly prohibited by statute. This is often done in the trust instruments of family foundations. However, as previously stated, no matter how broad the power to deal with himself or wide the relief from liabilities contained in a trust instrument, a donor may not relieve a trustee from responsibility for willful and deliberate violation of his fiduciary obligations, for gross negligence, for actions taken in bad faith or dishonestly, or for acts from which he has profited personally. Considerations of public policy dictate this rule.[5]

2. *The duty not to delegate to others the doing of acts which he can reasonably be required to perform.*[6] In essence, this rule states a personal duty on the trustee to administer the trust. His must be the final responsibility and ultimate source of all decisions. He may delegate the performance of administrative tasks to others, may employ counsel, attorneys, accountants, or stock brokers to handle certain matters, and may entrust them with the property of the trust, but he must maintain at all times full responsibility for their acts.

In *Attorney General* v. *Olsen,*[7] a recent Massachusetts case, trustees

---

[1] See Scott, Austin W., *The Law of Trusts, op. cit.,* sec. 170, for statutory references.

[2] Secs. 2229 to 2230.

[3] Ohio Rev. Code, sec. 2109.44.

[4] Sec. 5, adopted in North Carolina, South Dakota, Oklahoma, Louisiana, New Mexico, and Texas. See Table 1 of Appendix A, for references.

[5] *Browning* v. *Fidelity Trust Co.,* 250 Fed. 321 (3d Cir. 1918); *Matter of Andrus,* 156 Misc. 268, 281 N.Y. Supp. 831 (Surr. Ct. 1935). For further discussion see American Bar Association, "Report of the Subcommittee on Outer Limits of Trustee Powers," *Trusts and Estates,* vol. 101, 1962, pp. 553, 559ff.

[6] *Restatement of the Law of Trusts (Second), op. cit.,* sec. 171.

[7] 346 Mass. 190, 191 N.E.2d 132 (1963).

were charged with an improper delegation of duties by entering into an agency agreement with a bank that was to act as custodian of securities, advise the trustees concerning investments, and handle the bookkeeping details for the trust. The court held that this type of arrangement did not constitute an improper delegation of duties, noting that none of the trustees had much, if any, experience in the field of investments and that the trustees were consulted before investments were made and gave their approval before each transaction. "While a trustee cannot surrender to another his duties with respect to investments, he may seek advice of those better qualified."[1]

3. *The duty to keep and render clear and accurate accounts with respect to the administration of the trust,*[2] *and to furnish to the beneficiary on request at reasonable times complete and accurate information as to the administration of the trust.*[3] In some states the precise form of a trustee's account is prescribed by statute.[4] In the absence of statute, the rule is that a trustee must keep complete and accurate accounts of all receipts and expenditures, gains and losses, and allocations of funds to principal and income. He is required to make this information available to the beneficiary on reasonable request.

If a reasonable request for information is refused, the court may order a trustee to account to his beneficiaries. In the case of charitable trusts, an action for an accounting can be brought only by the attorney general or by the court on its own motion. The requisites for an action for an accounting were discussed in *State* v. *Taylor,*[5] a case involving a charitable trust created in 1939 to establish and endow a charitable institution. By the terms of the trust, the trustees were required to keep full and accurate accounts, to direct an audit of their accounts at the end of each fiscal year, and to publish a condensed statement of the condition and assets of the trust immediately thereafter in a local newspaper. In 1958 the attorney general of Washington wrote to the trustees requesting: a complete history of the trust, including records of income and distributions, all property, and changes in administration; legal actions relating to the trust; and present status. He also requested notification of future changes in administration. The trustees refused to supply the requested information, and the attorney general

---

[1] *Ibid.*, p. 134.
[2] *Restatement of the Law of Trusts (Second)*, *op. cit.*, sec. 172.
[3] *Ibid.*, sec. 173.
[4] For example, see the Uniform Trustees' Accounting Act, *op. cit.* See Table 1 of Appendix A for citations to states where this act has been adopted.
[5] 58 Wash.2d 252, 362 P.2d 247 (1961).

forthwith brought an action for an accounting. The attorney general's bill contained no allegation that the trustees had failed to follow the requirements of the trust instrument regarding accounts. The court dismissed the action on the basis that the letter from the attorney general was not a reasonable and proper request, and was insufficient to constitute a proper demand for a full-scale accounting, which is the prerequisite for court action. The court, however, refused to accept the arguments of the trustees that a showing of mismanagement or breach of trust was also a prerequisite for court action.

This duty to account may extend to the trustee's personal affairs and actions if they have a bearing on the trust property. It also extends to the administration of a corporate business managed by the trustee. For example, a New York court held in 1961 that where a trustee owned 56 per cent of the stock of two business corporations personally and held the balance as trustee of a charitable trust, he was required to account to the attorney general for the management of these business corporations. The court stated that the fiduciary duty extended not only to the trust estate but to the entire operations of the corporation.[1] This doctrine may well become important in cases involving family foundations that own stock in closely held corporations.

Complete relief from a duty to account is often written into trust instruments. In some instances these clauses have been interpreted as indicating an intention by the donor to give the entire interest to the trustee and therefore to negate the creation of any trust. In other cases, the courts have refused to recognize the provision and have required trustees to account.[2]

4. *The duty to exercise reasonable care and skill.*[3] This is the so-called prudent man rule first applied to charitable and private trusts alike in the case of *Harvard College* v. *Amory,* where it was stated that a trustee "must . . . observe how men of prudence, discretion and

---

[1] *Matter of Luce,* 224 N.Y.S.2d 210 (1961), affirmed mem. 17 A.D.2d 636, 230 N.Y.S.2d 45 (1962). See also *In re Hubbell's Will,* 302 N.Y. 246, 97 N.E. 2d 888 (1951) and Note, "The Trust Corporation: Dual Fiduciary Duties and the Conflict of Institutions," *University of Pennsylvania Law Review,* vol. 109, 1961, p. 713.

[2] See Scott, Austin W., *The Law of Trusts, op. cit.,* sec. 172. In the case of *Minot* v. *Attorney General,* 189 Mass. 176, 75 N.E. 149 (1905), a testator left his estate in trust for the benefit of charitable or worthy objects and included a clause releasing the trustee from any legal accountability. The court refused to recognize this as a beneficial gift to the trustees, but held that the trust failed for indefiniteness, since the gift to "worthy objects" could include gifts to a class broader than that authorized by the legal meaning of charity.

[3] *Restatement of the Law of Trusts (Second), op. cit.,* sec. 174.

intelligence manage their own affairs, not in regard to speculation, but in regard to the permanent disposition of their funds, considering the probable income as well as the probable safety of the capital to be invested."[1]

If a trustee has greater skill than others, he is under a duty to use such skill. Some cases hold corporate trustees such as banks to a higher degree of performance based on their particular qualifications and on the fact that they hold themselves out to the public as possessing extraordinary skill and receive compensation for such skill.[2]

A settlor may in the trust instrument relax or modify to a certain extent the requirement of care and skill ordinarily required of a trustee. It should be noted that such a clause will relieve a trustee from a duty which would otherwise be imposed on him. It differs, therefore, from the so-called exculpatory clauses, which relieve a trustee from liability if he does commit a breach of trust.

Investment of Trust Funds. In most jurisdictions, the standards as to investments of trust funds are governed by statutes. Most of these statutes recite the prudent man rule,[3] although several states require trustees to invest only in those securities enumerated in the statute and called the "legal list."[4] The New York statute provides that in addition to the types of securities listed as legal trust investments, trustees may invest in other securities including common and preferred stock in which a prudent man would invest, using up to 35 per cent of the market value of the trust property at the time of investment.[5] There are similar provisions in New Jersey[6] and Ohio.[7]

These statutes on the investment of trust funds vary in their application. Some extend to all fiduciaries, others to banks and trust companies. Some permit a settlor to enlarge or restrict investment provisions, his statements being controlling.[8]

In their practical application to specific situations, statutory requirements as to investments do give broad leeway to the trustees to use their discretion as to both individual purchases and the nature of the

---

[1] 9 Pick. 446, 461 (Mass. 1830).
[2] Scott, Austin W., *The Law of Trusts, op. cit.,* sec. 174.1, contains a discussion of the standards commonly imposed on professional trustees. See also Bogert, George G., and George T. Bogert, *op. cit.,* 1960, sec. 541.
[3] See, for example, Cal. Civ. Code, sec. 2261.
[4] See, for example, Iowa Code, sec. 682.23.
[5] N.Y. Pers. Prop. Law, sec. 21 (1).
[6] N.J. Rev. Stat., secs. 3A:15–12 to 3A:15–29 (60 per cent).
[7] Ohio Rev. Code, sec. 2109.371 (35 per cent).
[8] Table 1 in Appendix A contains a list of references to all state statutes dealing with investments.

investments. *A Trustee's Handbook* lists, however, nine types of investments generally considered improper for a trustee to acquire or to hold for an unreasonable period:

(1) Speculative investments. This includes any sort of purchase upon margin and any security which is bought at a substantial discount because of common doubt as to its eventual worth.

(2) Investments which are lacking in seasoned performance as to safety and yield.

(3) Investments as an individual or partner in carrying on a trade or business.

(4) Investments in any enterprise in which the trustee has a personal interest.

(5) Investments upon a temporary basis, that is to say, for quick turnover or sale at a profit.

(6) Investments in junior mortgages which because they are subject to a prior lien, might be suddenly extinguished without recourse.

(7) Investments in real estate which lies outside the state having jurisdiction over the trust. . . .

(8) Investments which are unproductive.

(9) Investments consisting of personal loans without security.

(10) Investments of a wasting nature.

(11) Investment in life insurance or annuity contracts. . . . [1]

If the trust instrument contains a clause that a trustee may invest "in his discretion" or as he "deems advisable," the effect of this clause will depend in part on the tradition of the state. If the investment rule is narrow, these words ordinarily mean that the prudent man rule will then become applicable. If the prudent man rule is in force, however, the phrase may not enlarge the trustee's powers.[2] The trust instrument, however, may go further and specifically permit "speculative" investments or investments not ordinarily considered proper for a trustee. In such a case, the courts are likely to interpret the provision strictly, although according to Scott, there is no rule of public policy that prevents the settlor from permitting the trustee to make speculative investments. The one case generally cited in support of this proposition, however, dealt with a trust where the settlor was also trustee and reserved a right to direct investments. The court discussed his powers in relation to the purposes of the trust, of which the ability to speculate was an integral part.[3] It is open to question whether a court would ex-

---

[1] Loring, Augustus, *A Trustee's Handbook*. Revised by James A. Farr. Little, Brown and Co., Boston, 1962, pp. 199–201.

[2] Scott, Austin W., *The Law of Trusts, op. cit.*, sec. 227.14; *Davis, Appellant*, 183 Mass. 499, 67 N.E. 604 (1903).

[3] *In re Greenhouse's Estate*, 338 Pa. 144, 12 A.2d 96 (1940).

tend such an interpretation to a trust for charitable purposes, however, where the public interest is so different.

Generally, in construing clauses enlarging powers or limiting trustee liability, the courts attempt to give a meaning consistent with the purpose and object of the trust.[1] The public nature of a charitable trust, and the fact that it may last in perpetuity, are strong arguments for the strict construction of any clause that permits excessive speculation with funds devoted to charitable purposes. It should also be noted that a provision enlarging the discretion of a trustee as to investments does not, of itself, relieve the trustee from his duty of loyalty.[2]

Diversification of Investments. One aspect of the application of the prudent man rule to trust investments is the question of diversification of risk. Common sense dictates that it is not prudent to keep too many eggs in one basket. The question of diversification is particularly important to trustees of the many charitable foundations to which donors have contributed large amounts of stock of a closely held corporation. Unfortunately, the cases do not make clear how far a trustee is subject to liability for failure to diversify investments. The requirement of diversification has been specifically recognized by the courts in some jurisdictions,[3] and has been imposed by statute in others.[4] The question has not been decided by the Court of Appeals in New York, but several lower court decisions have stated that failure to diversify is not of itself imprudent.[5]

Ordinarily a trustee is under a duty to dispose of improper investments which he receives at the time of creation. In just over half of the states, however, it is provided by statute that a trustee may retain investments received from the original donor even though they would not otherwise be proper.[6] These statutes have the effect of establishing

---

[1] See *Tuttle* v. *Gilmore,* 36 N.J.Eq. 617, 622 (1883).

[2] For general discussion of investment powers, see Curtis, Charles P., *The Modern Prudent Investor.* Joint Committee on Continuing Legal Education of the American Law Institute and the American Bar Association, Philadelphia, 1961.

[3] *Dickinson, Appellant,* 152 Mass. 184, 25 N.E. 99 (1890); *Pennsylvania Company for Insurance on Lives and Granting Annuities* v. *Gillmore,* 142 N.J.Eq. 27, 59 A.2d 24 (1948); *Knox County* v. *Fourth & First National Bank,* 181 Tenn. 569, 182 S.W.2d 980 (1944).

[4] Ind. Ann. Stat., sec. 31–507; Tenn. Code Ann., secs. 35–308, 35–309, 35–310; N.H. Rev. Stat. Ann., sec. 386:16; S.C. Code Ann., sec. 67–58.

[5] See *Central Hanover Bank & Trust Co.* v. *Clark,* 81 N.Y.S.2d 883 (1948) for review of other New York cases; Scott, Austin W., *The Law of Trusts, op. cit.,* sec. 228.

[6] For example, see N.Y. Pers. Prop. Law, sec. 21(6), which applies to all fiduciaries but adds the following provision: "provided such fiduciary exer-

different rules for the making and the retention of investments, but it should be noted that they do not relieve a trustee from his basic duty of prudence. A provision in the terms of the trust authorizing a trustee to retain securities in which the donor invested or which the donor has contributed to the trust does not justify the trustee in retaining them if such retention later becomes imprudent.[1]

Where the rule of diversification exists, it is applied less strictly to retention of investments than to the making of investments. If a trustee is specifically permitted by the terms of the trust to retain certain securities, the rule of diversification will not apply. In the case of *First National Bank of Boston* v. *Truesdale Hospital*,[2] a testator directed that a portion of his shares of stock in one company worth $500,000 should be established as a permanent trust fund for the benefit of a hospital. Shortly after the trust was established, the shares fell in value, but the court refused to hold the trustee guilty of a breach of trust by failing to diversify, since all investments had fallen in value at that time and the loss could not be attributed to a failure to diversify. The court stated that unless there was a fear for the safety of the specific investment, the trustee had a right to retain the trust fund in the form in which it was received.

Where a duty to diversify does exist, there are a number of factors which must be considered, such as a balance between various types of securities (particularly between fixed indebtednesses and equities and between various fields of enterprises), the maturities of respective investments, and the location of the enterprises.

Additional Duties. In addition to these basic duties of loyalty, diligence, care, and prudence other more specific duties are imposed on trustees as arising from the trust relationship. The trustee is under a duty to administer the trust,[3] take and keep control of the property,[4] preserve the trust property,[5] enforce claims,[6] defend actions,[7] and keep the trust property productive.[8] He must keep the property separate

---

cises due care and prudence in the disposition or retention of any such ineligible investment." See Scott, Austin W., *The Law of Trusts, op. cit.,* sec. 230, for citations.

[1] Scott, Austin W., *The Law of Trusts, op. cit.,* sec. 230.3.
[2] 288 Mass. 35, 192 N.E. 150 (1934).
[3] *Restatement of the Law of Trusts (Second), op. cit.,* sec. 169.
[4] *Ibid.,* sec. 175.
[5] *Ibid.,* sec. 176.
[6] *Ibid.,* sec. 177.
[7] *Ibid.,* sec. 178.
[8] *Ibid.,* sec. 181.

from his individual property,[1] use care in selecting a bank as a depository for trust funds, and properly earmark the deposit.[2]

An exception to the duty not to mingle funds (as well as to the duty not to delegate) has been made in recent years by the passage of statutes in most all the states authorizing trustees to make investments in so-called common trust funds. These funds have been granted exemption from federal income tax and, when administered by national banks, must conform to prescribed rules of the Federal Reserve Board of Governors covering their administration and the amounts which may be so invested. A Uniform Common Trust Fund Act has been approved by the Commissioners on Uniform State Laws and has been enacted in 29 states.[3] These funds have provided an effective means of securing diversification and ease of administration of the funds of small trusts.[4]

It should be noted that in England, by the terms of the Charities Act of 1960, a new duty was imposed on all trustees of trusts for charitable purposes, namely, "where the case permits and requires the property or some part of it to be applied cy près, to secure its effective use for charity by taking steps to enable it to be so applied."[5] There is no similar legislation in effect in any of the states, although the duty to administer a trust could well give rise to such an obligation.

Of far-reaching importance to trustees of charitable trusts is the question of whether they are under a positive duty to assure that they do not by their actions jeopardize the tax-exempt status of the trust. Some commentators have felt that this was implicit in the fiduciary concept, but it has not been the subject of either legislation or court decision. The Uniform Trustees' Powers Act, drafted and approved by the National Conference of Commissioners on Uniform State Laws in August of 1964 includes the following section:

> Section 3 (b). In the exercise of his powers including the powers granted by this Act, a trustee has a duty to act with due regard to his obligation as a fiduciary, including a duty not to exercise any power under this Act in such a way as to deprive the trust of an otherwise available tax exemption deduction or credit for tax purposes. . . .[6]

---

[1] *Ibid.,* sec. 179.

[2] *Ibid.,* sec. 180. See correspondingly numbered sections in Scott, Austin W., *The Law of Trusts, op. cit.,* for discussion.

[3] See Uniform Common Trust Fund Act, *Uniform Laws Annotated, op. cit.,* vol. 9, p. 223 ff., for citations and text.

[4] Annotation "Construction of the Uniform Common Trust Fund Act," *American Law Reports 2d,* vol. 64, 1959, p. 268.

[5] Stat. 8 & 9 Elizabeth II, c. 58, sec. 13(5).

[6] Uniform Trustees' Powers Act, *Handbook,* 1964, National Conference of Commissioners on Uniform State Laws, Chicago, forthcoming.

As explained by the executive director of the National Conference of Commissioners on Uniform State Laws, the purpose of this provision was "to avoid the possibility that ordinary trusts might inadvertently run afoul of some provision of the revenue laws because of the existence of unusual administrative provisions."[1] Its ramifications for charitable trustees may be even more far-reaching.[2]

Powers of Trustees

The law of trusts does not merely impose negative restraints; it also recognizes and upholds grants of power to trustees to carry out their duties. A trustee may execute any powers specifically conferred on him by the terms of the trust so long as they are not contrary to law or public policy. In addition, a body of rules grants powers that the courts consider necessary and appropriate to the accomplishment of the trust purpose. Ordinarily a settlor may forbid the exercise of powers which, without such express provision, would normally be inferred from the nature of the trust.[3] In some instances, however, under the doctrine of deviation, the court may disregard these prohibitions if their exercise will impair accomplishment of the trust purpose.

The powers ordinarily conferred by the law are closely related to the trustees' duties. For example, a trustee must make the trust property productive. Accordingly, he is granted by law a power to invest and reinvest.[4] Similarly, he has the power to incur expenses,[5] to lease[6] and to sell property,[7] to compromise, arbitrate, or settle claims,[8] and to vote stock so long as it is not done against the interests of the benefici-

---

[1] Dunham, Allison, "Uniform Laws on Estates," *Trusts and Estates*, vol. 103, 1961, p. 818.

[2] A problem is presented by the definition in section 1 of the act, which defines "trust" as "an express trust created by a trust instrument, including a will, whereby a trustee has the duty to administer a trust asset for the benefit of a named or otherwise described income or principal beneficiary or both." Specifically excluded are resulting or constructive trusts and a number of other specifically described relationships which "do not admit of general administration." None of these exclusions is clearly applicable to charitable trusts, although the requirement of a named or otherwise described beneficiary could be interpreted as excluding trusts for charitable purposes, where by definition the beneficiaries must be "indefinite." Dunham does give as an example of the operation of section 3(b) the prohibition in the tax laws on a charitable trust to loan money to the creator of the trust (see *ibid.*), but it may be necessary in certain jurisdictions to alter the definition section to make explicit the question of the application of the act to charitable trusts and corporate foundations.

[3] *Restatement of the Law of Trusts (Second)*, *op. cit.*, sec. 380.

[4] *Ibid.*, sec. 227.

[5] *Ibid.*, secs. 188, 380b.

[6] *Ibid.*, secs. 189, 380c.

[7] *Ibid.*, secs. 190, 380d.

[8] *Ibid.*, secs. 192, 380f.

ary.[1] When the settlor of a foundation created to be the recipient of donations of stock in his closely held business is both the trustee and an officer of the corporation, there may be serious questions as to his ability to act for the interests of the beneficiaries.[2]

The powers of trustees of charitable trusts may in some cases be more extensive than those of trustees of private trusts as a result of the indefinite duration of the charitable trust. This is particularly true of the power to make long-term leases. Where land is the subject of a charitable trust, the courts have granted power to sell, even where it was expressly forbidden by the terms of the trust. However, if no power to sell can be inferred expressly or by implication, a court order authorizing sale is required, and the attorney general is ordinarily a necessary party to the suit.[3]

In general, the powers to mortgage or to pledge securities are not as broad as the powers to sell or lease. It is improper for a trustee to mortgage or pledge property unless the authority can be clearly implied from the purposes of the trust or from specific provisions therein, such as those granting a trustee power to deal with the property in his own discretion.[4]

As in the case of sales, the court may disregard an express prohibition and permit the mortgaging of property if it is necessary to carry out the purpose of the trust. For example, the New York Real Property Law[5] permits the Supreme Court to authorize the sale or mortgage of real estate held for charitable purposes when the property has or is likely to become unproductive, has depreciated or is likely to depreciate in value, when it is advisable to raise money to improve or erect buildings upon the property, or when it is expedient for any other reason.[6]

---

[1] *Ibid.*, secs. 193, 380g.

[2] See Scott, Austin W., *The Law of Trusts, op. cit.*, sec. 193.1; and Sacks, Albert M., "Use and Misuse of the Private Foundation," *Proceedings* of the New York University Fifth Biennial Conference on Charitable Foundations, Edited by Henry Sellin, Matthew Bender and Co., New York, 1961, p. 217.

[3] *Congregational Church Union of Boston* v. *Attorney General*, 290 Mass. 1, 194 N.E. 820 (1935). *Trustees of Sailors' Snug Harbor* v. *Carmody*, 211 N.Y. 286, 105 N.E. 543 (1914). If the trust instrument expressly provides for a reversion of the property to the donor or his heirs in case of sale, the court will not permit the sale in spite of a change of condition. *Roberds* v. *Markham*, 81 F. Supp. 38 (D.D.C. 1948). Conditions of this type are usually strictly construed, however.

[4] See Annotation "Powers of Trustees of Charitable Trusts to Mortgage Trust Property," *American Law Reports*, vol. 127, 1940, p. 705.

[5] Sec. 113(4).

[6] See Scott, Austin W., *The Law of Trusts, op. cit.*, secs. 191, 191.2.

As trusts have come to be used for an ever-expanding variety of purposes, the powers of trustees have been expanded to make the trust device better suited to its modern use. In some states this has been accomplished through the enactment of statutes granting to trustees greater powers than those traditionally conferred by equity courts. They are generally applicable to trustees of charitable as well as private trusts.[1] Even where these statutes are in force, however, the trend is to write into trust instruments broad powers to deal with the trust property, as well as to limit as far as possible the liability of the trustees.

Uniform State Laws

The National Conference of Commissioners on Uniform State Law has drafted several Uniform Acts relating to trusts which have been adopted in various states.[2] The Uniform Fiduciaries' Act[3] deals with various situations in which it is sought to charge with liability for participation in a breach of trust third persons who have entered into transactions with a trustee or other fiduciary. The revised Uniform Principal and Income Act[4] is designed to provide a convenient and workable rule for this aspect of the administration of trusts and is applicable in the absence of express contrary intentions by the settlor. In most respects it follows the common law, although there are some exceptions. It has been enacted in four states and substantially copied in recent revision in New York. The Uniform Trustees' Accounting Act[5] establishes standardized procedures for trustee accounts and contains provisions regarding court supervision. The Uniform Trusts Act[6] is a codification of trust doctrine. The most recently promulgated of these Uniform Acts, The Uniform Trustees' Powers Act, seeks to extend the principle established in the prudent man investment statutes to the field of trustees' powers.[7] The Uniform Act for Supervision of Charitable Trustees is discussed in detail in Chapter VII. It should be noted that the various states often make changes in these Uniform Laws at the time of enactment. The laws do provide a certain mini-

---

[1] Fratcher, William F., "Trustees' Powers Legislation," *New York University Law Review,* vol. 37, 1962, p. 627, contains a listing and discussion of many of these statutory provisions.
[2] See Table 1 of Appendix A for listing and citations.
[3] *Uniform Laws Annotated, op. cit.,* vol. 9B, pp. 10 ff.
[4] *Ibid.,* pp. 365 ff.
[5] *Ibid.,* vol. 9C, pp. 273 ff.
[6] *Ibid.,* pp. 289 ff.
[7] Uniform Trustees' Powers Act, *op. cit.*

mum degree of uniformity but state legislatures often modify or omit certain sections before their adoption.

Exercise of Discretionary Powers by Trustees

Often a trust instrument confers broad powers of discretion on a trustee as to either the administration of the trust or the application of the funds. A wide grant of discretion as to the method of distributing funds in fulfillment of the charitable purpose is essential to the nature of foundations, although it may be present in certain other types of charitable trusts. Courts do not interfere with decisions of this nature unless it can be clearly shown that the exercise was not within the bounds of reasonable judgment. The duty of the court is not to substitute its own judgment for that of the trustee but to consider whether he has acted in good faith, from proper motivation, and within the bounds of judgment which appear to the court to be reasonable.

> In determining whether the trustee is acting within the bounds of a reasonable judgment the following circumstances may be relevant: (1) The extent of discretion intended to be conferred upon the trustee by the terms of the trust; (2) the existence or non-existence, the definiteness or indefiniteness of an external standard by which the reasonableness of the trustee's conduct can be judged; (3) the circumstances surrounding the exercise of the power; (4) the motives of the trustee in exercising or refraining from exercising the power; (5) the existence or non-existence of an interest in the trustee conflicting with that of the beneficiaries.[1]

The courts will not relinquish all powers to supervise a trustee no matter how broad a grant of freedom is incorporated in a trust instrument. For example, in the case of *Conway* v. *Emeny,* a testator, in creating a trust for the benefit of a museum, gave to the trustees "absolute" discretion to determine a certain matter. The court stated, "It is apparent from the presence of the word 'absolute' that she intended to give them considerable discretion. The use of the qualifying adjective, however, did not give unlimited discretion and the grant of authority, broad as it was, did not necessarily remove the trustees from judicial supervision."[2]

In decisions rendered in 1964 and 1965[3] the Massachusetts Su-

---

[1] Scott, Austin W., *The Law of Trusts, op. cit.,* sec. 187.

[2] 139 Conn. 612, 96 A.2d 221 (1953). See also *In re James' Estate,* 119 N.Y.S. 2d 259 and 130 N.Y.S.2d 691 (1953) involving a charitable foundation.

[3] *Copp* v. *Worcester County National Bank,* 347 Mass. 548, 199 N.E.2d 200 (1964); *Boston Safe Deposit and Trust Company* v. *Stone,* _____ Mass. _____, 203 N.E.2d 547 (1965).

preme Judicial Court reiterated the position that the exercise of even
the broadest of discretionary powers is still subject to supervision under principles of equity:

> Indeed, even with respect to very broad discretionary powers "a court of
> equity may control a trustee in the exercise of a fiduciary discretion
> if its acts beyond the bounds of a reasonable judgment or unreasonably
> disregards usual fiduciary principles, or the purposes of the trust, or if it
> fails to observe standards of judgment apparent from the applicable
> instrument." Such fiduciary powers cannot be used arbitrarily, capri-
> ciously, or in bad faith, but must be "exercised after serious and re-
> sponsible consideration, prudently, and in accordance with fiduciary
> standards." See *Copp* v. *Worcester County National Bank,* 347 Mass.
> 548 (1964)[1]

Exercise of Powers by Majority of Trustees

There is a very important difference between the administration of
charitable trusts and that of private trusts. In a private trust powers
can be exercised only with the concurrence of all the trustees; whereas
in a charitable trust, the affirmation of a majority is sufficient unless
there is a provision in the trust instrument requiring unanimity.[2] A
trustee who refuses to join with the majority in an action that constitutes a breach of trust is not liable for the consequences of the majority action, but he may have a duty to apply to the court to prevent
the action.[3]

Liability of Trustees for Breach of Trust

When a breach of trust is committed, the redress provided by law
will vary with the nature of the breach. In severe cases a court may
remove a trustee in a proceeding brought by the attorney general, or
by his cotrustees if there are any. In addition, if a trustee fails to dis-

---

[1] *Boston Safe Deposit and Trust Company* v. *Stone,* _____ Mass. _____, _____
N.E.2d _____ (1965). In this case the court expressed open disagreement with
the decision of the United States Court of Appeals for the First Circuit in *State
Street Bank and Trust Company* v. *U.S.,* 263 F.2d 635 (1st Cir. 1959) which
had been based on Massachusetts law and held that powers given to trustees
under the trust in question were so broad and all inclusive as to nullify effective
court supervision and to permit the trustee to shift the economic benefits of the
trust.

[2] Scott, Austin W., *The Law of Trusts, op. cit.,* sec. 383; *Restatement of the
Law of Trusts (Second), op. cit.,* sec. 383; *City of Boston* v. *Doyle,* 184 Mass.
373, 68 N.E. 851 (1903); *Morville* v. *Fowle,* 144 Mass. 109, 10 N.E. 766
(1887).

[3] *Sheets* v. *Security First Mortgage Co.,* 293 Ill. App. 222, 12 N.E.2d 324
(1937); *Heard* v. *March,* 12 Cush. 580 (Mass. 1853). *Comstock* v. *Dewey,* 323
Mass. 583, 83 N.E. 2d 257 (1949).

charge one or more of his duties, or otherwise falls below the standard of care required of him, the law seeks to place the beneficiary in the position that he would have occupied had there been no breach of trust. The liabilities imposed on the defaulting trustee are designed to attain this objective.[1] The trustee, therefore, is liable to account for the trust property and all of its proceeds. He is chargeable for any loss of the trust property arising from a breach of trust. A breach of trust may consist of a violation of any duty owing to the beneficiary. Ordinarily, it involves an act in which the trustee is personally at fault, but it can also consist of a failure to exercise the care and skill of an ordinary man of prudence which results in loss, even though the trustee has done the best he can. In general, reliance on legal counsel is not sufficient to relieve a trustee from liability.[2]

If a trustee has doubt as to his powers or duties, the law allows him to obtain instructions from a court. In following the instructions, he will be protected from a later charge of breach of duty. A trustee may present to the court any question involving a proper construction of the trust instrument or a determination between conflicting claims. The primary limitation on the use of this procedure is that the problem must be practical, not theoretical, and in need of prompt decision. If the question relates to an exercise of discretion, the court will not usually give instructions.[3] In a petition for instructions by trustees of a charitable trust, the attorney general is a proper party to the proceeding, and in many states he is a necessary party.[4]

If there has been a breach of trust, the beneficiaries of a private trust have three possible alternative remedies. They may charge the trustee (1) with any loss that resulted from the breach, (2) with any profits made through the breach, or (3) with any profits that would have accrued if there had been no breach of trust. Interest is awarded as a form of income not received, not as a penalty.

In the case of a trust for charitable purposes, the interest paid by a trustee will become part of the trust fund and be distributed in accordance with the purposes of the trust. In most cases, a trustee will be liable for simple interest, although in some cases of deliberate fraud or

[1] Loring, Augustus, *op. cit.*, p. 154.
[2] See Scott, Austin W., *The Law of Trusts, op. cit.*, sec. 201, and *The Restatement of the Law of Trusts (Second), op. cit.*, sec. 201, for further discussion.
[3] Scott, Austin W., *The Law of Trusts, op. cit.*, sec. 394; and *Kirwin* v. *Attorney General*, 275 Mass. 34, 175 N.E. 164 (1931).
[4] See Table 1 of Appendix A and Chapter VI.

a violation of express instructions, the court has required a payment of compound interest.[1]

The accountability of trustees is not confined to cases where there has been a breach of trust, however. The duty of loyalty requires that even when the trustee has committed no wrong through intention or negligence, and even if he is unaware of any moral fault, he is under an obligation to avoid possible conflicts of interest. Therefore, if he makes any personal profit through, or arising from, the administration of the trust, he is accountable to the trust for the amount he receives. For example, if a trustee receives a commission or bonus from a purchase or sale of trust property which is not itself improper, he must nevertheless pass the profit on the trust. If he buys with his own funds an encumbrance on the trust property, he is accountable for any profits he makes thereby.[2]

The remedies for breach of trust in the case of a charitable trust are equitable. They may include, in addition to restitution and accounting, a decree of specific performance, injunction, the appointment of a receiver, or the removal of the trustee. A trustee may also be guilty of a criminal offence such as embezzlement or larceny. Failure to comply with certain statutes requiring registration or licensing of trustees who are soliciting funds from the public for charitable purposes is in some states a criminal act.[3]

The power to remove trustees is, in a sense, the most extreme remedy the court can impose. The question of removal is ordinarily a matter for the exercise of a sound discretion of the court, and in deciding this type of case, the court will take into account all circumstances relating to the matter. The mere fact that a trustee has committed a breach of trust is not necessarily a ground for his removal. Serious breaches of trust will be remedied by removal, however, even if they were not committed dishonestly. Refusal or neglect to obey court orders has been held to be a ground for a removal action,[4] as have in-

---

[1] *Lewis Prichard Charity Fund* v. *Mankin Investment Co.,* 118 W.Va. 134, 189 S.E. 96 (1936); see also Scott, Austin W., *The Law of Trusts, op. cit.,* sec. 207.1, for list of cases.

[2] *Restatement of the Law of Trusts (Second), op. cit.,* sec. 203; Niles, Russell, "Trustee Accountability in the Absence of Breach of Trust," *Columbia Law Review,* vol. 60, 1960, p. 141.

[3] For example, Mass. Gen. Laws Ann., ch. 68 sec. 17, and N.J. Rev. Stat., sec. 2A:111–30.

[4] *Attorney General* v. *Garrison,* 101 Mass. 223 (1869); *Restatement of the Law of Trusts (Second), op. cit.,* sec. 107; and see Scott, Austin W., *The Law of Trusts, op. cit.,* secs. 107 and 387, for collection of cases.

stances of willful breach of trust, unfitness, long continued absence, or excessive use of the trustee's powers. The matter of removal is dealt with by legislation in many jurisdictions,[1] but in most cases these statutes merely set forth the powers of the court in general terms. This subject will be discussed further in Chapters VI and VII relating to enforcement procedures available to the attorney general as representative of the beneficiaries of charitable trusts. Furthermore, it should be remembered that an exculpatory clause may, to a certain degree, absolve a trustee from liability which would otherwise follow from a breach of trust.

Liability to Third Persons

It is often said that the chief disadvantage of forming a foundation as a trust is that the trustee is personally liable for all actions taken by him as trustee and legal actions may be brought against him personally.

Until recently the courts held that all obligations arising out of either contracts or torts made in the course of administration of a trust rested upon, and only upon, the trustee personally. If the trustee was not personally at fault, he was entitled to repayment, or indemnity, from the trust estate, but the legal action had to be brought against the trustee. In recent years, there has been a relaxation of this view, noticeable in court decisions and statutes alike, so that today it is possible under many circumstances for a plaintiff to bring an action in equity directly against the trust estate.[2] A trustee may be relieved of his personal liability by means of a provision in the contract specifically stating this fact. Often such a provision is included in the trust instrument itself, but the courts require that the other party to the contract have notice of the provision.[3]

If a trustee commits a tort during the course of administration of the trust, the question of the trustee's liability will depend upon whether the trustee himself was personally at fault. These cases are rare. The question of whether an injured party can also sue the trust directly is complicated by the fact that in some states property of charitable institutions has been held to be exempt from tort liability.

---

[1] See Scott, Austin W., *The Law of Trusts, op. cit.*, secs. 107 and 387, for citations.

[2] *Restatement of the Law of Trusts (Second)*, *op. cit.*, sec. 262; and Scott, Austin W., *The Law of Trusts, op. cit.*, sec. 262.

[3] Scott, Austin W., *The Law of Trusts, op. cit.*, sec. 262.2.

In these states no action can be brought against the trust property. In the states that do not grant immunity to charities, recovery is allowed out of the trust estate.[1]

Compensation of Trustees

Trustees of all trusts are permitted reasonable compensation for services rendered in the course of their administration of the trust, as well as remuneration of expenses incurred. The amount of a trustee's fee is often stated in the trust instrument, and, in fact, the English rule is that the trustee is not entitled to compensation unless the instrument so provides. There is no such restriction in the United States, however, where the matter is controlled by statute in almost all jurisdictions.[2] Most of these statutes merely provide that the court may direct compensation reasonable in amount, although some include a fixed schedule.[3] In certain states the statute refers only to executors but has been held by the courts to govern trustees as well.

In the case of charitable trusts, it is customary for corporate trustees to be compensated at a rate comparable to that of a trustee of a private trust. As a general rule, however, individual trustees of charitable foundations do not receive compensation other than reimbursement for expenses incident to meetings or for travel. F. Emerson Andrews' work, *Philanthropic Foundations,* contains a description of some of the exceptions to this general rule.[4] The observation of those who have examined reports from foundations submitted to the attorney general's offices of several states is that very few of the smaller, family foundations pay compensation to trustees, although no statistics are available. As Andrews reports:

> The weight of current opinion is against payment of trustees, though, as Dr. Young indicated, it is not a "black or white" decision. Where the duties are arduous and time-consuming compensation is defensible and may be desirable. Where such duties do not interfere seriously with the ordinary occupation, charitable trusteeship seems a proper voluntary contribution to the general welfare. A nonpayment policy also avoids any suspicion that the foundation may be a device for channeling tax-exempt income to family members or friends of the donor.[5]

---

[1] *Ibid.,* sec. 402.2.
[2] *Ibid.,* sec. 242.
[3] For example, N.Y. Civ. Prac. Law, sec. 1548, N.Y. Surr. Ct. Act, sec. 285a. See Loring, Augustus, *op. cit.,* Appendix I, p. 351, for a summary of the statutory provisions in the various states.
[4] Russell Sage Foundation, New York, 1956, pp. 84–87.
[5] *Ibid.,* p. 87.

CHAPTER IV

Foundations as Corporations

THE POPULARITY OF THE CORPORATE DEVISE for establishing charitable foundations can be attributed, in part, to the pervasiveness of the corporate form in American business life and to the familiarity of the creators of foundations with corporate operation. The corporation became popular in this country because it provided the means whereby large amounts of capital could be raised from investors whose ownership would be divorced from the responsibility of management and the liability for debt of the organization.

The most widely quoted definition of a corporation is that of Chief Justice Marshall in the case of *Trustees of Dartmouth College* v. *Woodward*.

A corporation is an artificial being, invisible, intangible, and existing only in contemplation of law. Being the mere creature of law, it possesses only those properties which the charter of its creation confers upon it, either expressly or as incidental to its very existence. These are such as are supposed best calculated to effect the object for which it was created. Among the most important are immortality, and, if the expression may be allowed, individuality; properties by which a perpetual succession of many persons are considered as the same, and may act as a single individual. They enable a corporation to manage its own affairs, and to hold property without the perplexing intricacies, the hazardous and endless necessity, of perpetual conveyances for the purpose of transmitting it from hand to hand. It is chiefly for the purpose of clothing bodies of men, in succession, with these qualities and capacities, that corporations were invented, and are in use. By these means, a perpetual succession of individuals are capable of acting for the promotion of the particular object, like one immortal thing.[1]

---

[1] 4 Wheat. 636, 4 L.Ed. 629, 635 (1819).

112

This definition may be more appropriate for a charitable corporation than for its business counterpart, since the primary reason for the increase in the use of corporations for business purposes was the limited liability it offered to shareholders.

The two most important elements in this definition are that a corporation exists only by virtue of law and that it is treated in law as an individual entity capable of acting in many respects as a single individual. The right to existence as a corporation can be granted only by an act of the state. As was noted earlier, the original "franchises" granted by the King and later by Parliament to certain groups of men were accompanied by privileges, usually a monopoly to trade in certain areas or to operate a local "public work" such as a ferry, or in the case of charitable corporations, freedom from taxation. Implicit in the act of the sovereign was the assumption that some return would accrue to the public good from the grant of corporate existence. As the law of business corporations developed, the concept of the public good became less predominant, and with wider recognition of the advantages of corporate organization, the requirements for creation were gradually liberalized by the legislatures.

During the period when general incorporation statutes were enacted to liberalize the method of creating corporations, there was uniformity among the states in the provisions adopted for incorporation of business organizations, but not in the provisions for charitable and other not-for-profit organizations. In some states, a section of the general business corporation act was applicable to not-for-profit corporations; in others, legislation regarding religious and educational corporations was separate from legislation for other types of nonprofit activities; and in still others, no mention of not-for-profit organizations appeared in the statute books at all. The last case is still true in Delaware, which was the leader in the development of business corporation law but has no significant statute for nonprofit corporations.

> General statutes relating to non-profit corporations now exist in almost endless variety. Some are elaborately designed as to scope, administration and regulation; others consist of a mere paragraph or so, wholly devoid of administrative and procedural guidance; while others are interwoven with business corporations in an over-all statute. This lack of uniformity or systematic approach to an important field of statutory law is probably attributable more to inattention than to the inherent difficulties of drafting a suitable general statute.[1]

---

[1] *Model Non-Profit Corporation Act*. American Law Institute, Philadelphia, 1952, p. 12.

A Model Non-Profit Corporation Act was prepared in 1952 by the Committee on Corporate Laws and the Committee on Non-Profit Corporations of the American Bar Association. It was revised in 1957 and again in 1964. It has been used as the basis for statutes in nine states.[1]

Requirements for the Creation of Charitable Corporations

The wide variety of the state laws relating to not-for-profit corporations makes it impossible to describe any specific rules regarding creation of a charitable corporation. Table 2 in Appendix A contains a summary of the legislative provisions in each state and some of the principal sources of state power to supervise corporations of this nature.

Unlike a trust, a corporation cannot come into existence without authorization from the state. Its existence depends upon a specific grant of authority from the sovereign. The method for receiving the authorization is today in almost all instances purely a matter of complying with a statutory requirement that certain papers be placed on file with an appropriate state official, usually the secretary of state. In some states, instruments must also be filed with an official in the county or district in which the office of the corporation is to be located. Usually five or more persons of legal capacity must sign the application, and certain basic information such as its purposes, powers, and the names and addresses of the directors, and the members, if there are any, must be included.

Upon receipt of the application and a filing fee, if one is required, in all but ten states a state official will automatically issue a charter or certificate of incorporation to the incorporators or their representatives. The corporation will then be in existence for all legal purposes. In several states, the appropriate state official is directed by statute to inquire as to whether the articles conform to law, and he may refuse to issue a certificate if they do not. This review is cursory, and while it does give some residual power to the secretary of state or commissioner of corporations, it cannot be considered in the nature of true supervisory power.

New York. Several states do have more stringent provisions regarding the creation of charitable corporations. The New York Member-

---

[1] *Ibid.* The Wisconsin, Ohio, North Carolina, Virginia, Alabama, Texas, Nevada, North Dakota, Oregon, Illinois, and Missouri acts are "quite similar." See Table 2 of Appendix A for citations.

ship Corporation Law contains the most detailed provisions regarding not-for-profit corporations. Four or more persons may form a membership corporation by filing a certificate of incorporation with the secretary of state together with a filing fee of $40. The certificate must be notorized and include specified information regarding the name of the corporation, its purposes, a statement of its nonprofit nature, the locality wherein its activities are to be conducted, the address of the corporate office, the number of directors or trustees or a stated maximum or minimum number, their residences, and a statement that two-thirds are citizens of the United States and at least one is also a resident of the state.[1]

Every certificate must have endorsed thereon the approval of a justice of the Supreme Court of the judicial district in which the office of the corporation is to be located. If the certificate specifies among its purposes, powers, or provisions any charitable or benevolent uses, purposes, or powers, five days' written notice of the application for judicial approval, accompanied by a copy of the proposed certificate, must be given to the attorney general. The statute provides that a justice may withhold approval if the name of the proposed corporation includes all or part of the name of a living person who has not executed the certificate.[2]

The extent of this judicial power to withhold approval has been the subject of some controversy. The earliest cases seemed to indicate that the judge was charged with determining from the statement in the certificate whether the proposed purposes were lawful. If he found the purposes to be lawful, the justice could not refuse approval. In several cases, however, evidence was heard as to the intent of the incorporators, and approval was withheld after a showing that the proposed purposes would be carried out in a manner contrary to public policy. For example, in *In re General von Steuben Bund, Inc.,*[3] the court upheld the decision of a justice that the organization would perpetuate a division of people into racial groups by uniting persons of German background or descent. This case has been criticized by several writers, who implied that the judges were exceeding their statutory power.[4]

Then in 1961, in the case of *Association for Preservation of Free-*

---

[1] N.Y. Membership Corp. Law, sec. 10.
[2] *Ibid.*
[3] 287 N.Y.S. 527, 159 Misc. 231 (1936).
[4] See Dwight, G.H.P., "Objections to Judicial Approval of Charters of Nonprofit Corporations," *Business Law,* vol. 12, 1957, p. 454.

dom of Choice v. *Shapiro,*[1] the New York Court of Appeals reversed a lower court action and held that a justice was not at liberty to grant or deny applications on his personal notion of what was contrary to public policy, but was limited solely to the question of whether the stated purpose was lawful. This case would seem to dispose, for the present, of the use of this statutory provision to control the purposes for which membership corporations may be formed, so long as they appear on their face to be legal.[2]

The court is also given the authority, notwithstanding prior approval by a justice of the Supreme Court, to order dissolution of a corporation if its name includes all or part of the name of a living person who had not executed the certificate.

Upon receipt of a fully executed certificate, the secretary of state signifies approval by signing or stamping and indexing the certificate. It is at this point that the corporate existence is said to begin.[3] Notice of this acceptance is sent to the attorney for the corporation, and a copy of the certificate is mailed to the clerk of the county in which the corporate office is located. This copy is kept in the county files and is the public record of incorporation which may be inspected by interested persons.[4]

Pennsylvania. The Pennsylvania Code also contains a provision requiring approval of an application for incorporation by the Court of Common Pleas of the county where the corporation is to be registered. The statute reads in part, "If the court shall find the articles to be in proper form and within the provisions of this act, and the purpose or purposes given in the articles to be lawful and not injurious to the community, and that the name is presently available for corporate use, as evidenced by a certificate from the Secretary of the Commonwealth, the court shall certify the articles approved."[5] If exceptions are filed, the court is authorized to appoint a master to report on the propriety of granting the application and to conduct hearings. Notice of the intention to apply to the court for a charter must be advertised once in two newspapers.

---

[1] 214 N.Y.S.2d 388, 9 N.Y.2d 376 (1961); rehearing denied 11 N.Y.2d 662 180 N.E.2d 898 (1962).

[2] See Vance, Arthur Charles, "Freedom of Association and Freedom of Choice in New York State," *Cornell Law Quarterly,* vol. 46, 1961, p. 290.

[3] State of New York, Opinions of the Attorney General, Albany, November 19, 1941.

[4] N.Y. Gen. Corp. Law, sec. 8.

[5] Pa. Stat. Ann., tit. 15, sec. 2851–207.

The power specifically granted to the court in this statute is broader than that in the New York Membership Corporation Law. There have been few reported cases challenging a judicial decision, however, and none more recent than *Application for Charter of the Conversion Center, Inc.*[1] decided in 1957.[2] In this case the Supreme Court reversed a lower court order which had refused a charter to the Conversion Center on the grounds that incorporation for the stated purposes, that is, to create a center to encourage religious conversion, would, in effect, place the blanket of approval of the court on such activity and "might well lead to a condition of unrest in the community. . . ." The upper court rejected this as a proper ground for denial of a charter. It stated that since the court's function was to determine whether the purposes, as set forth in the proposed articles, were lawful and not injurious to the public, the question was not one of placing a stamp of approval on the purposes but of determining the possibility of harm.

> Nothing in the purpose clause of the proposed incorporation or in the evidence adduced at the hearings indicates that the activities of the corporation would consist of or include acts inimical to the peace, good order or morals of society, but quite clearly the contrary. If the activities engendered reaction resulting in a breach of the peace, the sanctions of law are available. . . . But an interdiction based on nothing more than the possibility of some future transgression of the law is a violation of the applicable constitutional guarantees."[3]

In spite of this case, however, in the statutes of both Pennsylvania and New York there is a latent power to control incorporation which may have a restrictive effect on individuals seeking to create charitable corporations.

Massachusetts. The Massachusetts General Laws contain a specific chapter entitled "Corporations for Charitable and Certain Other Purposes," which governs the creation of charitable corporations as well as a wide variety of civic and social groups.[4] Before issuing a certificate of incorporation, the secretary of state is empowered to make an inquiry to the town or city of each of the proposed incoporators or officers to determine whether they have been "engaged in the illegal selling of alcoholic beverages . . . or in keeping places or tenements used for

---

[1] 388 Pa. 239, 130 A.2d 107 (1957).
[2] For discussion of earlier cases see Note "Judicial Approval as a Prerequisite to Incorporation of Non-Profit Organizations in New York and Pennsylvania," *Columbia Law Review*, vol. 55, 1955, p. 380.
[3] 130 A.2d 107, 111.
[4] Mass. Gen. Laws Ann., ch. 180.

illegal gaming or any other business or vocation prohibited by law, or are persons of ill repute, or whether any location to be occupied is unsuitable." On the basis of this report, the secretary of state may decide that the formation of the corporation "is or will be" to cover or shield any illegal business or practices or any business not within the scope of the expressed corporate purposes; and if he so finds, he must refuse the application.[1]

In addition, the articles of organization of any charitable corporation whose purposes are such that its personal property will be exempt from taxation must be referred to the Department of Public Welfare for investigation of the proposed purposes and the character of the incorporators. The Department of Public Welfare is required to conduct a public hearing after three weeks' notice of the scheduled date has been published in an appropriate newspaper. Following the hearing, the commissioner of the Department must make findings of facts as to the purposes, need, and suitability of the proposed corporation, and must approve or disapprove the application. This information is then forwarded to the secretary of state. If the report is favorable, the secretary must approve the charter application; if the report disapproves the application, he must refuse approval of the articles. A right of judicial appeal to the Supreme Judicial Court is then given to the applicants.[2]

The time involved in meeting these elaborate administrative prerequisites has served as a deterrent to some individuals, particularly when they are desirous of forming a charitable foundation before the end of a taxable year. Investigations by local officials are usually perfunctory in the case of foundations, their chief purpose being to provide a means of control over corporations which will be social clubs serving alcoholic beverages. There have been no recorded cases of appeals to the court from aggrieved parties seeking charters for charitable purposes, although the statute has been in force since 1901.

There are 12,000 active not-for-profit corporations in Massachusetts, but no record is kept of the number that would be considered by law to be charitable corporations. The secretary of state's office in Massachusetts approved charters for 475 nonprofit corporations in the fiscal year beginning July, 1962. This figure includes all charitable corporations whose charters were first approved by the Department of Public Welfare.

---

[1] Mass. Gen. Laws Ann., ch. 180, sec. 5.
[2] Mass. Gen. Laws Ann., ch. 180, sec. 6.

The secretary of state has adopted a literal wording of the statute governing incorporation procedure whereby only those applications which contain the word "charitable" are referred to the Department of Public Welfare for hearings. Therefore, an application to charter a foundation organized for religious purposes, for scholarships, or to conduct medical, scientific, or general research would not be subject to the hearing procedure.[1]

In 1963 the Department of Public Welfare held hearings on 64 applications for charters or requests for a substantive change in purpose of an existing corporation. An additional 74 applications were referred back to the secretary of state as not requiring the Department's approval. Many of these were requests from foundations for amendments which would require *cy pres* distribution of assets on dissolution, and were being sought to conform to requirements of the federal Internal Revenue Service. The others were declared not to be for charitable purposes in the narrow sense. All applications received that year were approved. The Department has established as conditions for approval that a proposed organization show that it has adequate financing and is sufficiently constituted to be capable of carrying out its purposes. These are not officially promulgated standards, however.

The failure to require hearings for those corporations whose purposes would be considered charitable under trust law has led to some divergence between these two departments. For example, a group of individuals desiring to create a nationwide organization to raise funds for scholarships had sought a charter that stated its purposes as "educational and charitable." Before taking final action, the Department of Public Welfare advised the group informally that it would not be properly organized to carry on its stated purposes and advised it to resubmit plans of operation. The group was unable to do so, and instead withdrew the application, deleted the word "charitable" from its charter, and subsequently received approval from the secretary of state.

South Carolina. South Carolina is the only other state where applications for charters of charitable corporations are referred to the Welfare Department. The statute requires that before the secretary of state may issue a charter the Department of Welfare must investigate the

---

[1] Information obtained from interviews with officials in Department of Public Welfare and Office of Secretary of State, Commonwealth of Massachusetts, State House, Boston, March, 1964.

merits of the proposed charitable corporation and recommend approval.[1]

California. California and Michigan each have two separate and distinct statutory methods for incorporating foundations. In California the choice of statute affects the future organization or the corporation, but not the enforcement procedures of the state. The General Non-Profit Corporation Law is similar to that found in other jurisdictions.[2] It gives wide latitude to the incorporators and members to prescribe the number of directors and their terms of office, and the conditions of membership. Section 10200 of the Corporation Code provides for the incorporation of "Corporations for Charitable and Eleemosynary Purposes." There must be 25 or more incorporators and no fewer than 9 nor more than 25 director-trustees whose terms of office may be for no more than six years. The articles may provide either that the board of trustees constitutes the corporation or that there also be a membership, in which case the by-laws must specify the terms and qualifications. The statute specifically permits provisions in the articles of incorporation for delegation of the management and investment of funds to a separate finance committee of no fewer than three board members or to a bank and trust company; it also allows investment in common trust funds. This section of the code specifically states that property and funds received by such a corporation shall "be held upon the trust that they be used for charitable and eleemosynary purposes."[3] Because of its restrictions, this section of the Corporation Code is not used as often as the less stringent provisions of the general nonprofit sections for incorporation of foundations.

Michigan. The Michigan corporation act contains special provisions[4] for the incorporation of foundations; however, the sections relating to nonprofit corporations generally also may be used for incorporation of foundations.[5] The provisions relating to foundations were first enacted in 1917.[6] Three incorporators are required. The purposes may be as broad or narrow as desired as long as they look toward the betterment of human welfare. The foundation is forbidden

---

[1] S.C. Code Ann., sec. 12–755.
[2] Cal. Corp. Code, secs. 9000 ff.
[3] Cal. Corp. Code, sec. 10206(c).
[4] Mich. Stat. Ann., sec. 21.1 ff.
[5] Mich. Stat. Ann. secs. 21.118 ff. For complete discussion see Boyer, Ralph, *Non-Profit Corporation Statutes:* A Critique and a Proposal, University of Michigan Law School, Ann Arbor, 1957.
[6] Mich. Stat. Ann., sec. 21.164 to 21.170.

to issue stock, but there is no statutory limit placed on the property which the corporation may hold. The trustees are free to expend income for their purposes, but investment of principal must follow the state law regarding investment by trustees.[1] The only statutory restriction on the initial organization of the corporation is that there be no fewer than 3 nor more than 15 trustees.[2] The decision as to whether to have other members, and the terms of office of both trustees and members, are to be prescribed in the by-laws. There is no specific method for dissolution, but power is given to the legislature to wind up a foundation and dispose of its assets for similar purposes if it is no longer able to serve the original purpose or if its funds are being diverted.[3] Use of the words "foundation" and "fund" is limited by the State Corporation Commission to Corporations organized under this section of the laws.

The act also includes a section enacted in 1952 which states:

> . . . Every corporation heretofore formed under any law of this state for benevolent or charitable purposes, and having no capital stock, shall be deemed to be a foundation within the meaning of this act and shall be subject to the provisions hereof excepting as such provisions may conflict with the articles and by-laws of any such corporation heretofore lawfully made and enacted pursuant to the act under which incorporated. But any such corporation may amend its articles and by-laws so as to bring itself in conformity with the provisions hereof.[4]

Incorporation under the general provisions for nonprofit organizations subjects the corporation to a limit on its property of not more than that necessary for carrying out the stated purposes. The act does permit the creation of a stock corporation, with stock of any amount up to $100 per share. No dividends may be paid, and the act states that on dissolution, excess assets may be distributed to members, although this provision is clearly inconsistent with Michigan law requiring *cy pres* application of charitable funds.[5] Shares and membership certificates may be transferable if it is so provided in the by-laws.[6] The board of directors must consist of at least three individuals, and if their term is for more than one year, one-third of the board must be elected every year.[7]

---

[1] Mich. Stat. Ann., sec. 21.165.
[2] Mich. Stat. Ann., sec. 21.167.
[3] Mich. Stat. Ann., sec. 21.168.
[4] Mich. Stat. Ann., sec. 21.169.
[5] Boyer, Ralph, *op. cit.*, p. 182.
[6] Mich. Stat. Ann., sec. 21.118.
[7] Gen. Corp. Act, Mich. Stat. Ann., sec. 21.125

Indiana. In Indiana also, there is a specific statutory provision for incorporation of foundations. The statute permits incorporation as a "foundation" or "holding company" to promote religious, educational, or charitable purposes.[1] The requirements for incorporation are similar to those in the Indiana not-for-profit act,[2] except that a minimum of five incorporators is required under the foundation act compared to the three required under the general act. The number of directors and their terms of office are similarly somewhat restricted. The chief advantage of incorporating under this statute is that the real property held by the foundations so created and used for the corporate purposes is automatically exempt from state taxation. In 1961 an amendment to the law provided a method for existing corporate organizations whose purposes were consistent with this section to accept the provisions of the act.[3]

States Permitting Stock Corporations. Creation of stock corporations is specifically allowed in Minnesota,[4] Pennsylvania,[5] and Iowa,[6] as well as in Michigan. Moreover, it is the accepted practice in those other states, notably Delaware, where the only method for incorporation is under the general business corporation law. In the formation of stock corporations, the articles of organization will usually contain a provision stating that the corporation is not organized for private profit and that no distribution of dividends to stockholders is contemplated.

It has been stated that the use of a stock corporation for charitable purposes represents a misconception of the concept of not-for-profit corporations,[7] and in some instances this is clearly the case. For example, an article on "Problems of Foundation Organization and Qualification"[8] states that since stockholders of foundations are subject to only light liabilities for the acts of the corporation while members of a membership corporation lack certainty regarding their liability, "some people who might be unwilling to act as members of a membership corporation, might very well be willing to act as stockholders of a

---

[1] Ind. Ann. Stat., secs. 25–1101 to 25–1111.
[2] Ind. Ann. Stat. secs. 25–508 ff.
[3] Ind. Ann. Stat., sec. 25–1112.
[4] Minn. Stat., sec. 317.08.
[5] Pa. Stat. Ann., tit. 15, sec. 2851–304.
[6] Iowa Code, sec. 504.10.
[7] Oleck, Howard L., *Non-Profit Corporations and Associations*. Prentice-Hall, Inc., New York, 1956, p. 6.
[8] Kramer, Jay O., in *Proceedings* of the New York University Second Biennial Conference on Charitable Foundations. Edited by Henry Sellin. Matthew Bender and Co., New York, 1955, p. 5.

stock corporation which is formed for the purposes of a charitable foundation."[1]

This same article suggests that a secretary of state may resist the filing of a certificate of a stock corporation designed to be a charitable foundation and recommends that the stock corporation be formed in Delaware and then qualified in the home state, a procedure which is easier than obtaining the original certificate. The propriety of such a suggestion is certainly open to question. This problem arises only in a minority of the states, however, as the great majority of not-for-profit corporation acts specifically forbid the issuance of stock and the payment of dividends.[2]

Reporting Provisions[3]

In 25 states the statutes relating to the creation of charitable corporations impose a duty to report at certain intervals to a state official on the status of the corporation. In 14 states the report consists of information as to the location of the corporation and a list of its current officers or directors; in 7 states it must contain financial information; and in 4 others, it consists of detailed financial reports submitted to the attorney general. Twenty-five states and the District of Columbia have no reporting requirements applicable to foundations, although an increasing number of these states, such as New York and Minnesota,[4] do have special provisions for organizations which solicit funds from the public. Failure to report for a certain specified number of years may result in a dissolution proceeding by the state.

Restrictions on the Amount a Charitable Corporation May Own or Take by Devise

The influence in this country of the English mortmain statutes may be seen in the provisions in some states restricting the power of corporations, charitable or not, to take property by devise unless specifically authorized to do so by their charter or by special act.[5] The effect of

---

[1] *Ibid.*, p. 9.

[2] For example, see *Model Non-Profit Corporation Act* (1964 Revision), *op. cit.*, sec. 26.

[3] See Table 2, Appendix A.

[4] N.Y. Soc. Welfare Law, sec. 481–83a; Minn. Stat. Ann., secs. 309.20 to 309.61. See Table 2, Appendix A, for further citations.

[5] Cal. Prob. Code, sec. 27; Mont. Rev. Codes Ann., sec. 91–104; N.Y. Deced. Est. Law, sec. 12; N.D. Cent. Code, sec. 56–02–05; Okla. Stat. Ann., tit. 84, sec. 45; S.D. Code, sec. 56.0205.

these statutes has been nullified, however, by provisions in the charters of incorporation specifically allowing such gifts.

A second type of statutory restriction limits the amount of property a charitable corporation may own. The majority of states have either no restriction or a statute permitting nonprofit corporations to hold only those amounts necessary for the carrying out of their corporate purposes. In Maine a charitable corporation other than a library, hospital, or school may not hold real estate valued at more than $500,000 or 10 per cent of the town's stated valuation, whichever is lower.[1] In Massachusetts the limit is $5 million unless authorized by special law to hold more;[2] in addition, religious corporations may not hold more than an amount earning $10,000 of income per year.[3]

The effect of these provisions has been greatly curtailed in some jurisdictions by the interpretation of the state courts of the wording of the particular statutes. In New York, the courts follow the narrow view first expressed in *Matter of McGraw*[4] that a bequest to a charitable corporation which is in excess of the permitted amount in its charter fails altogether, even though the legislature had amended the charter restriction prior to the action. A bequest in such a case reverts to the heirs of the testator. However, the rule in the majority of states, and according to some authorities,[5] the better view, is that expressed in the Massachusetts case of *Hubbard* v. *Worcester Art Museum*.[6] Here the court held that a bequest similar to that in the *McGraw* case was valid except as against the state. The court stated that an act of the legislature enlarging the property limit for the museum was effective to preclude any further state action and that even if the legislature had not acted, the court could appoint a new trustee to hold and administer the gift for the intended charitable purposes. In Rhode Island it is provided by a statute that when property given to a charitable corporation is in excess of the amount which it is entitled to take,

---

[1] Me. Rev. Stat. Ann., ch. 54, sec. 5; and ch. 57, sec. 3.
[2] Mass. Gen. Laws Ann., ch. 180, sec. 9.
[3] Mass. Gen. Laws Ann., ch. 68, sec. 9. See also Ariz. Rev. Stat. Ann., sec. 10–454; Ark. Stat. Ann., sec. 50–201; Ky. Rev. Stat., sec. 273090; Md. Constitution, Declaration of Rights, art. 38; Nev. Rev. Stat., sec. 86.160; N.H. Rev. Stat. Ann., sec. 306:10; N.D. Cent. Code, sec. 10–28–19; Ohio Rev. Code, sec. 1715.16; Pa. Stat. Ann., tit. 10, secs. 31–26, 71–73; R.I. Gen. Laws Ann., sec. 7–6–8; Vt. Stat. Ann., tit. 11, sec. 132; Va. Code Ann., sec. 57–12 (1950), amended by Act of 1958, ch. 423; W. Va. Code Ann., sec. 3495.
[4] 111 N.Y. 66, 19 N.E. 233 (1888).
[5] Zollmann, Carl F. G., *American Law of Charities.* The Bruce Publishing Co., Milwaukee, Wis., 1924, pp. 348–349.
[6] 194 Mass. 280, 80 N.E. 490 (1907).

the corporation shall take the property on a condition subsequent that it obtain from the legislature authorization to take and hold the property, but the application to the legislature must be made within one year.[1]

Indefiniteness of Beneficiaries

The rules concerning dedication to public purposes applicable to charitable trusts are also applicable to charitable corporations and are construed without distinction as to the form of the charity. The question of definiteness of the beneficiaries does not arise, however, at the time of creation, as is the case with a charitable trust which is to last in perpetuity. Incorporation under general not-for-profit laws is often undertaken for the purpose of creating organizations which will benefit only a limited class of members, such as a mutual benefit association, a social club, or a trade association. The charitable nature of the corporation, and therefore the question of beneficiaries, is considered by tax officials and by the courts in actions to determine disposition of the assets on dissolution or merger. The question of beneficiaries also arises whenever there is a question of compliance with laws imposing a duty on charitable entities to file reports with the state, such as the Massachusetts law applicable to all "public charities" incorporated within the Commonwealth[2] or the provision of the California statute for the supervision of trustees for charitable purposes[3] that defines a charitable corporation as "any nonprofit corporation organized under the laws of this State for charitable or eleemosynary purposes and any similar foreign corporation doing business or holding property in this State for such purposes."[4]

Duration

The essence of a corporation is its ability to endure forever by an inherent power of perpetuation. There is therefore no problem of the application of the Rule Against Perpetuities in the case of gifts to charitable corporations, although one may arise if there is a condition in the gift which could be exercisable at a period beyond that permitted by the rule. The rules in such a case, however, do not differ from those applicable to charitable trusts.

---

[1] R.I. Gen. Laws Ann., sec. 7–1–17; Scott, Austin W., *The Law of Trusts,* 2d ed., Little, Brown and Co., Boston, 1956, sec. 362.4.
[2] Mass. Gen. Laws Ann., ch. 12, sec. 8.
[3] Cal. Gov. Code, secs. 12580–12595.
[4] Cal. Gov. Code, sec. 12582.1.

If a settlor gives funds to trustees with a condition precedent that they form a charitable corporation at a specific time, or after the happening of a future event, such date or event must normally take place within the period of the Rule.[1] If the gift can be considered to be one to trustees for charitable purposes with a gift over to a charitable corporation to be formed at a later date, the courts do not apply the Rule, holding that the initial gift creates a valid charitable trust not subject to the Rule.[2]

Amendment and Merger

A distinction must be drawn between the power of the state to amend, merge, or dissolve a charitable corporation and the power of the directors or members to do so. As a general rule, once a charitable corporation has been created, changes which alter the contract of the corporation with the state, such as a change of purpose or of the special administrative procedures or limitations mentioned in the charter, may not be altered either by the legislature or by individuals acting for the corporation. The courts, however, have power to determine the application of the *cy pres* doctrine if there are to be changes of purposes, and they can permit certain administrative changes under the doctrine of deviation.

Amendments that do not alter the initial purposes of the corporation may be made by the corporation under a statutory power granted in all general incorporation statutes. The statutory requirements are precise; in most cases they follow the procedure for initial incorporation, but require in addition either a majority or two-thirds vote of the directors, or of the members if they have voting rights. The bylaws of some corporations may tighten the statutory requirements as to the required number of votes.

The Model Non-Profit Corporation Act requires that a two-thirds vote of all members having voting rights approve a resolution of the directors to amend the charter; and it states that if there are no members, or no members with voting rights, a majority vote of the board of directors is sufficient to authorize an amendment. In New York a majority vote of the members is required[3] and in Texas and Illinois, a

---

[1] Note "The Charitable Corporation," *Harvard Law Review,* vol. 64, 1951, pp. 1168, 1170.
[2] *Brigham* v. *Peter Bent Brigham Hospital,* 134 F. 513, 518 (1st Cir. 1904).
[3] N.Y. Membership Corp. Law, sec. 30.

two-thirds vote of the members, or if there are none, a majority of the directors, is necessary.[1]

The merger and consolidation of business corporations are common procedures that raise many problems concerning corporate holdings and acquisition of stock that do not arise in the case of charitable corporations. For the latter, state statutes specify methods for either consolidation or merger that are similar to procedures of amendment. If the proposed application will affect property held under restrictions or will alter purposes, court application of the *cy pres* doctrine is necessary.[2]

Dissolution

Unlike a trust, a corporation may be dissolved by act of those who direct its affairs, although dissolution, like creation, involves authorization by the state. Usually a vote of the board of directors is sufficient, although in some cases approval of the members may also be required. In the majority of states a *cy pres* application of funds on dissolution is required, but in most of them the administrative procedure is not designed to assure such a distribution.[3] As with the statutory procedure for amendment or merger, a majority vote, or in some cases a two-thirds vote, of the directors or members approving a resolution to dissolve and a plan for distribution of assets is required. Six states make no further requirement. The great majority of states do have a provision for the filing of the vote, a statement of debts and liability, and a plan for distribution of the corporation's assets with the secretary of state or another state administrative official and in some cases a county clerk.[4] In 10 states the plan must be filed with a court official; only 3 of these require judicial approval, however. In New York and Massachusetts judicial approval must follow a hearing of which notice must be given to the attorney general. In both of these states distribution of the assets of a charitable corporation must be made for other similar charitable purposes.[5] In Minnesota the authority to approve a petition for voluntary dissolution is placed in the county district courts, and the attorney general is specifically authorized to intervene in any

---

[1] Tex. Rev. Civ. Stat., art. 1396–4.02; Ill. Ann. Stat., ch. 32, sec. 163a33.
[2] Note "The Charitable Corporation," *op. cit.*, pp. 1179 to 1180.
[3] See p. 81.
[4] See Table 2, Appendix A.
[5] N.Y. Membership Corp. Law, sec. 55; Mass. Gen. Laws Ann., ch. 180, sec. 11A.

proceeding if it is in the public interest to do so.[1] However, there is no statutory provision requiring notice to the attorney general of such a proceeding, although the *cy pres* doctrine has been made applicable to charitable corporations. Rhode Island and Pennsylvania have similar procedures.[2]

In Texas and Connecticut directors are made personally liable for a distribution of the assets of an insolvent corporation or for a distribution that would render the corporation insolvent.[3] They are excused for liability only if they have used diligence, acted in good faith, or relied in good faith on financial statements of the corporation represented as correct by either the president, an officer in charge of the corporation's books or records, or a certified public accountant. The Texas statute also permits reliance on a written opinion from an attorney.[4] Procedure for voluntary dissolution of charitable foundations is, therefore, an area in which the states have failed to provide methods for assuring that the foundations' funds will continue to be used for charitable purposes.

Charitable corporations may also be dissolved involuntarily by action of the state in a proceeding, often entitled quo warranto, that may be brought by the attorney general or other state official. These proceedings usually require a showing of public injury or failure to comply with statutory requirements concerning the filing of reports.[5]

Accumulation of Income

The validity of provisions for the accumulation of income of charitable corporations is decided on the same basis as for charitable trusts. In some states the statutes regulating accumulations are applicable to all charitable dispositions. Until 1963, Arizona had explicit provisions concerning charitable corporations under which accumulations of income for charitable purposes for 21 years were allowed.[6] Until 1961, New York placed a statutory limit on the amount that could be accumulated by charitable corporations, but the provision has been repealed, and directions for accumulation are now valid subject to court supervision.[7]

---

[1] Minn. Stat., sec. 317.46.
[2] RI. Gen. Laws Ann., sec 7–6–13; Pa. Stat. Ann., tit. 15, sec. 2851–1001.
[3] Tex. Rev. Civ. Stat., art. 1396–2.26; Conn. Gen. Stat. Ann., sec. 33–455.
[4] Tex. Rev. Civ. Stat., art. 1396–2.26.
[5] See Table 2, Appendix A.
[6] Ariz. Rev. Stat. Ann., sec. 71–118; repealed by Laws of 1963, ch. 25.
[7] N.Y. Pers. Prop. Law, secs. 16, 16a, 12(2–b); N.Y. Real Prop. Law, secs. 61, 61–a, and 113(2–b).

Corporations Formed to Administer Charitable Trusts

In some instances charitable corporations are formed by trustees of a charitable trust after the trust has come into existence. Unless this is contrary to the express purposes of the settlor, trustees generally have the power to incorporate.[1] The provisions of the charter or articles of incorporation must conform to the provisions of the trust,[2] and the trustees will be governed by trust doctrine in their management of the property. In one case, the Massachusetts court refused to allow trustees to form a corporation where the charter provisions would result in the trustees' losing control of the trust.[3] The Franklin Foundation, Inc., formed by the trustees of the trust created under the will of Benjamin Franklin for the benefit of the city of Boston has been the subject of several court proceedings, and in each case the Massachusetts Supreme Judicial Court has disregarded the corporate entity on the grounds that "its purpose is to facilitate the administration and execution of the trust, not to relieve the individuals composing it from the obligations incident to their fiduciary obligation as managerial trustees."[4]

After property is conveyed by trustees of a charitable trust to a corporation formed to administer the trust, the trustees may be relieved of their duty to account to the courts as trustees, and future appointments may be made according to the provisions of the charter, not under the court supervision normally applicable to trustees.[5] This is the case whenever the gift includes a direction to form a charitable corporation or specifically permits trustees to incorporate at a later date if they deem it desirable; it may also apply in the absence of such directions.

In some jurisdictions there are separate statutory provisions for the incorporation of trustees of charitable trusts,[6] and in others the statutory powers of nonprofit corporations include the ability to receive funds to be held pursuant to a charitable trust created by will or instrument.[7]

---

[1] *Nelson* v. *Cushing,* 2 Cush. 519, 526–527 (Mass. 1848); La. Rev. Stat., sec. 9:2275.

[2] *Appeal of Vaux,* 109 Pa. 497 (1885); *Curran Foundation Charter,* 297 Pa. 272, 146 Atl. 908 (1929).

[3] *Shattuck* v. *Wood Memorial Home, Inc.,* 319 Mass. 444, 66 N.E.2d 568 (1946).

[4] *City of Boston* v. *Curley,* 276 Mass. 549, 562, 177 N.E. 557, 562 (1931).

[5] *Attorney General* v. *Olsen,* 346 Mass. 190, 191 N.E.2d 132 (1963).

[6] See, for example, Mich. Stat. Ann., sec. 21.149.

[7] For example, Mo. Rev. Stat., sec. 352.030; Cal. Corp. Code, sec. 10206(a).

Charitable Corporations—Trustees or Not?

The nature of a charitable corporation's interest in its assets has been the subject of conflicting decisions.[1] Today directors of charitable corporations are generally considered to be quasi-trustees. They are endowed with most of the attributes of regular trustees but freed from some of the more stringent supervisory powers of probate courts, particularly in relation to the appointment of trustees and accounting procedures.

The distinction was brought out in the leading case of *Brigham* v. *Peter Bent Brigham Hospital,* where the residue of an estate was left to trustees who were directed to manage the estate and accumulate income for twenty-five years, at which time they were to form a corporation to maintain a hospital. The court, in holding that a valid trust was created, went on to state:

> We should observe that the corporation contemplated by the will was not to hold in trust, in the technical sense of the word, the property which it might receive. It was to hold it for its own purposes in the usual way in which charitable institutions hold their assets. Such a holding is sometimes called a quasi-trust, and an institution like the one in question is subject to visitation by the state; but the holding does not constitute a true trust. On the transfer of the property devised by the fourteenth paragraph to a corporation as was anticipated, all technical trusts ceased.[2]

The basic problem raised by discussions of this nature is, of course, how far the application of trust rules should be foreclosed by the characterization of the interest of the corporation as absolute.

> The difficulty seems ultimately one of semantics: is the danger that the use of the word "trust" would cause an application of all the rules normally associated therewith so great as to outweigh the economy of mental effort in using a term which is in general valid, though modification of certain of its consequences would be necessary?[3]

The courts have gone both ways in their rationalization, depending on the interests affected; this is evident in the cases dealing with the availability of assets to meet creditors' demands. For example, in a Nebraska case where general creditors were attempting to assert claims

---

[1] See pp. 40 ff.

[2] *Brigham* v. *Peter Bent Brigham Hospital,* 134 Fed. 513, 517 (C.A. 1st Cir., 1904).

[3] Note "The Charitable Corporation," *Harvard Law Review,* vol. 64, 1951, p. 1173. Copyright © 1951 by the Harvard Law Review Association.

against the assets of a college, the court held that the endowment funds, although not technical trusts, were not accessible but that gifts without limitations were.[1]

In a case decided by the Delaware Supreme Court in 1963, this question arose in connection with the administration of a corporate foundation.[2] An action was brought by two members of the foundation against the foundation itself and two other members who were also officers and directors, charging that the action of the board of directors in agreeing to divide its assets and to donate 55 per cent of them to a newly created foundation organized for similar purposes was improper, since it was taken without a vote of the members and was contrary to the general rule that a trustee cannot divest himself of trust funds. The action had been agreed upon by a majority of the foundation board as a method of settling a disagreement over the operation of the foundation which had persisted for seven years following the donor's death.

In this case the court noted that it was sometimes important to determine whether or not a gift to a charitable corporation was an absolute gift to be used by the corporation for one or more of its corporate purposes, or a gift of such a nature as to make the corporation a trustee of a charitable trust. If there were no trust and no restrictions as to the disposition of the funds, the corporation would be under a duty to use the property solely for its corporate purposes and not to commit an ultra vires act. They found in this case that a charitable trust was not created.

> This being so . . . the test as to the legality of action taken by the governing board of the corporation is to be determined in accordance with principles of corporate law rather than the principles governing the fiduciary relationship between trustees of a technical trust and their trust.[3]

They ruled that, in a loose sense, the assets of a charitable corporation are trust funds, but that the extent and measure of the trust is to be determined from the certificate and bylaws of the corporation.

The court thereupon looked to the Delaware General Corporation Act which provides that the business of every nonprofit corporation shall be managed as provided in its certificate of incorporation. It

---

[1] *Hobbs* v. *Board of Education,* 126 Neb. 416, 253 N.W. 627 (1934).
[2] *Denckla* v. *Independence Foundation,* _____ Del. Ch. _____, 193 A.2d 538 (1963).
[3] *Ibid.,* p. 542.

found that the certificate of incorporation, as well as the by-laws of the foundation, gave to the members only the right to expel present members and to elect new members. Furthermore, the court found that the action of the directors was within their power to make grants to other charities, as stated in the certificate, so that they possessed, as a matter of law, sufficient authority to make the grant in question. Finally, as to the size of the grant, the court again stated that this was a question of degree to be left to the judgment of the board under "familiar principles of corporate law" and that the amount in question did not represent an abuse of their judgment.

It will be seen in the ensuing discussion that the outcome in this case was in actuality not different from what it would have been under trust doctrine, if the trust instrument had contained authorization for grants similar to that found in the certificate of incorporation.

The California statute regulating incorporation for charitable or eleemosynary purposes provides that properties held by the corporation shall nevertheless be held upon the trust that they shall be used for charitable and eleemosynary purposes.[1] The Massachusetts court stated a similar rule in a case dealing with property held by a not-for-profit college:

> The college is a charitable corporation and all of its property is held in trust in furtherance of the purposes for which it was organized . . . whether the gifts were made for some specified purpose of the college or unconditionally for any general purpose of the college, the petitioner holds the property in trust to carry out the terms and conditions under which it was given and accepted. Where no conditions were imposed by the donor, then it holds and must apply the property in carrying out the charitable object for which it was incorporated.[2]

Judicial or statutory language of this nature may, of course, foreclose arguments of defendant directors charged with breach of duty that a lesser standard should be applied to determination of their fiduciary duties than those of trustees.

Internal Organization of Charitable Corporations

Since a corporation is, in one sense, an association of individuals, it follows that certain legal rights and duties arise from the relationship of these individuals to the corporate entity. Membership in a business corporation arises through the purchase of shares of stock issued by

---

[1] Cal. Corp. Code, sec. 10206(c).
[2] *Wellesley College* v. *Attorney General,* 313 Mass. 722, 724, 49 N.E.2d 220, 223 (1943).

the corporation. Each share represents a part interest in the corporation's assets and entitles the stockholder to share in profits, participate in management, and receive a pro rata share of corporate assets on dissolution. Membership in certain not-for-profit corporations, such as social clubs or fraternal organizations, may give rise to similar privileges, the only exception being the right to share in profits.[1]

The only attribute of a shareholder or member applicable in the case of a charitable corporation, however, is the right to participate to some degree in the management of the corporation—that is, the right to vote for directors, although even this right is not always present. Most of the cases in which questions regarding the rights and liabilities of "members" of charitable corporations have arisen related to situations where the members participated in the charitable benefits bestowed by the corporation, such as "members" of a Young Men's Christian Association; in these cases, the questions have not been pertinent to the usual operation of foundations.[2]

In all states the initial incorporators of the foundation and the initial trustees or directors are required to be named in the articles of incorporation. Once the corporation is in existence, the incorporators as such have no further legal relationship to the corporation. In some states members must also be designated, and it is usual to name the incorporators as members. The charter may require that membership be either for a fixed term of years or for life unless the member resigns or is removed. Sometimes certificates of membership are issued which are transferable and may be bequeathed by will, although in other jurisdictions transfer is specifically prohibited. Illinois recently enacted legislation designed to prevent the sale of membership certificates.[3] The desirability of a statute specifically prohibiting this type of transaction came to light when a tax case was brought by the federal government against members of the corporation of a charitable hospital who had sold their certificates for $710,000, the buyers obtaining the sales price by mortgaging the hospital property.[4]

---

[1] *McAlhany* v. *Murray,* 89 S.C. 440, 71 S.E. 1025 (1911).

[2] *Leeds* v. *Harrison,* 7 N.J.Super. 558 (1950), 15 N.J. 82, 83 A.2d 45 (1951); 9 N.J. 202, 87 A.2d 713 (1952). *Dillaway* v. *Burton,* 256 Mass. 568, 153 N.E. 13 (1926). See Chafee, Zachariah, "The Internal Affairs of Associations Not for Profit," *Harvard Law Review,* vol. 43, 1930, p. 992; and Chafee, Zachariah, "Recent Developments in the Law: Judicial Control of Actions of Private Associations," *Harvard Law Review,* vol. 76, 1963, p. 983, for discussion of voluntary organizations where the problems may be similar.

[3] Ill. Rev. Stat., ch. 32, sec. 163a 7a.

[4] *Grace Sharf's Estate* v. *Commissioner of Internal Revenue,* 316 F.2d 625 (7th Cir. 1963) affirming 38 T.C. 15 (1962).

The requirements for membership are usually included in the bylaws of the corporation adopted by the original members. They may be in the charter, and in some states specific provisions for the appointment and succession of members must be in the charter.[1] In the majority of foundations being organized today, the members and directors are the same individuals, and election to the board of directors is done by the process of co-option, whereby the trustees elect themselves and membership on the board automatically carries with it status as a member of the corporation.[2]

Legal review of matters relating to the internal affairs of a corporation is difficult to obtain. The courts will, of course, intervene when there is a violation of statutory requirements. If the dispute relates to the internal affairs of the corporation, such as the expulsion of a member or the denial of a member's right to vote or participate, the courts will not take jurisdiction until the internal method for settling disputes specified in the corporation's legal instrument is exhausted or unless it is shown that the corporation delayed or denied a hearing or right of appeal. If all other resources are exhausted, the courts, under principles of equity, will nullify fraud, mistake, accident, or other inequitable conduct.[3]

Fiduciary Relations

The fiduciary relationship arises in many different situations, and although it is considered to be most intense in the trust, directors and officers of corporations are also fiduciaries. Their legal duties have been developed from the same principles as those applicable to trustees. In fact, in the earlier cases directors of all corporations were commonly said to owe a duty to the corporation as *cestui-que* trust similar to that which a trustee owes to his beneficiary.[4] Business reality required that in some instances a director be allowed greater freedom

---

[1] For discussion of different types of arrangements for elections of members and trustees, see Andrews, F. Emerson, *Philanthropic Foundations,* Russell Sage Foundation, New York, 1956, pp. 80–84; see also *Legal Instruments of Foundations,* compiled by F. Emerson Andrews, Russell Sage Foundation, New York, 1958, for specific examples of various provisions.

[2] *Ibid.*

[3] See Boyer, Ralph, *op. cit.*

[4] *Burden* v. *Burden,* 159 N.Y. 287, 54 N.E. 17 (1899); Dodd, E. Merrick, Jr., "For Whom Are Corporate Managers Trustees?" *Harvard Law Review,* vol. 45, 1932, p. 1145; Berle A. A., "Corporate Powers as Powers in Trust," *Harvard Law Review,* vol. 44, 1931, p. 1049.

than a trustee to deal with the corporation, particularly in making loans to assist the corporation, so that the rules were gradually relaxed. To-day in many instances the relationship of a director to both corporation and stockholders is similar to that of a trustee, but in the actual appli-cation of fiduciary rules to specific situations, corporate directors have greater latitude to deal with the corporation, to delegate authority, and to use standards of business judgment.

The courts have sought to formulate rules which would ensure the preservation and proper use of others' funds while at the same time taking cognizance of the fact that directors' actions are subject to scrutiny by stockholders with whom they share a profit motive. It has been argued that directors of charitable entities, being public-spirited citizens serving without compensation, should be held to standards of care that are less strict than those applied to the ordinary corporate director.[1] This attitude is evident in one or two court decisions,[2] but the majority of cases indicate that the courts look upon funds devoted to charitable purposes as the recipients of benefits from the state for which a high degree of care is required to assure that advantage is not taken of these state-granted privileges.

The *Restatement of the Law of Trusts (Second)*, in describing the duties of trustees of a charitable trust as similar to the duties of the trustees of a private trust, adds the following comment:

> In the case of a charitable corporation duties of a somewhat similar character rest upon the members of the controlling board, whether they are called directors or trustees. The extent of the duties is not always the same as the extent of the duties of individual trustees holding prop-erty for charitable purposes. It may be proper, for example, for the board to appoint a committee of its members to deal with the invest-ment of the funds of the corporation, the board merely exercising a general supervision over the actions of the committee.[3]

Reported cases dealing with the duties of directors of charitable corporations, particularly foundations, are scarce, and in some in-stances they conflict. They will be discussed under the same headings

---

[1] Taylor, J. Frederic, "A New Chapter in the New York Law of Charitable Corporations," *Cornell Law Quarterly*, vol. 25, 1940, pp. 382, 398; Note "The Modern Philanthropic Foundation: A Critique and a Proposal," *Yale Law Jour-nal*, vol. 59, 1950, pp. 477, 483.

[2] *Murdock* v. *Elliot*, 77 Conn. 247, 58 Atl. 718 (1904); *George Pepperdine Foundation* v. *Pepperdine*, 126 Cal. App.2d 154, 271 P.2d 600 (1954).

[3] *Restatement of the Law of Trusts (Second)*, American Law Institute, Phila-delphia, sec. 379, comment d., copyright 1959. Reprinted with the permission of the American Law Institute.

as those relating to duties of trustees. The comparable rule governing a business corporation will be presented with the case reports or statutes that relate to each particular duty. In many instances it is impossible to say what "law" will be applicable to charitable foundations. The rapid growth of foundations, particularly of the corporate type, is a recent development with which enforcement actions other than by the federal tax authorities have not kept pace.

1. *The duty of loyalty.* Self-dealing by trustees is flatly forbidden. A trustee who deals with trust property on his own without ratification by the beneficiaries is an insurer for losses incurred by the trust and is accountable for any gains. In the discussion of charitable trusts it was pointed out that since there are no beneficiaries to ratify, the strict rule against self-dealing is absolute unless relief is written into the trust instrument at the time of creation or is granted by a court of equity.

Directors of corporations are fiduciaries, and in most instances their duty of loyalty is analogous to that of trustees. The fiduciaries "must subordinate their individual and private interests to their duty to the corporation whenever the two conflict."[1] In the earlier cases the trust rule on self-dealing was affirmatively applied to directors of business corporations simply on the ground that they were fiduciaries.[2] This is the English rule.[3] Today, however, the absolute ban on dealings by a director of a business enterprise with his corporation has been relaxed. The standard applied by the courts is described as "the fairness test." It permits a director to deal with his corporation if a disinterested majority of the board approves the transaction and the contract itself is fair.[4] If the director participates in the vote, the transaction may be voidable by the corporation regardless of fairness or at the least the burden will be on the directors to show the fairness of the transaction. Of course if the vote is obtained through fraud or is unfair, the transaction is void.[5] This standard has been incorporated in the Connecticut Non-Stock Corporation Act.[6]

The most commonly cited case for the application of the fairness

---

[1] *Winter* v. *Anderson,* 242 App.Div. 430, 275 N.Y.S. 373 (1934).

[2] *In re Taylor Orphan Asylum,* 36 Wis. 534 (1875); *State* v. *Ausmus,* 35 S.W. 1021 (Tenn. Ct. Ch. Appeals 1895).

[3] *The Charitable Corporation* v. *Sutton,* 2 Atkyns 400, 26 Engl. Reports 642 (1742).

[4] Note "The Fairness Test of Corporation Contracts with Interested Directors," *Harvard Law Review,* vol. 61, 1948, p. 335; Ballantine, Henry Winthrop, *The Law of Corporations,* Callaghan and Co., Chicago, 1946, sec. 67.

[5] Ballantine, Henry Winthrop, *op. cit.,* sec. 68.

[6] Conn. Gen. Stat. Ann., sec. 33–455(b).

test to a charitable corporation in the absence of a statute specifically reciting it is *Kenney Presbyterian Home* v. *State*.[1] In this case two members of the board of trustees of a charitable corporation formed to administer a trust dealt with the corporation, one by selling mortgages and the other by selling fire insurance to the corporation. The court found that the trust was not subject to any additional expense because of the transactions, that the other trustees had passed on the transactions, that there was no evidence of negligence or carelessness, and no loss. The trustees were permitted to retain their commissions from both transactions. The court relied on the language of an earlier Washington case which held that when a trustee performs services of a nature properly chargeable as current expenses, there is no reason not to pay. However, it is questionable whether these transactions were merely services to the trust which ordinarily may be performed by a trustee.

In the more recent case of *Gilbert* v. *McLeod Infirmary*[2] two members of a charitable corporation successfully brought suit against the corporation and the chairman of the board to have a conveyance of a part of the corporation's property to the chairman declared void. The court held that although there was no evidence of fraud or fraudulent intent, the conduct of the director was not up to the high standard required of the fiduciary relationship. It based its decision entirely on corporate law, although it cited the rule that a director stands in a fiduciary relationship to the corporation. The outcome in this case, therefore, although based on corporate law, would not have been different had trust standards been applied.

There are other recent cases in which the court has discussed the duties of directors solely in terms of trustee standards. In *Eurich* v. *Korean Foundation*[3] the Illinois Supreme Court ordered the dissolution of a charitable corporation in order to prevent "illegal and oppressive" acts by the president, who had attempted to handpick a board which would allow him to invest the corporate funds in his own property in violation of the duty of a trustee to refrain from self-dealings. In *Voelker* v. *St. Louis Mercantile Library Association*[4] the Missouri court, in dismissing a suit brought by members of a library who charged breach of trust, stated that the defendant was a public charita-

---

[1] 174 Wash. 19, 24 P.2d 403 (1933).
[2] 219 S.C. 174, 64 S.E.2d 524 (1951).
[3] 31 Ill. App.2d 474, 176 N.E.2d 692 (1961).
[4] _____ Mo. _____, 359 S.W.2d 689 (1962).

ble corporation, which for the purposes of the suit would be considered subject to the principles applicable to a charitable trust.

Directors are also prohibited from engaging in transactions in which a conflict of interest could arise from their intimate knowledge of the corporation's affairs or from their position as director of the corporation. This ban has been likened to the rule that a trustee may not profit from any transaction arising from his relationship to the trust.

The rule was applied by the Wisconsin court in a suit by a nonprofit corporation against a trustee who was charged with causing the corporation to engage in numerous buying and selling transactions through a stock and bonds corporation of which he was the president and majority stockholder. The court required the defendant to return to the corporation the sum he received personally as a commission on one particular transaction that plaintiff was able to prove. It refused, however, to charge defendant for any additional amounts merely because he was a majority stockholder and officer without proof of personal profit to him or loss to the corporation.[1]

Corporate directors are also held accountable for any profit made as a result of appropriating corporate opportunities or trading in corporate shares,[2] but they are permitted to purchase at a discount a bond of the corporation and then enforce it for its face value or resell it for a profit. However, if the corporation is insolvent or if it failed to buy the claims for itself because of a director's actions, the director will be accountable for his profit. For trustees, however, the prohibition in similar cases is absolute.[3]

Certain aspects of the question of loyalty are dealt with by statute in some states. Thus it is common to find in corporation statutes prohibition against loans from the corporation to its directors.[4] The New York Membership Corporation Law[5] forbids a director or other officer from receiving directly or indirectly any salary, compensation, or emolument from the corporation, either as such officer or director or in any other capacity, unless authorized by the bylaws of the corporation or

---

[1] *Old Settlers Club of Milwaukee County, Inc.* v. *Haun,* 245 Wis. 213, 13 N.W.2d 913 (1944).

[2] Ballantine, Henry Winthrop, *op. cit.,* secs. 79 to 80; Hornstein, George D., *Corporation Law and Practice,* West Publishing Co., St. Paul, 1959, secs. 436 to 442.

[3] *Seymour* v. *Spring Forest Cemetery Association,* 144 N.Y. 333, 39 N.E. 365 (1895); Scott, Austin W., *op. cit.,* sec. 501.

[4] For example see *Model Non-Profit Corporation Act* (1964 Revision), *op. cit.,* sec. 27.

[5] N.Y. Membership Corp. Law, sec. 47.

by the concurring vote of two-thirds of all the directors. The statute then goes on to state:

> No director or other officer of a membership corporation shall be interested, directly or indirectly, in any contract relating to the operations conducted by the corporation, or in any contract for furnishing supplies thereto, unless authorized by the by-laws of the corporation, or by the concurring vote of two-thirds of the directors.[1]

In applying these statutes, the common law principle of fairness is still applicable. The effect of the statute is to tighten the ordinary requirement of approval by substituting a two-thirds vote of the directors for a majority vote.

2. *The duty not to delegate.* It is obvious that in the management of a business enterprise delegation of many functions by the board of directors to the officers and employees is not only desirable but necessary. The rule has developed that corporate directors may delegate most management duties provided they retain general supervision over the business. Directors may not, however, abdicate their duty to direct, and they may be chargeable with losses resulting from failure to participate.[2] They may not agree to place authority in one person or under one group of members, or agree that a director be only nominal. Every corporation has an inherent power to appoint an executive committee to act at times when the board is not in session even if the power is not specifically granted by statute.[3] Ordinarily the president of a corporation has authority to execute notes or ordinary commercial contracts for the corporation, but this rule has not been applied to not-for-profit corporations, and in order to hold the corporation liable, it is necessary to have proof of the authorization by the directors.[4]

The application of these principles to the trustees of a charitable corporation as members of its managing body was specifically made in the case of *Ray et al.* v. *Homewood Hospital, Inc.,*[5] where the court stated that there could be no dummy or nominal board of directors and therefore no delegation of a director's final responsibility to administer the corporation. This principle was also well illustrated in a

---

[1] Applied in *Knapp* v. *Rochester Protective Dog Association,* 235 A.D. 436, 257 N.Y.S. 356 (1932).
[2] Ballantine, Henry Winthrop, *op. cit.,* sec. 46.
[3] N.Y. Membership Corp. Law, sec. 20; Cal. Corp. Code, sec. 9401; Mich. Stat. Ann., sec. 21.13.
[4] Ballantine, Henry Winthrop, *op. cit.,* sec. 52; see *People's National Bank* v. *New England Home for Deaf Mutes, Aged, Blind & Infirm,* 209 Mass. 48, 95 N. E. 77 (1911).
[5] 223 Minn. 440, 27 N.W.2d 409 (1947).

Massachusetts case where directors of a charitable corporation set up a separate trust to which they turned over certain assets which had been donated for the general purposes of the corporation. The court declared such a delegation to be illegal on the grounds that the charter provided that the corporation should be the sole custodian and manager of its funds.[1]

In the operation of the usual charitable foundation the question of a power to delegate arises most frequently in connection with the choosing of investments. A trustee cannot delegate this function unless authorization is expressly given in the trust instrument, although he may seek the advice of investment counsel before making his choice. A charitable corporation, on the other hand, is generally permitted to assign the making of investments to a finance committee. The *Restatement of the Law of Trusts* (*Second*) uses the right to delegate the choice of investments as an example of the difference between the duties of a trustee of a charitable trust and those of the director of a corporation.[2] In California, the authority to establish a finance committee separate from the board, in addition to the power to delegate the management of finances to a bank or trust company, is specifically allowed to charitable corporations.[3] In all states, legislation permitting investment in common trust funds is also applicable to charitable corporations.[4]

3. *The duty to keep and render accounts.* A charitable corporation's duty to keep and render accounts differs in its source from that of a trustee, but is similar in its stringency. The initial sources of a duty to keep accounts are the statutes in each state. These require directors not only to keep accounts, but, in most jurisdictions, to report to the members or board of directors at least once a year.[5] These statutes often contain a detailed list of the items to be included in such reports which is similar to that required for trustee accounts.

The annual report of a charitable corporation must be available for inspection by members, if they differ from the board, and the right of directors to inspect all records of the corporation is also usually a statutory right.[6] In a New York case in 1949, however, the court spe-

---

[1] *Massachusetts Charitable Mechanic Association v. Beede,* 320 Mass. 601, 70 N.E.2d 825 (1947).

[2] *Restatement of the Law of Trusts* (*Second*), *op. cit.,* sec. 379(d).

[3] Cal. Corp. Code, sec. 10204.

[4] See pp. 144 ff. as to investment duties of directors.

[5] For example, Md. Ann. Code, art. 23, sec. 49; Okla. Stat., tit. 18, sec. 544; Utah Code Ann., sec. 16–6–10; N.Y. Membership Corp. Law, sec. 46.

[6] *Javits* v. *Investors League, Inc.,* 92 N.Y.S.2d 267 (1949).

cifically stated that section 46 of the Membership Corporation Law does not require the directors to file an account, the contents of which are without limitation but merely a report, which may be limited.[1]

The Model Non-Profit Corporation Act does not require the directors to make annual reports, but does specify that the corporation shall keep correct and complete books and records of account and minutes of all its proceedings, and requires that all books and records be open to inspection by any member or his agent or attorney "for any proper purpose at any reasonable time."[2]

When a corporation holds certain funds as trustee, it may be under additional duties to account. A Pennsylvania statute provides that the directors of a charitable corporation shall keep accounts of all trust funds separate and apart from other funds of the corporation and shall, unless the terms of the trust provide otherwise, make an annual report to the members concerning these funds.[3]

Where gifts are given to a charitable corporation by will or otherwise to be used for the general charitable purposes of the corporation, or with restrictions which are within the power of the corporation to follow, the corporation does not usually need to qualify in court as a trustee or to give bond. This specific issue was raised in the case of *American Institute of Architects* v. *Attorney General*.[4] A Massachusetts resident had left the residue of her estate to The American Institute of Architects, a New York charitable corporation, upon trust to maintain scholarships for advanced study by deserving architects and students of architecture. The court held that the corporation did not hold the property subject to a technical trust and was therefore not subject to the laws of Massachusetts requiring appointment and qualification of a trustee by the Massachusetts Probate Court.

There have been similar recent holdings in other jurisdictions,[5] although in a Pennsylvania case the orphan's court directed that funds for an endowment of an incorporated school should be paid to the school as trustee so that the court might retain jurisdiction.[6]

Whether or not a charitable corporation is declared in a particular instance to be a technical trustee, it is nevertheless subject to the pow-

---

[1] *Hamilton et al.* v. *Patrolmen's Benevolent Association,* 88 N.Y.S.2d 683 (1949).

[2] *Model Non-Profit Corporation Act* (1964 Revision), *op. cit.,* sec. 25.

[3] Pa. Stat. Ann., tit. 15, sec. 2851–306.

[4] 332 Mass. 619, 127 N.E.2d 161 (1955).

[5] *In re Estate of Bicknell,* 108 Ohio App. 51, 160 N.E.2d 550 (1958).

[6] *Wanamaker Trust,* 7 Fiduciary Reporter 486 (Pa. 1957).

ers of an equity court, and on proper demand by the attorney general or a proper party, may be ordered to account in the same manner as a trustee.[1] There may also be a statutory source of court power to compel accounts. For example, in New York the courts of general jurisdiction are specifically given a visitorial power which may be invoked by any member or creditor.[2]

This duty to keep and render accounts has been supplemented in several states by the requirement of annual financial reports to the attorney general,[3] and, of course, exists along with the duty discussed earlier to render reports to the secretary of state or other state official.[4]

4. *Reasonable care and skill.* The standard of care applied to directors of corporations has been described as that degree of care and diligence which ordinary prudent men prompted by self-interest, would exercise under similar circumstances.[5] There have been other expressions of this standard, but Ballantine explains that the difference is more of words than of actual substance.[6]

Unlike the obligation of loyalty, the obligation of responsibility (or care and diligence) is proportionate to the circumstances. "What would be slight neglect in the case of a quantity of iron might be gross neglect in the case of a jewel."[7] This rule has been made applicable to all directors, whether or not they receive compensation.

> One who voluntarily takes the position of director and invites confidence in that relation; undertakes . . . with those whom he represents or for whom he acts, that he possesses at least ordinary knowledge and skill, and that he will bring them to bear in the discharge of his duties. . . . It matters not that the service is to be rendered gratuitously.[8]

Thus, the standard which will be used by a court when asked to determine whether there has been a breach of the duty of care by a director is not essentially different from that used to determine a similar breach by a trustee. It is a standard which allows a great deal of lee-

---

[1] *Healy* v. *Loomis Institute,* 102 Conn. 410, 128 Atl. 774 (1925); *Brown* v. *Memorial National Home Foundation,* 158 Cal. App.2d 448, 329 P.2d 118 (1955), certiorari denied 358 U.S. 943 (1958), 3 L.Ed.2d 352, 79 S.Ct. 353 (1959).

[2] N.Y. Membership Corp. Law, sec. 26; *Re Green,* 10 Misc.2d 557, 177 N.Y.S. 2d 933 (1957).

[3] See Chapter VII.

[4] See p. 123.

[5] Hornstein, George D., *op. cit.,* sec. 445.

[6] Ballantine, Henry Winthrop, *op. cit.,* sec. 63.

[7] *Hun* v. *Cary,* 82 N.Y. 65, 71 (1880).

[8] *Ibid.;* see also *The Charitable Corporation* v. *Sutton,* 2 Atkyns 400, 26 Engl. Rep. 642 [1742].

way to the court, based as it is on the facts of the particular situation and the nature of the enterprise. In the cases dealing with commercial enterprises the courts have so applied the standard of care that mere "negligence," which would subject a trustee to liability, is not considered as serious a deficiency in a director.[1]

The standard is generally higher when applied to directors of banks or to similar positions where there is responsibility for the care of personal property. Where charitable funds are involved and the ultimate purposes of directors and trustees are the same, there is no reason to assume that the form of organization would alter the courts' attitude toward the standard of care.[2] The Pennsylvania court discussed this question in *Groome's Estate*,[3] saying that a board of trustees has no attributes of shareholders of a business corporation, but merely the position of trustees to whom the court would apply the standards governing trustees in determining the requirement of a duty of care.

The federal court for the District of Columbia also applied the trustee standard to directors of a charitable corporation, stating that the trustees "stood" in a fiduciary relation to both the corporation and its unknown beneficiaries and that a failure to inform themselves of the value of certain stocks which were sold far below their true value constituted "a failure to exercise the caution, care and skill which a man of ordinary prudence would exercise in dealing with his property," thereby constituting a breach of trust.[4]

The Minnesota case of *Ray et al. v. Homewood Hospital, Inc.*[5] discussed earlier has been cited as holding that the corporate standard of care is applicable to charitable corporations. The court in that case said that trustees of a charitable corporation, as members of the managing body, are charged with the same fidelity in the performance of their functional duties as the directors of a private business corporation. They have a fiduciary responsibility to administer their office and act for the corporation according to their best judgment, and in so doing they will not be controlled by the court for a reasonable execution and performance of duties. The case dealt, however, with the legality of an agreement that some of the directors would not par-

---

[1] Hornstein, George D., *op. cit.*, sec. 445; *Spiegel* v. *Beacon Participators* 297 Mass. 398, 8 N.E.2d 895 (1937).
[2] Note "The Charitable Corporation," *op. cit.*, pp. 1174 ff.
[3] 337 Pa. 250, 11 A.2d 271 (1940).
[4] *U.S.* v. *Mt. Vernon Mortgage Corporation*, 128 F. Supp. 629 (D.D.C. 1954). affirmed in 98 App. D.C. 429, 236 F.2d 724 (1956); cert. denied 352 U.S. 988 (1957).
[5] 223 Minn. 440, 27 N.W.2d 409 (1947); see the discussion on p. 139.

ticipate in the management of the corporation; it therefore stands as a precedent concerning delegation of duties rather than as a determination of the duty of care.

Investments. The prudent man rule is applicable to the investment of funds by a charitable corporation[1] unless there is a specific statute requiring a different standard. In those states which do not follow the prudent man doctrine, but limit investments by trustees to a "legal list," the question of whether the statutory limitations on investments are applicable to charitable corporations is a matter of court interpretation. Scott states that if the statute is not considered applicable, the directors of a charitable corporation will be held to the prudent man rule.[2] For example, the Ohio court held that a cemetery corporation was not limited by the statute regulating investments by trustees, but was bound to act with prudence.[3] An oft-cited case for this rule is *Graham Brothers* v. *Galloway Woman's College*[4] where, due to the circumstances of the depression, an investment which would otherwise have been improper was held not to be a violation of the prudent man rule.

The equity powers of the court are sufficient to permit a deviation from investment restrictions in a trust under which a charitable corporation was organized, or in the terms of a gift to a charitable corporation, when necessary owing to change of circumstances.[5]

A New York statute permits a membership corporation to make investments "in such mortgages, bonds, debentures, shares of preferred and common stock and other securities as its directors shall deem advisable," unless restricted by the terms of a specific gift,[6] thus giving a wider discretion than that afforded to trustees. Of course, the prudent man standard of care will govern the decisions of the directors as to what is "advisable."[7]

In Pennsylvania directors of a charitable corporation are given the power to invest funds, including those received on specific trusts, "in

---

[1] *Restatement of the Law of Trusts (Second)*, op. cit., sec. 389, comment b.
[2] Scott, Austin W., *op. cit.*, sec. 389.
[3] *Freeman* v. *Norwalk Cemetery Association*, 88 Ohio App. 446, 100 N.E.2d 267 (1950).
[4] 190 Ark. 692, 81 S.W.2d 837 (1935).
[5] *John A. Creighton Home for Girls' Trust* v. *Waltman*, 140 Neb. 3, 299 N.W. 261 (1941).
[6] N.Y. Membership Corp. Law, sec. 27.
[7] *Application of Arms*, 193 Misc. 427, 81 N.Y.S. 2d 246 (1948); *Restatement of the Law of Trusts (Second)*, op. cit., sec. 227, comment p; see also p. 148 re restrictions on power to lease, mortgage, and so forth.

such investments as they in the honest exercise of their judgment may, after investigation, determine to be safe and proper investments."[1] In Michigan the prudent man rule is made specifically applicable to non-profit corporations for charitable purposes,[2] while charitable foundations[3] and foundations holding funds as trustees[4] are governed by the laws regulating investments by trustees.

The Nebraska statute governing trustee investments specifically exempts incorporated religious, charitable, or eleemosynary institutions, the board of trustees of any college or university, and any endowment fund of a college or university.[5] It would probably not be applicable to a corporate foundation. In West Virginia[6] and Tennessee[7] the prudent man rule is recited in the statutes regarding investment of funds given in trust to charitable corporations. In Kansas, while the prudent man rule is applicable to all fiduciaries,[8] charitable, educational, and eleemosynary corporations and organizations are also specifically authorized to invest in shares of saving and loan associations which are under state or federal supervision; whereas such investments are legal for trustees only when permitted by the court.[9]

There are also some statutes specifically authorizing investment by charitable corporations in common trust funds, or permitting collective investments.[10]

The questions of whether separate funds held by a charitable corporation may be mingled in the making of investments and whether the shares of the fund and its income may be allocated according to the various purposes for which they were donated have caused interest, particularly among the universities.[11] The *Restatement of the Law of Trusts* (*Second*) takes the position that such mingling is proper unless otherwise provided by the terms of a donation, but there have

---

[1] Pa. Stat. Ann., tit. 15, sec. 2851–306.
[2] Mich. Stat. Ann., sec. 21.127.
[3] Mich. Stat. Ann., sec. 21.165.
[4] Mich. Stat. Ann., sec. 21.154.
[5] Neb. Rev. Stat., sec. 24–601.
[6] W. Va. Code Ann., sec. 4216(1), (2a).
[7] Tenn. Code Ann., sec. 48–1108.
[8] Kan. Gen. Stat. Ann., sec. 17–5004.
[9] Kan. Gen. Stat. Ann., sec. 17–5002.
[10] See for example, Cal. Corp. Code, sec. 10250; N.H. Rev. Stat. Ann., sec. 292.18 (1955); Me. Rev. Stat. Ann., ch. 25, sec. 273–B (hospitals); Pa. Stat. Ann., tit. 15, sec. 2851–318A; Vt. Stat. Ann., tit. 16, sec. 3641 (educational institutions); W. Va. Code Ann., sec. 4216(2).
[11] See Blackwell, Thomas E., "The Charitable Corporation and the Charitable Trust," *Washington University Law Quarterly,* vol. 24, December, 1938, p. 1; Daines, Harry C., "Theory and Procedure for Pooled Investments in Colleges and Universities," *Journal of Accounting,* vol. 69, 1940, p. 114.

been no reported cases dealing specifically with the question.[1] This is not, of course, a problem which is likely to arise in the operation of an average foundation.

Additional Duties. The administrative duties of trustees are all applicable to directors, including the duties to administer the trust, take and keep control of property, preserve the trust property, enforce claims, defend actions, and make the trust property productive. The need to keep property separate from that of the individual trustees is not a problem, since assets of a charitable corporation are owned in the name of the corporation, and contracts made by the corporation are made in the name of the corporation, not in the name of the individual directors.

Powers

The concept of a corporation as a separate legal person entitles it to certain constitutional protections. It may not be deprived of liberty without due process of law, nor denied the equal protection of the laws. The application of the constitutional prohibition against impairment of contract to corporate charities made by the Supreme Court in the *Dartmouth College* case has been discussed,[2] but it should be noted that the court reached its conclusion by treating the corporation as a person who was party to the contract.

Corporations possess under law all the powers of a natural person which are reasonably necessary for the accomplishment of their proper purposes, with the exception of those specifically forbidden by statute, the federal and state constitutions, or the terms of their charters. General corporation statutes in all states give certain powers to corporations. The courts also imply others which are regarded as incident to corporate existence. These latter are conferred by the mere creation of the corporation. They include:

1. Right to corporate succession, or the right to continuing existence irrespective of changes in membership.

2. Capacity to sue and be sued, and to grant and receive in the corporate name.

3. Capacity to purchase, hold and convey real and personal property for the corporate objects and in the corporate name.

4. Authority to have a seal and use it as a symbol to authenticate documents.

---

[1] *Restatement of the Law of Trusts (Second), op. cit.,* sec. 389, comment c.
[2] See pp. 112–113.

5. Authority to make bylaws not inconsistent with law to govern itself.

6. Power to elect or appoint officers and agents and fix their compensation.

7. Power to remove officers in proper cases.[1]

Among the powers of corporations that may be specified by statute are the abilities to borrow and secure obligations by mortgage or pledge, to make loans for the corporate purposes and to indemnify any director or officer for expenses actually and necessarily incurred by him in connection with the defense of any action in which he is a party by reason of his position as director.

The Model Non-Profit Corporation Act[2] enumerates each of the powers listed above and adds the powers to lend money to employees other than officers or directors, to make charitable donations unless prohibited by the articles of incorporation, to cease corporate activities and surrender the franchise, and "to have and exercise all powers necessary or convenient to effect any or all of the purposes for which the corporation is organized."

The exercise of any of these powers must at all times be in furtherance of and consistent with the purposes of the corporation. In the case of a foundation it is, therefore, questionable whether the power to make loans to employees would be considered consistent with the charitable purposes. A general power to mortgage property, lend and borrow money, or make other specific types of investments may be further limited by other statutes or case law in a particular jurisdiction.[3]

The Treasury Regulations require that the articles of an organization seeking exemption contain no express powers which would allow the organization to engage to any substantial extent in activities that in themselves are not in furtherance of one or more exempt purposes.[4] Furthermore, they warn that powers may not be stated which are inconsistent with the exempt purposes. Tax commentators therefore recommend that no mention of powers be included in the charter or articles of incorporation; or, if state practice requires that they be mentioned, they should be preceded by an introductory statement that: "For the purposes set forth in the purpose

---

[1] Ballantine, Henry Winthrop, op. cit., secs. 82 to 88.
[2] (1964 Revision), op. cit., sec. 5.
[3] See p. 148.
[4] Treas. Reg. 1.501(c)(3)–1(b) (1) (b).

clause of the articles, the corporation shall have the following powers."[1]

> Since the principal inquiry by the Service in ruling upon a new organization is the intention of its creators, the express recitation of powers that can take it into non-exempt activities creates a serious question as to whether the creators of the organization intend to stay within the limits of the tax law.[2]

These rulings serve as a useful warning to directors at the time of creation that their powers are limited to furtherance of the foundation's purpose. If a question of liability should arise for the doing of unauthorized acts, such a ruling may limit the possibility of using the defense of honest mistake.

Comparison of the specific powers of directors with those of trustees reveals that in the actual operation of a foundation there is little difference. Thus the powers to invest and reinvest, incur expenses, lease and sell, compromise, arbitrate or settle claims, and vote stock would all be inferred from the nature of a foundation's purposes. Generally there is a restriction on business corporations against binding the corporation by a contract as surety or guarantor and thereby lending its credit to a third party solely for his accommodation or benefit.[3] This limitation holds unless it can be shown that such act was for the benefit of the corporation or that it was specifically authorized by the terms of the charter. There is small likelihood that such an act would be held proper for a charitable foundation.

The powers of a charitable corporation to sell, lease, or mortgage realty have been limited by statute in some jurisdictions. Generally these restrictions require a two-thirds vote of the directors or members authorizing a mortgage or lease. In Michigan a mortgage is proper only if authorized by the bylaws and a vote of shareholders or members.[4] The New York Membership Corporation Law requires a two-thirds vote of the directors for any purchase, sale, mortgage, or lease of real property.[5] It also states that the sale, mortgage (other than a purchase money mortgage) or lease of more than five years of real property is not permitted without approval of the court. The majority of states,

---

[1] Eaton, Berrien C., Jr., and collaborators, "How to Draft the Charter or Indenture of a Charity so as to Qualify for Federal Tax Exemption," *Practical Lawyer,* vol. 8, October, 1962, pp. 13, 21.

[2] *Ibid.*

[3] Ballantine, Henry Winthrop, *op. cit.,* sec. 87.

[4] Mich. Stat. Ann., sec. 21.128; Ala. Code, tit. 10, sec. 241 (two-thirds of members or majority of directors); Pa. Stat. Ann., tit. 15, sec. 2851–308 (majority of members).

[5] New York Membership Corp. Law, sec. 21.

however, permit such transactions without further restriction.[1] In *Emmerglich* v. *Vogel*,[2] it was held that a cemetery corporation, being a charitable trust, could not mortgage property except as security for the purchase price. Only rarely will there be a distinction in result in cases involving powers of this nature if they are based on corporate law rather than on trust principles.

Discretionary Powers

The powers of an equity court to control the discretion of corporate fiduciaries are as extensive as they are in regard to trusts. In most states the directors of charitable corporations, just as trustees, may bring a petition for instructions to determine their duties or powers whenever they are in doubt as to a specific action.[3] Although a New York case has been cited as leaving this matter in doubt in that jurisdiction, it is likely that this case could be explained on the grounds that the request did not meet the requirements generally imposed by the courts before they will issue instructions; namely, it lacked a specific pending question.[4] In jurisdictions that treat directors of charitable corporations as trustees in determinations of their duty and power, a petition for instructions as to their fiduciary powers is likely to be permitted.

As with trustees of a charitable trust, the board of directors of a charitable corporation ordinarily acts by a majority vote, although the articles, the bylaws, or a statute may provide otherwise.[5]

Ultra Vires Contracts

There is a doctrine peculiar to corporations which holds that when a corporation performs an act or enters into an agreement that is outside the scope of its express or implied powers, the act, or agreement, is held to be ultra vires[6] and may be challenged on that ground in certain cases. Formerly, when a corporation entered into an ultra vires

---

[1] Cal. Corp. Code, sec. 10206(d).

[2] 131 N.J. Eq. 257, 24 A.2d 861 (1942).

[3] *Arkansas Baptists State Convention* v. *Board of Trustees*, 209 Ark. 263, 189 S.W.2d 913 (1945); *Trustees of Princeton University* v. *Wilson*, 78 N.J. Eq. 1, 78 Atl. 393, 395 (1910).

[4] *Trustees of Sailors' Snug Harbor* v. *Carmody*, 77 Misc. 494, 137 N.Y.S. 968 (1912), reversed on other grounds 158 App. Div. 738, 144 N.Y.S. 24 (1913), affirmed 211 N.Y. 286, 105 N.E. 543 (1914).

[5] N.Y. Membership Corp. Law, sec. 46, regarding contracts with directors requiring two-thirds vote.

[6] That is, "beyond the powers granted."

contract, either party could avoid liability under the contract and refuse to carry it out. Today, however, most courts have restricted the use of this defense, and if the contract has already been carried out, neither party can object. If it has not been carried out in any way by either party, they are both prohibited from enforcing it or suing for damages. However, the courts do not agree as to the result if the contract has been performed by one party only. A majority of states hold that it should be rescinded and both parties put back in their original position. In some states, however, the court will require that the contract be completed.[1]

Liabilities of Directors for Breach of Duties

Directors are liable to their corporation for any loss suffered by it as a result of their fraudulent design. They are also liable to the corporation for gross negligence, and there is no need to show that they have benefited from the negligence or that their services were gratuitous. They are not liable for losses suffered as result of poor judgment if there is no evidence of a breach of the duty of care. Directors, like trustees, are also free from liability for the wrongful acts of their co-directors if they did not concur in the act or if it did not come about through their negligence in attending to their duties. The *Restatement* applies this rule to charitable corporations: "A member of the controlling board of a charitable corporation does not incur a liability unless he himself is at fault."[2]

Ordinarily, the ability to hold a director of a business corporation responsible for negligence and mismanagement (that is, breach of the duty of care) depends on the ability of the corporation to show that the act of the director probably caused the loss and the damage suffered. This means that the corporation, or anyone suing to recover for the corporation, must show that the exercise of due care would probably have prevented the loss. The rule has been criticized as unduly lenient, and some authorities proposed that it be made similar to the rule which applies to a charge of breach of the duty of loyalty—

---

[1] Ballantine, Henry Winthrop, *op. cit.*, sec. 92. The liability of directors to the corporation for unauthorized acts will be discussed in the following section on liability of directors. It should be noted that a wrongful act of a serious nature may be grounds for an action by the attorney general of the state to revoke the corporate charter.

[2] *Restatement of the Law of Trusts (Second)*, *op. cit.*, sec. 386, comment c. This is the only statement of the duties of directors of charitable corporations in the section on duties of trustees of charitable trusts.

that is, the burden should be placed on the director to excuse himself and show that the loss probably would not have been avoided even if he had exercised due care and diligence.[1]

The charters or bylaws of some corporations contain exculpatory clauses which change the burden of proof in cases of violation of the duty of loyalty so that the plaintiff must show unfairness. It is also possible to add a clause to the bylaws which states that a director is not disqualified from dealing with the corporation because he is a director. However, the rule that it is against public policy to relieve a fiduciary from liability for acts performed in bad faith applies to directors of corporate charities as well as to trustees.

If a corporate director commits an ultra vires act, the corporation may hold him liable if he has acted willfully or negligently in exceeding the charter limitation. If directors have acted with prudence and the excess occurred by mistake, they are not usually liable to the corporation, although there have been cases which have held that ignorance or mistake is not a defense, nor is the fact that the directors acted on advice of counsel.[2]

In the case of a charitable corporation, the right to bring suit to enforce the duties of directors is available to the corporation as well as to the attorney general, who is acting for the beneficiaries, the public. The remedies are similar to those which may be brought against a trustee. If the defendant director is found guilty of a breach of his duties, he may be removed;[3] the court may order an accounting and restitution, issue an injunction to restrain threatened or future misconduct, rescind an improper contract, or require the defendant to pay to the corporation profits improperly received or to make good losses resulting from his misdeeds.

A further action open to the courts in cases involving corporations is an action to dissolve the corporation and transfer its assets to another corporation. This was done in the case of *Eurich* v. *Korean Foundation*,[4] the court stating that it was the best method of achieving the charitable purposes for which the foundation was originally created and for which gifts were made to it. In *Brown* v. *Memorial Na-*

---

[1] Ballantine, Henry Winthrop, *op. cit.*, sec. 63b; and Fletcher, William Meade, *Cyclopedia of the Law of Private Corporations,* Callahan and Co., Chicago, 1950, secs. 1029, 1035, 1041, 1047.
[2] Ballantine, Henry Winthrop, *op. cit.*, sec. 92.
[3] *Nugent* ex rel. *Lingard* v. *Harris,* _____ R.I. _____, 184 A.2d 783 (1962); *Commonwealth* ex rel. *Marshall* v. *Beeman,* 299 Ky. 26, 184 S.W. 117 (1945).
[4] 31 Ill. App.2d 474, 176 N.E.2d 692 (1961).

tional Home Foundation[1] the court did not dissolve the corporation, but ordered the transfer of all of its assets to another charitable corporation, thereby achieving the same result. In *State* ex rel. *Tacoma Boys Club* v. *Salvation Army*[2] the court took similar action after a showing of mismanagement by the defendant corporation.

If an enforcement action is brought by the corporation or by some members of the board against other directors, and the attorney general is not made a party, there is great likelihood that the arguments to the court will be made on the basis of corporate law. If the court should decide to accept these arguments, the instance in which the degree of liability is lesser for a director than a trustee is when there is an alleged violation of the duty of loyalty arising from a contract by the defendant director with the corporation, for if the director can prove fairness and authorization by a disinterested majority of directors, he may be relieved from liability. On the other hand, if the charge is one of breach of the duty of loyalty because of a conflict of interest whereby the director has profited from an appropriation of a corporate opportunity which the corporation sought to obtain or would have obtained, the basis for decision is not different, and the director will be held accountable for profit he received.[3] These cases are so rare, however, that it is difficult to predict any future trends. If the law is to develop consistently, both the enactment of statutes similar to the California provisions that the property held by charitable corporations is held in trust[4] and a forceful presentation to the courts of the need for a single standard for all charitable fiduciaries are necessary.

Liability to Third Persons

When a contract is made by a charitable corporation, the directors who have negotiated it are considered agents of the corporation and not parties to the contract. This means that the directors or officers have no liability to the other party to the contract for their acts unless they have neglected to disclose that they were acting for the corporation. If they had no authority to act for the corporation, and the corporation did not hold them out to have such authority, the corporation will not be liable, but the directors will be. Personal liability is imposed

---

[1] 158 Cal. App.2d 448, 329P.2d 118 (1955), certiorari denied 358 U.S. 943 (1958), 3 L.Ed.2d 352, 79 S.Ct. 353 (1959).

[2] 47 Wash.2d 113, 286 P.2d 709 (1955).

[3] See Niles, Russell, "Trustee Accountability in the Absence of Breach of Trust," *Columbia Law Review,* vol. 60, 1960, p. 141.

[4] Cal. Corp. Code, secs. 9505 and 10206(c).

only if the directors did not possess authority and the corporation did not hold them out as having it. These rules are based on agency law and apply to all situations involving employers and employees. They have been further narrowed for charitable corporations in some instances. For example, the New York Membership Corporation Law[1] states, "In the absence of fraud or bad faith the directors of membership corporations created under or by a general or special law shall not be personally liable for its debts, obligations or liabilities."[2] The statute is notice to all parties to a contract with a membership corporation that their only remedies are against the corporation and they may not hold directors liable for any act done for the corporation without showing that the director has been guilty of fraud or bad faith. The Pennsylvania Code, however, contains the more common provision, which merely recites that neither directors nor officers shall be personally liable for the debts, liability, or obligations of the corporation.[3]

The question of tort liability of charitable corporations has probably received more attention and been the subject of greater litigation than any other issue involving charitable funds. Ordinarily such liability arises from the operation of a charitable institution, particularly a hospital or occasionally an educational institution, church, or home. There is a conflict of authority on the question, but the trend today is away from the immunity doctrine. In any case, it is usually made applicable only to operating institutions, and it would be a rare and unusual circumstance under which a charitable foundation would be in a position to attempt to rely on it.

An officer or director of a corporation is ordinarily personally liable for all torts which he authorizes or directs or in which he participates, notwithstanding the fact that he was acting for the corporation and not on his own behalf. He will not be held liable, however, for the torts of other officers, agents, or employees acting for the corporation merely because of his office.

Compensation of Directors

The question of the compensation of directors of a charitable corporation is the same as that for trustees, although there may be no statutory provisions fixing any schedule of fees for the former. The custom is also the same. Generally, in the case of a charitable corpo-

---

[1] Sec. 46.
[2] See also, for example, Cal. Corp. Code, sec. 9504.
[3] Pa. Stat. Ann., tit. 15, sec. 2851–509.

ration which operates an institution, the trustees will not receive fees, and salaries will be paid to the executives who direct the day-to-day operations of the institution. There is ordinarily no ban against such an executive's also serving as a trustee. The one caveat in all questions of compensation is that fees must be based on the reasonable worth of services and must not be a disguise for a distribution of profits.[1]

Corporation versus Trust

Comparisons of the trust and the corporation as a form of organization for a foundation must therefore be made at several levels. At the moment of creation there are major differences in procedure: the formation of a trust is largely unsupervised and that of a corporation is subject to varying degrees of control, all states requiring some resort to state action and some form of registration with a state agency. In several states the choice of form will dictate limitations on the right of the foundation to hold property or to accumulate funds, but the restrictions on property holdings are not usually burdensome and in some instances may be modified by legislative act.

The degree of state supervision during the life of the charity may also vary with the form. Testamentary trusts are generally subject to continuing court supervision; inter vivos trusts may be completely free; and corporations may be under the supervision of a state administrative office. All are subject to the enforcement duties of the attorney general, although in some jurisdictions the duty to report to that office will vary depending on the legal form.

It is possible for the draftsman of a trust instrument to write its provisions so that the differences between the powers and the duties of trustees and those of corporate directors are minimal or nonexistent. However, in the absence of any of these provisions in a trust instrument, there are possible differences between the powers and duties of trustees and directors. Although the standard of care for trustees is no higher than that of corporate directors, when viewed in terms of the purposes of the organization, prohibitions relating to self-dealing and conflict of interest may not be as stringent for corporate directors. The most striking differences arise in the duties of personal management, whereby trustees are not permitted to delegate authority, to transfer the management of their trust, or to resign their position without approval of a court.

---

[1] Bogert, George G., and George T. Bogert, *The Law of Trusts and Trustees.* 2d ed. West Publishing Co., St. Paul, 1964, sec. 364.

The extent to which these requirements are different for corporate directors, however, varies in great degree from state to state. In those states where the courts or the statutes view a charitable corporation's interest in its property as being in the nature of a trust, no differentiation in fiduciary duties is made on the basis of form. There are cases in other states where the courts, rejecting or ignoring this doctrine, have looked to the law of business corporations to decide questions relating to charitable corporations. In these cases the result has been that the liability of corporate directors appears less than that of trustees. There are very few of these cases, however, and, in contrast, there appears to be a growing awareness of the need for developing a common set of fiduciary principles for directors and trustees alike. Finally, in the area of investment powers, in those states where there is a so-called legal list of proper trustee investments, corporate directors are generally afforded the wider latitude of the prudent man rule; in other states no difference exists.

It is in the areas of amendment and termination of a charity and appointment and resignation of fiduciaries where the greatest variances arise. Directors are elected by the corporation "members" or their fellow directors for short terms or for life. They may vote to vary the administrative provisions of the corporation or even to terminate and dissolve the organization, although they may not divert the funds from the general charitable purposes to which they were initially devoted. They may resign with the merest of formalities, and their successors may be chosen without any contact with the state.

Trustees, on the other hand, may neither amend the terms of the trust nor terminate it unless expressly authorized by its terms or by judicial action, and the courts will rarely consent to amendments or termination except under certain specific circumstances, and then only following a full judicial hearing. Again, unless specifically provided in the trust instrument, a trustee may not resign without court permission, and his successor must be appointed by a court. He may be removed only by the court, and then only on a showing of misbehavior or of action inimical to the trust. A corporate director, on the other hand, may be removed not only by a court, but under certain circumstances by vote of his fellow directors or by failing to be reelected.

It is the rare trust instrument which does not include some, if not all, of the provisions whereby these differences between trustees and directors are removed. The aim, of course, is to assure that the duties and the liabilities of directors and trustees are not so burdensome as to make the position of fiduciary completely undesirable. There is an outer limit to the extent to which this may be done, however. In all states either the courts or the legislatures have adopted the rule that no fiduciary, whether director or trustee, can be excused from gross or willful negligence or misconduct.

It is often said that the principal advantage of the corporate device is the insulation of its directors from personal liability. It should be evident from the foregoing discussion that this is not necessarily true. Since directors and officers are fiduciaries, they may be liable for breaches of fiduciary duty rather like trustees, whether or not trust standards are applied to them. Both trustees and directors are responsible to third parties for personal torts, and both are liable for contracts made in their own name for undisclosed principals. Trustees may escape liability on contracts by including this stipulation in the contract, and officers and directors are not generally liable on contracts made in the name of the corporation. Exculpatory clauses will be as effective for trustees as directors in excusing them from liability for negligent investments or other breaches of duty. Moreover, the tendency of recent judicial decisions has been to steadily raise the standards of conduct of directors. "Honesty and loyalty are insisted upon as strictly for a director as for an ordinary trustee."[1]

The comparison of the liabilities of directors and trustees has been summed up by one authority as follows: "In short, board membership in charitable foundations, whether corporate or trust, does not ordinarily involve much personal liability either for the actions of the organization or the safety of its funds. The net advantage of the corporate form, if any, is slight; and in this respect, as well as most others, any advantage can probably be neutralized by careful drafting of the creating instrument."[2]

The need for a single standard applicable to all charitable fiduciaries cannot be overemphasized. The detailed description of the nature of the rights and duties which arise from the trust and corporate concepts indicates that reliance has been placed on the nature of the fiduciary relationship to guarantee the proper management of charitable funds. Before attempting to assess the wisdom of this reliance, it is necessary to consider a third set of rules which define the obligations of charitable fiduciaries—those imposed by the federal tax laws. Al-

---

[1] Hornstein, George D., *op. cit.*, sec. 446.
[2] Eaton, Berrien C., Jr., "Charitable Foundations, Tax Avoidance and Business Expediency," *Virginia Law Review,* vol. 35, 1949, pp. 809, 828.

though they apply uniformly to corporations and trusts alike, the effect of the sanctions vary according to the form of the foundation. More important is the fact that the tax laws impose some duties on fiduciaries that are different from those imposed by the state laws. These substantive provisions will be discussed in the following chapter.

CHAPTER V

The Internal Revenue Code

THE INFLUENCE OF TAX CONSIDERATIONS on the activities, as well as the creation of charitable foundations, is amply attested to by the extensive periodical literature devoted to the tax aspects of charitable funds.[1] The grant of tax exemption to charitable entities and the allowance of tax deduction for charitable contributions represent an attitude of positive governmental encouragement of philanthropy which has been present in the American tax system since its inception. It was not until twenty years ago, however, that a rapid growth in the number and assets of charitable foundations became apparent. Congress at that time enacted the first requirement that foundations and certain other exempt organizations file information returns so that "a thorough study of the information contained in such returns" could be made with a view toward legislation.[2] From that date, the Internal Revenue Service has been actively involved in the regulation of foundations, and its influence on the activities of foundations has come to be a predominant one.

The increase in income tax rates during and after World War II led some tax planners into a search for what have become ever more complicated schemes for manipulating foundations for private purposes. The methods employed involved foundations in business and other

---

[1] See American Bar Association, Section of Real Property and Trust Law, "Report of the Committee on Charitable Trusts [Moses W. Rosenfeld, Chairman]," *Trusts and Estates,* vol. 103, 1964, p. 954, for an annotated bibliography of initial references prepared for attorneys with limited experience in the organization, operation, and functioning of charitable trusts.

[2] U.S. Congress, House of Representatives, Committee on Ways and Means, *Report* to accompany H.R. 3687. 78th Congress, 1st Session, House Report 871, Government Printing Office, Washington, 1944.

activities which, until that time, had not been considered the traditional methods of producing income for charitable enterprises. The principal operations of concern to the Revenue Service included: (1) corporations commonly known as feeders that operated as businesses but distributed all of their profits to a charitable organization and claimed exemption based on this "destination of income"; (2) foundations engaged in charitable activities but also undertaking various income-producing activities in furtherance of, or to support, charitable programs; and (3) organizations established for charitable purposes but subject to varying degrees of control by private interests whereby the accumulated income or earnings of the tax-exempt organization could be used to business or personal advantage.[1]

Prior to 1950 the Revenue Service had directed its activities toward assuring that the requirements for tax exemption were being met. The courts, however, had held that a certain amount of business activity was not sufficient to constitute grounds for revocation of exemption, regardless of whether it was related to the activities of the charitable organization.[2] They had also rendered conflicting decisions as to whether the mere existence of a charitable destination of income was sufficient to constitute grounds for exemption. Then, in 1948, a congressional investigation was made of the activities of Textron, Inc., a business organization charged with having taken advantage of a controlled foundation's tax-exempt status to accumulate large amounts of income for subsequent use in the acquisition of other enterprises or the financing of business transactions on a preferential basis.[3]

The Revenue Act of 1950[4] contained a series of restrictions on the activities of foundations designed to remedy the abuses brought to light

---

[1] Sugarman, Norman, and Harlan Pomeroy, "Business Income of Exempt Organizations," *Virginia Law Review,* vol. 46, 1960, pp. 424–438, especially p. 427.

[2] *Trinidad* v. *Sagrada Orden de Predicadores,* 263 U.S. 578, 582 (1924). See also Keir, Loyal E., "What Is Charity: Statutory Definitions; Exclusively; Lobbying," *Proceedings* of the New York University Fourteenth Institute on Federal Taxation, Matthew Bender and Co., New York, 1956, p. 19.

[3] U.S. Congress, Senate, Subcommittee of the Committee on Interstate and Foreign Commerce. *Hearings,* "Investigation of Closing of Nashua, N.H. Mills and Operations of Textron, Incorporated." 80th Congress, 2d Session, Government Printing Office, Washington, 1948, 1949, pts. 1 and 2; Comment "The Modern Philanthropic Foundation: A Critique and a Proposal," *Yale Law Journal,* vol. 59, 1950, p. 477, contains a summary of this investigation and of the activities of Royal Little and Textron, Inc., that served to bring the problem before Congress. See also "A Correction to the Textron Story," *Yale Law Journal,* vol. 59, 1950, p. 1121.

[4] See Rev. Act. of 1950, tit. 3, 64 Stat. 947.

in the congressional hearings, as well as to clarify the law relating to the business activities mentioned above.

The new law did not change the basic structure of the exemption provisions of the Code; it merely added four restrictions on foundation activity:

1. A tax was imposed on the net income of organizations carrying on charitable activities and also engaging in a trade or business, when the business activity was *not substantially related* to the exempt purposes and *regularly* carried on.[1]

2. An organization whose primary purpose was the carrying on of a trade or business for profit was defined as a feeder corporation, and the exemption for such organization was removed, regardless of the fact that all of its income was payable to a charitable organization.[2]

3. Accumulations of income that were unreasonable or used improperly were banned in the case of certain types of exempt organizations, particularly foundations.[3] Violation of this provision was made a ground for denying exemption for the taxable years of its occurrence.

4. Certain transactions between exempt organizations and their creators and substantial contributors, or members of their families or corporations controlled by them, were labeled "prohibited transactions" and became grounds for denial of exemption to certain types of organizations, particularly foundations.[4]

A discussion of the specific Revenue Code provisions used to regulate foundation activities should be prefaced with the statement that the provisions make no differentiation based on the form, corporate or trust, of the foundation. However, the effect of the revocation of exemption may differ according to the form of the organization. Once tax exemption is removed, an organization is subject to the same taxes as its nonexempt counterpart. Thus, a corporation is allowed a deduction for 5 per cent of its taxable income which is distributed to charity[5] and is taxed on remaining income at the flat rate of 22 per cent on the first $25,000 of taxable income and 50 per cent on the rest in 1964, 48 per

---

[1] Now Int. Rev. Code of 1954, secs. 511 to 514 and 681(a).
[2] Now Int. Rev. Code of 1954, sec. 502.
[3] Now Int. Rev. Code of 1954, secs. 504 and 681(c).
[4] Int. Rev. Code of 1954, secs. 503 to 504 and 681(b)(2). Excluded from the provisions of secs. 503 and 504 are churches, schools, hospitals, and charities that are supported by contributions from the public, sec. 503(b).
[5] Int. Rev. Code of 1954, sec. 170(b)(2).

cent after 1964.[1] It is also allowed the 85 per cent deduction for dividends received.[2]

A trust, on the other hand, is allowed to deduct an unlimited amount for contributions from gross income where the contributions are paid or permanently set aside for charity.[3] However, in cases where there is a loss of exemption due to participation in a prohibited transaction or to an accumulation of income that is unreasonable or used in an improper manner, or where the trust is taxed on a portion of the trust income ascribed to unrelated business, the charitable deduction is similar to that permitted an individual taxpayer—20 per cent of the taxable income or 30 per cent if the contribution is to a church, school, or hospital, to a governmental unit for public purposes, or to an organization that receives a substantial part of its support from the public or a governmental unit.[4] This seeming advantage for a trust may be obliterated, however, if the Internal Revenue Service treats the trust as an association and thus subjects it to corporate tax rates.

Another basis for differentiation between a trust and corporation in the tax laws arises in connection with charitable activities carried on outside the United States. It also relates to the eligibility of contributions for deduction. A business corporation is not allowed a deduction for a charitable contribution to a trust or to a chest, fund, or foundation that is not incorporated if the gift is to be used outside the United States; it is not so limited in the case of contributions to charitable corporations, however.[5] No explanation for this inconsistency has ever been put forth, so that it remains a "quirk" in the law. A trust instrument may specify that no funds received from corporations will be spent outside the United States and may set up separate accounts to handle these contributions; but the fact that this procedure entails considerable additional bookkeeping may explain some of the instances where the corporate form is preferred.[6]

---

[1] Int. Rev. Code of 1954, sec. 11, as amended by Public Law 88–272, 88th Congress, 2d Session, February 26, 1964, sec. 121, 234(a).

[2] Int. Rev. Code of 1954, sec. 243.

[3] Int. Rev. Code of 1954, sec. 642(c).

[4] Int. Rev. Code of 1954, secs. 681(a), 681(b)(2), 681(c), and 512(b)(11), as amended by Public Law 88–272, 88th Congress, 2d Session, February 26, 1964, sec. 209(a)(f); adding Int. Rev. Code, sec. 170(b)(1)(A)(v) and (vi).

[5] Int. Rev. Code of 1954, sec. 170(c)(2).

[6] This matter of foreign activities of charities is further regulated in the Code by means of a limitation on both individual and corporate contributions. Deduction is allowed only when the recipient is "created or organized in the United States or any possession thereof or under the law of the United States,

Operational and Organizational Tests

The primary weapon of the Internal Revenue Service for enforcement of the duties of foundation fiduciaries has been the statutory definition of exempt organizations contained in section 501(c)(3) of the Internal Revenue Code,[1] particularly the requirements that the foundation be "organized and operated" exclusively for exempt purposes and that no part of its net earnings inure to the benefit of any private shareholder or individual. The Internal Revenue Service has used this language to regulate foundations both at the time of application for exempt status and during the life of a foundation.

Although, technically, under the tax laws a foundation has no need to obtain a Service ruling that it is an exempt organization, as a practical matter determination of exempt status is necessary in order to assure donors that they will be allowed to deduct charitable contributions from their personal income or corporate tax. In 1954 the Internal Revenue Service ruled that all organizations seeking exemption would thenceforth be required to file an application and receive a ruling from the Service that they had qualified for tax-exempt status.[2] Certain operating institutions such as hospitals, schools, religious organizations and publicly supported charities were entitled to a tentative advance ruling as to their status, but foundations were required to have "operated" for one year before exemption would be granted.[3] The foundation was required to file a private income tax return if one became due during the one-year period.[4] However, once an exemption was granted, it applied retroactively, and contributions made during the period in most cases received the same retroactive treatment. By this ruling, the Treasury in effect divided the definition section into two parts and made each (that is, organization and operation) the basis for separate tests to be applied in deciding whether exemption would be granted.

---

any state or territory, the District of Columbia, or any possession of the United States." Interpretation of this provision has been troublesome. The Service requires that the domestic organization exercise some control over the manner in which contributed funds are expended abroad and has refused to allow deduction where the charity was characterized as a mere "conduit." Int. Rev. Code of 1954, sec. 170(c)(2)(A). Rev. Rul. 63-252, 1963-2 Cum. Bull. 101. For discussion see Eaton, Berrien C., Jr., "Charitable Foundations Making Grants Abroad," *Tax Law Review,* vol. 17, 1961, p. 41.

[1] See pp. 65–66 for the limitations on purposes imposed by this section.
[2] Treas. Reg., secs. 601.201(k), 1.501(a)–1, 1.501(c)(3)–1(b)(1)–(v), and 301.6104–1(b)(1)(ii)(f).
[3] Rev. Rul. 54–164, 1954–1 Cum. Bull. 88, 89.
[4] Treas. Reg., sec. 1.6033–1 (c); Rev. Rul. 54–393, 1954–2 Cum. Bull. 125.

These tests are now commonly referred to as the "operational" and "organizational" tests.

A series of regulations issued by the Treasury Department in 1959 spelled out in considerable detail the Department's attitude toward the requirements for organization and operation of a charitable organization. Included were certain standards that were required to be met under the so-called organizational test. They have been described as coming close to "providing 'a blueprint' for the preparation of the basic documents of a charitable corporation or charitable trust."[1] Of course, a resort to the courts might achieve a determination of tax exemption if a foundation's initial application were to be rejected by the Internal Revenue Service, but the practical effect of the Treasury regulation on almost all foundations is that of a uniform requirement or "blueprint."[2]

In regard to the powers and duties of charitable fiduciaries, these regulations impose certain limitations on the drafters of foundation charters or trust instruments.[3] One of the most important relates to the question of unrelated business activities, prescribing that the creators must not expressly empower the organization to engage in, or carry on, otherwise than as an insubstantial part of its operation, activities which in themselves are not in furtherance of one or more exempt purposes.[4] An example provided by the regulation states that an organization empowered to engage in a manufacturing business does not meet the organizational test regardless of its stated charitable purposes.[5]

In the area of trustees' duties, the Revenue Service has objected to broad exculpatory clauses, since they would excuse a trustee from any violations of the prohibited-transactions or unreasonable-accumulations sections or of any other section of the Code on the basis of which an exemption could be denied or withdrawn. For example, a clause that the trustee "should not be answerable for loss from investments made in good faith," would be acceptable, but adding to this "and for any cause whatsoever except his own willful misconduct" might well result in denial of exemption.[6]

---

[1] Eaton, Berrien C., Jr., and collaborators, "How to Draft the Charter or Indenture of a Charity so as to Qualify for Federal Tax Exemption," *Practical Lawyer*, vol. 8, October, 1962, pp. 13–38, and November, 1962, pp. 87–103 (quotation is from p. 15 of October issue).
[2] See p. 66.
[3] See p. 147 re powers, and pp. 72 ff. on dissolution provisions.
[4] Treas. Reg. 1.501 (c)(3)–1 (b)(1)(b) 1959.
[5] Treas. Reg. 1.501(c)(3)–1 (b)(1)(iii) 1959.
[6] Eaton, Berrien C., Jr., and collaborators, "How to Draft . . . ," *op. cit.,* November, p. 93.

The one-year operational test was intended to provide an opportunity for the Service to obtain a limited view of an organization's activities. This result was not achieved, however, since contributors were reluctant to take the chance of having their charitable deductions disallowed. Most organizations "limped along for the required twelve months, doing nothing wrong and still not really doing anything right," as one Internal Revenue Service official described the situation.[1]

In December, 1963, the Internal Revenue Service announced the recision of the twelve-month operational requirement, provided the organization could show affirmatively and in sufficient detail in its exemption application and supporting documents that it was "clearly exempt" within the requirement of the law under which exemption was claimed. The department did reserve the right to require a record of actual operation in certain cases where the Internal Revenue Service considered it warranted.[2]

The cases that have come before the courts on charges of a violation of the "organizational and operational" tests exemplify a wide variety of alleged abuses by charitable foundations. As is the case with many legal actions, a plaintiff will charge the defendant with as many potential violations as possible, and each will be argued by both parties. In tax cases it is customary for the Commissioner to rely primarily on one section of the Code but to introduce complementary arguments based on other sections. The court in its decision may pick and choose among them for its rationale, may single out one as the basis for decision or rely on several.

Cases that deal with charitable foundations, therefore, usually involve questions of both the definition section and the specific provision enacted in 1950, depending on the facts involved and the approach taken by the Internal Revenue Service. The situation is further complicated because the remedies available to the Commissioner are not only those in the sections relating to tax exemption, but cover the entire Revenue Code. For example, attacks on a practice of some foundations commonly referred to as "boot strap" acquisitions have been directed at the exempt status of the foundation, at the questions of whether the transfer was a completed sale, whether certain rents were

---

[1] Rogovin, Mitchell, "Revenue Service Audit Program," *Proceedings* of the New York University Sixth Biennial Conference on Charitable Foundations. Edited by Henry Sellin. Matthew Bender and Co., New York, 1963, p. 236.
[2] Rev. Proc. 63–30, 1963–2 Cum. Bull. 769.

entitled to be business deductions, and whether an individual was entitled to treat the transaction as a capital gain.[1]

The Internal Revenue Service has used the organizational test to challenge foundations that were indirectly benefiting donors. Some of these were discussed in Chapter II. In some instances the Service rulings followed the case law on validity of charitable purposes, particularly where the class of beneficiaries was larger than that of the donor's relatives or employees, and the benefits to be given were uniform for all recipients. Most of the court decisions, however, are based on both the operational and organizational requirements, however. For example, denial of an exemption to a company-sponsored foundation was recently upheld when it was shown that scholarship benefits that could be awarded only to employees of the founder corporation had actually been given primarily to the son of a man who was an employee, director, and stockholder of the corporation. Here, the organizational test might have been met, but the operations of the foundation belied the stated purposes.[2]

The operational test requires a showing that the primary or predominant purpose of the foundation is its charitable activities. Using this as the basis for decision, the courts have refused to uphold denials of exemption by the Internal Revenue Service in several cases where transfers of stock were made to a controlled foundation on conditions that annuities be granted to the donor, certain sums be paid to him, or that certain loans be made to him or others. The courts have used the foundation's benefit from the transaction, the existence of a fair price or terms, and the lack of evidence of a great number of such transactions to show that the foundation was operated *predominantly* for exempt purposes and that the private benefits were *incidental* to that purpose.

However, several extreme cases have resulted in loss of exemption. For example, in *Randall Foundation, Inc.* v. *Riddell*[3] the court denied exemption to a family foundation on the basis that it "was a business and not a charitable organization," thereby applying the operational test. This family foundation had invested heavily and traded actively in oil stocks, had mingled foundation assets with those of the donor,

---

[1] Young, Donald C., "Donor Foundation Dealings," *Proceedings* of the New York University Twenty-second Institute on Federal Taxation, *op. cit.*, 1964, pp. 965, 995–996.
[2] *Charleston Chair Co.* v. *U.S.*, 203 F. Supp. 126 (E.D. S.C. 1962).
[3] 244 F.2d 803 (9th Cir. 1957).

who acted as broker for the foundation, and had made minimal charitable contributions. The donor claimed that he had been accumulating income to finance the establishment of a home for underprivileged boys. The court did not rely on the accumulation section, but its decision has been interpreted to indicate that the accumulation provisions would be applicable in the case of speculations with corpus since such speculation is inconsistent with the requirements of the operational test.[1]

Evidence of a series of transactions involving donor benefit or substantial activity of a speculative nature may be sufficient to permit revocation of exemption, but only the most extreme cases have met the requirement.[2] It has been argued that since the Congress in 1950 did not see fit to outlaw completely all business activities and all donor foundation transactions, and specifically permitted those which were insubstantial, or at arm's length, the courts should not read more into the statute than the clear implication of these words and should permit a certain number of activities which by themselves are noncharitable or, at the most, suspect. The extent to which a charity may engage in unrelated business without defeating its qualification for exemption remains one of the most important unresolved problems of the tax laws relating to exempt organizations.

Unrelated Business Income

The objective of the 1950 provision imposing a tax on "unrelated business income" of exempt organizations and the taxation of "feeders" was the elimination of the competitive advantages of exempt organizations over taxable business. Since the Congress did not prohibit all business activities, but merely imposed a tax on certain of them, it became necessary to distinguish among those organizations that should be denied exemption entirely, those that would retain exemption but be subject to tax on some unrelated business income, and those that would remain entirely exempt even though they pursued certain business activities that would be taxable if not related to the charitable purpose.[3]

There were actually three types of business activities against which the sections on "unrelated business income" were directed. The first

---

[1] See Karst, Kenneth L., "The Efficiency of the Charitable Dollar: An Unfulfilled State Responsibility," *Harvard Law Review,* vol. 73, 1960, pp. 433, 440.

[2] *Stevens Bros. Foundation, Inc.* v. *Commissioner,* 324 F.2d 633 (6th Cir. 1963); *Donald G. Griswold,* 39 T.C. 620 (1962).

[3] Sugarman, Norman, and Harlan Pomeroy, *op. cit.,* p. 430.

and most obvious was the unrelated business operated by an exempt organization. The Code now taxes at business corporation rates that portion of a foundation's net income over $1,000 coming from such a business less the 5 per cent deduction for charitable contributions allowed to all corporations. Specifically exempted from the provision, however, are dividends, interest, annuities, royalties, and, in general, rents. The problem, of course, has been to determine what is "a business" and "unrelated." Rent is exempt, but if a foundation manages an apartment building as well as rents it, is it then a business? The question remains unresolved. Similar problems have arisen in connection with trading in royalties and patents.[1] Finally, it has been charged that many foundations are actively engaged in the banking and real estate business, thereby coming within the exemption for passive investments such as interest, but skirting close to the "primary purpose" prohibition.[2]

The second practice that had caused concern was the "lease-back," whereby a foundation buys property with borrowed funds, leases the property back to the seller or another, and pays off the loan and interest from the tax-free rent. Sections 512 to 514 now place a tax on such rentals if the business lease is for more than five years and the foundation has borrowed funds in order to acquire or improve the property, with certain exceptions.[3]

The reasons for congressional restriction on the sale and lease-back were three: a fear that large amounts of property would be transferred to tax-exempt organizations and thereby create an erosion of the national tax base; an underlying fear of unfair competition; and a feeling that such investments were not proper for foundations. As is the case in many instances when new tax laws are passed to stop particular abuses, certain individuals sought methods by which to achieve the original objectives of the newly restricted transaction and yet avoid the specific prohibitions. Thus it has been asserted that since 1950 many purchases have been made of property with tenants peculiarly suited to the premises, and that leases of five years or less have been concluded and renewed to fit the exemptions.

An extreme example of this type of legal ingenuity, however, is now known as the "boot strap" acquisition. In general, this type of

---

[1] Brookes, Valentine, "Foundations and Their Tax Problems," *Taxes*, vol. 41, 1963, pp. 742, 752, includes a discussion of both problems.

[2] Rogovin, Mitchell, *op. cit.*, p. 246.

[3] Int. Rev. Code of 1954, sec. 512(b)(2) and (3).

transaction involves the transfer of a closely held business to a foundation in return for a fixed price payable out of the earnings of the business. The seller is entitled to reclaim the business if there is a default in the payment. As part of the plan, the business will be operated by a separate corporation organized by the seller and the foundation jointly, with the stock of the corporation usually owned by relatives of the seller and employees of the business. The corporation then leases the business property from the foundation for five years in return for a rental which comprises most (often 80 per cent) of the profits of the business. The seller and his associates are usually hired by the new corporation on a salary basis to manage the business, which is carried on as before.

The tax advantages from such an arrangement have been described as follows: (1) payments to the seller will be taxed as capital gains; (2) the foundation's exemption will not be impaired; (3) the new operating corporation will be treated as a separate entity so that the seller will not be taxed on its income nor will the foundation need to pay a tax on unrelated business income; and (4) the rental payments of the operating corporation are deductible as a business expense.[1]

By the end of 1963 the Internal Revenue Service had attempted to revoke exemptions, deny capital gains treatment to the seller, or deny the rent deduction to the operating company in more than 15 cases involving one or more aspects of a boot strap acquisition, but it had achieved very limited success in maintaining its position on appeal to the courts. The sole case in which the government prevailed in the denial of an exemption involved a transaction where the purchase price was nearly four times greater than the fair market value of the assets, and the case included other evidence that the transaction was not conducted "at arm's length." The court concluded that the transaction was a sham and that there was private inurement.[2] An important consideration in this case was the fact that the business was conducted by the foundation, not an operating corporation. In the other cases, the courts have generally found that the prices were in excess of the amount that would be obtained from a taxpayer, that the investments were reasonable, and that there were therefore insufficient grounds for any of the government's positions.

The Commissioner did not acquiesce in the boot strap transaction

---

[1] Young, Donald C., *op. cit.*, p. 996.
[2] *Kolkey* v. *Commissioner of Internal Revenue,* 27 T.C. 37, 56 (1956), affirmed 254 F.2d 51 (7th Cir. 1958).

cases and in 1964 appealed an adverse decision of the 9th Circuit in the case of *Commissioner* v. *Brown*[1] to the United States Supreme Court. The issue in this particular case was whether the seller should be allowed capital gains treatment for the sale of stock of his controlled corporation to a foundation. The Supreme Court, with three justices dissenting, affirmed the holdings of the Court of Appeals and Tax Court.[2] The decision was based primarily on the grounds that there was nothing in the tax laws to indicate that risk-shifting from a seller to a buyer is a necessary concomitant of a sale and therefore of capital gains treatment. It was evident from its decision, as well as from the dissenting opinion, that the court was reluctant to tamper with an aspect of the Internal Revenue Code which has ramifications far beyond those in the exempt-organization field. The decision represented a major setback to the government's attempts to limit what was characterized as a scheme that involved "trading on tax-exemption," and Treasury officials announced that they were considering the introduction of special legislation to deal with the definition of capital gains, rather than awaiting congressional action on the Treasury's broad recommendations to control foundations, one of which would prohibit such arrangements.

These Code provisions relating to the business activities of foundations have been criticized on the basis of both the wording of the specific provisions and the basic premise on which they rest, namely, that a certain amount of business activity is not in itself improper for a foundation. The Treasury in 1965 gave official support to the latter point of view.

> Serious difficulties result from foundation commitment to business endeavors. Regular business enterprises may suffer serious competitive disadvantage. Moreover, opportunities and temptations for subtle and varied forms of self-dealing—difficult to detect and impossible completely to proscribe—proliferate. Foundation management may be drawn from concern with charitable activities to time-consuming concentration on the affairs and problems of the commercial enterprise.[3]

---

[1] *Commissioner of Internal Revenue* v. *Brown*, 325 F.2d 313 (9th Cir. 1963), _____ U.S. _____, 15 A.F.T.R.2d 790 (1965). See *University Hill Foundation*, T.C. Docket 73993; *Isis Windows, Inc.*, 22 T.C.M. 837 (1963); *Oscar B. Stahl*, 22 T.C.M. 996 (1963).

[2] 325 F.2d 313 (9th Cir. 1963), affirming 37 T.C. 461 (1961). _____ U.S. _____, _____ S.Ct. _____, 12 Am. Fed. Tax R.2d 6095 (1965).

[3] U.S. Congress, Senate, Committee on Finance, *Treasury Department Report on Private Foundations*. 89th Congress, 1st Session. Committee Print, February 2, 1965, p. 7.

The solution recommended by the Treasury was that all foundations be prohibited from owning, either directly or through stockholdings, 20 per cent or more of any business unrelated to their charitable endeavor. Furthermore, it suggested that restrictions be placed on three classes of financial activities closely related to the business area. Specifically, it proposed that (1) all borrowing be prohibited unless clearly for the purpose of carrying on the foundation's exempt function; (2) lending be confined to categories "clearly necessary, safe and appropriate" for fiduciaries,[1] and (3) any kind of trading and speculation with any of a foundation's assets be directly proscribed.

Others have suggested less restrictive measures, for example, that the exemption of five-year business leases be revoked; that borrowing be limited; that foundations be prevented from engaging in what amounts to a real estate rental or a loan business, or from trading in royalties and patents; and that they be specifically prevented from conducting "applied" research in competition with commercial firms. It has also been suggested that these activities not be absolutely prohibited, but added to those now considered "unrelated business" activities and thus subject to tax, leaving the foundation's exemption intact. Other commentators, as well as the Treasury, have recommended that a percentage limitation be placed on the ownership of business, although the amount of the limitation has varied from 3 to 50 per cent.

Feeder Corporations

The 1950 legislation relating to so-called feeder corporations represents the single instance in which Congress flatly withdrew exempt status from an activity that had previously been given this benefit. Section 502 states:

> An organization operated for the primary purpose of carrying on a trade or business for profit shall not be exempt under section 501 on the ground that all of its profits are payable to one or more organizations exempt under section 501 from taxation. For purposes of this section, the term "trade or business" shall not include the rental by an organization of its real property (including personal property leased with the real property).[2]

The term "feeder corporation" was originally given to enterprises owned by exempt organizations that did not dispense any charity but

---

[1] *Ibid.*, p. 9.
[2] Int. Rev. Code of 1954, sec. 502.

merely produced income for the parent charity. Before 1950 the practice was actually more common for charitable institutions other than foundations. The device was used for two reasons: it isolated the parent charity's other funds from exposure to the hazards of business; and it provided a dual tax benefit for the parent, since the feeder subsidiary paid no corporate or income taxes and the parent charity paid no tax on dividends received. Probably the best-known example of a feeder corporation was the macaroni company operated as a feeder for a university. The Tax Court had actually ruled that this corporation was not entitled to exemption at the time of the 1950 congressional hearings,[1] but in other cases exemption had been upheld on the theory that the "destination of income" was the support of charitable purposes.[2] The congressional action was designed to settle the question once and for all.

The wording of section 502 has been questioned by some writers on the ground that the test prescribed does not differ in practice from that in the sections of the taxation of unrelated business income. To date, however, the section by itself has not caused as much controversy as the other parts of the 1950 act. The one area of uncertainty relates to the exclusion of feeder corporations that rent real estate and provide services therefor. As this section complements the "organized and operated" requirements, however, it remains part of the entire problem area of the effect of business activities on the exempt status of an organization.

Unreasonable Accumulations and Misuse of Income

The descriptions in Chapters III and IV of the legal nature of charitable trusts and corporations included a discussion of the state laws that regulate accumulations of income. In general, these state laws limit only those accumulations that are "against public policy." As this standard has been interpreted by the courts, it has come to mean those accumulations that under all the circumstances are unreasonably long or not reasonably certain of ascertainment.[3]

Prior to 1950 there were no statutory restrictions on accumulation in the tax laws, although the Internal Revenue Service had used as

---

[1] *C. F. Mueller Co.*, 14 T.C. 922 (1950) reversed, 190 F.2d 120 (3d Cir. 1951).

[2] *Trinidad v. Sagrada Orden de Predicadores*, 263 U.S. 578 (1924); *Commissioner of Internal Revenue v. Orton*, 173 F.2d 483 (6th Cir. 1949).

[3] *Restatement of the Law of Trusts (Second)*, American Law Institute, St. Paul, 1959, sec. 401.

one basis for challenging the exemption of a few foundations an assertion that improper accumulations were evidence that the foundation was not organized and operated for charitable purposes. This view had not been upheld by the courts, however.

The act of 1950 reflected the approach of the Internal Revenue Service in these cases by specifically making certain transactions involving accumulation grounds for revocation of exemption. Specifically, section 504a of the Internal Revenue Code now provides that exemption will be denied if income accumulations during the taxable year or any prior year:

> (1) are unreasonable in amount or duration in order to carry out the charitable, educational or other purpose or function constituting the basis of exemption . . . (2) are used to a substantial degree for purposes or functions other than those constituting the basis for exemption. . . ; or (3) are invested in such a manner as to jeopardize the carrying out of the charitable, educational, or other purpose or function constituting the basis of exemption.[1]

The prohibition, therefore, applies to amount and duration, as well as to the use of the income so accumulated. It is not a blanket proscription against any accumulation and does not extend to use of principal. It should also be noted that in the case of testamentary trusts containing a mandatory provision for accumulation, if the provision is valid under state law, the tax law prohibition relating to amount and duration applies only to accumulations occurring after the expiration of the period of the Rule Against Perpetuities.[2] For the purpose of this section, the definition of income is the same as that used in other parts of the revenue laws to determine income of business corporations.[3]

This section of the Internal Revenue Code has now been in effect for fourteen years. It has been the subject of several Treasury regulations and four Internal Revenue Service rulings, as well as a number of court decisions, but the negative nature of the statutory wording and the use of the word "reasonable" have led to great uncertainty as to the actual scope of the prohibition.[4]

Treasury regulations issued since 1950 have primarily restated the

---

[1] Int. Rev. Code of 1954, sec. 504(a).
[2] Int. Rev. Code of 1954, secs. 504(a) and 681(c).
[3] Treas. Reg. 1.504–1(c).
[4] Mulreany, Robert, "Permissible Accumulations," *Proceedings* of the New York University Sixth Biennial Conference on Charitable Foundations, *op. cit.*, p. 174.

Code provisions. They have clarified the status of gains received from the sale or exchange of donated assets or property held for investment by holding in effect that gains are not considered accumulations if they are reinvested within a reasonable time in property which is to be held for the production of income[1] and that gains occurring before the donation of property are not attributed to the foundation.

The first published rulings of the Internal Revenue Service have been described as "rather limited and conservative and not very indicative of a general policy of the Internal Revenue Service."[2] They have permitted accumulation in two instances for short periods to formulate a new program and to replace grants previously made from capital,[3] held that contributions could ordinarily be considered additions to capital and not income,[4] and that commitments for a project that would require several years to complete could be transferred to a reserve account and charged against income for the year in which the project was approved.[5]

The third source of interpretation of the prohibition against unreasonable accumulation is the record of court decisions where the Internal Revenue Service has challenged a foundation's tax-exempt status on the grounds of violation of this section of the Code, particularly the first prohibition as to unreasonableness of amount or duration. The cases have given some indication of what constitutes unreasonableness in terms of particular fact situations, but to date they have not developed a single formula for application of the statute.

The first case, *Samuel Friedland Foundation* v. *U.S.*[6] was based in part on charges by the Commissioner of unreasonable accumulation of income. The foundation had accumulated $39,000 of income during a two-year period as part of a plan to raise $500,000 during a seven-to-eight-year period to construct a medical research building at Brandeis University. The court held that the plan did not violate the Code provisions, stating that the test for application of the accumulation section was whether the foundation had a concrete program for accumulation of income which would be devoted to a charitable purpose and whether, in the light of existing circumstances, the plan could

---

[1] Treas. Reg. 1.504–1(b)(1) and Reg. 1.504–1(c).
[2] Mulreany, Robert, *op. cit.*, p. 163.
[3] Rev. Rul. 54–137, 1954–1 Cum. Bull 289 and Rev. Rul. 54–227, 1954–1 Cum. Bull. 291.
[4] Rev. Rul. 58–535, 1958–2 Cum. Bull. 270.
[5] Rev. Rul. 55–674, 1955–2 Cum. Bull. 264.
[6] 144 F.Supp. 74 (D.C.N.J. 1956).

reasonably be achieved within the time proposed by the foundation.[1] The formula laid down in the *Friedland* case has been used by various federal courts to approve accumulations,[2] and the decision has been described as the best reasoned of the cases dealing with accumulations. Its use, however, has not yet produced any uniformity in result. This is best illustrated by a comparison of several more recent cases.

In *Shiffman Foundation,*[3] the foundation had used its sole asset of $1,000 to purchase real estate for $1,150,000 by borrowing $750,000 from an institutional lender as a first mortgage, $250,000 from one of the founders, and making up the balance from advance rentals from one tenant. The property was then leased back to the original seller.[4] The court held that the investment was sound and not speculative and that the use of net profit to pay off indebtedness was neither an unreasonable accumulation nor an accumulation for nonexempt purposes. The court noted that once the indebtedness was paid off, the entire net income would be available for the charitable purposes of the foundation, that it was paid off within five years, and that during that same period the foundation distributed almost $250,000 to exempt organizations. It also stated that the holding of title to the property was not the operation of an unrelated business, but a passive investment more like the ownership of stock, since the foundation had hired a management company to operate the property.[5]

The *Shiffman* case was distinguished a year later by the Court of Appeals in the case of *Erie Endowment* v. *U.S.*[6] where the court upheld the revocation of exemption of a foundation created as an inter vivos trust in 1935 with a mandatory direction to accumulate a certain percentage of the income each year until the fund was worth $10 million. The court, applying the test formulated in the *Friedland* case, pointed out that the accumulation was not for specific charitable purposes, merely general, and that the contributions that were made were

---

[1] In this decision the court also formulated a test in regard to speculative investments which is discussed on p. 176.

[2] *Truscott et al.* v. *U.S.*, _____ F. Supp. _____, 58–1 U.S.T.C. paragraph 9515 (D.C. E.D. Pa. 1958); *Hulman Foundation* v. *U.S.*, 217 F.Supp. 423, (D.C.Ind. 1962) ($1.4 million was accumulated over a fourteen-year period for construction of a civic auditorium).

[3] 32 T.C. 1073 (1959) (Acquiesced 1960–1 Cum. Bull. 5).

[4] A case with similar facts and a similar outcome decided in the same year was *Tell Foundation* v. *Wood*, 58–1 U.S.T.C. paragraph 9111 (DC. Ariz. 1959).

[5] Even though the management company was a partnership consisting of one of the founders and a member of his family.

[6] 202 F.Supp. 580 (W.D. Pa. 1961) affirmed 316 F.2d 151 (3d Cir. 1963).

to organized charities and not for programs initiated by the foundation.[1]

The most recent case, *Danforth Foundation* v. *U.S.*,[2] is the only
one to date where the sole issue was the question of accumulation. The
foundation, since its inception in the 1920's, had regularly accumulated a part of its annual income, so that it had acquired a substantial
capital fund by 1950 when section 504 was enacted. Shortly before
1950 the foundation had decided to obtain a full-time director to develop a program for the foundation, but it did not complete negotiations to hire a particular individual until 1951. In 1951 and 1952 the
foundation continued to make accumulations while its new director
assisted in the development of a program of activity. The Service revoked the foundation's exemption for these years on the ground of
unreasonable accumulation. This action was upheld by the federal
District Court, which held that plans for charitable expenditures were
required under the Code to be relatively specific and that "some activity" directed toward reaching a program-planning stage of development was found to be inadequate. The court stated that "the record is
absent of any showing of an attempt to relate the programs to anticipated income" and further observed that there was no possibility of
using the large amounts of income accumulated in the past years for
the programs which were presented to the court.

These cases have dealt with that part of section 504 which prohibits
accumulations that are unreasonable in amount or duration. Section
504 also prohibits the use of accumulations for purposes or functions
not constituting the basis for exemption, or their investment in such
a manner as to jeopardize the carrying out of the charitable purpose.
Neither the regulations nor the legislative history provide a clarification of these sections, and there have been no published rulings on
them to date.

The questions of speculation and the nature of foundation investments have arisen, however, in a number of cases where the charges
against the foundation were based on several grounds. In the *Friedland* case a formula was proposed for application of section 504a (3),
as was a formula for 504a (1) already discussed. The court stated:
"The test is not whether any one or two investments made with ac-

---

[1] Other factors in the *Erie* case which may have influenced the court were that
some of the accumulated income for the periods in question was invested in
loans to the founder, his family, and a business which he controlled.

[2] 222 F.Supp. 761 (D.C. Mo. 1963). This case has been appealed.

cumulated income were likely to founder, but whether whatever loss was apt to occur would imperil the capability of the organization to carry out its charitable purposes."[1]

Three years later the Tax Court proposed a different test for evaluating foundation investments in the case of *John Danz Charitable Trust*.[2] It held that exemption would not be denied when the investment activity was not "so speculative as to subject its funds to a significant risk of loss." Karst thinks that the phase "significant risk of loss" presumably meant that exemption would be lost if the risk taken was substantial, regardless of its amount, so that it was a more severe restriction on charitable investments than the formula of the *Friedland* case.[3]

Sections 504(a)(2) and (3) have not been relied on by the Internal Revenue Service as much as the other provisions of the 1950 act. Unless the Congress amends these sections, there are indications that they may be used to attempt to establish a basis for denying exemption to foundations engaged in wildcatting or other speculative investments involving a high risk of loss.[4] They may also be used in the future as a basis for attacking the boot strap transactions.[5] In any case they provide a catch-all type of power enabling the Service to attack investments of income.

These administrative rulings and court decisions have been described in detail because they offer excellent examples of several important aspects of attempts to use the tax laws to prevent diversion of charitable funds or their use for private gain. It has already been noted that the application of the accumulation provisions represents a departure from the traditional formula applied by the state courts to determine the validity of accumulation provisions in a trust instrument or corporate charter. This is particularly so in regard to the requirement that there be a specific program for which the accumulation is being made. The prohibition against accumulations has, therefore, imposed a greater restriction on the donors of charitable funds than have the laws of property that relate to charitable dispositions.

The accumulation provisions of the tax law actually represent a compromise between two points of view held by the members of Congress who drafted the Revenue Act of 1950. The House version

---

[1] 144 F.Supp. 74, at 93–4 (D.C. N.J. 1956).
[2] 32 T.C. 469 (1959), affirmed 284 F.2d 726 (9th Cir. 1960).
[3] Karst, Kenneth L., *op. cit.*, p. 440.
[4] Brookes, Valentine, *op. cit.*, p. 742.
[5] Young, Donald C., *op. cit.*, pp. 1000 ff.

of the act would have subjected to tax, with certain exceptions, that portion of the investment income of foundations which was not paid out on or before the fifteenth day of the third month following the close of the taxable year.[1] This view was rejected by the Senate as too inflexible and injurious to many worthwhile exempt projects.[2] The Senate committee did not dispute the existence of abuses of the tax-exempt provisions to build up accumulations, but felt that public disclosure of all accumulations would encourage distribution and reveal the extent of the problem, if indeed one existed.[3] In conference, these opposing views were reconciled into what is now section 504 of the Code, but the exact intent of the provision was never explained.[4]

The attitude of the Internal Revenue Service and the courts toward section 504 has been expressed as follows: "The purpose of exemption is to give relief to organizations which serve the public in a capacity which relieves the public treasury. Accumulating income does nothing to relieve the burdens of government."[5]

In 1964 Congress reiterated this philosophy in the course of amending the sections of the Internal Revenue Code that permit an unlimited contribution deduction to certain donors. In order to be eligible to receive such a contribution, a recipient foundation must spend 50 per cent of the contribution within three years for its charitable purposes and during that period must also expend all of its net income for the same purposes.[6]

The Treasury has recognized that the standards established in the accumulation sections are "inadequate as well as difficult and expensive to administer," and lead to uncertainty for tax officials and foundation managers alike.[7] The Department has recommended a return to the provision contained in the House version of the 1950 Revenue Act

---

[1] U.S. Congress, House of Representatives, Committee on Ways and Means, *Revenue Act of 1950: Report* to accompany H.R. 8920, 81st Congress, 2d Session. House Report 2319, 1950, pp. 40, 115–125.

[2] U.S. Congress, Senate, Finance Committee, *Revenue Act of 1950: Report* to accompany H.R. 8920, 81st Congress, 2d Session. Senate Report 2375, 1950, p. 34.

[3] Revenue Act of 1950 as reported by U.S. Congress, Senate, Finance Committee, sec. 341, printed in *ibid.*

[4] U.S. Congress, House of Representatives, Committee on Ways and Means, *Revenue Act of 1950: Conference Report*, 81st Congress, 2d Session. House Report 3124, 1950, p. 15.

[5] *Danforth Foundation* v. *U.S.*, 222 F.Supp. 761 (D.C. Mo. 1963).

[6] Revenue Act of 1964, sec. 209(b)(2) and (3); adding Int. Rev. Code, sec. 170(g)(2) and (3).

[7] U.S. Congress, Senate, Committee on Finance, *Treasury Department Report on Private Foundations, op. cit.,* p. 25.

and proposed that foundations be subject to a requirement of mandatory distribution of all current net income. The newer proposals would allow a foundation a year in which to budget and plan the distribution, however. They would also permit a five-year carryforward if the foundation had, during a prior period, expended amounts in excess of its income; and they would permit accumulations necessary to accomplish a clearly designated purpose for a reasonable period of time specified in advance by the foundation. A complementary provision in the Treasury's 1965 recommendation reflected a recognition that a mandatory payout-of-income provision would not answer the problem of the indirect accumulations that occur when a foundation retains or invests in assets providing little or no income. The Department suggested the enactment of an "income equivalent provision" whereby foundations would be required to disburse an amount equal to the greater of actual foundation net income or a fixed percentage of assets. The minimum level of charitable expenditures would be a percentage comparable to the yield on invested funds held by similar organizations such as universities. The percentage would be determined by the Secretary of the Treasury under his regulatory authority and would be subject to revision from time to time.

Those who most fear the growth of foundations have recommended a twenty-five-year limit on the life of all foundations. Another proposal has been that all capital gains be treated as ordinary income and thereby be subject to any restrictions on accumulations. Another view is that it is not the accumulation itself which is improper, but the uses of the funds which are retained. These critics suggest a proscription against speculation and business investments, or some other attempt to control investment practices, rather than any specific limitation on accumulation beyond the standard of "unreasonableness." Far less drastic than many of these suggestions would be still another proposal that the accumulation of unreasonable amounts of income no longer be grounds for removal of tax exemption, but that any such amounts themselves be subject to tax.

It may be seriously questioned whether accumulation per se is as undesirable as it seems to be to some of the commentators. It is legitimate for government to require that foundation income be devoted to the purposes for which tax exemption is permitted, and not held back to be used for the private purposes of a donor or other private individuals. Accumulating income to better serve charitable purposes at a future date through the production of greater sums of money or to permit the formulation of a plan to better distribute the income available would seem to be legitimate; yet under the present laws few foundations or even prospective donors are willing to risk such activities for fear of Service disapproval and the possibility of extensive litigation or loss of exemption.

The fact that the tax laws neither impose uniform standards nor permit foundations to develop freely is evident from the history of the accumulations section. Whether any of the proposed reforms would meet these objections would depend as much on the manner in which they are administered as on the nature of the restrictions that are enacted. It is to be hoped, however, that the Congress will not inadvertently force all foundations to serve as immediate conduits of funds, thereby severely restricting their ability to anticipate the ever-changing needs of society.

Prohibited Transactions

The fourth set of provisions[1] of the 1950 act contains a list of transactions which, if entered into by the foundation and certain proscribed parties (the creator, a substantial contributor, a member of the family of either, or a corporation controlled by such contributor or creator), will cause the foundation to lose its tax exemption for at least one taxable year. The transactions include any in which an organization:

(1) lends any part of its income or corpus, without the receipt of adequate security and a reasonable rate of interest. . . .

(2) pays any compensation, in excess of a reasonable allowance for salaries or other compensation for personal services actually rendered. . .

(3) makes any part of its services available on a preferential basis . . .

(4) makes any substantial purchase of securities or any other property, for more than adequate consideration in money or money's worth, . . .

(5) sells any substantial part of its securities or other property for less than an adequate consideration in money or money's worth; or

(6) engages in any other transaction which results in a substantial diversion of its income or corpus. . . .[2]

The House version of what became the Revenue Act of 1950 contained more drastic provisions. It would have denied a charitable deduction for a gift of stock where the foundation receiving it and the

---

[1] Int. Rev. Code of 1954, sec. 503.
[2] Int. Rev. Code of 1954, sec. 503(c).

corporation issuing it were controlled by the donor or his family, and would also have prohibited all loans, purchases, and sales with such a person or with officers of the corporation.[1] The Senate disagreed, feeling that the restrictions were too harsh.[2] The section as finally enacted expresses a philosophy of permitting such transactions so long as the two parties deal "at arm's length."

It has been suggested that this list of abuses was already embraced by the private inurement clause of section 501(c)(3), and that prior to 1950 evidence of frequent or substantial transactions of this sort would have resulted in loss of exemption.[3]

The Revenue Act of 1964 has compounded the problem by adding to the Code another list of prohibited transactions which are somewhat closer to fiduciary law. However, they are applicable to an infinitesimally small group of individuals who, because they had met certain standards, were permitted an unlimited charitable contribution deduction. These standards were that in the year of the contribution and in eight of the ten preceding taxable years, the income taxes and charitable contributions were in excess of 90 per cent of the donor's taxable income computed without the deduction for all charitable contributions, personal exemptions, and net operating loss carrybacks.

The 1964 provision places several restrictions on the availability of this unlimited deduction. Among them is a provision that no deduction for gifts to private foundations will be allowed if during the contributing year, the three years before, and the three years after, the foundation receiving the contribution:

(a) lends any part of its income or corpus to;

(b) pays compensation (other than reasonable compensation for personal services actually rendered) to;

(c) makes any of its services available on a preferential basis to;

(d) purchases more than a minimal amount of securities or other property from; or

(e) sells more than a minimal amount of securities or other property to, the donor of such contribution, any member of his family . . . , any employee of the donor, any officer or employee of a corporation in which he owns (directly or indirectly) 50 per cent or more

---

[1] See sec. 333(a) of H.R. 8920, 81st Congress, 2d Session, 1950; and U.S. Congress, House of Representatives, Committee on Ways and Means, *Revenue Act of 1950: Report* to accompany H.R. 8920, *op. cit.*, pp. 43–44, 131, 380, 412–413.

[2] U.S. Congress, Senate, Finance Committee, *Revenue Act of 1950: Report to* accompany H.R. 8920, *op. cit.*, pp. 483, 510.

[3] Young, Donald C., *op. cit.*, p. 980.

in value of the outstanding stock, or any partner or employee of a partnership in which he owns (directly or indirectly) 50 per cent or more of the capital interest or profits interest.[1]

These transactions are described as "disqualifying" rather than "prohibited" transactions. They make the prohibition against loans absolute; it holds regardless of fairness of rate of interest or adequacy of security. They prohibit any but minimal sales or purchases of securities, as opposed to the section 503 ban on "substantial" purchases and sales without adequate consideration. Finally, they provide a different definition for "related parties," including partnerships, but they do not define stock ownership as explicitly.

The number of individuals who may be eligible to take advantage of this unlimited deduction provision is small; but since the number of foundations that may desire to be eligible to receive such a contribution is potentially larger, the standards of the disqualifying transaction section may have a wider influence on foundation activities.

The fact that the provisions of both the prohibited transaction section and the disqualifying transactions section are applicable only to certain closely related persons is an important limitation to their effectiveness. In the case of the prohibited transactions section, an even more serious objection is that the ban on these dealings is not absolute. An Internal Revenue Service official has pointed out that the standards in this section—that is, that loans must be at a "reasonable" rate of interest and with "adequate security," and that purchase and sales transactions must be for "adequate consideration"—are hardly fiduciary standards. Moreover, it is most difficult for the Service to police all such transactions to ensure that arm's length formalities are observed in transactions which are not, inherently, at arm's length.[2]

A final objection must be made. It relates to the influence of the specific statutory prohibitions on the attitude of fiduciaries to their duties. The prohibited transactions section is universally applied and is fairly easily understood, in contrast to property laws restricting the activities of fiduciaries, which vary from state to state and are rarely as explicitly defined. It is easy to mistake the tax law prohibitions for the outer limits of fiduciary duties. That they are not should be obvious. What is prohibited to donors or substantial contributors in the Revenue Code is prohibited by fiduciary law to all trustees and direc-

---

[1] Revenue Act of 1964, sec. 209(b); adding Int. Rev. Code, sec. 170(g)(4).
[2] Rogovin, Mitchell, *op. cit.*, p. 241.

tors. The duty of loyalty is violated whenever any trustee or director acts for the benefit of a third party and not for the trust or corporation. The tax law prohibitions are applicable only when there is a disadvantage to the charity, such as a purchase or sale by the charity for more or less than adequate price. The law of trusts flatly forbids self-dealing without ratification by the beneficiary; the law of corporations forbids self-dealing that is unfair and not approved by a disinterested majority of the directors. Both forbid the expropriation of opportunities and the realization of private profit from transactions made in the course of administration of the foundation.

In its 1965 Report to the Congress, the Treasury gave official recognition to these limitations and underscored the difficulties of enforcing them. It recommended the enactment of an absolute ban on self-dealing for substantial contributors, officers, directors, or trustees of foundations, or parties related to them; the only exception would be payment of reasonable compensation for services and purchases of incidental supplies. The definition proposed by the Treasury would expand the list of individuals covered by the prohibited transactions section by adding corporations in which the donor or members of his family own 20 per cent or more of the stock of a corporation which is a substantial contributor to the foundation, and business corporations controlled by the foundation.[1]

Other suggestions for revision of the prohibited transactions section would not extend the list of parties to include all fiduciaries but merely expand the list of unrelated parties to encompass the estates of the donors and the parent organization of a subsidiary whose stock is contributed by a donor fiduciary. It has also been proposed that the list of proscribed transactions be expanded to include the use of foundation funds for accommodations-type transactions for friends of the fiduciaries and the use of a foundation's voting power in proxy fights in which the fiduciary donor may have a private interest. Some commentators advocate an exception to the ban on donor-foundation dealings to permit a foundation to purchase property from the donor when its market value is clearly ascertainable and the price offered to the foundation is substantially less than the market value. The Treasury Report specifically discussed the advisability of permitting these so-called "bargain sales" but concluded that such an exception would

---

[1] U.S. Congress, Senate, Committee on Finance, *Treasury Department Report on Private Foundations, op. cit.*, pp. 22–23.

give undesirable benefits to donors and would be exceedingly difficult to administer.[1]

Donor Control

The prohibited transactions section of the Internal Revenue Code was originally designed to minimize the problems of donor control of foundations. It is now evident that they do not reach many instances of donor advantage.

> Transactions between a donor and his foundation do not necessarily advance the exempt purposes of the foundation merely because they do not provide any direct benefit to the donor. Such transactions may shackle the foundation with unneeded goods and services, and require it to spend an inordinate amount of time (and money) in arranging its business affairs. Moreover, indirect benefits are available to the donor from such transactions which are not blocked by the section.[2]

Among the indirect benefits are the sale or gift and lease-back, the boot strap acquisition, the donation of property subject to an annuity, the creation of a foundation to make grants with a preference for employees or relatives, the use of a foundation to help a donor in proxy fights or to buy up stock of a competing business which the donor cannot buy himself.

Professor Sacks strikes at the heart of the drawbacks of the prohibited transactions legislation. While he believes that certain aspects of donor control of foundations may be clearly legitimate (among these he names a desire to level contributions or to use a foundation as a means of passing a business on within a family), he also suggests that there arc means of accomplishing this without permitting the donor and his family to retain control over the foundation's funds or activities. He suggests two conditions which ought to be met by any legislation.

> First, all transactions between related persons or organizations ought to be avoided, except perhaps such as are inherent, as the payment of compensation for services. Secondly, the activities of the foundation ought not to be distinctly beneficial to any related person or organization. I doubt that these conditions can be satisfied in cases where the donor has given to his foundation stock control of one or more corporations and proceeds to manage both.[3]

[1] *Ibid.*, p. 22.
[2] Young, Donald C., *op. cit.*, p. 983.
[3] Sacks, Albert M., "Use and Misuse of the Private Foundation," *Proceedings* of the New York University Fifth Biennial Conference on Charitable Foundations, *op. cit.*, 1961, pp. 203–215.

Karst has proposed a series of measures designed to minimize donor control which meet the criteria specified by Sacks. Karst suggested a definition of donor control based on a "voting control rule" similar to that in the sections of the Internal Revenue Code dealing with grantor trusts[1] and tied to a provision denying deductions for contributions from a donor to his controlled foundation.[2]

The Treasury Report of 1965 took a different approach. In addition to the amendments to the prohibited transactions section, it recommended that no income tax deduction be permitted for the donation of an interest in property over which the donor and related parties retain control until either (1) the foundation disposes of the asset or devotes the property to active charitable operations, or (2) the donor control over the business or property terminates. Control by a donor over the business or other property interest would be presumed if the donor and related parties owned either a 20 per cent equity interest or 20 per cent of the voting power of the corporation.[3]

The advantage of this proposal is that it obviates the problem of defining donor control of a foundation, which is a more difficult matter to determine than that of control of a business entity. There are some who feel, however, that it is unnecessarily restrictive since it would discourage gifts of stock in a company controlled by a donor to any foundation, whether or not he was even a member of the managing board. The Treasury Report recognized the force of this argument and suggested a modification of the proposal whereby the deduction would be postponed only if the contributing donor also exercised "substantial influence" upon the foundation. The Report stressed the difficulties entailed in defining "substantial influence" and in enforcing such a provision. However, it also expressed the belief that the gift of an interest over which the donor retained control was not a sufficiently clear and definite present gift to warrant a present tax deduction.[4] It was left to the Congress to weigh the merits of both proposals.

This same Treasury Report contained a further proposal relating to donor control. Based less on objections to the personal advantages to donors than on the problems arising from the perpetual existence of foundations and the possibilities for narrowness of view and paro-

---

[1] Int. Rev. Code of 1954, sec. 671–78.
[2] Karst, Kenneth L., "The Tax Exemption of Donor Controlled Foundations," *Ohio State Law Journal*, vol. 25, 1964, p. 183.
[3] U.S. Congress, Senate, Committee on Finance, *Treasury Department Report on Private Foundations, op. cit.*, pp. 41–43.
[4] *Ibid.*, pp. 44–45.

chialism in their management, it would require that after a foundation has been in existence for twenty-five years, its donor and related parties should compose no more than 25 per cent of its managing board. The definition of related parties for the purpose of this proposal would be confined to members of the donor's family, persons with whom the donor has a direct or indirect employment relationship, and persons with whom the donor has a continuing business or professional relationship. Finally, after the twenty-five-year period, the newly constituted board would be empowered to dissolve the foundation and distribute its assets in accordance with its purposes.

Foundation "Abuses"

The use of a foundation to further the personal economic interests of an individual contributor and the entry of foundations into certain business ventures represent departures from the concepts of permissible fiduciary actions traditional during the preceding centuries. The charitable trusts of the eighteenth century were created almost exclusively as testamentary trusts, so that the problem of donor control and donor advantage were not present. Being primarily trusts, fiduciary duties were usually well defined and more easily followed. Trust instruments were written so as to guarantee as much as possible that the donor's wishes would be observed by trustees over whom the donor would have no control.

The income tax laws have provided a new incentive for creating and controlling foundations during an individual's lifetime. Today, foundations are created in many cases as estate planning devices or as means of securing tax advantages for a donor and his family, rather than from a desire to establish in perpetuity the funds to carry on a favored charitable enterprise, perhaps coupled with a desire to perpetuate a family name. The entry of foundations into business enterprises has also arisen in part from these same personal motives, but it has also come about because of the ability of foundations to realize large financial returns from certain business investments, particularly where it is possible to offer to private individuals advantages not available through dealings with nonexempt sources.

Not all of the dealings with donors or business activities of foundations can be considered abuses of either tax privileges or the laws of fiduciary duty, yet there is no doubt that certain foundation operations have been highly questionable. No reliable evidence exists of the extent of wrongdoing, but even if it represents a bare minimum of all foundation actions, the effectiveness of the laws must be measured against their ability to stem the abuses while at the same time not unduly hampering legitimate foundation activity.

The recent charges of abuse have been directed primarily against certain specific foundation practices, notably self-dealing through foundations, and unfair competition with business enterprises particularly for interest and rental income. They have also been directed against speculative investments, unreasonable accumulations, manipulation of leases, donations of nonincome-producing property and overvaluation of donated property.[1] At the same time, attention has been focused on the premise that underlies the subsidy involved in tax exemption. The role of foundations in both the economic and social structure is once again being questioned. To date, however, the attention of Congress, the Treasury, and most tax writers has been directed primarily toward devising measures to deal with specific abuses. The problems they are attacking are in essence the same as those that existed in 1950, although the suggestions for reform are made in the light of almost fifteen years of experience with the restrictions enacted at that time. Suggestions for reform are also strikingly similar to those discussed in earlier decades. While some would have a fairly far-reaching effect on foundations, they are all designed to modify or supplement specific provisions of the Internal Revenue Code rather than change the basic structure of the exemption sections. The reformers, therefore, face problems of definition and administration that must be solved within the existing framework of laws designed primarily to raise revenue for government.

Each of the proposals discussed in previous sections of this chapter raises at the outset the question of definition. For example, an easy answer to the problem of business and financial activities would be to say that foundations should be limited to "passive" investments, and forbidden any business activities. But what is a passive investment? Receipt of rental income has traditionally been considered a proper "passive" source of income for trust property, but what if the entire funds of a foundation are so invested and the foundation then must manage the property? How much of an investment in individual small loans is sufficient to characterize a foundation as a banker, and how

---

[1] For examples, see *ibid.;* U.S. Congress, House of Representatives, Select Committee on Small Business, *Chairman's* (Patman) *Report,* "Tax-Exempt Foundations and Charitable Trusts: Their Impact on Our Economy," First Installment, 87th Congress, 2d Session, Committee Print, December 31, 1962; and Karst, Kenneth L., "The Tax-Exemption . . . ," *op. cit.*

much trading in the stock market should warrant the tax officials' characterizing a foundation as an investment company? If on the contrary some business activity is to be permitted, what standards can be used to decide specific situations? The term "related" which now appears in the Revenue Code has been defined as something more than "relevant" but less than "necessary." Application of such a standard cannot produce much uniformity. Should the phrase "necessary" be substituted? Would a prohibition against "commercial" activities be more easily administered?

One of the recent suggestions has been to place a ban on "speculation" similar to that which appears in the accumulations section. There is some feeling that the tax laws are not appropriate to police investment practices. Is it possible to enforce a ban on "speculation"? One possibility is the adoption of a "legal list" of investments; another is the incorporation of a version of the prudent man rule into the tax laws, accompanied by a provision requiring diversification. This immediately raises the problem of administrability.

The regulation of donor control raises as many quandaries.[1] Just what is donor control? Should all donors be prohibited from acting as trustees of foundations to which they have made any contributions, or only those to which they have made substantial contributions; or should they be prohibited only from participating in financial affairs, but allowed to control the program of the foundation? If the substantial contributor is to be prohibited from serving as a fiduciary, what about members of his family, his attorney or accountant, or business associates? How far should the concept "related parties" be extended? When donations are made of stock in a closely held corporation, the question of "control" then turns to the extent of the donor's interest in the corporation and the per cent of ownership that is sufficient to be considered control. If the contributor happens to have a financial interest in the majority of enterprises in his home town, would it ever be possible to find any "independent" fiduciaries? Should limitations be applied to all cases where a donor acts as a fiduciary, or only when he "controls" the foundation? The problems of defining "control" are so difficult that any solution that obviates the need for definition has merit.

Proposals to revise the prohibited transactions and accumulations sections raise similar problems. The accumulations section, in addi-

---

[1] For a detailed discussion of this particular problem see Karst, Kenneth L., "The Tax-Exemption . . . ," *op. cit.*

tion, poses at the outset, a philosophical question, for the limitation of the right to revise goals and remake plans goes to the essence of the freedom of foundations to operate within the various fields of philanthropy.

Problems Raised by Regulation of Charities Through Tax Laws

Participation in business enterprises and speculation are often violations of the prudent man doctrine. Yet attempts by the tax authorities to stop them through removal of tax exemption have been rejected by the courts in all but the most extreme cases on the ground that Congress did not evidence any intent to prohibit all breaches of fiduciary duty. The legislative history supports this view. Furthermore, the reluctance of the courts to remove exemption in some cases can be attributed in part to a realization that the penalty demanded by law for violation of the tax statutes does not achieve the long-accepted purpose of enforcement actions against charities—the preservation of their funds and their dedication to the public benefit.[1] The problem was well stated by a writer discussing the effects of violation of the accumulation and prohibited transactions sections, but his point is equally relevant to other violations of other sections of the Revenue Code:

> It may be asked . . . whether the means selected "have a real and substantial relationship to the object to be attained" or whether the remedy as applied is unreasonable, arbitrary or capricious. Why in the case of accumulations is it necessary to disrupt the exempt organization unless there is an intentional violation that goes to the entire structure of the organization? Why may not the result be accomplished more effectively by requiring a discontinuation of the practice and the taxation of the income if it is found to be unreasonably accumulated?
>
> And a similar question may be asked as to the prohibited transactions. Suppose the overreaching of the insiders is a fraud of which the foundation is the victim, should not the remedies be aimed at the offender and the offense instead of penalizing the victim?[2]

Consideration of any proposals for reform, therefore, must be accompanied by consideration of appropriate sanctions. In general, denial of individual contributions and taxation or penalization of donors or fiduciaries who participate in illegal conduct is preferable to

---

[1] See Forer, Lois, "Revocation of Tax Exemption—Then What?" *Foundation News*, vol. 4, September, 1963, p. 7.

[2] Stern, Carl S., "Duties and Liabilities of Foundation Trustees," *Proceedings* of the New York University Sixth Biennial Conference on Charitable Foundations, *op. cit.*, pp. 5, 12.

taxation of the charitable entity. It might even be possible in some cases to impose a penalty tax on a person who has diverted foundation funds for his private benefit and to include a provision whereby the personal tax will be abated if he repays the funds to the foundation.

The heart of the problem actually lies in the fact that the tax laws are being relied on to police activities in a manner for which they are not suited. Enforcement of fiduciary duties of charitable directors and trustees by this means has led to a conflict between two legitimate interests of government: the encouragement of philanthropy and the need to assure that the tax laws operate uniformly so that the privileges of exemption are not abused. The process of the revocation of exemption and the subsequent taxation of foundation assets assures that the federal revenue is not depleted, but it does not further in any way the legitimate community interest in the preservation of funds devoted to philanthropy. Of course, Congress can always decide that the revenue considerations are paramount. Carried to an extreme, this view could result in withdrawal of all exemptions and a consequent diminution of all charitable contributions. There is no evidence of any widespread acceptance of this attitude, although the income tax deduction provisions for individual contributions have been manipulated to favor contributions to so-called "public institutions" over those to foundations. Prior to 1964, up to 20 per cent of a taxpayer's adjusted gross income could be deducted for contributions to all section 501(c)(3) organizations, and an additional 10 per cent was allowed for contributions to churches, schools, hospitals, certain medical research organizations, and certain organizations affiliated with state colleges and universities.[1] The 1964 act extended the availability of the additional 10 per cent deduction to include contributions to "governmental units" for public purposes and to organizations which receive a substantial part of their support from a governmental unit or from direct or indirect contributions from the general public.[2]

---

[1] Int. Rev. Code of 1954, sec. 170(b).

[2] Revenue Act of 1964, sec. 209(a), adding Int. Rev. Code, sec. 170(b)(1)(A)(v) and (vi). In January of 1965, the Service announced the guidelines to be followed to determine whether a trustee organization was "publicly supported" within the meaning of this section. A formula was adopted which defined "substantial support from the general public" as meaning one-third or more of all contributions for each of three of the last four years. In addition, in determining the one-third amount any gift from a single individual in excess of 1 per cent of the total amount received from public support would be disregarded. Internal Revenue Service, Technical Information Release 667, dated December 21, 1964, announcement 65–9, 1965–4. Int. Rev. Bull. 47, January 25, 1965.

The reasons for adoption of this provision are stated in the Report of the House Ways and Means Committee.

Your committee has concluded that greater uniformity in the availability of this additional 10-percent deduction is desirable because of the many beneficial activities that are carried on by various philanthropic organizations not now eligible for the 30-percent deduction. This is especially true of many cultural and educational organizations and major charitable organizations not now eligible for the 30-percent deduction.

Your committee is limiting the additional 10-percent deduction to organizations which are publicly or governmentally supported, however, and is not making this additional deduction available in the case of private foundations. These latter types of organizations frequently do not make contributions to the operating philanthropic organizations for extended periods of time and in the meanwhile use the funds for investments. The extra 10-percent deduction is intended to encourage immediately spendable receipts of contributions for charitable organizations. . . .

Types of organizations which generally will in the future qualify for the additional 10-percent deduction are those publicly or governmentally supported museums of history, art, or science, libraries, community centers to promote the arts, organizations providing facilities for the support of an opera, symphony orchestra, ballet, or repertory drama, and organizations such as the American Red Cross, United Givers Fund, etc.[1]

The 1964 act also contained a provision permitting individual taxpayers a five-year carryover for contributions to organizations qualified for the 30 per cent deduction, for taxable years, beginning December 31, 1963, whenever the amount of the contribution exceeds 30 per cent of the taxpayers adjusted gross income.[2] This provision removes one of the incentives commonly set forth for creating so-called conduit foundations—namely, a desire to be able to average charitable contributions from year to year.

The clear-cut attempt in the 1964 legislation to differentiate between foundations and those charitable organizations that are publicly supported foreshadowed the approach made by the Treasury Department in its report to the Congress on "private" foundations. Its recommendations were specifically limited to organizations that did not qualify to receive this 30 per cent contribution deduction.

---

[1] U.S. Congress, House of Representatives, Committee on Ways and Means, to accompany H.R. 8363. 88th Congress, 1st Session. House Report 749, 1963, p. 53.

[2] Revenue Act of 1964, sec. 209(c); adding Int. Rev. Code, sec. 170(b)(5).

It is evident that Congress is about to take a new look at the so-called "private" foundations. In order to evaluate any of the proposals for reform, however, it is necessary to measure not only their ability to stem the specific abuses at which they are directed, the appropriateness of the sanctions, and the feasibility of administration, but the overall effect of the provisions on philanthropic activity as well as on the entire economy of the country.

Fiduciary Law and Tax Law

The aim of both tax and fiduciary law is, of course, to assure proper management of charitable funds. It has two aspects, the definition of standards and the formulation of proper and effective means of enforcing these standards. For several centuries the standards which have been relied upon to assure proper management of charitable funds have developed from the concept of the fiduciary relationship. This relationship is based on certain fundamental principles that reflect the philosophy of the state, of which freedom of action is the most pervasive aspect. Freedom of choice as to methods as well as purposes has been given to a donor of charitable funds. The trust instrument is the starting point for any determination of the duties and powers of the trustee. It has been appropriately described as the "fountainhead" of the trustee's powers. The charter of a corporation serves a similar purpose for a corporation's directors, and the right to create a corporation has been granted as freely as the right to create a trust. These grants of freedom are but a reflection of a basic American view that the owner of property should be as free as possible to dictate its future disposition.

Freedom to use their best judgment in the everyday management of the charity's affairs has been given to fiduciaries. The laws that establish and define their duties are designed to create a web of ethical restraints around what would otherwise be a complete grant of power to deal with another's property. The needs of "public policy" are given as the rationale behind these restraints. The courts stand ready to enforce them, but in actual practice they are rarely called upon. "The very heart of traditional English law of fiduciaries has been the responsible trustee—the trusted trustee...."[1]

There is as yet no evidence that the concept of fiduciary duty is inadequate to protect society's interest in the management of charita-

---

[1] Karst, Kenneth L., "The Efficiency of the Charitable Dollar . . . ," *op. cit.,* p. 459.

ble funds. The requirements of honesty, diligence, the avoidance of conflicts of interest, and dedication to the purposes for which the funds were created are the minimum standards which can be asked of individuals in the conduct of the affairs of charity. On the other hand, the fiduciary concept permits a freedom of action which is necessary if philanthropy is to continue to hold a place in the American pluralistic society.

New practices, new economic situations, and new private interests have arisen which, in a sense, have put a strain on the adequacy of some of these traditional rules. Trust law has not imposed a restraint against a donor's acting as trustee and reciting in the trust instrument either greater powers than those granted by law or a broader relief from liability for breach of duty. Donor management of charitable trusts takes on a different aspect, however, when it is used to further the donor's private interest, regardless of whether the charity is immediately injured or helped. When these situations involve a breach of a trustee's duty of loyalty to the trust, including the act of placing oneself in a position where there is a conflict of interest, it may be necessary for the courts or state legislatures to devise an arbitrary rule that the courts will not give recognition to any clause in a trust instrument condoning the existence of such a conflict or relieving a trustee from liability for actions arising where a conflict exists. Scott has stated:

> There is a growing feeling that certain duties and certain standards of conduct are applicable to the relationship between trustee and beneficiary, and that they are so necessarily inherent in the relation that they cannot be dispensed with by any provision in the trust instrument.[1]

Recent discussions of the duties of corporate directors evidence a similar attitude.[2] So long as there is this inherent possibility for growth and change to meet new situations, a continued reliance on the fiduciary concept is warranted as the starting point for a determination of what are proper activities of foundation trustees.

The position of the tax laws is that of a complementary set of rules existing along with fiduciary law. Both combine to focus on foundation management. Whenever the two conflict or impose inconsistent standards, therefore, the possibilities for abuse are magnified. However, there is no reason for these standards to diverge, even if at certain points the aims of the tax laws differ. The first concern of both is

---

[1] Scott, Austin W., *The Law of Trusts*. 2d ed. Little, Brown and Co., Boston, 1956, sec. 222.3.
[2] See p. 135.

to assure devotion to purpose. The tax laws must, however, prevent unfair competition with private interests. The fiduciary standards for investment would seem to contain the basis for meaningful restrictions, particularly if the proscription against speculation is added to a requirement concerning diversification. The basic problems of donor control all involve a conflict of interest for which the prohibitions against self-dealing that stem from a fiduciary's duty of loyalty again provide a starting point.

Assessment of specific rules or determination of the exact points at which one of these sets of laws should supersede the other cannot be considered in a vacuum, however. The mechanics of administration and enforcement are integral parts of any substantive laws. Furthermore, the likelihood of affirmative legislative action on any specific proposals cannot be ignored. Both of these considerations must be examined before it is possible to reach any conclusions as to the optimum methods for assuring public accountability of foundations. It is these considerations that will be discussed in the succeeding chapters.

CHAPTER VI

Agencies for State Supervision

Philanthropic activities have flourished in western democratic society in part because of an attitude of positive encouragement by the state. Despite theoretical arguments as to the extent to which foundation funds should be considered public or private, there is no dispute that the government's interest in the efficiency and effectiveness of philanthropic operations is a paramount one. The interest of the government arises from two major sources: the interest of the state in insuring that tax privileges granted by the state are not being abused, and the position of the state as representative of the public, which is the ultimate beneficiary of these funds. The assignment to the state of the role of representative of the beneficial interest of all charitable funds has its historic roots in the concept of the king as *parens patriae,* or father of his country. To understand the nature of this role, one must first examine certain aspects of the Anglo-American legal system. The functions of laws are twofold: they define the rights and duties of all individuals; and they provide the machinery through which these rights and duties may be enforced. The role of the courts is to act as arbiter in disputes, applying general legal principles and rules to specific situations and placing the force of the state behind their observance.

The Courts

The broad range of equity powers held by the courts give to the judiciary an inherently predominant position in the determination of the affairs of charity. Judicial decisions have framed the categories of valid

194

charitable purposes. They have defined the limits of trustees' powers and the extent of their duties. Even when these powers must be carried out within the framework of the most extensive legislatively enacted codes of law, the courts still have a wide area for interpretation. Through their power to settle accounts, they have drawn the lines governing proper investments. It is the courts which appoint new trustees and in some cases new directors, order corporate dissolution or force transfer of corporate property, determine the extent of trustees' discretionary powers, and direct the framing of schemes for *cy pres* dispositions.

Most of these matters are heard in the probate courts or in trial courts having equity jurisdiction where the procedural rules governing appeal are such that the lower court judges' findings of fact are given great weight and are rarely reversed without a showing that they were "plainly wrong."[1] Therefore, it is primarily at the lower level of the court system that the affairs of charity are determined.

Broad as the powers of the courts are in theory, they are only rarely called into action in practice. The average charitable foundation comes into existence and functions without any contact with a court. Inter vivos trusts and charitable corporations can be created without reference to judicial power in almost all jurisdictions.[2] Testamentary trusts come within the purview of the court at the time of creation, but unless the heirs dispute the validity of the disposition, the court merely acknowledges the filing of the instrument and the transfer of funds to the trustee at the close of the probate proceedings. Even in those jurisdictions where there is a duty placed on trustees of testamentary trusts to file accounts periodically with the court, the court's contact with the trustees is rarely more than routine. There is no procedure for identifying trustees who are remiss in their duty to account. Furthermore, the matter of allowance of accounts by the courts is in itself almost automatic. The courts do not have their own auditors to review accounts,[3] and unless objection is made by an interested party, approval is granted without question.

Conscientious trustees do seek instructions from the court when

---

[1] Loring, Augustus, *A Trustee's Handbook*. Revised by James A. Farr. Little, Brown and Co., Boston, 1962, p. 215.

[2] The exceptions in regard to corporations are New York and Pennsylvania, where judicial approval is a prerequisite to obtaining a corporate charter. See pp. 115 ff.

[3] With the exception of Indiana, where an audit section in each court passes on accounts. Ind. Ann. Stat., sec. 31–712.

there is a question as to their duties. They will also request a *cy pres* application of trust funds when their purposes can no longer be carried out. But laws are only as effective as the public desires them to be. Without observance by the majority, or active enforcement by public officials, the mere existence of a law can be almost meaningless. A striking example of this situation is found in Vermont, where all trustees holding funds for benevolent, charitable, humanitarian, or philanthropic purposes, incorporated or unincorporated, are required by statute to file accounts annually with the probate court for the district where the trustee resides. Failure to file for two successive years constitutes a breach of trust, and the probate court is required to report such failures to the attorney general or state's attorney, who "shall take such action as may be appropriate to compel compliance with this chapter."[1] Correspondence with three judges of probate in Vermont, however, revealed that there is little if any compliance with this statute. A judge of probate in Rutland stated:

> I have never known of a trustee filing an annual report pursuant to 14 VSA Sec. 2501. I do not know of a trust officer of a trust company, or of an individual trustee, who does so. I believe the statute is just ignored.

A judge from Burlington stated that to his knowledge there had never been a prosecution for failure to file. The only compliance reported was by cemetery associations and trustees of a few testamentary trusts. The reasons for failure lie in the facts that without any further means of identifying these trusts at the time of creation, it is impossible to tell where there is delinquency, and that the statutes provide for no administrative machinery or appropriation of funds to carry out the task of reviewing those reports that are filed.

The situation in Vermont is not unique, and it indicates a serious drawback to the use of the courts to assure enforcement, a task not traditionally placed with the judiciary and therefore unsuited to its method of operation and organization.

Equity power over charitable corporations has been attributed to two factors: (1) the existence of a trust for indefinite beneficiaries implicit in every charitable gift; and (2) the power of visitation over all corporations arising from the power to create them, which resides with the state. The latter concept originated under the Roman law and

---

[1] Vt. Stat. Ann., tit. 14, secs. 2501 and 2502.

was adopted by the English kings.[1] It has been further supplemented today by statutes enacted in every American jurisdiction which grant to the court the power to dissolve a corporation on a showing of certain actions that were in excess of the corporation's powers or purposes or were injurious to the public welfare. Today, therefore, the courts have a dual source of power over charitable corporations.

The powers of any court to act are further limited by the fact that they may adjudicate only disputes brought to their attention by opposing parties and that they are confined to the issues raised by these parties. One exception to this rule is recognized in some jurisdictions in the United States; it permits the court, under equity power, to act in certain circumstances on its own motion or sua sponte. The power is invoked only rarely, however. The Supreme Court of Massachusetts explained the nature of its exercise in a case involving the power of the court to remove a fiduciary:

> Ordinarily courts properly remain inactive unless and until judicial action is required by some party in accordance with recognized practice. But courts have a wide inherent power to do justice and to adopt procedure to that end. Where a court has once taken jurisdiction and has become responsible to the public for the exercise of its judicial power so as to do justice, it is sometimes the right and even the duty of the court to act in some particular sua sponte.[2]

Aside from this extraordinary jurisdiction, however, the Anglo-American judicial system relies on an individual's self-interest to assure compliance with the law. The existence of ascertained individuals who will look after their own interests is a basic component of all fiduciary relationships. The laws are so framed that reliance is placed on the beneficiaries of a private trust or on the shareholders of a business corporation to call into action the enforcement machinery of the courts. The trust developed as a legal device only after the Chancery Courts recognized the rights of beneficiaries and agreed to enforce them. Today the existence of a beneficiary capable of looking after his own interests is, in fact, a prerequisite to the validity of a private trust.

---

[1] Pound, Roscoe, "Visitorial Jurisdiction Over Corporations in Equity," *Harvard Law Review,* vol. 49. 1936, p. 369.

[2] *Quincy Trust Co.* v. *Taylor,* 317 Mass. 195, 57 N.E.2d 573 (1944). See also Scott, Austin W., *The Law of Trusts,* 2d ed., Little, Brown and Co., Boston, 1956, sec. 200.4.

The Attorney General

The rationale used by the courts to confer validity on a trust for charitable purposes was that the beneficiary was the public at large. Practicality dictated, however, that the amorphous mass of individuals could not properly perform the functions of a private beneficiary motivated by obvious and natural self-interest. The need for a situs for the enforcement power was answered, therefore, well before the passage of the Statute of Elizabeth, by considering that it was lodged in the King, the *parens patriae,* and carried out by his chief legal officer, the Attorney General. In the language of trusts, this power is described as the power of enforcement, and implies the duty to oversee the activities of the fiduciary who is charged with management of the funds, as well as the right to bring to the attention of the court any abuses which may need correction. Thus, a duty to enforce implies a duty to supervise (or oversee) in its broader sense. It does not, however, include a right to regulate, or a right to direct either the day-to-day affairs of the charity or the action of the court. This enforcement duty of the state extends to all funds held for charitable purposes, whether or not a formal trust has been created.[1]

The duty of the attorney general to "enforce the due application of funds given or appropriated to public charities . . . and prevent breaches in the administration thereof," to quote from a section of the Massachusetts General Laws first enacted in 1849,[2] is stated in most textbooks as an absolute duty and is recognized in almost all of the states either by statute or judicial decision. In 22 states it is recited by statute. In 22 others it has been declared by the courts to be an inherent power of the office of attorney general.[3] In Tennessee and Virginia the enforcement duty is conferred by statute on the district or prosecuting attorneys of the county.[4] In Florida the common law duty of the attorney general to enforce charitable trusts has been diminished by a statute enacted in 1957 which names the local state's attorneys as representatives of all unknown and unascertainable beneficiaries of charitable trusts in proceedings brought under that section of

---

[1] *Toler et al.* v. *Leila Toler Convalescent Home,* 236 Ark. 24, 364 S.W.2d 680 (1963).

[2] Acts of 1849, ch. 186, sec. 8.

[3] See Table 1, Appendix A.

[4] Tenn. Code Ann., sec. 28–2802 to 28–2803, 2809; Va. Code Ann., sec. 55–29.

the Florida laws which prescribes the procedure for court accountings by testamentary trustees.[1]

In Idaho there was dictum in a case decided in 1938[2] to the effect that the attorney general of that state, unlike his counterparts elsewhere, had no duties concerning charitable trusts. The court realized the problem created by this situation when it stated:

> If the sixth paragraph of this will [creating a charitable trust] should be upheld, and the trustee therein named should be derelict in the duty sought to be imposed upon him, we doubt that his misconduct could be brought to the attention of a court, because of the lack of a proper party plaintiff.[3]

The Idaho legislature in 1963 attempted to rectify this situation by amending the powers of the attorney general to include the common law powers of supervision and enforcement of charitable funds. The statute reads as follows:

> Subsection 4. To supervise non-profit corporations, corporations, charitable or benevolent societies, person or persons holding property subject to any public or charitable trust and to enforce whenever necessary any non-compliance or departure from the general purpose of such trust and, in order to accomplish such purpose, said non-profit corporations, corporations, charitable or benevolent societies, person or persons holding property subject to any public or charitable trust are subject at all times to examination by the attorney general, on behalf of the state, to ascertain the condition of its affairs and to what extent, if at all, said trustee or trustees may have failed to comply with trusts said trustee or trustees have assumed or may have departed from the general purpose for which it was formed. In case of any such failure or departure, the attorney general shall institute, in the name of the state, any proceeding necessary to enforce compliance with the terms of the trust or any departure therefrom.[4]

A second statute enacted that same year requires that "whenever any estate involves, or may involve a charitable trust, the probate court shall at the time of distribution of said estate, forward to the attorney general of the state of Idaho a certified copy of said decree of distribution of the estate which involves or may involve said charitable trust."[5]

---

[1] Fla. Acts of 1957, ch. 57–149, now Fla. Stat., sec. 737.251.
[2] *Hedin* v. *Westdala Lutheran Church,* 59 Idaho 241, 81 P.2d 741 (1938).
[3] *Ibid.,* pp. 250–251.
[4] Idaho Session Laws, ch. 161, 1963 (S.B. 221).
[5] Idaho Code Ann., sec. 15–1132A (1963 Supp.), S.B. 222, Acts of 1963.

But there still remain states where even today there is no clear-cut statement, either in judicial decisions or by statutes, that the duty to enforce charitable funds rests on the attorney general or another public officer. In Alaska and Utah there is no indication in the reported cases as to whether the attorney general has the power to enforce charitable funds. Nor is this role conferred by statute. In Louisiana charitable enforcement is definitely considered not to be one of his duties, nor is it delegated to any other state official.

Generally the attorney general's duty to enforce charities extends equally to corporations and trusts. The enforcement power in regard to corporate charities exists in addition to the statutory power (granted in all but three states[1]) to bring an action to dissolve a corporation for certain violations.[2] Usually the dissolution proceeding is called a "proceeding quo warranto" (by what warrant). Among the grounds usually recited as sufficient to warrant involuntary dissolution are: (1) abuse of corporate powers (misuser); (2) failure to exercise corporate powers for a fixed number of years (nonuser); (3) fraud practiced on the state in procuring the corporate franchise; (4) failure to file an annual report for a given period of years; (5) failure for a specified period to appoint and maintain a registered agent or to notify a state officer after change of registered agent.[3]

Exclusion of the General Public

The common law not only conferred supervisory powers and duties on the attorney general to enforce charitable funds, it excluded other members of the general public from so doing. The reasons for this exclusion were based not on a denial of the public's interest, but on the purely practical consideration that it would be impossible to manage charitable funds, or even to find individuals to take on the task, if the fiduciaries were to be constantly subject to harassing litigation. The rule developed that a person who was unable to show an interest other than as a member of the community would not be recognized by the courts as having capacity to maintain a suit for enforcement of a charity. His remedy was to bring the facts before the attorney general and try to induce him to bring the suit. The attorney general was permitted to designate such a person a "relator," and to permit him to

---

[1] Georgia, no statutory provision; Va. Code Ann., sec. 13.1–256, Corporation Commission; Wash. Rev. Code, sec. 7.56.020, attorney of county.

[2] See Appendix A, Table 2, for references.

[3] See, for example, *Model Non-Profit Corporation Act* (1964 Revision), Handbook D, American Law Institute, Philadelphia, 1964, sec. 51.

bring the suit and to pay the costs of litigation. An attorney general could, in fact, require the individual's agreement to pay all costs as a condition for bringing suit.

There has been some question as to whether a person with no standing to enforce a charitable fund himself could compel the attorney general to bring suit for enforcement.[1] The better view is that an action such as mandamus to compel an attorney general to bring enforcement proceedings or allow the use of his name by others cannot be brought;[2] nor can an action be brought to force him to reconsider a decision not to bring suit without a showing that his decision was capricious or not based on legitimate considerations of policy.[3]

This question of the availability of an action of mandamus to compel an attorney general to reconsider a decision not to bring suit against a charity was raised in the case of *Ames* v. *Attorney General*,[4] the only American decision on the subject to date. The plaintiffs, a group of alumni of Harvard College, had requested the Massachusetts attorney general to bring a suit, in which they would act as relators, against the president and fellows of Harvard in their capacity as trustees of the Arnold Arboretum. The purpose of the suit was to prevent the trustees from carrying out a plan to remove from the Arboretum premises to the college a large botanical library and herbarium. The plaintiff's view was that this act would constitute a breach of trust. The attorney general, after a hearing, decided that the proposed transfer was within the trustees' discretion, and refused to permit the plaintiffs to proceed in his name. The plaintiffs then brought suit against the attorney general to attempt to compel him to reconsider his decision on the basis of the law as they viewed it, but the court held that the attorney general's decision was not judicially reviewable and dismissed the case. Karst points out that the plaintiffs made no attempt to force the attorney general to bring the suit, but merely requested that he reconsider his decision, thereby coming within the rule that permits mandamus actions to compel a "ministerial," as opposed to a "discretionary," act by a public officer. He infers from the court's refusal to grant

---

[1] Lees, John G., "Governmental Supervision of Charitable Trusts," in *Current Trends in State Legislation* (1956–1957). University of Michigan Law School Legislative Research Center, Ann Arbor, 1957, pp. 609, 621.

[2] Scott, Austin W., *op. cit.*, sec. 391.

[3] For an excellent discussion of this problem, see Karst, Kenneth L., "The Efficiency of the Charitable Dollar: An Unfulfilled State Responsibility," *Harvard Law Review*, vol. 73, pp. 433, 449.

[4] 332 Mass. 246, 124 N.E.2d 511 (1955).

this relief that it would not compel the attorney general to commence a suit to enforce the charity.[1]

In a dictum in the case of *Longcor* v. *City of Red Wing*,[2] decided by the Minnesota court in 1940, the court did suggest that if the attorney general, after an adequate showing, had refused to act, an action might have been maintainable by a private person, but this represents an exception from the general rule.

A Wisconsin statute provides that an action to enforce a charitable trust may be brought in the name of the state by any 10 or more interested parties on their own complaint if the attorney general refuses to act; it also provides that the term "interested party" shall include a donor or a member or prospective member of the class for whose benefit the trust was established.[3]

It would appear that this same rule is applicable in the case of actions against charitable corporations. For example, in a 1964 case in New York, members of the public were precluded from maintaining an action to rescind the charter of a charitable corporation after the attorney general refused to bring or sanction such an action.[4]

Interested Parties

Although members of the general public are not recognized by the courts as proper parties to bring suit against a charity for breach of duty, it should not be inferred that the attorney general's power of enforcement is exclusive. When a charitable trust is created for a group of beneficiaries who are ascertainable at a given particular time although they may not be ascertainable over a longer period, these individuals have been recognized by the courts as proper parties to bring enforcement actions. The general rule is that a person must be able to show that he is entitled to a benefit from the trust beyond the benefit to which members of the public in general are entitled.[5]

---

[1] Karst, Kenneth L., *op. cit.,* p. 450. This case is not yet finished, however. With a change in administration, a new attorney general permitted the plaintiffs, known unofficially as "The Friends of the Arnold Arboretum," to proceed as relators in his name. The case has been pending before the Single Justice Session of the Supreme Judicial Court of Massachusetts since 1958. *Attorney General* ex rel. *Ames* v. *President and Fellows of Harvard College,* Equity No. 68735.

[2] 206 Minn. 627, 289 N.W. 570 (1940).

[3] Wis. Stat., sec. 231.34.

[4] *People* v. *American Society for Prevention of Cruelty to Animals,* 20 A.D. 2d 762, 247 N.Y.S.2d 487 (1964).

[5] *Restatement of the Law of Trusts (Second).* American Law Institute, St. Paul, 1959, sec. 391, comment b.

Where a trust has been established for the needy of a particular town or parish, the courts have allowed suits to be brought by the town officials, church wardens, or even residents or church members acting on behalf of themselves and other potential beneficiaries. There are records of cases of this sort in the Calendars in Chancery which were brought prior to the enactment of the Statute of Charitable Uses in 1601, as well as more recent examples.[1] The clearest case of a party having a special interest, of course, is that where there is a trust for the benefit of a charitable corporation. It is well settled that in such a situation the corporation can maintain a suit against the trustees for enforcement.[2]

How far the courts will go to stretch this concept of interest depends in part on the circumstances of the case and the gravity of the alleged action, and in part on the attitude of the court. In the case of *Day* v. *City of Hartford*[3] it was held that a citizen taxpayer of a city could maintain a suit to enjoin the city from destroying two bridges given to it; and in a New York case[4] the court refused to dismiss an action brought against a school by three pupils and the parents of other pupils, since the attorney general had been made a party and had requested a declaration of rights. In another New York case the court refused to dismiss a suit for enforcement of a charitable trust brought by a person having no special interest, on the ground that the court on its own initiative could enforce such a trust under its statutory authority to control gifts, grants, and bequests for educational purposes.[5]

The problem faced by the courts in deciding the grounds on which to permit standing as an interested party to bring suit to enforce a charity is, of course, the need to strike the difficult balance between the desire to assure that abuses will be corrected and the desire to permit fiduciaries to function without unwarranted abuse and harassment. Theoretically, the attorney general can serve the function assigned to him. Only when he fails will the courts feel compelled to broaden the class of parties who may take over his role. Of course, there are cases where the legislature has spoken so as to alter this balance, but they are rare. One example is the Wisconsin statute mentioned previously.

---

[1] See Scott, Austin W., *op. cit.,* sec. 391 for citations.
[2] *Harvard College* v. *Amory,* 9 Pick. 446 (Mass. 1830).
[3] 16 Conn. Supp. 228 (1949).
[4] *Elliott* v. *Teachers College,* 177 Misc. 146, 31 N.Y.S.2d 796 (1941), affirmed 264 App. Div. 839, 35 N.Y.S.2d 761 (1942), affirmed 290 N.Y. 747, 50 N.E.2d 97 (1943).
[5] *Application of Herman,* 177 Misc. 276, 30 N.Y.S.2d 448 (1941).

Another example is a Massachusetts statute that permits a suit by taxpayers to enforce gifts made for charitable purposes to any city, town, or other subdivision. The attorney general must, however, be notified of the action and given leave to intervene.[1] This is a specialized type of enactment, however. In the case of the modern American foundation, if the attorney general does not act, there is no other potential beneficiary capable of doing so, and abuses will remain uncorrected if he is in default of his duty.

In the situations discussed thus far, the interest of the person seeking standing to enforce a charity has been that of a beneficiary. There are other interests, however, that are sufficient to allow a court to confer standing to commence action. One of several trustees may bring a suit to enforce a charitable trust or compel the redress of a breach.[2] Similarly, a director may bring action on behalf of a charitable corporation against a codirector.[3] There are cases where a successor trustee has been permitted to bring suit upon learning of a predecessor's breach of duty.[4] It would seem that an analogy could be made to the case of a successor director of a charitable corporation, but in 1954 the District Court of Appeals of California refused to allow a nonprofit corporation to sue its founder and former director, his wife, and five other former directors to recover over $3 million which they charged had been dissipated over an eleven-year period through speculation and mismanagement.[5] The decision was severely criticized by Karst.

> It is as plainly wrong on the question of capacity as it is wrong in its general approach to money which has been given to charity. The reason for the frequently seen statement that the attorney general alone can enforce a charitable trust is of course that the charity needs to be protected from constant harassment by meddlesome individuals who have no interest in the charity except as members of the public. This is sound but quite inapplicable to enforcement by the fiduciaries who are both few in number and charged with the duty of managing the charity's affairs.[6]

---

[1] Mass. Gen. Laws Ann., ch. 214, sec. 3.
[2] *Eurich* v. *Korean Foundation*, 31 Ill. App.2d 474, 176 N.E.2d 692 (1961).
[3] *Gilbert* v. *McLeod Infirmary*, 219 S.C. 174, 64 S.E.2d 524 (1951).
[4] *Shattuck* v. *Wood Memorial Home, Inc.*, 319 Mass. 444, 66 N.E.2d 568 (1946).
[5] *George Pepperdine Foundation* v. *Pepperdine*, 126 Cal. App.2d 154, 271 P.2d 600 (1954), rehearing denied, 126 Cal. App.2d 164.
[6] Karst, Kenneth L., "The Efficiency of the Charitable Dollar: An Unfulfilled State Responsibility," *Harvard Law Review*, vol. 73, p. 444. Copyright © 1960 by the Harvard Law Review Association.

The Supreme Court of California gave tacit recognition to this criticism by quoting extensively from the Karst article in a decision rendered in August of 1964[1] upholding the right of 3 trustees of a charitable corporation to bring suit against the 23 remaining trustees and the attorney general to enforce the breach of a charitable trust. The lower court had dismissed the suit on the basis of the holding in the *Pepperdine* case that the plaintiffs had no capacity to bring the action and that the complaint did not set forth a threatened breach of a charitable trust. The Supreme Court specifically rejected defendants' contention that the fact that the charity was a corporation required the application of a rule different from that which would apply to a charitable trust, and concluded that the *Pepperdine* case was disapproved "to the extent it is contrary to this opinion."

As to the members of a charitable corporation, or shareholders if such are permitted by statute, there are cases in which suits by members against the corporation's directors have been permitted on the theory that the relationship gives rise to the same rights and liabilities as those arising from the relationship between directors and stockholders of a profit corporation.[2] However, in other cases the courts have refused to confer the right to sue, stating that the issues of proper management or breach of fiduciary duty involve not the members' private interest as members but matters in which only the public interest, as represented by the attorney general, is directly concerned.[3]

In *Voelker* v. *St. Louis Mercantile Library Association,*[4] a recent Missouri case, the court refused to permit a suit for breach of trust brought against the directors by the members of a charitable corporation that operated a library. The court held that the members' rights were confined to participation in the charitable use conferred by the corporation upon all of the public, that membership did not confer a pecuniary interest similar to that of a member of a business corporation, and that the action should have been brought by the attorney general. The reasoning of this case would deny to the member of a foundation the right to enforce the directors' duties, but as Karst points out, in a typical postwar family foundation the members of the corpo-

---

[1] *Holt* v. *College of Osteopathic Physicians and Surgeons et al.,* _____ Calif. _____, 394 P.2d 932 (1964).
[2] *Leeds* v. *Harrison,* 7 N.J. Super. 558, 72 A.2d 371 (Ch. 1950).
[3] *Dillaway* v. *Burton,* 256 Mass. 568, 153 N.E. 13 (1926).
[4] _____ Mo. _____, 359 S.W.2d 689 (1962).

ration are the same as the directors, and thus for most legal purposes
the fiduciaries *are* the corporation.[1]

The Power of Visitation

Another source of enforcement power was placed under the common law in the donors or founders of charities. Following the Roman law terminology, at one time a distinction was made between the *fundatio incipiens,* the granting of the charter by the state, and the *fundatio perficiens,* the donation of funds by individuals. The *fundators perficiens* were given the right to enforce the faithful execution of the charity. They were permitted not only to prescribe rules for the management and administration of the trust at the time of the donation, but to specify methods for the government and control of the trustees, for the inspection of their proceedings, and for the correction of abuses.[2] Similarly, where an individual founded and gave property to a charitable corporation, he was allowed to reserve or confer on others a power of visitation. As described in an early Massachusetts case,[3] this was a power and duty to hear and determine all differences of the corporation among themselves and generally to superintend the internal government of the body, taking as a guide the rules laid down by the founder. So long as the visitor did not exceed his province, his decision was deemed final, but he would be subject to prosecution and removal in an action by the attorney general for acts that were in excess of his powers.

The visitorial power did not extend to heirs unless expressly reserved, and in most cases such reservations were narrowly construed, the attitude of the court being that the interests of heirs were usually inimical to that of the charity.

Today the right of a donor or his heirs to sue to enforce a charitable trust is rarely recognized.[4] In Maryland, however, the relatives of a testator or founder are given, by statute, the right to enforce gifts to educational or charitable corporations,[5] and in Wisconsin the donor of a trust is considered an "interested party" for the purposes of the statute which permits 10 interested parties to bring suit for enforcement when the attorney general refuses to act.[6]

---

[1] Karst, Kenneth L., *op. cit.,* p. 445, n. 46.

[2] Zollmann, Carl F. G., *American Law of Charities.* The Bruce Publishing Co., Milwaukee, 1924, p. 418.

[3] *Nelson* v. *Cushing,* 2 Cush. 519, 530 (1848).

[4] Scott, Austin W., *op. cit.,* sec. 391; Karst, Kenneth L., *op. cit.,* p. 445.

[5] Md. Ann. Code, art. 16, sec. 125.

[6] Wis. Stat., sec. 231.34.

The reservation of a visitorial power has also fallen into disuse, although the Bogerts state that it would still seem to exist in the United States unless abolished by statute.

> The exact status of the doctrine of visitation in modern American law is not perfectly clear. It seems to be a relic of earlier times which has not been expressly abolished by statute in most states and has been occasionally recognized by decision. It is not believed, however, that it is a feature of charitable trust administration which is extremely practical or desirable under present conditions.[1]

Karst argues for permitting a founder to sue, pointing out that he is the one person, other than the fiduciaries, who knows and cares the most about the charity's operations. He raises serious objection to the visitorial power, however, because of its tendency to undercut the responsibility of charitable fiduciaries.[2]

Of course, if a founder has a property interest in the administration or operation of the charity, as for example when he has made a charitable gift on a condition which, if met, will result in a reversion of the property to his estate, then he or his heirs or personal representative can maintain a suit to recover the property. In such a case these individuals will be attempting to enforce rights adverse to the trust, not seeking to enforce it. The same rule applies where there is a contingent gift to another charitable institution.[3]

In a recent case which raised the question of the nature of an adverse interest, the Supreme Court of Oregon dismissed a complaint of mismanagement brought against trustees of a testamentary charitable trust by the employees and managers of a newspaper who were given by the terms of the trust a preference to purchase the stock of the paper held by the trustees in the event that they were to be sold. The court held that the plaintiffs' interest was not sufficient to maintain an enforcement action.[4]

The right of a donor who is not a founder to bring enforcement action has consistently been denied by the courts.[5] Following the analogy to the rights of founders to sue for enforcement, Karst has suggested consideration of legislation permitting substantial donors a similar right, but with several safeguards. He would include a requirement

---

[1] Bogert, George G., and George T. Bogert, *The Law of Trusts and Trustees*. 2d ed. West Publishing Co., St. Paul, 1964, sec. 416.
[2] Karst, Kenneth L., *op. cit.*, p. 446.
[3] *Trustees of Dartmouth College* v. *City of Quincy*, 331 Mass. 219, 118 N.E. 2d 89 (1954).
[4] *Agan* v. *United States National Bank*, 227 Ore. 619, 363 P.2d 765 (1961).
[5] Zollmann, Carl F. G., *op. cit.*, p. 420.

that the donor have contributed a certain dollar amount or a certain percentage of the charity's total contributions for a recent period. The donor-plaintiff would be required to post security for costs, including counsel fees, which would be paid to the fiduciaries if they prevailed in the suit. He would also be compelled to present the case to the attorney general, argue his view at a public hearing, and receive an adverse determination before proceeding on his own. Furthermore, Karst recognized that the plaintiff should be prevented from receiving any private gains for his action, such as a settlement for withdrawing the action, although he would favor the allowance of counsel fees to the plaintiff, if successful.[1]

Conferring a right of action on cofiduciaries and successor fiduciaries does afford a measure of protection for the public interest in the enforcement of charitable funds, but it is a limited one. All too often in modern foundations the donor is one of a small number of fiduciaries; and in many cases the entire board of trustees, or at least the majority, will be members of one family. Furthermore, the danger of being found to have had a contributory role in the breach of duty, either through acquiescence or neglect, may well deter many cofiduciaries. Conferring an enforcement right on a founder or substantial contributor, if accompanied by the safeguards suggested by Karst, would be of value in some instances. How widespread its use would be, however, is seriously open to question. It would perhaps have great merit in those situations where an attorney general is completely inactive or unreceptive to the pursuit of his duties in regard to charities.

Parties to Suits Involving Charity

An important adjunct to the question of who may bring an enforcement action against a charity is the problem of what parties must be joined when a suit involving a charity is before the court. If an enforcement action is brought by the attorney general, ordinarily it is brought against the trustees or corporate directors, or some of them. If the action is a petition for application of the *cy pres* doctrine, the heirs will also be required to be defendants, since they may have a right to the property if the court refuses to apply the doctrine and declares that the trust fails.

When an action is brought by the trustees or directors of a foundation, the question of parties is more complicated. It is necessary to

---

[1] Karst, Kenneth L., *op. cit.*, pp. 446 ff.

distinguish in this discussion between those who are considered "necessary" parties and those who may be deemed "proper" parties. A final court decree is binding only on those who have been joined in the action and have been afforded a chance to state their position. Once joined, they may not later question the decision by bringing another action on their own or by attempting to raise the same question in a suit on another, although related, matter. In other words, a question once decided by an appellate court, or by a lower court, and not taken by the parties to an appeal, is res judicata as regards those who were joined and as regards all matters shown to have been put in issue or to have been necessarily involved and actively tried and determined.[1] The term "necessary party" refers to individuals who will be so closely affected by the outcome of litigation that it would be inconsistent with equity and good conscience to permit judicial action without their receiving notice and being given the opportunity to participate. The term "indispensable parties" is also used to designate such persons.

In all states where the attorney general is recognized as having a duty to represent the public interest in the enforcement of funds devoted to charity, he is considered a necessary party to all actions brought to enforce the duties of charitable fiduciaries or to uphold the charitable intent. Tudor's classic treatise on charitable trusts states the rule as follows:

> The Attorney-General, as representing the Crown, is the protector of all the persons interested in the charity funds. He represents the beneficial interest; consequently, in all cases in which the beneficial interest requires to be before the court, the Attorney-General must be a party to the proceedings.[2]

This requirement that the attorney general be a "necessary" party to certain actions involving charitable interests may be imposed by statute[3] or by court rule[4] or precedent.[5] The Massachusetts Supreme

---

[1] *Restatement of the Law of Judgments*. American Law Institute, St. Paul, 1942, sec. 84.

[2] Tudor, Owen Davies, *The Law of Charitable Trusts*. 5th ed. Sweet and Maxwell, Ltd., London, 1930, chap. 12, sec. II.

[3] N.Y. Pers. Prop. Law, sec. 12(3); N.Y. Real Prop. Law, sec. 113(3); Tex. Rev. Civ. Stat. Ann., art. 4412a (Laws 1959, ch. 115); Ga. Code Ann., sec. 108.212; Minn. Stat. Ann., sec. 501–12; Okla. Stat., tit. 60, sec. 175.18; Wis. Stat., sec. 317.06(4); Neb. Rev. Stat., sec. 24–612.

[4] N.J. Superior Court Civil Practice Rules 4:117–6.

[5] *Pruners' Estate*, 390 Pa. 529, 136 A.2d 107 (1957); *Dickey* v. *Volker*, 321 Mo. 235, 11 S.W.2d 278 (1928); *Trustees of New Castle Common* v. *Gordy*, 33 Del. Ch. 196, 91 A.2d 135 (1952); *Thurlow* v. *Berry*, 247 Ala. 631, 25 S.2d 726 (1946); *State* ex rel. *Emmert* v. *University Trust Co.*, 74 N.E.2d 833 (1947) reversed on other grounds 227 Ind. 571, 86 N.E.2d 450 (1949).

Judicial Court has from its earliest cases read the statute conveying enforcement duties on the attorney general[1] as meaning that he is a required party to a broad category of actions involving charitable interests.[2]

> No proceeding in regard to a public charity, no matter how general the assent of those beneficially interested, would bind him if not made a party; nor can any proceeding in regard to a public charity to which he has been made a party be invalidated by those beneficially interested, but having no peculiar and immediate interests distinct from those of the public.[3]

This requirement was, in effect, restated by the legislature in 1954 when a statute requiring compulsory reporting to the attorney general by all public charities was enacted. The legislation included a section stating: "The attorney general shall be made a party to all judicial proceedings in which he may be interested in the performance of his duties under section eight. . . ."[4] Similar provisions in the statutes expanding the attorney general's supervisory powers have been enacted in California,[5] Ohio,[6] Rhode Island,[7] Iowa,[8] Oregon,[9] New Hampshire,[10] Texas,[11] and Michigan,[12] although some are restricted to certain types of actions.

There is no uniformity, however, either in these statutes or in the court decisions regarding the type of proceeding in which the attorney general will be declared indispensable. In Massachusetts the courts have interpreted the statutory provision very broadly, and the attorney general must be given notice of the probate of every will that includes a charitable gift, so that he participates at all stages of the proceedings for probate of wills and accounts of executors, as well as actions involving trusts.[13]

In New York statutory interpretation requires the attorney general's participation in suits involving petitions for instructions, construction

---

[1] Mass. Gen. Laws Ann., ch. 12, sec. 8.
[2] *President and Fellows of Harvard College* v. *Society for Promoting Theological Education,* 3 Gray 280 (Mass. 1855).
[3] *Burbank* v. *Burbank,* 152 Mass. 254, 25 N.E. 427 (1890).
[4] Mass. Gen. Laws Ann., ch. 12, sec. 8G (Stat. 1954, ch. 529).
[5] Cal. Gov. Code, sec. 12591; and Cal. Prob. Code, sec. 328.
[6] Ohio Rev. Code Ann., sec. 109.25.
[7] R.I. Gen. Laws Ann., sec. 18–9–6.
[8] Iowa Code, sec. 682.49.
[9] Ore. Rev. Stat., sec. 128.710.
[10] N.H. Rev. Stat. Ann., sec. 94:3.
[11] Tex. Rev. Civ. Stat., art. 4412a.
[12] Mich. Stat. Ann., sec. 26.1200(1), (4).
[13] *Budin* v. *Levy,* 343 Mass. 644, 180 N.E.2d 74 (1962).

of wills, approvals of compromises, settlement of accounts, and *cy pres* applications. The attorney general's participation is also specifically required by the statutes providing for court approval of the sale or mortgage of real property by charitable corporations, as well as for their creation and dissolution. The Surrogate's Courts of New York, however, have ruled that the attorney general is not a necessary party to a proceeding where there is a specifically named charitable beneficiary, such as a corporate institution. An unsuccessful attempt was made in 1962 to obtain legislation to amend the Civil Practice Act and the Surrogate's Courts Act to include wording similar to that in the Tilden Act that the attorney general "represents the sole inherent and statutory power of the ultimate beneficiaries of a charitable trust," thereby insuring that he would be considered a necessary party to all proceedings in which a charitable beneficial interest was involved. Despite the failure to pass these amendments, the attorney general's office is a party to approximately 3,500 cases per year in New York.

In California, where the statutory requirement for participation by the attorney general is broad, the courts have nevertheless held that he is a necessary party to probate of a will only when the gift creates a trust and the trustee is not a California resident or corporation, or is not named in the trust. This is also the position taken by the courts in Nebraska[1] and Kansas.[2]

The Illinois court in an early case stated that the attorney general was an indispensable party when the trustees were charged with a wrong, but that in other situations, if the gift were to named trustees, the attorney general was not a necessary party.[3] Recent cases reflect a more liberal view, however.[4]

In New Hampshire, where the attorney general's powers over the administration of charitable trusts are exceptionally broad, the court nevertheless held in a 1947 case that he was not a necessary party to a case involving compromise of a will.

Whether the Attorney General should be notified concerning such claims involves questions of policy and procedure on which the Legislature has remained silent. If notice to the Attorney General and his

---

[1] *Rohlff* v. *German Old People's Home et al.,* 143 Neb. 636, 10 N.W.2d 686 (1943), criticized by Scott, Austin W., *op. cit.,* sec. 391.

[2] *Trautman* v. *De Boissiere Odd Fellows' Orphans' Home & Industrial School Association,* 66 Kan. 1, 71 Pac. 286 (1903).

[3] *Newbury* v. *Blatchford,* 106 Ill. 584 (1882).

[4] *Kolin* v. *Leitch,* 343 Ill. App. 622, 99 N.E.2d 685 (1951); *Holden Hospital Corp.* v. *Southern Illinois Hospital Corporation,* 22 Ill.App.2d 150, 174 N.E.2d 793 (1961); *Hinckley* v. *Caldwell,* 35 Ill. App.2d 121, 182 N.E.2d 230 (1962).

approval are necessary, it will require legislative authority therefor. We know of no decision which requires the Attorney General's approval of all Probate proceedings or the actions of executors in administering the estate before the charitable trust is in existence.[1]

Legislation was enacted in 1959, however, under which the attorney general was made a necessary party to any agreement between an executor, creditors, legatees, or heirs at law whenever such agreement may directly or indirectly affect a charitable interest.[2]

The Pennsylvania court has taken an opposite view from that of New Hampshire, stating in several cases that the attorney general must receive notice of *all* matters involving charities.[3] Following these decisions, each of the local orphan's courts promulgated rules, in cooperation with the attorney general's office, to facilitate administration of the requirement. The office receives from 50 to 100 notices each month and participates in all cases where the charitable interest is not represented by a named charitable beneficiary such as a corporation.

In a Texas decision in 1941 the court held that the attorney general was not a necessary party to a suit to construe a will bequeathing property to a public charity where the bequest was to named trustees for the benefit of an unincorporated charitable foundation, although it added that he was a necessary party to proceedings affecting validity, administration, and enforcement when the public interest was involved.[4] Legislation modifying this rule was enacted in 1959, however. The attorney general was made a necessary party to suits for termination, *cy pres* application, and construction, or to will contests involving "charitable trusts," which for the purpose of the act are defined as "all gifts and trusts for charitable purposes."[5] A judgment rendered without service of process on the attorney general in any suit referred to in this article is void and unenforceable, and settlements or compromises of suits are binding only if the attorney general is a party and joins in the agreement. It is interesting to note that section 6 of the statute states:

> It is the purpose of this Article to resolve and clarify what is thought by some to be uncertainties existing at common law with respect to the subject matter hereof. Nothing contained herein, however, shall ever

---

[1] *Burtman v. Butman,* 94 N.H. 412, 54 A.2d 367 (1947).
[2] N.H. Laws 1959, ch. 16, amending N.H. Rev. Stat. Ann., ch. 556.
[3] *Pruner's Estate,* 390 Pa. 529, 531, 136 A.2d 107 (1947); *Garrison's Estate,* 391 Pa. 234, 137 A.2d 321 (1958).
[4] *Miller v. Davis,* 136 Tex. 299, 150 S.W.2d 973 (1941).
[5] Tex. Rev. Civ. Stat., art. 4412(a).

be construed, deemed or held to be in limitation of the common law powers and duties of the Attorney General.[1]

The Ohio Charitable Trusts Act contains a provision similar in its wording to the Texas statute. Two lower court decisions, however, have limited its applicability to situations where charitable trusts have already been created, holding that the attorney general is not a necessary party either to a will contest[2] or to an action to construe a will containing provisions for the creation of a charitable trust.[3] In a third case, decided by the court of appeals of a different county, the court reached the opposite conclusion in an action to construe a will.[4] The Supreme Court of Ohio has not, as yet, been called upon to make any interpretation of the section.[5]

When an action is brought by trustees of a private trust seeking settlement or allowance of their accounts, the ordinary court procedure is to require written notice to named and ascertainable beneficiaries; publication in a newspaper if there are unknown beneficiaries; and appointment by the court of a guardian ad litem, who is a neutral third party, to represent the rights of unborn or unascertainable beneficiaries. If no objection is made, the accounts are then allowed without a hearing. Where a charitable interest is involved, unless the beneficiary is a named charitable corporation, there is a problem of assuring proper review, unless the courts or state statutes include this type of proceeding in the category of actions for which written notice to the attorney general is required. Otherwise, the adversary procedure is insufficient to protect the charitable interest. The jurisdictions which require such written notice to the attorney general are in the minority, however; and in some, notice will be required as regards trusts where the charitable interest is vested, but not where it is contingent or is a remainder interest following the termination of one or several life estates. The need for review in these situations, however, is no less acute. Several states do have statutes specifically requiring that a copy of all accounts be mailed to the attorney general. Indiana,[6] Wisconsin,[7] and Nevada,[8] for example, are states where this rule is followed. The

---

[1] Tex. Rev. Civ. Stat., art. 4412(a).
[2] *Spang* v. *Cleveland Trust Co.,* 1 Ohio Op.2d 288, 73 Ohio L. Abs. 164, 134 N.E.2d 586 (1956).
[3] *Baily* v. *McElroy,* 89 Ohio L. Abs. 289, 186 N.E.2d 213 (1961).
[4] *Blair* v. *Bouton,* 15 Ohio Op.2d 474 (1956).
[5] See pp. 290 ff.
[6] Ind. Ann. Stat., sec. 31–712.
[7] Wis. Stat., secs. 317.06 and 317.16(1)(b).
[8] Nev. Rev. Stat., sec. 165.010–250.

Vermont situation described earlier represents the opposite extreme.

In Virginia, where the attorney general does not have primary responsibility for enforcement, the legislature has adopted a procedure whereby the judges of each court having jurisdiction over probate of wills appoint a commissioner of accounts who has general supervision of all fiduciaries, including trustees. It is the commissioner's duty to make all *ex parte* settlement of accounts, review fiduciaries' bonds, receive inventories, and report to the court on account of the transactions of all such fiduciaries.[1] Trustees of charitable trusts are required to settle accounts with him annually.[2] This would seem to be adequate substitute for the attorney general, in theory, and it is at least preferable to the situation in other states where no provision whatsoever is made for representation of charitable interests.

"Proper" Parties

The determination of whether the attorney general is a *proper* as distinguished from a *necessary* party to a proceeding involving a charity is even more difficult. By definition, a "proper" party is one with no interest in the controversy between the immediate litigants, but with an interest in the subject matter which may be affected during the course of the suit. A proper party may be joined by the plaintiff in any action. When charitable fiduciaries bring suit, a failure to join the attorney general may result in a failure to resolve all the issues in the case, but will not prevent the attorney general from raising them in a subsequent action.

Occasionally, an attorney general has requested permission of the court to intervene in a case involving a charity to which he was not made a party. In certain categories of cases the courts have denied this right. But there is no clear-cut rule on which decisions have been based. If a suit is brought by trustees or directors seeking to enforce a contract or to obtain damages for a tort, or if a suit of a similar nature is brought against them, the attorney general is neither a necessary nor a proper party.[3]

Usually, actions to enforce corporation membership rights fall into the same category, but, again, the rule is not absolute. For example, in the case of *Leeds* v. *Harrison* a group of members and nonmembers of a Young Men's Christian Association brought suit against the cor-

---

[1] Va. Code Ann., secs. 26–8–9 to 26–8–17.
[2] Va. Code Ann., sec. 55–29.
[3] Scott, Austin W., *op. cit.*, sec. 391.

poration, charging that one of the requirements for membership was inconsistent with the corporate charitable purposes. The court required that the attorney general be joined in the action to represent the indefinite beneficiaries of the corporation.[1]

The outcome of cases of this nature will often depend on the general attitude of the court toward the role of the attorney general. A Kentucky case denied the right of the attorney general to intervene in a suit involving the compromise of a will;[2] yet the Massachusetts court in a case with similar facts declared that he was not only a proper but a *necessary* party and refused to render judgment until he was joined.[3] In a recent federal case decided on the basis of New York law, the court permitted a motion by the attorney general to join in an action by the settlor of an inter vivos trust to require the trustees to account and pay over to him the corpus and income.[4]

Possibly the most striking example of a failure to consider the attorney general as a party is the case of *Cocke* v. *Duke University, et al.,* decided in 1963 by the Supreme Court of North Carolina.[5] In that case the trustees of the Duke Endowment, a charitable trust, brought a petition requesting authority to make investments prohibited by the indenture of trust. The beneficiaries were named in a section of the indenture wherein the trustees were directed to distribute the net income annually as follows: 20 per cent was to be retained and added to principal until the total aggregate of such additions amounted to $40 million; the remaining 80 per cent was to be divided so that 32 per cent of it would be distributed to Duke University; 32 per cent to hospitals in North or South Carolina; and varying lower percentages to three named universities, organizations and institutions aiding orphans in North and South Carolina, needy and deserving preachers, widows and orphans of deceased Methodist preachers, projects to build churches in rural areas of North Carolina, and projects to maintain and operate similar churches.[6] The lower court had appointed a guardian at litem to represent all "minors, incom-

---

[1] *Leeds* v. *Harrison,* 7 N.J. Super. 558 (1950), 15 N.J. Super. 82, 83 A.2d 45 (1951); 9 N.J. 202, 87 A.2d 713 (1952).
[2] *Commonwealth* v. *Gardner,* _____ Ky. _____, 327 S.W.2d 947 (1959).
[3] *Budin* v. *Levy,* 343 Mass. 644, 180 N.E.2d 74 (1962); see also *In re Roberts' Estate,* 190 Kan. 248, 373 P.2d 165 (1962).
[4] *Grace* v. *Carroll,* 219 F.Supp. 270 (D.C. S.D. N.Y. 1963).
[5] 260 N.C. 1, 131 S.E.2d 909 (1963); see p. 92 for further discussion of this case.
[6] See *Legal Instruments of Foundations,* compiled by F. Emerson Andrews, Russell Sage Foundation, New York, 1958, p. 91, for a copy of the trust indenture.

petent persons, unknown persons, corporations associations and entities and all other persons, corporations associations and entities whether now in being or hereafter coming into being who may now have or might hereafter acquire an interest in the subject matter of this suit."

In another order, the lower court found that two specific hospitals, a children's home, two churches, a minister, and "Mary Jane Walton, and Mary Jane Walton, general guardian of Patricia Jane Walton, were members of the different classes of beneficiaries named in the indenture; and the members of the several classes were so numerous that it was impracticable to bring all potential beneficiaries before the court."[1] These defendants were accordingly directed to represent their respective classes. The guardian ad litem filed a demurrer, which was overruled, and later excepted to the lower court's action granting the trustees' request, claiming as one cause of error that the court lacked authority to act because all potential beneficiaries had not been personally served with process and had not voluntarily submitted themselves to the court's jurisdiction. The Supreme Court ruled that the lower court action appointing representatives of all beneficiaries was proper under North Carolina law, noting the impossibility of naming approximately 2,240 individuals or associations which might be selected as beneficiaries and finding that they were all appropriately represented.

No mention of the attorney general appears in the decision. It is, of course, just because of the impossibility of naming potential beneficiaries that the common law conferred on the attorney general a representative role in actions of this nature. It is not known why the trustees did not name the attorney general of North Carolina, who is directed by statute to assure the enforcement of funds donated to charity,[2] and has been named a proper party defendant in several suits involving charitable trusts.[3] The *Cocke* decision, therefore, represents an exception to what would seem to be the law of North Carolina as well as to the practice and rules of the vast majority of states.

The foregoing discussion of parties indicates the importance of the attitude of the courts of a particular state toward the attorney general's role, for the courts have it within their power to force an attorney general to participate actively in the affairs of charity. A comparison

---

[1] *Cocke* v. *Duke University, et al.,* 260 N.C.1, 131 S.E.2d 909, 912 (1963).
[2] N.C. Gen. Stat., sec. 36–23.1.
[3] For example, *Brandis* v. *McMullan,* 229 N.C. 411, 50 S.E.2d 7 (1948).

of the experience in a state such as Massachusetts or Pennsylvania with that in Kentucky or Idaho (prior to 1963) brings this out most clearly.[1]

Statutes of Limitations and Laches as Bars to Action

In the case of private trusts, an action for breach of trust may be barred if the beneficiaries have consented to the breach, acquiesced in it, or failed to bring suit against the trustees for so long a time and under such circumstances that it would be inequitable to hold the trustees liable.[2] This last circumstance is described in law as "laches." It is a principle of equity and subject to the flexibility of many equitable doctrines. The primary limitation on its use is that it will be applied only if the beneficiary knew or reasonably should have known of his cause of action. In the case of charitable trusts, the doctrine of laches is not usually applicable to actions against a trustee to recover misappropriated funds. As the Massachusetts Supreme Judicial Court has said:

> Generally it is true that no length of time of division from the plain provisions of a charitable trust will prevent its restoration to its true purposes.[3]

Similar holdings are to be found in decisions of the courts of California,[4] Texas,[5] and the District of Columbia.[6]

A further restriction on the time in which suits may be brought is to be found in the statutes of limitations of all states and the federal government. Although the first statutes of limitations enacted in this country applied only to actions at law and not to proceedings in equity, the removal of the distinction between equity and law in many states, and the wording of the particular statute of limitations in still others, has led to the extension of the provisions of these statutes to both types of actions in all but a few jurisdictions.[7] When a statute of

---

[1] See Bogert, George G., and George T. Bogert, *op. cit.,* sec. 411, for additional cases and discussion.

[2] *Restatement of the Law of Trusts (Second), op. cit.,* secs. 216, 218, 219.

[3] *Trustees of Andover Seminary* v. *Visitors,* 253 Mass. 256, 298, 148 N.E. 900 (1925).

[4] *Brown* v. *Memorial National Home Foundation,* 162 Cal. App.2d 513, 329 P.2d 118 (1958).

[5] *Wm. Buchanan Foundation* v. Shepperd, 283 S.W.2d 325 (Tex. Civ. App. 1955), reversed by agreement of parties, 155 Tex. 406, 289 S.W.2d 553 (1956).

[6] *Mt. Vernon Mortgage Corporation* v. *U.S.,* 98 U.S. App. D.C. 429, 236 F.2d 724 (1956).

[7] Note *Harvard Law Review,* vol. 63, 1950 pp. 1177, 1215.

limitations applies to cases involving breach of fiduciary duty, an exception is made to its unequivocal operation, and the period of the statute starts to run only after a defendant knew or reasonably should have known of the facts which constituted a breach of duty. A similar exception is made in cases of fraud. Both exceptions have obvious roots in the doctrine of laches.

The applicability of statutes of limitations to actions involving charitable trusts has not been clearly decided in many jurisdictions. Scott states that neither laches nor the statute of limitations is an absolute bar to actions brought to recover charitable funds that have been misapplied.[1] This was the holding of the Federal Court for the District of Columbia in the case of *Mt. Vernon Mortgage Corporation* v. *United States,* and it has also been stated by the Massachusetts court. Bogert explains that the exception arose because of "the indefinite nature of those persons who are to be benefited by a charity, and the probability that breaches of trust may easily be unnoticed by the Attorney General or any interested party, unless there is a record of all existing charities and periodic accountings are strictly enforced."[2]

This quotation has led to some speculation as to whether the filing of financial reports with the attorney general in compliance with the provisions of a supervisory statute is sufficient to start the running of a statute of limitations with respect to those matters included in the report, or whether the filing of reports would even constitute sufficient notice to the attorney general to warrant a finding of laches if he delayed bringing suit for an unreasonably long period of time. Fear of such an effect, combined with apprehension that an attorney general's staff may not be adequate to review reports properly, has been given by some state officials as the reason for opposing registration and reporting statutes. On the other hand, it is the rare breach of fiduciary duty which will clearly appear on the face of a report filed with the state.

In England all trustees, including trustees of charitable trusts, are entitled to plead the statute of limitations as a defense to suits brought after six years have elapsed since the action in question, but the statute is specifically inapplicable to claims of fraudulent breach of trust and to actions to recover trust property the trustee has received and converted to his own use. However, if the misapplication of charitable funds was due to honest mistake only, the trustees will not be com-

---

[1] Scott, Austin W., *op. cit.,* sec. 392.
[2] Bogert, George G., and George T. Bogert, *op. cit.,* sec. 399.

pelled to refund payments made wrongfully before action was brought
or before they received notice that their conduct was open to question.
Keeton comments that "To hold otherwise, it has been said, would
ruin half the corporations in the Kingdom, and would also operate as a
serious discouragement to those contemplating undertaking the office
of a charitable trustee."[1]

The sparsity of cases dealing with this subject has caused uncertainty in many states. In California, in spite of the language of the
Brown case and several others, a lower court accepted the statute of
limitations as a defense to a suit brought in 1963 by the attorney general against trustees for misapplication of funds occurring over a period of ten years. The state has appealed the decision. A similar situation occurred in Illinois in 1964. Uncertainty as to whether an action
will be barred by the statute impedes enforcement efforts and gives
fiduciaries no assurance of their rights. Legislation to settle this question may be desirable in certain states.

The Legislature

The power of the courts other than the U.S. Supreme Court to mold
and modify law has inherent limitations. Judges make law "intersti-
tially," to quote Justice Holmes, building on principles and precedent.
They fill gaps and make small adjustments, but only rarely do they
take bold strides. Cases presented to them usually involve narrowly
defined situations, and the chances to make sweeping changes are almost nonexistent. Being inherently conservative, the courts only rarely
and slowly modify or change existing law.

The determination of broad community policy through the enactment of laws and through the creation of the specific executive, administrative, and judicial machinery to administer them is the function
of the legislative branches in the United States and England. Therefore
the legislature must be considered to have a more fundamental power
to alter the course of charitable dispositions.

Legislative power is limited by the federal and state constitutions,
but it is generally broad enough to supersede, alter, revise, or reject
judge-made law. The legislature can establish the arbitrary dividing
lines so essential to a system of laws. An example is the enactment of
a law that specifies the range of trustees' fees, perhaps in terms of
percentages; another would be a law that lists the specific categories

---

[1] Keeton, George W., *The Modern Law of Charities*. Sir Isaac Pitman and
Sons, London, 1962, p. 208.

of investments proper for a trustee. Furthermore, only the legislature can work out broad and sweeping solutions to problems covering an entire class of related situations and at the same time create new methods for administration of these solutions.[1]

In most states the laws of trusts are drawn from the common law and are to be found in decisions of the state Supreme Court. In a few states, notably California, Georgia, Montana, North Dakota, Oklahoma, South Dakota, Texas, and Louisiana, the legislatures have attempted to reduce this common law of trusts to statutory form and to publish it as a code. In all of these states, however, with the exception of Louisiana, the common law is still drawn upon to interpret the code as well as to supplement it wherever it is silent.

Furthermore, it is the state legislatures that write the tax laws, conferring exemption for charitable funds under certain circumstances which they have defined. They prescribe procedures for creation and dissolution of corporations. In some jurisdictions they are specifically granted power to investigate the affairs of charitable corporations.[2] In Michigan it is the legislature that may determine disposition of property on dissolution of charitable corporations, but this is the sole exception to the general rule.[3] In all states the power of the legislatures to conduct investigations for the purpose of gaining information in regard to the need for legislation extends over the entire range of charitable activities.

The chief restrictions on the legislative power to enact provisions replacing common law rules are the prohibitions in the United States Constitution against impairment of contracts and deprivation of property without due process. These restrictions usually apply to attempts to terminate trusts or corporations, or to modify charitable purposes. The enumeration of fiduciary duties and powers, however, does not usually involve these constitutional restrictions, and the legislature may freely regulate such provisions as the duty to account, the amount of trustees' compensation, the regulation of trust investments, and the determination of allocations between principal and income.

One particular aspect of these constitutional restrictions raised by the enactment of statutes affecting charitable dispositions is their retro-

---

[1] See Hurst, J. Willard, *The Growth of American Law: The Law Makers,* Little, Brown and Co., Boston, 1950; and Houghteling, James L., and George G. Pierce, *The Legal Environment of Business,* Harcourt, Brace and World, New York, 1963, chap. 5.

[2] Minn. Stat. Ann., sec. 300.63; S.D. Code, sec. 11.0106.

[3] Mich. Stat. Ann., sec. 168.

active effect. There is no constitutional restriction against a statute having a retroactive effect so long as it does not thereby impair a contract already made or violate the due process clause. A statute that has a prospective effect only does not run afoul of this proscription. Therefore if the wording of the statute is unclear as to its intended effect, the question of legislative intent often arises. The result of a court determination that the statute has a retroactive effect may be that the statute will be unconstitutional in its entirety.

The power of the legislature to establish procedures for enforcement is as extensive as that to determine substantive law. Although in some states the creation of state courts is circumscribed by the state constitution, the legislatures in all states have the power to allocate jurisdiction, designate venue, fix the number and length of terms of court, create, modify, and abolish remedies, and regulate court procedure. It is within the power of the legislature, therefore, to decide which courts have jurisdiction over charitable funds and the extent of this jurisdiction.

The legislature may also determine how broad the authorization of the attorney general will be to enforce the administration of charitable funds; or it can remove this duty from him altogether and place it in a different state official, create an entirely separate agency to regulate charitable funds, or adopt any combination of these arrangements. It is only when the state constitution and the legislature have remained silent concerning the duties of the attorney general and the standing of other parties that the courts are able to adopt or reject the common law rules concerning enforcement of the rights of charitable beneficiaries.

The drawbacks to reliance on the courts to change existing law have been described. The legislature, too, is limited in its freedom to make major changes and innovations in ways that go beyond the constitutional restrictions and may often be decisive when it comes to enacting specific proposals. The limitations stem from the very nature of the legislative process. Since the major focus of legislators is on the operation and financing of government and on keeping in touch with their constituents, persuasive and articulate pressure is needed to induce them to take any action on matters affecting private transactions and relationships. The existence of organized and vociferous opposition to new measures often results in no action whatsoever.

Attempts to increase the supervisory powers of the attorney general in various states by means of legislative enactment provide excellent examples of the limits on effective action by the legislature. Various attorneys general who were aware of their duties in regard to charitable funds, but felt inadequately equipped to fulfill them, have introduced legislation to augment their powers. The New Hampshire legislature, the first to enact such legislation, rejected bills in 1940 and 1942, and finally enacted legislation in 1943 following a decision of the Supreme Court in regard to a charitable trust in that year. In that decision the court stated:

> A somewhat obscure situation exists in the relation of the State's Attorney General to charitable trusts. The duty of his office to enforce them admits of no question. The beneficiaries of such trusts are the public or a part of the public, and an individual as a member of the public has rights only as a relator to the Attorney General. But the office is unorganized and unequipped to enforce such trusts in a comprehensive scheme under supervisory arrangement. The result is that the office acts only in sporadic instances when complaint is made or instructions sought, with the further result that the trustee's errors of commission are more difficult to remedy by redress than are errors of omission by correction. When the trust fund or property is not given to an institution as trustee for its own benefit, but the trustee has discretionary powers in administering the trust, as here, the occasion for supervision as an implement of enforcement seems especially demanded.[1]

The director of the Division of Charitable Trusts in New Hampshire has introduced legislation to extend the coverage of this act to charitable corporations and foundations several times. He described the reasons for rejection as follows:

> a) the continued opposition of bank trust officers and corporate trustees; b) the archaic belief that a charitable corporation or foundation is the beneficiary rather than merely the administrative machinery to handle funds for the benefit of the indefinite public; c) a conservative complacency with the status quo; and d) an unwillingness to increase the cost of supervision at a time when the administration was pledged to no new taxes, although supervision, well understood, provides the greatest dollar value in financial returns for the public benefit.[2]

A similar situation in Texas is described by Bogert.[3] There, church groups objected to the bill until an amendment was adopted exempting

---

[1] *Souhegan National Bank* v. *Kenison*, 92 N.H. 117, 122, 26 A.2d 26 (1942).

[2] D'Amours, Ernest R., "Charitable Trusts: New Hampshire's Experience with Supervision and Enforcement," *New Hampshire Bar Journal*, vol. 5, July, 1963, pp. 217, 219.

[3] Bogert, George G., "Proposed Legislation Regarding State Supervision of Charities," *Michigan Law Review*, vol. 52, 1954, pp. 633, 647.

their funds. Certain trustors of charities expressed fear that the legislation was bureaucratic and that the attorney general would "interfere and meddle" if the proposed statute was adopted. Corporate trustees were favorable so long as remainder interests to charity were excepted until they became vested in possession. In 1959, the Texas legislature did pass what could be considered a compromise requiring the participation of the attorney general in certain suits involving charities. The more usual situation in the case of conflicting claims, however, is that the legislature takes no action whatsoever. This was the case in Arizona, Indiana, Wyoming, and Pennsylvania when the Uniform Act for Supervision of Trustees for Charitable Purposes was introduced.[1] The Uniform Act was submitted to the legislature of Washington in 1963. According to information supplied by Attorney General Thornton, it aroused little interest, either in support or in opposition, and died in committee. When reintroduced in 1965, it became the subject of an interparty political dispute and again failed of passage.

In Massachusetts, a bill to increase the supervisory powers of the attorney general was first suggested in 1936 by Attorney General Dever. It was not formally presented to the legislature at that time, but in 1945 Attorney General Bushnell introduced a statute similar to that in force in New Hampshire. It was referred by the legislature for opinion to the Judicial Council, which reported:

> If this is not a new "bureau" of enormous size and scope of authorized activities, capable of practical expansion of assumed power with all the possible, conceivable, and proverbial "insolence of office" which the imagination of some *future* officials in the department may suggest, we do not know what it is. We do not believe that any such inquisitorial establishment of official "super-trustees" or permanent, official "guardians ad litem" for all the religious, educational, and charitable institutions in Massachusetts should be created, or imposed upon the taxpayers of Massachusetts, most of whom have only very indirect or remote interests in most of the trusts. . . . While appreciating the sincerity of the recommendations, we see no reason for believing that public charitable trusts in general are not properly administered by the trustees to *whom the creators of the trusts assign their administration.* . . .
>
> We think the fundamental trouble with the proposals is a sincere but exaggerated misconception of the nature and extent of the necessary

---

[1] Taylor, Eleanor K., "Accountability of Charitable Trusts," *Ohio State Law Journal,* vol. 18, 1957, p. 157.

and proper functions of the office of the Attorney General as the *representative* of the public interest in these trusts.[1]

This recommendation was sufficient to settle the issue concerning the attorney general's powers for almost ten years. The same Report contained a recommendation of the Council that a duty be placed upon the executor of each estate to notify beneficiaries of charitable bequests "whose addresses are known to him" within three months after the allowance of a will and his appointment. This bill was not enacted, however. It should be noted that at that time directors of charitable corporations[2] and trustees of charitable trusts[3] were required to file annual financial reports with the Department of Public Welfare, so that the introduction of a requirement to report to the attorney general did not represent as radical a change as it would in other states. Not until 1954 was legislation passed imposing a duty on all public charities to report to a Division of Public Charities in the Office of the Attorney General. An exception for charities with religious purposes answered the principal objection to the act put forth at the time.[4]

In contrast to these examples, the Rhode Island legislature itself created a commission to study the laws with respect to charitable trusts;[5] this action followed nationwide publicity engendered by a United States Senate investigation of the activities of a Rhode Island industrialist and two foundations that he organized.[6] The recommendations of the Commission were embodied in a bill passed in 1953 establishing a trust registry.[7]

The political climate and the political problems peculiar to each state will, of course, influence the attitude of the legislature toward regulation of charitable funds, just as toward any other questions. There is sufficient evidence, however, to conclude that general lack of interest can be overcome only by forceful presentation from several

---

[1] Judicial Council of Massachusetts, "Twenty-first Report," *Massachusetts Law Quarterly,* vol. 30, December, 1945, pp. 42, 46.

[2] Mass. Gen. Laws Ann., ch. 180, sec. 12.

[3] Mass. Gen. Laws Ann., ch. 68, sec. 15.

[4] Laws of Mass., Acts of 1954, ch. 529.

[5] State of Rhode Island and Providence Plantations, Special Commission to Study the Laws of This State with Respect to and Governing Charitable Trusts, So-Called, *Report* to His Excellency Governor John O. Pastore, January 25, 1950, Wm. Brown Co., Providence, R.I., 1950.

[6] U.S. Congress, Senate, Subcommittee of the Committee on Interstate and Foreign Commerce, "Investigation of Closing of Nashua, N.H., Mills and Operations of Textron, Incorporated. 80th Congress, 2d Session," Government Printing Office, Washington, 1948.

[7] Now R.I. Gen. Laws Ann., secs. 18–9–1 ff.

sources. In Ohio the attorney general, the banking interests, and the judiciary combined to support enactment of reporting provisions;[1] and in Illinois the Trust Committee of the Chicago Bar Association assisted the attorney general in a successful attempt to amend the Illinois Uniform Act for Supervision of Trustees for Charitable Purposes in 1963.[2] In sum, unless these political realities are taken into account in assessing new solutions to the problem of supervising foundation activities that require legislative action, the proposals may be meaningless.

Supervision by Other State Agencies

In addition to the office of the attorney general, several other executive agencies of state government exercise supervisory powers over charitable foundations. Administrative control over many foundations is exercised in the first instance through the state agencies that grant corporate charters and oversee corporate activities. The primary purpose of present-day corporation chartering laws is not regulatory, although they were originally conceived of as providing that function. These laws are more in the nature of enabling acts, and they were designed to afford an easy means for the state to confer authority on businessmen to organize and operate their businesses, large and small, with the advantage of the corporate mechanism. Gradually the concept of general chartering provisions was extended to include not-for-profit organizations. All of the statutes were drawn with a view toward facilitating the act of obtaining a corporate charter. The difficulties of using them to regulate the purpose and nature of charitable corporations have been illustrated by the experiences of New York and Pennsylvania.[3]

The mandatory reporting provisions contained in the corporation statutes of all states represent a second source of supervisory power over corporate foundations.[4] In all but a few states, however, corporations are required to report no more than a list of current officers and their addresses. Even in states where greater information is required, no separation of charitable from other not-for-profit corporations is made, and little if any evaluation of either the contents of the reports or their veracity is undertaken. The fact that failure to file may result in involuntary dissolution has actually created situations where dis-

---

[1] Klapp, Ralph, and Neva Wertz, "Supervision of Charitable Trusts in Ohio," *Ohio State Law Journal,* vol. 18, 1957, p. 181.
[2] See discussion on pp. 267 and 332.
[3] See pp. 115 ff.
[4] See Table 2, Appendix A.

solution of charitable corporations by the state has been done without any guarantee of *cy pres* distribution of funds, or even any investigation of the disposition of funds before the corporation became inactive.

Although in most states it is the attorney general who, on recommendation by other state officials, brings actions for dissolution of inactive corporations, he rarely has information as to whether a particular corporation was created for charitable purposes, and ironically it may be he who requests court action to dissolve a corporation without *cy pres* proceedings. Provisions for dissolution represent the area wherein the state regulatory powers are completely inadequate to achieve a suitable aim. The states lack adequate administrative arrangements and even the machinery for the cooperation between state agencies that would be necessary to assure proper disposition of funds on termination.

The states also lack adequate administrative machinery for enforcing provisions that impose restrictions on the fiduciary duties of corporate directors such as those forbidding loans to corporate officers and directors or a distribution of dividends to members or directors. In several states the secretary of state is given specific authority to propound interrogatories to any corporation formed under the provisions of the not-for-profit corporation act, so long as they are reasonable and proper, to enable him to ascertain whether the corporation has complied with all provisions of the act.[1] These statutes usually provide that answers to interrogatories shall be confidential and that the secretary of state shall certify to the attorney general any answers which disclose violations of law. In other jurisdictions, this power to examine the affairs of corporations is given to the attorney general, the legislature, the governor, or a combination of these.[2] They are rarely called into action, however.

Basic to any series of legislatively enacted safeguards is the establishment of responsibility in one state office to see that they are properly administered. Fragmentation, however, is the prevailing situation; usually an attorney general is given the duty of enforcement, but super-

---

[1] *Model Non-Profit Corporation Act* (1964 Revision), *op. cit.*, sec. 87; Conn. Gen. Stat. Rev., sec. 33–439; Ill. Rev. Stat., ch. 163a, sec. 97; N.C. Gen. Stat., sec. 55A–79; N.D. Cent. Code, sec. 10–28–05; Mo. Rev. Stat., sec. 335.480.

[2] Wis. Stat. Ann., sec. 182.220 (the governor may request the attorney general to investigate and present findings to legislature); Minn. Stat. Ann., sec. 300.63 (similar to Wisconsin but legislature may also conduct examination); Nev. Rev. Stat., sec. 81:340 (attorney general); S.C. Code Ann., sec. 12–745 (attorney general); S.D. Code, sec. 11.0106 (legislature).

vision or mandatory reporting provisions are placed in a separate executive office, and no provision is included for cooperation or communication.

In some states administrative responsibility has been further fragmented by statutes that require a degree of supervision by welfare officials. The chartering procedures in Massachusetts and South Carolina represent the extreme of decentralization through their requirements that the welfare board pass on all applications for charters of charitable corporations. In other states a welfare board or commissioner of institutions is required to approve applications for chartering certain charitable corporations, usually specific types of operating institutions.[1] Aside from the power to approve charter applications, state departments of health and welfare also have certain duties to supervise institutions that receive state aid or grants.[2] In Oklahoma the commissioner of charities and corrections is responsible for inspecting all eleemosynary institutions, hospitals, and homes for the aged at least once a year;[3] and all such institutions must file an annual financial report with him. In no instance, however, are powers of this nature extended to include supervision of the operation of foundations.

It is interesting to note that almost all of the provisions requiring participation of state welfare agencies in chartering procedures originated at or before the turn of the century. In Massachusetts, for example, the Department of Public Welfare, which was originally known as the Board of State Charities, exercised supervisory power over institutions receiving public subsidies from its creation in 1863. In 1899 all corporations granted tax exemption were required to file an annual report with the Board,[4] and in 1930 this requirement was extended to trustees of charitable trusts.[5] The investigatory power relating to issuance of corporate charters was passed in 1901.[6] Reports of the department at first listed organizations whose applications for charters were disapproved as well as those approved. Starting in 1929, the department report listed only the number of rejections. Abstracts of the financial reports of the corporation as well as aggregate figures were included in these reports. A 1928 statute permitted the depart-

---

[1] N.J. Rev. Stat., sec. 15:1–15; Ill. Rev. Stat., ch. 23, sec. 2025.
[2] For example, Me. Rev. Stat. Ann., ch. 25, sec. 5.
[3] Okla. Stat. Ann., tit. 74, sec. 171.
[4] Laws of Mass., Acts of 1899, ch. 259.
[5] Laws of Mass., Acts of 1930, ch. 209.
[6] Laws of Mass., Acts of 1901, ch. 405.

ment upon request or with its consent to make an annual inspection or investigation of a charitable corporation.[1]

This legislation remained in force in Massachusetts until 1954 when a bill was enacted enlarging the supervisory duties of the attorney general and requiring mandatory annual financial reports from all charitable organizations to his office. It was the depression and the resulting increase in state and federal funds for public welfare purposes, in addition to the passage of social security legislation, that caused a change of both emphasis and function for the welfare department and a concomitant diminution of attention to privately operated charitable organizations. The same experience was evident in South Carolina and Illinois.[2]

The provisions in the early Massachusetts legislation, particularly those requiring annual financial reports and granting investigatory powers to the public welfare department, foreshadowed the current approach to supervision of charitable organizations by the attorneys general and are of interest for this reason.

Solicitation of Charitable Funds

Welfare departments, the attorneys general, the secretaries of state, and the clerks of courts in some states have been given supervisory powers over one phase of charitable activity which, although not of direct concern to foundations, may have an indirect effect on their operation, particularly if they make grants to soliciting organizations. Supervision of the solicitations made by charitable organizations has traditionally been conducted by cities and towns. A growing awareness of the need for broader regulation of this type of activity at the state level has been in evidence in recent years, however. Twenty-six states have now enacted specific legislation dealing with this matter. In 17, annual or special financial reports are required from soliciting organizations, and separate reports are called for from paid solicitors or promoters. The special reports usually must be submitted before and after the undertaking of a campaign. Twenty-one states require either a license or registration before solicitation may be undertaken. In three states, Illinois, Ohio, and Massachusetts, reports must be filed with the attorney general; this means that a double reporting requirement is imposed on certain charitable organizations. In Massachusetts and Ohio, regulation of solicitation is conducted by the same state of-

---

[1] Laws of Mass., Acts of 1928, ch. 155, sec. 34.
[2] See Taylor, Eleanor K., *Public Accountability of Foundations and Charitable Trusts.* Russell Sage Foundation, New York, 1953, p. 72.

ficials who administer the statutory provisions requiring registration and reporting to the attorney general by foundations and charitable trusts. In Illinois, the attorney general's office maintains two separate divisions to administer these programs. A bill introduced in the Washington legislature in 1965 encompasses both the regulation of solicitations and the supervision of trustees.[1]

A preliminary study sponsored by The Rockefeller Foundation in 1960–1961, which received national attention, suggested the need for further regulation of all health and welfare agencies, although it did not specify methods.[2] One of the most important results of this study was the impetus it gave to the organization of a joint committee of the National Health Council and the National Social Welfare Assembly to draft a proposed Uniform Standards of Accounting and Financial Reporting for Voluntary Health and Welfare Organizations.[3] The adoption of such uniform standards is a basic prerequisite to any meaningful supervision, or even public scrutiny, of the reports of voluntary organizations. The standards adopted by the group were developed with the hope that government regulatory authorities could use them in connection with statutory requirements for filing financial reports.

Supervision of Bank and Trust Companies

Charitable trusts that are managed by bank and trust companies acting either as fiduciaries or as custodians of trust funds are subject to a degree of supervision under statutes in all states, as well as under federal laws, that require an annual audit of all accounts. In some states the banking laws include special sections relating to trust funds. For example, Indiana specifically makes it a routine duty of the state superintendent of banks to check all trusts, trust funds, and trust and estate accounts held in possession and control of banks.[4] Provisions in Ohio relate specifically to trust funds that have been held by a bank in its fiduciary capacity and not invested,[5] and the Mississippi statute

---

[1] See pp. 255 ff.

[2] *Voluntary Health and Welfare Agencies in the United States:* An Exploratory Study by an Ad Hoc Citizens Committee, Study Director, Robert H. Hamlin, M.D. The Schoolmasters Press, New York, 1961.

[3] *Standards of Accounting and Financial Reporting for Voluntary Health and Welfare Organizations,* National Health Council, New York, 1965. See also *Viewpoints on State and Local Legislation Regulating Solicitation of Funds from the Public,* National Health Council, New York, 1965.

[4] Ind. Ann. Stat., sec. 5–1025.

[5] Ohio Rev. Code Ann., sec. 1111:23.

requires separation of assets and the maintenance of separate books and records of all assets held in a fiduciary capacity.[1]

Supervision of this nature assures that there will be no malfeasance in the investment of funds, but it does not assure that the funds will be devoted to charitable purposes. There have been instances of banks serving as trustees of charitable funds so small that they produce only enough income to cover the trustee's annual charges. In one such instance, in Massachusetts, this practice continued for fifteen years, at which time the bank filed its accounts for allowance in court and the attorney general was cited and supplied with copies of the accounts. He was able to bring a *cy pres* petition and have the funds transferred to an operating charitable institution. Supervision under the banking laws, therefore, has the same disadvantage as supervision by state agencies which perform this function as one minor part of a larger function. There is neither responsibility for, nor focus on, the particular problems that relate to the management of charitable funds.

Tax Authorities

State tax authorities have a less pervasive influence on charitable activities than does the federal counterpart. This is due in part to the nature of state taxes, particularly in those states without an income tax. Exemption from real property tax is usually confined to operating institutions and does not affect the ordinary foundations, which must generally pay state and local property taxes on the real estate they own unless the property is used for their charitable purposes. The right to claim deduction for contributions to charitable organizations in computing state income or death taxes, however, raises the question of the nature of the charitable organization. Determinations under state tax law depend on the wording of the state statute as interpreted by the state tax officials and state courts. Cooperation between these officials and other branches of state government is rare. An appeal from an adverse ruling by state tax authorities is, of course, heard by the courts.

In almost all jurisdictions the attorney general's office serves as legal counsel for all actions involving the state, so that it is conceivable that an attorney general's duty to represent the state's interest in taxation will conflict with his duties to enforce charitable funds. Procedural conflicts can be solved, however, by having the state agency involved appoint its own attorney, or use one of its own legal officers to

---

[1] Miss Code Ann., sec. 5198.

represent it in such a situation, leaving the attorney general free to represent the charitable interest. More often, however, the charitable gift in such cases is to a named charitable corporation capable of representing its own interests, so that there is not as great a need for the attorney general to intervene to protect the charitable interest.[1]

Arizona is the only state that requires the filing of tax returns from exempt organizations. Its statute covers all charitable organizations except religious and educational corporations, charitable organizations supported by funds from the government or general public, and organizations whose gross income does not exceed $25,000.[2] Since Arizona is one of the states where the attorney general's powers over charitable funds are undefined, the existence of a reporting requirement of this nature serves as the sole restraint on the operation of foundations.

Cooperation between the offices of the attorney general and the state tax officials is implicit in a section of the Uniform Act for Supervision of Trustees for Charitable Purposes as enacted in California, Michigan, and Oregon. It requires all agencies of the state receiving applications for tax exemption of any charitable trust subject to the act to file annually with the attorney general a list of all applications received in that year.[3] Furthermore, in California and Oregon, failure to file annual reports with the attorney general in compliance with the Supervision of Trustees for Charitable Purposes Act is made a mandatory ground for removal of tax exemption for the year or years in which the charity is in default.[4] It is obvious that statutory provisions requiring this type of cooperation increase the efficiency and effectiveness of administration.

Independent Boards for Charity Supervision

Karst, in an article written in 1960, proposed the creation of specific and independent state boards of charity to bear primary responsibility for supervising charitable activities and administering the various state controls over their operation. His enumeration of the duties of such a board provides a useful catalogue of the possibilities for effective state action.

---

[1] See, for example, *James E. Carroll* v. *Commissioner of Corporations and Taxation,* 343 Mass. 409, 179 N.E.2d 260 (1961).

[2] Ariz. Rev. Stat. Ann., sec. 43–144.

[3] Cal. Gov. Code, sec. 12594; Mich. Stat. Ann., sec. 26.1200(14); Ore. Rev. Stat., sec. 128.730.

[4] Cal. Revenue and Tax Code, sec. 23703; Ore. Rev. Stat., sec. 128.740.

The proposed board would:
(1) replace the attorney general in his supervisory capacity, by
  (a) maintaining a registry of all charities operating in the state,
  (b) collecting and evaluating periodic reports to be required of all charities required to register, perhaps with some exemptions,
  (c) investigating possible breaches of fiduciary duty, and
  (d) calling abuses of fiduciary responsibility requiring remedial action directly to the attention of the proper court;
(2) advise and consult with charity managers in
  (a) planning for future programs of operation and selection of projects, and
  (b) organizing the management and investment of funds;
(3) take responsibility for effectuating new schemes for the operation of obsolete charities and the consolidation of charities of uneconomical size;
(4) administer a statewide system of control over the solicitation of funds, which would either coordinate or supersede municipal control;
(5) cooperate with tax officials, both state and federal, by reporting to them abuses which appear to call for withdrawal of tax exemption.[1]

This proposal is similar in concept to one formulated by the Harvard Legislative Research Bureau that was never formally published but was described in an article of 1957.[2] The scope of the Harvard proposal, however, is limited to charitable trusts, and does not include any duties relating to charitable solicitations, let alone the important area of charitable corporations.

Both of these suggestions are derived from the English experience where responsibility for supervision is placed with an independent Board of Charity Commissioners. The English method of supervision has many features pertinent to a study and assessment of the situation in the United States. Before describing them, however, it is necessary to examine the actual extent of enforcement and supervision carried on in the offices of the attorneys general in the 50 states, since the trend in this country has been toward continued reliance on this office as the focus for enforcement at the state level. No state has considered the establishment of an independent board for charity supervision, and all attempts to increase state action have, to date, centered on enlarging the scope of the attorney general's authority.

---

[1] Karst, Kenneth L., "The Efficiency of the Charitable Dollar: An Unfulfilled State Responsibility," *Harvard Law Review*, vol. 73, pp. 433, 449. Copyright © 1960 by the Harvard Law Review Association.
[2] Taylor, Eleanor K., "Accountability of Charitable Trusts," *op. cit.*

CHAPTER VII

The Role of Attorney General

Despite the existence of a variety of sources for the supervision of foundations at the state level, described in Chapter VI, almost all of the American states accept the common law doctrine and place primary reliance on the attorney general to secure enforcement of charitable funds. In theory, this power of enforcement, derived as it is from the court's ultimate power to redress breaches of duty and to order deviations, modifications, or *cy pres* dispositions, is sufficient to justify this reliance.

The range of the court actions that an attorney general may bring is broad.[1] He may request accountings, removal of trustees, dissolution of corporations, forced transfer of corporation property, or a combination of these. He may ask the court to force charitable fiduciaries to restore losses caused by breach of duty and to return profits made in the course of administration of the trust. He may seek to enjoin trustees from further wrongdoing or from continuing certain specific actions. Furthermore, transactions involving a breach of the duty of loyalty may be voided at the option of the attorney general unless he decides that it is in the public interest to affirm them. The attorney general, as well as trustees, may bring actions requesting modification or deviation from the terms of a trust, or *cy pres* application of funds.

---

[1] See Chapters III and IV for examples of these actions. Also *Restatement of the Law of Trusts (Second)*, American Law Institute, St. Paul, 1959, secs. 379 to 392; Bogert, George G., and George T. Bogert, *The Law of Trusts and Trustees*, 2d ed., West Publishing Co., St. Paul, 1964, secs. 391 to 430; Scott, Austin W., *The Law of Trusts*, 2d ed., Little, Brown and Co., Boston, 1956, secs. 379 to 392; *American Law Reports Annotated 2d*, vol. 75, 1961, p. 444, and vol. 86, 1962, p. 1375.

At least a few cases in almost every jurisdiction have involved one or more of these actions. In many of the early ones, the action was frequently brought by the attorney general at the relation of private individuals, but today the attorney general acts on his own in many cases. It should be noted, furthermore, that even in those cases where the courts have refused to grant the relief requested, they have questioned neither the right of the attorney general to bring the action nor the power of the court to grant the relief requested upon a proper showing.[1]

Surveys of Extent of Supervision by Attorneys General

Several references have been made to recent legislation in 10 states that supplements the common law enforcement duty of the attorney general with specific powers to obtain continuing information as to the financial affairs of certain charities and to investigate situations that may require court action. In six additional states attempts have been made to increase the participation of the attorney general in court proceedings that involve charitable interests. In all other states, however, the attention of the attorneys general to charitable affairs has been minimal, and rarely have their offices had dealings with charity. This observation has been clearly established by three surveys made in the past two decades of the extent of the activity in connection with charitable funds carried on by the state attorneys general.

In 1947 the Council of State Governments sponsored the circulation to all attorneys general of a questionnaire requesting information as to their powers, duties, and operations in regard to the supervision of charitable trusts. The 33 replies received were supplemented by responses to a second questionnaire circulated in 1952 to 18 states whose attorneys general have enforcement duties in respect to public and charitable trusts. The results of both surveys were included in a volume on *Public Accountability of Foundations and Charitable Trusts*.[2] As of 1952, only New Hampshire had enacted legislation supplementing the common law enforcement duties of the attorney general with certain supervisory powers. Of the other states, only four reported "some" provision for keeping the attorney general informed as to the need for his assistance in charitable cases, whether for securing ap-

---

[1] See, for example, *State* v. *Taylor,* 58 Wash.2d 252, 362 P.2d 247 (1961); *Attorney General* v. *Olsen,* 356 Mass. 190, 191 N.E.2d 132 (1963); *Buell* v. *Gardner,* 168 App. Div. 278, 149 N.Y.Supp. 803, 153 N.Y.Supp. 1108 (1914).

[2] By Eleanor K. Taylor. Russell Sage Foundation, New York, 1953, pp. 143 ff.

proval of the appointment or removal of trustees, the application of *cy pres,* or a holding that trustees are liable for breach of trust.[1] In the remaining states responding to the questionnaire, it was evident that the office of the attorney general had little or no involvement in charitable cases. Furthermore, only three states—Florida, Indiana, and Vermont —reported that they were considering the advisability of legislation, despite the fact that officials in nine other states replied that the present machinery was inadequate.

In 1959 a report of the American Bar Association's Committee on Charitable Trusts contained a review of the extent of accountability of charitable trustees.[2] In addition to the six states which had by then enacted statutes requiring registration of charitable trusts and reports to the office of the attorney general, Nebraska, New Jersey, and Pennsylvania were characterized by the Committee as "active" states. The Committee found that in the great majority of states the attorney general took action with respect to charitable trusts only when he was notified or joined as a party to the action.

The report also contained a survey of state requirements imposed on trustees to file accounts with the courts at periodic intervals. The Committee noted that:

> The experience in New Hampshire and Rhode Island indicates that compulsory reporting by the trustees of charitable trusts, with certain exceptions, and rather close supervision by the Attorney General's office, has produced results for the benefit of the public substantially outweighing the costs involved.

They concluded that because of the rapid growth of charitable trusts in the United States, "further study should be made of the need and most appropriate methods for regulating charitable trusts."[3]

Again in 1961, the American Bar Association Committee on Charitable Trusts reported on an attempt to review the situation in the various states.[4] The report was based on answers to a questionnaire sent to the attorney general of each state requesting information as to the basis of his authority to supervise and intervene in matters related to charitable trusts and foundations, statistics as to the number and type

---

[1] Connecticut, Nevada, New Hampshire, and North Carolina.
[2] Ball, Ralph K., "Accountability of Charitable Trustees," *Trusts and Estates,* vol. 98, 1959, p. 970.
[3] *Ibid.,* p. 971.
[4] Knecht, Lawrence G., "Report of the Committee on Charitable Trusts and Foundations [of the American Bar Association Section of Real Property, Probate and Trust Law]," *Trusts and Estates,* vol. 100, 1961, p. 895.

of cases in which his office was involved in 1960, information as to the number of new corporations or foundations formed, a description of the nature of any reports submitted to the office, and a report of the staff and budget of the office available for this work. Answers were received from 36 states. Because information was not received from a number of "very important states, including California and New York (outside New York City), and apparently no data were available in Illinois. . . ,"[1] the Committee reported that it had not attempted any specific statistical analyses but had merely endeavored to point out some of the factors that seemed to them significant.[2]

The Committee concluded that in only six states was there any indication of activity having to do with incorporated charities and that the total number of court cases involving charitable corporations in which the attorney general had participated was "a mere 16." The remainder of the investigations and litigation reported to them involved charitable trusts, and of these the vast majority seemed to be testamentary. Initiative for involving the attorney general came from other parties, rather than from that office, by a ratio of 10 to 1. Only in New York City, Ohio, Minnesota, and New Hampshire did it appear that the attorney general had taken any initiative of his own to investigate charitable activities. The states singled out as being among those with the most activity were Connecticut, Minnesota, New Hampshire, Ohio, Pennsylvania, and Rhode Island. The report ascribed inadequate staff and budget in the offices of the attorneys general for this type of work as one of the major reasons for the lack of activity.

> It would appear that in only six states were there any individuals assigned to this work on a full-time basis. It was obvious that by and large this entire area of activity has been regarded as one which *had* to be done under certain circumstances but generally there was no feeling that this is a special field of activity which required the allocation of adequate manpower.[3]

It concluded with a recommendation for a detailed study of the actual activities carried on in the offices of the attorneys general to provide sound basis for conclusions that the members did not feel competent to draw on the basis of the data then available. The following possible conclusions were listed:

---

[1] The other states not included in the survey results were Arizona, Delaware, Hawaii, Idaho, Kansas, Massachusetts, Missouri, Montana, Pennsylvania, Tennessee, Utah, Washington, the District of Columbia, and Alaska.
[2] Knecht, Lawrence G., *op. cit.*
[3] *Ibid.,* p. 896.

a. No legislative action is needed, but perhaps some encouragement to the various Attorneys General and some assistance for them in getting the necessary budget funds to support their activities in this area.

b. Further legislation on the state level. We are thoroughly aware of the Uniform Supervision of Trustees for Charitable Purposes Act, but we are also aware that it has been enacted only in California to date and that there seems to be but little interest elsewhere in its enactment. A detailed study might really *prove* the advisability of enacting it, or might indicate areas in which the Uniform Act might be improved.

c. Regardless of the foregoing, we are sure that those who create these charitable organizations, the beneficiaries of them, and all taxpayers (who in the final analysis are footing part of the bill) are truly entitled to know more about what is going on than is known now —and a thoroughgoing study would at least disclose some of the presently hidden parts of the picture.[1]

One of the greatest drawbacks to a statistical study of the nature of that done by the American Bar Association is that few states keep records according to the categories under which the Committee requested information. The situation in Massachusetts affords an example. Although the attorney general possessed wide powers to supervise charitable trusts and foundations and his office was among the most active in supervising charitable funds and participating in court proceedings, his staff could not complete the A.B.A.'s questionnaire because there were no readily available means of identifying the nature of specific cases.

Nevertheless, the information contained in responses to the questionnaires presented a realistic picture of the situation in a majority of the states and confirmed the general lack of interest in this field of activity.[2] For example, the attorney general's office in West Virginia replied that the office had not in the past supervised or intervened in charitable matters. South Dakota reported that the attorney general had no authority over charitable funds, although chapter 429 of the Acts of 1955, entitled "Charitable Trusts," does contain a section specifying that "the Attorney General shall represent the beneficiaries in all cases arising under the chapter, and it shall be his duty to enforce such trusts by proper proceedings in the Courts."[3] A similar reply was received from Oklahoma, although in this case there would appear

---

[1] *Ibid.*

[2] Information obtained from answers to questionnaire circulated by the American Bar Association Committee on Charitable Trusts and Foundations, made available by Lawrence G. Knecht, Cleveland, Ohio, Chairman of the Committee.

[3] S.D. Code Ann., sec. 59.0603.

to be both judicial and statutory authority for the attorney general's participation in cases involving charitable trusts.[1]

The special counsel to the attorney general of Louisiana replied that, although the attorney general had no authority to supervise, he did render advisory opinions concerning the construction and application of the Louisiana Trust Estate Law.[2] In Virginia that office performs a similar function through the rendering of advice to the commonwealth's attorneys on the execution of their duties imposed by law, one of which is the enforcement of charitable trusts. The answer stated that there had been no actions in 1959 or 1960, and that the attorney general does not participate in cases involving charities. It should be noted, however, that he is permitted by statute[3] to request the court to appoint trustees of charitable trusts, if none has been appointed, and to participate to assure compliance with gifts for charitable, literary, or educational purposes to bodies corporate or incorporate.

The list of inactive states as disclosed in the replies also includes Alabama, Arkansas, Colorado, Florida, Kentucky, Mississippi, Montana, Nebraska, New Mexico, Nevada, North Carolina, North Dakota, and Wyoming. The attorneys general of Nebraska and North Dakota did point out that trustees were required to make regular reports to the district courts.[4] The Wyoming answer revealed that the state examiner was charged with making annual inspections of all trusts,[5] but contained no further comments. In none of these states did the attorney general receive information as to the creation of charitable corporations. The Nevada attorney general noted that he was authorized to examine the affairs of nonprofit corporations in order to ascertain their condition, determine whether there was compliance with law and with the terms of any trusts being administered, and take necessary action to correct any noncompliance by officers and directors.[6] The reply added that the attorney general did not have sufficient personnel to supervise.

The states singled out in the Committee Report as among the most

---

[1] See *Phillips* v. *Chambers*, 174 Okla. 407, 51 P.2d 303 (1935); and Okla. Stat., tit. 60, sec. 175.18, which provides that the attorney general must be notified of actions of contract against trustees of charitable trusts and given a right to intervene.

[2] La. Rev. Stat., secs. 9–2271 ff.

[3] Va. Code Ann., sec. 55–29.

[4] Neb. Rev. Stat., secs. 24–607, 24–612; N.D. Cent. Code, sec. 59–04–17.

[5] Wyo. Stat. Ann., sec. 9–104.

[6] Nev. Rev. Stat., sec. 81.400.

active were Connecticut, Minnesota, Georgia, Indiana, Maine, Maryland, New Jersey, Vermont, and Wisconsin. In Connecticut the attorney general is charged by statute with representing "the public interest in the protection of any gifts, legacies or devises intended for public or charitable purposes."[1] The reply stated that the attorney general had no investigatory power except when a complaint was made, citing *Healy* v. *Loomis Institute*.[2] The office reported that it had been made a party to litigation in 18 cases in 1960, but had initiated none. It participated in 12 cases involving *cy pres,* 2 requests for deviation, 6 for construction of instruments, and 5 accountings (of which one was contested and 4 involved termination). Of the types of charities involved, 15 were testamentary trusts, 7 were corporations, and none was an inter vivos trust. The office was the sole opponent in 10 cases. No records were available as to the number of charitable trusts or corporations created during that period, no notice was received of petitions for allowance of accounts, and no copies were received of the required initial or annual reports to the probate courts if there were other parties in interest besides the attorney general. Two part-time assistant attorneys general were reported to be assigned to charitable affairs.

Minnesota reported that the attorney general's office was a party to 24 *cy pres* cases, 4 requests for deviation, 20 routine accountings, 2 requests for construction, and 3 requests for removal of trustees. In 1960, an intensive study by the attorney general of Minnesota of the affairs of the Sister Kenny Foundation disclosed that less than 50 per cent of contributed funds were applied for research or hospital purposes.[3] This case received nationwide attention and led to the passage in Minnesota of legislation requiring registration and the filing of annual financial reports by charities that solicit funds from the public.[4] However, there is no general provision in that state requiring that the attorney general be supplied with information as to the creation or continuing status of other charities. It was reported that one staff attorney devoted half of his time to charitable affairs.

Georgia, Indiana, Maine, Maryland, New Jersey, Vermont, and Wisconsin each reported participation in from 2 to 20 cases involving charitable funds in 1959 or 1960. The office of the attorney general in

---

[1] Conn. Gen. Stat. Rev., sec. 3–125.
[2] 102 Conn. 410, 128 Atl. 774 (1925).
[3] *Sister Elizabeth Kenny Foundation* v. *National Foundation,* _____ Minn. _____, 126 N.W.2d 640 (1964).
[4] Minn. Stat., sec. 309.50 ff.

New Jersey, although involved in only 5 litigations in 1960, reported participation in 100 routine accountings by testamentary trustees, only 1 of which was contested. This participation is required by New Jersey Court Rule.[1] One attorney is assigned part-time to the work. In Wisconsin, where there is a similar rule,[2] the attorney general reported participation in 30 routine accountings in 1959 and 40 in 1961, but no further activity with respect to the operation of charitable trusts or corporations.

In Indiana it is the practice of some trustees and directors to file with the attorney general copies of annual court accountings accompanied by notice of the court's approval. Under Indiana law these reports are verified and passed upon by the audits sections of the courts.[3] The procedure in the attorney general's office is to review and file them. It is the staff's observation that the reports do correctly reflect the nature of the expenditures. Approximately 20 reports are received annually; one assistant attorney general is assigned to review them and to participate in litigation when there is a contested proceeding or the attorney general is made a party.

The value of this American Bar Association report lies in the fact that it is based on direct information from those involved. It therefore underscores most clearly the conclusions reached in the prior Bar Association studies and held by most commentators[4] that in the states there is neither adequate knowledge of the existence of charitable trusts and foundations nor sufficient supervision of their activities to assure that funds for charitable purposes are actually being devoted to those purposes.

Bogert and Scott have attempted to explain this lack of supervision. Scott attributes it to the fact that "the attorney general is charged with a great many duties which have nothing to do with the enforcement of charitable trusts."[5] Bogert thinks that part of the problem has been a lack of knowledge as to how to proceed.

> In the great majority of states there was no provision as to how the enforcing officer should perform his duty—no direction, for example, that he proceed in any particular way to collect information regard-

---

[1] Supreme Court Civil Practice Rules 4:117–6 and 4:99–7.
[2] Wis. Stat. Ann., sec. 317.06.
[3] Ind. Ann. Stat., sec. 31–712.
[4] See Bogert, George G., and George T. Bogert, *op. cit.,* sec. 411; Scott, Austin W., *op. cit.,* sec. 391, and Karst, Kenneth L., "The Efficiency of the Charitable Dollar: An Unfulfilled State Responsibility," *Harvard Law Review,* vol. 73, 1960, p. 433.
[5] Scott, Austin W., *op. cit.,* sec. 391.

ing existing charities and performance or breach of them; and rarely was any obligation fastened on other public officials to aid the attorney general in his work in the field of charities or was it made the duty of trustees for charity to register and report to this officer.[1]

Both men have concluded that without legislation to supplement the attorney general's common law powers there is little likelihood that the attention of an attorney general to charitable affairs will be more than "sporadic."[2] Further support for this view comes from a comparison with England, where as early as 1601 Parliament, in the enactment of the Statute of Charitable Uses, provided for the creation of ad hoc commissioners to inquire into the administration of charitable trusts. In more recent times, Parliament created the permanent Board of Charity Commissioners which supplements the enforcement duties of the attorney general with broad supervisory and quasi-judicial power.

Not until 1943 was any attempt made in the United States to enact legislation that would enable an attorney general to deal more effectively with the supervision and enforcement of charitable trusts. In the twenty-year period following the enactment in New Hampshire of a Charitable Trusts Act, nine additional states adopted similar legislation; a Uniform Act for Supervision of Trustees for Charitable Purposes was promulgated; and in New York, Pennsylvania, Texas, Hawaii, and Washington a Division of Charitable Trusts has been established in the office of the attorney general to participate actively in certain categories of court proceedings involving charitable funds. It is interesting to note that in three of these states the establishment of an active program of supervision has resulted in action by the attorney general to obtain even broader statutory powers. To date, however, these attempts have not been successful.

Supervision of Charities Without a Registration and Reporting Statute

New York. The duty of the attorney general as representative of the ultimate beneficiaries of dispositions for charitable and religious purposes contained in wills, trust agreements, deeds, and corporate purposes was first recognized by the Colonial Courts of the Province of New York.[3] This role was reaffirmed in the Tilden Act which con-

---

[1] Bogert, George G., "Proposed Legislation Regarding State Supervision of Charities," *Michigan Law Review,* vol. 52, 1954, pp. 633, 639.
[2] Scott, Austin W., *op. cit.,* sec. 391.
[3] *Williams* v. *Williams,* 8 N.Y. (4 Seld.) 525, 553 (1853).

ferred validity on charitable trusts and directed the attorney general to enforce them.[1] There is also in New York a so-called fiduciary act which is part of the General Corporation Law. It permits the attorney general on behalf of the people of the state to bring action against one or more directors or officers of a corporation to procure judgment for the following relief:

a. to compel defendants to account for their conduct
b. to pay to the corporation funds lost or wasted through neglect, or failure to perform, or violation of duties
c. to suspend a defendant from office for abuse of his trust
d. to remove a defendant from his office
e. to set aside a transfer of property
f. to enjoin such a transfer[2]

In addition, the attorney general must be given at least five days' notice and a chance to review applications for charters of membership corporations before they are approved by a justice of the Supreme Court.[3] He is a necessary party to all actions for dissolution or consolidation of charitable corporations[4] and to those for applications by corporations to sell or mortgage real property, or to other special proceedings wherein charitable beneficiaries have an interest.[5]

The Division of Charitable Trusts and Escheat in the office of the attorney general in New York is staffed by eight men. They participate in approximately 4,000 cases a year, half of which relate to questions of distribution to charity under wills. For example, in 1964 the office made the following classification of actions in which it participated: fiduciary accountings, 1,250; construction of wills and trust instruments, 200; probated wills, 900; applications for incorporation and related matters, 575; mortgage or sale of real property of charitable corporations, 400; escheat, 1,025.

Many of these cases present no serious problem, and, after examination, the attorney general's office merely certifies no objection; but many others entail extensive investigation and participation in litigation to protect the charitable interests. For example, in one case a will presented for probate contained a gift of two-thirds of a residuary estate of $3 million to benefit a charitable foundation, and one-third to three individuals—the testatrix's lawyer, her accountant, and her in-

---

[1] N.Y. Pers. Prop. Law, sec. 12; N.Y. Real Prop. Law, sec. 113.
[2] N.Y. Gen. Corp. Law, secs. 60, 61.
[3] N.Y. Membership Corp. Law, sec. 10.
[4] N.Y. Membership Corp. Law, secs. 55 and 56.
[5] N.Y. Real Prop. Law, sec. 113(4) and (5).

vestment counselor. The attorney general's office, proceeding on the theory that the gift to these men was questionable in view of their fiduciary capacity, investigated and found a prior will under which the entire estate went to the foundation. The staff also found that the three individuals were the sole directors of the foundation. Objections to the second will were filed, and members of the attorney general's office tried the case. A settlement was subsequently made which contained a provision that the board of the foundation be increased by nine members appointed by the attorney general with the court's approval, thereby effectively removing control of the foundation from these men.

Many of these New York cases have involved questions of the proper distribution of extraordinary dividends, the payments of fees, and the apportionment of taxes in estates and trusts where there is a vested remainder for charity following one or several life estates. Particular attention has been given to trust accounts of this nature to assure protection of the charitable interests. The office has also been involved in several cases wherein stock of a closely held corporation has been left to a family foundation, often one originally created by the decedent. Several cases have concerned questionable valuations of stock of this nature as well as instances where fiduciaries have been in conflict of interest.

In all cases relating to corporate dissolution or consolidation, the attorney general has required that the directors submit, with their petition, an accounting for at least the last six years of existence. Several such accountings have revealed questionable activities by directors and have led to corrective actions. The Charitable Trusts Bureau also cooperates with the attorney general's Charity Fraud Bureau, which handles all complaints and actions relating to the improper solicitation of charitable funds.

In 1964, in an effort to expand its information sources, the attorney general's office requested the United States Treasury Department to furnish it with notice of all revocations of tax exemption of New York charitable funds, particularly foundations. The office received excellent cooperation from Revenue Service personnel, but found in most instances that the notice of revocation came too late for effective state action.

Prior to 1964 the attorney general's office in New York had been reluctant to sponsor legislation to require all charitable foundations and trusts to register and file periodic reports, primarily because there had been no assurance that sufficient funds would be made available to administer the program; the office had considered it unwise to undertake so great a task unless it could be done properly. In 1964, however, the attorney general requested one of his assistants to make a detailed study of the supervisory legislation in effect in other states and to consider the advisability of drafting a bill suitable for introduction in New York.

This study resulted in a decision to obtain legislation similar to the Uniform Supervision of Trustees for Charitable Purposes Act. A bill was drafted that would apply to all trustees and corporations holding funds or administering property for charitable uses and purposes except religious and educational charities and hospitals. It contained a provision imposing a filing fee equal to one-fifth of one per cent of the gross income of each charity to accompany periodical reports that would be filed with the attorney general. It also contained explicit requirements making the attorney general a necessary party to legal proceedings that involve charitable funds, whether or not the charitable interest was vested in use.

This bill was introduced to the Senate and the Assembly of the State of New York in May of 1965[1] shortly before adjournment, and was expected to be considered during the 1966 session. The 1,594,000 New York foundations listed in *The Foundation Directory, Edition 2* hold 56 per cent of the assets of all foundations listed in the *Directory*. It is estimated that a large proportion of the smaller foundations in the country are also situated in that state. The application of a state registration and reporting requirement to these foundations would represent a major extension of the scope of state supervisory programs and would undoubtedly influence the future course of enforcement in those states that do not have active programs of supervision.

Pennsylvania. The Uniform Act for Supervision of Trustees for Charitable Purposes was rejected by the Pennsylvania General Assembly in 1955,[2] and a bill that would have combined supervision of solicitation with the creation of a registry of all charitable organizations and the imposition of reporting requirements was rejected in 1961.[3] Nevertheless, the attorney general's office in that state has carried on an active supervisory program within the limits of the information available. This information comes from two primary sources: notice to the

---

[1] State of New York, Assembly, Print 7010, May 17, 1965.
[2] State of Pennsylvania, House Bill No. 1085 (1955).
[3] State of Pennsylvania, House Bill No. 1603 (1961).

attorney general of all proceedings involving charitable trusts, required at the direction of the Supreme Court of that state as recited in a 1958 case;[1] and notice of applications for charters for charitable corporations.[2] In addition, in 1956, a search of probate records was made in several courts; it revealed several instances of dormant funds which have since been reactivated.[3]

One deputy attorney general is assigned to charitable matters. At one time charitable trust matters were handled in Philadelphia, but since 1963 they have been conducted from the attorney general's office in the state capitol at Harrisburg. The deputy attorney general works on a statewide basis, reviewing all notices, wills, accounts, and petitions. Two special assistant attorneys general assist him, one on cases arising in Philadelphia and the four adjacent counties, and one on those in Allegheny County. When a case requiring the personal attention or intervention of the attorney general arises in any of the other courts, the matter is customarily turned over to a local attorney who acts for the office on a fee basis. The deputy attorney general appears with this local attorney whenever the problems are of major importance. In some instances, the court has requested his appearance to expedite the decision-making process.

Almost all of the county orphans courts have adopted a court rule, originally drafted in 1958 by the attorney general, under which at least fifteen days' written notice to the attorney general of every proceeding involving a charitable trust must be mailed to the attorney general's office in Harrisburg, accompanied by a copy of the account, petition, or other pleading; a copy of the will or trust instrument; information as to the caption of the case; a statement of the nature of the proceeding; the name of the donor, settlor, or testator and of the charities which may be affected; and the name and address of the counsel for any charities involved that are to be represented. The attorney general's office has prepared forms containing spaces for all of the required information for use by attorneys.

The type of problems most frequently encountered by the attorney general's office in Pennsylvania, and the actions usually taken, include:

1. Legacies or contingent remainders to named charity. The office assures that the legatee has received notice.

---

[1] *Garrison's Estate,* 391 Pa. 234, 137 A.2d 321 (1958).
[2] See pp. 116–117.
[3] See Forer, Lois, "Forgotten Funds: Suggesting Disclosure Laws for Charitable Funds," *University of Pennsylvania Law Review,* vol. 105, 1957, pp. 1044, 1052.

2. Contingent remainders for indefinite charitable purposes. Periodic review is attempted to determine whether the contingency has occurred, but lack of time and personnel has prevented the establishment of a regular system of review.

3. Compromises or settlements. In many cases, organized charities have been fearful of bad publicity which might result from a contest; the attorney general's office has entered such cases to oppose unmerited claims.

4. Questions of validity of gifts for unspecified charitable purposes. The office has been successful in sustaining gifts "for worthy purposes" or "for benevolent purposes" in several instances.

5. Cy pres and deviation. The actions here are similar to those described in detail elsewhere.[1]

6. Fees. When extraordinary fees are requested, the office requires that the request be made a part of the court record, thereby affording the court a basis on which to make a decision.

7. Excessive accumulations. The office makes a regular practice of intervening to assure distribution of funds for charitable purposes.

In addition, the attorney general's office has initiated actions to assure proper application of funds and the availability of the charitable benefits to the public. In one, the directors of a museum were prevented from excluding members of the public.[2] In another, a foundation was required to desist from distributing its funds as supplemental fringe benefits to its trustees. In a third case, foundation trustees were required to account, and a receiver was appointed to take possession of and title to whatever assets remained following bankruptcy of a foundation and removal of its federal tax exemption.[3] Several cases involving improper self-dealing by trustees have also been discovered and corrected.

A leading case in regard to accumulation of funds was decided by the Supreme Court of Pennsylvania in 1964 following extensive litigation in which the attorney general's office assisted the charitable corporation, which was to be the ultimate recipient, in presenting the arguments for a deviation from the provisions for accumulation. The court ruled that the provisions for accumulation, which were to continue for 400 years, were unreasonable, and held them void as un-

---

[1] See Chapter VIII.
[2] *Commonwealth* v. *Barnes Foundation*, 398 Pa. 458, 159 A.2d 500 (1960).
[3] See Forer, Lois, "Revocation of Tax Exemption—Then What?" *Foundation News*, vol. 4, September, 1963, pp. 7 ff.

necessary, charitably purposeless, and contrary to public policy as well as to the testator's primary charitable intent. The immediate application of income for the benefit of the homes designated to be the ultimate beneficiaries was ordered.[1]

The attorney general of Pennsylvania is appointed by the governor. Three attorneys general were appointed between 1961 and 1964, and the consequent turnover in personnel assigned to charitable matters has hampered the activities of the office. As with New York, however, the Pennsylvania experience illustrates the range of activities that can be undertaken by an attorney general interested in enforcing charitable funds but operating without benefit of a registration and reporting statute.

Texas. The program for enforcement established in Texas affords a third example of supervision of charities without a registration and reporting statute; it is more limited in its effect than the others because Texas lacks statutory provisions regarding the accountability of fiduciaries. Testamentary trustees are bound only by common law duties to account and are not under the jurisdiction of the probate courts.[2] Similarly, the only requirement regarding reports from directors of charitable corporations is that the secretary of state may require a statement of existence not more than once every four years.[3] Furthermore, corporations may be created and dissolved without state supervision. Under the terms of a statute enacted in Texas in 1959, however, the attorney general is considered a necessary party to all court proceedings directly or indirectly involving charitable trusts, and the term "charitable trust" is defined so that it includes corporations.[4]

In 1961, the attorney general of Texas established in his office a Division of Charitable Trusts to handle all matters arising under this statute and to carry out his common law duties of enforcement. One assistant attorney general has been assigned to this Division and devotes full time to the work. At any one time there are approximately 20 cases pending involving charitable matters. The assistant's duties take him to all the counties in the state. He receives occasional assistance with cases arising in Austin, Houston, or Dallas, but generally handles all matters personally. The majority of cases relate to will con-

---

[1] *In re James' Estate,* 414 Pa. 80, 199 A.2d 275 (1964), affirming 31 D. & C. 1 (1963).
[2] Tex. Rev. Civ. Stat., art. 3290; see also Appendix A, Table 1.
[3] Tex. Rev. Civ. Stat., art. 1396–9.01.
[4] Tex. Rev. Civ. Stat., art. 4412a; see also p. 212.

tests, although some are petitions for instructions and requests for *cy pres* or deviation.

The cases which come to his attention include some where the statutory notice may not be applicable; this is true because the newness of the statute has caused attorneys in Texas to cite the attorney general whenever there is even a remote possibility of his having an interest, rather than take the risk that the proceeding will be void.

The one case decided by the Texas Supreme Court to date that has interpreted the 1959 statute was *Akin Foundation* v. *Trustees for the Preston Road Church of Christ*.[1] A motion for declaratory judgment had been filed to construe the terms of a charitable bequest contained in a will. The trial court held that the issue was not a proper one for declaratory judgment, and the plaintiffs appealed. The Texarkana Court of Appeals, on its own motion, held the trial court proceeding null and void because the attorney general had not been joined, and remanded the case for further proceedings.

One of the most important cases in which the attorney general's office has participated since 1961 is *William Mark Rice University et al.* v. *Waggoner Carr, Attorney General of Texas, et al.* This suit was brought by the trustees of Rice University to remove restrictions prohibiting the admission of Negro students and the charging of tuition, both of which were contained in the original indenture of trust executed in 1891 under which the University was established. The trial court applied the doctrines of *cy pres* and deviation and relieved the University from the two requirements on the ground that they rendered impracticable the development of the University as an educational institution of the first class. Certain intervenors, primarily alumni of the University, opposed the changes at the trial level, and have filed an appeal which is now pending. The attorney general's position was in support of the trustees' petition.

A second matter of major interest in Texas involved extended litigation and several suits, two of which are of primary importance. One is a controversy over membership in the Kennedy Memorial Foundation, a corporate foundation created by a testatrix before her death; the second, a proceeding in the probate court contesting the will of the same testatrix by which she left the bulk of a vast estate to the foundation. The attorney general has been active in both cases. In the controversy over membership rights, he has taken the position that the

---

[1] 367 S.W.2d 351 (Tex. Civ. App. 1963).

members named in the original charter are the validly elected trustees of the foundation and that certain actions taken by the testatrix after the foundation was created were improper and made under undue influence. In the will contest case, he has appeared in support of the will. The litigation was expected to continue for several years, but the outcome will have an important bearing on the question of a donor's ability to control a charitable corporation, a subject not at present clear under Texas law.

In 1960 and 1961, the attorney general's office in Texas undertook a survey of all known charitable foundations in Texas in an attempt to obtain information as to the amount of funds devoted to charitable purposes in the state, and to produce information that could form the basis for a presentation to the legislature of the need for a registration and reporting statute. A list of all organizations that filed Form 990–A with the Internal Revenue Service's Texas office was compiled with the help of Service personnel, and in September, 1960, 1,600 letters were sent out requesting the following information: a copy of the instrument creating the foundation; a list of trustees or directors; an enumeration of the purposes of the organization; and financial reports for the years 1958, 1959, and 1960, including a detailed schedule of assets, income, and charitable distributions.

The office rested its authority for this request on two bases: the visitorial power of the attorney general over all corporations, which under Texas law includes the power to request any information from any corporation, business or charitable, and carries with it the sanction of automatic dissolution for failure to answer;[1] and the common law powers of the attorney general over all charitable funds, which, it was considered, carried sufficient authorization to demand the information. Only 3 foundations objected to the request; 235 did not respond, and of these, 65 were found to be extinct; 425 were ruled to be noncharitable although not-for-profit corporations on the basis of their reply. Of the remaining 910 foundations, reports were received for 850. The large foundations sent complete audits; many others filed photostats of Form 990–A; and some of the smallest sent a letter stating the financial data for the years requested.

A part-time employee was hired to tabulate the information from these reports in terms of capital assets, income, and charitable distributions. His work was discontinued in 1962 following a change of ad-

---

[1] Tex. Rev. Civ. Stat., art. 1302–5.05.

ministration. The completed tabulations covered 675 of the 850 foundations filing returns. They indicated assets of $403,370,850, income of $73,357,000, and distributions of $55,344,000, but the attorney general's office thought that the figure for total assets was low, either because assets were given at book value or because some of the largest known foundations in Texas were not included in this partial listing.[1]

No further work has been done on this survey, nor have the files been examined to ascertain the existence of any situations needing further action. The information was not obtained for this purpose originally, and the personnel have been inadequate to review it even if the task were felt to be desirable. The files are consulted for additional information about the charities that come to the attorney general's attention from other sources.

In 1964 the attorney general requested his staff to prepare new legislation to increase his supervisory powers. A draft bill prepared by them was circulated among several of the banks and bar associations throughout the state for comment and was submitted to the legislature in 1965. In its original form it contained a novel approach to the concept of a supervisory program. With certain exceptions, trustees and directors of all charitable trusts and corporations not dependent upon public solicitations for their funds, would have been required to file annually with the attorney general the following information: (1) a statement of the primary purpose of the charity, (2) the approximate value of its assets, (3) the names of its officers and trustees, and (4) the address of the location of its books and records. All books and records were to be expressly available for examination at the written request of the attorney general who would be empowered to employ auditors to make personal examinations. The cost of these examinations was to be borne by the charity at a per diem fee equivalent to that paid for examination of state banks. Failure of a trustee or director to comply with the reporting or examination provisions would subject him to a penalty not exceeding $100 for each day that the failure persisted.

These provisions reflected the desire expressed by several bank trustees and foundation officers to be free from additional filing requirements. They also reflected the preference of the attorney gen-

---

[1] Information supplied by Assistant Attorney General J. Gordon Zuber, Office of the Attorney General, Austin, Texas.

eral's staff for personal audits rather than reliance on reporting provisions as a method of supervision.

Following the introduction of this bill in the legislature, however, the attorney general received many complaints from foundations that had not been consulted previously. They were fearful that the investigatory powers were too broad and could be used to discriminate against certain foundations. The trustees of one Texas foundation arranged a meeting for members of the attorney general's staff, representatives of the Internal Revenue Service, and a number of foundation directors to effect a compromise. The Service personnel explained the changes made in Form 900-A for 1964, and it was agreed that a requirement that copies of Form 990-A be filed with the attorney general would provide his staff with adequate information and at the same time not unduly increase the burden on fiduciaries.

These decisions were incorporated into an amended bill. It applied to "all charitable trusts and all charitable foundations over which the State of Texas has jurisdiction and the Attorney General has enforcement or supervisory powers." The definition of charitable trusts followed that in the Uniform Supervision of Trustees for Charitable Purposes Act, but added a provision making it specifically applicable to trusts with vested charitable remainders. Charitable foundation was defined as, "any nonprofit corporation organized under the laws of this State one of whose purposes shall be the receipt of gifts and the dispensing of services or funds for purposes of public charity and any foreign corporation doing business or holding property in this State for such purposes." Exempt were federal or state operated institutions; trusts or foundations that receive substantially all their support from religious or fraternal organizations, from membership dues or fees, or from the operation of a nonprofit facility; cemetery or burial associations; trusts or foundations dependent primarily on public solicitation; and trusts or foundations administering assets of a religious organization.

The bill called for establishment of a public register of charitable trusts and foundations containing the names, addresses, and purposes of the reporting charities. All other information required to be filed under the act was declared to be classified and its disclosure was stated to be a misdemeanor. In addition to filing an initial statement and supporting documents, and annual copies of Form 990-A, trusts and foundations subject to the act would be required to furnish the attorney general with any notices from the Internal Revenue Service proposing disallowance of tax exemption, any final notices of disallowance, copies of amendments to pending instruments, any audits which the foundation may have had made, additions or changes in the governing board, material changes in value of assets, and all notices or papers relating to any legal proceeding involving the foundation. Failure to file any of this information within stated periods prescribed in the bill would subject the directors or trustees to a penalty not exceeding $100 for each day of failure after thirty days following notice from the attorney general of the delinquency.

The amended bill established a sliding scale of fees. Foundations and trusts the reasonable fair market value of whose assets was less than $25,000 were exempted from any payments. All others were subjected to an initial fee of $25. Those with assets of $25,000 to $500,000 were required to pay an annual fee of $10; for those with assets in excess of $500,000, the annual fee was set at $25. The original bill had contained a provision whereby the fees would automatically be earmarked for the use of the attorney general to maintain the registry and examine reports. This was deleted and a statement that these funds "may" be earmarked for the attorney general's use was substituted.

The amended bill also contained a provision granting to the attorney general a right to examine books and records of the trusts and foundations similar to that which he currently holds to examine the records of corporations. He would also be empowered to conduct whatever investigations were necessary for proper supervision within the scope of the act.

Unchanged in the amended bill was a provision granting the attorney general the power to institute suit for the removal of any officer, director, or trustee of a charitable trust or foundation for misfeasance, nonfeasance, or malfeasance in office, or for their limited disqualification or suspension on the ground of conflict of interest. Authority would also be given to the court to replace any fiduciary so removed if the trust indenture, charter, or bylaws did not provide a suitable method, or if replacement was not made within a reasonable time. In the case of suspension or disqualification for conflict of interest, the court could appoint a new trustee or director for the duration of such period of time as the conflict continued and could limit the authority of the appointee to areas in which the conflict exists.

The amended bill passed the House of Representatives on May 11, 1965, but the Senate failed to consider it before adjournment.

Since no call for a special session of the legislature was anticipated, further action was postponed until the next regular session in 1967.

The entire history of the attempted passage of this bill warrants further attention. It received the strong support of the attorney general and, in its final form, of many of the large foundations. Furthermore, the bill itself contained novel provisions that could serve as models for other states.

Hawaii. The attorney general of Hawaii has set a precedent among the states by requiring the submission of accounts of charitable trusts to his office under his powers as *parens patriae.* Both testamentary and inter vivos trusts are involved. Accounts are reviewed by an assistant attorney general, and where necessary, corrective measures may be recommended. There are certain trusts which, by their terms or under statute, require annual court approval of accounts. These trusts file a petition with the court, which then refers it to the attorney general, who selects a master. Upon receipt of the master's report, the attorney general prepares his own report and submits it to the court for disposition. The attorney general's office also participates in bills for instructions, petitions for deviation and *cy pres,* and requests for approval of appointment of trustees. The office has not, as a practice, reviewed reports from charitable corporations. This may be the result of a 1942 decision of the Hawaii Supreme Court that the attorney general could not be made a party defendant in a suit for misuse of funds that was brought against a charitable hospital by trustees of a trust directed to pay part of the net income to the hospital.[1] Although this decision is open to question,[2] it has not been reversed, and it has thus limited the power of the attorney general in that state in relation to corporate charities.

At present, accounts are received from 20 trusts each year. No search has been made for additional trusts that should be filing, nor has the office made any comments about a possible expansion of its activities. The primary importance of this program is that Hawaii is the only state in which the role of the attorney general as *parens patriae* has been interpreted in such a way as to give to him the power

---

[1] *Hite* v. *The Queen's Hospital,* 36 Hawaii 250 (1942).

[2] "This seems erroneous. It would seem that the trust was charitable, with the corporation merely a conduit through which the charitable benefits reached the community, and that the Attorney General should have been held a proper party either as the enforcer of charitable trusts, or as a proper agency to compel corporations to use their funds for their corporate purposes." Bogert, George G., and George T. Bogert, *op. cit.,* sec. 411, footnote 29.

to require receipt of reports on a regular basis. It is possible that this interpretation would be valid in other states as well, but this would depend to a degree upon the statutes and case law in the various states particularly in regard to any statutory powers conferred upon the attorney general.

Hawaii is also unique in having a statutory provision by which, in any proceeding involving a trust that is wholly or partially charitable and in which the attorney general has been cited by the court as a necessary or proper party, the court is empowered to require "the payment of all reasonable and necessary expenses incurred by the attorney general for the protection of the beneficial interests in, or for the proper conduct of, such proceedings."[1] The award may be made from the principal or income of the trust, or both, so long as it is reasonable in amount. In no other jurisdiction is an allowance of costs to the attorney general permitted. The existence of such a statute does assure that an attorney general's participation will not be hampered by lack of funds. It is against the common law tradition, however,[2] and would most likely not be viewed with favor in the majority of the states.

Washington. A Department of Charitable Trusts was first established in the attorney general's office in Washington in the 1950's, but its efforts to establish an active program of supervision have been hampered by lack of specific power. The courts of Washington are not at present required to notify the attorney general of proceedings involving charitable trusts; moreover, the attorney general's appearance is not necessary unless the question is clearly one of improper administration. A bill that would have imposed an accounting requirement on charitable trustees was introduced in 1959, but it died in committee. The attorney general then attempted to secure voluntary reporting, but he met with the problems of the lack of information on existing trusts, and a reluctance by trustees to supply more than a minimum amount of information and the refusal by most to submit periodic reports.

A decision of the Washington Supreme Court in 1961[3] implied by dicta that the attorney general had the right to maintain an action against trustees of a charitable trust concerning the course of administration of the trust without alleging mismanagement or breach of trust.

---

[1] Hawaii Rev. Laws, sec. 340–8.
[2] See *Thatcher* v. *City of St. Louis*, 343 Mo. 597, 122 S.W.2d 915 (1938).
[3] *State* v. *Taylor*, 58 Wash.2d 252, 362 P.2d 247 (1961). See also pp. 96 and 234.

However, the court refused to order an accounting in that case because it found that the attorney general's demands were unreasonable. The outcome of this case made the attorney general naturally reluctant to press for more imformation from individual trustees without statutory authority. Nevertheless, in 1962, he required all bank and trust companies and court clerks to supply him with information as to the existence of charitable trusts. His office received excellent cooperation from both sources, and approximately $8 million in charitable trust funds was reported.

The information obtained from this survey provided the impetus for a decision to introduce legislation to require trustees to register and report to the attorney general on a regular basis. In 1963 a version of the Uniform Supervision of Trustees for Charitable Purposes Act was introduced to the legislature.[1] The bill was accompanied by a statement prepared by the attorney general which contained information as to the operation of the Uniform Act in other states, and an estimate that an amount in excess of $100 million was held by charitable trusts in Washington. It received widespread publicity in newspapers throughout the state, and was supported by most of the charitable organizations. The bill was approved without change by an almost unanimous vote of the Senate in the closing days of the regular session, but since it reached the House at the close of the session, it was not acted upon. A bill relating to charitable solicitation also failed of passage in that year.

In 1965 the attorney general's office prepared legislation that combined the Uniform Act and the solicitation bills introduced in 1963. The purposes of the act were declared to be:

(a) To prevent deceptive and dishonest statements or conduct in the solicitation of funds by persons or organizations in the name of charity.

(b) To require full public disclosure of all material facts relating to persons and organizations soliciting funds for charitable purposes in the state of Washington and the nature of such charitable purposes.

(c) To facilitate public supervision over the administration of charitable trusts and similar relationships, clarifying and implementing the powers and duties of the attorney general with relation thereto.[2]

The definition section included the term "trustee" as defined in the Uniform Act, but excluded banks supervised by the supervisor of banking of the state of Washington, the Comptroller of Currency of

---

[1] State of Washington, Senate Bill No. 316, 38th Regular Session (1963).
[2] State of Washington, Senate Bill No. 93, 39th Regular Session (1965), sec. 1.

the United States, or the Board of Governors of the Federal Reserve System. The provisions for regulating soliciting organizations and professional fund-raisers[1] were similar to those in legislation now in effect in Illinois, New York, and Connecticut.[2] Section 13 required the attorney general to establish and maintain a register or registries of charitable organizations registered under the solicitation provisions, and in addition, or as a part of such register, a register of trustees of charitable trusts. Annual reports were to be required of these trustees.

The bill stated that the "wilful refusal by a trustee to make or file any report, to perform any other duties expressly required by this act, or to comply with any valid rule or regulation promulgated by the attorney general under this act, shall constitute a breach of trust." In addition, the act of knowingly making a false statement in any registration statement or report required by the act would constitute a felony; other violations of the act not otherwise provided for would be deemed gross misdemeanors. The bill also required the courts to give notice to the attorney general of judicial proceedings affecting or dealing with charitable trusts, a provision similar to that in the Michigan version of the Uniform Act. Finally, it was provided that if a court should refuse to enforce an order of the attorney general made after investigation and hearing, the court would be required to state its reasons clearly in the record, and the action would be subject to review by the Supreme Court.

A novel feature of this bill was a provision imposing fees to defray the cost of administering the act. In the case of charitable trusts an act stated:

> For initial filing of a trust instrument and inventory, a fee measured by one-half of one percent of the net value of the corpus of each trust, provided that such filing fee shall be not less than fifteen dollars nor more than two hundred fifty dollars as to any individual trust; and for each annual report of such trust filed thereafter with the attorney general, a fee measured by one-tenth of one percent of the net value of the trust corpus, provided that such annual filing fee shall be not less than ten dollars nor more than one hundred dollars.[3]

After the bill had been filed, objections from certain trustees led to a reduction of this amount to one-twentieth of one per cent of the net

---

[1] *Ibid.*, secs. 3 to 12, 21 to 23.
[2] See pp. 228–229 and Appendix B.
[3] State of Washington, Senate Bill No. 93, 39th Regular Session (1965), sec. 25.

value and the deletion of any reference to a minimum fee. The maximum amounts were not changed.

This bill failed of passage in the regular session. In the special session that followed, it was approved by the Senate, but became the subject of a party dispute in the House. Its passage was blocked when a minority group managed to delay action so that it would have required a two-thirds vote for approval. As a compromise, the legislature did enact a concurrent resolution directing the legislative council to conduct an interim study of the need for legislation to regulate solicitations and to consider the provisions of the draft legislation. The council was directed to report its findings to the next legislative session.[1]

If enacted, this legislation would have been the first in any state to combine regulation of solicitation with supervision of foundations and other charitable trusts. It is similar in this regard to legislation that was introduced in Pennsylvania in 1961 but failed of passage and has not been revived to date. The actual scope of the program established under the bill would not differ from that in Massachusetts. It does, however, present a model for amendments to legislation in states that regulate solicitations but do not attempt to supervise charitable trusts and foundations.

The provisions of the act relating to fees may also be of future importance. Attempts to impose even minimum fees for filing reports have met with serious objections in most states. Massachusetts is the only one that collects a fee ($3.00) with periodic reports, and complaints have been received from time to time that this fee is excessive. A bill was introduced in 1961 in California that would have imposed filing fees determined annually by the attorney general on the basis of the amount needed to defray the reasonable expense of administering the Uniform Act.[2] The fees were to be apportioned among all trusts and corporations in accordance with their annual income, but in no case were they to exceed $100 per year; moreover, any trust or corporation receiving an annual income of less than $5,000 was to be exempt. The bill met with serious objection. The Texas bill described above was also designed to provide fees sufficient to support the administration of a supervisory program. Provisions of this nature may well be the only method of overcoming the almost universal problem of lack of funds to establish adequate supervisory programs.

---

[1] State of Washington, House Concurrent Resolution No. 30, 39th Extraordinary Session (1965). Passed April 26, 1965.
[2] State of California, Senate Bill No. 934 (1961).

Increasing the Powers of the Attorney General by Registration and Reporting Statutes

The first state to take any concerted legislative action to increase specifically the powers of the attorney general was New Hampshire. In 1940 the attorney general of that state recommended adoption of a statute designed to grant to his office some of the powers held by the Charity Commissioners in England, particularly in connection with establishment of a registry, the imposition of annual reporting requirements, and a grant of investigatory powers.[1] The bill was rejected in 1940 and 1942; but following an almost unprecedented statement of support by the New Hampshire Supreme Court in 1943, it was passed.[2]

The New Hampshire legislation set a pattern that has been followed in nine other states. The second state was Rhode Island,[3] where legislative action followed the recommendations of a special committee established by the legislature itself to investigate the affairs of a Rhode Island enterpreneur who was charged with taking advantage of the tax-exempt status of several charitable trusts to further his private business interests.[4] South Carolina and Ohio both enacted statutes similar to New Hampshire's in 1953,[5] and in 1954 Massachusetts followed.[6]

Also during the early 1950's the National Association of Attorneys General and the National Conference of Commissioners on Uniform State Laws collaborated in the drafting of a Uniform Act for Supervision of Trustees for Charitable Purposes suitable for introduction in the several states. The interest of the attorneys general was aroused by an address at their 1946 annual meeting in which the attorney general of New Hampshire described the experience in that state with the registration statute.[7] In 1951 the National Association of Attorneys

---

[1] State of New Hampshire, Office of the Attorney General, *Biennial Reports* for the periods July 1, 1936 to June 30, 1938 and July 1, 1938 to June 30, 1940. State House, Concord, N.H. (mimeographed).

[2] N.H. Laws 1943, ch. 181; see also pp. 221 ff.

[3] Public Laws of 1950, ch. 2617.

[4] This same scheme had been the subject of an investigation by the United States Congress in 1948 that led to the amendment of the tax-exempt provisions of the Internal Revenue Code in 1950. See U.S. Congress, House of Representatives, Committee on Ways and Means, *Revenue Act of 1950: Report* to accompany H.R. 8920, 81st Congress, 2d Session, House Report 2319, Government Printing Office, Washington, 1950, p. 42.

[5] S.C. Laws 1953, No. 274; Ohio Laws 1953, amended Sen. Substitute Bill 196.

[6] Laws of Mass., Acts of 1954, ch. 529.

[7] National Association of Attorneys General, *Conference Proceedings*. Secretariat of the Council on State Governments, Chicago, 1946, p. 91.

General formally requested the National Conference of Commissioners on Uniform State Laws to "consider this subject for study and development of suggested state legislation."[1] At its 1952 convention the Association received from the Commissioners a tentative draft of legislation. It passed a resolution requesting the Commissioners to develop legislation in alternative forms, one containing a provision for mandatory reporting, the other leaving to each attorney general the decision as to whether to require reports in special cases.[2] As reported by Bogert, the principal argument against a permissive bill was that the common law power and duty of the attorney general to enforce the public interest in charitable trusts carried with it the power to take such actions as will enable him to obtain and record information, so that a merely permissive act was unnecessary, except as a suggestion of how to proceed.[3]

The Commissioners prepared two drafts, however, and, at the convention of the following year, the attorneys general adopted a resolution stating their desire to extend to the Commissioners their considered view that such model legislation "should contemplate mandatory rather than optional reporting by trustees and should place the mandatory duty of regulation upon a state regulatory agency."[4] The Uniform Act was finally adopted at the annual meeting of the commissioners in 1954, and it was subsequently approved in August of that year by the House of Delegates of the American Bar Association.[5]

The first state to adopt the Uniform Act was California, which enacted it in 1955 on an experimental basis for a two-year period.[6] The act was then extended to 1959[7] and thereafter was finally made permanent.[8] In 1959, Iowa also adopted an act modeled on the earlier legislation in Rhode Island.[9] The Uniform Act was adopted in Michigan[10] and Illinois[11] in 1961, and in Oregon in 1963,[12] bringing to 10 the number of states with registration and reporting statutes. During

---

[1] *Ibid.*, 1951, p. 184.
[2] *Ibid.*, 1952, p. 155.
[3] Bogert, George G., *op. cit.*, p. 645.
[4] National Association of Attorneys General, *op. cit.*, 1953, p. 198.
[5] Uniform Supervision of Trustees for Charitable Purposes Act, *Uniform Laws Annotated.* Edward Thompson Co., Brooklyn, N.Y., 1957, vol. 9C, p. 208.
[6] Cal. Stats. 1955, ch. 1820.
[7] Cal. Stats. 1957, ch. 2024.
[8] Cal. Stats. 1959, ch. 1258.
[9] Iowa Laws 1959, ch. 364.
[10] Mich. Public and Local Acts 1961, Public Act 101.
[11] Ill. Laws 1961, S.B. 297.
[12] Ore. Laws 1963, ch. 583.

this same period it was introduced in Arizona, Indiana, Wyoming, Texas, Pennsylvania, and Washington, but failed of passage.[1]

Charities Affected by New Legislation

In spite of the existence of a Uniform Act, the specific provisions included in the state supervisory statutes vary widely. The most difficult drafting and interpretation problems have arisen in connection with the coverage of the act. The New Hampshire legislation uses the *Restatement* definition of a charitable trust,[2] but it specifically exempts (1) inter vivos trusts until such time after the death of the settlor or donor as the charitable or public purpose expressed in such trust becomes vested in use or enjoyment and (2) charitable corporations holding property or funds for their charitable purposes.[3] Thus the act is effective only as to testamentary trusts and certain inter vivos trusts after the death of the donor, but contains no provisions for identifying these trusts at the time of creation.

The Rhode Island legislation also employs the *Restatement* definition of a charitable trust,[4] but the exemption provision states:

> The provisions of this chapter shall not be applicable to charitable, religious and educational institutions holding funds in trust exclusively for their own charter or corporate purposes nor to trusts in which the charitable interest is contingent upon the happening of an uncertain future event; provided, however, that upon the happening of said event vesting the charitable interest such trust shall thereafter be subject to all the provisions hereof.[5]

This language has been construed by the attorney general as exempting institutions of a charitable, religious, or educational nature holding funds in trust exclusively for their own charter or corporate purposes, but not foundations organized as corporations. To date, this interpretation has not been challenged by any corporation.

The wording of the Ohio act follows the language of the Rhode Island act defining charitable trusts and excluding charitable, religious, and educational institutions; but it adds in the exempt category "trusts until such time as the charitable, religious or educational purpose expressed in such trust becomes vested in use or enjoyment" and "insti-

---

[1] Taylor, Eleanor K., "Accountability of Charitable Trusts," *Ohio State Law Journal*, vol. 18, 1957, pp. 157, 165.

[2] *Restatement of the Law of Trusts (Second)*, *op. cit.*, sec. 348.

[3] N.H. Rev. Stat. Ann., sec. 7:21.

[4] R.I. Gen. Laws Ann., ch. 18–9–4.

[5] R.I. Gen. Laws Ann., ch. 18–9–15.

tutions created and operated as agencies of the state government or any political subdivision thereof."[1] The language of this section caused immediate problems, primarily because in 1954 the Ohio court had held that for the purpose of exemption from inheritance tax an institution for public charitable purposes was established upon the distribution to trustees for public charitable or educational purposes of funds given in trust for such use.[2] The attorney general ruled informally that for registration purposes he was interpreting the word "institution" to be synonymous with "corporation," and that therefore nonprofit corporations need not register funds held for general corporate purposes; he acted on the ground that any other interpretation would render the act nugatory.[3]

In 1960 the attorney general announced that the earlier decision of that office excluding all corporations from the act was incorrect. He stated that henceforth registration would be required of:

> . . . all charitable organizations—including corporations—operating in this state which have been or will be filing Forms 990A with the Internal Revenue Service. Such charitable trusts are further identified as those which have qualified, or are to be qualified, as exempt charitable organizations under the provisions of Section 501 (c) (3) of the "Internal Revenue Code of 1954 as Amended" and not exempted from filing annual returns under Section 6033 (b) of such Code.[4]

The information release contained the following explanation:

> This information is released to secure registration under Section 109.26, R.C., of those corporations not yet registered which are included under the provisions of Section 109.23, R.C.
>
> Many incorporated charitable trusts have already registered; others have not, due to advice in the early days of the Charitable Trusts Act that registration of corporations was not required. It is now recognized that exclusion of all corporations was incorrect.
>
> Section 109.23, R.C., defines Charitable Trust to include "any fiduciary relationship . . . subjecting . . . the . . . corporation . . . by whom the property is held to equitable duties. . . ." The last sentence of this section provides for exclusion of "institutions holding funds in trust or otherwise exclusively for their own purposes." "Own purposes" is the key phrase. An incorporated charitable foundation, for example, has as its purpose the equitable duty of holding funds in trust for distribution

---

[1] Ohio Rev. Code Ann., sec. 109.23.
[2] In re Estate of Oglebay, 162 Ohio St. 1, 120 N.E.2d 437 (1954).
[3] Klapp, Ralph, and Neva Wertz, "Supervision of Charitable Trusts in Ohio," Ohio State Law Journal, vol. 18, 1957, p. 181.
[4] State of Ohio, Mark McElroy, Attorney General, Information Sheet No. 2, Form CT–4 Columbus, Ohio, March 30, 1960 (mimeographed).

to named charitable purposes; therefore, there is no identifiable *"own purpose"* to qualify for exclusion under Section 109.23, R.C., as would occur when donors make outright gifts to such charitable institutions as churches, hospitals, or colleges.[1]

In January, 1963, following a change of administration, the newly elected attorney general announced a return to the original interpretation of the act, so that thereafter corporate foundations would not be required to comply with the reporting provisions.

The South Carolina statute applies to "trustees of charitable trusts," but then exempts churches, cemeteries, orphanages operated in conjunction with churches, nonprofit colleges or universities, school districts, and banking institutions that act as trustees under the supervision of the State Board of Banking Control or federal banking agencies.[2]

In direct contrast to all of these provisions, the Massachusetts act is applicable to all "public charities within the Commonwealth" as well as to foreign corporations engaged in charitable work or raising funds in the Commonwealth, with the sole exception of "any property held for any religious purpose by any public charity incorporated or unincorporated."[3] The term "public charity" has been defined in regulations promulgated by the attorney general as follows:

> those endeavors commonly regarded as constituting a public charity and shall include, without limitation:
> A. Any corporation which constitutes a public charity organized under Chapter 180 of the General Laws of Massachusetts or created by special act of the General Court.
> B. Any Trust which constitutes a public charity, whether created by will or inter vivos instrument including:
>   1. A Trust where the current distribution of principal or income or any part of either is left to the discretion of the trustee, limited to benefit other charitable organizations, limited to benefit a stated charitable purpose, or limited to benefit one named charitable organization.
>   2. A Trust where the trustee has no discretion as to distribution of principal or income or any part of either, and current distribution is to be made, according to the trust instrument to a named charitable organization or organizations, or beneficiaries named by independent persons under the terms of the trust instrument.
>   3. A Trust where the trustee has the obligation or the discretion to

---

[1] *Ibid.*
[2] S.C. Code Ann., sec. 67–85.
[3] Mass. Gen. Laws Ann., ch. 12, sec. 8F.

accumulate the income until a stated condition or time is met, and then distribute either principal, or income, or both in any of the manners described in paragraph . . . B 1, or . . . B 2 above.

C. Any other voluntary association or undertaking which constitutes a public charity.[1]

A major problem of the drafters of the Uniform Act was the definition of the charities that would be subject to the requirements of a supervisory statute. At the annual meeting of the Commissioners in 1953, considerable time was devoted to the discussion of this problem, and each of the variations just described was considered.[2] Strong opposition was voiced to the inclusion of charitable corporations to which property has been given with a request that it be applied to one particular corporate purpose and not for general corporate purposes. Objection was also made to the inclusion of operating institutions such as schools or colleges, hospitals, and religious institutions, whether any of these holds funds in trust or otherwise for charity or for general or specific corporate purposes. A motion to remove religious and educational institutions from the act failed by a narrow vote. As to other charitable corporations, the language proposed was taken from the New Hampshire act. The chairman noted during discussion that the draft was a compromise and that the reason for omitting all corporate charities was political. He noted that the attorneys general had been kept advised of the status of the draft, that they had voiced no objections, and that actually some of them had expressed approval. He concluded that the attorneys general, as a body, must feel that there was a strong likelihood that they could obtain passage of the act as it was presented to them, and that therefore it would be undesirable to extend the coverage. At this same meeting it was voted to require annual reports from trusts for charitable purposes only when the charitable interest was vested in enjoyment.

When the act came before the Commissioners for final approval in 1954, its name was changed from the "Uniform Supervision of Charitable Trusts Act" to the "Uniform Act for Supervision of Trustees for Charitable Purposes," reflecting a feeling that its coverage was

---

[1] Commonwealth of Massachusetts, Department of the Attorney General, *Regulations of the Director of Public Charities.* State House, Boston, filed with the Secretary of State on July 26, 1962 (mimeographed).

[2] See *Proceedings* in Committee of the Whole, Uniform Supervision of Charitable Trusts Act, National Conference of Commissioners on Uniform State Laws, Chicago, August 17–22, 1953 (mimeographed).

broader than just charitable trusts.[1] The draft, however, excluded religious, educational, and hospital institutions despite the 1953 vote. The subcommittee members reported their feeling that the subject of these institutions was too controversial and should therefore be excluded from the act. They may have been influenced in part by the views of Professor Bogert, which were expressed in an article in the *Michigan Law Review* published in 1954 just prior to the meeting. He listed six possible categories of charitable agencies which could be brought within the supervision of the act:

    a. Individuals, banks and trust companies holding property under living or testamentary trusts for charity.

    b. Individuals, banks and trust companies holding property in trust for charitable corporations.

    c. Charitable corporations to whom property has been given absolutely under an agreement that it will be applied to one particular corporate purpose but not for corporate purposes in general and not to be held in trust.

    d. Property held absolutely and not in trust by membership corporations or corporations not-for-profit.

    e. Property held by community trusts.

    f. Property held by community chests.

    g. Funds raised for charitable purposes as a result of a campaign or drive and held by individuals or unincorporated associations, and not covered by the preceding classification.[2]

He noted that the two questions of judgment involved in deciding which organizations should be covered were: whether or not the dangers of neglect and abuse were substantial and equal in all cases; and assuming differences in degree of danger, whether or not, for the purpose of overcoming political opposition, it would be expedient to limit coverage to the agencies within which there are frequent and important dangers and to exclude from the act the agencies where the danger is slight. Bogert's conclusion was:

> In the opinion of the writer it would be wise to limit the original application of the act to cases (a), (b), (c), and (g) above, where the dangers of inactivity and dormancy are greatest, and to exclude the other cases from the scope of the act, where the chances of neglect and abuse are relatively slight. This choice would, it is believed, enhance greatly the chances of wide adoption of the act, would eliminate perhaps four-fifths of the evils of the present system, and would build a foundation

---

[1] *Ibid.*
[2] Bogert, George G., *op. cit.*, pp. 652 ff.

on which the act could be extended after the plan had proved itself, if experience showed that an extension was desirable.[1]

The Uniform Act, as finally adopted by the Commissioners, applies to all trustees holding property for charitable purposes over which the state or the attorney general has enforcement or supervisory powers. Sections 2 and 3 state:

> Section 2. Definition of Trustee. "Trustee" means (a) any individual, group of individuals, corporations, or other legal entity holding property in trust pursuant to any charitable trust, (b) any corporation which has accepted property to be used for a particular charitable corporate purpose as distinguished from the general purposes of the corporation, and (c) a corporation formed for the administration of a charitable trust, pursuant to the directions of the settlor or at the instance of the trustee.
>
> Section 3. Exclusions from the Act. This act does not apply to the United States, any state, territory, or possession of the United States, the District of Columbia, the Commonwealth of Puerto Rico, or to any of their agencies or governmental subdivisions, to an officer of a religious organization who holds property for religious purposes, or to a charitable corporation organized and operated primarily for educational, religious or hospital purposes.[2]

This language has caused considerable difficulty. Clause (b) of section 2 is the most difficult to interpret. In clauses (a) and (c) of section 2 the word "trust" is used to describe the nature of the ownership of property, but it is omitted in clause (b). Since the word "trust" is not used, the language could be taken to mean that it includes more than those situations where a donor has made an absolute gift to a charitable corporation but the corporation has indicated its intention to apply the funds to a particular purpose. It may also include those instances where the donor has expressed in precatory language a desire to have the property applied to a particular purpose; in this case the corporation would be placed in the anomalous position of being required to report on the disposition of the funds even though it was under no legal obligation to apply them to the specific purposes and would otherwise be exempted from the operation of the act.[3]

Further difficulty is caused by the fact that in those jurisdictions in

---

[1] *Ibid.*, p. 653.

[2] Uniform Supervision of Trustees for Charitable Purposes Act, *op. cit.* Reprinted in Appendix B.

[3] See discussion in Lees, John G., "Governmental Supervision of Charitable Trusts," *Current Trends in State Legislation (1956–1957)*, University of Michigan Law School Legislative Research Center, Ann Arbor, 1957, pp. 609, 648.

which the funds of charitable corporations have been construed by the courts to be held "in the nature of a trust" or to be "quasi-trusts," it is impossible to determine whether the language of clauses (a) and (c) would require reporting by all charitable corporations not specifically exempted as being for educational, religious, or hospital purposes. Furthermore, when trustees of a charitable trust subsequently receive court permission to incorporate, a question arises as to whether they are then holding their property in trust within the meaning of the act.

The most cogent objection to the language of the Uniform Act, however, is that it tends to perpetuate, and even accentuate, the view that a distinction should be made between the duties of directors of charitable corporations and the duties of trustees. This distinction, based as it is on form rather than function, permits possibilities for evasion that are inimical to the public interest. This is particularly true in the case of foundations.

California recognized the deficiency in the wording of the Uniform Act in 1959 when it re-enacted the statute on a permanent basis.[1] The act was amended so that it became applicable to "all charitable corporations and trustees holding property for charitable purposes." An added section defined charitable corporations as "any nonprofit corporation organized under the laws of this State for charitable or eleemosynary purposes and any similar foreign corporation doing business or holding property in this State for such purposes."[2] The Oregon act adopted the same language.

In Illinois the attorney general, in regulations promulgated in June of 1962, held that the language of the Uniform Act required the registration and reporting of any corporation, business or charitable, which has accepted property for charitable purposes, including all Illinois not-for-profit corporations which administer funds for charitable purposes, with respect to such funds, unless the corporations specifically come within the act's exclusions for corporations or trusts holding property for educational, religious, hospital, or cemetery purposes. He explained this section as follows:

> In my view, clause (b) of Section 3 subjects to the Act's coverage all charitable corporate foundations operating in Illinois. . . . Clause (b) is susceptible of the interpretation that the words "particular charitable corporate purposes as distinguished from the general purpose of the corporation" indicate that only those charitable corporations which ac-

---

[1] Cal. Stats. 1959, ch. 1258.
[2] Cal. Gov. Code, sec. 12582.1.

cept property for a particular purpose specified by the donor are subject to the Act's coverage and that when such corporations solicit funds for general charitable purposes, they are immune from the Act's coverage. The administration of funds solicited by charitable corporate foundations for their general purposes was a special object of concern to our General Assembly, and I do not believe that the General Assembly meant to exempt funds in the hands of such corporations from the Act's coverage.

No sound reason exists for including in the Act's coverage trustees of trusts created by trust instruments and excluding those created by the transfer of funds to a corporation organized under a corporation act and whose charter creates a trust for charitable beneficiaries.[1]

This regulation was successfully challenged in a lower court in Illinois by a charitable corporation which had been requested to file under the act.[2] The attorney general filed an appeal, but also sponsored a bill in the Illinois legislature to amend the act. This bill was passed on July 15, 1963, rendering the judicial proceeding moot.[3] The Illinois act now applies to "Any trustee defined in section 3, holding property of a value in excess of $4000."[4] In section 3, the term "trustee" is now defined as "any individual, group of individuals, corporation or other legal entity holding property for any charitable purpose."

The Michigan act also adopted the language of the Uniform Act. The attorney general has ruled that corporate foundations are required to register and report, but, as in Illinois, he has received resistance from certain foundations. A bill to amend the act was introduced in the 1963 session of the legislature, but failed of passage.

Just prior to the adoption of the Uniform Act by the Commissioners on Uniform State Laws, the American Bar Association's Committee on Charitable Trusts presented as its 1954 report a critique of the proposed act wherein they predicted that the sections dealing with coverage and definitions might cause confusion.[5] The Committee wondered whether the words "individual" and "corporation" were broad enough to include all those who administer property for charitable purposes. They questioned the use of the phrase "for a particular charitable corporate purpose," and suggested that if its meaning was so obscure as to justify them in posing the question, it could only lead

---

[1] Clark, William G., "The New Charitable Trust Act," *Illinois Bar Journal,* vol. 50, 1962, pp. 753 ff.
[2] *Abeles Foundation* v. *Clark,* District Court, Cook County, No. 62C–7307.
[3] Ill. Laws 1963, p. 1462.
[4] Ill. Rev. Stat., ch. 14, sec. 52.
[5] Wynn, James O., "Accountability of Trustees of Charitable Trusts," *Trusts and Estates,* vol. 93, 1954, p. 938.

to future controversy. They also had doubts as to the meaning of the term "not for the purposes of the corporation in general." They thought that a literal interpretation would place a corporation created for the general or sole purpose of charity entirely outside the purview of the statute. This was the problem faced in Ohio in that same year.

The predictions of this Committee have been borne out. No other sections of the Uniform Act have caused as much difficulty as these definition and exemption sections. Karst went so far as to state that "this is one case in which the Commissioners should amend their law to conform to a change made by an individual state."[1] In 1963 the Commissioners reconstituted a Committee on Charitable Trusts which reviewed the act and voted to recommend a change in these sections. No action has been taken to implement this decision, however.

The Uniform Act for Supervision of Trustees for Charitable Purposes

One of the principal substantive provisions of the Uniform Act is section 4[2] which provides that the attorney general shall establish and maintain a register of trustees subject to the act and authorizes him to conduct whatever investigations shall be necessary and to obtain from public records, court officers, tax authorities, and the like whatever information shall be necessary to establish and maintain the register.

Section 5 imposes a duty on every trustee subject to the act who has received property for charitable purposes to file with the attorney general, within six months after any part of the income or principal is authorized or required to be applied to a charitable purpose, a copy of the instrument providing for his title, powers, or duties. Charities already in existence are required to file within six months of the time the act takes effect.

Section 6 imposes a duty on trustees to file periodic written reports, under oath, with the attorney general. Determination as to the contents of these reports and the time of filing are placed within the discretion of the attorney general, who is required to promulgate rules and regulations relating to the nature of the reports, the time for filing, and the manner and execution thereof. He may classify trusts and other relationships concerning property held for charitable purposes as to purpose, nature of assets, duration of the trust, amount of assets,

---

[1] Karst, Kenneth L., *op. cit.*, p. 457.
[2] For complete text, see Uniform Supervision of Trustees for Charitable Purposes Act, *op. cit.*, pp. 210–215. Reprinted in Appendix B.

amounts to be devoted to charitable purposes, and nature of trustee or otherwise; and he may establish different rules for different classes to the end that

1. he shall receive reasonably current, periodic reports as to all charitable trusts or other relationships of a similar nature, which will enable him to ascertain whether they are being properly administered, and
2. that periodic reports shall not unreasonably add to the expense of the administration of charitable trusts and similar relationships.[1]

An account filed by a trustee in any court which substantially complies with the rules and regulations may be filed as a report required by the section.

The attorney general is authorized by section 7 to make additional rules and regulations, and by section 8 to investigate transactions and relationships of trustees subject to the act to ascertain whether or not the property held for charitable purposes is being properly administered. To this end he may require individuals to appear and give information under oath and to produce papers and other evidence. Safeguards regarding notice of hearing, and a provision conferring on the attorney general a subpoena power, subject to court supervision, are included in section 9.

Section 10 requires that the register, copies of instruments, and reports be open to public inspection, subject to reasonable rules and regulations. Section 11 states:

The Attorney General may institute appropriate proceedings to secure compliance with this act and to secure the proper administration of any trust or other relationship to which this act applies. The powers and duties of the Attorney General provided in this act are in addition to his existing powers and duties. Nothing in this act shall impair or restrict the jurisdiction of any court with respect to any of the matters covered by it.

In section 12, the act is declared to apply regardless of any contrary provisions of any instrument.

The final sections, 13 and 14, are aimed at giving the attorney general information as to the creation of charitable funds. They require that the custodian of records of courts having jurisdiction over charitable trusts furnish copies of such papers as the attorney general may require. In addition, every state officer, agency, board, or commission that receives applications for tax exemption from any charitable trust

---

[1] *Ibid.*, sec. 6b.

or other similar relationship in which the trustee is subject to the act shall annually notify the attorney general of all such applications.

The American Bar Association Committee's critique of the Uniform Act made only minor comments as to these provisions. The members did point out that the task of implementing the creation of the registry would be of major proportions in the older states, and they wondered whether, without a specific duty and administrative implementation of this duty, the attorney general would receive necessary information from other state officers.[1] They also questioned the lack of sanctions for fiduciaries who failed to comply. The possibility of providing for withdrawal of tax exemption for failure to file documents was suggested.[2]

The drafters of the Uniform Act were clearly influenced by the statutes already in force in New Hampshire, Rhode Island, and Ohio, and followed the format of those acts by placing the registry in the office of the attorney general and conferring duties on him rather than on a separate commission or on another state official. Bogert suggested that it would be better to provide for the creation in the attorney general's office of a position known as the Supervisor of Charitable Trusts to which an assistant attorney general could be assigned than to leave the duty of establishing such a position to the attorney general alone; but this was not accepted.[3] The lack of sanctions on trustees for noncompliance was explained by Bogert as resulting from the fact that they are in all likelihood unnecessary, since willful violations would probably be grounds for removal of the trustees or forfeiture of their fees in any case. The act's omission of any requirement that fees be established for filing reports was deliberate and was based on the Commissioners' feeling that this was a matter to be left to the states. Also specifically omitted were provisions requiring that the attorney general be an indispensable party to court actions and proceedings affecting or dealing with charitable trusts, and that he approve of compromise agreements, judgments, or settlements involving or affecting a charitable trust. These provisions had been a part of the second tentative draft of the Uniform Law,[4] but were omitted in the final version. The Uniform Act as adopted in Michigan does contain a provi-

---

[1] Wynn, James O., *op. cit.,* p. 939.
[2] *Ibid.*
[3] Bogert, George G., "Proposed Legislation . . . ," *op. cit.,* p. 655.
[4] See Special Committee on Uniform Act for Supervision of Charitable Trusts, *Report,* National Conference of Commissioners on Uniform State Laws, Chicago, 1953, secs. 10, 11 (mimeographed).

sion requiring that the attorney general be given notice and a copy of petitions for accountings for the disposition or distribution of the assets of charitable trusts; and it states that the court may not pass upon such petitions without proof that such notice was given.[1]

The Uniform Act also omits specific provisions defining the situs of trusts to be covered by the act, as well as means for relieving the burden of trustees who may be required to file different reports in several states. Finally, the act makes no attempt to establish standards for fiduciaries of charitable funds, nor does it specifically prevent a settlor from relieving fiduciaries from personal liability, as the Rhode Island statute does.

The purpose of all of the Uniform Acts adopted by the Conference of Commissioners on Uniform State Laws is to make the laws of those states that enact them as consistent with one another as possible. In a field such as charity, it is assumed that variations in state practice as well as in substantive state law will require the modification of certain specific provisions in any proposed act. This has, of course, been the case with the Uniform Act for Supervision of Trustees for Charitable Purposes. With the exception of its poorly drafted definition and exemption sections, it contains the basic elements for the establishment of an effective supervisory program. It is to be hoped, however, that the faulty sections will be amended before they are enacted in any other states.

---

[1] Mich. Stat. Ann., sec. 26.1200(6).

CHAPTER VIII

State Supervisory Programs
in Action

Prior to the final promulgation of the Uniform Supervision of Trustees for Charitable Purposes Act in 1954, five states had adopted legislation designed to increase the common law enforcement duties of the attorney general by granting him power to establish an active program of supervision. The operation of these programs has varied from state to state owing in part to the language of the enabling legislation, in part to differences in the facilities available to the administrators, and in part to variations in the size and number of the charitable endeavors in the state. Each of the programs of these five states is described in this chapter. The Iowa program is also included, although the legislation establishing it was passed in 1959, because it followed the language of the Rhode Island statute rather than that of the Uniform Act.

New Hampshire

The legislation passed in New Hampshire in 1943 was the first that placed a positive duty on trustees of certain charitable trusts to make periodic reports to a state official on the administration of their trusts. Immediately after the passage of this act, the attorney general's office undertook a survey of the records in the probate courts of the state to discover all wills that provided for the creation of charitable trusts. Almost $9 million in 900 trust estates were recorded, the funds ranging in amount from $100 to $3 million. The survey uncovered "loose and distracted administration" in an estimated 25 per cent of the cases.[1]

This study took two years to complete. It entailed, in addition to the search of probate records, the preparation of a register and a file for each trust describing the nature of the charity, the amount involved, the terms of the trust, the charitable beneficiaries designated, the investment provisions, the names and addresses of the trustees appointed, the amount of bond furnished and the name of the surety, and the date of the last account.

Letters were sent to all trustees advising them of their duty to furnish reports, and a report form prepared by the attorney general was included. This form was based on the standard form for trustees' accounts used in New Hampshire. It required details as to amount of principal; amounts received on account of principal; payments or deductions from principal, including losses, sales, and expenses; a detailed schedule of all assets; income in the hands of trustees according to their last report; amounts received on account of income; payments from income for the expenses of operating the trust; amounts paid to beneficiaries with their names and addresses; compensation of trustees; a recapitulation; the date a last court account was filed; and the amount and name of the surety bond. The notarized signatures of the trustees certifying the truth and accuracy of the report were required. This form is still used in New Hampshire, and has been copied or used as the basis for report forms in several other states.

Each report received was personally examined by the director of charitable trusts. He has described the general results of this inspection as follows:

> This initial examination produced very beneficial results. Generally speaking, the main effect was not so much to correct criminal or bad faith administration as to substitute active operation for passive waiting. Dormant funds came to life again; efficiency and economy were promoted; probate accounts increased in number and were more complete—some trustees not having reported for periods ranging from five to twenty years; undistributed income was turned over to the intended charities; the prudence of investments improved, with corpus no longer speculatively sacrificed to income where life tenants were involved; charges for expenses and fees were controlled; the bad practice of in-

---

[1] State of New Hampshire, Office of the Attorney General, *Biennial Report* for the period July 1, 1942 to June 30, 1944. State House, Concord, N.H. (mimeographed).

come accumulation was arrested; petitions by trustees for instructions increased, especially where changes in circumstances created doubts as to what should be done; there was a flood of petitions for deviation and cy pres application—all of this with resulting encouragement to charity-minded benefactors. Unfortunately, a few funds had been lost or commingled beyond tracing.[1]

The director of charitable trusts estimated in 1963 that approximately $110 million of charitable funds in 1,500 trusts were being supervised and enforced by his department. Of these, 20 were inter vivos trusts, and the remainder were testamentary.

The office became actively involved in enforcement, so that its participation in court proceedings increased markedly. The new activity was due in part to the provision in the 1943 legislation requiring that the attorney general be made a party to matters concerning charitable trusts.[2] From 1950 to 1962, the attorney general participated in 344 cases involving charitable interests submitted to and adjudicated by the courts of New Hampshire. Most of these cases involved attempts to reactivate dormant trust funds by petition to the court for application of the *cy pres* doctrine or for deviation. For example, a bequest of nearly $1 million, which had to be used within twenty years to build a school if it was to enjoy the accretion of another testamentary fund of $250,000, was reactivated two years before the termination date. A large high school was built with $400,000, and remainder was placed in a trust as an endowment fund for the school. In another case accumulated income of $150,000 of a trust created for hospital purposes was used to increase hospital facilities in the designated town, and the trust was reactivated. Trustees of a trust that had been dormant and without accounting for more than twenty years were required by the court to sell real estate that was found to be unproductive and wasteful. The sale brought $50,000, bringing the total fund to $150,000, all of which was used for the purpose of the trust.

The New Hampshire office also cooperated with the attorneys general of Massachusetts, New York, and Illinois on three separate cases involving New Hampshire decedents or gifts for New Hampshire residents. In one, a ten-year report was obtained from trustees in Illinois,

---

[1] D'Amours, Ernest R., "Charitable Trusts: New Hampshire's Experience with Supervision and Enforcement," *New Hampshire Bar Journal,* vol. 5, July, 1963, pp. 217, 220.
[2] N.H. Rev. Stat. Ann., sec. 17:29.

and programs were established to distribute income to New Hampshire charities according to the terms of the trust.[1]

Several of the cases involving charitable interests in which the director of charitable trusts participated were decided by the Supreme Court of New Hampshire. In *Orr* v. *Moses*,[2] the court held that the provision of a testamentary trust permitting use of the net income and as much of the principal as shall be necessary for the support and comfort of a widow during her lifetime did not authorize invasion of principal for gifts that merely contributed to the widow's happiness and peace of mind; the decision thereby preserved a large proportion of a remainder gift for charitable purposes. In another case involving construction of a will, the court protected a charitable interest of $350,000 by upholding the attorney general's contention that the class of heirs at law who were named as beneficiaries should be given a restricted interpretation.[3]

These results are all the more striking in that, although all testamentary trustees are required by New Hampshire laws to account to the courts annually, prior to the 1943 legislation, the courts were not required to notify the attorney general of these proceedings and only did so in some instances.

The New Hampshire legislation states that the attorney general shall make such rules and regulations as may be reasonable and necessary to secure records or other information for the operation of the registry and for the supervision, investigation, and enforcement of charitable trusts.[4] Regulations promulgated on February 6, 1957, require that reports be submitted by every fiduciary holding funds that shall or may be used for charitable purposes, including trusts in which there are one or more interested life tenants and those where the charitable remainder is contingent. However, upon application to the director of charitable trusts, a trustee may be excused from the duty to report annually and directed to report at less frequent intervals if (a) the remainder charitable interest is so remotely contingent that vesting of the same appears almost negligible and (b) if the charitable interest is very small.

---

[1] See State of New Hampshire, Office of the Attorney General, *Biennial Reports* for years 1942 to 1964, *op. cit.*, for further details.
[2] 94 N.H. 309, 52 A.2d 128 (1947).
[3] *Merchants National Bank* v. *Berry*, 101 N.H. 496, 148 A.2d 280 (1959).
[4] N.H. Rev. Stat. Ann., sec. 7:22.

The regulations also provide that a copy of an account or report made to the probate court is acceptable to meet the statutory requirements[1] if it contains all the information specified. Final probate accounts must show the assets of the trust at their market value; and the principal and income accounts must be distinctly and separately stated. The regulations also prohibit postponement of payment of trustees' compensation unless a good reason is shown. They require trustees to file a copy of the applications for income tax exemption required under the Internal Revenue Code.

The statute also grants the attorney general broad powers to conduct investigation of charitable trusts at any time to determine whether they are administered in accordance with law and with the terms and purposes thereof. To date, the office has not found it necessary to conduct any formal investigation of this nature.

The continuous supervision of charitable funds is carried on by the director of charitable trusts of the state of New Hampshire, who is appointed by the governor with the advice and consent of the council for a term of five years. He acts under the supervision of the attorney general, and he possesses and may exercise all the common law and statutory rights, duties, and powers of the attorney general in connection with the supervision, administration, and enforcement of charitable trusts.[2] The director personally supervises the examination of all reports filed, consults with trustees as to their duties, and handles court proceedings. The office staff consists only of the director and a registrar, although they have received assistance occasionally from clerks or law students.

Assistance to fiduciaries as well as beneficiaries is considered an important part of the director's duties:

> A supervisory office also serves as an information center and clearing house for advice to trustees which sometimes makes it unnecessary for them to undertake formal proceedings for instructions. Frequent consultations are held informally concerning the administration of a trust at the request of trustees themselves. Oft times the office is asked by trustees to prepare petitions to the court in order to save expense on small trusts. Accounting assistance is provided in numerous cases where the income from a trust does not seem to justify retaining the services

---

[1] N.H. Rev. Stat. Ann., sec. 7:28.

[2] N.H. Rev. Stat. Ann., sec. 7:20, as amended by Acts of 1949, sec. 39:1, and Acts of 1951, sec. 246:2. Under the provision of the statute as originally enacted, the attorney general was empowered to appoint an assistant attorney general to carry out the provisions of the act.

of an accountant or where an examination of the reports presents a vague or ambiguous picture after long years of trust management.[1]

The files of the office have been classified according to the purpose of the trusts, the names of trustees, and alphabetically, so that it is possible to obtain information as to the beneficial nature of the registered charitable trusts. In 1962, a directory of trusts created for broad charitable uses and for scholarships was published to meet numerous requests for information. The original supply of 500 was exhausted, but no funds were available for publication of reprints or supplements. The regulations state that records of any charitable trust in the register may be inspected at reasonable times by any person who can show that his interest as a member of the beneficiary public may be directly or indirectly affected by the administration of such trust.

The director of charitable trusts has also been active in drafting and submitting legislation to improve the operation of the act and the administration of charitable trusts. In 1947 the scope of trusts covered by the act was increased to include inter vivos trusts following the death of the settlor and the vesting of the charitable interest.[2] This was a compromise with an original draft which would have included all inter vivos trusts from the date of creation. Several attempts have also been made to include corporate foundations, but have failed of passage, as did a 1959 bill to require the filing of inter vivos trust instruments at the time of creation and the imposition of a positive duty on the trustees of these trusts to notify the director of the existence of a charitable trust at the death of a settlor.

In 1955 two statutes drafted by the attorney general's office to lessen the burdens and expenses of administering smaller estates were enacted. One act authorizes the judges of probate to appoint suitable persons to serve as public trustees at the court's pleasure. The public trustees are under a duty to administer small charitable funds that the court can assign to them whenever it is found that the practical difficulty or unreasonable expenses involved in administering such a trust would tend to defeat its purposes. The trustees are permitted to establish common trust funds for the investment of these trusts.[3] The second statute authorizes a judge of probate to permit the filing of a bond, without sureties, in estates of $5,000 or less.[4] The office of public trus-

---

[1] D'Amours, Ernest R., "The Benefits to Fiduciaries from the Supervision of Charities," *New Hampshire Bar Journal,* vol. 2, April, 1960, pp. 161, 167.
[2] N.H. Laws 1947, ch. 94.
[3] N.H. Laws 1955, ch. 183; N.H. Rev. Stat. Ann., sec. 565:2a–c.
[4] N.H. Laws 1955, ch. 20; N.H. Rev. Stat. Ann., sec. 564:1.

tee, although long in existence in England, has not been created else-where in the United States.

The requirement that notice be given to the attorney general of court proceedings involving charitable interests was expanded in 1959 so that the attorney general is now considered a necessary party to any agreement between executors, creditors, legatees, or heirs-at-law when-ever such agreement may directly or indirectly affect a charitable interest.[1] This legislation was drafted following a holding of the New Hampshire court that, although the attorney general was an indispen-sable party in the enforcement and supervision of charitable trusts, his approval was not required for an executor's settlement by compromise of claims against an estate, even though it might indirectly affect a residuary charitable trust created therein.[2] In 1963, the director pre-pared and introduced legislation to broaden the scope of the *cy pres* doctrine.[3]

The New Hampshire Act for Supervision of Charitable Trusts im-poses a duty on all registers of probate to forward such copies of pa-pers and such information as to the records and files in his office relat-ing to charitable trusts as the attorney general shall request, and requires them to notify the attorney general as soon as possible after the probate in common form of any will containing clauses creating a charitable trust.[4] In practice, this statutory requirement is not widely observed. By informal agreement, the inheritance tax department of the state does supply the director with the names of estates involving charitable trusts created by will. The attorney general's office is in contact from time to time with the State Tax Commission in connec-tion with the annual reports of town trust funds. When these funds are invested in common trust funds, the town trustees are required to file with the attorney general's office a copy of the annual report filed with the Tax Commission.

The attorneys general of New Hampshire have rightly been singled out as deserving "great credit for the pioneer work they have done in establishing a model system of supervision and enforcement" of char-itable trusts.[5] Working with a minimum staff and budget, the director and registrar have not only made impressive contributions to the ad-

---

[1] N.H. Laws 1959, ch. 16; now N.H. Rev. Stat. Ann., sec. 556:27.
[2] *Burtman* v. *Butman,* 94 N.H. 412, 54 A.2d 367 (1947).
[3] See pp. 76–77.
[4] N.H. Rev. Stat. Ann., sec. 7:29.
[5] Bogert, George G., "Proposed Legislation Regarding State Supervision of Charities," *Michigan Law Review,* vol. 52, 1954, p. 641.

ministration of charitable trusts in New Hampshire but have assisted officials in other states in drafting supervisory legislation and establishing offices. The benefits to the public from the revival of dormant trusts are obvious, but no less important is the valuable assistance given to fiduciaries in the administration of their duties.

> . . . the role of the office in policing the administration of charitable trusts, in prodding delinquents and in pushing the dilatory is a significant factor in the whole context of beneficial supervision and enforcement without the necessity of going to court. Indeed, the mere existence of a watching and watchful sentinel insures alertness.[1]

The primary drawback to the program in New Hampshire, recognized by its director as well as by the Supreme Court of the state,[2] is the failure of the legislature to include within the scope of the reporting provisions certain charitable corporations, particularly corporate foundations. In an older state, such as New Hampshire, with a long history of judicial support of charitable trusts, there is great need for supervision to prevent dormancy and accumulation; and this has been attested to by the results of the supervisory program. The omission of corporate foundations from the purview of the reporting provisions not only enables fiduciaries of certain foundations to escape duties imposed on trustees; it also omits the area in which, according to most authorities, the greatest possibilities for abuse lie.

Rhode Island

On April 24, 1950, the Rhode Island legislature passed An Act Establishing a Division of Charitable Trusts,[3] which incorporated recommendations made by a Special Committee to Study the Laws of This State with Respect to and Governing Charitable Trusts, So-Called. The Committee, created by resolution of the state legislature in 1949, had examined the Rhode Island statutes and case law relating to charitable trusts, conducted public hearings in September of 1949, and had submitted a report to the governor that contained a summary of its findings and recommendations for legislation.

The report noted that, at the outset, the Committee had felt a need to define "charitable trusts so-called," for the purpose of its work.

---

[1] D'Amours, Ernest R., "Charitable Trusts . . . ," *op. cit.,* p. 227.

[2] "We fully recognize the desirability of reasonable control by the State over charitable trusts and charitable corporations and the substantial advances made here in this direction commencing in 1943." *Portsmouth Hospital* v. *Attorney General,* 104 N.H. 51, 178 A.2d 516 (1962).

[3] R.I. Public Laws of 1950, ch. 2617.

> Much confusion has been caused by the misuse and misunderstanding of the terms charitable corporations, charitable trusts, charitable foundations, but in each there is always found a triangular composition consisting of a moving party, or creator; an individual, group of individuals, or non-business corporation which manages the fund, and a class which is the recipient of the benefits of the fund. It is this triangular relationship that the Committee has considered in its study, irrespective of whether this relationship was set up by an indenture, a will, or the formation of a corporation.[1]

This definition obviated the need to distinguish between charitable trusts and charitable corporations. The report briefly reviewed the pertinent Rhode Island laws and concluded that there was little or no supervision or enforcement of charitable trusts in that state. In Rhode Island, unlike many other states, the trustees of testamentary trusts are under no duty to file accounts with any court, nor must their appointment receive court approval if they are named in the trust instrument.[2] Charitable corporations must file biennially a list of directors and the current address of the corporation, but need not submit a detailed financial accounting.[3]

The Committee reported that it was the unanimous opinion of those testifying before them that some type of trust registration was essential to enable the attorney general to carry out his duty of supervision and that, in addition, there must be annual accounting by trustees. Differences of opinion were expressed as to whether the registry should be open to the public, those against it fearing that trustees might be inundated with requests for contributions and that some donors might be reluctant to establish trusts if their existence became public knowledge. The Committee also heard requests from certain specific groups which desired to be exempt from the registration requirements.

The Committee recommended that legislation be enacted establishing a Registry of Charitable Trusts administered by a director of charitable trusts under the supervision of the attorney general. The one exception to the registration requirement which they suggested was that trusts with a contingent charitable interest not register until the event which vested the charitable interest took place. Also recommended were a requirement that trustees account annually to the di-

---

[1] State of Rhode Island and Providence Plantations, Special Committee to Study the Laws of This State with Respect to and Governing Charitable Trusts, So-Called, *Report,* to His Excellency Governor John O. Pastore, January 25, 1950. Wm. Brown Co., Providence, 1950, p. 5.
[2] R.I. Gen. Laws Ann., sec. 18–6–3.
[3] R.I. Gen. Laws Ann., sec. 7–6–14.

rector of charitable trusts and a grant to the director of broad investigatory powers backed by adequate sanctions. The Committee found no justification for creating a separate board of charitable trusts, believing that the supervision could be adequately and inexpensively performed by a single administrative office accountable to the attorney general.

All of these proposals were incorporated into the 1950 legislation. The chairman of the Special Committee was appointed to be the first holder of the office of Director, or as it was titled in the statute, Administrator of Charitable Trusts, and served in that position until 1962. On November 1, 1950, the attorney general promulgated rules and regulations for the operation of the register. They established a Division of Charitable Trusts in the Department of the Attorney General and a Register of Charitable Trusts. December 31, 1950, was set as the date on or before which the trustee or trustees of each charitable trust, established or active in the state, should file with the Division a statement showing:

(1) Whether such charitable trust was established by will, deed, indenture or other instrument, and the name of the testator or settlor.
(2) The name and address of the trustee or trustees.
(3) The name and address of the present charitable beneficiary or beneficiaries.
(4) The name and address of any future charitable beneficiary or beneficiaries.
(5) The value of the trust as of the latest appraisal and the date of said appraisal.

Charitable trusts becoming effective or active within the state after that date were required to file a registration statement within thirty days. A filing fee of $5.00 to accompany each registration statement was required by the statute and the regulations, and forms were made available from the attorney general's office. The regulations exempted from registration charitable institutions, contingent charitable interests, and charitable trusts having a value of less than $3,000.

As of December 31, 1963, 508 trusts were registered. They had an appraised value of over $88 million. In 303 trusts, with total assets of approximately $52 million, the charitable, religious, or educational interest was presently being enjoyed. In the remaining 205, with assets of approximately $36 million, the charitable interest had not come into being and was awaiting either the death of some living noncharitable beneficiary or the happening of some future event.

None of the office files is classified according to the purposes of the trusts, but a running tally of assets devoted to particular purposes is kept. During 1963, disbursements to charitable beneficiaries amounted to a little over $4 million.[1] The registration statement used in Rhode Island contains categories similar to those required in New Hampshire, except that a report of income received and disbursed is necessary only when a charitable beneficiary has an interest in the net income or when principal funds are paid to or used for the benefit of the life beneficiary. If there has been a change of beneficiaries or trustees during the period covered by the reports, details are requested as to the names and addresses, the cause for change, and the manner in which it was accomplished. The report must be signed and certified, but the signatures need not be notarized.

These reports are reviewed by the administrator of charitable trusts with the assistance of one clerk. No auditors, accountants, or investigators are used. To date, the administrator has been able to rectify abuses without resort to court action. A failure to file reports for two years will result in a court action to remove the trustees, but it has not been found necessary to move against trustees in that way. No formal investigations have been undertaken. The only category of cases in which the attorney general has regularly conferred with trustees has been in regard to accumulations of cash.

Under the terms of the 1950 legislation, the attorney general is deemed to be an interested party to all judicial proceedings affecting, or in any manner dealing with, a charitable trust or with a trustee who holds in trust property given, devised, or bequeathed in whole or in part for such purposes. Notice must be sent to him of any such proceeding.[2] The practice established by the courts since the enactment of this legislation has been for the clerk to mail a card to the attorney general notifying him of the offering for probate of any will that contains provisions for establishing a charitable trust, although the attorney general need not receive formal notice until the trust comes into being at the conclusion of probate. In 1962 the attorney general's office participated in 19 matters in the Superior and Supreme Courts; in 1963 the figure was 20. The courts consider the attorney general to

---

[1] State of Rhode Island, Office of the Attorney General, Division of Charitable Trusts, *Annual Report of the Administrator of Charitable Trusts* for the period January 1, 1963 to December 31, 1963, Providence, R.I., 1964 (mimeographed).

[2] R.I. Gen. Laws Ann., sec. 18–9–5.

be a necessary party to cases involving compromise of will contests where the will creates a charitable trust.[1]

In 1951 the original act was amended to provide that the administrator of charitable trusts may be designated a special assistant attorney general who shall act in cases involving charitable trusts.[2] Appropriations for the Division have at all times been included within the budget for the Department of the Attorney General. In both 1963 and 1964, the governor excluded any appropriation for the Charitable Trust Division and suggested its abolition and the transfer of its administration to the regular office of the attorney general, which is staffed by 14 attorneys. Each time, the attorney general objected to this suggestion, and the legislature voted appropriations that have permitted continuation of the Division as a separate office. In 1963 the appropriation amounted to $13,164, of which $12,675 was for personnel service and $489 was for operating expenses, including postage, telephone, telegraph, and printing costs. In the 1964 budget the total division allocation was $14,300, of which $12,675 was for salaries.

It should be noted that the Rhode Island Division of Charitable Trusts has undertaken no survey of charitable trusts in the state similar to that made in New Hampshire. Although the division does cooperate with the state tax department on determinations of charitable gifts and receives regular notice of the creation of charitable trusts under wills, it has not undertaken any search of records in the probate courts, the office of the secretary of state, or the local office of the Internal Revenue Service. Lack of staff is the primary reason for failure to undertake such a survey.

The distinctive features of the supervision program in Rhode Island stem primarily from the smallness of the state. The administrator knows a great number of the trustees and has been able, through personal conferences, and even telephone calls, to maintain a close and continuing contact with the trustees of the trusts under his jurisdiction. Since there was no statutory requirement for any form of accounting by trustees prior to the passage of the act, the reporting requirement had a stronger impact on trustees and directors than it would otherwise have had.

The substantive laws of Rhode Island relating to trustees' duties and powers, particularly in connection with investments, were of par-

[1] *Leo* v. *Armington,* 74 R.I. 129, 59 A.2d 371 (1948).
[2] R.I. Public Laws of 1951, ch. 2852.

ticular interest to members of the Special Committee that proposed enactment of the registration statute. The Committee found that although under the common law in Rhode Island the investment powers of trustees of charitable trusts were governed by the prudent man rule, there was statutory authority permitting the creator of an inter vivos charitable trust to grant to trustees far broader powers.[1] This provision had permitted the creation of what the Committee termed a "novel legal arrangement referred to and described as a trust, formally and mechanically functioning as a trust, yet in its more vital aspects essentially and distinctly different from what is accepted as the 'classic' type of charitable trust."[2] They characterized this new arrangement as a "child of the tax laws," referring to it as the "Little-Type" charitable trust after one of its originators and its chief proponent at the Committee hearings. The indenture of a "Little-Type" trust agreement gave unrestricted investment powers to trustees, whose first duty was to build up the fund through "investments in situations such as aggressive businessmen would personally make," and was specifically designed to permit trading in securities on margin and participating in so-called risk ventures in Rhode Island, none of which would be permissible under the prudent man doctrine. The Committee Report expressed a fear that unconscionable creators and trustees might dissipate a "Little-Type" trust, not only of the original contributions, but of tax savings as well, by using the trust funds in times of weak prosperity to bolster the creator's private financial position. The Committee concluded:

> The question before your Committee thus resolves down to whether this novel departure from customary charitable trust practice actually serves the public interest. After careful study the Committee concludes that in its present form it does not.[3]

The Committee recommended the enactment of a statute providing that regardless of any language of the trust instrument, the attempted exoneration of a trustee of an inter vivos trust from liability for failure to exercise reasonable care, diligence, and prudence shall be deemed contrary to public policy.[4] Their recommendation was em-

---

[1] See R.I. Gen. Laws Ann., sec. 18–4–2.

[2] State of Rhode Island and Providence Plantations, Special Commission to Study the Laws of This State . . . , *op. cit.*, p. 13.

[3] *Ibid.*, p. 13.

[4] *Ibid.* The Committee quoted the following provisions from the Rhode Is-

bodied in the 1950 legislation in section 14.[1] The prohibition, however, does not apply to testamentary trusts or to inter vivos gifts to a charity or charitable institution.

The Committee also heard testimony concerning the desirability of enacting legislation requiring trustees to distribute a certain portion of income to beneficiaries annually and limiting the life of all charitable trusts to twenty-five years. It recommended no legislative action on either suggestion, however, pending the outcome of a study by the officer charged with supervision of charitable trusts.

> In the administration of most charitable trusts there is a substantial annual distribution and the time may come when a minimum percentage of distribution will be required by law. But for hundreds of years creators have established trusts which contemplated accumulations for long periods before the funds would grow large enough to fulfill their purposes. We do not think the evidence brought before the Committee justifies interfering with this practice at this time.[2]

No recommendations to reconsider these proposals have been formally made since the Committee hearings in 1949. The amendments to the Internal Revenue Code enacted by the United States Congress in 1950, particularly the section that deals with accumulations of income,[3] have to a certain extent rendered restrictive legislation of this nature unnecessary.

The administrator of charitable trusts in Rhode Island has not found any cases to date in which it has been necessary to call trustees to account for improper investments. The staff thinks that the mere fact that the substantive laws were tightened in 1950 may have been sufficient to discourage further speculative activity by foundations organized or operating in that state.

---

land Charities Trust (a foundation), stating that temporary success is hardly a reason practically to exonerate charitable trustees from all responsibility: "No trustee hereunder shall be required to give any bond or other security for the faithful performance of his duties as trustee. No one of the trustees shall be answerable or accountable for any act or omission of any prior trustee, nor for any act of any cotrustee or cotrustees in which he shall not have participated or concurred, nor for any moneys, estate, or property which shall not have come to his own personal possession or control, nor for any loss which shall occur except by his own willful act, neglect, or default, nor for the speculative or venturesome character or the extent of an investment or transaction or for the absence of diversification or risk in respect to the property in trust."

[1] R.I. Gen. Laws Ann., sec. 18–9–14.
[2] *Ibid.,* p. 14.
[3] Int. Rev. Code of 1954, sec. 504.

Ohio

The Ohio Charitable Trusts Act was passed in 1953. Impetus had come originally from the attorney general, whose office drafted the legislation. He stated that prior to 1953 not more than an estimated 5 per cent of all charitable trusts in Ohio came to his attention, that he was rarely notified of suits involving charitable interests, and that without legislation providing the means necessary for acomplishing his common law duties in respect to charitable trusts, he could not function.[1]

The language of the Ohio act follows the pattern of the Rhode Island legislation, but differs from it in several important aspects. Several exclusions were listed in the first section which contains definitions.[2] Unlike the Rhode Island and New Hampshire acts the statute does not apply to charitable trusts until they become vested in use or enjoyment, so that there is no supervision of the administration of these funds during the period in which private individuals may be receiving the beneficial interest.[3] The act permits the attorney general to appoint such assistants as may be necessary to administer its provisions, but does not create a specific position in his office. Trustees are required to report biennially instead of annually;[4] failure to register is made a criminal offense subject to a fine of not less than $500 nor more than $10,000, or imprisonment of not less than one month nor more than one year, or both.[5] Powers are not specifically granted to the attorney general either to make investigations or to subpoena witnesses; instead, the auditor of the state is required to undertake these tasks at the request of the attorney general.[6]

Another important difference is in the wording of the section making the attorney general a necessary party to certain types of actions involving charitable funds. The act states:

> The attorney general is a necessary party to and shall be served with process or with summons by registered mail in all proceedings, the object of which is: (A) To terminate a charitable trust or distribute its assets to other than charitable donees; (B) Depart from the objects or purposes of a charitable trust as the same are set forth in the instru-

---

[1] Klapp, Ralph, and Neva Wertz, "Supervision of Charitable Trusts in Ohio," *Ohio State Law Journal,* vol. 18, 1957, pp. 181, 182.
[2] See p. 260.
[3] Ohio Rev. Code Ann., sec. 109.23.
[4] Ohio Rev. Code Ann., sec. 109.31.
[5] Ohio Rev. Code Ann., sec. 109.99.
[6] Ohio Rev. Code Ann., sec. 109.32.

ment creating the trust, including any proceeding for the application of the doctrine of cy pres, or (C) Construe the provisions of an instrument with respect to a charitable trust. A judgment rendered in such proceedings without service of process upon the attorney general is void, unenforceable, and shall be set aside upon the attorney general's motion seeking such relief. The attorney general shall intervene in any proceeding affecting a charitable trust when requested to do so by the court having jurisdiction of the proceedings, and may intervene in any proceeding affecting a charitable trust when he determines that the public interest should be protected in such proceeding. No compromise, settlement agreement, contract or judgment agreed to by any or all parties having or claiming to have an interest in any charitable trust is valid if the compromise, settlement agreement, contract, or judgment modifies or terminates a charitable trust unless the attorney general was made a party to all such proceedings and joined in said compromise, settlement agreement, contract or judgment; provided, that the attorney general is expressly authorized to enter into such compromise, settlement agreements, contracts, or judgments as may be in the best interests of the public.[1]

This language is far more restrictive than that found in some other jurisdictions. It should be noted, however, that under the sections of the Ohio Code relating to dissolution of corporations, the attorney general is a necessary party to actions brought by corporations or trustees to determine disposition of assets of charitable corporations.[2]

Following passage of the legislation in 1953, the attorney general established in his office a division of charitable trusts under the direction of an assistant attorney general. A one-page bulletin summarizing the requirements of the act and directing attention to the registration provisions was prepared and sent to members of the bar and all bank and trust companies in the state.

At the end of 1954, 734 trusts had been registered, with an approximate value of $204 million. By December 31, 1956, the figure had increased to 910 trusts with a value of more than $224 million.[3] The director reported in 1957, however, that there was no way of knowing "whether there is still a backlog of such trusts which have not as yet been registered."[4] As of January 1, 1965, the number of trusts in the register had risen to 1,777, of which 99 had been registered during 1964 and 102 in 1963.[5] No estimate is available as to the value

---

[1] Ohio Rev. Code Ann., sec. 109.25.
[2] Ohio Rev. Code Ann., sec. 1702.49.
[3] Klapp, Ralph, and Neva Wertz, *op. cit.,* p. 185.
[4] *Ibid.,* p. 186.
[5] Information obtained in interview with Assistant Attorney General Neva Wertz, April, 1964.

of these trusts, nor is it known how many of them are corporations which, following a decision of the attorney general in 1964, are no longer required to report.[1]

The office requires the submission of a registration form similar to that adopted in New Hampshire and Rhode Island, and a copy of the trust instrument. No official form has been devised for biennial reports. The office accepts any reasonable accounting which shows in detail the assets, liabilities, income, expenditures, and disbursements for charitable purposes. Many trustees file copies of reports made to the Internal Revenue Service on Form 990–A. No fees are required. The attorney general has promulgated no regulations and has set no definite annual date for filing reports, having interpreted the statute as requiring reports every other year on the date of the registration.

The office is currently staffed by one assistant attorney general who devotes full time to charitable matters, one administrative assistant who reviews all biennial reports and maintains the register, and one stenographer. Records are kept in a simple numerical file according to the permanent file number assigned to each trust. A cross-index system is used, and all trusts are indexed by the names of both the donor and the trustees. No files on records are kept according to the purposes of the trusts or according to their legal form, nor are tabulations made of financial data. An informal check of delinquent accounts is kept, and letters are sent out periodically to remind trustees of the duty to file when they appear to be in default. If a new trust is registered which was in existence prior to 1953, the attorney general will request an accounting for every year since 1953 if it is possible to comply.

The assistant attorney general in charge of charitable matters reviews all initial registrations and examines any biennial reports that his assistant indicates are questionable. A complete file of reports for a trust is examined when it appears that corpus is being depleted or that the trustees' fees are excessive. Communications to trustees are usually by letter.

From 1958 to 1962, the office conducted several informal investigations of foundation activities. One of these involved an attempt by the settlor of an inter vivos trust, who had retained the power to appoint trustees, to force a bank trustee to invest in a corporation of which he owned the controlling stock. When the bank refused, the settlor transferred the trust to a New York bank. The Ohio attorney general's office, in cooperation with the attorney general's office in New York,

---

[1] See pp. 260 ff.

was able to maintain supervision of the trust funds to assure that they were not improperly invested. The office also participated informally in negotiations to sell the principal asset of a large foundation in an attempt to assure that a fair price was received.

Participation in litigation involving charitable trusts increased markedly following passage of the Charitable Trusts Act in October of 1953. The office reported that the attorney general was named a party defendant in 14 cases in 1953, 25 cases in 1954, and 30 in 1955 and in 1956;[1] the number remained at 30 until 1960 when it rose to 60. In 1961 it was 45; in 1962, 48. In 1963, 40 new cases were docketed, and 31 pending cases were closed. In 1964 the figure for new cases rose to 59. The assistant attorney general in charge of the division in 1963 and 1964 estimated that more than half of the time spent on charitable affairs was devoted to these litigations. Personal court appearances are made on an average of two full days per month. In a state as large as Ohio, with 88 county courts, it is necessary to file briefs in many cases in lieu of appearing personally. Preparation of these briefs, as well as the pleadings for all cases, requires the major time of the assistant attorney general.

Although the statute provides for notification to the attorney general of the probate of wills creating or purporting to create a charitable trust,[2] in practice this requirement is not widely observed. The lower courts, however, do require petitioners to observe the provisions of the act requiring that the attorney general be made a party to certain proceedings.[3] The majority of cases in which the attorney general has been cited as defendant have involved construction of wills or requests for declaratory judgment. In many of them a request for termination has been made by heirs of the settlor, and had the attorney general not presented the case for upholding the charitable interest or requested application of the doctrine of *cy pres* or deviation, the charitable gift would have been lost. When a charitable corporation has also been named as a defendant, the office has cooperated with the trustees whenever possible. Although trustees of testamentary trusts in Ohio are required to account annually to the court, the attorney general does not receive notice of these proceedings unless another party contests the account. In such a case, certain courts will require his participation.

The wording of the 1953 legislation has created several problems

---

[1] Klapp, Ralph, and Neva Wertz, *op. cit.,* p. 187.
[2] Ohio Rev. Code Ann., sec. 109.30.
[3] Ohio Rev. Code Ann., sec. 109.25; see pp. 286–287.

for the attorney general. Although consideration has been given to amending the act at various times since 1957, and a bill containing several amendments was presented to the legislature in 1963, the only amendments enacted merely made stylistic changes in conjunction with a revision of the entire Ohio Code.[1]

The definitions in section 109.23 have caused the greatest difficulty, not only because of the problem of interpreting their application to charitable corporations mentioned earlier, but because they imply an exclusion of the exempt charities from the entire purview of the attorney general. The act reads as follows:

> As used in sections 109.23 to 109.33, inclusive, of the Revised Code, "charitable trust" means any fiduciary relationship with respect to property arising as a result of a manifestation of intention to create it, and subjecting the partnership, corporation, person, or association of persons by whom the property is held to equitable duties to deal with the property for any charitable, religious or educational purpose.[2]

It has been argued that this language removes certain charitable trusts and all property held by charitable institutions from the operation and effectiveness of the entire Charitable Trusts Act, thereby diminishing, rather than increasing, the common law powers of the attorney general. Just such an interpretation was given to the act by one of the common pleas courts in 1956, which held that the attorney general was not a necessary party to a will contest case, the purpose of which was to determine whether a certain writing proposing to create a charitable trust was, in effect, the last will of the testator.[3] In that same year, however, the court of appeals of a different county reached an opposite result.[4] The question was again raised in the case of *Baily* v. *McElroy*,[5] which involved construction of a will purporting to create a charitable trust. Following extended litigation in the lower courts, the Court of Appeals held, on June 25, 1963, that the will was valid, that it created a charitable trust so that section 109.25 of the Charitable Trusts Act of Ohio was applicable, and that the attorney general was a proper party to further proceedings therein.[6] A motion filed by

---

[1] State of Ohio, House Bill No. 1 (1960), effective January 10, 1961.

[2] Ohio Rev. Code Ann., sec. 109.23.

[3] *Spang* v. *Cleveland Trust Co.,* 1 Ohio Op.2d 288, 73 Ohio Law Abstracts 164, 134 N.E.2d 586 (1956).

[4] *Blair* v. *Bouton,* 15 Ohio Op.2d 474 (1956).

[5] *Baily* v. *McElroy,* 89 Ohio Law Abstr. 289, 186 N.E.2d 213 (1961).

[6] Court of Appeals, 1st Appellate District, Warren County, No. 260, filed June 25, 1963.

one of the defendants to certify the case to the Supreme Court was overruled.

This same section became the ground of contention in another case which reached the Supreme Court of Ohio, when, in 1960, the attorney general was named a party defendant under the provision of section 109.25 in a suit brought by the Ohio Society for Crippled Children and Adults, Inc.[1] The Society requested the Court to declare that a farm devised to it for use as a home for crippled children was a gift in fee simple, and that provisions in the will that the farm should be used as the home and not sold or leased were void. The attorney general filed an answer claiming that the will created a charitable trust under which the Society had an enforceable obligation to use the property for the purposes intended by the testator. He denied the Society's allegation that the farm was no longer practicable for use as a home, but asserted that if the court should rule otherwise, the doctrine of *cy pres* should be applied. The Society then moved to have the court declare that the attorney general was not a necessary party to the action on the grounds that the Society was exempt from the Charitable Trusts Act under section 109.23, which excludes institutions holding property exclusively for their own purposes.

The lower court ruled that the attorney general was a necessary party to the action and that the trustees held the farm under an enforceable duty to use it for the purposes set forth in the will, but the court gave no opinion as to the application of the doctrines of *cy pres* or deviation. The Society appealed to the District Court of Appeals, which reversed the lower court and held that the devise was of a fee simple title unaffected by any other language in the will. The court did not reach the question of whether the attorney general was a necessary party to this type of action. The attorney general then appealed to the Supreme Court, which reversed the decision of the Court of Appeals and held that the gift was subject to an enforceable condition. The only mention of the question raised as to the standing of the attorney general came in the first paragraph of the decision where the Court stated that the attorney general had been made a party defendant to the action and had filed a brief.

In each of these cases the language in sections 109.23 and 109.25 has been used by adverse parties as the basis for a position that the attorney general's enforcement powers over charitable funds have been

---

[1] *Ohio Society for Crippled Children & Adults, Inc.* v. *McElroy*, 175 Ohio St. 49, 191 N.E.2d 543 (1963).

limited by the exemption provisions of the act and by the categorization of proceedings listed in section 109.25. The attorney general has countered in his briefs in both the *Baily* and *Ohio Society for Crippled Children* cases that the act merely supplements the common law powers which existed before passage of the act of 1953.

These problems have arisen because of poor draftsmanship. Unless the Ohio act is amended or the Supreme Court states unequivocally that the 1953 legislation does not alter the common law powers, the attorney general's effectiveness will be open to attack and thereby diminished. The bill that failed of passage in 1963, in addition to bringing corporate foundations within the purview of the act, would have clarified the situation by making the exemption provisions applicable only to the section wherein registration and reporting requirements are imposed. It would also have added a sentence stating explicitly that the powers of the attorney general under the common law remain in effect.

The assistant attorney general in charge of charitable trusts is assigned the duty of maintaining a file of registration reports received from certain organizations that solicit charitable funds from the public. The Ohio statute regulating solicitation[1] places a duty on any group, association, partnership, or corporation which intends to solicit contributions for a charitable purpose in the state to file with the office of the attorney general or the local county clerk of courts, on forms provided by the office of the attorney general, certain information as to the purpose of the solicitation and the names of individuals connected with it. Each organization so registered must also file an annual financial report of its activities for the prior year. Professional fund raisers and solicitors must register personally, and the former must also supply a $5,000 bond. Exemption is made for religious organizations, educational and other charitable corporations soliciting from their own members, and any organization that expects its expenditures for solicitation to be less than $500 per year.

The registration forms and reports are maintained in a separate file. As of March, 1964, approximately 160 registrations were on file in the office of the attorney general, and an unknown number had been filed with local clerks of court. A series of reporting forms have been prepared by the office. The attorney general's office does not feel it has any duty or authority to supervise solicitations. The reports are

---

[1] Ohio Rev. Code Ann., secs. 1716 ff.

reviewed by the assistant attorney general and then filed. Health and welfare organizations that solicit funds from the public have not been required to file reports under the provisions of the Charitable Trusts Act.

It would appear that the potentialities for active supervision of charitable funds in Ohio have not been fully realized. This has resulted from a lack of adequate staff and the problems encountered in interpreting the act. The figure of 1,777 charitable trusts seems low when compared with that of 1,500 registered in the far less populated state of New Hampshire where the exemption provisions are now similar.[1]

Some survey of either court records or the files of the Internal Revenue Service would be in order to determine how many trusts have not complied with the act, and the office should attempt to secure their registration. It would also seem necessary to delve more closely into the operations of the trusts. Only striking irregularities or arithmetic mistakes are brought to the attention of the assistant attorney general. Greater use of the state auditor might also be advisable. It is obvious, however, that one attorney cannot perform this entire program. Prior to 1963, two attorneys were assigned to charitable matters, and they felt handicapped by a lack of staff. The use of student law clerks for certain routine functions could take some of the burden if it is administratively impossible to assign another assistant attorney general to the work. The participation of the attorney general in litigations has unquestionably contributed to the preservation and proper disposition of charitable funds in Ohio, but this result appears to have been achieved at the expense of attention to the great number of charitable trusts that exist without contact with the courts.

South Carolina

The legislation passed in South Carolina in 1953 is the briefest statute attempting to establish a registry of charitable trusts. It states:

Section 67–81 The trustees of charitable trusts in existence on July 1, 1953, or thereafter created, under the laws of this State, shall file a certified copy of the trust instrument with the Attorney General within ninety days after such date or within sixty days after the creation of the trust, whichever is later.

Section 67–82 Trustees of charitable trusts shall submit an annual report to the Attorney General, which shall include a complete financial

---

[1] *The Foundation Directory, Edition 2,* Edited by Ann D. Walton and Marianna O. Lewis, Russell Sage Foundation, New York, 1964, p. 16, lists 396 large foundations in Ohio, only 24 in New Hampshire.

statement relating to the trust property during the preceding year, a summary of the acts of the trustees in their capacity as such, the name and address of each trustee, and, if a trustee is a corporation, the name and address of each director and officer thereof. The first report submitted shall include an itemized statement of the property which passed into the hands of the trustees upon the creation of the trust, and every report shall include a statement of the trust property in the hands of the trustee both at the beginning and the end of the year for which the report is made.

Section 67–83 Upon the failure of the trustees to discharge their duties under this chapter, or when it appears that the trustees are not properly discharging the duties imposed upon them by the trust, the Attorney General shall bring an action to compel their compliance with this chapter or to compel them to discharge the duties imposed upon them by trust, as the case may be.

Section 67–84 The Attorney General may make such rules and regulations, relating to the time for submission of, and the information to be contained in, the reports required by this chapter.[1]

A final section entitled "Exemptions" has been described previously.[2]

The administration of the act has been minimal. The office of the attorney general in South Carolina is small, and since 1959 it has been involved in litigation arising from a large interstate highway construction program. Consequently, no lawyer has been assigned to the field of charitable trusts on a permanent basis.

Eighteen trustees have filed copies of trust instruments and annual reports with the office of the attorney general in compliance with the act. The attorney general himself and clerical personnel have examined the reports, but only cursorily. The attorney general reports that no actions have been taken to assure compliance with the act and that he is not aware of any violations of the law or omissions or cases of improper performance of trustees' duties. In one instance an inspection of returns from a trustee indicated that small loans had been made to the trustee on several occasions. After consultation with the trustee, the practice ceased.[3]

The 1953 legislation appears as part of the section of the South Carolina Code relating to the validity of charitable trusts and to the jurisdiction of the courts of probate and common pleas over charitable trusts. This section also contains a requirement that trustees appointed

---

[1] S.C. Code Ann., sec. 67–81.
[2] See p. 262.
[3] Information obtained from Daniel R. McLeod, Attorney General, State of South Carolina, 1964.

by the court make annual returns to the judges of probate.[1] The attorney general does not consider that this provision carries with it a requirement that notice be given to his office of petitions for allowances of accounts. Trustees' fees are fixed by statute, and in one instance where a petition requesting allowance in excess of the statutory fees was brought, the attorney general was made a party and participated in the proceeding.

The attorney general's duties to enforce the application of funds given or appropriated to public charities within the state and to prevent breaches of trust in the administration thereof have been part of the statutory law in South Carolina since 1868,[2] but only recently have actions involving its application been brought before the Supreme Court of the state. The case of *Watson* v. *Wall*[3] in 1956 clearly established that the attorney general has the right to intervene in a case where the public interest in a charitable bequest is shown to exist. In this case the matter had been heard at the trial level without the knowledge of the attorney general; but on appeal to the Supreme Court, his office petitioned for leave to intervene. The Court subsequently adopted the attorney general's position with respect to the construction to be given to the will in question.

Thereafter, the case of *Furman University* v. *McLeod*[4] was brought to determine the proper construction to be given to certain deeds whereby land had been conveyed for the purpose of maintaining a school. The decision in that case held that the attorney general was the only proper defendant to a case involving a charitable trust where no private rights by way of reversion or reverter existed.

The only other recent case that has been reported in which the attorney general was made a party defendant involved a decision relating to apportionment of stock dividends, the distribution of which affected a remainder gift creating a charitable trust.[5]

The attorney general of South Carolina has expressed concern about a conflict between his duties to enforce charitable funds and those as attorney for the South Carolina Tax Commission. The conflict has arisen in two recent situations. In one case, the evidence at

---

[1] S.C. Code Ann., sec. 67–57.2.
[2] S.C. Code Ann., sec. 1–240.
[3] 229 S.C. 500, 93 S.E.2d 918 (1956).
[4] 238 S.C. 475, 120 S.E.2d 865 (1961).
[5] *Cothran* v. *South Carolina National Bank of Charlestown*, 242 S.C. 80, 130 E.2d 177 (1963).

the trial court level supported the Tax Commission's position that the corporation in question was not in actuality a charity, but had been created as a subterfuge. To prevent the necessity of bringing an action to revoke the charter, a settlement was made under the terms of which a portion of the taxes were paid and the charter of the alleged charity was voluntarily surrendered. In the second case, which has not come to a final determination, the attorney general has been faced with a situation where both positions seemed reasonably arguable. A possible solution is to have a special attorney appointed to represent one of the two sides.

No program of active supervision of charitable trusts has been instituted in South Carolina primarily because the legislature has failed to appropriate sufficient funds to maintain the necessary personnel. In turn, the lack of any specific provision in the charitable trust act calling for the establishment of a registry or the creation of a specific administrative position in the office of the attorney general has made it difficult for the attorney general to request additional funds from the legislature. The South Carolina experience provides another example of the futility of passing legislation without including specific financial support to carry it out. Interest in the program exists in that state, and there is some indication that it will receive greater attention in the future, but to date the program has made no great impact on the administration of charitable funds in that state.[1]

Massachusetts

The Massachusetts General Court passed legislation in 1954 to increase the attorney general's supervisory powers over trustees and directors of charitable organizations. This act had far less impact on charitable fiduciaries than have the statutes in the states previously described, for prior to this time trustees and directors had been under a statutory duty to file annual reports with the Department of Public Welfare, and many of the probate courts required that the attorney general be notified of matters involving charitable funds. Nevertheless, it was felt that additional legislation was necessary to assure

---

[1] *The Foundation Directory, Edition 2, op. cit.,* lists 36 foundations with assets of $31,175,000 meeting the size requirement of the *Directory.* Since no interpretation of the statute has been made in terms of its application to charitable corporations, it cannot be assumed that all of them should be filing reports with the attorney general. Nevertheless, it is reasonable to assume that there are more than 18 trusts in that state which fall within the terms of the statute.

proper supervision. For example, in 1938, the attorney general had reported that:

> The Provisions of G.L. (Ter. Ed.) Chap. 68, sec. 15, which were originally inserted by St. 1930, c. 209, would seem to require every trustee holding funds in trust for any charitable purpose, not required to report elsewhere, to file yearly reports with the Department of Public Welfare. In practice, however, the statute has been construed in the main, although no authority seems to exist for the interpretation, as requiring reports only from trustees holding funds to be devoted to those purposes comprehended within the meaning of the word "charitable," which includes aid to the poor and sick, the widows, the aged and the orphans. This construction relieves trustees holding funds for the undoubted legal charitable purposes of education, religion, public improvements, etc., which constitute a large proportion of all the charitable trust funds, from any supervision whatsoever.[1]

In 1945, the attorney general had included in his Report the following statement:

> In the report of Attorney General Austin for the year 1837 there appears a reference to the subject of charitable trusts and in the period of over 100 years that has passed since then it is doubtful if any attorney general has ever felt that he has been able to fulfill his duties in this field in a manner satisfactory to himself.[2]

The difficulty, he felt, was similar to that in other jurisdictions, and stemmed from the fact that the attorneys general had neither sufficient information about charitable funds nor sufficient personnel to enforce the application of the funds, even if the necessary information had been available.[3]

This 1945 report also contained the one published description of a survey of funds left for charitable purposes by wills in Massachusetts which was made from 1936 to 1939 under the direction of the previous attorney general, Paul Dever.[4] Dever had obtained an appropriation from the federal Works Progress Administration to support in part the salaries of 53 individuals who compiled from the records in each probate court in the state lists of all wills that contained funds for permanent charitable purposes. Over 350,000 wills were examined;

---

[1] Commonwealth of Massachusetts, Office of the Attorney General, *Annual Report* for the period December 1, 1937 to November 30, 1938, Public Document 12, State House, Boston, 1938; also noted in *Massachusetts Law Quarterly,* vol. 30, May, 1945, pp. 22, 25.

[2] Commonwealth of Massachusetts, Office of the Attorney General, *Annual Report* for the period December 1, 1944 to June 30, 1945, *op. cit.,* 1945.

[3] *Ibid.*

[4] *Ibid.,* p. 24.

pertinent provisions were copied onto permanent record cards; lists of trustees were compiled; and the charities were organized and indexed according to certain purposes. The survey indicated that there were 26,451 estates in which 50,928 separate bequests for charitable purposes had been made in Massachusetts up to the year 1935. It also showed that many fiduciaries under wills were not filing accounts with the probate courts or the Department of Public Welfare in accordance with law.

Letters were sent to trustees and executors to obtain information as to these trusts. The replies revealed dormant funds amounting to $7,614,000, loose methods of administration, and improper investment procedures. The office attempted to rectify these situations, but the survey of probate records was continued by the next administration only to the extent of examining all wills filed in Suffolk County, which comprises the city of Boston, for the period from July 1, 1935 to December 1, 1937, and a sampling of wills in the other counties of the state.

In Attorney General Bushnell's Report for 1945 this information was combined with an analysis of the different types of cases relating to charitable trusts which required the attention of the attorney general from December 1, 1943 to November 10, 1944. During this period, 963 different matters pertaining to charitable trusts were handled by the office. The breakdown by categories was as follows:

1. Petitions for allowance of will   134
2. Petitions for instructions   46
3. Petitions for sale of real estate   43
4. Petitions for amalgamation   1
5. Petitions for allowance of accounts   677
6. Petitions for approval of settlements   13
7. Petitions for application of doctrine of cy pres   2
8. Petitions for the appointment and removal of trustees   40
9. Miscellaneous petitions[1]   7

The attorney general concluded that these matters "represent but a small portion of the charities in the Commonwealth which should be receiving attention."[2] He recommended enactment of a statute similar to that in force in New Hampshire but no legislative action was taken.[3] However, in 1948 the legislature did attempt to increase the participa-

---

[1] Ibid., p. 27.
[2] Ibid., p. 33.
[3] See discussion on p. 223 concerning the reaction of the Judicial Council to this proposal.

tion of the attorney general in cases involving charities by requiring the registers of probate to notify him of the creation or enlargement of any estate or fund for charitable purposes by any instrument filed with the register. This act also attempted to secure compliance with the reporting requirement imposed on charitable corporations by providing that failure to file reports with the Department of Public Welfare for two successive years would make them subject to dissolution at the suit of the attorney general who was to be notified of such failure by the Department.[1]

In 1954 a bill containing most of the provisions in the act presented to the Judicial Council nine years previously was drafted and sponsored by the attorney general, and was passed by the General Court. It called for the establishment of a Division of Public Charities in the Department of the Attorney General. The Division was directed to perform the duties imposed on the attorney general by chapter 12, section 8, of the General Laws, the section stating the common law duties of the attorney general in respect to funds given or appropriated to public charities in the commonwealth. The new statute prescribed that the attorney general designate an assistant attorney general as director of public charities to serve as the executive and administrative head of the division.[2] The director, in turn, was authorized to appoint and remove, subject to the approval of the attorney general, such accounting, investment, clerical, and other experts and assistants as the work of the division might require.[3] The act contained no directive to establish a registry. Every charitable corporation established, organized, or chartered under laws other than those of the commonwealth, was required to file with the division a certified copy of its charter, articles, or certification of incorporation, and its constitution or bylaws before engaging in charitable work or raising funds in the state. Failure to comply was made subject to a fine of not more than $500 and a suit by the attorney general to restrain the violation or the transaction of any business while the violation continues.[4] This provision is unique to the Massachusetts act.

Section 8F required the trustee or trustees or governing board of every public charity, including those referred to in section 8E, to file a written report annually. The act specified that the report should state:

---

[1] Laws of Mass., Acts of 1948, ch. 354.
[2] Mass. Gen. Laws Ann., ch. 12, sec. 8C.
[3] Mass. Gen. Laws Ann., ch. 21, sec. 8D
[4] Mass. Gen. Laws Ann., ch. 12, sec. 8E.

... the names and addresses of the trustees, or if the public charity is an organization, the name and address of the organization and the names and addresses of the members of its principal governing board and of its principal officers, and if the organization is a corporation, the statute under which it was incorporated; the aggregate value of endowment and other funds, the aggregate value of real estate, and the aggregate value of tangible personal property held and administered by the public charity for charitable, educational, benevolent, humane or philanthropic purposes or for other purposes of public charity, all as shown by the books of the public charity at the end of said fiscal year, and the aggregate income and the aggregate expenditures of the public charity for such fiscal year.[1]

Written reports furnished by a charity to interested parties, or copies of probate accounts filed with the courts were deemed acceptable to meet the filing requirement. Exemption from this section was made for property held for any religious purpose by any public charity incorporated or unincorporated. The act imposed a filing fee of $3.00 for each report and stated that failure to file for two successive years was grounds for such action by the Division as may be appropriate to compel compliance.

The Division was granted authority, subject to application to, and with approval of, a judge of a probate court or a justice of the Supreme Judicial Court, to examine all books and records and investigate the administration of any public charity. The director was granted power to require attendance and testimony of witnesses who could be duly sworn and required to give testimony under the penalties of perjury.[2] The director was also given the right to formulate rules and regulations with reference to filing reports and conducting examinations and investigations, subject to approval of the governor and the executive council. This was the usual procedure for promulgation of rules and regulations by state agencies.[3] The act contained a section discussed earlier which required that the attorney general be made a party to all judicial proceedings in which he may be interested in the performance of his duties under section 8.[4] Finally, the provision of the General Laws defining the duties of the Department of Public Welfare with regard to receipt of reports and investigation of charities was repealed.

Following passage of this legislation, all files in the Department of

---

[1] Mass. Gen. Laws Ann., ch. 12, sec. 8F.
[2] Mass. Gen. Laws Ann., ch. 12, sec. 8H.
[3] Mass. Gen. Laws Ann., ch. 12, sec. 8I.
[4] Mass. Gen. Laws Ann., ch. 12, sec. 8G; see also p. 210.

Public Welfare were transferred to the new Division of Public Charities in the office of the attorney general, which was staffed by a director
and several clerical workers. Forms were printed which required information according to the categories listed in the statute. The director ruled unofficially that the term "public charity" did not include
a trust under the terms of which the trustees' duties were confined to
management of the property and payment of income or principal or
both to established charitable institutions over which the trustee had
no control. Furthermore, the Division agreed to an interpretation
whereby the term "public charity" was not applicable to a trust until
its funds were appropriated for charitable purposes, thereby exempting from the reporting provisions any remainder bequests, whether
vested or contingent, until such time as the intermediate estates had
terminated. The attorney general continued to be considered a necessary party to all judicial proceedings involving charitable bequests
which are remainder interests or contingent, so that copies of accounts
were filed with him when they were presented to the court for allowance. Accounts of inter vivos trusts did not, of course, come within
his purview until the charitable interest vested.

In 1958 and 1959 the Division of Public Charities undertook an
investigation of probate records in six counties in an effort to determine whether any funds left for charitable purposes were dormant and
should be activated. Law students were hired for two succeeding sum-
mers to undertake this task. More than $5 million of dormant charita-
ble funds were discovered and reactivated. These included a trust of
approximately $1 million established for general charitable purposes,
another of like amount for the benefit of crippled children, and a third
for scholarships for students from two large public high schools. In
each case action was brought to have new trustees appointed by the
court. In the case of the fund for crippled children, the court ordered
that half of the income be accumulated until it was sufficient to build
a hospital, as required by the terms of the will, and the other half be
used annually to support medical research in the designated field. The
new trustees, who were presidents of three local colleges, have since
supported a wide variety of research projects dealing with the physical
and emotional aspects of the treatment of handicapped children.

During the same period, a listing of charitable corporations organized under chapter 180 of the General Laws was made from records
in the office of the secretary of state in an attempt to assure that all
corporations subject to the filing requirements were complying with

the statute. A letter was also prepared and mailed to all city and town solicitors requesting lists of all known charitable organizations within their particular communities, as well as copies of city or town financial reports containing information in regard to charitable funds administered by them. The reporting form was revised in 1959 to include requests for more detailed information as to each of the statutory categories. By the end of 1959, a total of 2,252 public charities were filing annual reports with the division.

In 1960 the attorney general requested two members of the staff of Brandeis University to conduct a survey of the activities of the Division of Public Charities with an eye toward assessing and improving the operation of the Division. Their report contained four major recommendations:

> First: a detailed inventory of all funds currently reporting to the Division to gather further information on the method of creation, administration and purpose of these funds; and a compilation of this information in a Master File.
> Second: a revision of the form currently used for annual reports, to give more detailed information about financial activities and the means by which the charitable purposes are being implemented.
> Third: preparation and distribution of a booklet containing information on all charities currently reporting to the Division.
> Fourth: expansion of current efforts to discover funds which were not reporting; exploration of the feasibility of amending the existing law to extend the authority of the Attorney General over certain funds not currently included under Chapter 12.

A supplementary appropriation was obtained from the General Court to carry out these recommendations with an expanded staff.

As a first step, the attorney general appointed an Advisory Committee on Public Charities composed of 30 members and including leaders from the fields of philanthropy, law, accounting, and social work, and representatives from the law schools in the area. This group, working primarily through small committees, gave advice and recommendations on such phases of the new program as the revision of forms, the compilation and distribution of the *Directory,* the problems arising from solicitation by charitable organizations, and the drafting rules and regulations for the Division. They also consulted on certain policy matters in which the attorney general was interested. As an example, they discussed and proposed recommendations concerning a Bill in Equity filed by the trustees of a fund established under the will of Benjamin Franklin to provide loans to young artificers under certain specific conditions during a two-hundred-year period. No loans had been made since 1886, and the trustees had requested permission of the Supreme Judicial Court to apply the funds *cy pres* for loans to medical students and residents. Following the recommendation of the Advisory Committee, the attorney general's answer requested the court to broaden the scope of the plan so that loans could be made to those in training in other technical sciences and crafts. The final decree of the Supreme Judicial Court embodied this suggestion.

The Division, in June of 1961, published a *Directory of Public Charities in Massachusetts,*[1] which listed all charities filing reports with the Division alphabetically and by purpose. A grant for this project was donated by the Permanent Charity Fund of Boston. The *Directory* was distributed to all public libraries in the state, to city and town clerks, to the probate courts, and, on request, to individuals. A mimeographed supplement was published in 1963.

In April of 1965 a second edition, entitled *Directory of Foundations in Massachusetts,*[2] was published. Financed again by a grant from the Permanent Charity Fund of Boston, it contained detailed information on grant-making organizations reporting to the attorney general in a format similar to that of *The Foundation Directory.* It also included a statistical table and a comprehensive catalog of foundations with special purposes and geographical or other restrictions.

Prior to publication of the *Directory,* a complete analysis of all charities reporting to the Division was undertaken. A new office file was compiled which listed the charities by purpose, and included the names of the principal directors, the total assets, and the amounts of charitable donations. The file has been used by many individuals seeking sources for donations or potential beneficiaries, as well as by members of other state departments.

For the first time, the assets of charitable funds, including total figures and a breakdown of these totals according to charitable purpose were computed. The classification system that was adopted for the files and the *Directory* contains 49 separate categories of public charitable purposes grouped under the following headings: Civic, Conservation and Animal Care, Crime Prevention and Legal Aid, Clubs and Societies, Cultural, Direct Aid, Education, Fund-raising Organ-

---

[1] Howard, Lawrence C., and Marion R. Miller, editors, Commonwealth of Massachusetts, Boston, 1961.

[2] John J. Roche, editor, Commonwealth of Massachusetts, Boston, 1965.

izations, Health—General, Health—Specific Areas, Missionary Work, Old Age, Patriotic and Fraternal, Youth, and Foundations and Funds. The last category includes: (a) organizations established for religious, charitable, and scientific purposes; (b) organizations which may make payments only to other charitable organizations; and (c) organizations which are required to pay funds over to specifically named charitable organizations. Approximately $182 million is held by organizations in the first and second of these categories, and $57 million, by those in the third. The total assets of all charitable organizations filing with the Division of Public Charities was estimated at $3 billion, of which $1 billion was held by educational institutions and an additional $500 million by hospitals and clinics. At the time these statistics were compiled, annual reports were often made in terms of book value, so that the actual figure is probably considerably higher.

The Directory of Foundations published in 1965 includes those charities listed in the earlier editions as Foundations and Funds, and all other charities whose assets are available for other charitable organizations, for needy individuals, or for specialized programs that are of interest to the public. However, very small funds and foundations whose principal assets were less than $10 thousand or whose income was less than $1,000 were excluded. Approximately 1,200 of the 4,000 public charities in the commonwealth met the criteria. Their net assets were estimated at $366 million book value. Income from these foundations in 1963 was $37 million and during that period they made grants of $30 million. The *Directory* noted that:

> The seven million dollar discrepancy between income and grants is owing to the fact that the total income of many operating charitable organizations was included, notwithstanding the fact that the grants only constituted a small fraction of total expenditures. Therefore, the bulk of seven million dollars in question was used in providing services to the public.[1]

Office procedures were also revised during 1961–1963. Addressograph plates were made for all funds; and the staff undertook a preliminary investigation of the use of automatic data processing with the financial reports, but concluded that such a step was not necessary to handle the present number of charitable funds reporting.

After the master list for the *Directory* had been compiled, a second phase of the work commenced: the comparison of this list with that of the exempt organization file of the local office of the Internal Revenue

---

[1] *Ibid.*, p. xi.

Service. As a result, over 1,000 additional charitable funds were located and notified of the reporting requirements.

A measure of the success of this search for new charitable funds was evident from the figures supplied by the state auditor on the collection of the $3.00 fee which must accompany each financial report. For the period from January 28, 1960 to November 18, 1960, $6,270 was collected; for the period from November 18, 1960 to November 8, 1961, during which this intensive search was started, the figure rose to $11,448. As of January 1, 1965, the Division was receiving reports from approximately 4,000 public charities.

Revision of the form for filing financial reports was a major task of the Division and a subcommittee of the Advisory Committee. In 1961, a new form with a format similar to Form 990–A of the federal Internal Revenue Service was adopted; except for the inclusion of certain categories of information relating to liabilities and expenses for solicitation of funds, it required the same information.[1] The director reported in 1962 that the form was well received by the charities since it simplified bookkeeping and management of records.[2]

The regulations promulgated by the Division of Public Charities in 1962 were drafted with the aid and advice of members of the Advisory Committee. Article I deals with the term "public charity" in terms of legal framework and provides a guide to the meaning of the exemption for property held for religious purposes. An informal ruling by the Division in 1954 that trusts for the benefit of named charitable organizations did not constitute "public charities" was formally reversed. Article II grants exemption from the report-filing requirement to charities which pay their total income to a department or agency of the state, city, or town, and to charities whose trustees are elected or appointed by members of state departments and whose accounts are audited by the state. It contains guides for determination of conflicts of law problems in respect to charities created outside the state or administered in part outside the state. The language of the Restatement of Conflicts of Law in regard to trusts was adopted, so that reports must be filed by all charities "within the Commonwealth" except those previously described as exempt. The regulations state:

Determinations as to the inclusion of any public charity within the section shall be made by the Director and shall be based on evidence as to

---

[1] This form (Mass. Form 12) is reprinted in Appendix C.

[2] Commonwealth of Massachusetts, Office of the Attorney General, *Annual Report* for the period January, 1961 to May, 1962, *op. cit.,* 1962.

the place where the public charity was created, the language of the instrument or corporate charter, the domicile of the trustees or directors, or the settlor, or the charitable beneficiaries, the location of the property and the place where the business is conducted.[1]

Article III contains detailed provisions for investigatory proceedings.

Also during 1962, the General Court enacted three bills prepared by the Division of Public Charities with the assistance of members of the Advisory Committee. The bills were designed to supplement and improve the 1954 act. A new section was added which in effect created a registry of charitable trusts by requiring the trustees and directors of every public charity organized or operated within the commonwealth to file with the Division a copy of its charter, articles of organization, agreement of association or instrument of trust, and a copy of its constitution and bylaws, within thirty days following the date of its creation.[2]

The second bill gave broader power and greater flexibility to the Division in relation to the information required in the annual reports. Although the forms used by the Division during the period from 1959 to 1962 requested detailed financial information, the legislative authorization extended only to aggregate figures. No complaints had been received from trustees or directors about the attempted extention of power, and, of course, the attorney general could at any time require the examination of all books and records. Nevertheless, the Division felt it extremely desirable to obtain statutory authorization to require necessary information. This amendment simply added to section 8F the following words: "each aggregate figure required being accompanied by an itemized statement on forms provided by the director, of the component parts of such aggregate assets, income and expenditures."[3]

The third bill was designed to clarify the statutory machinery for dissolution of charitable corporations and to guarantee that any funds involved would continue to be used for charitable purposes. Prior to the enactment of this bill, charitable corporations seeking dissolution used the procedure in chapter 155 of the General Laws which applied to business corporations and provided no guarantee for *cy pres* appli-

---

[1] Commonwealth of Massachusetts, Department of the Attorney General, *Regulations of the Director of Public Charities,* State House, Boston, filed with the Secretary of State on July 26, 1962, art. 2.3 (mimeographed).
[2] Laws of Mass., Acts of 1962, ch. 401; now Mass. Gen. Laws Ann., ch. 12, sec. 8J.
[3] Laws of Mass., Acts of 1962, ch. 425.

cation of funds. In several early cases, the Massachusetts Supreme Judicial Court had stated that the provisions of chapter 155 did not apply to public charities and it was felt that a clarification was in order. Two other factors led to the drafting of this legislation. One was the feeling of the Division that the power to bring action to dissolve inactive public charities should clearly rest with the attorney general, as overseer of all charitable funds. The second was that many individual Massachusetts charitable corporations were having trouble obtaining tax-exempt status from the federal Internal Revenue Service because the Service considered that the Massachusetts case law did not state with sufficient clarity the requirement that funds donated to a charitable corporation are required to be applied *cy pres* on dissolution.

The new statute[1] contains two methods for dissolution, one to be used by a charitable corporation which contemplates dissolution, the second to be used by the attorney general where a corporation has failed to file reports to his office for two years or where he is convinced that a charitable corporation is inactive and that its dissolution would be in the public interest. This act became effective in August, 1962, and by that date there had been 16 requests for action by the attorney general under section 2 or for advice on using section 1. The attorney general has since sought dissolution before the Supreme Judicial Court in several other cases involving large sums of money.

Since 1958, the staff of the Division of Public Charities in Massachusetts has consisted of at least two assistant attorneys general, one of whom has served as the director, a legal clerk, an executive secretary, and a secretary-clerk. Each summer one or two third-year law students have also been assigned to the Division. Although all assistant attorneys general in Massachusetts are permitted to carry on private law practice, the job is, in effect, a full-time occupation. The chief problem in terms of staff has been the Division's inability to obtain permanent auditors and investigators. At one time a member of the state police was assigned to the Division to do investigatory work, but now an investigator is available only for particular cases on request from the attorney general. The same situation applies in respect to auditing personnel.

Since its creation in 1954, the Division has had five directors, three of whom served for periods of at least two years. This turnover has been due, in part, to the fact that the office of attorney general in Mas-

---

[1] Mass. Gen. Laws Ann., ch. 180, sec. 11A.

sachusetts has been elective with a two-year term. Each attorney general appoints approximately 35 assistants, legal clerks, and some of the administrative personnel. In January of 1963 a leading member of the Massachusetts bar and former teacher of trusts and probate law accepted a special appointment as director on a temporary basis. Under his direction, a study of solicitation laws in the 50 states was undertaken, and new legislation was drafted to improve the supervision of charities that solicit funds from the public. The next director was the one assistant attorney general on the staff who was under the state civil service laws; he had served in the office for more than twenty-five years. By this appointment, the attorney general intended to place in the position the one person who would not be subject to the political vagaries of the office, thereby giving some measure of stability to the supervision of charities. Although from time to time consideration has been given to the advisability of proposing legislation to make the position of director of public charities a permanent position under the state civil service laws, the attorneys general have thought it inadvisable to make this exception to their appointive power.

Investigation of the misapplication of charitable funds is the primary responsibility of one of the assistant attorneys general assigned to the Division. Routine procedure has consisted of evaluation of all financial reports filed with the Division, first by the executive secretary, then by an attorney. Each year approximately 150 inquiries are sent out as a result of the first scrutiny. They generally comprise the following categories: loan questions, accumulations, inadequate returns on investments, incomplete reports, or small charitable expenditures. Many cases are settled by the first letter, but others are marked for further investigation or administrative hearing. Loans to and from charities are very carefully perused to see that there is compliance with the law in regard to self-dealing. In two separate cases it was discovered that charitable trusts were paying the premiums on insurance policies on the life of the settlor, but the policies were not irrevocably the property of the trust, and these situations were rectified. Trustees of several funds accepted recommendations to diversify investments, and many that had accumulated an unwarranted amount of income were persuaded to distribute it to charitable beneficiaries.

The Division has also conducted special investigations into alleged irregularities brought to its attention by reliable outside sources. Often these investigations have revealed only a dispute between two conflicting factions of a charitable organization. In one instance, however, a valid complaint led to action by the attorney general to prevent an unauthorized sale of property donated for charitable purposes. In another, the Division cooperated with the directors of a charitable hospital to prevent an illegal sale of securities of a closely owned company held by the charitable corporation.

The Division has felt that the routine informal inquiries are as important in their overall influence on all charitable organizations as on those immediately affected. In many cases where ignorance has led to abuses, the matter has been easily and willingly rectified. Only in rare instances have individuals purposefully used charitable funds to their own advantage. The policy of the Division, therefore, has been to attempt to take care of routine matters without undue publicity, since it is understood that bad publicity may, in the long run, discourage the growth of philanthropy.

Massachusetts is the only state in which the statutory power of the attorney general to conduct formal investigations, subpoena records, and examine witnesses has been used to any great extent. It is interesting to observe that the power to conduct investigations in Massachusetts is limited by a requirement that the attorney general first obtain approval from a judge of a probate court or a justice of the Supreme Judicial Court, a limitation not found in the statutes of other states. Approximately 10 such court approvals have been obtained since the effective date of the act in 1954.

The formal investigations have related to diverse problems: several involved improper solicitation of charitable funds; one related to misapplication of trust funds; and one arose from a dispute over the election of directors of a charitable corporation. In 1962 the director obtained permission to conduct an investigation of an allegedly improper sale of property held under a ninety-nine-year lease by an inactive charitable corporation; at the same time, he obtained an injunction against the sale pending the outcome of the investigation. In another case, the power to subpoena books and records was crucial to the prevention of a complete diversion of an estate left by will to carry on a school. The attorney general was able to obtain the appointment of a new administrator of the estate and to arrange to have an established institution assume the school's charter and continue its operations as part of its larger educational program.

The scope of charitable endeavors in Massachusetts, as represented in the reports received from public charities, is far broader than that of any other state. This fact has created certain problems, one of which relates to the nature of the reports which must be required, and another to the difficulty of comparing these different types of operations. The value of receiving reports from so-called "operating institutions," however, has been amply demonstrated. One striking result was the discovery that four different corporations, originally established through testamentary bequests of funds, and in some cases of real property, with directions to build either a hospital, a home for the aged, or a community center, had failed to build a facility. In two other cases, homes for the aged were being operated on such a small scale that large amounts of income had of necessity accumulated. In one of these cases, the director of public charities was able to persuade the trustees to request permission for *cy pres* application of more than 75 per cent of the income of a fund of $1 million. Under the terms of the decree of the probate court, the directors are continuing to operate a small home for aged men, and are empowered to use the remaining 75 per cent of the income to make direct grants or support other charitable organizations engaged in research in problems relating to geriatrics. In another case, action was brought and a decree obtained under the terms of which the trustees turned over their fund to a large hospital in the area intended to be served by the original trust. The fund has since been used to build and endow an addition to the hospital. In most of these cases, the trustees have cooperated with the attorney general in bringing these actions, but there is no indication that any change would have been made without initial impetus from the state.

Participation in litigation affecting charitable funds represents the second major aspect of the activities of the division. An assistant attorney general has been assigned to review all wills, executors' and trustees' accounts where there are charitable bequests, and miscellaneous petitions. Routine office procedure does not provide a tabulation of the types of cases handled, but a special computation made in 1962 indicated that the attorney general had participated in 1,273 cases during that year. These break down as follows: 579 petitions for allowance of trustees' accounts; 198 petitions for final allowance of executors' and administrators' accounts; 19 for appointment or removal of trustees; 353 cases pertaining to probate of wills; 51 petitions for sale of real estate; 29 petitions for instructions (usually involving questions of *cy pres*); and 44 miscellaneous petitions. In an attempt to simplify the paper work involved in this phase of its duties, in 1963 the Division discontinued mailing notices to the court when the attorney general did not care to be heard. At present notice is sent only when the attorney general has objections and desires to participate in the proceedings.

A third aspect of the work of the Division of Public Charities in Massachusetts is the regulation of charitable solicitations. Prior to 1964, the Massachusetts statute regulating solicitation of funds[1] was similar to that of Ohio, except that there was no bonding requirement for solicitors. However, unlike the situation in Ohio, the solicitation of funds by charitable organizations, except those for religious purposes, is considered to be under the supervisory powers of the attorney general, and all soliciting organizations come within the reporting requirement of section 8F. At one time, reports from solicitors and professional fund-raisers, as well as the reports required both prior to and at the close of a solicitation, were kept in the Criminal Division of the Department of the Attorney General, although investigations were conducted under the direction of the Division of Public Charities. In 1962, all records of charitable solicitations were reviewed and consolidated with the financial reports required of these charities under chapter 12, section 8F. This move facilitated the evaluation of both types of reports. It was recognized, however, that the statutory provisions relating to solicitations were unclear and inadequate. In 1963, the Division reviewed the existing legislation in the 50 states and drafted a bill establishing a licensing and bonding requirement for charitable organizations and paid solicitors intending to solicit funds in the state. This bill was passed by the General Court in July of 1964.[2]

A second bill drafted at the same time and approved on June 5, 1964, contained amendments dealing with annual financial reports. It amends section 8F by the addition of provisions explicitly requiring information as to the cost of administration, the cost of solicitation, the costs of programs designed to educate or inform the public, funds or properties transferred out of state with explanation as to the recipient and purpose, and a certification of an independent public accountant that he has examined the books of the charity and finds the financial statement correct (if the public charity has a gross income of $5,000 or more or investment income of $1,000 or more).[3]

---

[1] Mass. Gen. Laws Ann., ch. 67, secs. 18 ff.
[2] Laws of Mass., Acts of 1964, ch. 718, effective January 1, 1965.
[3] Laws of Mass., Acts of 1964, ch. 449, amending Mass. Gen. Laws Ann., ch. 12, sec. 8F.

The act further requires that the reports be signed by two authorized officers, including the chief fiscal officer, and verified under oath. Reports by parent organizations must include information as to all affiliates. A new paragraph made the act of knowingly filing a false report subject to a fine of not more than $1,000, or imprisonment for not more than one year, or both. A new reporting form was devised immediately to meet the requirements of the new statute, although it did not alter the general format adopted in 1962.[1] The Division also issued a pamphlet containing the text of the new legislation, a brief explanation of its provisions, and a foreword by Attorney General Edward W. Brooke that acknowledged the counsel and support of the scores of charitable organizations in the state that had endorsed the bills and aided in obtaining their passage.

The Division of Public Charities also made arrangements in 1964 to receive immediately copies of all applications for charters of not-for-profit corporations from the secretary of state's office. If the application indicates that the organization's purposes are "charitable" in the broad legal sense, a form letter is sent to the directors advising them of the registration and reporting requirements of chapter 12 and including forms for annual reports. The Division also cooperates actively with both the state Commission on Taxation and the local Internal Revenue Service office in the exchange of information. Several additional surveys of the federal reports have been made since the initial work in 1961. Personnel in the attorney general's office have confirmed the impression of some commentators that many charitable funds are operating without tax exemption from the federal government and without having filed under federal law.

It should be noted that in addition to its duties in regard to charitable organizations, the Division of Public Charities, acting for the attorney general, represents the commonwealth of Massachusetts in all court proceedings involving public administration and estates of absentees. It reviews approximately 1,000 petitions from public administrators each year. The proceedings usually involve petitions for appointment of public administrator, approval of accounts, sales of real estate, and distribution and collection of funds escheating to the state.

The Massachusetts program of supervision has been constantly enlarged and improved during its ten-year lifetime. Although the staff of the Division of Public Charities is larger than that of any other state

---

[1] This form (Mass. Form 12) is reprinted in Appendix C.

except California, it is still not adequate, particularly with respect to specialized personnel such as auditors and investigators. With the enactment of new legislation relating to organizations which solicit funds, the Division will require additional help to meet the demands of both the new and the existing programs.

Even without auditing personnel, however, the attorneys in the office have been able, with the assistance of a well-trained executive secretary, to maintain a great degree of supervision of charitable activities, correcting misuse and activating dormant funds.

Furthermore, Massachusetts has made an important contribution to the concept of supervision through its program of active cooperation with trustees and directors of charitable funds and with the general public. Close contact with those groups most directly affected by regulation has long been recognized as an effective administrative device. The establishment of the Attorney General's Advisory Committee, the publication of two directories, and the revision of reporting forms to conform with those required by the federal government were each considered means whereby government could encourage philanthropic activities. They were devised in the belief that alert administration and enforcement entails more than securing mere statutory compliance, and that the attorney general's duty extends to providing service to charitable organizations and their beneficiaries. The potentialities of such a program have not yet been fully realized, but the start made in Massachusetts has already been followed in several other states and is worthy of wider acceptance.

Iowa

A Charitable Trusts Act was passed by the legislature of Iowa in 1959.[1] It follows the language of the Rhode Island act except that it contains no sections dealing with the appointment by the attorney general of an administrator of charitable trusts. Immediately upon passage of the act, however, the attorney general adopted rules and regulations that established in the Department of Justice a Register of Charitable Trusts. One assistant attorney general was assigned to handle all charitable trust matters. A registration form and a reporting form adapted from those used in Rhode Island are currently in use. The office prefers to use these forms rather than probate accounts, because they are uniform and easily filed. Trusts are indexed alphabetically but filed by number according to the date of registration.

---

[1] Iowa Laws 1959, ch. 364; now Iowa Code Ann., secs. 682.48 to 682.59.

The Register of Charitable Trusts, which is open to public inspection, contains a condensation of the information included in the registration statement, a listing of the date on which each annual report is received, and the value of the trust given in the report. The files of annual reports are not available for public inspection. As of January, 1965, 404 trusts were registered. Of these, 21 had registered in 1964, 23 in 1963, 10 in 1962, 27 in 1961, and the remaining 323 from the effective date of the act to December 31, 1960. No separate tabulations of the trusts are made by the office according to charitable purposes or other categories.

In 1960, however, a study of this information was made by a private individual.[1] He reported that as of March 21, 1960, there were 256 charitable trusts registered, with an approximate value of $28 million. Four of these held funds of more than $1 million, the largest being valued at $3.2 million. The smallest trust had a principal of $43. One hundred twenty-five had been created by will, 9 by deed, and 122 were not listed, but presumably were either corporations or inter vivos trusts. It should be noted that in Iowa, as in Rhode Island, the language of the exemption provisions has been interpreted as being confined to operating institutions, so that corporate foundations are required to file.

The trusts were also analyzed according to purpose, with the following findings: aid to the poor, 39; educational, 49; religious, 56; governmental, 8; cemetery, 19; health, 20; charitable, religious, and educational,[2] 63; aid to other tax-exempt organizations, 6; miscellaneous, 17. Finally, an attempt was made to analyze the trusts according to the type of trustee: 108 funds were held by individual trustees (in 45 of these at least one trustee had a name in common with the name of the trust and presumably was the donor or a member of his family); 141 were held by banks; and 7 by other corporations.[3]

All reports are reviewed by the assistant attorney general assigned to charitable matters. Upon receipt of a report, an acknowledgment is sent by return mail with two copies of report forms to be used the following year. The assistant attorney general checks from time to time to assure that reports have been received when due, but has not devised a routine system for finding delinquents. No search of other

---

[1] Craig, Arlo F., Jr., "Charitable Trusts in Iowa," *Drake Law Review,* vol. 9, May, 1960, p. 90.
[2] That is, foundations organized under the Int. Rev. Code, sec. 501(c)(3).
[3] Craig, Arlo F., Jr., *op. cit.*

sources has been made to locate funds that should be reporting. At the time the act was passed, a letter went to all members of the state bar notifying them of its provisions, but no further effort has been made to publicize the provisions.

Prior to passage of this legislation, the courts in Iowa customarily notified the attorney general of litigations involving charitable funds but not of routine requests by trustees for the allowance of accounts. The requirement that trustees of testamentary trusts file accounts annually with the courts, however, has always been strictly observed. Since passage of the legislation, trustees have made a practice of submitting their accounts to the attorney general prior to filing a motion for allowance. If the attorney general's office has objections, it will then file an appearance and may submit written objections.

The attorney general has brought no actions on his own motion involving charitable funds since 1959, although he has actively participated in several cases relating to dormant trust funds and construction of wills creating charitable trusts. For example, in *In re Ditz's Estate*[1] he intervened in a suit challenging the validity of a will establishing a charitable trust for the benefit of charities to be selected by the trustees. The bequest was upheld. In another case, the attorney general intervened in an action brought by citizens of a town named as beneficiary of a dormant trust of $350,000 created under the terms of a will probated more than fifty years previously. The lower court held that the citizens were not proper parties but that the intervention of the attorney general was sufficient to permit the case to be heard. The court decreed the appointment of new trustees and held that the fund should be used for scholarship purposes for citizens of the town.

In a third case, a testamentary trust left to the "Iowa State Public School Fund," for use by children of the public schools in grades one, two, and three to promote lung development and the teaching of vocal music was challenged by the heirs of the testator. The attorney general's position upholding the charitable gift was accepted by the Supreme Court of Iowa, which found that a charitable trust was created, and directed application of the funds for assisting music programs in the schools.[2] In later proceedings to close the probate of the estate, the attorney general intervened and was successful in reducing excessive fees charged by the executor-trustees.

In 1963 the legislature adopted a complete revision of the Iowa

---

[1] 254 Iowa 444, 117 N.W.2d 825 (1962).
[2] *Eckles* v. *Lounsberry,* 253 Iowa 172, 111 N.W.2d 638 (1961).

Probate Code. The revision had been prepared by a Special Probate Committee of the Iowa State Bar Association, first appointed in 1958 to review the existing body of probate law in that state and make recommendations for its improvement. One of the recommendations of the Committee was the repeal of the Charitable Trusts Act of 1959 and the substitution of the following section:

> Charitable Trusts—Copies of Wills to Attorney General. When a will creating a charitable trust has been admitted to probate, or when any instrument establishing a charitable trust has been filed with the clerk, the clerk shall forthwith mail a copy of such will or instrument to the attorney general. At any time, the attorney general may investigate for the purpose of determining and ascertaining whether or not such estate or trust is being administered in accordance with law and with the terms and purposes thereof, and may, at any time, make application to the court for such orders therein as may appear to be reasonable and proper to carry out the purposes of the trust. The words "charitable trust" as used in this section shall mean any fiduciary relationship with respect to property arising as a result of manifestation of an intention to create it and subjecting the person by whom the property is held to equitable duties to deal with the property for charitable, educational or religious purposes.[1]

The Special Probate Committee's comments indicated that this change had been made with the advice of the attorney general. The legislature rejected the recommendation, however, refusing to repeal the Charitable Trusts Act. It did add a section to the new Probate Code providing that the attorney general, at any time after the issuance of letters testamentary, may request notice of all hearings in any estate, and may, with the approval of the court, intervene in behalf of the public interest. Furthermore, the court, on its own motion, is empowered to direct a fiduciary to give notice of hearings to the attorney general.[2]

A second section of the new code that will affect testamentary charitable trusts provides for the creation of a trust register: each county clerk of court must treat every trust created by will as a separate proceeding with a separate docket number;[3] on May 1 and November 1 of each year he is required to notify any fiduciary and his attorney of any delinquent inventory or report due by law, and he must also notify the court on July 1 and January 1 of each year of all delinquent reports

---

[1] Quoted in *1963 Iowa Probate Code*. West Publishing Co., St. Paul, 1963, p. 32 (special publication of the New Code with explanations).
[2] Iowa Probate Code, sec. 43, as inserted by Acts of 1963 (60 G.A.) S.F. No. 165.
[3] Iowa Probate Code, sec. 28.

on which notice was given and no report was filed.[1] Under a separate section, the court is empowered to remove dilatory trustees.

The Special Committee's proposal to repeal the 1953 Charitable Trusts Act resulted from the opinion that review of annual reports was not a proper function of the attorney general's office and that the trust register should be located in the offices of the county clerks of court. An additional proposal considered by the Special Committee, but not submitted to the legislature, would have required the clerks to forward to the attorney general such inter vivos charitable trust instruments as the attorney general might require, in addition to a copy of every trust created by will. Even with the added provision for inter vivos trusts, however, the recommendation would have fallen far short of supplying the attorney general with information about all foundations, particularly corporations.

No changes in office procedure have been made since the new Probate Code became effective on January 1, 1964. The attorney general's staff has felt that the limited personnel available to handle charitable matters makes it difficult to attempt a thorough program directed at all possible abuses by charitable fiduciaries, so that it is better to concentrate on a more limited number of objectives. Since 1959, the office has focused primarily on court proceedings involving charitable gifts, particularly dormant trusts. This emphasis was re-evaluated following the enactment of the Probate Code, and because there has been a change of administration in the office, new programs are likely to be developed in the near future.

Since the Register in Iowa is small, even the limited staff should be able to administer a meaningful program of continuous supervision that is directed at correcting some of the more flagrant abuses, particularly in the area of breach of fiduciary duty. The establishment of a program of cooperation with the federal Internal Revenue Service would be a likely first step. Two factors argue for such action. First, the new Probate Code gives the attorney general extremely explicit weapons with which to handle problems of self-dealing and proper investment. Section 155 of the new Code codified existing law by stating:

> No fiduciary shall in any manner deal with himself, except on order of court after notice to all interested persons, and shall derive no profit other than his distributive share in the estate from the sale or liquidation of any property belonging to the estate.

---

[1] Iowa Probate Code, sec. 32.

And a section defining breach of duty, adapted from the Model Probate Code, provides:

> Every fiduciary shall be liable and chargeable in his accounts for neglect or unreasonable delay in collecting the credits or other assets of the estate or in selling, mortgaging or leasing the property of the estate; for neglect in paying over money or delivering property of the estate he shall have in his hands; for failure to account for or to close the estate within the time provided by this Code; for any loss to the estate arising from his embezzlement or commingling of the assets of the estate with other property; for loss to the estate through self-dealing; for any loss to the estate arising from wrongful acts or omissions of his cofiduciaries which he could have prevented by the exercise of ordinary care; and for any other negligent or willful act or nonfeasance in his administration of the estate by which loss to the estate arises.[1]

The second fact that makes an expansion of supervision desirable is that the Iowa law relating to the creation and dissolution of corporate charities is one of the most permissive of any state. Charitable corporations can be created on a stock or membership basis, and a charter may be obtained by merely filing the required papers with the secretary of state. No annual reports need be submitted to the state. A corporation may be dissolved by the filing of a letter with the secretary of state signed by two of the officers and notarized. The secretary of state's office keeps no separate record of the purposes for which not-for-profit corporations are chartered, but they estimate that approximately 200 corporate foundations were created during 1963 and 1964. Although no automatic procedure has been established for notifying the attorney general's office of the creation of these corporations, or of any others that might fall within the provisions of the Charitable Trusts Act, a member of the attorney general's office does check the files of the secretary of state from time to time to obtain the names of newly created corporations. Unless the attorney general takes the initiative in following the activities of these corporations, however, they may be dissolved, and the charitable funds distributed, without any oversight by authorities of the state.

---

[1] Iowa Probate Code, sec. 160.

CHAPTER IX

The Uniform Act in Operation

CHAPTER VIII CONTAINED A DESCRIPTION of the programs for the supervision of charities in the six states that followed the lead of New Hampshire in adopting legislation empowering the attorney general to obtain information about the operation of certain charitable trusts and corporations, and to correct abuses in their administration. In 1954 a Uniform Supervision of Trustees for Charitable Purposes Act was adopted by the Commissioners on Uniform State Laws. It was designed to provide a model for any state wanting to adopt a program similar to those described in Chapter VIII.[1] Modified versions of the Uniform Act are in force in California, Michigan, Illinois, and Oregon, and their operations are described in this chapter.

California

California became the first state to adopt the Uniform Supervision of Trustees for Charitable Purposes Act, when the legislature enacted the law in 1955 for a two-year trial period.[2] Prior to the expiration date, the period was extended an additional two years.[3] In 1959 the legislature made certain amendments and put the legislation on a permanent basis.[4]

Little action was taken following the original passage of the act, largely because the statute contained no enforcement provisions or

---

[1] The Uniform Supervision of Trustees for Charitable Purposes Act is reprinted in full in Appendix B.

[2] Cal. Stats. 1955, ch. 1820.

[3] Cal. Stats. 1957, ch. 2024.

[4] Cal. Stats. 1959, ch. 1258.

penalties for noncompliance, and because no specific appropriations were made to finance the establishment of a registry. In June of 1957 interest in the establishment of an active program of supervision revived. The attorney general appointed Frederick Auforth, a man experienced in business and accounting, to make a survey of charitable trust matters and to recommend procedures for administering the act. One year later the attorney general created the position of Registrar of Charitable Trusts, under the supervision of the chief assistant attorney general, and appointed Mr. Auforth to fill the post.

In the meantime, files from San Francisco and Los Angeles had been consolidated in the Sacramento office of the attorney general, report forms had been redesigned, and information sources explored. A major source of information was the Franchise Tax Board, which made available 12,000 record cards for tax-exempt corporations. The Internal Revenue Service Cumulative Bulletin of exempt organizations was also employed. New registration and reporting forms were mailed to trustees in March of 1958.

By the close of 1958, 1,214 charitable trusts with corporate, individual, or cotrustees had registered. They held capital funds worth $324 million and had donated $96 million to charity in that year. An additional 486 trusts had registered, but were ruled exempt from the annual filing requirement because they were subject to the jurisdiction of the superintendent of banks of the state of California or the Comptroller of Currency of the United States.[1]

An additional 1,545 charitable organizations had been requested to register. Of these, 731 were registered, 95 were ruled exempt, 124 were found to be inactive, 273 claimed exemption, 198 had ignored requests, and an additional 124 had not registered for various reasons. Of the 731 charitable organizations registered, 194 complied with a first request, 361 required two letters, and 176 required three or more. The registrar of charitable trusts, in his report for 1958, stated that there were 595 known organizations that undoubtedly should register but owing to the "unfortunate wording of the Act and because there are no enforcement provisions. . . ," had refused to comply.[2] The work during 1958 had been carried on by the registrar of charitable trusts with the assistance of a secretary, a stenographer-clerk, and an accountant.

---

[1] Cal. Gov. Code, sec. 12586(a).
[2] State of California, Office of the Attorney General, *First Annual Report of the Registrar of Charitable Trusts,* State Capitol, Sacramento, Cal., December 31, 1958 (mimeographed).

It is apparent from this report for 1958 that some confusion remained in the minds of certain members of the attorney general's staff as to whether the attorney general had authority under the Uniform Act to question the administration of a trustee, or whether his sole function was to create a register or file of trusts. Nevertheless, the report listed several cases wherein trustees were questioned and irregularities corrected. In one case, a trustee of a corporate charitable trust who had been investing funds in a trading account at a loss of $219,050 agreed to release custodianship of investments to the trust's bank and subject the trust's account to the supervision and direction of the bank's investment committee. In another case, an attempted sale of real estate and distribution of the assets among the officers of a charitable corporation was forestalled, the directors were forced to resign, and new officers were elected. In addition, the report listed 63 trusts with capital valued at $34 million that required further investigation, 19 cases under investigation in the Los Angeles office of the attorney general, and 33 cases that had been closed during the period of the report. The registrar recommended that the Charitable Trusts Act be made permanent with certain amendments.

The legislation adopted in 1959 put the Uniform Act on a permanent basis and included several of the recommendations of the registrar. Most important was the proposal that the act clearly include within its scope all charitable corporations and charitable trusts.[1] The act clarified the exemption for charitable institutions by stating that it applied to "a charitable corporation organized and operated primarily as a religious organization, educational institution or hospital"; thus, it replaced the wording of the Uniform Act, which states, "a charitable corporation organized and operated primarily for educational, religious, scientific or hospital purposes." Additional language was added requiring that the attorney general be made a party to all proceedings to modify or terminate any trust of property for charitable purposes. Another new requirement was that any person who offers for probate any instrument that establishes a testamentary trust of property for charitable purposes or who records any inter vivos trust of property for charitable purposes furnish a copy of the documents to the attorney general.

In 1961 the enforcement power of the attorney general was enlarged through the enactment of a provision that:

---

[1] See p. 266.

(a) No exemption shall be allowed under this article to any charitable corporation as defined in Sections 12582.1 and 12583 of the Government Code for any year or years for which it fails to file with the Attorney General, on or before the due date, any registration or periodic report required by Article 7 (commencing with Section 12580) of Chapter 6, Part 2, Division 3, Title 2, of the Government Code.

(b) The exemption shall be disallowed under this section only after the Attorney General has notified the Franchise Tax Board in writing that a charitable corporation subject to the provisions of subdivision (a) has failed to file any such registration or periodic report on or before the due date thereof.

(c) If an exemption is disallowed under this section, such exemption may be reinstated when the registration or periodic reports are filed; however, any such charitable corporation shall pay the minimum tax provided for by Section 23153 for any year or years for which its exemption was disallowed under this section.

(d) No exemption shall be disallowed under this section for income years commencing before January 1, 1962.

(e) The Franchise Tax Board may make any regulations which it deems necessary to effectuate the purposes of this section.[1]

No additional amendments to the Uniform Act have been made, but in 1963 the legislature did amend the California Probate Code by adding a provision requiring notice to the attorney general of any instrument offered for probate that involves or may involve a testamentary trust for charitable purposes where none of the designated trustees resides in the state. The notice must be accompanied by a copy of the petition and the will.[2]

This amendment codified the practice in many of the local courts. It is not as extensive as either the statutory language or the practice in many other states, limited as it is to trusts where there is no resident trustee designated. The primary drawback to an exemption of this type is that in some cases, particularly if there is a will contest or a question of construction, a designated trustee, such as a named charitable corporation, may not feel it worthwhile to advance the necessary legal expenses, or, for policy reasons, may not wish to litigate with a decedent's family. Furthermore, it has been found that when the contest occurs prior to administration of a will, banks, as well as many individuals, ordinarily refuse to take legal action to uphold the will on the grounds that they have not as yet been designated as trustees and their obligations do not arise until after the will has been admitted for probate. Moreover, in some instances a designated corporate trustee

---

[1] Cal. Stats. 1961, ch. 2112, adding sec. 23703 to the Cal. Rev. and Tax Code.
[2] Cal. Stats. 1963, ch. 984.

has argued that the language of the will was merely precatory, and did not create a trust or even an enforceable right to hold the property for the purpose stated. The attorney general has intervened in several such cases to uphold the trust, but he has been limited by the fact that he has had to learn of the proceedings on his own initiative. In 1961 a bill was submitted to the legislature requiring notice in all cases, but it failed of passage.

Immediately following the effective date of the 1959 legislation, the organization of the Charitable Trusts Division was redefined, and its relationship to the attorney general's office was clarified. Because of geographical and population factors, it was necessary to spell out these administrative arrangements in precise detail. The attorney general of California, who is elected for a four-year term, is the active head of the Department of Justice, which is staffed by 200 attorneys. One of the assistant attorneys general was named as chief of the Trust and Trade Practices Unit. At present his headquarters are in San Francisco, where he has the aid of a deputy attorney general on a half-time basis, and one investigator. The office in Los Angeles is staffed by one deputy attorney general who devotes full time to charitable matters, two others who give half time, and one full-time investigator. Adequate clerical staff assists these offices. All of the positions are under the state civil service program, and the attorneys may not engage in private practice. In the Sacramento office of the Department of Justice, a deputy attorney general works part-time on charitable trust matters and serves as legal counsel to the registrar.

The Registry of Charitable Trusts is located in Sacramento. It is a separate office under the administrative direction of the registrar, who is appointed by the attorney general and operates under the general supervision of the assistant attorney general in charge of the Trusts and Trade Practices Division. The staff of the Registry includes three auditors and five secretaries. The auditors are assigned to the Registry on a two-year basis under a unique contractual arrangement with the Audits Division of the Department of Finance. Thus, the attorney general's office has the services of exceptionally well-trained and qualified auditors who have made the state service their career. The arrangement resulted from the discovery that individuals of the competence required were less willing to take a position with the Registry, where there is little possibility for advancement, than with the Department of Finance. It went into effect at the close of 1961, and has proved extremely effective. The expense of operating the Registry is estimated at approximately $85,000 a year, not including the salaries or expenses of investigators or other members of the attorney general's staff.

A Register of Charitable Trusts was formally established in 1959. It consists of a card index file containing information for each registrant as to the registration number, trust name and address, donor, purpose, initial capital, date created, trustees, attorney, beneficiaries, classifications as to legal form, and financial information taken from the annual reports as to amount of capital, income, expenditures (including distribution of funds in the categories of religious, educational, medical, scientific, and charitable purposes) and amounts accumulated.[1]

In addition, two separate sets of files are maintained. One, designated the Public File, contains the registration certificate, a copy of the instrument establishing the trust or corporation, copies of each periodic report, and copies of all court orders or judgments that affect the administration of the trust. Any document having contents not entirely for charitable purposes is withheld from this file. These public files are open, on request, for public inspection. Because of the large number of individuals seeking information on charitable trusts in the office, the Registry also maintains separate notebooks listing all trusts with similar purposes and including the information contained on the registration cards. Public use of the Registry has been constant. In 1962 the files were examined to the extent of 225 visitor days; in 1963 the figure was 271 visitor days.

The second set of files, designated the Department File, contains all papers, that are not included in the public file, such as correspondence, departmental memoranda, reports of investigations, work papers, and a trust analysis sheet on which the auditor's reports are made.

The functions of the registrar include: (1) maintaining the register and files; (2) obtaining new registrations, furnishing trustees with forms for annual reports, and reminding them of the provisions of the act; and (3) examining and analyzing all documents and reports to determine their adequacy. In connection with new registrations, the registrar receives from the Franchise Tax Board monthly lists of tax exemptions granted to charitable corporations. The Registry also receives copies of all court papers forwarded to the attorney general which involve the creation of new testamentary or inter vivos trusts.

---

[1] The California Registry Card is reprinted in Appendix C.

Further information is gathered from the Internal Revenue Service as to newly exempted organizations.

The Registry has developed a series of form letters to facilitate correspondence. It includes requests for registration, requests for articles of incorporation, trust instruments or bylaws, follow-up letters for unanswered requests for registration statements or delinquent periodic reports, acknowledgments of registration of charitable trusts, and receipt of report forms.

The initial registration form requests, in addition to information as to legal form, the date of creation, legal provisions, and names and addresses of officers or trustees, a detailed description of *all* assets and liabilities, including cash on hand and in banks, name and number of invested securities at cost or book value, personal and real property, and the names and addresses of recipients of benefits. The form must be executed and signed by one of the trustees or, in the case of a corporation, by an authorized officer.[1] This is the registration statement that must be filed by corporate trustees that are subject to the jurisdiction of the state banking authority or the federal government. Although the statute requires merely the filing of a copy of the articles of incorporation or other instrument providing for the trustees' title, powers, or duties, almost all bank and trust companies in the state have filed the registration statement and supplied the requested financial information.

The Uniform Act states that the registration must be filed "within six months after any part of the income or principal is authorized or required to be applied to a charitable purpose."[2] In April of 1962, following numerous inquiries as to the application of this provision to wills or other instruments that establish a remainder over for charitable purposes, the attorney general announced that trusts with charitable remainders need not register until the termination of prior estates and the vesting of the remainder interest. However, since a copy of any will offered for probate that contains a charitable remainder must be filed with the Registry, a separate section of the files was created to handle these instruments until the termination of the prior estates.

The periodic report forms, which must be signed and certified, require information similar to that called for on the registration statement. Separate schedules of financial conditions and operations that provide a complete disclosure of the activities of the organization

---

[1] The California Registration Statement is reprinted in Appendix C.
[2] Cal. Gov. Code, sec. 12585.

during the reporting period must be submitted. The regulations state that they must contain the following:

(a) A list of all assets and money on hand at the beginning and ending of such year. Securities in an investment portfolio with a total valuation in excess of $100,000 shall be scheduled on a form provided by the Attorney General.

(b) A list of all gains or losses from assets sold and investments made during the year, including statement of moneys derived from any sale and money placed in each investment.

(c) A statement of all receipts and income during the year, contributions, gifts or grants giving amount and source.

(d) A detailed statement of all disbursements and expenses during the year.

(e) A statement of the purposes for which the distributions, donations or payments have been made giving the name, address and amount disbursed to each recipient of benefits under the Charitable Trust.[1]

The regulations permit the filing of a probate court account which substantially complies with the contents required in lieu of the form supplied by the attorney general; they also allow the submission of a copy of information returns made to the state taxing authority or a copy of Form 990–A of the Internal Revenue Service, provided these are accompanied by all required exhibits and schedules.[2]

Where individuals serve as cotrustees or cofiduciaries with trustees exempt from filing, such as a bank or trust company, the individual must report annually on the actions taken to carry out the trust in which the exempt trustee did not participate and of which he has no record.[3] If there is no reportable act during any particular year, the regulations require that a periodic report must be filed with a statement of "No Activity."[4]

In 1961 the attorney general sponsored legislation which would have required a filing fee based on the assets of the charity. It failed of passage, however, and has not been reintroduced.[5]

The registrar examines each new registration form before it is filed and prepares a trust analysis sheet.[6] Each periodic report is referred to an auditor for examination and confidential analysis of such consid-

[1] Cal. Admin. Code, tit. 11, subch. 4. Regulations adopted pursuant to the Uniform Supervision of Trustees for Charitable Purposes Act, sec. 306.
[2] Ibid., sec. 308.
[3] Ibid., sec. 309.
[4] Ibid.
[5] State of California, Senate Bill No. 934 (1961); see p. 257.
[6] The California Trust Analysis Sheet is reprinted in Appendix C.

erations as the adequacy of assets investments; the nature and extent
of operating expenses; sources of income, and, where appropriate,
the methods and costs of solicitation; legality of investments; the propriety and adequacy of annual disbursements of income and capital
under the trust documents; conflict of trustees' interests; the possibility
of *cy pres* application of neglected or dormant funds in appropriate
cases; eligibility for tax exemption as a charitable trust or corporation;
and any illegality or actionable impropriety in the administration of
trust affairs.

These reports are reviewed by the registrar, who may authorize requests for supplemental additional information but may not inquire
further into the propriety of any acts or indicate approval or disapproval of any course of action of a registrant. A firm policy decision
of the office requires that all of the registrar's inquiries and requests
for information during the course of an investigation be made to the
trustees or appropriate officers of a corporation, not to their attorneys or accountants. Responses to these inquiries containing factual
representations must be made over the signature of the trustees or
officers.

The principal objective of these examinations and analyses is to determine whether there is a basis for further investigation of seeming
irregularities. The term "investigation" means, in this connection, any
inquiry other than requests by the registrar for supplemental or clarifying information. At this stage Registry personnel must confer with
the legal staff of the attorney general before proceeding. An investigation docket is maintained, and a card is prepared and given a "charitable trust investigation number." Copies are sent to the chief of the
Department, the deputy attorney general in Sacramento, and the head
of the departmental office where the investigation may be conducted.
It is the practice of the registrar and his assistants to prepare letters
and, in some cases, an outline of a course of investigation, which are
forwarded with this card. The assistant attorney general, after consultation with the registrar, then makes the assignment for investigation, often back to the registrar's office, and in other cases to the attorneys in the area offices or to other available personnel. Provision is
made for periodic review of the investigative docket.

A second docket is maintained which contains information as to
any court proceedings initiated by the attorney general, or to which he
has been made a party, or wherein he has filed an appearance. The
routine for handling litigations is substantially similar to that for in-

vestigations except that the matters are handled by the legal staff exclusively. In addition to these formal procedures, the Registry personnel have devised a system for flagging the files that require periodic scrutiny or may be suitable for investigation at a later date.

These administrative procedures have been described in detail because California is the only state in which the administrative functions have been separated from the legal procedures. It has the largest state registry, which contained as of January 1, 1965, 6,245 charitable trusts and corporations, and an additional 550 potential registrations that had not been finally processed. The office has maintained annual statistics as to total registrations. The year 1963 was the first since the establishment of the Registry that there had been a decrease in both the monthly and annual rates of registration.

> The registration rate rose from a monthly average of 80 in 1961 to 146 in 1962. During 1963 it declined to an average of 78. This is undoubtedly the result of having passed the peak of the work-load resulting from the establishment of the Registry in 1959 and the beneficial effects of the statutory amendment enacted in 1961.[1]

To date the provision of the California Code relating to withdrawal of tax exemption for failure to file has not been invoked. The mere existence of this statutory provision has apparently been sufficient to assure compliance with the act, since it is estimated that present registrations comprise 90 per cent or better of those presently required to register.

The record of both the number and the result of investigations and litigations made by the office attests to the effectiveness of the procedures for analysis of registration and reports. The statistics are as follows: 216 formal investigations were undertaken during the period from July 1, 1959 to December 31, 1964. The office initiated or became a party to 176 court cases. In 1963 alone, 24 investigations and 31 cases were commenced. The office has adopted a policy of not reporting publicly on the details of numerous matters concerning the administration of charitable trusts and corporations that can be or have been resolved by administrative action, believing that it is necessary to protect trustees who have not been willfully delinquent and to uphold the image of charitable activities whenever it is warranted.

Many of the investigations have related to problems of income ac-

---

[1] State of California, Department of Justice, *Year-End Report on Charitable Trust Activities*. State Capitol, Sacramento, December 15, 1963 (mimeographed).

cumulation, nondiversification of investment portfolios, and the use of charitable funds to control profit-making enterprises in which the donor has retained personal control. For example, the attorney general recently investigated the affairs of a foundation where all of the members of the board of trustees were also the directors of a large business corporation of which the foundation owned the controlling interest. The assets of the business corporation had increased tremendously since the creation of the foundation, but its income had remained small, as had its charitable activities. The attorney general, through negotiation, was able to secure the resignation of more than half of the common directors and the substitution of independent trustees not personally involved in the affairs of the business corporation. In another instance, the attorney general's office was able to obtain an agreement to a reduction of clearly unreasonable fees and charges made by trustees of a charitable trust.

It is the policy of the Registry to request information from trustees who appear to have been accumulating more than the equivalent of one year's income at any time during a five-year period unless the instrument contains a specific provision for accumulation. If the trustees present a specific program that will require the accumulation of a stipulated sum of money over a reasonable period, and under which 50 per cent of current income is spent annually, the office will take no further action beyond following the progress of the trust's affairs to assure that at the end of the specified period steps are taken to distribute the accumulated funds.

Much of the litigation has resulted in the revival of dormant funds and the application of the *cy pres* doctrine. Negotiations with one inactive corporation that had held $80,000 contributed for cancer research for more than five years resulted in the transfer of the funds to another institution active in the field. In a similar case, where $6,000 of matured government bonds contributed during World War II for the benefit of war veterans had never been used, the attorney general successfully brought an action requesting the court to appoint new trustees and authorize them to develop a program to use the funds for the benefit of the community in which they were initially raised.

Many cases have involved situations similar to those found in Ohio and New Hampshire, where the heirs of a decedent attacked a will containing provisions for the creation of charitable trusts. Often excessive attorney's fees appear in these cases, and the attorney general's office has been able to move successfully for their reduction. The office successfully opposed attempts by a trustee of a $1 million trust fund to invest in speculative real estate not authorized by the terms of the trust instrument. The office appears regularly in cases involving dissolution of charitable corporations to assure the disposition of their assets for similar charitable purposes. In one of these cases a donor attempted to force the return of a $52,000 donation, but was prevented from so doing and ordered by the court to transfer the assets to a hospital. In another action brought by the attorney general, $20,000 paid to an official of a charitable institution was returned when it appeared that the circumstances under which it was paid involved self-dealing.

Many of the cases handled in the area office of the attorney general have been brought to its attention through private individuals. This is particularly true of matters involving solicitation of funds and disputes among directors of charitable organizations. In the latter cases, the attorney general takes action if the dispute has risen to the point where it is detrimental to the normal operation of the organization or will jeopardize its assets. One example of this type of situation involves a foundation with assets of more than $12 million and has to do with a novel question of first instance. A court proceeding has been brought to validate an election to fill three vacancies on a five-man board of directors of a California not-for-profit corporation. The two remaining trustees have been unable to agree upon successors to three directors who died within a short period of time. The attorney general has intervened to request that if the court should decline to validate the election in dispute, it appoint on its own motion directors to fill the vacancies, so that the corporate activities and purposes would not be wholly frustrated. This case is currently pending.

One of the most important activities of the attorney general's office has been the preparation of a study and analysis of the information contained in the Registry files. Financial support for this project was received from Russell Sage Foundation in the spring of 1964, and the study was immediately begun. It has two major objectives: (1) to disclose the nature and dimensions of charitable organizations at work in the most populous state of the union, and (2) to devise a system for the annual compilation of a continuing series of significant statistics and data that would accurately reflect the evolution and growth of private charitable organizations of all types. The Foundation plans to publish the results of the survey and a description of the methods adopted so that the system can be extended to other states with similar reporting provisions.

Information for this study is being obtained from the reports filed with the Registry of Charitable Trusts as to the nature, purpose, and structure of each charity; its control with reference to the persons or authority to which it is directly responsible; the source of its funds; the nature and extent of its assets and investments, income and expenditures. The data have been transferred to computer punch cards to be processed by the staff and equipment already operating in the California Department of Justice.

In connection with the commencement of this project, an ad hoc committee composed of civic leaders with experience and a demonstrated interest in charitable work met with representatives of certain organizations operating within the framework of the charities movement in June of 1964 to consider and recommend specific statistical and other information to be obtained from the study that would be of value for public dissemination in the state.

The question of solicitation of funds for charitable purposes is one of the areas needing immediate attention in California. Unlike many of the states which require registration and reports from charitable organizations, California has, at present, no statewide requirement for the licensing or registration of organizations that solicit funds from the public. These organizations are considered to come under the Uniform Act, and their annual reports are reviewed by the Registry staff as part of its normal duties. Approximately 100 municipalities or counties in California have established some type of permit or license requirement for those engaged in charitable solicitation. In fact, the administration of such a program in Los Angeles County is considered to be a model of its kind.[1] However, organizations that operate on a statewide basis or in a major portion of the state have met serious administrative difficulties and attendant expenses as a result of duplication of effort and the minor variations in requirements from one municipality to another. To the personnel in the Registry of Charitable Trusts, there appear to be problems peculiar to this field that require specific treatment. The staff has considered preparing a statute that would provide regulation on a statewide basis, but it has preferred to await the results of the Russell Sage Foundation project so that the

---

[1] See Karst, Kenneth L., "The Efficiency of the Charitable Dollar: An Unfulfilled State Responsibility," *Harvard Law Review*, vol. 73, 1960, pp. 433, 465.

decision can be made in terms of the number, size, and relative importance of these organizations and the extent of their activity.

The attorney general did prepare and sponsor legislation enacted in 1963[1] making it a criminal offense to make a false statement of fact, either willfully or negligently, in connection with the solicitation of charitable funds from the members of the public. The purpose of this legislation was to fill what was considered to be a gap in the California Penal Code under which only the willful act of making a false statement was actionable. It was designed to provide local enforcement officers as well as the attorney general with a means of regulating fraudulent solicitations.

The program established in California for the administration of the Uniform Act is the largest of any currently in existence. It is a model of efficiency and exemplifies the results that can be achieved with an adequate and diversified staff. No other state has defined as clearly the goals of a supervisory program and the methods for their achievement. With the commencement of the project sponsored by Russell Sage Foundation and the establishment of an Advisory Committee, a new phase of activity has been entered which should prove beneficial not only to those states currently administering supervisory programs but to any which contemplate their establishment.

Illinois

The course of the program for supervision of charitable trusts in Illinois since the passage in 1961 of a Charitable Trust Act[2] illustrates the problems that can arise from statutory language which is unclear or susceptible of differing interpretations. The Illinois act follows the language of the Uniform Supervision of Trustees for Charitable Purposes Act, although it is not so titled. As explained in Chapter VII, soon after its effective date of July 31, 1961, the attorney general announced his interpretation that the act was applicable to charitable corporations other than those supervised by religious organizations or organized and operated for educational or hospital purposes or for the purpose of operating cemeteries or homes for the aged. This interpretation was officially pronounced in rules and regulations promulgated on January 30, 1962.[3]

---

[1] Cal. Crim. Code, sec. 532(d).

[2] Ill. Laws 1961, S.B. 297.

[3] State of Illinois, Office of the Attorney General, Charitable Trust Division, Regulations promulgated by Attorney General William G. Clark, Springfield, Ill., January 30, 1962, rule 2.

Immediately thereafter, three charitable corporations brought suit against the attorney general, claiming that the act was unconstitutional and that the plaintiff corporations were not "charitable trusts" within a proper construction of the act. The trial court's finding that the act was constitutional but that the corporations were not trusts was appealed by both parties. Briefs were prepared by the attorney general's office, and oral arguments were presented during the January term of the Supreme Court in 1963. Action by the Illinois legislature amending the act rendered this proceeding moot.[1] It nevertheless diverted a large amount of the time and energy of the available staff of the Charitable Trust Division from the large task of establishing the Registry.

The Illinois Charitable Trust Act differs from the original Uniform Act in several particulars other than the definition of trustees. One unique provision makes it applicable only to those trusts with a corpus of more than $4,000. Another relieves trustees from the periodic reporting provisions whenever the trust is the subject matter of an adversary proceeding pending in a court of competent jurisdiction in the state. Upon commencement of such proceeding, the trustees are required to file a report with the attorney general informing him of that fact, the title and number of the case, and the name of the court. They must also notify him upon entry of a final decree.

In 1963 a statute regulating the solicitation of funds for charitable purposes was passed.[2] Under this legislation, charitable organizations soliciting funds from the public must register and must file an annual report to a separate division of the attorney general's office established to administer the act. On March 13, 1964, the rules and regulations promulgated in January, 1962, were amended to include changes made necessary by the passage of the 1963 act and some 1964 amendments. The regulations relating to the Charitable Trust Act provide that any legal entity required to file periodic reports under the solicitation act on the long annual report form (those organizations raising more than $10,000 per year) shall not be required to file under the Charitable Trust Act for any year in which it submits an affidavit stating its compliance with the solicitation statute. The regulations also specifically permit the filing of an account that has been approved by any court,[3] an audit by a certified public accountant,[4] or an annual

---

[1] See p. 267.
[2] Ill. Rev. Stat., ch. 23, secs. 5101 ff.
[3] *Reg.*, rule 7(g), as specified in the Charitable Trust Act, sec. 6c.
[4] *Reg.*, rule 7(h).

statement by a bank or trust company acting under an agency account if the account, audit, or statement contains substantially the information required on the periodic report form.[1] It should be noted that copies of probate accounts may be filed only if they have received court approval. In other states, there is no requirement of court approval prior to filing with the attorney general.

The regulations call for the establishment of a Division of Charitable Trusts in the Office of the Attorney General. The Division, in turn, is directed to establish and maintain a Registry of Charitable Trusts in the offices of the attorney general in Springfield and a subregistry in the Chicago office containing files for charitable trusts maintained in the counties of Cook, Lake, McHenry, and DuPage.[2] Ninety per cent of all the charitable trusts registered have been established in these four named counties.

The regulations also clarify the exemption for trusts with assets under $4,000 by stating that assets shall be determined at fair cash market value and that in the case of fluctuating assets, if the fair cash market value is in excess of $4,000 on any day of the fiscal or calendar year of the trust, or if the receipts and/or disbursements of the trust exceed $4,000 during any such year, the trust is then subject to the act.[3]

The Illinois regulations relating to vested remainders,[4] unlike those of California, provide that property is received for application to charitable purposes whenever it is held for those purposes or whenever there is a vested remainder for charitable purposes. If a vested remainder is preceded by a life estate, then a registration statement, a copy of the instrument, and annual periodic reports must be filed unless the trustee is a bank and trust company, in which case there is no duty to file the periodic reports. The regulations also provide that the attorney general may waive the requirement as to annual reports from time to time, and that upon written request, the written instrument defining the trust may be marked and held confidential and not open for public inspection until such time as the charitable remainder vests in possession.

Bank and trust companies authorized to accept and execute trusts in Illinois, as well as individuals acting as cofiduciaries with such bank

---

[1] *Reg.*, rule 7(1).
[2] *Reg.*, rule 1.
[3] *Reg.*, rule 2(c).
[4] *Reg.*, rule 5(c).

or trust companies, are required by the regulation[1] to file the registration statement and a copy of the written instrument of trust but are specifically excused from completing paragraph 5 of the registration statement, which requests a detailed statement of the assets of the trust.

Although the Registry is maintained in Springfield, the main office of the Division of Charitable Trusts is located in Chicago. In Springfield, one assistant attorney general is assigned to charitable matters. Upon receipt of a new registration, the charity is entered in the Registry and a charitable trust number is assigned. All forms must be submitted in quadruplicate. One is stamped "received" and returned to the trustees. Two are kept in Springfield, one in a master file according to number, and the other in a file according to county. The fourth is forwarded to the Chicago office with a copy of a registration card that contains the name of the trust, information as to the trustees, and the trust number. These cards are filed alphabetically. The Chicago office maintains a general file containing all registration statements and periodic reports, and an alphabetical card file. Neither office keeps a special file according to charitable purposes. Total assets of registered trusts are tabulated periodically.

The duties of the assistant attorney general in the Springfield office include, in addition to maintaining the Registry and supervising the handling of registrations and reports, the original scrutiny of all reports coming from the counties handled by his office, which represent approximately 10 per cent of the total number of registrants. He refers any questionable reports to the Chicago office for consultation, and may conduct investigations if requested to do so. He also handles all court proceedings in the counties within his jurisdiction which relate to charitable matters.

The Chicago office is staffed by the director of the Charitable Trust Division, two assistant attorneys general, a certified public accountant who shares this assignment with the attorney general's inheritance tax department, and one secretary. One of the assistant attorneys general makes an initial check of all reports and registrations from the four counties under the jurisdiction of the office. He then refers the reports to the accountant for review. The accountant records his comments on a prepared mimeographed form, and refers all recommendations for further inquiry or investigation to the director of the Division. The office has prepared a memorandum listing 50 items to be checked

---

[1] *Reg.*, rule 6.

during the analysis of all reports; it is as thorough as any used in the states. Investigators assigned to the attorney general's office are available as needed for the Charitable Trust Division, and field audits have been made by the attorneys and the auditors on several occasions.

The Division maintains close communication with the attorney general and with his first assistant, who must be consulted before the office undertakes any investigations or participates in litigation. The attorney general's term of office is four years. Assistant attorneys general are appointed by him and must serve full-time. The current director has served since the creation of the Division, but the assistants have changed during that time. For a short time, one of the assistant attorneys general was also qualified as a certified public accountant, and gave valuable assistance to the Division.

The forms adopted by the attorney general of Illinois for statements of registration and periodic annual reports, as well as the trust analysis sheets used by the office, are very similar to the ones used in California. Unique to Illinois, however, is a schedule-of-securities form which provides for the listing of all transactions but also requires specific information as to diversification of common stock, including percentages for each of 21 categories. The form was prepared with the assistance of a group of certified public accounts in Chicago, and has proved extremely helpful for the comparison of reports.[1]

As of January 1, 1965, there were 3,083 charities registered with the Division of Charitable Trusts in Illinois with assets of approximately $700 million, and it was estimated that an additional $700 million was being held in trusts for which bank and trust companies were the trustees.

The Illinois statute does not require that the attorney general receive notice either of cases involving charitable interests or of the filing of accounts by testamentary trustees, nor are testamentary trustees required by law to obtain periodic court approval of their accounts. In the so-called lower counties of the state, many attorneys have made a practice of submitting their accounts to the attorney general for approval, but in other areas, attorneys rarely make him a party to these proceedings. Even without a statutory requirement, however, the assistant attorneys general appear in court proceedings to which the attorney general has been made a party on an average of two days a

---

[1] The Illinois Periodic Report and Securities Analysis Sheet are reprinted in Appendix C.

week. In 1963 they initiated or intervened in 25 actions, several of which involved construction of wills or requests by trustees for *cy pres* or deviation.

The probate records have not been scrutinized to locate trusts that should be registered. The Illinois Chamber of Commerce and the Chicago Welfare Association assisted the Division to obtain lists of known charities at the start of the registration, and the secretary of state's office has supplied the names of all not-for-profit corporations organized for charitable purposes, as well as copies of all charters currently being granted.

The laws of Illinois require the participation of the attorney general in proceedings for involuntary dissolution of not-for-profit corporations, but these cases are handled by a separate department of the attorney general's office. This Division has not, to date, established any regular liaison with the Charitable Trust Division to assure *cy pres* application of charitable funds. The Inheritance Tax Department, a part of the attorney general's office, regularly notifies the Charitable Trust Division of all bequests made to charity, including those where the will provides for the creation of a trust for charitable purposes. Copies of the registration form and a notification letter are sent immediately to the named trustees or the executor. The Charitable Trust Division has, of course, worked closely with the newly established Charitable Solicitation Bureau.

As in the other states, the greatest part of the work of supervision is carried on through letters, telephone communications, and personal conferences with trustees and has not yet involved any litigation. Members of the attorney general's staff consider that they have received excellent cooperation from individual trustees who, with few exceptions, have appeared desirous of correcting irregularities.

In one instance, communication with trustees in connection with capital assets valued at approximately $500,000 that were producing no income revealed that the asset was land. The land was subsequently sold, and the proceeds were invested so as to produce a 4 per cent return, which is now being distributed for charitable purposes. Several reports have disclosed fairly large sums of money deposited in checking accounts. Following inquiry, they were either placed in savings banks or invested so as to produce income for the charitable purposes. Investigation of one report revealed that a trustee had been buying and selling stock through a trading account, entering into 59 different transactions in one year, and holding some stock issues for only one day. Following consultation with the attorney general's staff, the trustee ceased this improper amount of activity.

One of the major problems of the Division has been the large number of donor-controlled foundations owning stock in a family business where the rate of return on income has been no more than 1 to 2 per cent over a long period of time; in two instances there was no report of income received. Inquiries by the Charitable Trust Division resulted in an increase in dividends in several cases, although two have been earmarked for further investigation and possible litigation. The Division questions all loans made to, or received from, fiduciaries, as well as all instances of accumulation of income, although it has not established a policy standard such as that used in California.

Several inquiries have gone to bank and trust companies following receipt of the initial registration, where the statement indicated that no distributions were being made for charitable purposes. Members of the Division feel that the exemption for these trustees is a serious drawback to the effectiveness of their program.

In one of its most important actions, the Division of Charitable Trusts initiated litigation in 1963 against the directors of a charitable hospital who had sold corporation membership certificates and personally received $710,000. The certificates carried with them the right to elect the directors of the hospital, so that the sale was in effect a sale of all of the hospital property. The action was brought to obtain restitution of the amounts received. It has been opposed on the ground of the statute of limitations and the fact that the Illinois corporation law did not at the time prohibit such a transaction. Soon after this transaction came to light, the attorney general sponsored legislation, enacted in July of 1963, that specifically prohibits the sale of membership certificates of charitable corporations. The directors of the hospital now contend that the enactment of legislation was evidence that transactions of this nature were not improper prior to 1963. The attorney general's position, on the other hand, is that the act merely codified common law provisions of equity applicable to all charitable funds. The case has been heard at several equity sessions of the Illinois Circuit Court, and no final determination is expected for several years.

Unlike its counterparts in some of the other states, the Illinois Charitable Trust Division seems to be understaffed in terms of secretarial and clerical assistants. Therefore, the attorneys have been diverted from investigations and the preparation of litigation to routine inquiries as to the accuracy of figures or to follow-ups on delinquent reports. The lack of supplementary staff has also held in abeyance plans to establish a file of trusts according to purpose, as well as a regular system for following up on delinquent reports. However, form letters similar to those used in California have been adopted, and they do ease the situation to a certain extent. The appointment of a registrar or at the least an executive secretary would improve the efficiency of the Division. In spite of its deficiencies and the initial difficulties encountered in the application of the act, much has been accomplished in the first four years of the supervisory program in Illinois. The Registry is well established, and the task of providing continuous supervision of charitable funds appears to be operating effectively. Furthermore, the office has received excellent cooperation from the Chicago Bar Association, the Chamber of Commerce, and other civic groups, and this has created an atmosphere wherein the Division can best assist in the accomplishment of charitable purposes.

Michigan

The Uniform Supervision of Trustees for Charitable Purposes Act became effective in Michigan on September 8, 1961. The first section of the act states:

> It is hereby declared to be the policy of the state that the people of the state are interested in the administration, operation and disposition of the assets of all charitable trusts in the state; and that the attorney general shall represent the people of the state in all courts of the state in respect to such charitable trusts. This act applies to all trusts and trustees holding property for charitable purposes over which the state or the attorney general has enforcement or supervisory powers.[1]

This language, in effect, conferred new powers on the attorney general, for before its passage the prosecuting attorney of the county had been charged with representing uncertain or indefinite beneficiaries and enforcing trusts for their benefit.[2] The Michigan act is similar to the Uniform Act in almost all respects. It does contain a section requiring that notice be given to the attorney general of any petition for disposition or distribution of the assets of any trust, and of the rendering of any account of a charitable trust to a court. The act directs the attor-

---

[1] Mich. Stat. Ann., sec. 26.1200(1).
[2] Mich. Stat. Ann., sec. 26.1192; *In re Powers' Estate,* 362 Mich. 222, 106 N.W.2d 833 (1961).

ney general to examine any such petition or account, permits him to register approval or disapproval thereof and to appear in court to contest the action, and prohibits court action without proof of compliance with the provision for notice.[1] This section was amended in 1962 to extend the time of mailing from twenty-four hours after filing to sixteen days before a hearing date has been set.[2]

In 1963 an attempt to amend the act so that it would clearly be applicable to charitable corporations other than institutions and religious bodies failed of passage,[3] as did a bill filed in 1964 that would have exempted trusts administered by a corporate trustee or cotrustee subject to the supervision of the state banking commission or the comptroller of currency of the United States.[4] This amendment, which had been prepared by private individuals, was opposed by the attorney general. The assistant attorney general who appeared before the Judiciary Committee at a public hearing explained that the objections to the amendment arose primarily from the experience of the attorney general's staff in reviewing annual reports; they had observed that the bank and trust companies functioned very well in terms of investment policy but that where there was a duty to select charitable beneficiaries or to carry out specific directions of a testator they did not perform as effectively.

The supervision of charitable trusts in Michigan is conducted by members of a Charitable Trust Division established in the office of the attorney general.[5] The Division is under the control of an assistant attorney general designated by, and serving at, the pleasure of the attorney general. The current head of the Division also serves as state public administrator, a statutory position appointed by the governor upon the recommendation of the attorney general.[6]

One assistant attorney general and two secretaries are assigned to the Division. There are no permanent investigators or auditors, but the Division has been able to call on other offices of state government for assistance on special cases, in particular, the Municipal Finance Division, the State Department of Revenue, the State Police, and, in one instance, the Michigan Board of Nursing. Division members think

[1] Mich. Stat. Ann., sec. 26.1200(6).
[2] Public Acts of 1962, No. 6.
[3] State of Michigan, Senate Bill No. 1240, 72d Legislature (1963).
[4] State of Michigan, Senate Bill No. 1135, 72d Legislature (1964).
[5] State of Michigan, Office of the Attorney General, Charitable Trust Rules and Regulations, Lansing, Mich., Effective February 14, 1964, rule 14.1, sec. 1.
[6] Mich. Stat. Ann., sec. 27.2754(1).

they need a trained auditor or an additional attorney with training in accounting, and they contemplate that the legislative appropriation for the office of the attorney general for 1966 will be sufficient to secure this additional personnel.

The Registry of Charitable Trusts in Michigan is maintained in Lansing. The registration statement that has been adopted contains categories similar to those of the California and Illinois forms. It makes no mention of charitable corporations on its face, but a note on the back acknowledging this fact provides directions for adaptation if the charitable trust is a corporation. In the case of trusts, copies of the will or instrument creating the trust and the trustee's first inventory and last account or report must be submitted. Corporations must supply similar information as well as a copy of the most recently filed Internal Revenue Service form.

No official form has been prepared for periodic reports. The regulations state that periodic reports, which must be filed annually, shall disclose information relating to:

(a) Market value of the trust at the beginning and at the close of the report period. If the market value is not readily available then the ledger or book value of the trust may be substituted.

(b) Investments of the trust, including identification of the securities, real estate and other investments, and the actual income or rates of return received from each investment. Changes in investments or reinvestments occurring during the report period should be indicated.

(c) Income received from investments, including a statement of losses or gains resulting from sale, transfer or exchange of assets.

(d) Disbursements from income or corpus of the trust, including details of trustees fees, attorney fees, administration expenses, and grants or payments made to beneficiaries or recipients, identifying each beneficiary or recipient and the amount each received.

(e) A statement indicating whether or not a creator of the trust or a contributor to the trust or a trustee, in his individual capacity, or a person related either by consanguinity or by affinity to such creator, contributor or trustee, has entered into any transaction involving the purchase, sale, transfer, or loan of any of the trust's assets. In the event of such a transaction, a complete detailed explanation must be set forth in the statement.

(f) The complete details relating to all such transactions whereby a trustee, employees of a trustee, or persons related to the trustee, or related to employees of a trustee, either by consanguinity or by affinity, have personally benefited from operation and management of the trust or received any part of the income or corpus of the trust (other than the normal and reasonable trustee fee), must be disclosed in a statement accompanying the report.

C. It is recognized that present methods of reporting by the trustee to the court having jurisdiction of the trust or to the federal internal revenue service or to other interested persons or entities in respect to the operation of charitable trusts will disclose most of the information requested to be submitted. Verified copies of such reports will be acceptable as the required report to be made to the charitable trust division of the office of the attorney general, provided that a supplemental information statement is attached indicating such of the above stated required information as may not be part of the report required to be filed with such court or the federal internal revenue service. The statements required by section 3 B(e) and section 3 B(f) above are required to be made a part of the periodic report to the charitable trust division and shall be under oath.[1]

These reports must be filed not later than one year after any part of the income or principal is authorized or required to be applied to a charitable purpose, and must be submitted annually thereafter on that date. In the case of charitable remainders, therefore, no report need be filed until the charitable interest has vested, but a registration statement must be filed within two months following the date of creation of the trust. A grace period of three months is granted for filing annual reports. The decision not to require reports on specific forms was made in an attempt to ease the burden on trustees. The majority of reports received are copies of the federal Form 990–A. No filing fees are required.

The files in the Lansing office include, in addition to a loose-leaf registration book, three notebooks wherein all trusts are listed alphabetically, by trustees' names, and by number according to county. Three card files are also kept—one alphabetically, a second listing all trustees, and a third by purpose. Each trust is given a registration number which is preceded by the year of registration. Folders containing registration statements, periodic reports, and correspondence are filed according to these numbers. As of January 1, 1965, 1,905 trusts were registered; they held assets valued at approximately $2.9 billion. The current market value of the combined trust assets was estimated by the attorney general's office as in excess of $5 billion.

Although one file contains the names of the trusts grouped according to similar purposes, no tabulations of assets have been made according to purpose. In 1962 a directory of charitable trusts with assets of more than $25,000 was prepared with the cooperation of the Michigan Welfare League and was distributed on a limited basis. There

---

[1] *Ibid.*, rule 14.3, secs. 3B, 3C.

are no plans for future distribution. The files of the Registry have not been used by the public to as great an extent as in Massachusetts or California. This may be due in part to a requirement in the attorney general's regulations that they may be used only with specific permission of the director of the Charitable Trust Division given after receipt of a written request stating the reasons for inspection.

The assistant attorney general in Lansing peruses all reports and registration statements. He holds weekly conferences with the head of the Division, at which time they review any questionable reports and make decisions as to further action. Both men make court appearances, and both hold conferences with trustees or directors. Although a few corporate foundations have resisted reporting, claiming that the language of the act does not apply to not-for-profit corporations holding property for general corporate charitable purposes, no actions have been brought to test the attorney general's ruling, either by his office or by corporate directors. The attorney general hopes that clarifying amendments will be enacted, thereby obviating the necessity of extended litigation such as has occurred in Illinois.

The Division analyzes reports in much the same way as do the offices in Massachusetts and Illinois. On several occasions it has written to charities listed as beneficiaries in foundation reports to ascertain whether the gifts were received. One such inquiry revealed that funds donated for aid to medical students were being used to finance a research project; the situation was thereafter corrected. Reports showing loans to fiduciaries or accumulations of income are questioned immediately by means of letters requesting further information. Several on-the-spot audits have been made; no formal hearings have been held, however.

In addition, the Division has not initiated any litigation, although it has intervened in several court proceedings. In one of these, a dispute between an executor and the trustees of a foundation over control of the voting stock of a business corporation of which the foundation was the majority stockholder brought to light the fact that the foundation trustees were furthering their private interests at the expense of the charity. The attorney general's office was able to negotiate a settlement which included the resignation of the trustees and appointment of independent fiduciaries, as well as the sale of the business at a fair price. In this case an important consideration in the negotiations was a desire to assure that the sale of the business be made to a buyer who would not liquidate the company, thereby closing the sole industry of a small town.

In another case the attorney general's office succeeded in obtaining the resignation of trustees who were in conflict of interest because of their positions as trustees of a foundation that owned controlling stock of a business of which they were officers. The salary of these officers had risen from $25,000 per year to $83,000 per year after they became directors of the foundation. At the start of these negotiations one attorney was representing the foundation as well as the business corporation. The attorney general required the foundation to obtain independent counsel and secured a final settlement that included provision for election of independent trustees.

The laws of Michigan require an annual accounting by trustees of testamentary trusts, and under the provisions of the Uniform Act the attorney general must receive notice of these actions as well as of actions to dissolve corporations or distribute assets of charitable trusts. The courts also generally require that notice be given to the attorney general of cases involving charitable gifts, including will contests and requests for construction. Notice is not given of petitions for appointment of trustees.

The attorney general, through intervention in petitions for allowance of accounts, has succeeded in obtaining court orders for distribution of accumulated income, *cy pres* application of dormant funds, removal of restrictive investment provisions, and in several instances, reduction of excessive trustees' fees. In one case, $99,000 had been accumulated during a period of thirty-seven years by trustees of a trust established to provide magazine subscriptions for a designated prison and to support a home for children. The subscriptions had been bought each year, but the trustees had taken no further action. Following the attorney general's intervention, a *cy pres* petition was brought and a decree obtained permitting the trustees to make gifts and provide outings for children two to four years old whose parents were in prison.

An example of dilatory action by a trustee appeared in an account filed in 1961 which showed $44,090 undistributed income from a trust valued at $484,189, created to aid children in a particular town. The trustee replied to a letter from the attorney general that he had been accumulating these funds for use in case of a national disaster or a severe break in the stock market which he expected immediately. The accumulated funds have been turned over, by court order, to a social service agency for distribution to needy children, and arrangements have been made for the agency to suggest distributions of income in the future. In another case of dormancy, following action by the attorney general, a fund of $1.5 million left in trust to build a hospital was used to finance the building of a new wing to a hospital in the area designated by the settlor.

In many instances the attorney general's office has cooperated with trustees in the presentation of petitions to the court requesting modification of trust provisions that were no longer feasible. An interesting example was the attorney general's support of a petition to permit the continuation of a trust created for a twenty-five-year period which contained no provision for the disposition of surplus funds left at the end of that period. The fund was created to provide maternal health services and make grants to other institutions for similar programs. No other organizations that were carrying out the services provided by this fund had been found. During the twenty-five-year period, the capital value of the fund, which initially was a gift of General Motors Company stock valued at $250,000, had grown to $358,000. In 1961, $93,764 had been spent for charitable purposes. A court decree was obtained permitting the trustees to continue their programs until 1987 unless the corpus was expended prior to that date.

An opposite position was taken by the attorney general, however, in a case involving a trust created to construct and maintain a home for the aged with directions that if the funds were insufficient to carry out this purpose, the income should be used to pay stipends to elderly people who would be qualified to enter the home once it was built. No home was built, although in 1963 the assets of the trust were valued at approximately $7 million. The trustees brought a petition requesting application of the *cy pres* doctrine to permit them to disregard the direction to build a home and to continue instead their policy of granting stipends to elderly people so that they might continue to stay in their own homes. In this instance the attorney general's office, after consultation with members of the University of Michigan Law School, concluded that the *cy pres* doctrine, as defined by the Michigan courts, was inapplicable. The attorney general's position opposing the petition was upheld by the court.[1]

Because of difficulties with the definition of the word "trustee" contained in the Uniform Act, no attempts have been made to secure compliance by the charitable corporations commonly referred to as health and welfare organizations which derive their support from public solicitations. These organizations are subject to regulation and

---

[1] For further examples see Feldman, Irving, Charitable Trusts: "What's Happening to the Money?" *The Detroit Lawyer,* vol. 33, 1965, p. 37.

supervision by the Michigan Department of Social Welfare. The statute regulating solicitations[1] requires the charitable organizations to obtain a license from the department; the license may be issued upon receipt of a financial report for the previous fiscal year and a statement of the purposes of the solicitation. The rules and regulations adopted by the Social Welfare Commissioners contain several interesting provisions.[2] A report prepared and certified by a certified public accountant is required of all organizations that received more than $15,000, from solicitation; if the amount received was less, a detailed statement sworn to by two or more officers is accepted. All organizations must show sound financial accounting and that all moneys expended have been applied to the carrying out of the announced purpose for which the agency was organized or the solicitation was held.

The regulations also state that no organization, regardless of its statement of purposes, shall be considered to be formed for a charitable purpose and therefore eligible to receive a license: (1) "where more than one-third of the members of the board of directors (or trustees) consists of persons who either are receiving remuneration from the organization, institution, association or corporation or have spouses, parents or children so receiving";[3] or (2) "if dividends are distributed to members or stockholders," or (3) "if, upon dissolution, the net assets are to be so distributed in whole or in part."[4]

To date there has been no attempt to establish a continuing liaison between the Department of Social Welfare and the attorney general's office, although some organizations licensed to solicit funds in Michigan do file reports with the Charitable Trust Division.

The centralization of supervision in the attorney general's office in Michigan has given a new focus to the enforcement of charitable funds not present when this duty rested on the county district attorneys. Since the passage of the Uniform Act, the supervisory program has been active and aggressive, and there can be no doubt of its impact on trustees and directors of all types of charitable funds. The staff of the Charitable Trust Division is convinced that the Uniform Act should be clarified so as to remove questions about the act's coverage. The office might engender support for amendments, which has not been forthcoming to date, through cooperation with local bar associations

---

[1] Mich. Stat. Ann., secs. 16.71 ff.
[2] Supplements 22, 24, and 28 of the 1954 Compilation of the State Administrative Code.
[3] State of Michigan, Social Welfare Commissioners, Regulations, rule 400.244.
[4] *Ibid.*, rule 400.245.

and trade or civic groups. The general efficiency of the Division would be greatly increased by the availability of auditors and investigators to permit the staff attorneys to devote more time to legal considerations. In addition, the entire area of cooperation with federal officials remains to be explored. Nevertheless, the concrete results achieved by the attorney general's office during the three years in which the Uniform Act has been in effect are evidence of the benefits of this program to the public.

Oregon

An amended version of the Uniform Act passed by the Oregon legislature, became effective on September 2, 1963. The attorney general provided the impetus for passage of this legislation following the revelation of a land promotion scheme in that state which involved several charitable foundations. He ordered his staff to survey the charitable funds in Oregon to analyze the extent of supervision under existing law, and to engage in correspondence and consultation with the other states that had enacted supervisory legislation. The drafters of the legislation relied heavily on the experience in the California Registry, and they prepared the act in close cooperation with the Oregon com missioners on uniform state laws. The bill was submitted to the legislature in 1963 with a report containing the results of the attorney general's study. The report concluded that supervision of tax-exempt charitable trusts and similar organizations by the courts, by the state, and by the federal government was quite limited.

In the course of the study, members of the attorney general's staff first attempted to ascertain the extent and amount of bequests and gifts to charitable trusts and other exempt organizations. The State Tax Commission had no data on this subject. A review of the files of the State Treasury Department indicated that since 1950, 21 institutions and funds had received testamentary bequests of $100,000 or more. These bequests were not totaled, but it was estimated that they amounted to at least several million dollars, including two totaling $270,000 in 1961. Listed assets of charitable bodies reporting to the Internal Revenue Service and reports for testamentary trusts submitted to the probate court of Multnomah County in 1961 or 1962 amounted to $30 million.

The report stated that there was no practical method of determining whether all organizations engaged in tax-exempt activities were submitting reports to either of these governmental authorities. It was found that the Multnomah County probate court list of trusts contained testamentary trusts worth some $12 million and that not all of them had submitted reports to the Internal Revenue Service. One foundation with listed assets of $5.3 million in 1962 had not filed a 1961 or 1962 return according to the Internal Revenue Service.

The report also contained the observation that although the State Tax Commission requires fiduciaries to file reports, no administrative machinery existed to determine whether all reports were submitted, and in any case their contents were confidential. The report further stated that the Inheritance and Gift Tax Division approved exemptions for bequests to tax-exempt organizations, but made no attempts to determine whether the bequests were used for tax-exempt purposes. At the county level, available evidence indicated that reports were received and filed in a routine manner, and no audits were made to determine their compliance with applicable statutes, nor were any reminders sent to delinquent trustees. Furthermore, practice varied in different counties. In one county, the clerk of the court maintained a designated list of testamentary trusts; in other counties, he did not.

Two hearings were held by the legislature on the bill. The attorney general, a state tax commissioner, the state treasurer, and one of the commissioners on uniform state laws appeared in its support. The bank and trust companies did not oppose the bill, and approved of the provision in the act permitting the submission of copies of trustees' accounts filed with the probate court. The bill passed the House on May 10, 1963, by a vote of 50 to 9, with one excused; and it passed the Senate with two amendments on May 30, by a vote of 24 to 6. One amendment, proposed by a large railroad company, modifies the definition of "charitable corporation" so that the mere making of grants or donations to institutions or beneficiaries within the state of Oregon, or the investigation of applicants for such grants or donations, does not constitute doing business in the state.[1] The most interesting change, made by the House, consisted of the deletion of all sections under which the attorney general was empowered to make rules and regulations necessary for the administration of the act, leaving him only the ability to classify trusts and establish rules concerning the execution, time, and nature of the reports. It is not anticipated that these deletions will restrict the administration of the act.

The Oregon act follows the language of the California Supervision

---

[1] Ore. Rev. Stat., sec. 128.620(1).

of Trustees for Charitable Purposes Act in almost all particulars. It provides for disallowance of tax exemption for failure to file reports, but does not exempt from reporting trusts supervised by state or federal banking authorities. The bill also contains a new section amending the Oregon statute relating to solicitation of funds; it imposes a duty on the county clerks of court to forward to the attorney general duplicate copies of financial reports filed with them by organizations that solicit funds in the state and collect more than $250 in any year.

Appropriations to administer the act were not requested prior to its passage. After the close of the legislative session, the attorney general made an application for funds to the State Emergency Board, but the request was refused owing to lack of funds and uncertainty over the outcome of a then-pending election on a tax increase. The outcome of this initiative election was the defeat of the 1963 revenue law. As a result, it forced cutbacks and precluded the possibility of an allocation to develop a Registry. The attorney general has assigned one assistant attorney general to the position of registrar of charitable trusts on a part-time basis, although he hopes that in the future there will be sufficient funds to appoint a nonlawyer to this position, who will operate under the supervision of an assistant attorney general assigned to charitable affairs. The current registrar is assisted by one secretary. Discussions are now being conducted with the State Tax Commission to explore the possibility of obtaining auditing personnel on a basis similar to that in California. There is no feeling that an investigator is needed, since personnel from cooperating agencies can be made available for special cases.

Soon after the passage of the bill in the spring of 1963, the attorney general appointed an advisory committee to assist in establishing the Registry. The committee is composed of seven individuals representing organizations interested in and affected by the act, one of the commissioners on uniform state laws, a representative of the state bar experienced in probate matters, a representative of the bank and trust companies, an officer of the Oregon Association of Certified Public Accountants, a member of the Oregon Judicial Council, a representative of the State Tax Commission, and a representative of the State Treasury Department's Inheritance and Gift Tax Bureau.

With the advice of this committee, the attorney general decided to adopt a simple registration form similar to that used in California and to require that the annual reports be a copy of the Internal Revenue Service Form 990–A with all schedules and statements or a copy of a probate accounting. These requirements have been incorporated into regulations prepared by the attorney general.

An initial mailing of registration forms went out to a list of 400 exempt organizations, the names of which were obtained from the Internal Revenue Service, the State Tax Commission, the Corporation Commission, and from the list compiled from the records of the probate courts during the initial survey of charitable trust funds. As of January 1, 1965, 337 charities had registered, and 50 letters had been returned marked "unknown." Follow-up letters were sent to the remaining charities. The registrar has reviewed each registration form received. The forms received have been filed alphabetically and will also be filed by purposes.

Much of the attention of the Division in this initial phase has been directed toward making rulings on the application of the act to specific charitable funds. The office has arranged to have the State Inheritance and Gift Tax Department supply a monthly list of new charitable trusts established by will or gift and it is negotiating a similar arrangement with the Corporation Commission. The major source of information, however, has been the local office of the Internal Revenue Service, and it is expected that close cooperation and communication with this office will continue.

The preliminary examination of files in the Internal Revenue Service revealed approximately 13 foundations that appeared to warrant closer examination. One report indicated a family foundation with gross income of $23,500 and expenses of $12,000, making grants of $4,800; another with a gross income of $58,000, expenses of $47,400, and grants of $8,100; and a third with gross income of $219,200 had expenses of $193,100 and grants of $15,200. In one instance the supervisor of the Inheritance and Gift Tax Division of the state treasurer's office reported to the attorney general that a family foundation was purchasing beef carcasses, supposedly for distribution to missions in one community. Actually, the choicest cuts were being kept by the foundation donor's family. In a second case referred by the Inheritance Department, it was found that a corporate foundation had acquired large numbers of art objects which were being kept in the homes of the corporation's officers and had never been exhibited in museums or placed on public display.

Under the provisions of the Oregon Uniform Act, the attorney general is now considered a necessary party to proceedings to modify or terminate a charitable trust or corporation. He is not required under

Oregon statutory law to participate in petitions for allowance of accounts; the requirement that he receive periodic reports from testamentary trustees will have a new impact on the administration of these trusts in Oregon. Prior to passage of the act, the attorney general's office was only rarely cited in proceedings involving construction of wills or compromises. It is expected that the practice will become more widespread in the future.

There is less case law relating to charitable trusts and corporations in Oregon than in most of the other states where there are supervisory programs, and the attorney general and his staff expect to play an active role in the development of this law, particularly as it relates to foundations. They are developing critera for evaluation of reports and actions with the assistance of the advisory committee.

Although the Oregon program has not been in existence long enough to allow an assessment of its operation, it promises to be a highly successful supervisory program.

CHAPTER X

Agencies for Federal Supervision

THE INFLUENCE OF THE FEDERAL GOVERNMENT on all charitable funds, and on foundations in particular, stems primarily from its taxing powers. Theoretically, it could have arisen through the enactment of substantive laws affecting the creation and operation of many charitable endeavors, possibly all but the very smallest, but such an extension of control has not occurred nor is this likely. Charitable activities remain creatures of the states; the laws governing their creation, their right to continuous existence, their freedom of operation, the limitations on their holdings, and the conditions for their dissolution are determined at the state level. Although at one time it was customary to seek a federal charter for foundations, this practice is almost nonexistent today. Federal control over the creation of foundations, as debated in the early 1900's when The Rockefeller Foundation sought a charter from Congress, has become an item of historical interest only.

The fact that federal jurisdiction over foundations is limited to the drafting and administration of the tax laws, and their interpretation in the federal courts, does not mean that the federal role is unimportant. It is, on the contrary, the primary source of supervision of charitable foundations in the United States today. One reason is, of course, the uniformity in the application of these laws, but another stems from the methods used for their enforcement.

The substantive provisions of the federal tax law have been described in Chapter V. The present chapter deals with the methods by which these substantive laws are enforced. Federal supervision of foundation activities has three major aspects. The Congress itself per-

352

forms a dual role—conducting investigations to obtain information on which to determine whether changes in law are advisable, and enacting substantive provisions to bring about these changes. Second, the federal government exerts power over charitable activities through the Treasury, which both prepares legislative proposals and implements congressional actions by the promulgation of regulations. The Internal Revenue Service, a branch of the Treasury Department, has the direct responsibility for administering the laws and regulations. Third, the federal courts interpret the laws and regulations and determine their constitutionality. The judiciary, thereby, holds the ultimate power, although it deals directly with only the minority of foundations that become involved in litigation.

The Congress

Just as at the state level, the legislatures play an important role in determining the substantive provisions of law and the agencies that will supervise and direct their application, at the federal level the Congress of the United States decides these matters. Congress is limited, in theory, only by the Constitution; but in practice, again as in the states, political considerations, pressures from individual groups, and the internal organization of each house of the legislature are major factors determining when and how any particular legislative action will be taken. The constitutional provision that revenue bills originate in the House of Representatives has meant that the House Ways and Means Committee wields tremendous power; to a major degree, it has shaped the entire pattern of taxation in the United States. This is true in spite of the fact that the tax legislation may have had its formal origins in a message from the President or initiative from Congress as a whole. In the American congressional tradition, the tax writing committee often prefers to follow its own ideas rather than adopt the President's suggestions. Consequently, its role is considered to be "of greater significance"[1] than that of the President.

The process of considering, drafting, and adopting tax legislation follows a fairly regular path in the Congress. It is usually initiated after a decision by the Ways and Means Committee to consider tax legislation, which may follow a special message from the President or recommendations in his economic report or budget message. The

---

[1] Harvard Law School, International Program in Taxation, World Tax Series, Wm. Sprague Barnes, Director, *Taxation in the United States.* Commerce Clearing House, Chicago, 1963, sec. 1/5.2.

Committee itself decides on the timing and the course of action, however. The customary first step is a public hearing. The Secretary of the Treasury is usually the first witness; he is followed by other government officials and interested members of the public. Witnesses representing foundation interests have occasionally testified at these hearings; they were notably present at the hearings on the revenue revisions of 1950,[1] and in 1947[2] when the proposals to tax business income of foundations were discussed. As early as 1942 representatives of the Treasury made proposals to the Committee to limit the business activities of foundations, although the Committee recommended no action on them at that time.[3]

The Ways and Means Committee's interest in tax problems is not confined to years in which a major tax revision is being considered. In 1959, for example, it sponsored a series of panel discussions on "Income Tax Revisions," one of which was devoted to tax-exempt organizations. Several experts in this area of tax law participated and submitted prepared papers.[4] The meetings were not intended to deal with specific proposals, but were an attempt to delineate major areas needing future revision. In 1964 the Senate Finance Committee and the House Ways and Means Committee requested the Treasury to examine the activities of foundations for possible tax abuses and report its conclusions and recommendations to the Committees. The Treasury Report, filed in February, 1965, was expected to serve as the basis for committee hearings and future revisions of the Internal Revenue Code.[5]

The Congress is assisted by several groups of experts throughout the entire process of drafting and enacting tax legislation, and the influence of these men is often considerable. The staff of the Joint

---

[1] U.S. Congress, House of Representatives, Committee on Ways and Means, *Hearings, Revenue Revision of 1950.* 81st Congress, 2d Session, Government Printing Office, Washington, 1950.

[2] U.S. Congress, House of Representatives, Committee on Ways and Means, *Hearings, Revenue Revisions, 1947–1948.* 80th Congress, 1st Session, 1948, pt. 5.

[3] U.S. Congress, House of Representatives, Committee on Ways and Means, *Hearings, Revenue Revision of 1942.* 77th Congress, 2d Session, 1942, vol. 1.

[4] See U.S. Congress, House of Representatives, Committee on Ways and Means, *Income Tax Revision:* Panel Discussions, 86th Congress, 1st Session, 1959; and *Tax Revision Compendium;* Compendium of Papers on Broadening the Tax Base, Submitted to the House Committee on Ways and Means in Connection with the Panel Discussions on the Same Subject to Be Conducted by the Committee on Ways and Means Beginning November 16, 1959, 3 vols.

[5] U.S. Congress, Senate, Committee on Finance, and House of Representatives, Committee on Ways and Means, *Treasury Department Report on Private Foundations.* 89th Congress, 1st Session, Committee Print, February 2, 1965.

Committee on Internal Revenue Taxation, a permanent congressional committee, performs a major role in advising on technical matters, as does the Treasury's tax staff. A third group is composed of members of the staff of the House and Senate Legislative Counsels, who are responsible for the translation of policy decisions into proper legislative language. The Ways and Means Committee and the Senate Finance Committee also have permanent staffs of tax experts familiar with their members' predilections and interests. The reports of these two committees that accompany all revenue bills contain the only official explanation of the provisions and the reasons for their inclusion. Later interpretations of tax statutes by the Treasury, the Internal Revenue Service, and the courts often rely on these reports.

After introduction in the House, each revenue bill follows the usual procedure for enactment of legislation, except that debate, by tradition, is carried on under a "closed rule" whereby only amendments sponsored by the Ways and Means Committee are permitted. No similar limitations on debate or amendments are made in the Senate, and changes are often made from the floor. Although conference committee proceedings are held in executive session, a report is prepared which gives some indication of the reasons for final modifications.

An example of the modifications that may occur before a proposed change of a particular section of the Internal Revenue Code is finally accepted is to be found in the history of amendments to the so-called unlimited charitable deduction provisions enacted in 1964.[1] The President's tax message for 1963 contained a request for repeal of this section of the Code on the grounds that it permitted a handful of high-income taxpayers to escape all tax liability and that it had resulted in an annual $10 million depletion of revenue. Statistics were presented relating to 19 taxpayers who took advantage of the provision in the period from 1958 to 1960.[2] The Ways and Means Committee made no mention of the subject in either the bill or its Report. The Senate Finance Committee, however, proposed an amendment that had been drafted at its request by the Treasury. The amendment would have added a new subsection that would, in effect, have made the unlimited charitable contribution deduction available only for contributions to publicly supported organizations and not to foundations. This amend-

---

[1] Revenue Act of 1964, sec. 209(b).

[2] U.S. Congress, House of Representatives, Committee on Ways and Means, *Hearings, President's 1963 Tax Message,* 88th Congress, 1st Session, 1963.

ment was adopted by the Senate.[1] In conference, the Senate proposal was revised to permit contributions to foundations under certain specific circumstances, and a section was added containing grounds for denial of the deduction based on a set of new limitations on donor-foundation transactions. These limitations are similar to certain proposals contained in the revenue bill that had been adopted by the House in 1950.[2] In 1964 the Senate also added to the House bill a provision permitting individual taxpayers a five-year carryover for certain charitable contributions.

This interplay between the two houses of Congress and the consequent revision and redrafting of tax legislation is typical. It is noteworthy that during the past twenty years, the House of Representatives has generally drafted the stricter versions of limitations on foundations, and the Senate has tended to dilute them.

Congressional Investigations

As important to foundations as the adoption of substantive laws, particularly since World War II, has been the investigation of their activities by three separate congressional committees. The use of the congressional investigatory power has expanded since the early years of the twentieth century. It reached a height during the 1950's, and remains a great source of authority, extending to all matters relating to the conduct of government and the spending of public money, and including the right to subpoena witnesses and require them to testify on pain of being found in contempt of Congress.

Congressional investigations may serve several functions. They enable legislators to acquire information and to follow the course of administration, but they are also used to form and direct public opinion. It is this last function which has been expanded in recent years, as Congress has made investigations into such areas as civil liberties, the concentration of economic power, labor and business practices, lobbying, campaign expenditures, and subversive activities. Unfortunately, this function has on occasion been abused, particularly by individual congressmen seeking personal gain or private advantage. Although in 1957 the Supreme Court stated unequivocally that the provisions of the Bill of Rights applied to investigations of all forms of governmental

---

[1] U.S. Congress, Senate, Committee on Finance, *Final Report, Revenue Act of 1964*, 88th Congress, 2d Session, Senate Report 830, 1964, p. 59.
[2] U.S. Congress, House of Representatives, *Conference Report, Revenue Act of 1964*. 88th Congress, 2d Session, House Report 1149, 1964, pp. 3–5.

actions,[1] Congress may still demand information from a witness and place him on what is, in effect, public trial, even though a court may later refuse to uphold a "conviction for contempt" if he refuses to testify.[2]

The first major congressional investigation of foundation operations was undertaken by the Senate Industrial Relations Committee in 1915. In 1948 the Committee on Interstate and Foreign Commerce of the Senate, as part of an investigation into the economic situation of the textile industry in New Hampshire, looked into the operations of an industrialist, Royal Little, who had been charged with using tax-exempt foundations created by him to finance several of his business ventures.[3] The Committee Report contained a description of the methods by which Mr. Little was able to obtain risk capital for certain ventures and to buy at substantially lower prices both stock and fixed assets of certain companies that he wanted to obtain. It also was charged that he had entered into leaseback arrangements on other property at high rentals that were deductible by the business companies and provided additional capital for the foundation to reinvest in further ventures.

The Committee Report recommended an amendment of the Internal Revenue Code to prevent a recurrence of this type of arrangement by requiring that no trust receive tax exemption "unless during the taxable year it has actually paid to charitable beneficiary 85 per cent of its gross income received in such taxable year."[4] A bill incorporating this provision was introduced in the Congress during the 1949 session[5] but was not adopted.

The investigation did focus congressional attention more firmly on foundations, however, and the provisions enacted in 1950 represented the culmination of efforts to impose limitations on the business activities of foundations.

---

[1] *Watkins* v. *U.S.,* 354 U.S. 178, 77 Sup. Ct. 1173 (1957).

[2] See Barth, Alan, *Government by Investigation,* Viking Press, New York, 1955.

[3] U.S. Congress, Senate, Committee on Interstate and Foreign Commerce, *Hearings.* 80th Congress, 2d Session, 1948; U.S. Congress, Senate, Committee on Interstate and Foreign Commerce, *Report.* 81st Congress, 1st Session, Senate Report 101, 1949. For summary, see Note "The Modern Philanthropic Foundation: A Critique and a Proposal," *Yale Law Journal,* vol. 59, 1950, pp. 477 ff., 1121.

[4] U.S. Congress, Senate, Committee on Interstate and Foreign Commerce, *Report.* 81st Congress, 1st Session, Senate Report 101, 1949, pp. 23–24.

[5] Senate Bill 1408, 81st Congress, 1st Session, 1949.

The Cox Committee. In 1952 a Select Committee to Investigate and Study Educational and Philanthropic Foundations and Other Comparable Organizations Which Are Exempt from Federal Taxation was created, and its powers and duties defined, by a resolution of the House of Representatives. The Committee was

> authorized and directed to conduct a full and complete investigation and study of educational and philanthropic foundations and other comparable organizations which are exempt from Federal income taxation to determine which such foundations and organizations are using their resources for purposes other than the purposes for which they were established and especially to determine which such foundations and organizations are using their resources for un-American and subversive activities or for purposes not in the interest or tradition of the United States[1]

The chairman of the Committee was Representative E. E. Cox of Georgia. Upon his death in December of 1952, he was succeeded by Representative Brooks Hays of Arkansas. In the course of its study the Committee sent questionnaires to more than 1,500 organizations, interviewed 200 persons, and communicated by letter with approximately 200 additional individuals. It held public hearings on eighteen days between November 18 and December 30, 1952, and called 39 witnesses to the stand. It also made a study of the available literature on foundations. A special questionnaire was sent to the larger foundations containing approximately 120 inquiries. The replies received from 54 foundations contained an unprecedented source of information on all aspects of foundation operations, and they were used as the basis for a study of the operating principles of foundations.[2]

The Committee Report can be considered in two parts. The first, which described foundations in terms of their growth rate, their role in modern society, and their present and future needs concluded with the following statement:

> We have referred briefly to the past accomplishments of foundations and the importance of their role in modern-day life. It appears that the present need for foundations is even greater than it has been in the past

---

[1] U.S. Congress, House of Representatives, Select (Cox) Committee to Investigate and Study Educational and Philanthropic Foundations and Other Comparable Organizations Which Are Exempt from Federal Income Taxation, *Final Report*. 82d Congress, 2d Session, House Report 2514, 1953, p. 2.

[2] Kiger, Joseph C., *Operating Principles of the Larger Foundations*. Russell Sage Foundation, New York, 1954. The appendix to the volume contains a copy of the questionnaire.

and that there is great likelihood that the need will prove an increasing one in the future. Despite the vast sums being poured by Government into the various fields formerly occupied by foundations and into fields in which the foundations and Government are cotenants or at least co-adventurers, the need for the basic research so largely supplied and supported by the foundations continues to increase. Every new headland of human knowledge which is won opens up new vistas to be explored. As each mountain peak of discovery is scaled, vast new areas are laid open to exploration. Aside from the pressing needs of national security there are ever-widening and lengthening avenues of knowledge that require research and study of the type and kind best furnished or assisted by foundations. The foundation, once considered a boon to society, now seems to be a vital and essential factor in our progress.[1]

The second part of the Report dealt with 12 questions compiled from complaints and criticisms of foundations that had come to the Committee's attention. They related principally to whether foundation funds had been diverted from their original purposes, and the extent to which they had been involved in subversive activities. Other questions related to charges that foundation trustees were "absentee landlords," that they were controlled by an interlocking directorate of individuals from the northern and mid-Atlantic states; that they had shifted the center of gravity of colleges and other institutions to a point outside the institutions themselves; and that they had favored internationalism.[2] Finally, the Committee addressed itself to the question of accountability. It mentioned the problems of donor control and the use of foundations to evade income tax, but reported that it had made no attempt to find answers, regarding these problems as matters for consideration by the Committee on Ways and Means, and suggested that they were of sufficient importance to warrant further inquiry.[3]

As to the first series of questions relating to subversive activities, the Committee concluded:

> The foundations, for the most part, have made no secret of their mistakes and have stated frankly that in recent years they have recognized the increasing need to be constantly alert to avoid giving unintended aid to subversives.
>
> The committee believes that on balance the record of the founda-

---

[1] U.S. Congress, House of Representatives, Select (Cox) Committee to Investigate and Study Educational and Philanthropic Foundations and Other Comparable Organizations Which Are Exempt from Federal Income Taxation, *Final Report, op. cit.*, pp. 4–5.

[2] *Ibid.*, p. 5.

[3] *Ibid.*, p. 13.

tions is good. It believes that there was infiltration and that judgments were made which, in the light of hindsight, were mistakes, but it also believes that many of these mistakes were made without the knowledge of facts which, while later obtainable, could not have been readily ascertained at the time decisions were taken.[1]

It found that the idea that the office of trustee of a large foundation was a sinecure, involving little work but great power, was misinformed. It did suggest that a wider geographical distribution of directors would go far toward establishing greater public confidence in foundations.[2] No opinion was ventured as to the question of foundation power shifting the center of gravity from colleges and other institutions.[3] The Committee's view as to foreign expenditures by foundations was that international activities and foreign expenditures were motivated chiefly by consideration of the welfare of the American people and as such were "entirely praiseworthy."[4]

Finally, the criticisms relating to accountability of foundations were answered in the recommendations contained in the Report that:

> 1. Public accounting should be required of all foundations. This can best be accomplished by amendment of the existing laws in substantially the form herewith submitted as appendix A, to which we direct the attention of the Eighty-third Congress.
> 2. That the Ways and Means Committee take cognizance of our finding that the maintenance of private sources of funds is essential to the proper growth of our free schools, colleges, churches, foundations, and other charitable institutions. We respectfully suggest that the committee reexamine pertinent tax laws, to the end that they may be so drawn as to encourage the free-enterprise system with its rewards from which private individuals may make gifts to these meritorious institutions.[5]

This recommended act was never adopted, possibly because provisions for public disclosure of information contained in returns from tax-exempt organizations in categories substantially similar to those listed by the Cox Committee had been authorized in the Revenue Act of 1950,[6] and had been implemented by subsequent Treasury revisions of Form 990–A.

The Reece Committee. On July 27, 1953, the House passed a Reso-

---

[1] *Ibid.*, p. 8.
[2] *Ibid.*, pp. 10–11.
[3] *Ibid.*, p. 11.
[4] *Ibid.*, p. 12.
[5] *Ibid.*, p. 13.
[6] Rev. Act. of 1950, sec. 341, now Int. Rev. Code of 1954, sec. 6033(b).

lution that was similar to the one under which the Cox Committee was established but added the categories of political purposes, propaganda, or attempts to influence legislation to those studied by the Cox Committee. The Resolution directed that a report be filed by January 3, 1955, and funds were appropriated for its implementation.[1] Congressman B. Carroll Reece of Tennessee, who had been a member of the Cox Committee, had sponsored the Resolution and was appointed chairman of what was described as the Special Committee to Investigate Tax-Exempt Foundations and Comparable Organizations. The Special Committee conducted 16 sessions of public hearings between May 10 and June 17, 1954.[2] Andrews has provided a summary of these sessions:

> Of the 12 witnesses, the 11 first heard were Mr. Reece, three members of his paid staff with extensive reports, two Treasury Department witnesses on technical tax questions, and five general witnesses unconnected with foundations. The thesis supported by the general witnesses and the staff testimony appeared to be that great changes had occurred in America in the direction of socialism and collectivism, with one of the witnesses holding that even the federal income tax was a socialist plot to destroy the government; these changes were aided, it was alleged, through a "diabolical conspiracy" of foundations and certain educational and research organizations. During a final four hours and twenty minutes one rebuttal witness was heard, though even he was not a representative of a foundation, but of one of the accused research organizations. Then the stormy sessions were suddenly ended by a strictly party vote.[3]

From the outset, the Committee members were divided in their attitudes toward the conduct of the hearings, as well as their content, and the Final Report was signed by only three of the five members, and one of the signers in effect negated his signature by submitting a statement that concluded: "Nothing has transpired in the proceedings of the present committee to cause me to alter or modify the views I expressed in the Cox Committee report. I take this opportunity to again re-affirm them."[4]

---

[1] U.S. Congress, House of Representatives, *Resolution No. 217*, 83d Congress, 1st Session, adopted July 27, 1953.

[2] See U.S. Congress, House of Representatives, Special (Reece) Committee to Investigate Tax-Exempt Foundations and Comparable Organizations, *Hearings*. 83d Congress, 2d Session, 1954, pts. 1 and 2.

[3] Andrews, F. Emerson, *Philanthropic Foundations*. Russell Sage Foundation, New York, 1956, p. 345.

[4] Statement by the Honorable Angier L. Goodwin, congressman from Massachusetts, reprinted in *Ibid.*, p. 346.

The Report concluded with 14 findings charging that foundations had power and influence so great that they might eventually control a large part of the American economy, and that they were characterized by interlocking control by a professional class of administrators. Although the Committee stated that foundation activity was clearly desirable when operating in the natural sciences and making direct donations to religious, educational, scientific, and other institutional donees, it found that foundation activities in the social sciences were cause for alarm, particularly since the research had been empirical, as opposed to theoretical, and thereby threatened the basic moral, religious, and governmental principles of the country. It stated that foundations had displayed a distinct tendency to favor political opinions to the left, had led education toward the promotion of collectivism, affected foreign policy and education in things international, and, finally, had directly supported "subversion."[1]

The Report contained a review of the testimony received at the hearings as well as a 189-page appendix that consisted of an alphabetical listing and detailed discussion of persons or agencies "whose names had appeared in the body of the Report in a distinctive kind of type indicating that they had been cited by the Attorney General of the United States or by various other government agencies for having associations and affiliations of a questionable character."[2]

The majority's conclusions have been characterized as relatively mild in the light of its findings.[3] They specifically did not recommend the abolition of all foundations or the removal of their tax-exempt status. They did recommend a continuing investigation of what they considered unfinished work. Specifically, they suggested that the manpower of the Internal Revenue Service be increased so that foundation activity could be watched more closely; that there be full public access to Form 990–A's; and that a ten-to-twenty-five-year limit be placed on the life of all foundations. They further recommended that the accumulations provision of the Internal Revenue Code be amended to give foundations two to three years in which to distribute each year's income, but requiring all income to be paid out within that period and all capital gains to be treated as income and subject to the rule on accumulations. Finally, they recommended that restrictions be placed on

---

[1] U.S. Congress, House of Representatives, Special (Reece) Committee to Investigate Tax-Exempt Foundations and Comparable Organizations, *Report.* 83d Congress, 2d Session, House Report 2681, 1954.

[2] *Ibid.*, pp. 227 ff.

[3] Andrews, F. Emerson, *op. cit.*, p. 345.

corporation-controlled foundations, and that the denial of exemption for engaging in subversive or political activity, be made retroactive unless the trustees and directors resigned forthwith.

Several proposals were suggested to the Ways and Means Committee for further consideration. They included a requirement that there be a trustee appointed by a government agency on every foundation board, or a limit on the term of office of trustees; the enactment of a provision under which a private citizen could bring a proceeding in the federal courts to compel the attorney general to take action against a foundation; further study of the so-called prohibited transactions; a denial of tax exemption to any foundation that holds more than 5 or 10 per cent of its capital in the securities of one enterprise; and a complete exclusion of political activity and lobbying. Other proposals called for consideration of prohibitions against subversion and the limitation of income or principal spent abroad by foundations to 10 per cent.

Two members of the Committee filed a minority report that opened with the following statement:

> The minority does not agree with the report submitted by the majority. It not only disagrees with that report but earnestly believes that it should never be published.[1]

They charged the majority with prejudgment, stating that its report contained false statements, half-truths, and misleading information. The conduct of the Hearings was characterized as unfair, undemocratic, and directed toward justifying conclusions arrived at in advance. The minority concluded in part:

> The proceedings and the majority report evidence the tragedy of the men and women of the committee's staff who, having lived and prospered under freedom, yet do not believe in due process and American fair play; who fear the thinkers and those who dare to advance the new and the unaccepted; who believe that universal education for our people can be risked only if the teachers and their pupils accept their doctrine and are shielded from the mental contamination of other thoughts and beliefs. They would deny the right of individuals to seek truth without limit or restriction.[2]

It was signed by Representatives Wayne L. Hays and Gracie Pfost.

The effect of both of these investigations on foundation activities is difficult to gauge. There was much contemporaneous criticism in

---

[1] *Ibid.*, p. 421.
[2] *Ibid.*, pp. 431–432.

the press of the conduct of the Reece Hearings. Andrews felt that the results were salutory for those few foundations that needed prodding on their responsibilities as public trusts, and that review of policies by many trustees and their staffs, as well as the development of a sense of common interest under violent attack, had been stimulated. He stated that although damage had been done in terms of reaction of the head-line-reading public, little evidence existed that the serious and un-founded charges of the Reece Committee were being taken seriously by any considerable group, or that restrictive legislation was impend-ing.[1]

In 1962, Waldemar A. Neilsen, president of The African-American Institute and former executive of The Ford Foundation, wrote that the two congressional investigations of the 1950's had "not achieved much." He stated that the Reece Committee conducted "the most totally mismanaged Congressional investigation of the McCarthy pe-riod." He also asserted that the investigations had caused the larger foundations to become exceedingly cautious in their programs.[2] Fear that this would happen was, of course, expressed in the Minority Re-port. Ten years later this very caution was being put forth as a ground for criticism of foundation operation.

The direct effect of these investigations on Congress and the state governments is easier to measure than the effects on foundations. No major amendments to the Internal Revenue Code relating to tax-exempt organizations were enacted after the 1950 amendments. In the states, there is no evidence that the activities of either the Cox Committee or the Reece Committee led directly to any legislation similar to that which can be traced from the 1948 and 1950 Hearings to the enactment of supervisory legislation in Rhode Island. Acts similar to the Rhode Island legislation were adopted in Ohio and South Carolina in 1953, and in Massachusetts in 1954, and the publicity engendered from the congressional hearings may have affected the at-titude of individual state legislators, making them receptive to this type of legislation. However, the great impetus for state legislation came from the reports of achievements in New Hampshire after pas-sage of a reporting statute. The drafting of the Uniform Act had been requested by the National Association of Attorneys General in 1951 following a report at their annual meeting by the New Hampshire at-

---

[1] Andrews, F. Emerson, op. cit., pp. 346–347.
[2] Neilsen, Waldemar A., "How Solid Are the Foundations?" New York Times Magazine, October 21, 1962, p. 27.

torney general. More important, foundation activity was not the major focus of any of these acts. This fact is evident in the failure of all of them, with the exception of Massachusetts, clearly to include foundations organized in the corporate form. The adoption of the Uniform Act in California in 1954 was the only legislative action taken soon after the publication of the Reece Committee Report, but not until 1959 was it amended to include corporations and adopted on a permanent basis.

The Patman Investigation. In 1955, soon after the close of the Reece Hearings, Dean Rusk, then president of The Rockefeller Foundation, refuting charges that the congressional investigations had intimidated foundations, made the following statement:

> I do not believe that foundations and their trustees have been intimidated by the events of the past two years. And I have no doubt but that ten or twenty years hence, whenever the next round of investigation comes, we shall have an interesting list of controversial items for consideration. Just which ones they shall be, we have no way of knowing, for that will depend upon the predilections of the investigator.[1]

As early as 1961 his predictions were borne out. Shortly before the recess of the Eighty-seventh Congress, the Select Committee on Small Business of the House of Representatives decided to make a study of the impact of tax-exempt foundations on the American economy. In January of 1962 the Committee passed an authorizing resolution to that effect. The impetus for this investigation came from Committee Chairman Wright Patman of Texas, who had already conducted a preliminary survey as an individual member during 1961. His "preliminary survey" had entailed requests to more than 500 foundations for certain information as to their operations. Each foundation was asked to supply copies of exemption applications, Internal Revenue Service letters granting exemption, tax returns for the years 1951 through 1960 (either Form 990–A or Form 1041–A), accountants' financial statements, investment portfolios, information on directors, trustees, and officers, and other financial and legal information.

In December of 1962 Congressman Patman submitted an Interim Report, subtitled "Chairman's Report to the Select Committee on Small Business," which described the information compiled from these documents. Two of its chapters dealing with income, assets, liabilities,

---

[1] Rusk, Dean, "Building a Professional Staff," *Proceedings* of the New York University Second Biennial Conference on Charitable Foundations, Edited by Henry Sellin. Matthew Bender and Co., New York, 1955, pp. 178–179.

and net worth of these 500 foundations had been inserted in the issues of the *Congressional Record* for July 23, 1962 and August 20, 1962.

The introduction to the Report contained a statement of its purpose and the methods used. Congressman Patman stated that the task of obtaining information from the foundations had been a struggle, entailing four or five letters to many foundations and in some instances a reminder of the Committee's subpoena powers. Seventeen subpoenas were finally issued. However, he also stated that "After several months, we have most of the material on 534 organizations for this 10-year period, or some portion thereof, if the foundation was created after 1951."[1] The direct questionnaires were sent after it was decided that information in the files of the Internal Revenue Service was inadequate. All data were recorded in categories by Congressman Patman's staff but tabulations and charts were compiled by the General Accounting Office of the United States Government. The work of the director of the Study, H. A. Olsher, and one consultant, J. S. Seidman, a partner in a New York certified public accounting firm was acknowledged.

The statistics compiled from the questionnaires were presented in seven tables covering the following categories:

1. Gross receipts: 534 foundations.

2. Data regarding corporations in which certain foundations failed to report their ownership of 10 percent or more of each class of the corporation's stock.

3. Data regarding foundations' ownership of 10 percent or more of any class of stock of any corporation, as reported on the Internal Revenue Service Form 990A.

4. The Ford Foundation—List of notes receivable as of February 1, 1962, representing participations in private placements.

5. Assets: 534 foundations.

6. Liabilities, net worth, and accumulation of income: 534 foundations.

7. State-by-state breakdown: 534 foundations—number of foundations under study; total receipts; expenses plus contributions, gifts, grants, scholarships, etc., total assets, total net worth.[2]

---

[1] U.S. Congress, House of Representatives, Select Committee on Small Business, *Chairman's* (Patman) *Report*, "Tax-Exempt Foundations and Charitable Trusts: Their Impact on Our Economy," First Installment, 87th Congress, 2d Session, Committee Print, December 31, 1962, p. 2.

[2] *Ibid.*

The congressman's observations and findings were contained in the body of the Report. He called initially for an immediate moratorium on foundation tax exemptions for the following reasons:

1. Laxness and irresponsibility on the part of the Internal Revenue Service.

2. Violations of law and Treasury regulations by far too many of the foundations encompassed in our study.

3. The withdrawal of almost $7 billion from the reach of the tax collectors for taxable years 1951 through 1960. This amount represents the total receipts of only 534 out of an estimated 45,124 tax-exempt foundations.

4. The rapidly increasing concentration of economic power in foundations which—in my view—is far more dangerous than anything that has happened in the past in the way of concentration of economic power.

5. Foundation-controlled enterprises possess the money and competitive advantages to eliminate the small businessman.[1]

He stated that the Internal Revenue Service had reported an increase in the number of foundations from 12,295 at the close of 1952 to a total of 45,124 at the end of 1962, and charged that there may be hundreds or thousands of others that operate without the knowledge of the Treasury.

The Report contained 17 sections of recommendations, which can best be grouped under five headings: business operations of foundations; accumulations; contributions to foundations; private benefits; and federal supervision. In regard to business activities, Representative Patman recommended that foundations be prohibited from engaging in business, directly or indirectly, and that a foundation which controlled a business should be deemed to be engaged in that business for tax purposes. He suggested bans on commercial money-lending and borrowing, and prohibition of foundation ownership of more than 3 per cent of the stock of any corporation as well as the denial of the right to vote the stock. Furthermore, he called for the establishment of standards for foundation behavior in proxy fights, and for taxation of any income that was received from trading or speculating in securities or was acquired from assets for which the foundation incurred substantial obligations.

In the area of accumulations, it was recommended that all founda-

---

[1] *Ibid.,* p. 1.

tions should be limited to a twenty-five-year life and be required to distribute such amounts of income and principal each year as would result in a complete distribution of all assets, holdings, and interests at the end of the twenty-five-year period. All contributions and capital gains should be treated as income for the purpose of computing accumulations. In cases where a foundation controlled a corporation, the income of the foundation should be added to that of the corporation to determine amounts accumulated, and an accumulated earnings tax should be put on the income of the corporation.

As to contributors' taxes, the Report recommended that no deduction for income tax purposes be allowed for contributions to a controlled foundation until they were actually used for charity. Until so used, any income earned should be taxed to the donor. Congressman Patman called for limiting the amount of charitable deductions to the lesser of cost or fair market value of property contributed, and for treating any charitable gifts made by corporations that could be considered partnerships for tax purposes as contributions of individual shareholders. Finally, he recommended that foundations and donors be prohibited from soliciting or accepting contributions from suppliers or users of goods and services.

With respect to gift and estate taxes, the Report asked for the exclusion of amounts left to foundations from the adjusted gross estate in computing the marital deduction, and application of rate brackets so that gifts to foundations would be treated as part of taxable gifts or estates.

The recommendations relating to private benefit were that the use of foundation funds to assist employees of controlled corporations be prohibited, that an arm's length relationship be required for all foundation dealings, and that the formation or availability of a foundation for tax avoidance be made a basis for denial of exemption. A converse recommendation was that controlled corporations be denied a deduction for contributions to the controlling foundation.

The last of the 17 sections of recommendations related to federal supervision and consisted of ten specific suggestions:

(a) Consideration should be given to a regulatory agency for the supervision of tax-exempt foundations. . . .

(b) A penetrating review of every application for tax exemption is needed. . . .

(c) All matters relating to the granting or denial of tax exemption, as well as revocations and penalties, should be made public.

(d) The full content of foundation tax returns should be open to public inspection.

(e) A national registry of all foundations should be published annually.

(f) The tax returns of foundations should require disclosure of amounts spent for instigating or promoting legislation, or political activities, or amounts paid to other organizations for the purpose.

(g) The returns should likewise require disclosure of amounts spent for TV, radio, and newspaper advertising.

(h) The returns should call for a description of all activities, directly or indirectly engaged in by the foundation, in which commercial organizations are also engaged.

(i) The program of field auditing returns of foundations should be greatly expanded.

(j) Stiff penalties and revocation of tax exemption for improper or insufficient reporting would help curb abuses.[1]

These recommendations are presented in detail for two reasons. One is that a majority of them are strikingly similar to recommendations made in the earlier congressional investigations, particularly that of the Reece Committee.

Second, the Interim Report received widespread coverage throughout the country and had an immediate effect on the administrative branch of the federal government. In August of 1962 the President announced that he was considering Congressman Patman's charges and was appointing a White House Task Force to study whether tighter administration by the Internal Revenue Service or new legislation was needed.[2] In the summer of 1963 the Treasury named an advisory group of private individuals interested in and directly concerned with foundation activity to provide information on the operations and investment practices of foundations.

This reaction within the Internal Revenue Service was even more specific. In 1961, prior to publication of the Patman Report, the Commissioner of Internal Revenue had formulated a "New Directions" program directed primarily toward encouraging and achieving more effective voluntary compliance by all taxpayers. Specifically, the program included revision of information report forms and an expanded audit program. As a result of Congressman Patman's survey, each of these programs had specific application to tax-exempt organizations.

---

[1] *Ibid.*, pp. 134–135.
[2] *Foundation News,* vol. 3, November, 1962, p. 5.

Form 990–A was revised in 1962 and 1963. The scheduled audits for these organizations were increased from 2,000 to 10,000 per year, and plans were commenced for the creation of a master file of exempt organizations to be based on a questionnaire sent to all organizations that were on the Service records.[1]

In the spring of 1963 the Internal Revenue Service also established an Exempt Organization Council composed of a member of the Commissioner's personal staff, a member of the office of the chief counsel of the Internal Revenue Service, as well as representatives from the technical organization and compliance branches of the Service. Council members were directed to review and recommend an overhauling of procedural and substantive positions, to coordinate all existing projects, to identify other problems, and to recommend policy positions directly to the Commissioner.

On October 16, 1963, Congressman Patman released the second installment of his report.[2] Of its 407 pages, 324 were exhibits of correspondence and documents pertaining to the business transactions of several foundations controlled by a New York industrialist, David G. Baird. Chapter 2 was devoted to these foundations, and Chapters 3 and 4 contained information as to stock transactions of three other New York foundations. Only two of the three foundations established and managed by David G. Baird were active when this report was issued, and they were scheduled to be dissolved and their assets distributed to other charitable organizations within the year. The third had been inactive since 1954 and was in the process of final liquidation.[3]

A third installment of the Patman Report was released on March 30, 1964, and was subtitled "Subcommittee Chairman's Report to Subcommittee No. 1, Select Committee on Small Business." This Report contained three pages of text describing the "Destructive Effect on Our Tax Base" of the disposition of the estate of Alfred I. DuPont and of its affiliate, The Nemours Foundation and 326 pages of tables and exhibits. The letter of transmittal described the report as follows:

Laid bare here for the first time is the detailed anatomy of one of America's great fortunes—a fortune that will one day slip away forever

---

[1] See pp. 396–397, 406 for discussion of each of these programs.

[2] U.S. Congress, House of Representatives, Select Committee on Small Business, *Subcommittee Chairman's* (Patman) *Report to Subcommittee No. 1,* "Tax-Exempt Foundations and Charitable Trusts: Their Impact on Our Economy," Second Installment, 88th Congress, 1st Session, Committee Print, October 16, 1963.

[3] *New York Times,* Sunday, October 20, 1963, p. 77, col. 1.

from the payment of any income taxes. By this dramatic example we will contribute to an understanding of the ever-increasing erosion of our tax base.[1]

Four other examples were given, in short paragraphs, three of which were acknowledged as having been included in earlier charges of Treasury laxness.

Congressman Patman held public hearings in the summer of 1964. He called as witnesses the Secretary of the Treasury, the former Commissioner of Internal Revenue who had resigned during July of 1964, and his successor, and the Acting Chairman of the Securities and Exchange Commission. The sessions were conducted by Congressman Patman and H. A. Olsher, director of the Foundation Study. Other members of the subcommittee appeared only briefly. Each witness made a prepared statement describing the activities of his respective agency or department in connection with tax-exempt organizations. The questions directed at the witnesses by the congressman consisted primarily of requests for opinions or greater detail on many of the issues raised in the three reports to the Subcommittee. Representative Patman did query the Secretary of the Treasury as to the need for a separate regulatory agency to supervise foundation operations, suggesting specifically the General Accounting Office. The Secretary declined to comment on the advisability of establishing a regulatory agency, but stated that the General Accounting Office would not be appropriate in any case.[2]

The Patman investigation had elements of the best and the worst use of the congressional investigatory power. Reforms in the Internal Revenue Service procedure for dealing with tax-exempt organizations were long overdue, and although the need had been recognized by Service personnel before the start of the investigation, much credit must be given to Representative Patman for accelerating their implementation. The Treasury decision to increase the amount of public information on foundation activities and the expansion of the Service audit program were the most valuable results of the pressures brought by the Subcommittee. Although the full extent of its influence could not be seen until the Congress dealt with specific legislative proposals

---

[1] U.S. Congress, House of Representatives, Select Committee on Small Business, *Subcommittee Chairman's* (Patman) *Report to Subcommittee No. 1,* Third Installment, 88th Congress, 2d Session, Committee Print, March 20, 1964, p. iii.

[2] U.S. Congress, House of Representatives, Select Committee on Small Business, *Hearings Before Subcommittee No. 1 on Foundations,* "Tax-Exempt Foundations: Their Impact on Small Business," 88th Congress, 2d Session, 1964, p. 61.

relating to tax-exempt organizations, the new focus on Treasury supervision was sufficient to justify congressional attention to the problem.

On the other hand, the Subcommittee reports, the congressman's statements, and some of the charges made at the public hearings went far beyond the area of the Subcommittee's immediate concern, which was foundation impact on small business. One writer has charged that the reports were basically ultra vires.

> The evidence submitted in connection with the impact of foundations upon the small business community is sketchy, to say the least. The investigation procedure likewise extended well beyond the restrictions of the Executive Order and Regulations relating to the matter.[1]

This same writer criticized the publication of the first and second Patman Reports on the grounds that they were "neither reports of a Committee to the House, nor of the Subcommittee to the Committee, but merely reports of a chairman to his own subcommittee," and were therefore only the opinion of a single individual, based on preconceived ideas and "correlating only such unrelated and, at times, immaterial facts as supported the preconception."[2]

One of the members of the Subcommittee issued a similar objection, stating further that the failure to afford to the foundations any public opportunity to refute the charges made against them, or to place their justifications on the printed record, amounted to "an indictment without a chance to respond or an indictment without even being advised that a party is under indictment or possibly to be indicted. . . ."[3]

Criticism was also leveled at the content of the reports and the specific recommendations contained therein.[4] The recommendations were called inconsistent and confusing.[5] In some instances they were based on mistakes of facts. The most widely criticized mistake of this nature was the statement that "According to the figures compiled for us by the Internal Revenue Service, there were 45,124 foundations

---

[1] Powell, Roger I., "The Patman Report and the New Reporting Requirements," *Proceedings* of the New York University Twenty-second Annual Institute on Federal Taxation. Matthew Bender and Co., New York, 1964, pp. 921, 923.

[2] *Ibid.*, p. 922.

[3] Representative William H. Avery, *Congressional Record,* 87th Congress, 2d Session, Monday, August 20, 1962, pp. 16007–8.

[4] See, for example, Reicher, John E., "Foundations and the Putman Committee Report," *Michigan Law Review,* vol. 63, 1964, p. 95.

[5] Krasnowiecki, Jan Z., and Alexander Brodsky, "Comment on the Patman Report," *Pennsylvania Law Review,* vol. 112, 1963, pp. 190, 192.

at the close of 1960."[1] This figure was, in actuality, the number of Form 990–A returns filed by *all* organizations using the form in that year, so that it included many charitable organizations that did not fall within the generally accepted view of foundations, such as hospitals, educational organizations without student bodies, orphanages, homes for old people, and so forth. Treasury officials estimated that approximately 25 per cent of the reports filed on Form 990–A are from foundations; this figure corresponded with estimates made by The Foundation Library Center that there were approximately 15,000 foundations at the end of 1961.[2]

Finally, some observers expressed the fear that because the extent of the misdealings detailed in the Report was unknown, the remedies would be unnecessarily harsh and would damage the structure of legitimate foundation operations to an extent not warranted by the actual situation. In this connection it was felt particularly misleading to rely on the statistics contained in the first Patman Report as to the relationship of foundation contributions to income, since the tables included capital gains in computing all figures for income, a practice contrary to Treasury regulations as well as universally accepted accounting procedures for charitable endeavors.

At present, the only practical answer to the abuse of the congressional investigatory power is pressure by individuals on their own congressmen to require responsible behavior. The executive branch of the federal government reacted responsibly to the Patman investigation, accepting valid criticisms and acting on them positively. Wherever this same effect was achieved by individual foundations, the result was also positive. Of particular value was the reminder to foundations that tax-exempt status is not a matter of right, and that the act of creating a foundation imposes on the donor a responsibility to the public which cannot be ignored.

The Role of the Treasury

The Treasury Department plays a dual role in the management of the nation's financial affairs. The Secretary of the Treasury is responsible for formulating and drafting proposals that reflect the President's policies, and for assisting in attempts to secure their passage. Second,

---

[1] U.S. Congress, House of Representatives, Select Committee on Small Business, *Chairman's* (Patman) *Report, op. cit.*, p. v.

[2] McGreevy, Michael, "Review of Rulings and Forms for Reporting," *Proceedings* of the New York University Sixth Biennial Conference on Charitable Foundations, 1963, pp. 175, 200.

the Treasury directs the operation of the Internal Revenue Service, participating in all of its major policy decisions and actions, approving regulations and published rulings, and assisting and cooperating on legal as well as legislative matters that affect the Revenue Service. A measure of the closeness of the Department and the Service may be seen from the fact that the chief counsel of the Internal Revenue Service is also an assistant general counsel of the Treasury Department. He is appointed by the President with the advice and consent of the Senate, serves as legal adviser to the Commissioner of Internal Revenue on all matters pertaining to the administration and enforcement of tax laws, and is, in turn, directly responsible to the general counsel of the Treasury.

The interaction of Treasury staff members and the Congress has already been described. Within the Treasury Department, problems relating to foundations and other charitable organizations are the responsibility of members of the Exempt Organization Section of the Office of Tax Legislative Counsel. This group, in addition to drafting legislative proposals, prepares report forms and formulates policy decisions in regard to the regulations and rulings of the Commissioner that relate to exempt organizations. Members of this office attended the five meetings of the Treasury's Informal Advisory Committee on Foundations which were held in 1963 to discuss specific problem areas where legislative action might be desirable. The Treasury has also, on occasion, retained private attorneys experienced in the field of exempt organizations to prepare analyses of certain problems.

Treasury Department Report on Private Foundations. In January of 1964, the Senate Finance Committee and the House Ways and Means Committee requested the Treasury to prepare a report on the adequacy of the 1950 amendments to the Internal Revenue Code in remedying abuses by exempt organizations, including determinations as to whether the legislation needed strengthening from a policy or administrative point of view, and whether new abuses had developed which required correction by legislative or administrative action.

In preparation for the study, the Treasury Department undertook a survey of approximately 1,300 foundations. They were picked by a random sampling method to include 100 per cent of all foundations with assets of $10 million or more, 25 per cent of those with assets of from $1 million to $10 million, 10 per cent of those in the $100,000 to $1 million range, and 5 per cent of those with assets of $100,000 or less. The foundations in the survey were chosen from information furnished by the Internal Revenue Service and The Foundation Library Center. Each foundation was asked a series of questions relating to the nature of its assets, the composition of its managing board, and its participation in transactions between its officers, contributors, and related parties.

The Treasury's Report was submitted to the Congress on February 2, 1965. It contained an appraisal of the place and value of foundations in the United States; a detailed analysis of problems raised by foundation activity; and six major recommendations for reform of the tax laws, as well as several additional ones. A 45-page Appendix contained the findings of the 1964 survey, pertinent tables of information relating to the size and growth of foundations, and a brief description of Internal Revenue Service administrative activity.[1]

The Treasury Department's appraisal of foundations dealt specifically with three broad criticisms that had been directed at foundations. The charge that the interposition of foundations between a donor and active charitable pursuits entailed undue delay in the transfer of benefits to society was declared to possess "considerable force," but it was also considered to be capable of solution by a legislative measure of special designation and limited scope.[2]

The charge that foundations were becoming a disproportionately large segment of the national economy was characterized as lacking factual basis:

> While the available information is far from definitive, it suggests that, since 1950, foundation wealth has not grown appreciably faster than other segments of the economy which have substantial investments in common stocks. The existing restrictions on charitable deductions for contributions to foundations would seem to provide a significant restraint upon abnormal growth. Hence, there would appear to be little present factual basis for the assertion that foundation lives should be limited because foundation wealth has become disproportionate.[3]

The third criticism of foundations discussed in the Report was that foundations represent a dangerous concentration of economic and social power. The Treasury concluded that, for the present, this was being amply met by foundations themselves.

As a result of its investigation, the Treasury Department concluded that the preponderant number of foundations perform their functions

---

[1] See p. 45.
[2] U.S. Congress, Senate, Committee on Finance, *Treasury Department Report on Private Foundations, op. cit.,* p. 13.
[3] *Ibid.,* pp. 13–14.

without tax abuse.[1] Evidence of abuse by a minority of foundations, however, was felt sufficient to warrant new legislation.

> Since the Federal tax laws have played a significant part in the growth of foundations, an unavoidable responsibility rests upon the Federal government to do what it reasonably can to insure that these organizations operate in a manner conducive to the fulfillment of their purposes. The Treasury Department does not, however, recommend that any separate Federal regulatory agency be created to supervise foundations. Rather, the Department is of the view that the effort should be made to frame the tax laws themselves to curb abuses.[2]

Although the Report delineated six specific problems and contained recommendations to meet each one, all were directed at two general situations. Each of the proposals reflected an attempt to curb the benefits available to donors who control foundations, although the first and fourth dealt specifically with pecuniary benefits and the sixth was concerned with the less tangible possibilities for individual benefit and parochialism. In addition, the Treasury was concerned with the extent to which foundations have become involved in business enterprises and have thereby placed taxable business at a competitive disadvantage. This concern was specifically reflected in its third and fifth recommendations.

The titles used in the Report to describe these six major problems were (1) self-dealing, (2) delay in benefit to charity, (3) foundation involvement in business, (4) family use of foundations to control corporate and other property, (5) financial transactions unrelated to charitable functions, and (6) broadening of foundation management. Recommendations for legislative action to deal with each one were made. They were stated in broad terms, however, and no draft bills were submitted with the Report.[3]

The second major concern of the Treasury Department, which is reflected to some degree in each of its recommendations and is focused on specifically in the third and fifth, was the extent to which foundations have become involved in business enterprises, thereby placing taxable business at a competitive disadvantage and diverting the attention of foundation directors from their proper concerns and functions.

The recommendations made by the Treasury Department to deal with what were classified as "additional problems" were as follows:

---

[1] *Ibid.*, p. 2.
[2] *Ibid.*, p. 14.
[3] See Chapter V for a summary of these recommendations.

(1) deductions for donation of certain classes of unproductive property should be postponed until the assets are either made productive, disposed of, or applied for charitable uses; (2) the amount of the deduction for donations to foundations should be reduced by any amounts of income they would have generated to the donor if they had been sold rather than donated; (3) technical changes should be made in certain of the provisions of the estate tax laws that now give an unfair advantage to decedents making contributions to foundations; (4) more appropriate sanctions for failure to file information returns should be enacted.

The statistics compiled in the Treasury's survey indicated the reasons for the emphasis in its Report on the problems of donor control and business activities. The statistics on donor control obtained from the survey indicated that in slightly over two-thirds of all foundations the donor or persons related to him made up 50 per cent of each foundation's managing trustees. When the statistics taken from the sample 1,300 foundations were extrapolated to provide an estimate of the data for all foundations, they indicated that of 14,850 foundations, in 10,990 donor-related influence over investment policy was 50 per cent or more; in 810 this influence was over 33 per cent but not over 50 per cent; in 100 it was over 20 per cent but not over 33 per cent; and in 2,420 it did not exceed 20 per cent.[1]

In regard to the business involvement of foundations, the Report stated that of the approximately 1,300 foundations surveyed, about 180 reported ownership of 10 per cent or more of at least one class of stock of a business corporation. Of these, 109 held 20 per cent or larger interests and 40 owned 100 per cent interests. Forty-three of the 180 owned 10 per cent or more of the stock of two or more corporations.[2]

On the question of accumulation of income, the survey indicated that in 1962 approximately one-fourth of all foundations did not expend for charitable purposes an amount equal to the net ordinary income (that is, total income, excluding capital gains, less the expenses incurred in earning that income).[3]

Finally, although borrowing was estimated to account for only 2.5 per cent of the total assets of foundations, the specific instances of

---

[1] U.S. Congress, Senate, Committee on Finance, *Treasury Department Report on Private Foundations, op. cit.,* p. 85.

[2] *Ibid.,* p. 31.

[3] *Ibid.,* p. 26.

borrowing to further private, rather than charitable, purposes was felt to be of sufficient import to warrant the proposed restrictions.[1]

Although the Treasury admitted that the sample used for the survey was small, the estimates were felt to be of sufficient value to indicate the major problem areas. They were complemented in several instances by statistics contained in the Patman Report on 435 foundations, as well as by data from several independent studies.

All of these statistics are open to certain criticisms. Throughout the Treasury Report foundations were discussed in terms of the number falling into various categories, but no indication was given of the amount of assets held by the foundations falling within each. However, meaningful discussions of the extent of any abuse can only be made in terms of the amount of total assets, or of income, loans, or distributions that are involved rather than solely on the number of foundations. For example, although 700 foundations may have expended less than 25 per cent of their ordinary income for charitable purposes, it is quite possible that this 5 per cent of all foundations surveyed represented less than one-half of one per cent of all foundation income. Another example is to be found in the statistics dealing with foundations that have certain degrees of donor-related influence over investment policy. It was found that this influence was under 20 per cent in only 2,420 of a total of 14,850 foundations. However, the assets of these 2,420 foundations are almost certainly larger than the assets in all of the other categories, since many of the largest foundations are in this "less than 20 per cent" category.

A second problem raised by the Treasury's use of statistics is that several conclusions were based on information taken from a single year's operation and were, thereby, distorted. For example, the Report indicated that in 1962 one-fourth of all foundations did not expend an amount equal to their net income. This statement is misleading unless some indication is also given of the record of each of these foundations for several years. In connection with this question of charitable expenditures, it should also be noted that foundations that expended 80 to 100 per cent of income at the end of one given year fall into a far different category from those which expended 50 to 60 per cent, yet the tables grouped together all foundations expending 50 to 100 per cent of their income and separated out those below 25 per cent from the lower half. Finally, it is unfortunate that the survey

---

[1] *Ibid.*, p. 45.

grouped together the 4,910 foundations whose assets range from $100,000 to $1 million since the management and investment practices of the smaller ones are usually far different from those whose assets are close to a million dollars. These criticisms, of course, highlight the need for a broadened and continuing study of foundation management practices.

The Report was far milder in its criticism of foundation abuse than the Patman Reports, although the major recommendations were similar in approach to several of the congressman's proposals. However, the Treasury's specific rejection of a twenty-five-year limit on the life of foundations and its proposals to regulate accumulations of income reflected philosophical attitude toward the role of foundations different from that of the congressman.

Certain important aspects of the question of federal supervision of foundations were not dealt with in the Report. A footnote to the introduction stated that "provisions designed to insure compliance with existing rules will need to be reexamined to determine their adequateness to the task of seeking compliance with the rules proposed in this report."[1] It was also noted that effective enforcement was dependent upon adequate information and that changes would be necessary to assure that all foundations subject to the new rules would be required to file information returns. These were the only references in the Report to changes in methods of enforcement.

The Report also lacked any indication of whether certain specific standards and proscriptions should be spelled out in legislation or dealt with under the Treasury's regulatory powers. Certain of the proposals mentioned standards that were not sufficiently specific to permit any evaluation in terms of suitability or ease of enforcement. Finally, the Report did not attempt to deal in any detail with the question of how to treat foundations operating under agreements of trust or corporate charters that contain provisions inconsistent with the Treasury's proposals and that may not be subject to amendment.

The greatest omission, however, was in the important area of sanctions: the only one specified related to the penalties for failure to file information returns, although the proposal to postpone deduction for contributions of stock in a corporation controlled by the donor would, of course, carry its own sanction. It was not clear, therefore, whether the Treasury favored any attempts to make the sanctions for evasion

---

[1] *Ibid.*, p. 3.

of either its new proposals or existing laws more appropriate for the preservation of philanthropic funds, or whether it preferred continued reliance on the existing sanctions of denial of tax-exempt status and, in limited instances, denial of deductions for prior contributions.

Despite these omissions, and regardless of whether the Congress accepts any of its specific recommendations, the Treasury Department Report on Private Foundations represents a carefully prepared, well-reasoned study of foundations that will have an important place in all further debates over the relationship of foundations to government.

Promulgation of Regulations. There are four sources of law that must be examined to ascertain all taxpayers' federal tax liability on any matter—statutes, court decisions, regulations, and administrative rulings. Regulations are promulgated by the Treasury Department as Treasury decisions, although they are originally prepared by the Internal Revenue Service in cooperation with Treasury officials. These tax regulations are specifically authorized by law and have the force and effect of law in the dealings of all taxpayers with the Treasury Department and the Service.

Proposals for new Treasury regulations are first published as proposed regulations in the *Federal Register*. A period of thirty days follows, during which interested parties may submit views, data, and arguments concerning the proposals. Final promulgation may occur immediately following the expiration of this thirty-day period, although in some cases the proposed regulation is revised or republished. For example, regulations proposed in February of 1959 relating to the definition of "exempt purposes" included an example of "scientific purposes," but no specific definition of this category. Complaints were filed during the thirty-day period about this omission, and the regulations were promulgated with a statement that the example had been eliminated and that a proposed regulation on scientific purposes would subsequently be published.[1] This was done in December of 1959,[2] but further complaints led to the withdrawal of this proposal on November 14, 1960, and the publication of a third revision, which was finally promulgated on January 5, 1961.[3]

The importance of Treasury regulations cannot be overemphasized. They may be challenged by a taxpayer in a proceeding brought before

---

[1] T.D. 6391, 1959–2 Cum. Bull. 139.
[2] 25 Fed. Reg. 9587 (1959).
[3] T.D. 6525, 1961–1 Cum. Bull. 186.

the Tax Court or the Court of Claims to contest a deficiency, or in a suit for a refund in the federal district courts. Although they are not controlling on the courts, they may not be overruled unless the court finds that they are arbitrary or capricious, or contrary to the intent of Congress. Otherwise, the regulations have the same authority as law, binding on taxpayers and the Internal Revenue Service alike. Instructions on tax returns have the weight of regulations.

The authority of the Treasury Department to issue regulations is, in effect, a quasi-legislative power. It is a necessary adjunct to the taxing process and, when properly utilized, should keep litigation to a minimum. Following the intent of Congress is not always easy to do, however, and this has been particularly true of the regulations relating to the business activities of exempt organizations. Under the "organizational test,"[1] no more than an "insubstantial" amount of unrelated business activity may be permitted in the organization's charter or it will not qualify for exemption. However, the regulation defining the "operational test,"[2] embodies both a primary-activity test and an insubstantial-activity test; whereas section 1.501(c)(3)–1(e) retains the primary-purpose test, permitting substantial business operations in furtherance of exempt purposes if the primary purpose is not the carrying on of an unrelated trade or business. This internal inconsistency in the regulations has created problems for both the Service and the tax-exempt organizations; yet without further congressional definition of the extent to which business activities should be permitted before exempt status may be denied, it is likely that the regulations will remain inconsistent.

The Internal Revenue Service

Organization. On a chart of the organization of the administrative branch of the federal government, the Internal Revenue Service appears as a subdivision of the Treasury Department, but it is in most respects a self-contained department with overall responsibility for administering and enforcing the tax laws. The Commissioner is appointed directly by the President. His executive authority extends over the entire organization, with the exception of the chief counsel and the director of practice who are directly responsible to the Secretary of the Treasury.

The functions of the Service are divided into six major areas, each

---

[1] Treas. Reg. 1.501(c)(3)–1(b)iii.
[2] Treas. Reg. 1.501(c)(3)–1(c).

headed by an assistant commissioner. They are administration, compliance, data processing, inspection, planning and research, and technical. Each department has some contact with exempt organizations, although the compliance and technical divisions, through their responsibilities for audits and preparation of rulings, deal most closely with this area of tax law.

Since the government reorganization of 1952, the Internal Revenue Service has operated at three levels—national, regional (8 offices), and district (58 offices). Foundations have most of their contact with the district offices where applications for exemption are filed and audits originate; certain cases are immediately referred to the national office, and others ultimately receive final determinations at the national level. The responsibility of each level of organization can be seen most clearly in relation to each of the various functions of the Service that relate to exempt organizations—issuance of rulings, examination of information returns and audits, and legal determinations and proceedings.

Rulings. Rulings are statements in writing to a taxpayer that interpret and apply the Internal Revenue Code and Treasury Regulations to specific fact situations and state a conclusion as to the tax consequences of that particular transaction or situation. They are issued from the national office of the Internal Revenue Service by letter and are commonly called "letter rulings." When a ruling has wide application or value as a precedent, it is published in the weekly *Internal Revenue Bulletin* and is then captioned a "Revenue Ruling." It does not have the force and effect of a Treasury decision but, unlike a letter ruling, does provide a publicly recorded precedent to be used in the disposition of other cases and may be relied upon when the facts and circumstances in other cases are substantially the same as those on which the ruling was based.[1] Furthermore, revisions or modifications of these published rulings are usually made only prospectively, unlike many revisions or modifications of letter rulings.

Also published in the *Bulletin* are certain rulings relating to the procedural aspects of tax administration. They are entitled Revenue Procedures and contain summaries of the internal practices and procedures of the Service. Revenue Procedures issued in 1962[2] cover in detail the procedure and requirements for obtaining rulings or determination letters on tax-exempt status.

---

[1] Rev. Proc. 62–28, 1962–2 Cum. Bull. 496, 50b.
[2] Rev. Proc. 62–30, 1962–2 Cum. Bull. 512.

Certain rulings may also be issued by the District Directors of Internal Revenue; these also apply the law, regulations, and published rulings to a particular set of facts. They have the same legal effect as letter rulings, but are distinguished from those issued from the national office by their title of determination letters. They are issued only when it is possible to answer a request on the basis of clearly established precedent and when they do not cover any new or unusual questions.

Service policy has placed two major limitations on the issuance of rulings; they will not be issued if the nature of the question is inherently factual, or if it represents an obvious tax avoidance scheme. Within these limits, their promulgation is designed, as is that of the regulations, to clarify the statutory provisions and to minimize litigation.

The ruling process has been described as the basic instrument for the administration of the exemption provisions of the Internal Revenue Code;[1] and the procedures and limitations that apply to income, estate, and gift taxes have been modified in certain respects to make the process more suitable to this function. In the case of exempt organizations, the primary modification has been an exception to the policy against the issuance of rulings on factual questions. Thus, determination of the exempt status of an organization is made by the Internal Revenue Service in the form of a ruling, despite the fact that it is basically a factual question. Furthermore, the issuance of a determination letter or favorable ruling on exempt status represents an administrative determination on which the organization and certain donors may rely so that, until revoked, it carries a presumption that qualification for exemption continues. Revocation of rulings of this type are not usually made on a retroactive basis.[2]

It should be noted that nothing in the Internal Revenue Code itself requires an organization to obtain a ruling to the effect that it is exempt. Without a ruling or court decision, however, the status of an organization remains uncertain. It must file regular income tax returns, and deduction of contributions will be questioned by the Service. The organization may not advertise its exempt status, and it will not be included in the cumulative list of exempt organizations published by the Service. Therefore, although government officials generally

---

[1] Rogovin, Mitchell, "Tax Exemption: Current Thinking Within the Service," *Proceedings* of the New York University Twenty-second Annual Institute on Federal Taxation, pp. 945, 947.

[2] See pp. 401 ff.

remind the public that exemption is granted by the statute, not the Internal Revenue Service,[1] in practice it is the Service that makes this determination for most foundations; and it is the Service that has established, through regulations and revenue procedures, the definitions of exempt purposes and the procedures for obtaining such a determination.[2]

From 1954[3] to December, 1963, twelve months of active operation were required before the Service would issue a ruling to most organizations seeking tax-exempt status. Under procedures established in December of 1963, however,[4] an application for exemption on Form 1023, together with the proper accompanying documents and information, may be filed immediately following creation with the office of the district director where the principal place of business or principal office of the organization is located. The required documents include the organization papers setting forth the powers and purposes of the foundation and a separate, more explicit statement of purpose. Financial information for each accounting period prior to the date of application must be included. Also required is a statement of the actual and proposed operation of the organization which must be sufficiently detailed for the Service to reach the conclusion that, if followed in practice, the organization will meet the "operational test" of the Internal Revenue Code. In addition, the application may include a request for a determination that the organization is "publicly supported," within the meaning of the Internal Revenue Code, and thereby exempt from filing Form 990–A and eligible for inclusion in the 30 per cent-charitable-contribution-deduction class. All of this information is of public record unless, upon request of the organization, the Service determines that certain information that relates to any trade secret, patent, process, style of work, or apparatus of the organization would, if publicized, adversely affect either the organization itself or the national defense.[5]

If the case for exemption is factually clear and there are no questionable legal issues involved, the district director may issue a determination letter. Approximately 50 per cent of all exemption applications received from foundations are processed in this manner,

---

[1] See McGreevy, Michael, *op. cit.;* and Rogovin, Mitchell, *op cit.*
[2] See pp. 64 ff.
[3] Rev. Rul. 54–164, 1954–1 Cum. Bull. 88.
[4] Rev. Proc. 63–30, 1963 Int. Rev. Bull. 52, 512.
[5] Int. Rev. Code of 1954, sec. 6104(a)(1)(B).

although they are subject to review by the national office, which in some cases may take exception. If requests for exemption are forwarded to the national office and acted upon favorably, a determination letter is then sent directly to the applicant. Approximately 95 per cent of field cases are approved on post-review, and the Service has indicated that it is considering conducting post-review on a sample basis alone.[1]

These ruling letters are not open to public inspection. They usually contain merely the statement that the organization has been ruled exempt under a particular section of the Internal Revenue Code. During 1963 and 1964, the Exempt Organization Council of the Service was considering the possibility of revising the ruling letters so that they would be specifically tailored to the requests for exemption and would include the material facts on which the Service relied in making its determination, as well as appropriate conditions or caveats as to activities inimical to exempt status. Rulings of this type would be considered "executory contracts," and continued recognition of exempt status under them would be dependent upon the organization's living up to their terms.[2]

When an organization protests a determination made by the district director because it has been found nonexempt or exempt under the wrong category, the case will be reviewed by the district director. If his decision is unfavorable, the case is then referred to the national office, and the applicant is informed of a right to a conference. The organization may then have to amend the statements in the application or the articles of organization, or file a new application showing evidence that it has changed its activities. However, except where exempt status is refused because the organization engaged in a prohibited transaction under section 503, a new application may be filed immediately.

Approximately 12,000 applications for exemption are received by the Service each year. It is estimated that 10 per cent of these are from foundations. Approximately 4,000 determination letters are reviewed by the national office, 1,200 of these being issued immediately from that office. The number of adverse rulings issued at the national office during the period from January, 1960 to July, 1962 was 231, but this did not include cases where adverse determinations were made at the district office level and no protest was filed, nor those where an

---

[1] Rogovin, Mitchell, op. cit., p. 954.
[2] Ibid., p. 950.

organization was requested to amend its charter or make other adjustments as a condition to a favorable ruling.[1]

The second type of Revenue Service ruling that may affect exempt organizations relates to the consequences of specific transactions and their effect on an organization's tax-exempt status. The authority of the district directors to issue rulings of this nature is generally limited to situations involving completed transactions affecting a return required to be filed in his district, and on which the Service position is clear. All other rulings of this type are made in Washington.

The national office issues rulings on both prospective and completed transactions, subject to the following limitations: no rulings and determinations are issued with respect to the consequence of a transaction occurring in a year for which a return was already filed, nor on questions affecting future returns if an identical issue is involved in a return already filed. Ordinarily the policy prohibiting issuance of rulings on inherently factual questions is applicable to requests from exempt organizations. For example, a request relating to the existence of a prohibited transaction that depended primarily on the market value of property or the reasonableness of compensation would be refused. Unpublished rulings on specific transactions may be modified or revoked at any time, although ordinarily this action will not be applied retroactively to the organization that requested the ruling, unless it was based on misrepresentations.[2]

The number of published rulings in the exempt organization field has been less than in other areas of tax law primarily because of the factual nature of the cases. One of the proposals studied by the Internal Revenue Service Exempt Organization Council was the feasibility of increasing the number of published rulings, thereby furnishing better guidelines for future determinations by both Service personnel and the exempt organizations. The Commissioner of Internal Revenue announced in July, 1964, that during the previous three and one-half years the Service had published in the *Internal Revenue Bulletin* 41 revenue rulings, revenue procedures, and announcements relating to exempt organization matters.

Record-Keeping Requirements. Foundations are subject to federal as well as state requirements relating to the keeping of records and the filing of returns. The Internal Revenue Code requires all organizations exempt from tax but required to file an annual return to "keep such

---

[1] McGreevy, Michael, *op. cit.,* pp. 184–185.
[2] See Rev. Proc. 62–28, 1962–2 Cum. Bull. 496, 506.

permanent books of account or records, including inventories, as are sufficient to establish the amount of gross income, deductions, credits or other matters required to be shown by such person in any return of such tax or information."[1] Furthermore, in connection with both ruling applications and audits, an organization may be called upon to furnish a "record of operations"[2] that would show in specific detail its activities, financial and otherwise.

Until an organization has received a ruling that it is exempt, it must file annual income tax returns and pay any taxes due.[3] When the twelve-months' operation rule was in effect for all foundations, this requirement posed a problem for some organizations,[4] but with the amendment of this requirement, the problem of filing need not arise, except where action on a request for exemption is delayed for more than a year.

Information-Reporting Forms. Annual reporting by exempt organizations was not required until 1942, when the Treasury Department by administrative action imposed a requirement that annual information returns be filed by all tax-exempt organizations.[5] Some organizations protested the Treasury's authority to impose such a requirement, and compliance was poor. In 1943 the Treasury sought specific statutory authority to require reports of financial status from most types of exempt organizations.[6]

It was not until 1950, however, that these reports were made available to the public[7] and Form 990–A was published. This form consisted of four pages, the first two of which contained information required by the Treasury for its purposes, and the latter two of which contained information required by Congress to be disclosed to the public. Not open for public inspection were the detailed schedules of "other income," depreciation and depletion, miscellaneous expenses, the names of the recipients of contributions, and the answers to a series of questions relating to the organization and operation of the organization.

---

[1] Int. Rev. Code of 1954, sec. 6001; Treas. Reg. 1.6001–1(a).

[2] Rev. Proc. 62–30, 1962–2 Cum. Bull. 512; and Rev. Proc. 63–30, 1963–2 Cum. Bull. 769.

[3] Treas. Reg. 1.6033–1(c) (1958).

[4] See Sugarman, Norman, and David R. Fulmer, "The Requirements and Techniques for Filing Tax and Information Returns," Proceedings of the Fifth Biennial New York University Conference on Foundations, op. cit., 1961, pp. 169, 171–172.

[5] T.D. 5125, 1942–1 Cum. Bull. 101; and T.D. 5177, 1942–2 Cum. Bull. 123.

[6] Rev. Act of 1943, sec. 117; see also McGreevy, Michael, op. cit., p. 191.

[7] Rev. Act of 1950, sec. 341; now sec. 6033(b) of the Code.

Revisions of this form were made in seven of the twelve years from 1950 to 1962. The changes reflected primarily the Treasury's attempts to make the form yield the information required of foundations in the Acts of 1950 and 1954. Among the significant changes were:

In January, 1954, the minimum amount of gifts from one individual for which an itemized schedule is required was lowered from $3,000 to $100.

In December, 1954, foundations were required to attach a detailed statement of the nature of their activities.
In November, 1955, the balance sheet was enlarged to include figures for the end as well as the beginning of the year.

In October, 1957, foundations were required to file a duplicate of their schedule of grants which could be attached to the public's copy.
In October, 1958, the line related to contributions, gifts, grants, etc., from the foundation's donors was included on the public's copy.

In October, 1960, foundations were permitted to file balance sheets prepared for other officials, such as those filed with any national, municipal or other public officer, in lieu of the one required on Form 990-A.[1]

Late in 1962, following publication of Congressman Patman's report and study by the Treasury Department of means for increasing accountability of foundations, the Department concluded that it had statutory authority to disclose to the public all information required on Form 990–A with the exception of the names of contributors. This decision was first published in the *Federal Register* on December 29, 1962,[2] and it became effective shortly thereafter.[3] Under the terms of this regulation, the following categories of information became public: officers' salaries, holdings of stock and other investments, accumulation of capital gains and other income, dealings and relationships with contributors, and the names and addresses of persons receiving grants and their relationship to benefactors of the organization. Form 990–A was then revised to reflect this decision.[4] The new form, published in May of 1963, was required for all taxable years ending on or after December 31, 1962. The form contained two parts. Part II actually required duplicate copies of the information available to the

---

[1] National Council of Community Foundations, Inc., Memorandum to Members, New York, September 5, 1962, p. 4 (mimeographed).
[2] Fed. Reg., vol. 27, no. 251, p. 12953.
[3] Treas. Reg. 1.6033–1(a) as amended by T.D. 6645, 1963–1 Cum. Bull. 269.
[4] McGreevy, Michael, *op. cit.,* p. 192.

public; one copy was to be retained in the district where the return was filed and the other, forwarded to Washington.

One of the major complaints voiced by foundations against Form 990–A has been against the balance sheet. Prior to the 1963 revision, the form for this balance sheet was the same as that used for business enterprises. It requested figures as to net worth that were completely inappropriate for charitable endeavors, whether they were trusts or nonstock corporations. The 1963 revision omitted the questions as to net worth, but retained the rest of the balance sheet and required a statement of total liabilities and net worth. Prior to the 1963 revision, an organization was permitted to substitute a copy of a balance sheet used for reporting to state or municipal agencies; thereafter it was required to use Form 990–A, although the instructions stated that if the form did not contain adequate entry spaces, an attachment, following the format and sequence of the boxes provided, could be added. The balance sheet did contain a new provision keyed to the categories on the income page relating to capital gains and losses. On both the income and balance sheet pages of the form it was made possible to attribute accumulations to ordinary income gains as distinguished from sale of assets, thereby recognizing the distinction permitted by the regulations under which capital gains, if reinvested, would be considered addition to corpus and not, therefore, subject to the prohibition against unreasonable accumulation of income.

The major changes appeared on the first pages where more detailed information was requested as to contributions received, charitable distributions, and expenses. A description of any gift to a foundation of more than $100 was required on a separate schedule along with the information previously required as to the name and address of the donor. The purpose of this new requirement was to provide a means for "flagging" gifts of property where it was possible for an inflated valuation to be claimed by the donor as a deduction from his personal tax.

As to distributions made by an organization, the names of the donees were required to be accompanied by their addresses, the amounts received, and information as to whether there was a specific relationship between the organization and the donee. Space was provided for reporting voted grants, which could be offset against accumulations.

The new form also reflected attempts to clarify the allocation of expenses by establishing four categories: (1) earning gross income,

(2) distributing earned or accumulated income, (3) raising and collecting principal, and (4) distributing principal. Each of these categories was to be broken down further into seven types of expenses, a step previously applicable only to expenses of earning gross income. Shortly after publication, a Treasury Department official publicly recognized the fact that these new requirements were causing a great deal of confusion, particularly for the small conduit type of foundation. He stated that further refinements might be needed but that the new schedule was still an improvement.[1]

No significant changes were made in the list of 15 questions at the end of the form, although a new question was added that reflected clearly the influence of some of Congressman Patman's charges and recommendations. It requested specific information, on an attached schedule, in all cases where investments in corporate stock at the close of the taxable year included 10 per cent or more of any class of stock of any corporation. The schedule was to list (1) the name of the corporation, class of stock, and whether the stock was voting or nonvoting; (2) the number of shares owned of each class at the beginning and end of the taxable year; (3) the total number of shares outstanding of each class; (4) the value of the stock as recorded in the books; (5) the date acquired; and (6) the manner of acquisition. Although this same information was required on the prior form, the request for it appeared only in the instructions and not in connection with any specifically noted line of the form and, as McGreevy noted, "the requirement appears to have been frequently ignored."[2] Discussing all of the 16 questions, he also stated:

> There appears to be a tendency in some circles to take the position that the Service is entitled to enquire only about transactions which clearly jeopardize an organization's tax-exempt status and that questions which go beyond this point may be mentally revised before being answered or even disregarded. It seems evident from the legislative history of section 6033(a) of the Code that this is an untenable position.[3]

The problem of faulty filing of Form 990–A has evidently been present since the form was first adopted. The former editor of *American Foundations and Their Fields*,[4] Wilmer Shields Rich, described her experience as the first person to conduct a nationwide transcrip-

---

[1] *Ibid.*, p. 196.
[2] *Ibid.*, p. 198.
[3] *Ibid.*
[4] 7th ed., American Foundations Information Service, New York, 1955.

tion and analysis of the information returns of foundations to the Treasury Department.

> Between 1951 and 1955 I had the interesting and enlightening experience of analyzing the returns of more than 6,000 foundations of Forms 990-A and 1041-A. In the course of this study I was confronted by incomplete returns, several hundred letters from foundation trustees resentful of the availability of information about their activities and occasionally cessation of filing returns. The high proportion of returns which were inadequately filled out prompted me in 1953 to report my findings to Norman Sugarman, then Assistant Commissioner Technical of the Bureau of Internal Revenue. He expressed interest but of course explained that lack of staff made it impossible for the Bureau to follow up every delinquent foundation.
>
> Nine years later, in the course of its second nationwide analysis of foundation returns to the Treasury Department, The Foundation Library Center continues to find inadequate completion of Form 990-A.[1]

The experience of state officials using Internal Revenue Service files in connection with a search for foundations in their jurisdictions has borne out these serious findings and also reaffirmed charges that many organizations do not even file forms.[2]

The only statutory penalty for failure to file information returns is a criminal one; it carries a maximum of one year's imprisonment and a $10,000 fine, and the Service has been reluctant to invoke such a strong sanction.[3] On occasion the Service has applied an administrative sanction by revoking the exemption of an organization refusing to comply. McGreevy reported in 1963 that one district director had revoked approximately 100 executive rulings during a short period of that year for failure to comply with the information reporting requirements and warned that this activity would be continued at an even greater pace unless reporting compliance improved.[4] In conformity with this policy, in 1963 the Service ordered all district offices to establish controls to ensure that Form 990–A returns were filed by all exempt foundations and that such returns were complete in all respects.[5]

In 1965 the Treasury recommended to the Congress that the sanction for failure to file information returns be revised to make foundations subject to a penalty of $10 for each day of delay beyond a pre-

---

[1] National Council of Community Foundations, Inc., *op. cit.*, pp. 3–4.
[2] See Chapters VII–IX.
[3] Int. Rev. Code of 1954, sec. 7203.
[4] McGreevy, Michael, *op. cit.*, p. 199.
[5] Rogovin, Mitchell, *op. cit.*, p. 248.

scribed filing date, up to a maximum of $5,000. It also recommended imposition of a similar penalty, with a similar maximum, for officers, directors, or trustees responsible for filing returns if, after notice from the Service of failure to make a complete and timely return, the defect was not remedied within a specified time.[1]

The 1963 form, issued in 1964, included only one major addition: a requirement that the organization list all of its directors, officers, and trustees, indicating the relationship of such individuals by blood, marriage, adoption, or employment to the creator of the organization, to substantial contributors, or to corporations controlled by such creators or contributors. The request was included in the instructions and did not appear on the face of the return. In July of 1964 Treasury officials stated that preliminary examination of the 1963 returns indicated that this new requirement had apparently been overlooked in many cases and that the Department was considering adding it to the face of the return.

Several substantive changes were made in the form for 1964 and a question was added asking whether the information required in the instructions was attached. For the first time all organizations were required to state their assets at market as well as book value. The information regarding stock holdings was expanded to include all holdings of 5 per cent or more in any one company, rather than 10 per cent, as on the earlier returns. Finally, the Report required a description of any borrowing and lending activities which totaled $5,000 or more, including information as to whether the transactions were made through an account with a securities broker or dealer. If there had been any receivables or debts in excess of $1,000 that were not connected with exempt activities or business activities, information as to the name of the donor or creator, the amount, the rate of interest if any, and the circumstances out of which the debt arose was also required.

Those foundations that receive unrelated business income of more than $1,000, as defined in the Internal Revenue Code of 1954, section 511, must also file Form 990–T. This form requires specific information as to the nature of the business operation, including compensation of officers, the amount of time devoted to the business of each, the percentage of the organization's stock owned by them, and their expense-account allowances. This form is not open for public inspection.

---

[1] U.S. Congress, Senate, Committee on Finance, *Treasury Department Report on Private Foundations, op. cit.,* p. 64.

The major problem for foundations that has arisen in connection with Form 990–T has been the question of whether this report should be filed, since the existence of unrelated business income is a factual determination not always clearly ascertainable. The Code provides that if an organization determines in good faith that it is an exempt organization and files a return as such under section 6033, but is thereafter held by the Service not to be exempt, the return filed is sufficient to start computation of the three-year statutory limit on prosecution applicable to all taxpayers. Prior to 1962, it was felt by some tax attorneys that the filing of a Form 990–A was sufficient to cover situations where a determination might later be made that the organization owed tax on unrelated business income.[1]

In 1962, however, the Service ruled that the filing of Form 990–A was not sufficient to preclude the running of the statute of limitations against the assessment and collection of tax on unrelated business income. In that year Revenue Ruling 62–10[2] held that the filing of an information return under section 6033 did not start the statute of limitations for an exempt organization where it had unrelated business income properly reportable on Form 990–T. This meant, in effect, that all returns back to 1950 were open to review and to assessment of tax should any unrelated business income be found. Foundations protested the unfairness of such a retroactive ruling, and the Service announced that it would reconsider its position.[3]

On May 4, 1964, Revenue Ruling 62–10 was formally amended[4] to limit the retroactive effect to the date the ruling was published, January 22, 1962, thereby limiting the holding of the ruling to those taxable years where the period of limitations would not normally have expired by reason of filing a Form 990–A before January 22, 1962. As an example, for a foundation filing Form 990–A on a calendar year basis, the period of limitation would by that date normally have expired for 1957 and prior years. The effect of this amendment, therefore, was to move the period that could be scrutinized forward from January 1, 1951, the effective date of the 1950 amendment of the Revenue Code creating the tax in question, for a period of nearly seven years.

For those organizations formed as trusts, if the governing instrument

---

[1] Int. Rev. Code of 1954, sec. 6501(g)(2).
[2] 1962–2 Cum. Bull. 305.
[3] Rogovin, Mitchell, *op. cit.,* p. 957.
[4] 1962–1 Int. Rev. Bull. No. 18.

permits certain amounts of gross income to be paid or permanently set aside for a deductible charitable purpose (as defined in section 170(c) of the Code) and the trust may therefore deduct such amount in computing its income tax,[1] a special form (Form 1041–A) must be filed[2] for any year in which the income is not required to be paid out by the trust instrument. On this form the trust must show that amount of the deduction which was paid out and that amount which was permanently accumulated; the amounts so paid out or accumulated in prior years; the amount paid out of principal in both current and prior years for charitable purposes; the income and expenses of the trust; and a balance sheet showing assets, liabilities, and net worth. Copies of this form, as revised in 1963, are available to the public in Washington and the district offices. Neither the Code nor the Regulations specify that trusts ruled to be exempt organizations under section 501(c)(3) are relieved from filing Form 1041–A, although the apparent purposes of the Code do not seem applicable. Many trustees, accordingly, do file Form 990–A and Form 1041–A for all years for which the net income was not required to be distributed currently.

Form 1023 is to be used for the applications for exempt status. Following the partial abolition of the twelve-month operating requirement in December of 1963, this form underwent a major revision; it is now designed primarily to elicit information indicating the activities in which the organization expects to engage in the future. The instruction folder was also revised and expanded to clarify the new ruling and reduce requests by the Service for additional information which had often been necessary in the past.

In a system of tax administration that is based primarily on voluntary compliance, such as that of the federal government, the information returns provided by the government are of primary importance in determining its success. If they are reasonably clear and well suited to the nature of the operations to be reported, compliance will be more readily obtained. The problem of devising report forms for exempt organizations is particularly complex, primarily because of the heterogeneous nature of the organizations comprising this category. One of the proposals of the Service's Tax-Exempt Organization Council was to consider establishing separate schedules attached to a basic form; this would recognize the differences between the various categories of exempt organizations and provide a return tailored to the

---

[1] Int. Rev. Code of 1954, sec. 642(c).
[2] Int. Rev. Code of 1954, sec. 6034.

particular activities of each.[1] Consultations between the Service and the states that accept a copy of Form 990–A in compliance with a state reporting requirement in the making of future revisions would also be of value. The revision of the Massachusetts report form in 1961 was designed to make it follow as closely as possible the federal form then in use, but no communications were held between Treasury officials and the Massachusetts Attorney General's Office when Form 990–A was later revised. Although the information necessary for a tax audit and that needed for a review by a state attorney general's office are not similar in all respects, the two offices have sufficient mutuality of interests to warrant greater cooperation.

Audits. The enforcement activities of the Internal Revenue Service center primarily on the auditing of tax returns, and it is in this area of activity that federal supervision of foundations differs most markedly from the state programs. Audit of federal tax returns is done on a sampling basis under well-defined procedures. Returns are classified by examining officers in accordance with criteria established at the national level designed to identify those returns warranting further examination either because of revenue potential, broad-range coverage for deterrent value, or to identify areas of abuse.

A field audit involves a personal examination of a taxpayer's records at a conference at which the Internal Revenue agent and the taxpayer are present. The taxpayer may be represented by an attorney or accountant. Guidelines for audit procedure have been prepared for all Service agents. The basic function of the agent is fact-finding; he has authority to examine books and records and summon witnesses and he may inquire as to matters for all years for which the statute of limitations has not run.[2] He may make recommendations for assessment of tax deficiencies or, in the case of exempt organizations, revocation or continuation of exempt status, or for imposition of a tax on unrelated business income together with the amount of that tax. If the taxpayer agrees with this determination and makes a decision not to appeal, the matter will be terminated at that level.

The audit of exempt organization returns is necessarily different from that of income, estate, or gift tax returns, where the examination centers primarily on analysis of the correctness of items listed as receipts or expenditures, and on whether all items required to be reported have been properly included in the return. In the case of a foun-

---

[1] Rogovin, Mitchell, *op. cit.,* p. 955.
[2] Int. Rev. Code of 1954, sec. 7602.

dation, the audit is directed toward determining whether the activities of the organization have been in conformity with its particular nature and purposes as well as with the provisions of law under which it is exempt.[1]

The Service attitude toward audits of exempt organizations underwent a major transformation between 1950 and 1963. The 1950 legislation had imposed a new set of standards for which guidelines needed to be prepared. The enactment in 1954 of a three-year period of limitations on assessments[2] further intensified this need, but the defeat of Service positions in court proceedings, particularly in relation to business activity, left certain areas of policy undefined. Furthermore, a major deterrent to proper audit of tax-exempt organizations had been what has been described as the "historical Service attitude" toward this activity.

> There had prevailed for some years, the belief that a Revenue Agent's accomplishments were to be measured by his dollar and case productivity. Wherever such a quota system prevailed in the field, exempt organizations audits were generally held to a minimum since these difficult and time consuming examinations were rarely "productive."[3]

The introduction in 1959 of the "organizational test" requiring that an organization's charter contain limits on its activities was designed, in part, to relieve the necessity for a continuing audit program, but by 1961 it was evident that this view was erroneous.[4]

The "New Directions" program of the Service, introduced in 1961, included several important changes in the audit program. The first was the expansion of the audits of exempt organizations to afford to them the same scope and depth as those afforded to audits of income taxes. The quota system was abolished, and the number of programed audits was expanded from 2,000 in fiscal year 1962 to 7,219 in 1963 and 10,262 in 1964. A two-week training program for field agents was initiated; their exempt organization handbook was revised and reissued; and tentative tax guidelines were prepared. The former Commissioner, testifying at the Patman Committee Hearings in July of 1964 reported that:

---

[1] Sugarman, Norman, and collaborators, "What to Do When the Revenue Service Agent Appears to Make an Audit: A Panel Discussion," *Proceedings of the New York University Sixth Biennial Conference on Charitable Foundations,* p. 251.

[2] Int. Rev. Code of 1954, sec. 6501(g)(2).

[3] Rogovin, Mitchell, *op. cit.* p. 237.

[4] *Ibid.,* p. 237.

During the period from February 1963 through May 1964, the Service examined 9,552 exempt organizations, including 1,851 private foundations and charitable trusts. This number represents but a small proportion of those it actually looked at as part of its normal classification process. . . .

Of these 9,552 examinations, field offices recommended 560 revocations and made 829 tax changes. Many technical errors and a few glaring abuses were found. But on the whole, despite the extremely light audit coverage that had prevailed in the past, the examinations indicated that most exempt organizations were in substantial compliance with the law. There were technical errors, but most seemed to be making an effort to comply.[1]

In addition, the attempt to check on delinquent returns resulted in the addition of approximately 50,000 new files.

Appeals from decisions made during an audit of income tax returns follow a routine pattern. If no agreement is reached between the taxpayer and the agent conducting the audit, the taxpayer may request an "informal conference" held at the district office with the agent and a reviewing officer who has authority to settle the matter. If this conference yields no agreement, the agent submits an official report to his superiors, and a formal statement, called a thirty-day letter, is sent to the taxpayer notifying him of an intent to adjust his tax status or liability. The title of this notice refers to the fact that, upon its receipt, an individual is given thirty days to appeal the decision to the Appellate Division of the Service, which operates at the regional level. If a settlement is not reached following a hearing with the Appellate Division, a formal notice of deficiency, or ninety-day letter, is then mailed; it states that at the end of ninety days the additional tax will be assessed. At this point the formal litigation process may commence if the taxpayer decides to appeal the Service decision. However, settlements may be made with the Appellate Division at any stage of a judicial proceeding.

The appellate procedure has been modified to a certain extent in cases involving exempt organizations. Under the provisions of Revenue Procedure 62–30,[2] if a district office concludes in the course of examining an information return or from any other source that a ruling or revocation letter should be revoked or modified, a written notice of the decision and the reasons for it are sent to the organization with a

---

[1] U.S. Congress, House of Representatives, Select Committee on Small Business, *Hearings Before Subcommittee No. 1 on Foundations,* "Tax-Exempt Foundations: Their Impact on Small Business," *op. cit.,* p. 64.

[2] Rev. Proc. 62–30, sec. 9, 1962–2 Cum. Bull. 512, 516.

statement advising it of its right to protest the proposed action by submitting a formal statement of facts, law, and arguments, and having an informal conference at the district office. If no protest is filed, or if the district director's decision is unchanged following reconsideration, the findings of the district director may be forwarded to the national office in the form of a request for "technical advice."

The procedure for obtaining "technical advice" has also been outlined in a revenue procedure.[1] Any organization or taxpayer may request such advice when there seems to be a lack of uniformity within the Service as to the disposition of a particular case, or when the issue is so unusual or complex that consideration by the national office is warranted. If the national office, after considering the question, concludes that the district director's actions should be upheld, the taxpayer or organization is granted a right to a personal conference to discuss the question, before a final decision is forwarded to the district. This procedure assures greater uniformity in the disposition of cases involving revocation of exempt status, and at the same time it facilitates the handling of these cases.

Litigation

Private individuals or organizations may appeal to the courts from decisions of the Internal Revenue Service in one of two ways. Following receipt of a ninety-day letter, the individual or organization may either pay the tax and pursue an appeal by filing a claim for a refund with the Internal Revenue Service, or he may immediately petition to the Tax Court for a hearing. Under the first alternative, the request for a refund may be subject to the same administrative procedure that follows an unfavorable audit decision—that is, opportunity for an informal conference, receipt of a thirty-day letter, filing of a formal protest, an appellate division conference if desired, and issuance of the statutory notice of claim disallowance (a second ninety-day letter). However, if the Service takes no action for six months following receipt of a refund claim, a court petition may be filed without waiting for the ninety-day letter.

The appeal may be to either the federal district courts or the Court of Claims. If the appeal is to the district court the taxpayer has a right to a jury trial. The major disadvantage to appealing to either court is, of course, that the tax must be paid beforehand.

---

[1] Rev. Proc. 62–29, 1962–2 Cum. Bull. 507.

Cases brought before the district court and the Court of Claims are tried by members of the Tax Division of the Department of Justice; those heard by the Tax Court are handled by the legal staff of the Internal Revenue Service. The Court of Claims is a separate court to which any claim against the United States government may be brought. At one time all claims for refunds, if under a certain amount, had to be brought in the Court of Claims, but the jurisdiction of the federal district courts has been enlarged to permit suits there, too.

The second method of appeal, which carries no prerequisite of payment, is appeal to the Tax Court. The Tax Court, first established in 1924 as the Board of Tax Appeals, is an independent 16-member administrative board. It functions as a court, however, in almost all respects, and its 16 members are designated as judges. Appeals to the Tax Court may be made only from decisions of the Commissioner as to specific years, but the jurisdiction of the court is not limited to review of the Commissioner's decision, and it may consider the tax liability for the period in question *de novo,* finding overpayment or an even larger deficiency. There are no juries, and hearings are held before a single judge whose report usually becomes the decision of the court. Cases that involve important issues, however, may be presented to the entire court for decision by the presiding judge.

The decision as to which court to use involves many considerations. One of them is the absence of jury trial in the Tax Court and Court of Claims. Blough has suggested that the question of jury trial may not be decisive, however.

> Jury trials have been rare in tax cases, indicating that the privilege is not an important factor in choosing the court, although the number of jury trials is increasing in some kinds of cases. Judging from its previous decisions, the taxpayer and his attorney may believe that the District Court would take a more favorable attitude toward the taxpayer on the issue involved than would the Tax Court. Some lawyers feel more at home practicing before one or another of the courts. In many cases there is a reluctance to pay the tax and sue for a refund because it is believed to be more difficult to achieve satisfactory settlement once the government has the money.[1]

Appellate Courts

Decisions of the district courts may be appealed to the United States Circuit Court of Appeals for the circuit in which the district court is

---

[1] Blough, Roy, *The Federal Taxing Process.* Prentice-Hall, Inc., Englewood Cliffs, N.J., © 1952, p. 188.

located. Appeals from the Tax Court are made to the circuit in which the collector's office with which the return was filed was located. They may be taken by private individuals or organizations or by the government, or by both. If the Commissioner loses a case in the Tax Court and decides not to appeal, he may announce whether or not he will "acquiesce" in the decision. A decision to acquiesce means that the Service has accepted the legal interpretation made by the court as the correct one to be followed in future cases. This may require a change in the regulations, and notification of acquiescence often signals such a change. A notification of nonacquiescence, on the other hand, indicates that the Service does not concur in the court's interpretation and that future cases on the same issue may be brought to determine if the Tax Court will change its mind, or that an appeal may be later taken from a similar decision to the circuit court.

Furthermore, the Commissioner is not bound to acquiesce in a single decision of the circuit court. If decisions in two circuits are conflicting, the Supreme Court will be likely to decide the issue. Since there are 11 circuits, it is theoretically possible to have conflicting decisions rendered and a Supreme Court determination which will settle the issue to a certain extent. However, as Blough points out, finality is never completely attainable.

> With eleven circuit courts of appeal it is impossible to know with reasonable finality what the law is until the Supreme Court has decided the issue, or a sufficient number of appellate courts have confirmed the Tax Court's interpretation. In a sense, of course, finality is never achieved, since the Supreme Court may review itself, or Congress in later legislation may, in effect, override the Court.[1]

The grounds on which a Court of Appeals may overrule the Tax Court or a district court are that (1) there was no opportunity for a fair hearing; (2) insufficient evidence was presented to support the findings of a lower court; or (3) the lower court erred in its interpretation of the statute in question or the Constitution.

Final appeal to the Supreme Court is not a matter of right, but is subject to the decision of that court to grant certiorari to hear any particular case. Generally, only cases raising issues on which there is a conflict of statutory interpretation among the circuits, a substantial constitutional issue, or a question deemed to be of great public importance will be granted certiorari. The first category is the one that

---

[1] *Ibid.*, p. 190.

occurs most frequently in the field of taxation. Supreme Court decisions involving exempt organizations have been rare; the most important case brought before it since 1950 was granted certiorari in 1964 and decided in April of 1965.[1] Cases decided by the Court of Claims may be appealed only on petition for certiorari to the Supreme Court, appeals are, therefore, exceedingly rare.[2]

Procedure on Loss of Exemption or Denial of Deduction

The federal tax laws provide two major sanctions for violation of the Internal Revenue Code by an exempt organization: loss of exemption to the organization, and denial of deductions to contributors. The grounds for loss of exemption may be that the organization (1) is disqualified under section 501(c)(3), for failing to meet the organizational test, having nonexempt purposes, or carrying on a trade or business or other violations of the operational test;[3] (2) has engaged in a prohibited transaction; (3) has been unreasonably accumulating income; and (4) has failed to file an information return.

One of the most important questions that arises following a decision to revoke an exemption is the determination of whether the revocation will be retroactive or prospective. The Regulations state that:

> Subject only to the Commissioner's inherent power to revoke rulings because of a change in the law or regulations or for other good cause, an organization that has been determined by the Commission or the district director to be exempt under section 501 (a) or the corresponding provisions of prior law may rely upon such determinations so long as there are no substantial changes in the organization's character, purposes, or methods of operation.[4]

This regulation was promulgated under the authority of section 2805 (b) of the Code, which permits the Secretary of the Treasury or his delegate to prescribe the extent, if any, to which any ruling or regulation shall be applied without retroactive effect. The courts, however, have held that once a policy such as that announced in section 1.501 of the regulations has been promulgated, there is an inherent limitation on the Commissioner's power to determine when an exception can be made. If the exemption ruling was based on an arguable question of law, and if the conduct of the organization was not such as to

---

[1] *Commissioner of Internal Revenue* v. *Brown,* 325 F.2d 313 (9th Cir. 1963); 15 A.F.T.R. 2d 790 (1965).

[2] Blough, Roy, *op. cit.,* p. 191.

[3] See Treas. Regs. 1.501(a)–1(a); 1.504–1(a) and 1.501(c)(3)–1.

[4] Treas. Reg. 1.501(a)–1(a)(2).

estop it from relying on the ruling and it did not misrepresent or conceal the activities relied on by the Commissioner to deny exemption, a retroactive revocation has been held to be an "abuse of discretion" and therefore invalid.[1]

Revenue Procedure 62–30[2] contains the grounds on which ruling or determination letters may be retroactively revoked. They are: (1) there has been an omission or a misstatement of a material fact; (2) the organization operated in a manner materially different from that originally represented; or (3) the organization engaged in a prohibited transaction for the purpose of diverting income or corpus from its exempt purpose, and the transaction involved a substantial part of its income or corpus. Furthermore, in cases where revocation is based on unreasonable accumulation of income or improper use of accumulated income, the date of revocation is held by statute to be the year or years in which the improper action occurred, which, of course, is a prior time.[3]

Upon revocation of exemption, the organization becomes subject to tax, but it may apply for reinstatement of its exemption. Where the revocation was based on disqualification under Internal Revenue Code, section 501(c)(3), a new application may be filed immediately. Where revocation resulted from a prohibited transaction or a forbidden accumulation of income, reinstatement can be effective only after the organization has been subject to tax for at least one full taxable year.[4] The regulations also require that the officers must submit, with the application, a written declaration made under penalty of perjury that the organization will not knowingly engage in a prohibited transaction or violate the accumulations provisions. Furthermore, if the revocation resulted from a prohibited transaction, the Commissioner must be "satisfied" that the organization will not knowingly violate the section in the future.

Revocation of exempt status does not necessarily mean denial of deduction to contributors. If exemption was revoked because of a failure to comply with the provisions of section 501(c)(3), the determination of retroactive denial of deductions will be subject to the same criteria as those applicable to revocations. In the case of revoca-

---

[1] See *Lesavoy Foundation* v. *Commissioner of Internal Revenue,* 238 F.2d 589 (3d Cir. 1956); and *Automobile Club of Michigan* v. *Commissioner of Internal Revenue,* 353 U.S. 180 (1957).

[2] Sec. 8.03, 1962–2 Cum. Bull. 512.

[3] Treas. Reg. 1.504–1.

[4] Treas. Reg. 1.503(d)–1(b); and Treas. Reg. 1.504–1(e).

tion based on the prohibited transactions section, contributors lose their right to claim deductions only for years following the year of publication of the revocation.[1] However, if a substantial donor or his family was a party to the transaction, he may be subject to denial of deduction for the year in which the transaction occurred.[2] In the case of forbidden accumulation of income, individual contributions will not be disallowed retroactively if the revocation of exemption was based solely on section 504.[3]

In actual practice, denial of exemption is rarely invoked retroactively, and even when it is, denial of deductions does not automatically follow. The Treasury Department and the Service have indicated some awareness of the inappropriateness of the sanctions in the Internal Revenue Code. In 1963 the Service adopted a policy of issuing warning letters to organizations that appeared to be violating Code provisions either inadvertently or mistakenly. If the warning is not observed, revocation of exemption will follow, but at the least an attempt is made to protect the charitable funds from the misfeasance of the fiduciaries. Another important change considered by the Service in 1963 was the imposition of a requirement that final returns be filed by organizations that are being dissolved, indicating their compliance with the requirement in the regulations that upon dissolution the funds will be used for other exempt purposes. Greater surveillance of dissolution proceedings is necessary at the federal level of government, as well as at the state level, as previously pointed out.

Federal and State Cooperation

Cooperation between the federal agencies and the state attorneys general charged with supervising foundations is difficult to achieve. This is true for several reasons. In the first place, there are no direct and continuing lines of communication between the attorneys general and either the Treasury Department, the Internal Revenue Service, or the Congress. Second, the Internal Revenue Code provisions relating to exchange of information compound the problem. Section 6103(b) (2) does include provisions whereby all income-tax returns shall be open to inspection by "any official, body, or commission, lawfully charged with the administration of any State tax law, if the inspection is for the purpose of such administration or for the purpose of obtain-

---

[1] Int. Rev. Code of 1954, sec. 503(e).
[2] Int. Rev. Code of 1954, sec. 1.503(e)–1(g).
[3] Int. Rev. Code of 1954, sec. 1.504(f).

ing information to be furnished to local taxing authorities," but again, only for the purpose of administration of local tax laws.

The duties of attorneys general do not ordinarily include the enforcement of tax laws, however. These officials cannot, therefore, obtain information such as that relating to the income returns of fiduciaries or trusts that have not obtained tax-exempt status or have had their tax-exempt status denied. If an attorney general thinks that there may be a violation of state tax law, he can, of course, refer the matter to the state tax authorities for investigation, but this is often not a practical method for assuring the proper application of charitable funds. The limitation on state officials with regard to corporate returns is not as restrictive; it applies to merely "the proper officers of any State," upon "request of the governor," although the regulations have added the requirement that it be a "tax officer."[1] Nevertheless, these sections of the Code do not permit the release of the type of information that would be of primary value to a state attorney general— that is, determination letters, and even more important, revocation letters and the supporting information on which they are based. In order to obtain information of this nature, the Code and other federal statutes require an executive order from the President.[2] Although certain investigative information would remain classified even with such an order, the revocation letter stating the grounds for action would become available upon request. The advantages to the state attorneys general of such an executive order are obvious; yet none has been promulgated, and without pressure from the states on the executive branch, it remains unlikely that any action will be taken.

Information returns from exempt organizations are, of course, public records, and they have been used by officials of certain states to compile master lists of charitable trusts and corporations. The major difficulty with the use of these records is that returns from exempt organizations are not segregated into categories at the revenue offices, so that the officials must inspect all of them in order to obtain information about the minority that may be "charitable." Experience by state officials attempting to use these records has varied from district to district, but most have been afforded excellent cooperation by revenue personnel; their chief difficulty has been that the files were not in good order.

On the other hand, Revenue Service personnel have made several attempts to enlist the aid of certain state attorneys general in the inves-

---

[1] Int. Rev. Code of 1954, sec. 6103(b)(1).
[2] Int. Rev. Code of 1954, sec. 6103(a)(1) and (2).

tigation or prosecution of fiduciaries who appeared to have violated not only the tax laws but substantive state laws relating to their fiduciary duties. In some of these cases, state action has been taken immediately, but in several others, the federal government has been unable to persuade the state attorney general to act, either because of lack of interest, a shortage of personnel at the state level, or in one instance, a local political situation. Such negative responses of course, make the Service wary of attempting to move too far in attempts at cooperation.

The type of problem that is raised by the lack of communication between the state and federal governments can be illustrated by a situation that arose in connection with one state's laws relating to dissolution of charitable corporations. Although there was precedent and language in several decisions of the state supreme court to the effect that the *cy pres* doctrine was applicable to funds of charitable corporations upon dissolution, the Internal Revenue Service denied the applications for exemption of several charitable corporations on the grounds that the charters in question did not require *cy pres* and the state law was not sufficiently clear. When this situation was brought to its attention, the attorney general's office concluded that although the case law was clear, the statutory provision for dissolution contained no supervisory provisions to assure *cy pres* distribution. A statute drafted to rectify the situation was passed by the legislature in 1963. The Internal Revenue Service was notified of this. Still, in the year following passage of the legislation, the state commissioner of corporations received requests for approval of amendments to the charters of approximately 600 charitable corporations to require *cy pres* distribution on dissolution. The corporations declared in their applications for amendment that the requests were being made on advice of the Internal Revenue Service. A situation of this nature, of course, makes a state official wary of attempting to achieve greater cooperation with federal officials.

There seem to be two needs, therefore. The first would be for the promulgation of an executive order by the President recognizing the authority of the state attorneys general to request information of the Internal Revenue Service regarding charitable organizations in their state to assist them in their enforcement duties. The second need, which is equally important, would be for the establishment of more direct methods of communication between the Service and the attorneys general. In certain areas of the country, all that may be needed is to supply the attorney general with the name of the Revenue Service employee who is responsible for exempt organization activities. In other areas, the states need to be apprised of the possible benefits of such cooperation. A start was made in the spring of 1964 when the Committee on Charitable Organizations of the National Association of Attorneys General held a seminar on supervision of charities at which representatives of the Treasury Department and the Internal Revenue Service discussed cooperation with federal agencies. This was the first such contact between the state attorneys general and the federal government in relation to charitable organizations, and it demonstrated not only the possibilities but the need for increasing cooperation in the supervision of charitable organizations.

A National Registry of Tax-Exempt Organizations

In the summer of 1964 the Internal Revenue Service sent a questionnaire to all tax-exempt organizations requesting information as to the nature of their operations and specifically asking each one to classify itself according to a list of the various types of organizations eligible for tax exemption. This represented the first step in a program to create a national register of tax-exempt organizations keyed to the Service's automatic data processing system. The initial phase of the project was designed to create a master list of all exempt organizations according to categories.

Upon completion of the first phase in 1965, the master file will be used to obtain statistics on the number of each different type of exempt organization in the nation as well as in the various geographical regions. It will also be used to detect delinquent filers, to obtain audit lists, and to supplement the list of organizations to which contributions are deductible. The initial appropriation for the project was $300,000, which represents a major financial commitment by the Service to the intensified audit program for exempt organizations.

The full potentials of this master file of exempt organizations are still being explored by the Service. The file could be utilized to obtain complete and continuing information on all phases of the operations of tax-exempt organizations and to chart their economic implications. Automated analysis of individual returns and groups of returns would provide a basis for legislation and administrative decisions. It would also open up various new possibilities for cooperation with the states. Use of information from this registry could provide the basis for establishing state supervisory programs and might even obviate the establishment of separate reporting requirements in each state. This would lessen the burden on trustees and directors and assure at the same time that both federal tax laws and state-imposed duties are met.

The Federal Government and "Charity"

There is no evidence that the Congress will reverse its historical attitude favoring philanthropy in general. Nevertheless, the investigations of tax-exempt foundations and the concrete provisions of the 1964 Revenue Act point toward a greater indulgence of the "publicly supported" charitable organization than of the so-called private foundation that is new to the federal government as well as to the laws of any of the states. One writer has hypothesized that the antagonism against foundations evidenced in the 1960's represented the latest manifestation of the traditional American fear of large concentrated wealth which has been focused, in turn, on the "big" industrialists, the "big" corporations, and the "big" labor unions. Foundations represent an easy target for such attacks, having no constituency to rise in their support, nor a united voice to speak in their defense.

The future position of foundations under the tax laws is, however, uncertain. The evidence from the Treasury Department and the Service indicates a desire to curb specific abuses without a major revision of either the tax laws or the basic pattern of supervision. If Congress goes no further, foundation growth will not be impaired. From the point of view of government, however, certain of the most basic problems of supervision will remain, since they stem primarily from the fact that tax laws are being used as a vehicle for regulating individuals for nonrevenue purposes. Although individual adjustments may result in the improvement of certain aspects, foundations will remain subject to a set of rules that are not always consistent with the basic concepts of fiduciary duty or state law, rules administered as but a small part of a vast system, the main focus of which is on matters foreign to, and in some instances even inimical to, the legitimate function of charitable endeavors.

In terms of administration, the basic problems stem from the size of the Revenue Service operation. The length and complexity of the Revenue Code itself, comprising 8,000 sections and levying more than 100 separate taxes, dictates the complexity of its administration. In the area of tax-exempt organizations alone, there are 17 different categories of income-tax exemptions contained in section 501 and numerous other subchapters of the Code. It has been estimated that each year the Service monitors the exemption of 400,000 principal organizations and 700,000 subsidiaries, 71,850 of which are listed in the *Cumulative Bulletin* as eligible to receive deductible contributions. Information returns were filed in 1962 by over 250,000 exempt organizations, of which approximately 15,000 met the description of foundation; yet these represent but a minor percentage of all returns filed that year.

To a great extent it has been possible to modify the administrative procedures of the complex federal supervisory operation to suit the specific questions entailed by the supervision of foundations. However, since the supervision of foundations cannot be completely divorced from the entire administrative program, it is subject to the complaints of impersonality, delay, and inefficiency leveled at one time or another at all administrative operations. The need for consideration of most local decisions by the national office does create greater uniformity of interpretation and assures consideration by qualified personnel. For the foundation in Oregon, Florida, or Massachusetts, however, it may mean the need to hire special counsel and to engage in extended and expensive negotiations. There is no solution to this dilemma.

The difficulty of administering the federal supervisory program has been compounded by the lack of a significant body of regulations and rulings that could provide a guideline for foundations. On the one hand, certain individuals have taken advantage of the situation by engaging in activities that are clearly beyond the limits of proper fiduciary actions under state law, whether or not they would be proper in terms of the Revenue Code; on the other hand, overly conscientious trustees and directors have refrained from certain activities that are clearly proper for fear of running afoul of the Revenue Service. The decision as to what constitutes reasonable accumulations affords an excellent example, and others can be found in connection with almost all of the sections of the exempt-organization provisions of the Code.

It will take some time before the programs adopted since 1961 are established and even longer before they are accepted at the lowest levels of administration. So long as the legal framework on which they are based is not radically altered, either by the Congress or the courts, federal supervision of foundations will undoubtedly be more effective in the future, and this, in turn, should diminish new pressures on Congress for greater restrictions. Since the only feasible alternative is the creation of a separate regulatory agency, it would appear wise to wait for concrete evidence of the success or failure of the improvements already initiated.

CHAPTER XI

The English Experience

THE METHODS devised for the supervision of charitable trusts in England have taken forms different from those found in any of the American states. The Statute of Elizabeth of 1601 set the pattern for future enforcement machinery by authorizing the creation of *ad hoc* commissions to investigate the management of charitable trusts. The Board of Charity Commissioners, which was created in 1853 and functioned until the passage of the Charities Act of 1960, served as the primary agency for supervision. Its duties were:

1. To inquire into the administration of charitable trusts.
2. To compel the production of the accounts of charitable trustees, and to audit them.
3. To facilitate the administration of charitable trusts, and to supplement the powers of trustees where these were defective.
4. To secure the safe custody and proper investment of charity property.
5. To control and, if possible, diminish the cost of legal proceedings taken on behalf of charitable trusts.[1]

The jurisdiction of the Commissioners extended over all charitable trusts and corporations except religious bodies, institutions for religious or charitable purposes wholly maintained by voluntary contributions, unendowed charities, certain named universities and colleges, and mixed charities (those maintained partly by voluntary subscriptions and partly by income from endowments). As for a mixed charity,

---

[1] Keeton, George W., *The Modern Law of Charities.* Sir Isaac Pitman and Sons, London, 1962, p. 176.

although the organization itself was considered within the Charitable Trusts Act, bequests and donations for general purposes were considered legally applicable as income and therefore exempt from jurisdiction. Although the Commissioners' jurisdiction extended originally to charities established for educational purposes, this jurisdiction was transferred in 1899[1] to the Board of Education and in 1944[2] to the Ministry of Education.

The duties of the Commissioners, therefore, combined advisory, administrative, and supervisory functions, particularly regarding the appointment or removal of trustees and the framing of schemes within the limit of the *cy pres* doctrine. The attorney general still represented the Crown as *parens patriae,* and it was to him that the Commissioners were directed to certify cases in which charitable funds were misapplied so that he might take proper legal action.

Supervision of Charities Prior to 1960

In actual operation, the work of the Charity Commissioners concentrated on the correction of abuses specifically called to their attention. They attempted no active supervision of all trusts. The legal requirement that trustees submit accounts to the Commissioners was generally ignored. It has been estimated that less than one-third of the trusts on the Commissioners' books submitted any type of accounts.[3] The Nathan Report suggested that this was due partly to ignorance on the part of trustees and partly to a shortage of staff, but principally to the absence of any specific penalty for failure to comply combined with a reluctance on the part of the Commissioners to bring contumacious trustees to court.[4] The Commissioners also reported that the accounts that were submitted were usually not audited professionally. They found the task of checking them so difficult and time-consuming that their work was often in arrears. Particularly frustrating was their inability to compel audits. They attributed their inability to enforce economical and efficient administration to this lack of power.[5]

The Nathan Committee concluded, however, that breaches of trust

---

[1] Stat. 62 & 63 Victoria, c. 33 (Board of Education Act 1899).
[2] Stat. 7 & 8 George VI, c. 31 (Education Act 1944).
[3] Committee on the Law and Practice Relating to Charitable Trusts, *Report.* Cmd. 8710. H.M. Stationery Office, London, 1952, p. 46, paragraph 184.
[4] *Ibid.*
[5] Owen, David, *English Philanthropy 1660–1960.* Belknap Press of Harvard University Press, Cambridge, Mass., 1964, p. 306.

of severe types were extremely rare and that irregularities were usually committed inadvertently, so that not more than six cases a year were referred to the attorney general. An underlying drawback to the entire plan of supervision, which led to a reluctance to refer cases to the attorney general, was the fact that the court procedures by which the attorney general would seek correction of the misapplication of funds were cumbersome, costly, and ill-adapted for the purpose.

The advisory duties of the Commissioners were also exercised only rarely. Under the provisions of the Charitable Trusts Act of 1853, the opinions of the Commissioners, when given formally under seal, were to be considered to be granting an indemnity to trustees who followed them, regardless of a later judicial order contradicting or altering their contents. The Commissioners were accordingly reluctant to give formal opinions without adequate investigation, but lack of an adequate staff severely hampered and delayed this phase of their work.

Finally, although the Commissioners did have the power to frame schemes for the administration of trusts which were no longer capable of being executed, the limitations of the *cy pres* doctrine laid down by the courts, combined with the fact that they could act on their own initiative only if a trust had income of less than £50 a year, created severe limitations on their effectiveness.

Reports of the Commissioners during the mid-nineteenth century indicated the frustrations they felt because of their limited powers. By the end of the century, the tone of the reports changed, however, reflecting a resignation to the status quo. Summarizing the work of the Commissioners in the first half of the twentieth century, Owen states: "What seems clear is that they had long ceased to be actively concerned with the broader questions of charitable endowments and how to improve their social utility."[1] The aim of both the Nathan Committee Report and the Charities Act of 1960 was to revivify the ability of government to assist and enhance charitable endeavors.

Provisions of the Charities Act of 1960

The Charities Act of 1960[2] reflected the influence of the criticisms contained in the Nathan Report. It repealed the entire Charitable Trusts Act and its amendments from 1853 onward, and replaced its system of administration with a more modern one; it did not, however, disturb the existing administrative pattern. Primarily it increased the

---

[1] *Ibid.*, p. 585.
[2] Stat. 8 & 9 Elizabeth II, c. 58 (1960).

powers of a newly reconstituted Charity Commission and, for the first time, it associated local authorities with the supervision of the charitable trusts within their areas.[1]

The Charity Commission is now composed of three members, two of whom must be barristers or solicitors, appointed by the Home Secretary. Certain specifically named organizations are exempted from all provisions; these are primarily educational and religious institutions plus certain trusts for educational or religious purposes. The jurisdiction over educational trusts of the Ministry of Education was not disturbed.

Registration of Charities

The Commissioners are charged with preparing and maintaining a register.[2] Charitable trustees must apply for registration, and entry upon the register is considered conclusive proof that the institution is a charity at the time of registration. The register is open to the public. Persons affected by registration may object or apply for removal, and they have a right of judicial appeal from the decision of the Commissioners. The Commissioners, on request, will render an opinion as to whether a gift will create a valid charitable trust before it is created. This is a valuable service to potential donors, particularly in view of the fact that an affirmative decision is binding for tax deduction and exemption purposes.

The statute exempts three categories of charities from the registration requirement: (1) any charity exempt from the provisions of the entire act; (2) any charity excepted by order or regulation of the commission; (3) any charity having neither permanent endowment nor income from property amounting to more than £15 per year, nor the use and occupation of any land; (4) any charity which is a registered place of worship. Charities falling within these categories may, however, request entry upon the registry at any time.[3]

The Commissioners began the task of registration on January 1, 1961. All charities created after that date become immediately liable for registration as of the date they were created. Charities that took effect prior to that date were not permitted to be registered, under the terms of the act, until a request to register was extended to them by statutory instrument. It was decided to extend the obligation in stages,

---

[1] See Owen, David., *op. cit.,* pp. 588–594, for the legislative history of the act.
[2] Stat. 8 & 9 Elizabeth II, c. 58 (1960), sec. 4.
[3] Stat. 8 & 9 Elizabeth II, c. 58 (1960), sec. 4(4).

one area of operation at a time. Regulations have exempted voluntary schools with no permanent endowment other than their premises and funds not representing permanent endowments which are being accumulated for the purpose of local units of the Boy Scout and Girl Guides Associations and which produce an income of more than £15 per year. Exemptions have also been extended to certain churches and evangelical groups not exempted by the act, and to hospitals. In 1960 the registration of charities wholly or mainly concerned with the advancement of religion was deferred until January 1, 1963, and then extended to January 1, 1964.

Registration of all other charities has proceeded by stages. Four Commencement Orders were made; each listed a date for registration of charities for the benefit of certain counties; and the final order included all charities not previously covered. The date for registration contained in the Fourth Order was February 28, 1963. By November 16, 1963, the Commissioners had received 29,000 applications for registration, and 28,267 charities had been registered.[1] This represents but a small fraction of the 200,000 trusts which the Nathan Committee estimated would eventually be registered.

The files of the Registry contain three categories: an alphabetical listing; a classification by objects, subdivided geographically; and a division according to counties receiving benefits that includes separate listings of trusts for specific smaller areas as well as charities with general purposes. An additional file, also open to public inspection, contains a copy of the founding instrument, copies of accounts for the prior three years, and copies of any schemes ordered. A separate list is kept of charities that declined to register voluntarily after they had been notified that they need not do so, and another is kept of those rejected, with the reason for the rejection.

The application for registration as a charity requests information as to the area of operation of the charity by (1) administrative county, rating authority, and civil parish if in a rural district; (2) the beneficial area; (3) the objects of the charity and the approximate annual income available for each; (4) a description of land and premises occupied for charitable purposes, as well as other land owned; and (5) information as to whether application was made for relief from income tax and the outcome of such a request. This statement must be accompanied by the governing instrument and a copy of the latest available

---

[1] Aldrich, Trevor M., "Finding Out About Charities," *Solicitor's Journal,* vol. 107, 1963, p. 977.

accounts. A form letter prepared to be sent with the registration application states:

> Where the accounts do not contain a detailed list of all investments and property held by the charity at the time of application for registration the Commissioners would be pleased to receive a separate statement giving this information but only if it can be prepared without undue difficulty.[1]

The Commissioners have prepared an elaborate classification system for charities consisting of nine major categories: General, Poverty, Charitable and Youth, Old Age, Health and Sickness, Social Welfare and Culture, Moral Welfare and Reform, Religious, Educational, and Miscellaneous. Each of these is broken down into specific listings. For the purposes of registration, annual income is to be listed according to brackets established by the Commissioners rather than shown precisely.

Procedures and Forms for Reports

Regulations promulgated in 1960 prescribe the information to be contained in statements and accounts filed with both the Charity Commissioners and the Ministry of Education.

> 1. Particulars of the assets, and the persons in whom they are vested, on the day of the year to which the charity's accounts are made up, distinguishing between assets forming part of the permanent endowment and other assets.
> 2. The approximate amount of the liabilities on that day.
> 3. The amount of the receipts in the year ending on that day, classified according to the nature of the receipt and distinguishing between receipts forming part of the permanent endowment and other receipts.
> 4. The amount of the payments made during that year, classified according to the nature of the payment and distinguishing between payments made out of the permanent endowment and other payments.[2]

An extremely detailed form prepared by the Commissioners[3] may be used, but a copy of an account normally prepared by a charity showing substantially the same information is acceptable in lieu of the government form. Form letters are sent to all charities immediately following registration or classification which contain directions for the preparation of accounts. Section 32 of the Charities Act requires all

---

[1] Charity Commissioners, Form R.E. 10.
[2] Statutory Instrument, 1960, No. 2425, The Charities Regulations (Statements of Account), 1960.
[3] See Appendix C, pp. 526 ff.

charities, without exception, to keep proper books and accounts and to preserve them for seven years. The same section requires the preparation of consecutive statements of accounts consisting of at least an income and expenditures statement for a period of not more than fifteen months and a balance sheet relating to the end of that period.

Regulations of the Commissioners in 1961 and 1962 excepted certain classes of charities from filing accounts annually. Form letters to this effect are sent to all charities immediately following registration or classification.

Educational charities that must register with the Ministry of Education are subject only to regulations promulgated by that department. The jurisdiction of the Ministry of Education extends to schools, colleges, scholarship funds, and quasi-educational foundations, including trusts for recreation, youth clubs, village halls, museums, and apprenticing foundations. The forms used by the Ministry are similar to those prepared by the Commissioners, but the two registries are run independently. The Ministry of Education office maintains only one public file; it contains the name of the charity, particulars concerning the governing instrument, the objects, beneficial area, land and premises occupied, income, and the name and address of the correspondent. Actual trust instruments may also be inspected on request. There is no classification by purpose or by geographical area. The Ministry of Education has refused to register charities on a voluntary basis.[1]

Investigatory and Corrective Powers of the Commissioners

The Commissioners have general power to institute inquiries with regard to charities, to order production of accounts and statements in writing, and to propound interrogatories.[2] They may also hold hearings and summon witnesses. Local authorities are given the power to contribute to the expenses of such inquiries where they relate to local charities within the authority's area. When the Commissioners propose to take action following an inquiry, they may publish a report of the inquiry.

The actions the Commissioners may take following an inquiry are specifically set out in the act.[3] When the Commissioners are satisfied that there has been either misconduct or mismanagement and that it is necessary to act to protect the charity, they may:

---

[1] Aldrich, Trevor, *op. cit.*, p. 977.
[2] Stat. 8 & 9 Elizabeth II, c. 58 (1960), secs. 6, 7.
[3] Stat. 8 & 9 Elizabeth II, c. 58 (1960), sec. 20.

1. Remove any trustee or officer or servant who is responsible for, or party to, the misconduct or mismanagement, or who by his conduct has contributed to or facilitated it. (The terms "misconduct" and "mismanagement" specifically include the employment for remuneration or reward of persons acting in the offices of the charity or for other administrative purposes of sums that are excessive in relation to the amount of property available for charitable purposes, not withstanding anything in the trust instrument.)

2. Make an order vesting the trust property in the Official Custodian for Charities, a new official created by the act, to function as trustee for certain cases provided in the act.

3. Order any bank or person holding money or securities on behalf of the charity not to part with them without approval of the Commissioners. (Failure to abide by such order is subject to criminal penalty.)

4. Restrict transactions into which the charity may enter, including payment of officers.

The Commissioners may also remove, on their own order, any trustee who has been convicted of a felony, has not acted or is unwilling to act, or who is abroad. They may appoint trustees to replace any individual removed by them, or where, because of vacancies, the existing trustees cannot apply for appointment. Furthermore, they may appoint additional trustees whenever they deem it necessary for the proper administration of the charity. The Commissioners may also suspend a trustee, officer, or agent for a period not longer than three months pending the consideration of his removal.

Judicial action may not be taken without notice to the trustees. Appeals from orders under this section may be taken by the attorney general, as well as by any charity official who is removed by the Commissioners.

The jurisdiction of the Commissioners, other than that explicitly stated in regard to appointment, discharge, or removal for misconduct, is the same as it was under the Charitable Trusts Act.[1] They therefore have concurrent jurisdiction with the High Court to establish a scheme for administration of a charity, or to vest or transfer property, or require or entitle any person to call for or make any transfer of property or any payment. The court may require the Commissioners to prepare schemes for administration.

---

[1] In force from 1853 to 1939.

The Commissioners' jurisdiction does not extend to determinations of title to property where there are adverse claims. The greatest limitation on their jurisdiction, however, is that it can be invoked only by the charity itself, or by a request of the court to prepare or settle a scheme for administration, unless the charity's annual income is less than £50 per year, in which case the attorney general, or any one or more of the trustees, or any person interested in the charity, or two or more inhabitants of the area of a local charity may make application to the Commissioners.[1]

The Commissioners may bypass the requirement that jurisdiction to establish schemes may be taken only after application from the charity or the court in cases where the trustees have unreasonably refused or neglected to apply, by ordering application to the secretary of state, who after hearing the trustees, may make application for them to invoke jurisdiction. One further extension of the Commissioners' jurisdiction is permitted in cases where schemes involve alteration of provisions made by Act of Parliament, or where schemes go beyond the general powers of the Commissioners. In such cases, they may settle the scheme and then forward it to the secretary of state who places it before Parliament for approval.

The right of the attorney general to bring legal enforcement proceedings in any court was not limited by the 1960 act. The parties who may also sue for enforcement are limited to the charity, any of the trustees, any persons interested in the charity, or any two or more inhabitants of the area of a local charity; and these parties may act only after receiving authority from the Commissioners.[2] If the Commissioners believe that the case can be dealt with by them, they may not grant such authority without special reason. The High Court of the Chancery Division may also grant authority to bring suit for enforcement if application has been made to the Commissioners and refused. The power of the Commissioners to give advice to trustees on any matter affecting the performance of their duties was reenacted, and a provision granting immunity to a trustee who acts on such advice was added.

Local Authorities

The association of local authorities with the administration and supervision of charities is one of the new features of the 1960 act that

---

[1] Stat. 8 & 9 Elizabeth II, c. 58 (1960), sec. 18.
[2] Stat. 8 & 9 Elizabeth II, c. 58 (1960), sec. 28.

had been suggested by the Nathan Committee.[1] The council of a county or borough is authorized to prepare and maintain an index of local charities which shall be open to public inspection. The Charity Commissioners, on request, must supply the local council with full information concerning any local charity registered with them. These same local authorities may, in cooperation with charitable trustees, carry out a review of the working of groups with similar objectives and make recommendations to the Commissioners concerning amalgamation or employment of joint offices or coordination of activities.

It was reported in November of 1963, that 61 of 62 counties, 82 of 83 county boroughs, 26 of 28 metropolitan boroughs, and 228 of 317 boroughs had passed resolutions calling for the establishment of local indices. The Commissioners had supplied the necessary information to 22 of these, and the Ministry of Education, to 1. The provisions in this section of the act have not been implemented sufficiently to make any evaluation of its effect. They have received widespread approval, however, as shown by the large number of local government units that have voiced interest.[2]

Additional sections of the Charities Act of 1960 authorize the Commissioners to establish Common Investment Funds.[3] Others provide for the protection of the term "Common Good Trusts" for use only by charities organized on a basis similar to the community trusts in the United States.[4] The Commissioners are authorized to sanction expansion of trustees' powers in connection with administration when they deem it expedient.[5] Complex restrictions on dealing with real property owned by a charity were repealed, but a provision was included stating that no property forming part of a permanent endowment shall be mortgaged or changed by way of security for loans, nor, in the case of land in England and Wales, shall be sold, leased, or otherwise disposed of without order of a court or of the Commissioners.[6] The restriction overrides any provision in a trust instrument, but permission is not required for a transaction for which authorization is expressly given by statute or by a legally established scheme, or one for the granting of a lease for less than twenty-two years. Additional provisions regulate the calling of meetings and the delegation of au-

---

[1] Stat. 8 & 9 Elizabeth II, c. 58 (1960), secs. 10, 11, 12.
[2] Aldrich, Trevor M., *op. cit.*, p. 978.
[3] Stat. 8 & 9 Elizabeth II, c. 58 (1960), sec. 22.
[4] Stat. 8 & 9 Elizabeth II, c. 58 (1960), sec. 31.
[5] Stat. 8 & 9 Elizabeth II, c. 58 (1960), sec. 23.
[6] Stat. 8 & 9 Elizabeth II, c. 58 (1960), sec. 29.

thority, and specify the evidence of removal of trustees by a charity board.[1]

Certain specific provisions relating to dissolution of incorporated charities were also enacted.[2] No corporate charity having power to alter its charter may do so in any way that could result in the body's ceasing to be a charity. The attorney general was also granted the power to bring a petition for court dissolution under the terms of the Corporations Act of 1948.

Finally, the Charity Commissioners are authorized to exchange information with the Commissioners of Inland Revenue, as well as other government departments and local authorities with regard to any institutions that have been treated as charities by any of them, in order to determine their status.[3]

In connection with exemption from income tax, in England the definition of charity is the same in regard to questions of taxes as those of validity and administration. In the case of Scottish charities, however, the Scottish law supplies the definition of charity for general purposes, but on questions relating to income tax, the English law is applicable. Just as there has been agitation for a new definition of charitable purposes to determine validity of gifts, so too, the tax authorities have asked for a new definition, and have from time to time requested one that would be applicable only for tax purposes, but no action has been taken. The question of local property taxation was dealt with in the Rating and Valuation Act of 1961, which grants relief of 50 per cent of the rate for property occupied by a charity and used wholly or mainly for charitable purposes if the charity is registered with the Charity Commissioners or the Ministry of Education.[4]

The English method for supervision of charities has, therefore, centered on the creation of an independent agency of government with quasi-judicial powers that it exercises concurrently with the courts, although there is a right of appeal to the courts from its actions. The advantages of such a quasi-judicial agency stem from the fact that court proceedings are far less easily available in England than in most of the jurisdictions in the United States and are apt to be more costly. The 1960 legislation reflects an attempt to improve the procedure that had prevailed in the preceding century, primarily through the es-

---

[1] Stat. 8 & 9 Elizabeth II, c. 58 (1960), secs. 32 to 34.
[2] Stat. 8 & 9 Elizabeth II, c. 58 (1960), sec. 30.
[3] Stat. 8 & 9 Elizabeth II, c. 58 (1960), sec. 9.
[4] Stat. 9 & 10 Elizabeth II, c. 45 (1961).

tablishment of a registry and a reporting system, the decentralization of the entire system through the association of local officials and the creation of local registries, and the grant of power to the Commissioners to remove trustees for misconduct or mismanagement and to correct abuses.

One of the major problems that has plagued English charity has been the large number of small trusts whose purposes have become obsolete and which have been mismanaged, or allowed to become dormant. The remedies in the Charities Act of 1960 were designed to simplify methods of dealing with this problem. The substantive provisions of the act relating to the *cy pres* doctrine form an integral part of this reform, as do the registration provisions and the grant of increased powers to the Commissioners in cases of maladministration. This problem is not as evident in the majority of American states. It has appeared more often in the older states such as Massachusetts and New Hampshire. The English experience suggests, however, that the maintenance of a registry is one of the most effective means of assuring the continued surveillance of charities to the end that the problems created by dormancy and obsolescence are not allowed to arise.

Investment of Trust Funds

Other examples of positive government action that may be of great assistance in the administration of charitable funds are the empowering of the Charity Commissioners to establish common investment funds, and the creation of an Official Custodian for Charities in whom property may be vested without cost to the trustees.[1]

Prior to the passage of the Charities Act of 1960 there had been an Official Trustee of Charity Lands and an Official Trustee of Charity Funds. They had been created by the Charitable Trusts Act of 1853[2] and were characterized by Owen as "one of the more serviceable branches of the Commission's Office and one which expanded steadily. . . ."[3] The 1960 act combined these two positions, and all funds formerly held by them were transferred to the Official Custodian for Charities. The position of Official Custodian usually is filled by one of the Charity Commissioners, and he is considered a corporation sole. Trustees of charitable trusts may vest title to trust property in the Official Custodian for safekeeping and investment without resort to the

---

[1] Stat. 8 & 9 Elizabeth II, c. 58 (1960), sec. 3.
[2] Stat. 16 & 17 Victoria, c. 137 (1853).
[3] Owen, David, *op. cit.,* p. 300.

court; they retain the right to execute the trust and manage and distribute the income. Problems and expenses occasioned by a change of trustees are thereby obviated. The procedure of vesting property in the Official Custodian has commonly been used by trustees of small trusts, but the Commissioners and the courts may also order trustees to vest trust property in the Official Custodian when framing a scheme or otherwise.

The laws of England have greatly restricted the investments which trustees can make, unless specifically relieved by the terms of the trust. The Nathan Report had recommended that the powers of charitable trustees be expanded to permit investment in company stocks and in shares on the London Stock Exchange, and that the Charity Commissioners be empowered to authorize the creation of common investment funds.[1] Only the latter recommendation was included in the Charities Act of 1960,[2] although it did provide that the Official Custodian for Charities could hold and manage assets of common investment funds. However, a Trustee Investments Act was passed in 1961 applicable to charitable and private trustees alike. It removed the existing restrictions on investment in common stock by permitting such investment of up to 50 per cent of the value of any trust fund.[3] The passage of this act raised serious problems for the Charity Commissioners. The difficulties have been explained as follows:

On the passing of the Trustee Investments Act in August 1961 the Commissioners faced a difficult problem. On the one hand if they were to open a common investment fund to all charities at that juncture it would have come at a moment when reorganization of the Official Custodian's department was in full swing. If on the other hand it were to be deferred or not made there was a risk that large quantities of undated gilt-edged securities would be thrown on an already saturated market by charities anxious to switch into equities: the effect on their finances might be catastrophic. It had been estimated that of the 40,000 separate charity accounts held by the Official Custodian no less than 16,000 had holdings of a nominal value of under £200 to £499, about 5,000 from £500 to £999, about 7,500 from £1,000 to £4,999, and about 3,500 over £5,000. It was clear that the 24,000 charities with less than £500 could not unaided achieve an effective spread of invest-

---

[1] Committee on the Law and Practice . . . , op. cit., chap. 8.

[2] Stat. 8 & 9 Elizabeth II, c. 58 (1960), sec. 22.

[3] This act also contained requirements of diversification, consideration of investments in terms of the trust's purposes, review of investments at regular intervals, and an obligation to seek advice of persons qualified in financial matters in connection with investments.

ment or reap the benefits of the Trustee Investments Act so as to protect both capital and income.[1]

The Commissioners established two common trust funds in 1962, the National Association of Almshouses Common Investment Fund and the Charities Official Investment Fund; and the Ministry of Education established a smaller one for prize funds managed by the Institute of Chartered Accountants. Following passage of the Investments Act, the Commissioners attempted to assess the demand for a Common Investment Fund for all charities whose assets were held by the Official Custodian by sending a circular to trustees.

> The response to the Commissioners' circular was unexpected. Within two months 36 per cent. of the trustees approached had replied; of those replying 30 per cent. expressed an intention to participate, 10 per cent. declined the invitation and 60 per cent. expressed interest. The holdings of those who notified actual willingness to participate at this juncture were roughly £2.7 million in undated "gilts," £0.77 million in dated "gilts" and £0.38 million in other securities. Calculations showed that even if only half of those who expressed interest ultimately decided to participate the immediate sums available for inclusion in the common investment fund would exceed £15 million. Further correspondence moreover indicated that other charities with larger funds might wish to enter and more than double this total at an early stage. The prospect of managing so large a fund posed entirely different problems from those involved in the £5 million fund which had been estimated as the probable initial figure.[2]

The Commissioners decided that the Official Custodian's department was neither properly constituted nor sufficiently experienced to undertake the management of such a large fund; moreover, they did not consider it proper to employ a commercial agency or private investment managers. However, the Investment Management Office of the Central Board of Finance of the Church of England had been administering a somewhat similar investment fund for the Church of England charities since 1958. The Commissioners entered into negotiations with this group, as well as with the government, and a plan was devised whereby a board of independent trustees would be appointed to be responsible for policy and control of the fund, assisted by a panel of paid investment advisers. The day-to-day work of the fund would be carried on by the Investment Manager's Office of the Central

---

[1] Giles, D.P.F., "Charities: Developments in Investment Policy," *The Law Journal, Annual Charities Review,* April 24, 1964, pp. 24, 28.

[2] *Ibid.,* pp. 28–30.

Board of Finance. A detailed plan for consultation and communication between the fund trustees and the Charity Commissioners was worked out, and the entire plan was framed into a scheme and established officially on December 4, 1962. In the first three months of its existence the fund received £5,999,251 in 5,344 accounts. One year later the number of accounts had risen to 8,965, and the assets contributed were approximately £14.5 million.[1]

The establishment of such a fund would not have been possible before passage of the 1960 act. Its advantages to the small charities are obvious. In a broader sense, it represents one of the major actions of the Charity Commissioners under powers conferred by the 1960 legislation of a type substantially different from any permitted to an administrative agency in the United States. With the rapid proliferation of foundations, particularly small family foundations, in the United States in this decade, it is not altogether unlikely that a need for similar powers may arise in some states in the not too distant future. New Hampshire has passed legislation permitting the creation of court-appointed trustees. The future of the English investment plan bears continuing scrutiny.

Canada

The Ontario Charities Accounting Act. Although a survey of the laws relating to charitable foundations in Canada is beyond the scope of this study, two acts adopted by the legislature of the Province of Ontario which relate to matters of interest to American lawmakers, both state and federal, are worthy of note. The first, adopted in 1950, is the Charities Accounting Act,[2] which creates, in a sense, a registry of charitable trusts and corporations. It requires that whenever, under the terms of a will or instrument in writing, real or personal property is or will be given to or vested in a person as executor or trustee for a religious, educational, charitable, or public purpose, he must give written notice thereof to the Public Trustee. The Public Trustee is an individual appointed by the lieutenant governor and treated by statute as a corporation sole. He performs certain duties in relation to the administration of estates and the question of escheats, as well as the duties specified in this act.[3]

The Accounting Act was amended in 1951, to state specifically

---

[1] *Ibid.*, p. 42.
[2] Rev. Stat. of Ontario, 1960, c. 52.
[3] Rev. Stat. of Ontario, 1960, c. 355.

that any corporation established for a religious, educational, charitable, or public purpose shall be deemed to be a trustee, and that its instrument of incorporation shall be deemed to be an instrument in writing within the meaning of the act.[1] Every executor or trustee coming within the act is placed under a duty to forward information, upon request, from time to time, to the Public Trustee concerning the condition, disposition, or other particulars of the property; the names and addresses of the executor or trustees, the administrator or manager of the estate or trust, and any business corporation owned or controlled by the trust.

The Public Trustee is authorized to request a judge of the Supreme Court to inquire into and determine any question relating to the failure to forward information provided by the act, and he may specifically inquire into and determine questions of control, of election of directors, or of ownership or management of a corporation controlled by the charity. The Public Trustee may also require the trustee to submit an account for audit to a judge of the Surrogate's Court. The act spells out the power of the judge to remove trustees, order restitution, issue injunctions or attachments, and give directions as to future investments, as well as his right to impose a fine or twelve months' imprisonment for failure to obey. The final section of the act states clearly, however, that it does not affect any existing equitable remedies.

A separate section of this act relating to solicitations permits any individual to file a complaint to the judge of any county or district court as to the manner in which a person or organization has solicited or procured funds or gifts from the public or dealt with them. The judge may order the Public Trustee to undertake an investigation and report in writing to the attorney general and the court. Fraternal and religious charities are exempted from this section of the act.

The Accounting Act includes, therefore, several provisions found in the English Charities Act and in many of the registration and reporting statutes, but it substitutes the Public Trustee for the attorney general or an independent board of commissioners. The remedies available to the court are spelled out with greater precision than in the statutes of the various states, and, as in England, the provisions are clearly and unequivocally made applicable to corporate foundations.

Control of Charitable Trusts in Ontario. The most novel part of the Accounting Act relates to the powers of the Public Trustee and the

---

[1] Stats. of Ontario, 1951, c. 10, sec. 1.

court to demand information as to the affairs of any corporations owned by a charity. These powers supplement the provisions of the Charitable Gifts Act, which was also enacted in 1950;[1] its passage followed a political dispute that arose in connection with the owner- ship by the Atkinson Foundation of the controlling interest in the Toronto *Daily Star*.[2] The Charitable Gifts Act has since been amended, but its essential provisions are unchanged. They are spelled out in section 2(1), as follows:

> Notwithstanding the provisions of any general or special Act, letters patent, by-law, will, codicil, trust deed, agreement, or other instrument, wherever an interest in a business that is carried on for gain or profit is given to or vested in a person in any capacity for any religious, charita- ble, educational or public purpose, such person has power to dispose of and shall dispose of such portion thereof that represents more than a 10 percent interest in such business.

The one exemption is for an interest in a business given to or vested in any organization of any religious denomination. "Person" is defined to include a corporation and the heir, executor, administrator, or other legal representative of a person to whom the context can apply ac- cording to law. A person is deemed to have an "interest" in a busi- ness if (1) he is a part owner, (2) he holds or controls, directly or indirectly, through a combination or series of two or more persons, one or more shares in a corporation that owns or controls or partly owns or controls the business, or (3) he holds or controls, directly or indirectly, or through a combination or series of two or more persons, one or more bonds, debentures, mortgages, or other security upon, or asset of, the business.

The time allotted in the statute within which an interest must be dis- posed of is ten years from the death of a testator, in the case of a will, and seven years after the date of the instrument in all other cases; but a judge of the Supreme Court may extend this period when it is in the interest of the charitable purposes to do so. In each year during a period in which the business interest is held by the charity, if it rep- resents more than a 50 per cent interest in a business, the person to whom it is given, the person controlling the management of the busi- ness, and the Public Trustee must jointly determine the amount of profits earned by the business, and the business is required to pay to

---

[1] Rev. Stat. of Ontario, 1960, c. 50.
[2] See for discussion Taylor, Eleanor K., *Public Accountability of Founda- tions and Charitable Trusts,* Russell Sage Foundation, New York, 1953, p. 110.

the charity any undistributed profits as so determined. An annual accounting must also be made to the Public Trustee; it must include particulars of amount of fees paid to any director and any salaries in excess of $8,000 paid to any person.[1]

Provision is also made whereby, with court approval, a person may acquire the interest being disposed of under the terms of the act, notwithstanding the fact that he is one of the fiduciaries or an officer of administration of the charity. The proceeds of any sale under this act must be invested only in investments authorized by the Companies Act, which regulates joint stock insurance companies; but the investment may in no case result in a holding of more than 10 per cent in any one business. The Treasurer of Ontario is granted power to appoint any person to investigate the activities of any business or charity subject to the act, and the attorney general or any person interested may apply to the Supreme Court to make any necessary orders to carry out its provisions. Finally, contravention of any provision is made a criminal act subject to a fine of not less than $100, nor more than $5,000, or to imprisonment for not more than one year, or both.

Canadian Income Tax Act. As in the United States, supervision of charities in Canada is the responsibility of the provincial courts and legislatures. The only provisions of the Canadian statutes that apply to these entities are, as in the United States, the tax provisions. The Canadian Income Tax Act, first adopted in 1947–1948,[2] contained an exemption for corporations and trusts organized wholly for charitable purposes. Decisions as to exempt status were made case by case, and there were no statutory standards. In 1951 the Income Tax Act was amended[3] to provide that exempt status for organizations that do not carry on charitable activities themselves (such as foundations) would apply only to corporations and trusts that met very explicit requirements. To be eligible for tax exemption a corporation must be organized exclusively for charitable purposes and no part of its income may be payable to or otherwise available for the personal profit of any proprietor, member, or stockholder. After June, 1950, it may not have acquired control of any other corporation,[4] carried on any business, or incurred any business debts other than obligations ordinarily incident

---

[1] Rev. Stat. of Ontario, 1960, c. 50, sec. 4.
[2] Stats. of Canada, 1948, c. 52.
[3] Stats. of Canada, 1950–1951, c. 51, sec. 20.
[4] The definition of control of a business includes ownership of more than 60 per cent of the outstanding shares. Canadian Income Tax Act, sec. 63.

to its operation such as rents and salaries. Finally, it must expend its income only for carrying on its own charitable activities, for grants to other exempt organizations, or for gifts to Canadian corporations that spent at least 90 per cent of their aggregate income for charitable purposes during the previous year. Certain exclusions from these provisions were made for corporations organized for charitable purposes prior to January, 1940.[1] The provision for exemption of charitable trusts is similar to that for corporations.[2]

These Canadian statutes contain far stricter limitations or foundation activities than are found in either the United States or England.[3] The bans on foundation control of business bear a striking similarity to proposals made from time to time in the United States for limiting donor-controlled foundations, the most recent of which have been the suggestion by Congressman Patman that foundations be prohibited from owning more than 3 per cent of the stock of any corporation and the proposal of the Treasury Department that a 20 per cent limitation be set.[4] However, the American proposals have all been based on changes in the federal income tax laws, and, to date, it has not been suggested that they also be included in the substantive state laws regulating charities. The administration of both the Canadian Income Tax Law and the Charitable Gifts Act of Ontario warrant further study.

---

[1] Canadian Income Tax Act, sec. (1)(f).
[2] Canadian Income Tax Act, sec. 62 (1) (g).
[3] See, however, McKellar, John D., "Charitable Foundations," *Canadian Bar Journal*, vol. 8, February, 1965, pp. 7–21, which suggests certain tax-saving devices available through the use of a foundation that would not be permissible under the Internal Revenue Code.
[4] See Chapter V.

CHAPTER XII

Prospects and Recommendations

THE GROWTH OF FOUNDATIONS in the United States and the rationale for their existence both stem from the nature of the democratic society in which they have developed. This view was well expressed by President Charles W. Eliot of Harvard in 1874 when he described the role of philanthropy in this country.

> The two nations in which endowments for public uses have long existed are the two free nations of the world. In England and the United States, the method of doing public work by means of endowments managed by private corporations has been domesticated for several centuries; and these are the only two nations which have succeeded on a great scale in combining liberty with stability in free institutions. The connection of these two facts is not accidental. The citizens of a free State must be accustomed to associated action in a great variety of forms; they must have many local centers of common action, and many agencies and administrations for public objects, besides the central agency of government. . . . To abandon the method of fostering endowments, in favor of the method of direct government action, is to forego one of the great securities of public liberty.[1]

The fostering of private endowment entails two basic approaches which are, in a sense, antithetical. It is not disputed that foundations need freedom in which to operate. Their unique contribution to American life is directly related to the diversity of the programs they have developed and supported. On the other side, however, the people, through government, must be assured of three conditions: (1) that

---

[1] Eliot, Charles W., "The Exemption from Taxation," reprinted in *Charles W. Eliot, The Man and His Beliefs.* Edited by William Allan Neilson. Harper and Brothers, New York, 1926, vol. 2, p. 707.

foundation funds are being devoted to the purposes for which they were donated; (2) that those who manage these funds are acting in the public interest; and (3) that the funds of foundations whose purposes are no longer socially useful are directed into fields where they will continue to serve society.

Preceding chapters have described the means devised by the state and federal governments to assure these three conditions. These are many and varied, but on the whole they furnish but a modicum of supervision and little, if any, actual regulation. In contrast, the English since the early nineteenth century have utilized a stringent, centralized system of supervision based on the premise that the freedom of operation of charitable trusts is at all times and in almost all respects subject to the oversight of a governmental body holding both administrative and judicial powers to rectify abuses.

In the 1950's the Nathan Committee conducted what was, in a sense, a public debate over the position of charitable trusts in English society. The Committee concluded that philanthropy's position in the "welfare state" was of sufficient value to warrant its further encouragement, but it also noted and emphasized a need for strengthening the machinery by which government supervised charitable activity. The Charities Act of 1960 represented an attempt to improve and enlarge the existing program of strict public accountability.

In the United States the debate over the position of philanthropy, as well as the ideal methods for achieving accountability, has not been resolved. In the meantime, philanthropic activities have grown at such a rapid pace that some critics have called for a curtailment of growth until methods for control can be devised and put into operation. Although this extreme view is held by only a small minority, it is indicative of both the nature of the debate and the fact that adjustments are forthcoming.

The wide amount of freedom within which charities have operated in the United States has been, in part, a reflection of the nineteenth-century philosophy of free enterprise and, in part, a result of a lack of public awareness of any need for supervision. The legal structure in all of the states has provided for some agency of government to supervise charitable activities. Almost all of the states have followed the English tradition and have placed the duty of enforcement in the hands of the state attorney general. The courts in all states are granted broad powers to determine the purposes to be accorded the privileged status of "charitable," and there are bases of power in both taxing authorities and officials who supervise corporate activities to enforce certain aspects of philanthropic activity. Along with these administrative provisions, there are substantive laws in every state defining both the duties and the powers of those who manage charitable funds.

Despite all of these state provisions, the fact remains that only since the expansion of the federal government's taxing authority has there been any widespread recognition of the interest of government in philanthropy; and only since then has there been any attempt on a nationwide scale to direct the growth of foundations or to limit the manner in which they operate. The fact that the impetus for increased supervision of foundations has come about through the enforcement of the federal tax laws has meant that the economic implications of foundations vis-à-vis private enterprises have been emphasized at the expense of consideration of methods for preserving the unique position and unique contribution of foundations as a separate institution of society. Insufficient attention has been given to devising means for assuring devotion to purpose and the efficient and faithful management of charitable funds. A series of separate, and at times disparate, rules and regulations have evolved in both state and federal law, and enforcement procedures have been fragmented. The current debate over methods for assuring accountability by foundations affords an opportunity to reconcile and unify these divergent strands of the law, to formulate meaningful standards for performance, and to devise methods for enforcement that recognize the needs of both accountability and freedom of action.

Uniformity of approach is, therefore, the first essential. This requires that the standards of the tax laws be made as consonant as possible with those of substantive state law. It also requires that all foundations be treated in the same manner, regardless of their form of organization. In short, a "law of charity" must be developed, containing a broad designation of those purposes that society will recognize as valid and thereby eligible for tax exemption, as well as the standards by which the managers of these charitable funds will be measured. Uniformity of enforcement procedures is less easy to attain than uniformity of law—unless, of course, the federal government should preempt the entire field of supervision. Such a drastic step appears at this time to be neither warranted nor likely to succeed. Uniformity of enforcement, therefore, requires a set of consistent requirements for the creation and dissolution of foundations, the extension of all supervisory programs to corporations and trusts on a like basis, and the establishment of procedures combining the mutual interests of the state and federal governments to eliminate unnecessary duplication and to provide a more effective application of sanctions.

Charitable Purposes and the Obsolete Purpose

Both state law and the Internal Revenue Code require a determination of those purposes which meet the definition of "charitable." To date, no attempt has been made to formulate an explicit definition of "charitable" beyond referring to the purposes included in the so-called common law definition and using them for analogies to contemporary needs. From time to time there have been pleas for a more exact formulation, but it has been generally concluded that this task is impossible. Philanthropic enterprises will continue to contribute to society only so long as they are able to meet new and changing conditions. No definition can fit such a situation unless it contains an "escape clause," thereby retaining the same flexibility as the common law definition.

Reliance must therefore be placed on an enlightened and farseeing judiciary to determine those purposes which meet the standard of service to society. It is fortunate that in the United States the great majority of individual judges have retained a sufficiently open-minded approach to permit such a system to work. The decision of the Congress and the federal tax administrators to follow this common law approach rather than create a separate federal law of charitable purposes represented a wise evaluation of the difficulties involved in the alternative course, as well of the desirability of retaining as much uniformity as possible between state and federal law.

The actual administration of the federal tax laws, however, requires a determination of validity for each new charity at the time of its creation. In contrast, under state law such decisions may never be required, particularly in the case of inter vivos trusts. The federal system therefore generates strong pressures toward uniformity. A premium is placed on the use of the safe, conforming language. Conversely, the unusual or advanced concept may require extra support by its proponents, and resort to the courts is often necessary before a favorable determination may be obtained. It is to be hoped that the drives for individuality of potential donors will be sufficiently strong to overcome temptations and pressures to take the easiest course, that of "tracking" the federal statute, when defining purposes. In part, responsibility rests on attorneys and tax advisers to prevent the narrowing of purposes because of a desire to meet most easily any federally imposed restraints.

The greatest responsibility lies, however, with the tax administrators, who must not lose sight of the philosophy behind the decision to permit freedom to donors to choose the purposes for their philanthropic projects in their desire to simplify their duties of supervision. The tax administrators have admittedly been given a difficult task, as is evident in their struggle to formulate standards by which to measure "scientific" or "educational" purposes. Congress has further increased the difficulties by attempting to prohibit "substantial" activity that involves carrying on propaganda, or otherwise attempting to influence legislation. Cogent arguments have been advanced to the effect that this prohibition should be removed. So long as it remains a part of the Internal Revenue Code, the problem of determining what is "education" and what is "propaganda to influence legislation" will unfortunately continue to be a source of trouble, and as attempts are made to establish enforceable standards, the area of permissible purposes must perforce be narrowed.

The determination of validity of purposes is closely allied to the problem of dealing with obsolete purposes. The administratively imposed requirement of the federal tax law that exempt status will not be conferred unless *cy pres* disposition of funds is mandatory has an extremely valuable effect in the states that have not adopted the *cy pres* doctrine or in which the courts have afforded it a very narrow scope. Far better would be the adoption by the legislature or judiciary in all states of provisions whereby all charitable gifts, unless subject to a specific limitation valid for only twenty-one years, would be subject to alteration whenever they become "obsolete, useless, prejudicial to the public welfare, otherwise sufficiently provided for, or insignificant in comparison to the magnitude of the endowment," to use the language of the Education (Scotland) Act of 1946.[1] There should also be provisions whereby small charities can be consolidated or their investments or administration pooled. Without laws encompassing these provisions, there can be no assurance of the growth of philanthropy or of its continued service to society, and the dead hand may gain undue power.

Fiduciary Standards

Substantive laws defining the duties and powers of trustees and directors in each state have been devised with the aim of establishing a

---

[1] Stat. 9 & 10 George VI, c. 72, sec. 119B.

high standard of conduct for those who deal with the funds of others. The laws defining the powers and duties of these individuals are based on the concept that a fiduciary has a duty to act for the benefit of the other party to the relation as to all matters within the scope of the relation. This is primarily a duty of loyalty, but it also requires that the fiduciary use reasonable care and skill in management and that he be at all times accountable for his actions. These basic duties are not too much to expect of those who manage funds devoted to public purposes. The case law in every state affords examples of the application of fiduciary standards to specific situations and provides a means of ascertaining their scope and limitations.

Recent criticisms of foundation activities have been directed toward speculation with charitable funds, the use of charitable funds to gain private advantage, the competition of foundations with private business enterprises, and the accumulation of vast sums of capital not being used for charity and not being taxed. Fiduciary law prohibits speculation and the use of trust funds to further private interests. It restricts the accumulation of funds and requires that they produce income that can and must be expended for the charitable purposes of the foundation. In the sense that it requires devotion to purpose, it may even set a limit on the amount or type of private business enterprise in which a charity may engage. In short, there is within the fiduciary concept a basis for correcting the major abuses of foundations that have developed in recent years.

An entirely separate facet of the law of trusts, however, operates to reduce the application of fiduciary concepts in certain situations. The duties and powers of trustees, as defined in the law of trusts, may be modified by the settlor of any trust at the time of creation, whether through enlargement of the trustees' powers or by use of "exculpatory clauses" excusing trustees from all but gross negligence or willful misconduct. The courts look first to the terms of a trust instrument to define both duties and powers, supplying them from trust law only when the instrument is silent.

Prior to the increase in the federal taxes, the customary method for creating charities was by means of testamentary trusts. The primary interest of their settlors was to set down fairly rigid standards for the behavior of fiduciaries who would be carrying out their beneficence long after the settlors were gone. If the settlors varied the terms of trust law, they made them stricter as often as they made them more lenient. Today, however, private individuals are attempting to take advantage of the favoritism shown to the creators of trusts by creating foundations during their life, naming themselves one of the trustees or the sole trustee, relieving the trustees of many of their legal duties, and granting them unlimited investment powers and as complete a freedom from liability as the courts of their state will permit. These settlors then proceed to manage the trust funds as if they were still their own, thereby often obtaining personal benefit.

A court might refuse to recognize any of the powers granted by such a settlor, and it might well ignore any exculpatory language on the basis that the trustee's purposes were inimical or inconsistent with the purposes for which the trust was created. No court has been squarely faced with such a decision in a case involving a modern foundation, however, and it is impossible to predict how individual judges would weigh the interests of settlors as against the interests of society. There is growing evidence of a judicial attitude that certain standards of conduct are so necessarily inherent in the fiduciary relation that they cannot be removed by any provision in the trust instrument, and this attitude would certainly lead to a decision that the public's rights are paramount.

A more positive method of assuring the application of fiduciary standards to all charitable trustees would be through legislation providing that no settlor may relieve a trustee or director of a charitable trust or foundation from his duties of loyalty, nor from the use of reasonable care, skill, and prudence. Legislation passed in Rhode Island in 1950 attempted to accomplish this by providing that:

> Regardless of any language in the agreement, deed or other instrument creating an inter vivos charitable trust, no trustee or trustees of such a trust shall be exonerated from liability for failure to exercise reasonable care, diligence and prudence.[1]

Such a provision does not, of course, prohibit self-dealing, and it therefore falls short of the optimum, but it is the most positive statement in any of the state laws of the limits on the right of a settlor of a charitable trust.

If trust law appears too lenient on the one hand, it also has aspects that may be too harsh. The corporate form for foundations became popular in part because some donors wished to escape the restrictions in trust law on delegation of fiduciary duties and on investment powers—particularly in those states where trust investments must be made in conformity with a legal list. It should be possible for trustees of char-

---

[1] R.I. Gen. Laws Ann., sec. 18–9–13.

itable trusts to manage their affairs in much the same way as do directors of charitable corporations. It is true that unanimity of decision is not required of charitable trustees, but provisions permitting the delegation of certain duties and a flexibility of management would also be desirable. In regard to investments, the prudent man rule, which applies to the directors of all charitable corporations, should be made the universal standard for trustees of all charitable trusts. A requirement of diversification of investments would be an additional safeguard of great value for trustees and directors alike, but it might cause such upheaval in the existing structure of charitable investments as to be unworkable. At the least, all charitable fiduciaries should be under a duty to make and keep the charities' funds productive, a duty that might in some instances lead to greater diversification.

The major problem raised by the increased popularity of the corporate form for foundations has been that, here again, the case law has not caught up with the new developments. Some attorneys argue that the fiduciary duties of corporate directors are not as strict as those of trustees; they often rely improperly on court decisions rendered when some of the states did not recognize the validity of charitable trusts to establish the basis for a difference. This problem must be solved by the development of a body of case law or by the enactment of legislation clearly stating that differences of form are immaterial in determining the duties of charitable fiduciaries.

A new formulation of the statutes under which charitable corporations are chartered is also advisable and of particular importance in some of the states. These statutes should make it clear that the issuance of stock is inconsistent with charitable endeavors, that membership certificates do not have the attributes of property rights, and that the creation of a corporation for charitable purposes generates a series of duties and powers that are not the same as those applicable to business corporations or even to other not-for-profit corporations. The aim of state laws designed to improve the management of charitable funds should, in short, be to place the most important components of the fiduciary relationship into each charitable endeavor.

When one turns to analysis of the federal tax laws, the aim should, in theory, be different from that of state law; it should be the prevention of abuse of the privilege of tax-exempt status and thereby the prevention of unfair competition by tax-exempt organizations with private taxable interests. As the tax-exemption provisions of federal law have been extended and revised, however, they have moved into what could be characterized as the traditional state fields, and they now place limits on certain aspects of the fiduciary relationship and set certain standards for fiduciary behavior. These limitations and standards are in many instances poorly defined and inconsistently applied. The prohibited transactions sections of the Code, for example, do not apply to private foundations, all charitable endeavors, or all fiduciaries, but merely to donors, their families, and certain closely related individuals. They contain poorly articulated standards that are in all instances less stringent than those of the law of fiduciaries. Restrictions on investment in the Code are open to the same criticism, and attempts by the Internal Revenue Service to curtail certain investment practices have met with a series of failures in the courts. Even worse, the 1950 amendments have not succeeded in correcting the abuses to which they were directed; in fact, they have in themselves created a new set of enforcement problems for the government.

Pressures are now being directed at Congress to revise and expand the Internal Revenue Code restrictions, particularly in regard to donor control and the business activities of foundations. Yet it appears unlikely that Congress will attempt a complete revision of the tax exemption sections of the Code, but will instead again adopt specific provisions directed at curing the most flagrant abuses. It is to be hoped that in the process of amendment, serious thought will be given to the basic question of whether the Internal Revenue Service is to enter into full-scale enforcement of fiduciary duty or is to confine its attention to certain specific aspects of the field.

This question immediately raises problems relating to methods of enforcement and sanctions. On the substantive side, however, whatever decision is reached will require attention to the problem of reconciling any newly imposed standards with those already in force under state law; for when the tax laws set up duties that are more lenient than those imposed through the operation of state law, they give a false impression to fiduciaries in those states where the only active supervision comes from the Internal Revenue Service, and they enlarge the problems of enforcement in those states that are attempting to provide active supervision of charitable affairs.

Problems of Enforcement

The Internal Revenue Service has only indirectly and quite reluctantly become the major source for government supervision of foundations in the United States. Its proper role is still not clear, nor have any real attempts been made either to separate or to consolidate the enforcement powers and programs of the states and the federal government. Since it appears unlikely that the interest of the federal government will abate, no matter what the role of the states may be in the future, it is necessary to inquire into the methods by which both of these sources of power can be put to the best use for improving the operations of foundations.

It must be recognized at the outset that it is entirely possible for the federal government to preempt the entire field of enforcement. This could be done, for example, by means of a statute granting tax exemption only to foundations chartered by the Congress or by a separate federal agency created to supervise foundation activity. Such a statute might lead to the dissolution and reorganization under federal law of almost all existing charitable corporations, a modification of as many trusts as the state courts would permit, and the creation of few, if any, new charitable foundations under state law.[1] In short, it might result in a complete upheaval of the existing pattern for the creation and administration of foundations. To go to the extreme, this same law could define permissible investments for foundations, procedures for management, and the number and type of trustees; and it could even require the participation of government officials in all decisions made by the foundation, whether related to management or to the disbursement of funds.

Putting aside the most extreme elements of such a proposal, the establishment of a separate federal agency to supervise foundations, or even all charitable activities, would have the advantages put forth for most federal programs—uniformity of standards and a centralized administration that could view the needs of the entire country and evaluate proposals for dealing with obsolescence and inefficiency from a central vantage point.

A second method by which the federal government could extend its supervision of foundations would be through expansion of the activities of the Internal Revenue Service. An extension of the Code provisions establishing more explicit limitations on foundation activities could well bring this about with no premeditated design. It is also conceivable that Congress could decide purposefully to rewrite the tax exemption sections of the Internal Revenue Code, providing both an explicit category of permissible purposes and a series of detailed standards for foundation investments and methods of management, in ad-

---

[1] Of course, a donor could decide that it would be better to pay a tax and retain this freedom from federal control. Under present laws, the amount of such tax would not necessarily be confiscatory, but this, too, could be changed.

dition to the existing prohibitions. The tax exemption sections of the Internal Revenue Service could be expanded, and its staff could make annual audits of all foundations. The advantages of such a development would be similar to those of a separate administrative agency, with the added features that there is already in existence a core of personnel familiar with foundation problems, an administrative system that has well-established procedures, and a nationwide organization. There is precedent for such a move in the establishment within the Revenue Service of the Alcohol and Tobacco Tax Division and in its activities in connection with control of the distribution of alcoholic beverages, the production of tobacco, and enforcement of the National Firearms Act.

The disadvantages to either the establishment of a separate federal agency or the expansion of the duties of the Internal Revenue Service stem from the fact that the administration of a nationwide program of supervision tends immediately toward the development of rigid standards that must be applied impartially and impersonally, with little room for adjustment for special situations. Such a tendency is already evident in the procedures required for appeal of decisions by the Service following audit of exempt organizations. A special problem posed by the use of the Internal Revenue Service is that the agency's primary focus is on obtaining revenue and it tends to treat any enterprises relieved from the tax burden as, by definition, suspect. The Service has acknowledged this problem as it has expanded its audit program of tax-exempt organizations. Any expansion of the Service's supervisory duties would increase the difficulty of obtaining personnel familiar with the special problems and special needs of foundations and other philanthropic endeavors.

It would be naive to assume that the federal government is going to curtail its existing programs of supervision of foundation activity. The growth of tax-exempt organizations and the concomitant interest of the Congress in assuring that they are not used for private advantage dictate an expansion rather than a curtailment. It is therefore fruitless to discuss state supervision as an alternative to federal supervision. It is, however, worthwhile to consider whether state programs of supervision can be utilized to complement federal programs, thereby relieving the federal government of some of its concerns, or at the least, relieving the Congress of a need to expand the tax provisions to all areas of foundation operation.

The major advantage of continued reliance on the states for supervision of charity stems from the effectiveness of the sanctions available under state law. Recalling the criteria for effective supervision, it is evident that the weapons available to the tax authorities fall far short of the goal of preserving charitable funds, and may even cause the extinction of some charities. The primary weapon of the tax authorities when there is a breach of fiduciary duty which results in violation of tax law has been withdrawal of exemption, taxation of the charity's assets, and possible imposition of tax on the fiduciary if he was a contributor. Willful violation or fraud may carry a criminal penalty. None of these sanctions serves to further the interest of either the general public or innocent contributors in preserving the funds for charitable use.

In direct contrast, the power of the state courts can be directed against the individual wrongdoers while at all times assuring the protection of the charitable funds. Charitable fiduciaries may be required to restore losses caused by their actions and even to turn over profits made in connection with dealings arising from their position. They may be ordered to stop actions which are wrongful, and they can be removed from their positions of trust. A public representative may void transactions that involve a breach of duty and are inimical to the charitable interests. Corporations that have been misused may be dissolved through state action, or their property may be transferred to another group of fiduciaries better equipped to manage them. None of these sanctions is now available under the tax laws, and in fact, once tax exemption is removed, the federal government no longer supervises a charity's activities so as to assure devotion to charitable purposes; its interest then becomes merely that of obtaining taxes which may be due.

Revisions of the sanctions in the tax laws can make them more appropriate, but it would require extensive revision of the Internal Revenue Code if the federal government is to supplement the states in the imposition of sanctions. Furthermore, such a revision would also require a major reworking of the legal structure in the states if local courts were to be deprived of their powers to determine validity of charitable purposes and to interpret and modify the legal instruments under which charities are created. Changes of such a far-reaching nature are justified only if there is no other workable alternative.

A state program of supervision need not be administered as formally as a nationwide program. There is not as great a need for rigid procedural methods and the delay they may occasion. Thus, the possibilities for advice and consultation which the state may afford to charitable trustees are greater.

Conversely, it must be recognized that political considerations are more likely to influence decisions made by state officials than federal officials; that the efficiency of administration will vary greatly from state to state, increasing the difficulties of obtaining uniformity; and that many of the state governments lack the financial resources to establish and carry on an effective administrative program of supervision.

None of these obstacles is insuperable, however, and it is surely desirable to attempt to improve state performance before abandoning it in favor of exclusively federal supervision. It is interesting to note that in 1960 the English, after more than one hundred years of a centralized system, adopted measures to increase local participation in the supervision of charitable trusts, in the belief that there were positive values to be gained thereby which could not otherwise be achieved.

The first step, however, should be a revision of the sanctions in the federal tax laws to make them more appropriate. The ideal would be to provide the Service with a wide variety of corrective measures similar to those currently available to the states. Included should be the power to force removal of erring fiduciaries, to direct fines or penalty taxes on individuals as well as on foundations, to terminate or dissolve foundations, and to obtain court orders requiring direct action such as divestiture of improper investments.

Furthermore, the Commissioner should be granted discretion to withhold action if the state has taken jurisdiction and is effecting a correction. This would create a basis for a truly cooperative effort and might well serve as an incentive for expanding some of the now dormant state programs. Finally, once tax-exempt status is granted to a charity, that charity should be placed under a continuing duty to file reports with the Service so long as it remains in existence, regardless of whether its tax-exempt status is subsequently revoked or whether it is subject to other penalties. An appropriate time for the enactment of measures of this nature would be in conjunction with congressional action on the proposals made by the Treasury Department in 1965 for amendments to the substantive provisions of the Internal Revenue Code relating to foundations.

If it is concluded that the role of the states in the supervision of charitable funds is to be continued, the inquiry must turn to the methods by which the states can best perform this function. It is now evident that mere reliance on the common law power of the state attorneys general to enforce charities is insufficient. The experiences in New York and Pennsylvania have also indicated that rigid control of chartering provisions is not adequate; nor is reliance on the traditional laws requiring trustees to account periodically to the courts and directors of charitable corporations to file some type of periodic statement with a state official who deals with all corporate entities. Some degree of supervision at the time of creation may be desirable, but it is no guarantee of continued proper performance, regardless of what terms and conditions may be included in a charter or instrument of trust.

An essential requirement for any state program is centralization of responsibility for charitable affairs in one agency or department. Courts have neither the machinery nor the personnel to compel compliance with statutes requiring submission of accounts until delinquents are brought to their attention. The administration of laws requiring periodic reports from corporations is usually carried on by officials who deal with all types of corporations; they are neither trained nor directed to give the special attention needed for scrutiny of charitable enterprises. State tax officials are charged with enforcement of provisions that are, in some instances, similar to those in the Internal Revenue Code, so that they might be considered a source for supervision. Not all states have an income tax, however; and even in those that do, the state tax administrators generally rely on federal determinations rather than challenge exemptions on their own.

There remain two major alternatives: (1) the enactment of legislation to increase the enforcement powers of the attorney general and supplement them with machinery for obtaining information about charities within his jurisdiction and administering an active supervisory program; (2) the creation of an independent state agency to replace the attorney general in his supervisory capacity and carry out a program similar to that of the English Charity Commissioners.

Legislation designed to enhance the ability of the attorney general to supervise charities has been embodied in a Uniform Act, which is now in force with various modifications in 10 states. The administration of these programs, described in detail in Chapters VIII and IX, is varied. It depends greatly on the scope afforded by the statutory language, the attitude of the individual attorney general, the amount of funds, and the consequent size of the staff assigned to carry on the program.

In the fifteen years since the enactment of the first of these programs in New Hampshire, sufficient experience has been gained to evaluate their efficacy and to suggest measures for their improvement. The programs have clearly demonstrated that there existed in each state a need for increased attention to the administration of charities that could not have been met without the supplementary power granted by the legislation. They have also demonstrated that an increase in the powers of the attorney general and the duties of charitable fiduciaries has not meant a usurpation of privately managed charity by government, a possibility feared by some critics of the Uniform Act. No attorney general now regulates the operation of charitable enterprises in his state, nor does it appear possible that he could do so under the terms of any of the legislation passed to date. In fact, the major criticisms of several of the acts are that they have not provided sufficient power to compel fiduciaries to account and that they have not provided means whereby the state can take measures to increase the efficiency of small trusts or assist in the modification of obsolete purposes without resort to prolonged and involved litigation.

These acts have been based on the premise that enforcement of charitable interests can come about only if the officer charged with the duty of enforcement is supplied with information as to the charities under his jurisdiction and the nature of their operations. Registration and reporting are the major components of the statutes, and no attempt has been made to spell out in any detail what is to be done with the reports once they have been filed. Just as with the administration of state and federal tax laws, reliance has been placed on self-assessment and self-audit, supplemented by some form of power to compel compliance with the registration provisions and to gain additional information.

Reliance on the judiciary to correct abuses has not been altered, nor have any major changes been made in the substantive laws defining the duties and powers of fiduciaries. These reporting laws have had more impact through their effects on the trustees and directors who have been confronted with the recognition of their public responsibilities by a duty to report to the state than they have had on the ability of the state itself to uncover abuse, although there are many examples of abuses that have been brought to light and corrected.

The discovery and reactivation of dormant charitable funds which has come about in the course of establishing the supervisory programs represents a great tangible achievement. Equally important has been the stimulation of a search for new methods to solve the problems of obsolescence and impracticability. Centralization of interest in charitable endeavors has led to the formulation and enactment of substantive laws designed to improve the administration of charitable trusts and corporations. Finally, through these programs, the potentialities for positive assistance by government to fiduciaries through consultation and mutual exploration for means for improving charitable operations have been realized. The establishment in Massachusetts and Oregon of advisory committees of private individuals to assist the attorneys general in the drafting of rules and regulations and in the administration of the statutes has increased the possibilities for success of these programs. More important, they have called attention to the positive aspects of a supervisory program which remain to be explored and developed.

Comparison of State Enforcement Programs

The statutes passed in the ten states have differed most strikingly in the language used to define the coverage of the reporting and registration requirements. The New Hampshire act was originally applicable only to testamentary charitable trusts; unfortunately it set a pattern that was adopted by the drafters of the Uniform Act and followed in several of the other states. The exclusion from the reporting requirements of the New Hampshire act of corporate charities and of inter vivos trusts until after the death of the donor drastically curtailed the effectiveness of the statute in reaching the areas of greatest abuse. In several of the other states the exemption provisions have been made applicable to other types of charitable endeavors, primarily hospitals, educational institutions, and homes for the aged. In contrast, the Massachusetts act applies to all public charities except those created for religious purposes. In several states exemption is permitted for charities having small permanent endowments. Few of the states have acts that apply to contingent or remainder interests for charitable purposes.

It is not possible to make out a reasonable case for exclusion of corporations solely on the basis of their form. There is a better argument for excluding charities that operate educational institutions, hospitals, or homes for the aged. In Massachusetts, however, where no such exclusion exists, certain of these institutions were found to have become dormant and their funds subject to misapplication—situations that came to light only as a result of the reporting requirement.

It is not easy to justify exclusion of trusts when the trustee is a professional bank and trust company except on grounds of political expediency. Experience in states where they are not excluded has clearly demonstrated that although the standards of management by bank trustees may be high, these institutions are often poorly equipped to handle the disbursement of special purpose funds and have been found accumulating income because they were "unable to locate suitable beneficiaries." The difficulty raised by an exclusion for religious organizations has been one of definition, particularly in regard to small sects or missionary groups whose religious aims may actually be secondary to their other charitable purposes.

One of the major purposes of any increase in supervision is to assist in assuring efficiency in the operation of charitable trusts and corporations. Many small charitable trusts in all of the states are earning only enough income to cover the expenses of their administration. Excluding them from the reporting requirements means that there is little likelihood that any action will be taken to consolidate them, or to pool their investments, or to secure *cy pres* application. The burden of reporting is no greater for these small charities; in fact, it may often be less than for their richer and larger counterparts. The exemption of small trusts or corporations is, for these reasons, a poor practice.

A large number of states have programs to supervise or regulate charitable organizations that solicit funds from the public. It is preferable to have these programs under the same direction as a program for supervision of charitable trusts and corporations; in this way, organizations can meet the annual reporting requirement of both statutes by filing one form, supplemented by reports at the time of a campaign in the case of the soliciting organizations. Those states that do not have a statute regulating solicitations should certainly make their supervision statutes applicable to these organizations, and should have forms that provide adequately for activities of this nature.

Finally, there is the question of whether registration and reporting should be extended to cover trusts that contain a charitable remainder that has not vested or a contingent charitable gift. In these situations, there is always the possibility that the beneficiary will bring pressure on the trustees to favor him over the charity. If the courts do supervise these trusts and if the attorney general is considered the representative of the charitable interest and made a party to the court accounting, this may be sufficient to warrant exemption from a duty to file periodic reports with the attorney general until the charitable interest vests in use or enjoyment. They should be registered upon creation, however.

Decisions in individual states as to the proper scope of the coverage of reporting requirements may depend ultimately on the availability of other agencies that can provide supervision, such as boards of education or health, and the wisdom of permitting decentralization in those specific areas. No matter what exemptions are decided upon by a state legislature, great care must be taken in the drafting of the provisions relating to both the coverage of the act itself and any specific exemption from registration or reporting lest the common law powers of enforcement of the attorney general be inadvertently narrowed in the process.

Provisions relating to the administration of the supervisory legislation have been a major source of concern to their drafters and a source of controversy among their proponents and critics alike. The difficulty has arisen because of the nature of the office of the attorney general. In many states the position is an elective office, in some, for merely a two-year term. Assistant attorneys general are often appointed by the attorney general, and a high rate of turnover of appointees is the result. In states where the statute does not require the establishment of a separate division to administer the charities program or the designation by the attorney general of a specific assistant to carry out these duties, or where the attorney general is unsympathetic to the concept of supervision or his office is understaffed, the attorney general can ignore or underplay his duties in this field or place them in the hands of an individual who has other, more pressing functions.

Six years after the passage of the original supervision act, New Hampshire enacted an amendment providing that the director of charitable trusts be appointed by the governor, although he would hold the title of assistant attorney general and function under the supervision of the attorney general. The Uniform Act is silent on this subject. Massachusetts, in contrast, requires the establishment of a Division of Public Charities in the office of the attorney general and the appointment by the attorney general of an assistant attorney general to serve as director of public charities. There is no simple answer to the problem of providing continuity in the administration of supervisory programs, since the problems are so different in each state. As a minimum, statutory language requiring the appointment of an assistant attorney general to serve as director of such a program and establishing a permanent division of charities in the office of the attorney general would seem to be required.

Even more important than the method for designating a director is the adequate staffing of his office. Every one of the ten states is plagued by this problem. In South Carolina administration of the reporting statute has been almost nonexistent owing to the attorney general's inability to obtain funds for an adequate staff to handle all of his duties, and to his decision that the charities program was the most expendable. New Hampshire, Rhode Island, Oregon, Iowa, and Ohio each have only one assistant attorney general assigned to charities (and with the exception of Ohio not on a full-time basis), and one administrative assistant. Since the attorney-director must prepare and conduct court litigations, the time remaining for scrutiny of reports, searching out delinquent trustees or directors, or locating dormant trusts is minimal and sporadic.

The greatest lack in staffing, however, has come from the failure of any state but California to provide a group of trained auditors to review accounts and reports and conduct spot-check audits. New Hampshire, Rhode Island, Iowa, and Oregon may be small enough states with few enough charities so that the addition of one more assistant attorney general, or preferably an auditor-investigator, would constitute a sufficient staff. In a state as large as Ohio, the assignment of only one assistant attorney general and one clerk to handle all charitable matters is clearly inadequate.

Although a few states require a fee at the time of registration, only Massachusetts imposes one with the annual report of $3.00, which does not approximate the cost of administration. In contrast, not-for-profit corporations pay a fee when filing most reports with corporation commissions or secretaries of state. In Massachusetts, for example, this fee is $5.00. No provision for fees was included in the Uniform Act for fear that it might be the cause of rejection by the legislatures. The act, presented to the Washington and Texas legislatures in 1965, provided that all reports would be accompanied by a fee proportionate to the funds of the charity, the scale to be set by the state with the aim of meeting the costs of administering the supervisory program. It has been argued that the imposition of a fee represents a diversion of charitable funds; yet if the failure of the states to provide supervision leads to withdrawal of tax-exemption, the diversion of charitable funds to government would be far greater. The use of fees to support a supervisory program may answer those who oppose this type of legislation because they are fearful of any additions to a state budget. It could also provide the means for assuring adequate staff for some of the existing programs and thereby meet one of their greatest needs.

The central feature of each of the statutes under discussion is the creation of a registry of charities and the establishment of a reporting system. It is now evident that the mere enactment of a duty to register and report is insufficient to create and maintain a registry. What is also necessary is that a positive duty be placed on court officials, state tax authorities, and state corporation commissions to supply to the attorney general on a regular basis information on all newly created charities coming to their attention.

After that, it is up to the charity division's staff itself to ferret out cases of noncompliance and dormancy. The most fruitful methods employed in the various states have been a search of probate records and the use of the files of the Internal Revenue Service. It has been found that exclusive reliance on the federal lists is not sufficient, however, particularly in the case of the many older trusts that have never obtained an exemption or have become dormant long before the enactment of the federal reporting laws. A search of probate records and corporation files is therefore extremely valuable, although time-consuming. Furthermore, in states where testamentary trustees are not under a duty to account periodically to a court, it may not be practical to trace the older trusts. Tax and probate records and corporation files are available to some extent in all of the states. Their use generally depends on the size of the staff which can be assigned to undertake the task. The use of law students in Massachusetts to conduct a search of probate records during the summer months is worthy of attention.

The omission in all of the state laws of a clearly defined sanction for use against trustees who fail to register or to file reports has been felt to be a drawback by several of the assistant attorneys general who have directed supervisory programs. They have requested the Commissioners on Uniform State Laws to consider amending the Uniform Act so that it would include provision for the imposition of a fine for failure to report. Another solution that is available to those states that have an income tax is a provision similar to that found in California and Oregon whereby failure to file for a certain period is made a ground for revocation of tax exemption. When the registration act is silent, the remedy is resort to a court of equity to compel compliance, but this may be an involved and time-consuming procedure. Imposition of a fine on erring fiduciaries would appear to be a better solution than taxation of the charity's property.

One may question why fiduciaries should file separate but similar reports with the state and federal governments, as well as with corporation commissions or probate courts in some instances. The objections of fiduciaries to the burden of multiple reporting requirements have been reduced by statutes allowing the attorney general a fairly wide latitude in the type of report to be required and permitting the submission of probate accounts, if they must also be prepared. A balance must be reached, however, between the desire to ease the burden of reporting on fiduciaries and the need to relieve the attorney general's staff of having to sift through a large number of diverse types of financial statements. The ideal would be to have the federal Form 990–A devised so that it would also meet the requirements of the state attorney general. The Service appears to be aware of this need, and it is to be hoped that the federal forms will not be further revised until this problem has been explored with the state attorneys general.

The American Bar Association Committee on Charitable Trusts in 1962 studied the report forms in use in eight of the states. It concluded that the use of alternative forms would be advisable so long as the following minimum information was provided:

1. Balance sheets for the beginning and end of the period.

2. Operating statements including all items of income; additional donations; compensation to trustees, officers, and directors; all other exempt items by categories; and all charitable distributions including an itemized schedule of recipients.

3. Schedules of all investments in categories such as real estate, securities, and other investments; the date of purchase; and both the book and market value. If during the period any investments were sold to or purchased from a founder, trustee, officer, director, or any party related to them, a separate schedule containing a detailed statement of the transaction would also be required.

4. Documents such as a copy of the instrument of trust, corporate charter or deed, to be filed upon initial registration; annual report of any amendments or revisions of the documents and changes in fiduciaries.

This appears to be a comprehensive list of the information required by an attorney general, except that it does not specifically include details as to any loans made to or from the charity, for which there should also be a separate statement.

It must be noted, furthermore, that although this enumeration is appropriate and adequate for charitable trusts and foundations, it is not sufficient to detail the operations of either fund-raising charitable organizations or operating institutions. Although the development of uniform accounting procedures for fund-raising groups has been the subject of study by several independent organizations, no final proposals have been adopted on a national basis, and a major problem for state officials charged with supervision remains. Efforts by the National Health Council and the National Social Welfare Assembly to formulate uniform standards for accounting and financial reporting for voluntary health and welfare agencies resulted in the publication of a formal proposal in 1965. This represented an important first step toward meeting the need for uniform reporting forms and procedures. In certain respects this problem is even more pressing than is the preparation of report forms for foundations and other charitable trusts, since these fund-raising and voluntary groups are not at present under any duty to file periodic reports with the federal government. Finally, once a supervisory statute is in operation, it should be possible to permit fiduciaries to stop reporting to state corporation officials and tax authorities, or other state agencies; at the least, these duplicate reporting requirements should be minimal.

Closely connected with the preparation of report forms is the power given to the attorney general under the Uniform Act and the statutes of all of the states except Oregon to promulgate rules and regulations relating to the operation and administration of the statute. This grant of power was not intended to lead to the establishment of a body of law similar to the Treasury Regulations and Rulings. Rather, its purpose and merit lie in its use for spelling out more explicitly than is advisable in a statute the administrative requirements for compliance with the registration and reporting sections, and for permitting changes in reporting requirements and possibly exemptions for certain groups. One place where this power can be used particularly effectively is in making adjustments for those charities that may be under a duty to comply with the reporting provisions of several states. It can also be used to assist the states and charitable fiduciaries in clarifying the coverage of the act.

The potential use by the public of the files of reports from charities has been considered one of the primary means of assuring proper administration of charitable funds. They must, therefore, be considered public records and open to public inspection. In California, Massachusetts, New Hampshire, and Michigan these records are also considered to have a positive public use, and they are consulted regularly by potential beneficiaries and donors. The creation of files that list charities according to their purposes is extremely valuable if they are to be used in this way. Several of the states permit the attorney general to make rules and regulations regarding the use of these files. The publication of directories in Massachusetts and New Hampshire has received widespread public support, and there has been no evidence to date of any misuse of these lists for private purposes. A ruling that information as to any of these trusts which may also be for the benefit of private individuals, or in which the charitable interest has not vested, or which are under investigation may be withheld from public inspection is a reasonable safeguard to private individuals.

A necessary adjunct to the registration and reporting requirement is the statutory provision in almost all of the states empowering the attorney general to conduct investigations and make inquiries into the administration of the charities under his jurisdiction, and to require testimony and compel the production of books and records. The legislation originally drafted for introduction to the Texas General Assembly in 1965 reflected the belief that the examination of books and records is the only meaningful method of supervision. This is admittedly an extreme view, and its validity cannot be ascertained until such a program is put into operation. In several other states the very existence of such a power is felt to be sufficient to overcome the reluctance of certain charities to cooperate with the state. Until there is evidence of abuse of this power by the attorney general, its potential use remains an important adjunct to proper enforcement.

One of the major failures of the Uniform Act, which must be classified along with the problem of its coverage as a major drawback to effective enforcement, lies in its failure to require that the attorney general be a necessary party to suits affecting charitable trusts and corporations and to compromise settlements, contracts, and judgments. The second tentative draft of the Uniform Act did contain such a provision, but it was omitted from the version finally approved. It is true that the courts in some jurisdictions have imposed such a requirement without legislative direction, but the practice varies widely from state to state and even within some states. The large enforcement programs in New York and Pennsylvania, where such a requirement exists without a registration and reporting statute, indicate the value of the provision. The requirement appears, in fact, to be a minimum one for all states, and it is therefore somewhat ironical that it is not present in several of the states which have enacted a registration statute.

Requiring participation of the attorney general in suits involving charitable interests is the best means for protecting the public interest in trusts that contain a contingent charitable gift or a charitable remainder. When the duty of trustees to file court accountings is strictly enforced, participation of the attorney general in these actions affords a better means of enforcement than the imposition of a duty to report to his office before the charitable interest has vested. It cannot be considered an adequate substitute for all registration and reporting requirements, however, since it omits from any regular surveillance both inter vivos trusts and corporate charities.

The failure of the laws in most of the states to provide machinery that would guarantee *cy pres* application of funds upon the dissolution of charitable corporations has been cited as one of the biggest loopholes in state law. The procedure best designed to meet this need is a requirement that all orders for dissolutions be made by a court, preferably the same court that has jurisdiction over charitable trusts, in a proceeding brought by either the charity itself or the attorney general but to which the attorney general is a necessary party. Court actions of this type must, therefore, be included among the suits to which the attorney general must be joined, as should suits requesting consolidation of corporations.

Finally, in the course of supervision many situations will be found which do not involve violations of state law but which may involve tax abuses, just as supervision to determine tax abuses will uncover breaches of fiduciary duty. A program of continuing cooperation among state and federal tax officials and the attorney general is necessary to improve the administration of all of these programs.

This completes the catalogue of the major components of a program of enforcement administered by a state attorney general, as it is now in force to some degree in nine[1] of the states. Bogert has suggested that consideration be given to the possibility of expanding the power of the attorney general even further to enable him to effect the consolidation of small charities or the pooling of their investments, and to grant him a limited power to form and apply *cy pres* schemes without resort to the courts. These powers have long been exercised by the Charity Commissioners in England with excellent results. As long as provision for appeal to a court were present, this grant of power would not seem to be excessive. It would provide an easier and

---

[1] South Carolina is omitted because there is no program of supervision, despite the existence of a statutory reporting requirement.

far less expensive method for meeting the problems of obsolescence than any now existing. The primary drawback would be the extra burden such provisions might place on an already understaffed office. Consideration of the enactment of any provisions of this nature should only be made if there is assurance of sufficient funds to handle additional duties.

A different approach to supervision of charitable trusts and foundations is to be found in legislation drafted by the office of the attorney general of Texas for introduction in that state. Initial reliance would have been placed not on financial reports prepared and filed by the charities, but on the direct examination of books and records by trained members of the attorney general's staff. All foundations would have been required to submit annual reports merely identifying themselves and their purposes. The attorney general would have broad power to conduct the audits, and the cost of examination would be borne by the foundations.

The success of such a program would depend in great part on the frequency and nature of the examinations. Such a program would undoubtedly assure the discovery of instances of malfeasance more effectively than a system based on perusal of voluntarily prepared financial reports. It lacks, however, the possibilities for positive cooperation with foundations and the public which are implicit in the registration and reporting statutes and which have been of great value in several states.

Alternatives to Supervision by an Attorney General

Each of the facets of a program of supervision could be administered by other agencies of state government. Karst favors the creation of separate State Boards of Charity.[1] His objections to retaining the supervisory programs within the office of the attorney general are that this office may be subject to political pressures that may operate to defeat certain enforcement efforts; that the high turnover of staff found in these offices reduces the effectiveness of the operation of a specialized program of this nature; and that the most important phase of the program is the auditing of reports, which is not basically the function of attorneys.

The merit of the first two of Karst's criticisms can be seen from the

---

[1] Karst, Kenneth, "The Efficiency of the Charitable Dollar: An Unfulfilled State Responsibility," *Harvard Law Review,* vol. 73, 1960, p. 433.

experiences of some of the states but not all of them. Political considerations have not, to date, seriously hampered specific enforcement efforts in any of the states, and it may be questioned whether an independent agency would be any more immune to pressures of this nature. However, changes in administration, noticeably in Ohio, Pennsylvania, and Texas, have altered the entire nature of their enforcement programs, as well as the personnel. On the other hand, this has not occurred in Rhode Island, New Hampshire, or California. Although Massachusetts has had several directors of public charities during a short period of time, the scope of the program has not been curtailed; instead conscious efforts have been made to improve its operation with each change in personnel.

As to the matter of administration, it is true that the first order of business in administration is the analysis and evaluation of reports and that this is properly the task of auditors and accountants. However, correction of abuse is ultimately the responsibility of the attorneys who present individual cases to the courts. They must establish the guidelines for analysis of reports in relation to the legal standards to which fiduciaries are held. California has devised an administrative scheme that recognizes the need for initial direction and final decision by a legal staff, but it has placed responsibility for maintaining the registry and examining the reports in a corps of clerks and auditors headed by a well-trained and highly competent nonlawyer. This appears to be an excellent alternative for the larger states where the justification for a separate agency is the strongest.

If the field of charity continues to grow at the pace it has in the past two decades, the establishment of separate Boards of Charity in some of the larger states will become, not only advisable, but highly desirable. For the present it must be said that the likelihood that this proposal will be accepted in any number of the states appears small.

Other alternatives include the use of state welfare, charity, or correction boards; state taxing agencies; or the courts. As Karst has pointed out, training in social work and government-supported charity administration may not be the ideal background for the supervision of privately managed charity.[1] The experience in Massachusetts indicates that the Welfare Board, pressed with vast responsibilities of its own, was more than willing to relinquish its duties in regard to supervision of privately operated charities to the attorney general when

---

[1] *Ibid.,* p. 481.

the supervisory legislation was passed in 1954. As for the courts, the administration of what is at heart a supervisory program is so remote from the traditional judicial function that serious doubts must be raised as to whether a transfer of supervision to the judiciary would be in any circumstance accepted or carried out. The imposition of administrative duties of this type on the judiciary represents too great a departure from the concept of separation of powers to warrant its adoption unless there is no other feasible alternative.

Political Considerations

Decisions as to who will administer an expanded supervisory program, like decisions as to whether there will be such a program, are basically political questions. The New Hampshire legislation was passed in 1945. By 1964 it had been copied in only nine other states and rejected by almost the same number of others. However, Congressman Patman's proposal to create a separate federal agency to regulate foundation activity has caused many individuals who are fearful of any expansion of government at the federal level to consider possibilities for expanding state supervision. Even more important has been the renewed interest in state programs among attorneys, legislators, and foundation spokesmen who have concluded that the states provide a better situs for supervision. Legal scholars have been unanimous in their support of state supervisory programs; the National Association of Attorneys General retains a continuing interest in their adoption; and the Uniform Act remains a proposal which the Commissioners on Uniform State Laws are directed to support in each state.

Nonetheless, there is little concrete evidence that the Uniform Act will be adopted by any large number of states in the immediate future. It remains to be seen whether the renewed interest in foundation activity generated by the congressional investigations and the Treasury Department studies will be translated into specific efforts to increase the amount of state action in the great majority of states where it is now essentially nonexistent.

Although enactment of legislation similar to the Uniform Act appears to be the most feasible method for increasing state supervision, it is possible that this may not remain the case. It is evident that the Internal Revenue Code will be subject to a series of changes designed to correct abuses by foundations, and that the audit activities of the Service will be further augmented. With the creation of the national registry of tax-exempt organizations and the transfer of information from Form 990–A to an automatic data processing system, the need for filing duplicate reports with the states could even be eliminated. Instead, the federal government could supply state officials with copies of all reports, or with those that suggest a need for investigation by state officials chosen on the basis of a series of criteria drawn up jointly by the states and the Internal Revenue Service. If this should come to pass, the necessity of obtaining legislative support for enactment of a reporting statute in each state would be obviated. There would remain, of course, the need to obtain funds to finance the state activity. The Texas proposal for state audit of charities financed by the charity itself might well provide the answer, although it must be recognized that the financial burden would not be spread equitably.

State supervision of foundations may also be expanded as an adjunct to programs for the regulation of improper solicitation practices. Recent amendments to the Internal Revenue Code have all favored the creation of "publicly supported" charities. Taxpayers receive a bonus for contributions to these charities, but not for gifts to so-called "private" foundations. Moreover, the publicly supported organizations are not required to file information reports with the federal government. The number of these organizations and the amount of funds they receive will undoubtedly increase sharply in the next few years. However, the evidence of abuses in the management of these funds has led an increasing number of states to adopt legislation designed to supervise their operations and in some cases to regulate their solicitation practices. These acts contain the basis for a supervisory program that could easily be expanded to cover nonsoliciting organizations. It must be recognized, however, that if the states are slow in correcting abuses by publicly supported charities, there will be pressure on Congress to increase the federal requirements, and the situation may then parallel what has occurred in regard to foundations.

A final possibility worthy of study is that the federal government provide some type of incentive to the states to improve their supervision of foundations and other charitable endeavors. Legislation granting the Service discretion to withhold federal sanctions if a state takes jurisdiction is a possibility that has already been mentioned. A more effective measure would be some form of financial incentive to the states to establish active programs of their own. A parallel for this may be found in the scheme of administration of the unemployment compensation laws whereby the federal government has enacted minimum standards and requirements for their administration, which, if adopted in any state, will result in a federal subsidy to the state to administer the program once the state program is established; and federal action is confined to assuring that its standards are observed. The parallel between supervision of charities and the administration of unemployment insurance laws is admittedly not very exact, particularly since there is no tax that can be collected and retained by the states to finance an administrative program. However, if the Congress should become convinced of the very real advantages of placing primary responsibility for the supervision of philanthropy in the states rather than in a nationally administered program, and could still be assured that federal revenue interests would not be hampered thereby, there is a chance for the formulation and adoption of such a measure.

Limitations on State Action

Determination of the best method for administering a program of accountability is only a first problem, and it is a far easier one to solve than the more basic but less tangible one of the nature of the program and the attitude of those who are to direct its operation. Legislation can merely supply the guidelines, providing safeguards against brash assumptions of control but sufficient power to permit the correction of abuse. It is here that the law must be made clear, defining reasonable limits for proper action as well as supplying methods for remedying its violation. However, as in all legal endeavors, the human factor must be taken into account. Certain administrators will appear too zealous, others too timid; it must be recognized that evaluations of their attitude will always reflect the bias of the critic. Some fiduciaries will continue to resist any interference with their freedom; others will be critical of any failure to make striking and immediately successful improvements.

It is important to understand the limitations of any program that represents a resolution of such conflicting goals as accountability and freedom of action. Individuals whose acts are unequivocally *mala fides* can file incomplete or even false reports. The imposition of a duty to account is not designed to uncover these acts. They require investigation, audits, and alert enforcement. On the other hand, the honest and well-intentioned, but inexperienced, naive, or even incompetent fiduciary must be assisted without being subjected to the enforcement procedures designed to correct flagrant abuse. Above all, the government officials who supervise charitable operations must remain constantly aware that their duty does not embrace the direction of charitable enterprises, but is limited to assuring the public that those who manage charitable funds are doing so with integrity and propriety.

Fulfilling the Public Trust

If the role of government is to remain thus limited, however, there is a concomitant responsibility upon the charitable fiduciaries themselves. This must start with the recognition of their position of public trust, which is generally accepted by the larger foundations, although still resisted by many of the smaller ones. Responsible foundation officials have advocated the adoption of programs to assure "accountability." Many of them provide tangible evidence of their adherence to the public trust concept by issuing voluntary reports on a regular basis. This practice has even been suggested as a substitute for a requirement that reports be made to the government, but more often it has been proposed as an ancillary duty.

For whatever reasons, an increasingly large number of foundations do issue voluntary reports. The reports vary widely in their content and may include, in addition to financial data, information as to the principles and philosophy of the foundation, its current programs and future plans, and its methods of administration. The first voluntary report issued by a foundation was made by the Peabody Education Fund in 1867. Other large foundations adopted the practice from their inception. In 1956 Andrews published data on the voluntary reports of 107 foundations which were published periodically, although he noted that the record was probably not complete.[1] His summary of the results of foundations reporting pointed out its limitations as a method of accountability:

> Looked at in terms of the whole foundation field, adequate public reporting is characteristic chiefly of the larger foundations and by no means universal among them. The practice is improving and spreading. Indeed, only a few specialists are now able to assemble and reasonably digest the reports already issuing in the mounting paper flood. Adequate reports from all foundations of substantial size would not proportionately increase public understanding and acceptance; more reports now appear than the general public can consume or desires to see. But each foundation has interest groups of its own, and perhaps a geographical

[1] Andrews, F. Emerson, *Philanthropic Foundations*. Russell Sage Foundation, New York, 1956, p. 312.

centralization. These groups need to be informed of its activities; when this is widely possible, public understanding will be much advanced.[1]

Still another method of self-regulation advocated for foundations has been the development of a "code of ethics." The Commissioner of Internal Revenue, in 1963, gave support to the formulation of such a code when he stated that a wholesome substitute for a series of harsh legislative provisions emanating from Congress would be "an effective plan of self-policing by foundations, similar to that already undertaken by certain other tax-exempt groups, most noticeably college fund-raisers and art museums." Specifically, he suggested five courses of action, four of which related to meeting the philosophical as well as the legal requisites of the public trust concept. The fifth was that:

> Foundations should give serious thought to the formulation of a specific code of conduct. I am not proposing a trade association, or the merging of individual identities into some sort of semi-collective entity. But the precise standards which foundations should observe, in commonly experienced situations, have yet to be articulated. It seems to me desirable that the foundations themselves make—and then observe—such a formulation. I believe such a recognized code would be a giant step forward in establishing the kind of meaningful program of self-policing I am advocating.[2]

The major difficulty in implementing this suggestion, of course, arises from the diversity of the groups which can be considered foundations, and the general lack of communication among the vast majority of them. It was not until 1949 that there was any degree of formal cooperation among foundations. Although there are several regional and local groups of foundations which meet periodically to exchange information and hear experts in fields of their interest, no formal organization of foundations has been established which would be in a position to formulate a code of ethics in any respects similar to those established by physicians or attorneys, or even fund-raising organizations. On the contrary, officials of many of the large foundations have studiously avoided the establishment of any organizational ties, partly from a fear that the charges of foundation interlock or of monopoly, raised in both the 1916 and 1954 congressional investigations, would thereby be substantiated, but also from a desire to preserve their individuality and freedom of operation. There are presently only two nationally oriented organizations in the foundation field: The

---

[1] *Ibid.*, p. 321.
[2] Caplin, Mortimer M., "Foundations and the Government: Some Observations on the Future," *Foundation News*, vol. 4, May, 1963, pp. 2–3.

Foundation Library Center and the Council on Foundations. Neither is constituted to speak for all foundations on questions relating to the ethics or professional standards of their directors, trustees, or employees.

The problems of the responsible foundations are obviously manifold and diverse. They tread a difficult path. They must preserve their individuality and their freedom to explore and initiate. Since they are not subject to the usual and well-recognized pressures toward efficiency which are placed on other institutions, and are neither engaged in the competition of the business world nor responsible to an electorate, they must ever recognize the unique and subtle responsibility accorded them. A positive decision has been made by society that the contributions of private philanthropy are of sufficient value to outweigh the consequences of assuring their totally pragmatic efficiency, for as Sacks has pointed out:

> If public regulation were to take the form of detailed and pervasive standards dictating the purposes and methods of operation of each charity, the cure might well be worse than the disease. The basic institutional values of philanthropy—freedom to try new and experimental programs, diversity of approaches, multiple centers of initiative— would probably be seriously diluted, if not destroyed.[1]

His solution is "the development of commonly understood and accepted standards of conduct, plus a willingness to engage in responsible and informed criticism of the actions of sister charities." He has called on the larger foundations to take the lead in encouraging this development of a professional tradition.[2]

Despite the difficulties of implementation, it must be concluded that there is great value in any and all public indications by foundations that they recognize their favored position and accept their public responsibilities. The public must, in a similar vein, accept the proposition that a certain latitude is essential for any institution whose value lies in its ability to experiment and pioneer in the entire range of problems facing mankind. The duty of government is both to the public and to the great number of responsible and dedicated individuals who direct the affairs of foundations. Government must guarantee to the public that standards of loyalty, diligence, and prudence are met; that charitable funds are not chained to the needs of the past but

---

[1] Sacks, Albert M., "The Role of Philanthropy: An Institutional View," *Virginia Law Review,* vol. 46, 1960, pp. 516, 526.

[2] *Ibid.,* p. 528.

are being directed to the solution of existing problems, and to the formulation of methods for meeting the needs of the future; and, finally, that foundations do not become vehicles of special privilege or position. Only as long as government fulfills this function will the public refrain from demands for greater control which may ultimately destroy the ability of foundations to make their unique contributions to society.

APPENDICES

APPENDICES

APPENDIX A. LEGAL REQUIREMENTS FOR CHARITABLE TRUSTS AND CORPORATIONS, BY STATE

TABLE 1. STATE LEGAL REQUIREMENTS: CHARITABLE TRUSTS

	1	2	3	4	5	6	7	8
			Duty to Account		Statutory Requirement of Notice to Attorney General in Suits Involving Charitable Trusts			
State	Statutory Reference	Uniform Laws[a]	Testamentary Trustees	Inter Vivos Trustees		Limit on Investments	Cy Pres	Power of Attorney General
Alabama	Code of Ala. (1958)	U.F.A., Tit. 19A, secs. 1 to 14. U.P.I.A., Tit. 58, secs. 75 to 87	None	None	None	Legal list (Tit. 58, secs. 47 ff.)	Yes (Tit. 47, sec. 145)	To enforce a public charity is a common law duty. *State v. Bibb*, 234 Ala. 46 (1937)
Alaska	Alaska Stat. (1962)	U.C.F.T.A., sec. 06.35.010	Trust cos. accountable to all interested parties (sec. 06.25.150)	None	None	None	No	No specific statement in case or statute
Arizona	Ariz. Rev. Stat. Ann. (1956)	U.F.A., secs. 14-1101 ff. U.P.I.A., secs. 14-1081 ff. U.C.T.F.A., secs. 6-281 ff.	May report or be compelled to report by Super. Ct. (secs. 14-1021 [Supp. 1964])	None	Representative of beneficiaries in suits to determine heirship if will creates a charitable trust and no trustee designated. (sec. 14-642 [Supp. 1964]	Generally governed by common law, other investments authorized by stat. (see sec. 14-1021 [Supp. 1964]) for example	No	No specific statement in case or statute other than as listed in 5
Arkansas	Ark. Stat. Ann. (1947)	U.C.T.F.A., secs. 58-106 ff. U.T.R.A., sec. 68-1701	None	None	None	Prudent man rule (sec. 58-302 [Supp. 1963])	Yes. See *Bossen v. Women's Christian National Library Assn.*, 216 Ark. 334 (1949)	Common law powers. See *State v. Van Buren School District No. 42*, 191 Ark. 1096 (1936)
California	West's Ann. Cal. Stat.	U.S.F.S.T.A. Corp. Code, secs. 30000 to 300010 U.C.T.F.A., Fin. Code, sec. 1564 U.P.I.A., Civ. Code, secs. 730 to 730.15 U.S.T.C.P.A., Gov. Code, secs. 12580 to 12595	Periodic financial reports to the atty. gen. (Gov. Code, sec. 12586 [1963]) May report or be required to report by the Super. Ct. (Prob. Code, secs. 1120 and 1121 [Supp. 1964])	Periodic financial reports to the atty. gen. (Gov. Code, sec. 12586 [1963])	Necessary party to termination or modification proceedings (Gov. Code, sec. 12491 [1963]), and to estates involving charitable trusts (Prob. Code, sec. 1080 [Supp. 1964])	Prudent man rule (Civ. Code, sec. 2261 [1954])	Yes. See *Estate of Peabody*, 154 Cal. 173 (1908)	May institute appropriate proceedings to secure compliance with uniform supervision law (Gov. Code, sec. 12591 [1963]). May investigate transactions to see if they comply with trust (Gov. Code, sec. 12588 [1963])

[a] See p. 478 for the Code to Uniform Laws.

TABLE 1. STATE LEGAL REQUIREMENTS: CHARITABLE TRUSTS (Continued)

| | | Duty to Account | | Statutory Requirement of Notice to Attorney General in Suits Involving | | | |
| 1 | 2 | 3 | 4 | 5 | 6 | 7 | 8 |
State / Statutory Reference	Uniform Laws[a]	Testamentary Trustees	Inter Vivos Trustees	Charitable Trusts	Limit on Investments	Cy Pres	Power of Attorney General
Colorado Colo. Rev. Stat. Ann. (1953)	U.C.T.F.A., secs. 14-18-1 to 14-18-6. U.F.A., secs. 57-1-1 to 57-1-14. U.P.I.A., secs. 57-4-1 ff.	Render ann. report to county ct. unless will provides otherwise (sec. 153-14-11 [Supp. 1960])	None	Necessary party to accountings if unknown beneficiaries (sec. 153-14-1)	Prudent man rule (secs. 57-3-1 to 57-3-4)	Judicially affirmed but not applied. See Fisher v. Minshall, 102 Colo. 154 [1938])	Is made a party to litigation. See Ireland v. Jacobs, 114 Colo. 168 (1945)
Connecticut Conn. Gen. Stat. (1958)	U.P.I.A., secs. 45-110 ff. U.T.A.T.A., secs. 45-173a	Unless excused in will or less than $2000, ann. report to prob. ct. (secs. 45-267 and 268 [Supp. 1963])	Community trusts ann. report to prob. ct. (sec. 45-82)	See col. 8	Prudent man rule (secs. 45-88 and 89 [Supp. 1963])	Yes. See sec. 52-498 and Duncan v. Higgins, 129 Conn. 136 at 140 (1943)	To represent the public in protection of gifts for public or charitable purposes (sec. 3-125). Investigatory power when complaint made. Healy v. Loomis Institute, 102 Conn. 410 (1925)
Delaware Del. Code Ann. (1953)	U.T.R.A., Tit. 6, sec. 1101 ff.	Report to county register of chancery no more than once in every two years unless waived by will (Tit. 12, secs. 3521 and 3522 [Supp. 1962])	Exempt except on order of ct. (Tit. 12, sec. 3521 [Supp. 1962])	None	Prudent man rule (Tit. 12, sec. 3301)	Yes, applied. See Delaware Trust Co. v. Graham et al., 61 A.2d 110 (Del. Ch. 1948)	Proper party in a suit involving the existence or administration of a charitable trust. See Trustees of New Castle Common v. Gordy et al., 33 Del. Ch. 196 (1952)
District of Columbia D.C. Code Ann. (1961)	U.C.T.F.A., secs. 26-701 ff. U.F.A., secs. 28-2301 ff. U.F.T.A., secs. 28-2321 ff. U.S.T.A., secs. 28-2901 ff.	None	If ct. supervised, must file ann. report (local Civil Rule 22 of the dist. ct.)	None	Rule 23 of U.S. Dist. Ct. for D.C. contains list and limitations	Judicially affirmed and applied. See Noel v. Olds, 138 F.2d 581 at 586 (1943)	To bring action on behalf of unknown beneficiaries of a charity. U.S. v. Mt. Vernon Mortgage Corporation, 128 F. Supp. 629 (1954)

[a] See p. 478 for the Code to Uniform Laws.

465

TABLE 1. STATE LEGAL REQUIREMENTS: CHARITABLE TRUSTS (Continued)

	1	2	3	4	5	6	7	8
			Duty to Account		Statutory Requirement of Notice to Attorney General in Suits Involving Charitable Trusts			
State	Statutory Reference	Uniform Laws[a]	Testamentary Trustees	Inter Vivos Trustees		Limit on Investments	Cy Pres	Power of Attorney General
Florida	Fla. Stat. Ann. (1964)	U.C.T.F.A., secs. 655.29 ff. U.P.I.A., secs. 690.01 ff. U.S.F.S.T.A., secs. 610.021 ff. U.S.T.A., secs. 614.01 ff. U.T.A.L., secs. 691.01 ff. U.T.R.A., secs. 673.01 ff.	Ann. financial report to ct. (sec. 737.12). Ct. may override provision in will waiving necessity of accounting (sec. 737.23)	Report to ct. only if trust instrument so provides (sec. 737.24)	State's atty. for judicial cir. represents unknown beneficiaries (sec. 737.251)	Prudent man rule (sec. 518.11 [1962]).	Yes. See *Lewis v. Guillard*, 61 Fla. 819 (1911)	To enforce trusts. See *State ex rel Landis v. S. H. Kress & Co.*, 115 Fla. 189 (1934); and *Jordan v. Landis*, 128 Fla. 604 (1937). Note also col. 5
Georgia	Ga. Code Ann. (1959)	None	*Ford v. Thomas*, 111 9a.493 (1900) exempts trustees of charities from ann. accounting	None	Necessary if decision involves rights of beneficiaries; may be solicitor gen. of cir. instead (sec. 108–212 [Supp. 1963])	Legal list (secs. 108–417 ff.)	Yes. See secs. 113–815 and 108–202	See col. 3
Hawaii	Hawaii Rev. Laws (1955)	U.F.A., secs. 189–1 ff.	Ann. acct. to ct. who appointed him unless prior trustee not required to report by stat. or instrument (sec. 340–4)	None	None	Prudent man rule (secs. 179–14 [Supp. 1961] and 340–6)	Not yet applied	Dicta in *Hite v. The Queens Hospital*, 36 Haw. 250 (1942) infers common law powers on atty. gen.
Idaho	Idaho Code Ann. (1948)	U.S.F.S.T.A., secs. 68–901 ff. U.C.T.F.A., secs. 68–701 ff. U.F.A., secs. 68–301 ff.	May report or be required to report to prob. ct. (sec. 15–1136 [Supp. 1963])	None		Prudent man rule (secs. 68–501 to 68–505 [Supp. 1959])	Undecided	To supervise and enforce charitable trusts and corps. (sec. 67–1401 [Supp. 1963])

[a] See p. 478 for the Code to Uniform Laws.

TABLE 1. STATE LEGAL REQUIREMENTS: CHARITABLE TRUSTS (Continued)

	1	2	Duty to Account		5	6	7	8
State	Statutory Reference	Uniform Laws[a]	3 Testamentary Trustees	4 Inter Vivos Trustees	Statutory Requirement of Notice to Attorney General in Suits Involving Charitable Trusts	Limit on Investments	Cy Pres	Power of Attorney General
Illinois	Ill. Ann. Stat. (1963)	U.C.T.F.A., ch. 16½, secs. 57 ff. U.F.A., ch. 98, secs. 234 ff. U.P.I.A., ch. 30, secs. 159 ff U.S.T.A., ch. 32, secs. 416 ff. U.S.T.C.P.A., ch. 14, secs. 51 to 64. U.T.R.A., ch. 121½, secs. 166 ff.	Periodic financial report to atty. gen. (ch. 14, sec. 57)		Required in adversary proceedings (ch. 14, sec. 57)	Prudent man rule (ch. 148, sec. 32 [1964])	Yes	May institute proceedings to secure proper administration of trust (ch. 14, sec. 59)
Indiana	Ind. Ann. Stat. (1949)	U.F.A., secs. 31–101 ff. U.S.F.S.T., secs. 31–901 ff. U.T.R.A., secs. 51–601 ff.	Ann. financial report to cir. ct. by trustees of property for benevolent purposes (sec. 31–712 [Supp. 1964])		Court to notify atty. gen. when breach of trust has occurred (sec. 31–712 [Supp. 1964])	Prudent man rule (sec. 31–507 [Supp. 1964])	Yes. See secs. 26–631 and 632; and Quinn v. Peoples Trust & Savings Co. 223 Ind. 317 (1945)	To maintain litigation involving public charitable trusts. See Boice v. Mallers, 121 Ind. App. 270 (1951)
Iowa	Iowa Code Ann. (1950)	U.C.T.F.A., secs. 633–126.1 ff. U.S.F.S.T., secs. 633–130 to 138. U.S.T., secs. 493A.1 ff.	Ann. financial report to ct. unless waived by will (sec. (633.700 [Supp. 1964]) Ann. financial report to atty. gen. (sec. 682.57)	Ann. financial report to atty. gen. (sec. 682.57 [Supp. 1964])	Yes (sec. 682.49 [Supp. 1964])	Legal list (sec. 682.23 [Supp. 1964])	Applied. See Lupton v. Leander Clark College, 194 Iowa 1008 (1922)	May investigate charitable trusts to see if they are being properly administered (sec. 682.53)

a See p. 478 for the Code to Uniform Laws.

TABLE 1. STATE LEGAL REQUIREMENTS: CHARITABLE TRUSTS (Continued)

		Duty to Account					
		3	4	5	6	7	8
	2	Testamentary Trustees	Inter Vivos Trustees	Statutory Requirement of Notice to Attorney General in Suits Involving Charitable Trusts	Limit on Investments	Cy Pres	Power of Attorney General
State 1	Uniform Laws[a]						
Kansas	Kan. Gen. Stat. Ann. (1949)	U.C.T.F.A., secs. 9-1609 and 9-1610. U.P.I.A., secs. 58-901 ff. U.S.F.S.T.A., secs. 17-4903 ff. U.T.A.A., secs. 17-5001 ff.	Ann. acct. with prob. ct. only if ct. or will demands accounting (sec. 59-1609)		None	Prudent man rule (sec. 17-5004 [Supp. 1961])	Yes. See *Forbes v. Board of Education,* 7 Kan. App. 452 (1898)	Has power to enforce. See *Trautman v. DeBoissiere Odd Fellows' Orphans' Home and Industrial School Association,* 66 Kan. 1 (1903)
Kentucky	Ky. Rev. Stat. (Supp. 1962)	U.P.I.A., secs. 386.180 ff.	Biennial financial report to county ct. (sec. 25.175)	None unless under control of ct.	None	Prudent man rule (sec. 386.020)	Yes	Has power to supervise the administration of established charitable trusts. See *Commonwealth v. Gardner,* 327 S.W.2d 947 (1959)
Louisiana	La. Rev. Stat. (1950)	U.F.A., secs. 9:3801 ff. U.P.I.A., secs. 9:2141 ff. U.P.L., secs. 9:2421 ff. U.S.F.S.T.A., secs. 9:3831 ff. U.T.A., secs. 9:2081 ff. U.W.L., secs. 9:2401 ff.	Ann. financial report to beneficiary and ct. (sec. 9:2088 [Supp. 1964])	None unless required by instrument or ct. (sec. 9:2088 [Supp. 1964])	None	Prudent man rule (sec. 9:2091 [Supp. 1964])	Yes (sec. 9:2331 to 9:2337 [Supp. 1963])	No specific statement in case or statute

[a] See p. 478 for the Code to Uniform Laws.

TABLE 1. STATE LEGAL REQUIREMENTS: CHARITABLE TRUSTS (Continued)

	1	2	Duty to Account		5	6	7	8
			3	4				
State	Statutory Reference	Uniform Laws^a	Testamentary Trustees	Inter Vivos Trustees	Statutory Requirement of Notice to Attorney General in Suits Involving Charitable Trusts	Limit on Investments	Cy Pres	Power of Attorney General
Maine	Me. Rev. Stat. Ann. (1954)	U.S.F.S.T.A., Tit. 13, secs. 641 ff.	Financial report every three years to judge of prob. (Tit. 618, sec. 400 [Supp. 1964])	Same as col. 3, unless excused by instrument, if trustee confirmed by ct. (Tit. 18, secs. 4051 ff. [Supp. 1964])	Yes	Prudent man rule (Tit. 18, sec. 4054 [Supp. 1964])	Yes. See Stevens v. Smith, 134 Me. 175 (1936)	To enforce the due application of funds given to pub. charities (Tit. 5, sec. 194 [Supp. 1964])
Maryland	Md. Ann. Code (1957)	U.C.T.F.A., art. 16, sec. 196. U.F.A., art. 37A, secs. 1 to 13. U.P.I.A., art. 75B, secs. 1 to 10. U.T.R.A., art. 95½, secs. 1 to 20.	Interested party may petition for trust to be administered under ct. jurisdiction and then must acct. ann. unless instrument provides otherwise (Md. Rules of Procedure 1372 and 1374)	Annual financial report to attorney general, (ch. 12, sec. 8F [Supp. 1965])		Prudent man rule in effect by common law. Authorized list (art. 49A, sec. 1 to 5)	Yes (art. 16, sec. 196)	To bring suit for enforcement of charitable trusts (art. 16, sec. 195)
Massachusetts	Mass. Gen. Laws Ann. (1958)	None	Ann. financial report to prob. ct. (ch. 204, sec. 1). Ann. financial report to atty. gen. (ch. 12, sec. 8F. [Supp. 1965])	Annual financial report to attorney general, (ch. 12, sec. 8F [Supp. 1965])	Required in all judicial proceedings regarding charities (ch. 12, sec. 8G)	Prudent man rule. See Harvard College v. Amory, 9 Pick. 446, 461 (Mass. 1830)	Yes	To enforce the due application of funds given to pub. charity (ch. 12, sec. 8)
Michigan	Mich. Stat. Ann.	U.C.T.F.A., secs. 23.1141 ff. U.S.T.C.P.A., secs. 26.1200(1) to (16)	Ann. financial report to prob. ct. (sec. 27.3178 (289)). Periodic financial report to atty. gen., (sec. 26.1200(6) [Supp. 1963])	Periodic financial report to atty. gen. (sec. 26.1200(6) [Supp. 1963])	Yes (sec. 26.1200 (1) and (6) [Supp. 1963])	Prudent man rule, with restricting list (secs. 26.85 [1957] and 27.3178(288) [1962])	Yes. See Gifford v. First National Bank, 285 Mich. 58 at 69 (1938)	To represent people of state to enforce charitable trusts, to investigate whether properly administered (secs. 26.1200(4) and (8) [Supp. 1963]

^a See p. 478 for the Code to Uniform Laws.

TABLE 1. STATE LEGAL REQUIREMENTS: CHARITABLE TRUSTS (Continued)

	1	2	3	4	5	6	7	8
			Duty to Account		Statutory Requirement of Notice to Attorney General in Suits Involving Charitable Trusts			
State	*Statutory Reference*	*Uniform Laws*[a]	*Testamentary Trustees*	*Inter Vivos Trustees*		*Limit on Investments*	*Cy Pres*	*Power of Attorney General*
Minnesota	Minn. Stat. Ann. (1947)	U.F.A., secs. 520.01 ff. U.S.F.S.T.A., secs. 520.21 ff. U.S.T.A., secs. 302.01 ff. U.T.R.A., secs. 522.01 ff.	Ann. accts. to dist. ct. when appointment of trustee of an express trust confirmed by ct. (sec. 501.34). Mandatory for testamentary trustees. (Rule 28 of Code of Rules for Dist. Ct.)		Yes (sec. 501.12 (3))	Prudent man rule (sec. 501.125)	Yes (sec. 501.12(3) and 501.12(5))	To represent beneficiaries and enforce charitable trusts (sec. 501.12(3))
Mississippi	Miss. Code Ann. (1942)	U.C.T.F.A., sec. 5198.5. U.S.F.S.T.A., secs. 5359–31 ff. U.S.T.A., secs. 5359–01 ff. U.T.R.A., secs. 5080–01 ff.	Trustee must report to chancery or cir. ct. when required to do so by law or creating instrument (sec. 1273–10 [Supp. 1962])		None	Prudent man rule (sec. 421.5 [1956])	Not yet applied	Common law power. See dicta in *Dunn Construction Co. v. Craig,* 191 Miss. 682 (1941)
Missouri	Mo. Stat. Ann.	U.C.T.F.A., secs. 363.225. U.F.A., secs. 456.240 ff. U.S.T.A., secs. 403.010 ff.	Those appointed by ct. must report to it ann. sec. 456.220). Others may be required to report (sec. 456.225 [Supp. 1964])		Required (sec. 456.225(4) [Supp. 1964])	Prudent man rule. See *St. Louis Union Trust Co. v. Toberman,* 235 Mo. App.2d 559 (1940)	Yes. See *Thatcher v. St. Louis,* 335 Mo. 1130 at 1142 (1934)	To enforce charitable trusts, see *Dickey v. Volker,* 321 Mo. 235 (1928)

[a] See p. 478 for the Code to Uniform Laws.

TABLE 1. STATE LEGAL REQUIREMENTS: CHARITABLE TRUSTS (Continued)

	1	2	3	4	5	6	7	8
			Duty to Account		Statutory Requirement of Notice to Attorney General in Suits Involving Charitable Trusts			
State	Statutory Reference	Uniform Laws[a]	Testamentary Trustees	Inter Vivos Trustees		Limit on Investments	Cy Pres	Power of Attorney General
Montana	Mont. Rev. Codes Ann.	U.C.T.F.A., secs. 5–1401 ff. U.P.I.A., secs. 67–1901 ff.	May acct. and dist. ct. may require accounting (sec. 91–4201 [1964])	None	None	Mont. Const. art. V, sec. 37, prohibits investment in private corps. (See Code, secs. 86–504 [1964] and 35–142 1961])	Undecided	Has common law powers to enforce trusts. See State ex rel Ford v. Young, 54 Mont. 401 (1918)
Nebraska	Neb. Rev. Stat.	U.C.T.F.A., secs. 24–601.01 and .02. U.S.F.S.T.A., secs. 24–621 ff. U.S.T.A., secs. 21–201 ff. U.T.R.A., secs. 69–701 ff.	May acct. and ct. may require accounting (sec. 24–607 [1956])	None	Required (sec. 24–612 [1956])	Legal list subject to ct. approval (sec. 24–601 [Supp. 1961])	Yes. See First Trust Co. v. Thompson, 147 Neb. 366, 370 (1946)	May bring action to enforce charitable trusts, In re Estate of Giblny, 147 Neb. 117 at 127 (1946), along with county atty. (sec. 30–240 [1956])
Nevada	Nev. Rev. Stat. (1963)	U.C.T.F.A., secs. 164.070 ff. U.F.A., secs. 162.010 ff. U.S.F.S.T.A., secs. 162150 ff. U.T.A.A., secs. 165.010 ff. U.T.A., secs. 163.010 ff. U.T.R.L., secs. 93.010 ff.	Ann. financial reports to dist. ct. (see secs. 165.040, 165.140, 165.230, 153.020, 164.020)		Required (sec. 165.230)	Prudent man rule (sec. 164.050)	Undecided.	See col. 5 and sec. 81.450.

[a] See p. 478 for the Code to Uniform Laws.

471

TABLE 1. STATE LEGAL REQUIREMENTS: CHARITABLE TRUSTS (Continued)

State	1 Statutory Reference	2 Uniform Laws[a]	Duty to Account		5 Statutory Requirement of Notice to Attorney General in Suits Involving Charitable Trusts	6 Limit on Investments	7 Cy Pres	8 Power of Attorney General
			3 Testamentary Trustees	4 Inter Vivos Trustees				
New Hampshire	N.H. Rev. Stat. Ann. (1955)	U.C.T.F.A., secs. 391:1 ff. U.T.A.T.A., sec. 563–A	Ann. acct. required to judge of prob. (sec. 564:19), and to the atty. gen. (sec. 7:28)	Ann. financial report to the atty. gen. after death of settlor (sec. 7:38)	Yes (see sec. 7:29)	Prudent man rule (sec. 564:18 as amended by Acts 1961, c. 94)	Yes. See *Trustees of Pittsfield Academy v. Attorney General*, 95 N.H. 2d. 5 (1948)	May investigate and take appropriate action (sec. 7:24)
New Jersey	N.J. Stat. Ann. (1953)	U.S.F.S.T.A., secs. 14–8–1 ff. U.F.A., secs. 3A–41 ff.	To acct. to ct. at least every three years (sec. 3A:9–3)	Encouraged but not required (sec. 3A:9–10 and 129 N.J.Eq. 377 [1941])	Required (Supper Ct. Civ. Prac. Rules 4:117–6 and 4:99–7)	Prudent man rule (sec. 3A:15–19) with limit to amount held in single place (sec. 3A:15–20 [Supp. 1964])	Judicially confirmed and applied. See *Wilber v. Owens*, 2 N.J. 197 (1949)	Common law duty to enforce pub. charities. See *Passaic National Bank & Trust Co. v. E. Ridgelawn Cemetery*, 137 N.J.Eq. 603 (1945)
New Mexico	N.M. Stat. Ann. (1953)	U.C.T.F.A., secs. 33–1–21 ff. U.F.A., secs. 33–1–1 ff. U.P.I.A., secs. 33–5–1 ff. U.T.A., secs. 33–3–1 ff. U.T.A.A., secs. 33–2–1 ff.	Ann. financial report to dist. ct. (sec. 33–2–3)	Ann. financial report to dist. ct. (secs. 33–2–13 and 33–2–22)	Required (sec. 33–2–22)	Prudent man rule (sec. 33–1–16)	Undecided	To represent interests of beneficiaries in charitable trusts (U.T.A.A. secs. 33–2–1 to 33–2–22)

[a] See p. 478 for the Code to Uniform Laws.

TABLE 1. STATE LEGAL REQUIREMENTS: CHARITABLE TRUSTS (Continued)

State	Statutory Reference	Uniform Laws[a]	Duty to Account		Statutory Requirement of Notice to Attorney General in Suits Involving Charitable Trusts	Limit on Investments	Cy Pres	Power of Attorney General
			Testamentary Trustees	Inter Vivos Trustees				
	1	2	3	4	5	6	7	8
New York	N.Y. Laws	U.S.F.S.T.A., Pers. Prop. Law, sec. 183.1. U.T.R.A., Pers. Prop. Law, chs. 50 ff.	May report to Surr. Ct. or sometimes Sup. Ct. or be required to report (Surr. Ct. Act, secs. 251 to 274) and for express trusts (Civ. Prac. Acts, secs. 1310 to 1319)	Sup. Ct. jurisdiction	Yes (see Pers. Prop. Law, sec. 12, and Real Prop. Law, sec. 113, and Surr. Ct. Act, sec. 54)	Prudent man rule Pers. Prop. Law (sec. 21) sets forth limitations	Yes (see Pers. Prop. Law, sec. 12(2), and Real Prop. Law, sec. 113 (2))	To enforce charitable trusts by proper ct. proceedings. (Pers. Prop. Law, sec. 12, and Real Prop. Law, sec. 113 (3))
North Carolina	N.C. Gen. Stat. (1950)	U.C.T.F.A., secs. 36-47 to 36-52. U.F.A., secs. 32-1 to 32-13, U.P.I.A., secs. 37-1 to 37-15. U.S.F.S.T.A., secs. 32-14 to 32-24. U.T.A., secs. 36-24 to 36-46. U.T.R.A., secs. 45-46 to 45-66.	Ann. acct. to clerk of Super. Ct. (secs. 36-19 and 36-20)			Prudent man rule. *Sheets v. J. G. Flynt Tobacco Co.*, 195 N.C. 149 (1928). (See also secs. 36-1 to 36-5.1)	Judicially affirmed. See *Brooks et al. v. Duckworth et al.*, 234 N.C. 549 (1951)	To bring action to enforce (sec. 36-20)
North Dakota	N.D. Cent. Code (1960)	U.S.F.S.T.A., secs. 10-18.1-01 ff. U.T.A.T.A., secs. 56-07-01 ff. U.T.R.A., secs. 41-18-10 ff.	File ann. report with dist. ct. if placed under supervision of ct. on application of trustee or beneficiary (secs. 59-04-02 and 59-04-17)		Yes (secs. 59-04-02 and 59-04-17)	Prudent man rule for trust cos. Legal list subject to ct. approval for all others (secs. 30-13-22 and 6-10-15)	Undecided.	Interested party to public or charitable trusts (sec. 59-04-02)

[a] See p. 478 for the Code to Uniform Laws.

TABLE 1. STATE LEGAL REQUIREMENTS: CHARITABLE TRUSTS (Continued)

	1	2	3	4	5	6	7	8
			Duty to Account		Statutory Requirement of Notice to Attorney General in Suits Involving Charitable Trusts			
State	Statutory Reference	Uniform Laws[a]	Testamentary Trustees	Inter Vivos Trustees		Limit on Investments	Cy Pres	Power of Attorney General
Ohio	Ohio Rev. Code Ann.	U.C.T.F.A., secs. 1117.01 ff. U.F.A., secs. 1339.03 ff.	Ann. financial report to prob. ct. (sec. 1719.05 [1964]) and biennial report to atty. gen. (sec. 109.31 [1953])		Necessary party to termination or modification proceedings (sec. 109.25 [Supp. 1964])	Prudent man rule as to 35%, legal list and other ct. approved items (sec. 2109.37 [Supp. 1964])	Yes	To enforce and restrain abuse of charitable trusts (sec. 109.24 [1953])
Oklahoma	Okla. Stat. Ann. (1963)	U.C.T.F.A., Tit. 60, sec. 162. U.P.I.A., Tit. 60, secs. 175.3, 175.26 to 175.36. U.T.A.T.A., Tit. 84, sec. 301.	Dist. ct. may require accting. (Tit. 60, sec. 175.23)		Required (Tit. 60 sec. 175.18)	Prudent man rule (Tit. 60, sec. 161)	Strong evidence it would be applied, but has not yet been applied. See In re Nuckols Estate, 199 Okla. 175 (1947)	
Oregon	Ore. Rev. Stat.	U.C.T.F.A., sec. 709.170 U.P.I.A., secs. 129.010 ff. U.S.T.C.P.A., secs. 128.610 ff.	Must render ann. report to atty. gen. (sec. 128.070 [Supp. 1965]) and periodic reports to atty. gen. 128.660 [Supp. 1965])		Necessary party to termination or modification proceedings (sec. 128.710 [Supp. 1965])	Prudent man rule (sec. 128.020 [Supp. 1965])	Yes. See In re Stouffer's Trust, 188 Or. 218 (1950)	To investigate transactions to see if comply with trust (sec. 128.680 [Supp. 1965])
Pennsylvania	Pa. Stat.	U.F.A., Tit. 20, secs. 3311 ff. U.P.I.A., Tit. 20, secs. 3470.1 to 3470.15.	May acct. and be required to acct. on termination (Tit. 20, sec. 320.981 [1950]), and may acct. at other times. See also col. 4.	Orphan's ct. may require accounting charitable trustees at any time. In re McKee's Estate, 378 Pa. 607 (1954)	Yes (Tit. 20, sec. 301.10 [1950]) re cy pres and Garrison's Estate, 391 Pa. 234 (1958) generally	Prudent man rule (Tit. 20, secs. 821.6 and 821.9; see also Tit. 20, secs. 821.2 to 821.20 [Supp. 1963])	Yes (Tit. 20 sec. 301.10 [1950])	Broad common law powers as did the atty. gen. under English law. See Commonwealth ex rel. Minerd v. Margiotti, 325 Pa. 17 (1936)

[a] See p. 478 for the Code to Uniform Laws.

474

TABLE 1. STATE LEGAL REQUIREMENTS: CHARITABLE TRUSTS (Continued)

	1	2	Duty to Account 3	Duty to Account 4	5	6	7	8
State	Statutory Reference	Uniform Laws[a]	Testamentary Trustees	Inter Vivos Trustees	Statutory Requirement of Notice to Attorney General in Suits Involving Charitable Trusts	Limit on Investments	Cy Pres	Power of Attorney General
Rhode Island	R.I. Gen. Laws Ann. (1956)	U.F.A., secs. 18-4-16 to 22. U.S.F.S.T.A., secs. 18-11-1 to 18-11-11.	Ann. financial report to atty. gen. (sec. 18-9-13). A trustee may apply to Super. Ct. for allowance of his account or accounts (sec. 18-6-3).		Yes (sec. 18-9-5)	Prudent man rule (sec. 18-4-2 [Supp. 1964])	Yes (sec. 18-4-1)	Common law and special stat. power to investigate (sec. 18-9-9)
South Carolina	S.C. Code Ann. (1962)	U.S.F.S.T.A., secs. 62-451 ff. U.T.A.T.A., secs. 19-295 ff.	All ct. appointed trustees to report to ct. ann. and allowance required (sec. 67-57.2); ann. financial reports to atty. gen. (sec. 67-82)		None	Legal list (sec. 67-58)	Not yet applied.	To enforce due application of funds given for charitable purposes (sec. 1-240)
South Dakota	S.D. Code (1939)	U.C.T.F.A., secs. 6.0901 ff. U.F.L., secs. 6.0701 ff. U.T.I.L., secs. 59.05.	Trustees of ct. supervised trusts to file report ann. and finally with cir. ct. (sec. 33.2606)		Yes (see col. 8)	Prudent man rule (sec. 6.0801 [Supp. 1960])	Yes (sec. 59.0603 [Supp. 1960])	To represent beneficiaries and enforce trusts by proper proceedings in the cts. (secs. 59.0603 [Supp. 1960])
Tennessee	Tenn. Code Ann. (1955)	U.C.T.F.A., secs. 35-402 ff. U.F.A., secs. 35-201 to 214. U.P.I.A, secs. 35-701 to 715. U.S.F.S.T.A., secs. 35-901 to 911.	State may bring action to require accounting (sec. 23-2802); Ct. of Chancery may compel testamentary trustee to report (See *Vaccaro v. Cicalla*, 89 Tenn. 63 [1890]); and resigning trustee to report (sec. 35-106)	None	None	Prudent man rule (sec. 35-320) with authorized list (secs. 35-301 to 324)	Applied in *Goodman v. State* 49 Tenn. App. 96 (1960)	County atty. to bring suit to enforce charitable trusts and secure proper administration
Texas	Tex. Rev. Civ. Stat. Ann. (1960)	U.C.T.F.A., art. 7425b-48. U.P.I.A., arts. 7425b-4 and 7425b-26 ff. U.S.F.S.T.A., art. 582-1.	None	None	Yes in actions to terminate, depart from purposes, construe and re wills (art. 4412a)	Prudent man rule (art. 7425b-46)	Yes (art. 4412a)	Common law powers, *Akin Foundation v. Trustees for the Preston Road Church of Christ*, 367 S.W. 2d 351 (Tex. Civ. App. 1963)

[a] See p. 478 for the Code to Uniform Laws.

TABLE 1. STATE LEGAL REQUIREMENTS: CHARITABLE TRUSTS (Continued)

	1	2	3	4	5	6	7	8
			Duty to Account					
State	Statutory Reference	Uniform Laws[a]	Testamentary Trustees	Inter Vivos Trustees	Statutory Requirement of Notice to Attorney General in Suits Involving Charitable Trusts	Limit on Investments	Cy Pres	Power of Attorney General
Utah	Utah Code Ann. (1953)	U.C.T.F.A., secs. 7-5-15 to 7-5-20. U.F.A., secs. 22-1-1 to 22-1-11. U.P.I.A., secs. 22-3-1 to 22-3-15. U.T.R.A., secs. 9-2-1 to 9-20.	Ann. and final accts. to ct. (sec. 75-12-30); allowance required on termination		None	Prudent man rule (sec. 33-2-1)	Judicially affirmed. U.S. v. Late Corporation of Church of Jesus Christ of Latter-Day Saints, 8 Utah 310 (1892)	
Vermont	Vt. Stat. Ann. (1958)	U.P.I.A., Tit. 14, secs. 3301 to 3313.	Ann. report to prob. ct. with copy to Dept. of Insts. (Tit. 14, sec. 2501)		None	Prudent man rule. See Scoville v. Brock, 81 Vt. 405, 70 Atl. 1014 (1908)	Yes (Tit. 14, sec. 2328)	To take action to compel compliance with reporting requirement (Tit. 14, sec. 2502). May apply for application of cy pres (tit. 14, sec. 2328, and common law powers)
Virginia	Va. Code Ann. (1964)	U.P.I.A., secs. 55-253 to 55-268. U.S.F.S.T.A., secs. 13.1-424 to 13.1-433	Ann. settlement of account with commissioner of accts. for county ct. (sec. 55-29 [1959] and sec. 26-17)		None	Prudent man rule (sec. 26-45.1); legal list (sec. 26-40)	Yes (sec. 55-31 [1959])	Commonwealth's atty. are to take action to enforce charitable gifts (sec. 55-29 [1959])
Washington	Wash. Rev. Code (1961)	U.C.T.F.A., secs. 30.28.010 ff. U.T.A.A., secs. 30.30. 010 ff. U.T.R.A., sec. 61.20. U.S.F.S.T.A., secs. 21.17.010 ff.	Ann. statement to beneficiaries required unless waived by settlor or beneficiaries, and may be filed, or be required to file it in Super. Ct. (secs. 30.30.020 and 30.30.040)		None	Prudent man rule (sec. 30.24.020)	Judicially affirmed but not yet applied	See discussion in State v. Taylor, 58 W.2d 255, 362 P.2d 249 (1961)

[a] See p. 478 for the Code to Uniform Laws.

TABLE 1. STATE LEGAL REQUIREMENTS: CHARITABLE TRUSTS (Continued)

	1	2	3	4	5	6	7	8
			Duty to Account		Statutory Require-ment of Notice to Attorney General in Suits Involving Charitable Trusts			
State	Statutory Reference	Uniform Laws[a]	Testamentary Trustees	Inter Vivos Trustees		Limit on Investments	Cy Pres	Power of Attorney General
West Virginia	W. Va. Code Ann. (1961)	U.C.T.F.A., secs. 4219(1) ff. U.P.I.A., secs. 3581(6) to (12). U.S.F.S.T.A., secs. 3142(30) to (40). U.T.A.T.A., secs. 4058(1) to (4).	Ann. report to commissioner of accts. (sec. 4185). Certain trustees to account less frequently (sec. 4187). Allowance required		None	Legal list requiring ct. approval (sec. 4216)	Yes (sec. 3502)	Can enforce. See dicta in *Goetz v. Old National Bank of Martinsberg*, 140 W.Va. 422, 845 S.E.2d 759 (1954)
Wisconsin	Wis. Stat. (1961)	U.C.T.F.A., sec. 223.055 U.F.A., secs. 112.01 to 112.05. U.P.I.A., secs. 231.40(1) to (12). U.S.F.S.T.A., sec. 112.06	Ann. acct. to county ct. required (sec. 317.06). Allowance required ann.	May account to county or cir. ct., sec. 231.36	Yes (sec. 324.18(1) (b))	Prudent man rule (sec. 320.01). See also *In re, Bletsch's Estate*, 130 N.W. 2d 275 (1964)	Yes (sec. 231.11 (7) (d))	To bring action to enforce a pub. charitable trust (sec. 231.34)
Wyoming	Wyo. Stat. Ann. (1957)	U.C.T.F.A., secs. 4-20 to 4-22. U.F.A., secs. 4-1 to 4-11 and 4-13 to 4-15. U.S.F.S.T.A., secs. 4-15.1 to 4-15.11.	None, except for banks acting as trustees (see sec. 13-98). Court may require accounting on affidavit of an interested party (sec. 4-33)		None	Legal list (secs. 4-16 and 13-102. [Supp. 1963]). The Wyo. Const., art. 3, sec. 38, forbids investment in private corps	Undecided by cts. and legislature	Common law powers.

[a] See p. 478 for the Code to Uniform Laws.

Code to Uniform Laws listed in Table 1

U.C.T.F.A.	Uniform Common Trust Fund Act	U.T.A.	Uniform Trusts Act
U.F.A.	Uniform Fiduciaries Act	U.T.L.	Uniform Trusts Law (same as above)
U.F.L.	Uniform Fiduciaries Law (same as above)	U.T.A.A.	Uniform Trustees Accounting Act
U.F.T.A.	Uniform Fiduciaries Transfers Act	U.T.A.L.	Uniform Trustees Accounting Law (same as above)
U.P.I.A.	Uniform Principle and Income Act	U.T.A.T.A.	Uniform Testamentary Additions to Trusts Act
U.S.F.S.T.A.	Uniform Simplification of Fiduciary Security Transfers Act	U.T.R.A.	Uniform Trust Receipts Act
U.S.T.A.	Uniform Security Transfers Act	U.T.R.	Uniform Trust Receipts (same as above)
U.S.T.C.P.A.	Uniform Supervision of Trustees for Charitable Purposes Act		

TABLE 2. STATE LEGAL REQUIREMENTS: CHARITABLE CORPORATIONS

State	1 Statutory Reference	2 Filing of Charter on Creation	3 Approval of Certificate by State Official	4 Reports	5 Attorney General's Power to Dissolve	6 Statutory Requirement for Distribution of Assets to Other Charitable Corporation on Dissolution	7 Notice to State Official of Voluntary Dissolution	8 Other Statutes and Notes
Alabama	Ala. Code, Tit. 10, secs. 203 to 263 (1958). Model Nonprofit Corp. Act	Judge of prob.	Yes, judge of prob. to see if it complies with chapter	None	Yes, special provision and quo warranto (Tit. 7, secs. 1133 to 1155)	Yes	Judge of prob.	Separate provisions for churches, educ. or benevolent societies (Tit. 10, secs. 124 ff.)
Alaska	Alaska Stat., secs. 10.20.010 ff. (1962). Nonprofit Corp. Act	Clerk of Super. Ct. and Dept. of Commerce	No	None	Yes, special provision (see col. 8)	None	Dept. of Commerce	Items 5, 6, and 7 taken from business corp. act (secs. 10.05.003 ff. [1962])
Arizona	Ariz. Rev. Stat. Ann., secs. 10-451 ff. (1956). Nonprofit Corp. Act	Corp. Commission and county recorders of every county where transacting business	Yes, corp. commissioner and Dept. of Pub. Welf. for "charitable agencies"	Ann. reports to Corp. Commission containing information it requires	Yes, special provision and quo warranto (secs. 12-2041 to 12-2045 [1956])	None	None	Separate provisions for corps. sole and fraternal and benevolent assns.
Arkansas	Ark. Rev. Stat. Ann., secs. 64-1901 to 1921. (Supp. 1963). Nonprofit Corps. and secs. 64-1601 ff. (Supp. 1963) Charitable Orgs.	Cir. ct.	Yes, cir. ct.	Report to sec. of state only if soliciting funds	Yes, quo warranto (sec. 12-713 [1956])	None	Sec. of state and county clerk (from business corp. act)	May incorporate under other laws (see sec. 64-1311 [1947])
California	Cal. Corp. Code, secs. 9000 ff. (1955). Gen. Nonprofit Corp. Law	Sec. of state and county clerks where it owns real estate. Atty. gen.[a]	Sec. of state if it conforms to law	Periodic financial reports to the atty. gen.[a]	Yes, special provision and quo warranto (Civ. Proc. 802 to 811 [1955])	Yes	Sec. of state and county clerk. Ct. disposes of assets on petition of atty. gen. or other interested party	Separate provisions for corps. for charitable or eleemosynary purposes (secs. 10200 ff. [1955]). The provisions of the Gen. Nonprofit Corp. Law apply, however, except as specifically provided otherwise. Also specific provisions for other kinds of corps. and foundations

[a] Required by Uniform Supervision of Trustees for Charitable Purposes Act.

479

TABLE 2. STATE LEGAL REQUIREMENTS: CHARITABLE CORPORATIONS (Continued)

State	1 Statutory Reference	2 Filing of Charter on Creation	3 Approval of Certificate by State Official	4 Reports	5 Attorney General's Power to Dissolve	6 Statutory Requirement for Distribution of Assets to Other Charitable Corporation on Dissolution	7 Notice to State Official of Voluntary Dissolution	8 Other Statutes and Notes
Colorado	Colo. Rev. Stat. Ann., secs. 31–19–1 ff. (1953). Corps. Not for Profit	Sec. of state and county recorders where corp. owns real estate	No	Ann. financial report to sec. of state	Yes, special provisions (in sec. 31–34–13 [1953])	None	Sec. of state and county clerk	Slightly different provisions for religious, educ. and benevolent societies (secs. 31–20–1 ff, [Supp. 1960])
Connecticut	Conn. Gen. Stat. Ann., secs. 33–419 ff. (1958). Nonstock Corp. Act	Sec. of state	Sec. of state, if it conforms to law	Nonfinancial biennial report to sec. of state. Ann. financial report if soliciting funds (secs. 17–210 ff. [Supp. 1964])	Yes, quo warranto (sec. 52–491 [1958])	Yes	Sec. of state	None
Delaware	Del. Code Ann., tit. 8, secs. 101 ff. (1953)	Sec. of state and county recorder	No	Ann. reports to sec. of state on capital in real estate and taxes paid thereon; or if exempt, why.	Yes, special provision and quo warranto (tit. 8, sec. 323 [1953])	None	Sec. of state and county recorder	None
District of Columbia	D.C. Code Ann., secs. 29–1301 ff. Nonprofit Corporation Act (1962)	Commissioners	Commissioners conform with law	None, unless soliciting funds (sec. 2–2106 [1961]); then to commissioners of D.C.	Yes, quo warranto (secs. 16–1601 to 16–1611 [1961]) and special provision	Yes	Apply to U.S. Dist. Ct. for D.C.	None
Florida	Fla. Stat. Ann., secs. 617.01 ff. (1956). Corps. Not for Profit Generally	Sec. of state	Sec. of state	Ann. reports to sec. of state, not financial unless soliciting funds, then to county clerk (sec. 617.24 [1956])	Yes, See *State ex rel. Landis v. S. H. Kress & Co.,* 115 Fla. 189 (1934)	None	Petition cir. ct.	Scholarship plans come under commissioner of banking. (secs. 617.50 *et seq.* [Supp. 1963])

ᵃ Required by Uniform Supervision of Trustees for Charitable Purposes Act.

TABLE 2. STATE LEGAL REQUIREMENTS: CHARITABLE CORPORATIONS (Continued)

	1	2	3	4	5	6	7	8
State	Statutory Reference	Filing of Charter on Creation	Approval of Certificate by State Official	Reports	Attorney General's Power to Dissolve	Statutory Requirement for Distribution of Assets to Other Charitable Corporation on Dissolution	Notice to State Official of Voluntary Dissolution	Other Statutes and Notes
Georgia	Ga. Code Ann., secs. 22–1801 to 22–1885 (Supp. 1963). The Corp. Act	Sec. of state	Super. Ct. judge to see the name not a duplicate and charter consistent with law	Ann. reports to sec. of state, not financial unless soliciting funds (sec. 35–1064 [Supp. 1963])	No	None	Sec. of state	See secs. 22–401 and 22–413 (1935) providing for incorp. of schools, charitable and literary orgs. Probably repealed by 1938 Corp. Act.
Hawaii	Hawaii Rev. Laws, secs. 172–16 ff. (Supp. 1961) Non-profit Corps.	Treas.	Treas.	Ann. financial reports to treasurer	Quo warranto provision (secs. 236–19 to 236–27) and treas. may dissolve under other special provisions	None	Treas.	None
Idaho	Idaho Code Ann., secs. 30–1101 ff. (1948) Religious, Social, and Benevolent Corps.	Sec. of state and county recorders where own real estate	Sec. of state	Ann. reports to sec. of state and county recorder including all wages paid; otherwise is not financial (secs. 30–601 ff. [Supp. 1963])	Yes, special provision; quo warranto provision allows county prosecuting atty. to bring action also (secs. 6–601 to 6–611 (1948))	None	Apply to dist. ct.	Note that most of the foregoing provisions come from applicable sections of the Business Corp. Code (secs. 30–101 to 30–165 [1948])
Illinois	Ill. Ann. Stat. (Smith-Hurd), ch. 32, secs. 163 ff. (1954) Gen. Not For Profit Act	Sec. of state and county recorder of deeds. Atty. gen.[a]	Sec. of state if conforms to law	Ann. reports to sec. of state (nonfinancial). Periodic financial reports to atty. gen.[a] Financial reports to atty. gen. if soliciting funds (ch. 23, secs. 5101 ff. [Supp. 1964])	Yes, special provisions in act (see col. 1)	Yes	Sec. of state and county recorder of deeds	Corps., if charitable, educ. etc., may be formed under special charter (see ch. 32, secs. 198 to 199a [1954])

[a] Required by Uniform Supervision of Trustees for Charitable Purposes Act.

TABLE 2. STATE LEGAL REQUIREMENTS: CHARITABLE CORPORATIONS (Continued)

State	1 Statutory Reference	2 Filing of Charter on Creation	3 Approval of Certificate by State Official	4 Reports	5 Attorney General's Power to Dissolve	6 Statutory Requirement for Distribution of Assets to Other Charitable Corporation on Dissolution	7 Notice to State Official of Voluntary Dissolution	8 Other Statutes and Notes
Indiana	Ind. Ann. Stat., secs. 25–507 to 25–553 (1960) Gen'l Not-for-Profit Corp. Act	Sec. of state and county recorder	Sec. of state if conforms to law	Ann. reports to sec. of state including some financial items	Yes, special provisions in act (see col. 1)	Yes	Sec. of state and county recorder	Foundations or holding cos. (secs. 25–1101 ff. [1960]), educ. insts. (secs. 25–3201 ff. [1960]), charity hospital assns. (secs. 25–3601 ff. [1960]), lodges, churches and societies (secs. 25–1501 ff. [1960])
Iowa	Iowa Code Ann., secs. 504.1 ff. (Supp. 1962). Corps. Not For Pecuniary Profit	Sec. of state and county recorder	Sec. of state	Ann. financial report from foundations to atty. gen. (sec. 682.57 [Supp. 1964]). See p. 000 for discussion.	Yes, special provision in Business Corp. Act (sec. 491.23 [Supp. 1964])	None	Sec. of state and county recorder	None
Kansas	Kan. Gen. Stat. Ann., sec. 17–2901 ff. (Supp. 1961). Corps. Not For Profit	Sec. of state and county register of deeds	None	None	Yes, also county attorney (from Business Corp. Act, sec. 17–706 [1949])	None	Sec. of state and county register of deeds	None
Kentucky	Ky. Rev. Stat., secs. 273.010 ff. (1962). Religious, Charitable, and Educ. Societies	Sec. of state and county clerk	None	If acting in fiduciary capacity must file annually with court	Yes, special provisions (secs. 271.590 and 415.010 [1962])	None	Sec. of state and county clerk	Nonstock Nonprofit Corp. Act (sec. 273.160 [1962]), contains generally the same provisions

a Required by Uniform Supervision of Trustees for Charitable Purposes Act.

TABLE 2. STATE LEGAL REQUIREMENTS: CHARITABLE CORPORATIONS (Continued)

State	1 Statutory Reference	2 Filing of Charter on Creation	3 Approval of Certificate by State Official	4 Reports	5 Attorney General's Power to Dissolve	6 Statutory Requirement for Distribution of Assets to Other Charitable Corporation on Dissolution	7 Notice to State Official of Voluntary Dissolution	8 Other Statutes and Notes
Louisiana	La. Rev. Stat., secs. 12:101 ff. (1950). Nonprofit Corp. Law	Sec. of state and parish recorder of mortgages	None	Ann. list of membership to sec. of state	Yes, special provisions in act (see col. 1)	Yes	Sec. of state and parish recorder of mortgages	None
Maine	Me. Rev. Stat. Ann. Tit. 13, secs. 901 ff. (1964) Corps. without Capital Stock	Sec. of state and Registry of Deeds	Atty. gen. approves for conformance to law and the register certifies	None	Yes (from Tit. 14, sec. 5402 [Supp. 1964] regarding profit corporations)	None	Notice given to atty. gen. and others as ordered by the court	None
Maryland	Md. Ann. Code, art. 23, secs. 132 to 138 (1957). Nonstock Corps.	State dept. of assessments and taxation and county clerk	State dept. of Assessments and Taxation	Report to comptroller only if receive state appropriation	Yes, special provision in act (see col. 1)	Yes	State dept. of assessments and taxation	Religious corps. (art. 23, secs. 256 to 314 [1951])
Massachusetts	Mass. Gen. Laws, ch. 180, secs. 1 to 29 (1958). Corps. for Charitable and Certain Other Purposes	Sec. of state and Atty. gen. (Supp. 1964)	Sec. of state and Dept. of Pub. Welf.	Ann. nonfinancial report to sec. of state and ann. financial report to atty. gen. (ch. 12, sec. 8F [Supp. 1964]; ch. 68, secs. 18 ff. [Supp. 1965])	Yes, special provision and quo warranto (ch. 246, secs. 6 to 13 [1958])	Yes	Atty. gen.	None

[a] Required by Uniform Supervision of Trustees for Charitable Purposes Act.

TABLE 2. STATE LEGAL REQUIREMENTS: CHARITABLE CORPORATIONS (Continued)

| State | Statutory Reference | Filing of Charter on Creation | Approval of Certificate by State Official | Reports | Attorney General's Power to Dissolve | Statutory Requirement for Distribution of Assets to Other Charitable Corporation on Dissolution | Notice to State Official of Voluntary Dissolution | Other Statutes and Notes |
	1	2	3	4	5	6	7	8
Michigan	Mich. Stat. Ann., secs. 21.1 ff. (1963). Gen. Corp.	Sec. of state and county clerk.[a] Atty. gen.[a]	Sec. of state if they conform to law	Ann. financial report to Mich. Corp. and Securities Commission. Ann. Financial report to Dept. of Soc. Welf. if soliciting funds (secs. 16.71 ff. [Supp. 1963])	Yes, quo warranto (secs. 27A.4501 ff. [1962]). Special provision for legislature by law to provide for dissolution of foundations	Yes	Mich. corp. and securities commission	Note: Secs. 21,164 to 21,170 (1963) contain special provisions for foundations
Minnesota	Minn. Stat. Ann., sec. 317.01. (Supp. 1963). Nonprofit Corps.	Sec. of state and county register of deeds	Sec. of state if they conform to law	Financial report to sec. of state only if soliciting funds (sec. 309.53 [Supp. 1963])	Yes, special provisions in act (see col. 1)	Yes	District ct. of county, but atty. gen. may intervene if in public interest to do so.	
Mississippi	Miss. Code Ann. secs. 5310.1 ff. (1956). Nonprofit Nonshare corps.	Sec. of state	Atty. gen. and gov.	Ann. report to sec. of state with some financial information	Yes, special provision and quo warranto (secs. 1120 to 1145 [1956])	None	Sec. of state	None
Missouri	Mo. Ann. Stat., secs. 355.010 ff. (Supp. 1964). General Not-for-Profit Corporation Law	Sec. of state and county recorder of deeds	Sec. of state if they conform to law	Ann. nonfinancial report to sec. of state	Yes, special provision in act (see col. 1)	Yes	Sec. of state and county recorder of deeds	See below for religious and charitable assns.
	Mo. Ann. Stat., sec. 352.010 ff. (1952). Religious and Charitable Associations	Sec. of state and county recorder of deeds	Circuit ct.	None	Yes, special provision that circuit attorney may also exercise in act (see col. 1)	Yes	Sec. of state	Note: These sections include incorp. trusts.

[a] Required by Uniform Supervision of Trustees for Charitable Purposes Act.

TABLE 2. STATE LEGAL REQUIREMENTS: CHARITABLE CORPORATIONS (Continued)

	1	2	3	4	5	6	7	8
State	Statutory Reference	Filing of Charter on Creation	Approval of Certificate by State Official	Reports	Attorney General's Power to Dissolve	Statutory Requirement for Distribution of Assets to Other Charitable Corporation on Dissolution	Notice to State Official of Voluntary Dissolution	Other Statutes and Notes
Montana	Mont. Rev. Codes Ann., secs. 15–1401 ff. (1955). Religious, Social and Benevolent Corps.	Sec. of state and county clerk	Sec. of state if they conform to law	None	Yes, special provision in act (see col. 1)	None	Sec. of state and county clerk	Separate provisions for religious corps., sole (sec. 15–1501 to 15–1507 (1955))
Nebraska	Neb. Rev. Stat., secs. 21–1901 ff. (Supp. 1961). Nonprofit Corp. Act	Sec. of state and county clerk. Sec. of state and county clerk if to convey real estate (see note 1, col. 8, for citation).	Sec. of state if they conform to law	Ann. nonfinancial report to sec. of state	Yes, special provision in act (see col. 1)	Yes	Sec. of state	Note 1: Applies to societies, charitable and fraternal (secs. 21–608 to 21–624 [1954]) Note 2: Separate provisions for religious corps. and hospital service corps.
Nevada	Nev. Rev. Stat., secs. 81.290 to 81.340 (1963). Nonprofit Corps. for Charitable and Eleemosynary Activities	Sec. of state and county clerk	Sec. of state	Ann. list of officers to sec. of state. Ann. financial report to sec. of state if nationwide or statewide org. and major support comes from the public (sec. 86.190 [1963])	Yes, quo warranto (sec. 35.020 and 35.030 [1957])	None	Sec. of state	Applies to religious, charitable, literary and scientific assns. (secs. 86.100 ff. [1963]). Also separate provisions for cooperative Assns., nonprofit cooperative corps. and corps. for advancement of state and local interests.
New Hampshire	N.H. Rev. Stat. Ann., secs. 292.1 ff. (1955). Voluntary Corps. and Assns.	Sec. of state and town clerk	None	None	Yes, special provision in act (see col. 1)	None	None	None

a Required by Uniform Supervision of Trustees for Charitable Purposes Act.

TABLE 2. STATE LEGAL REQUIREMENTS: CHARITABLE CORPORATIONS (Continued)

State	1 Statutory Reference	2 Filing of Charter on Creation	3 Approval of Certificate by State Official	4 Reports	5 Attorney General's Power to Dissolve	6 Statutory Requirement for Distribution of Assets to Other Charitable Corporation on Dissolution	7 Notice to State Official of Voluntary Dissolution	8 Other Statutes and Notes
New Jersey	N.J. Stat. Ann., sec. 15:1-1 ff. (1939). Not for Profit Corps. (General Provisions)	Sec. of state and recorded by county clerk	Commissioner of insts. and agencies (for insts.)	Ann. list of officers to sec. of state	Yes, quo warranto (secs. 2A:66-1 ff. [1952])	None	Sec. of state	Separate provisions for educ., historical, library and literary corps.; hospitals and similar insts., insts. of learning, patriotic societies, etc.
New Mexico	N.M. Stat. Ann., secs. 51-14-20 ff. (1962). Assns. not for profit	State Corp. Commission and county clerk	State corp. commission if conform to law	Ann. report to Corp. Commission containing information the Commission requires	Yes, or district attorney or Corp. Commission for failure to report	None	Corp. Commission (from gen. corp. law)	None
New York	N.Y. Membership Corp. Law	Sec. of state and county clerk	Justice of Sup. Ct. with notice to the atty. gen.	Report to comptroller if receive state appropriation. Report to Dept. of Soc. Welf. if solicit more than $25,000 or use paid solicitors (from Soc. Welf. Law [sec. 481 ff.])	Yes, on leave of court or direction of legislature	Yes	Ct. and sec. of state	Religious Corp. Law
North Carolina	N.C. Gen. Stat., secs. 55A-1 ff. (1960). Non-Profit Corp. Act	Sec. of state and recorded in Super. Ct.	Sec. of state	None	Yes, special provision in act (see col. 1)	Yes	Sec. of state who has it recorded in Super. Ct.	Separate provisions for religious societies and fraternal orders and societies

a Required by Uniform Supervision of Trustees for Charitable Purposes Act.

TABLE 2. STATE LEGAL REQUIREMENTS: CHARITABLE CORPORATIONS (Continued)

State	1 Statutory Reference	2 Filing of Charter on Creation	3 Approval of Certificate by State Official	4 Reports	5 Attorney General's Power to Dissolve	6 Statutory Requirement for Distribution of Assets to Other Charitable Corporation on Dissolution	7 Notice to State Official of Voluntary Dissolution	8 Other Statutes and Notes
North Dakota	N.D. Cent. Code, secs. 10-24-01 to 10-28-22 (1960). Nonprofit Corp. Act	Sec. of state	Sec. of state	None	Yes, special provision in act (see col. 1)	Yes	Sec. of state	Special provisions for religious corps., cemetery and fraternal corps. (sec. 10-28 [1960])
Ohio	Ohio Rev. Code Ann., secs. 1702.01 ff. (1964). Nonprofit Corp. Law	Sec. of state	Sec. of state	Certain charitable corps. must report to atty. gen. (sec. 109.31).* See page 000 for discussion. See also col. 8.	Yes, special provision and quo warranto (secs. 2733.02 to 2733.39 [1954])	Yes	Sec. of state	Incorporation of charitable trusts, to be enforced by county prosecuting attny. and to submit an annual financial report to the prob. judge (secs. 1719.01 ff. [1964])
Oklahoma	Okla. Stat. Ann., tit. 18 secs. 541 ff. (1953). Religious, Educational and Benevolent Corps.	Sec. of state	Sec. of state	If soliciting funds report to commissioner of charities and corrections (tit. 18, sec. 552.5 [Supp. 1964])	Yes, quo warranto (Tit. 12, sec. 1532 [1961]). Also sec. of state for failure to pay taxes	None	Sec. of state	Separate provisions for religious corps. and societies
Oregon	Ore. Rev. Stat., secs. 61.005 to 61.950 (1961). Nonprofit Corp. Law	Corp. commissioner and atty. gen.[a]	Corp. commissioner if it conforms to law	Nonfinancial report to corp. commissioner. Periodic financial reports to atty. gen. (Supp. 1965). Financial report to county clerks if soliciting (sec. 61.972 [1961])	Action by dist. atty. or proclamation of gov.	Yes	Corp. commissioner	

[a] Required by Uniform Supervision of Trustees for Charitable Purposes Act.

TABLE 2. STATE LEGAL REQUIREMENTS: CHARITABLE CORPORATIONS (Continued)

State	1 Statutory Reference	2 Filing of Charter on Creation	3 Approval of Certificate by State Official	4 Reports	5 Attorney General's Power to Dissolve	6 Statutory Requirement for Distribution of Assets to Other Charitable Corporation on Dissolution	7 Notice to State Official of Voluntary Dissolution	8 Other Statutes and Notes
Pennsylvania	Pa. Stat., Tit. 15, secs. 2851–1 ff. (1958). Nonprofit Corp. Law	Sec. of state and prothonothary of Ct. of Common Pleas	Ct. of Common Pleas. Some specific types of insts. require further approval	Ann. financial report to sec. of state if soliciting funds (Act. No. 337 of 1963)	Yes, quo warranto (Tit. 12, sec. 2022 to 2038 [1951])	Yes	Ct. of Common Pleas	
Rhode Island	R.I. Gen. Laws Ann., secs. 7–6–1 ff. (1956). Non-business Corps.	Sec. of state	Sec. of state	Nonfinancial biennial reports to sec. of state. Certain charitable corps. must report to the atty. gen. See p. 000 for discussion.	Yes, special provision (see sec. 7–5–17 [1956])	None	Super. Ct.	None
South Carolina	S.C. Code Ann., secs. 12–751 ff. (1962). Charitable, Soc., and Religious Corps.	Sec. of state and county clerk of mesne conveyances recorder	Investigated by Bd. of Pub. Welf., and in most cases also clerk of ct., sheriff, prob. judge, county treas., and county auditor	None	Yes, special provision (see secs. 12–22.1. to 12–22.15 [1956])	None	Sec. of state	None
South Dakota	S.D. Code secs. 11.1301 ff. and 11.1401 ff. (1939). Benevolent, Religious, Educ. and Cemetery Corps.	Sec. of state. Religious corps. must also file with register of deeds	None	None	Yes, quo warranto (secs. 37.0501 ff. [1939])	None	Cir. ct.	Note: Provisions for dissolution are in secs. 11.0901 ff. (1939)

ᵃ Required by Uniform Supervision of Trustees for Charitable Purposes Act.

TABLE 2. STATE LEGAL REQUIREMENTS: CHARITABLE CORPORATIONS (Continued)

State	1 Statutory Reference	2 Filing of Charter on Creation	3 Approval of Certificate by State Official	4 Reports	5 Attorney General's Power to Dissolve	6 Statutory Requirement for Distribution of Assets to Other Charitable Corporation on Dissolution	7 Notice to State Official of Voluntary Dissolution	8 Other Statutes and Notes
Tennessee	Tenn. Code Ann., secs. 48-1101 ff. (1955). Gen. Welfare Corps.	Sec. of state and county register	None	If soliciting funds, financial report to sec. of state (sec. 62-1504 [Supp. 1964])	Yes, quo warranto (secs. 23-2801 ff. [1955])	Yes	Sec. of state	Separate but similar provisions for religious corps., denominational schools and fraternal and patriotic orgs.
Texas	Tex. Rev. Civ. Stat. Ann., arts. 1396-1.01 to 1396-11.01 (1962). Nonprofit Corp. Act.	Sec. of state	Sec. of state if they comply with law	Sec. of state may require nonfinancial report every four years	Yes, special provision (sec. 1396-7.01)	Yes	Sec. of state	None
Utah	Utah Code Ann., secs. 16-6-18 ff. (Supp. 1963). Nonprofit corps.	Sec. of state	Sec. of state if it conforms to law	None	Yes	None	Sec. of state	Note: The 1961 Business Corp. Act (secs. 16-10-1 ff. [1962]) may impose further reporting requirements and provision regarding dissolution.
Vermont	Vt. Stat. Ann., tit. 11, secs. 1 to 552 (1958). (see also note 2 in col. 8.)	Sec. of state	Atty. gen. if it conforms to law	Ann. report to prob. ct. and Dept. of Insts. by incorp. trustees of property given for charitable purposes	Yes, or state's atty. for proper county	None	Sec. of state and tax commissioner	Note 1: Separate provisions for religious societies. Note 2: Most of the reported provisions are taken from the Gen. Corp. Law, which applies to nonprofit corps.
Virginia	Va. Code Ann., secs. 13.1-201 ff. (1964) Non-Stock Corp. Act.	Corp. Commission and county recorder of deeds	Corp. Commission if it complies with law	Ann. nonfinancial report to Corp. Commission	No, Corp. Commission	Yes	Corp. Commission	None

a Required by Uniform Supervision of Trustees for Charitable Purposes Act.

489

TABLE 2. STATE LEGAL REQUIREMENTS: CHARITABLE CORPORATIONS (Continued)

State	1 Statutory Reference	2 Filing of Charter on Creation	3 Approval of Certificate by State Official	4 Reports	5 Attorney General's Power to Dissolve	6 Statutory Requirement for Distribution of Assets to Other Charitable Corporation on Dissolution	7 Notice to State Official of Voluntary Dissolution	8 Other Statutes and Notes
Washington	Wash. Rev. Code Ann., secs. 24.04.010 ff. (1961). Nonprofit, Nonstock Corps. (see col. 8.)	Sec. of state and county auditor	None	None	No, prosecuting atty. of proper county under quo warranto provisions (secs. 7.56.010 ff. [1961])	None	Sec. of state and county auditor	Note: The reported provisions are the same for educ., religious, benevolent, fraternal or charitable societies (secs. 24.08.010 ff. (1961)) and for assns. for mutual benefit and educ., charitable, etc. purposes (secs. 24.16.010 ff. [1961])
West Virginia	W. Va. Code Ann., secs. 3016 ff. (1961)	Sec. of state	None	None	Yes, also prosecuting atty. under quo warranto provisions (secs. 5310 ff. [1961])	Yes	Cir. ct. of county	Note: No church, religious sect or denomination may be incorporated.
Wisconsin	Wis. Stat. Ann., secs. 181.01 ff. (1961). Nonstock Corp. Law	Sec. of state and recorder of deeds of county	None	Financial report to sec. of state if solicit funds (sec. 175.13 [1961])	Yes, special provision and quo warranto (sec. 294.04 [1961])	Yes	Sec. of state and register of deeds	Note: There are separate provisions for religious societies and fraternal societies
Wyoming	Wyo. Stat. Ann., sec. 17-122.1 ff. (Supp. 1963). Nonprofit Corps. (see col. 8.)	Sec. of state	None	None	Yes, quo warranto secs. 1-897 ff. [1957]	None	Sec. of state and county clerk	Note: Charitable, educ., religious, and other societies have similar provisions but must also file articles with county clerk (secs. 17-123 ff. [1957])

a Required by Uniform Supervision of Trustees for Charitable Purposes Act.

APPENDIX B. CERTAIN STATE ACTS, RULES, AND REGULATIONS

1. Uniform Supervision of Trustees for Charitable Purposes Act
2. Illinois Charitable Trust Act—Definitions and Exemptions
3. California Uniform Supervision of Trustees for Charitable Purposes Act—Exemption Provisions
4. Oregon Statute—Disallowance of Tax Exemptions for Failure to File Reports and Reinstatement of Exemptions
5. Illinois Rules and Regulations for the Administration of Charitable Trusts
6. Massachusetts Regulations—Investigatory Proceedings
7. Massachusetts Statute—Dissolution of Charitable Corporations

1. UNIFORM SUPERVISION OF TRUSTEES
FOR CHARITABLE PURPOSES ACT[1]

The text of this model act is presented in full as an aid to the discussion of its provisions in Chapters VII and IX. It should be noted that the failure of the act to include foundations organized as corporations represents a major omission. Attempts to rectify this fault have been made in California, Illinois, and Oregon. Following the text of the act, therefore, excerpts from the California and Illinois versions of the act are presented as illustrations of two different ways in which the definition and exemption sections have been modified.

AN ACT to implement the state supervision and enforcement of certain charitable trusts and similar relationships, and to make uniform the law relating thereto.

Be it enacted

SEC. 1. SCOPE OF ACT. This act applies to all trustees holding property for charitable purposes over which [the State or] the Attorney General has enforcement or supervisory powers.

SEC. 2. DEFINITION OF TRUSTEE. "Trustee" means (a) any individual, group of individuals, corporation, or other legal entity holding property in trust pursuant to any charitable trust, (b) any corporation which has accepted property to be used for a particular charitable corporate purpose as distinguished from the general purposes of the corporation, and (c) a corporation formed for the administration of a charitable trust, pursuant to the directions of the settlor or at the instance of the trustee.

SEC. 3. EXCLUSIONS FROM THE ACT. This act does not apply to the United States, any state, territory, or possession of the United States, the District of Columbia, the Commonwealth of Puerto Rico, or to any of their agencies or governmental subdivisions, to an officer of a religious organization who holds property for religious purposes, or to a charitable corporation organized and operated primarily for educational, religious, or hospital purposes.

SEC. 4. REGISTER OF CHARITIES. The Attorney General shall establish and maintain a register of trustees subject to this act and of the particular trust or other relationship under which they hold property for charitable purposes and, to that end, shall conduct whatever investigation is necessary,

---

[1] *Uniform Laws Annotated,* vol. 9C, 1957, pp. 210ff. Reproduced with the express permission of the Edward Thompson Co., Brooklyn.

and shall obtain from public records, court officers, taxing authorities, trustees, and other sources, whatever information, copies of instruments, reports and records are needed for the establishment and maintenance of the register.

SEC. 5. FILING COPIES OF INSTRUMENTS. Every trustee subject to this act who has received property for charitable purposes shall file with the Attorney General, within six months after any part of the income or principal is authorized or required to be applied to a charitable purpose, a copy of the instrument providing for his title, powers or duties. If any part of the income or principal is authorized or required to be applied to a charitable purpose at the time this act takes effect, the filing shall be made within six months thereafter.

SEC. 6. FILING OF PERIODIC REPORTS.

(a) Except as otherwise provided, every trustee subject to this act shall, in addition to filing copies of the instruments previously required, file with the Attorney General periodic written reports, under oath, setting forth information as to the nature of the assets held for charitable purposes and the administration thereof by the trustee, in accordance with rules and regulations of the Attorney General.

(b) The Attorney General shall make rules and regulations as to the time for filing reports, the contents thereof, and the manner of executing and filing them. He may classify trusts and other relationships concerning property held for a charitable purpose as to purpose, nature of assets, duration of the trust or other relationship, amount of assets, amounts to be devoted to charitable purposes, nature of trustee, or otherwise, and may establish different rules for the different classes as to time and nature of the reports required to the ends (1) that he shall receive reasonably current, periodic reports as to all charitable trusts or other relationships of a similar nature, which will enable him to ascertain whether they are being properly administered, and (2) that periodic reports shall not unreasonably add to the expense of the administration of charitable trusts and similar relationships. The Attorney General may suspend the filing of reports as to a particular charitable trust or relationship for a reasonable, specifically designated time upon written application of the trustee filed with the Attorney General and after the Attorney General has filed in the register of charitable trusts a written statement that the interests of the beneficiaries will not be prejudiced thereby and that periodic reports are not required for proper supervision by his office.

(c) A copy of an account filed by the trustee in any court having jurisdiction of the trust or other relationship, if the account substantially complies with the rules and regulations of the Attorney General, may be filed as a report required by this section.

(d) The first report for a trust or similar relationship hereafter established, unless the filing thereof is suspended as herein provided, shall be filed not later than one year after any part of the income or principal is authorized or required to be applied to a charitable purpose. If any part of the income or principal of a trust previously established is authorized or required to be applied to a charitable purpose at the time this act takes effect, the first report, unless the filing thereof is suspended, shall be filed within six months after the effective date of the act.

SEC. 7. RULES AND REGULATIONS. The Attorney General may make additional rules and regulations necessary for the administration of this act.

SEC. 8. INVESTIGATION. The Attorney General may investigate transactions and relationships of trustees subject to this act for the purpose of determining whether the property held for charitable purposes is properly administered. He may require any agent, trustee, fiduciary, beneficiary, institution, association, or corporation, or other person to appear, at a named time and place, in the county designated by the Attorney General, where the person resides or is found, to give information under oath and to produce books, memoranda, papers, documents of title, and evidence of assets, liabilities, receipts, or disbursements in the possession or control of the person ordered to appear.

SEC. 9. ORDER TO ATTEND. When the Attorney General requires the attendance of any person, as provided in section 8, he shall issue an order setting forth the time when and the place where attendance is required and shall cause the same to be delivered to or sent by registered mail to the person at least 14 days before the date fixed for attendance. Such order shall have the same force and effect as a subpoena and, upon application of the Attorney General, obedience to the order may be enforced by any court having jurisdiction of charitable trusts in the county where the person receiving it resides or is found, in the same manner as though the notice were a subpoena. The court, after hearing, for cause, and upon application of any person aggrieved by the order, shall have the right to alter, amend, revise, suspend or postpone all or any part of its provisions.

SEC. 10. INSPECTION OF RECORDS. Subject to reasonable rules and regulations adopted by the Attorney General, the register, copies of instruments and the reports filed with the Attorney General shall be open to public inspection.

SEC. 11. POWERS OF ATTORNEY GENERAL AND COURTS. The Attorney General may institute appropriate proceedings to secure compliance with this act and to secure the proper administration of any trust or other relationship to which this act applies. The powers and duties of the Attorney General provided in this act are in addition to his existing powers and duties. Nothing in this act shall impair or restrict the jurisdiction of any court with respect to any of the matters covered by it.

SEC. 12. CONTRARY PROVISIONS INVALID. This act shall apply regardless of any contrary provisions of any instrument.

SEC. 13. CUSTODIANS TO FURNISH COPIES OF INSTRUMENTS. The custodian of the records of a court having jurisdiction of probate matters or of charitable trusts shall furnish such copies of papers, records and files of his office relating to the subject of this act as the Attorney General requires.

SEC. 14. DUTIES OF TAX AUTHORITIES. Every officer, agency, board or commission of this state receiving applications for exemption from taxation of any charitable trust or similar relationship in which the trustee is subject to this act shall annually file with the Attorney General a list of all applications received during the year.

SEC. 15. UNIFORMITY OF INTERPRETATION. This act shall be so construed as to effectuate its general purpose to make uniform the law of those states which enact it.

SEC. 16. SHORT TITLE. This act may be cited as the Uniform Supervision of Trustees for Charitable Purposes Act.

SEC. 17. SEVERABILITY. If any provision of this act or the application thereof to any person or circumstance is held invalid, the invalidity shall not affect other provisions or applications of the act which can be given effect without the invalid provision or application, and to this end the provisions of this act are severable.

SEC. 18. INCONSISTENT LEGISLATION REPEALED. Sections . . . are hereby repealed, and all acts or parts of acts inconsistent with this act are hereby repealed.

SEC. 19. TIME OF TAKING EFFECT. This act shall take effect . . .

2. ILLINOIS CHARITABLE TRUST ACT—DEFINITIONS AND EXEMPTIONS[1]

SECTION 1. This Act may be cited as Charitable Trust Act.

SECTION 2. This Act applies to any trustee as defined in Section 3 holding property of a value in excess of $4,000.00.

SECTION 3. "Trustee" means any individual, group of individuals, corporation or other legal entity holding property for any charitable purpose.

SECTION 4. The Act does not apply to the United States, any State, territory or possession of the United States, the District of Columbia, the Commonwealth of Puerto Rico, or to any of their agencies or to any governmental subdivision; nor to a corporation sole, or other religious corporation, trust or organization which holds property for religious, charitable, hospital or educational purposes, for the purpose of operating cemeteries or a home or homes for the aged; nor to any agency or organization, incorporated or unincorporated, affiliated with and directly supervised by such a religious corporation or organization; nor to an officer, director or trustee of any such religious corporation, trust or organization who holds property in his official capacity for like purpose; nor to a charitable organization, foundation, trust or corporation organized for the purpose of and engaged in the operation of schools or hospitals, or for the purpose of operating a cemetery or cemeteries, or a home or homes for the aged.

---

[1] Ill. Rev. Stat., ch. 14, secs. 15ff.

497

3. CALIFORNIA UNIFORM SUPERVISION OF TRUSTEES FOR CHARITABLE PURPOSES ACT— EXEMPTION PROVISIONS[1]

12580. This article may be cited as the Uniform Supervision of Trustees for Charitable Purposes Act.

12581. This article applies to all charitable corporations and trustees holding property for charitable purposes over which the State or the Attorney General has enforcement or supervisory powers.

12582. "Trustee" means (a) any individual, group of individuals, corporation, or other legal entity holding property in trust pursuant to any charitable trust, (b) any corporation which has accepted property to be used for a particular charitable corporate purpose as distinguished from the general purposes of the corporation, and (c) a corporation formed for the administration of a charitable trust, pursuant to the directions of the settlor or at the instance of the trustee.

12582.1 "Charitable corporation" means any nonprofit corporation organized under the laws of this State for charitable or eleemosynary purposes and any similar foreign corporation doing business or holding property in this State for such purposes.

12583. This article does not apply to the United States, any state, territory, or possession of the United States, the District of Columbia, the Commonwealth of Puerto Rico, or to any of their agencies or governmental subdivisions, to any religious corporation sole or other religious corporation or organization which holds property for religious purposes, or to any officer, director, or trustee thereof who holds property for like purposes, to a cemetery corporation regulated under Chapter 19 of Division 3 of the Business and Professions Code, or to a charitable corporation organized and operated primarily as a religious organization, educational institution or hospital.

---

[1] Cal. Gov. Code, secs. 12580 to 12583.

4. OREGON STATUTE—DISALLOWANCE OF TAX EXEMPTIONS FOR FAILURE TO FILE REPORTS AND REINSTATEMENT OF EXEMPTIONS[1]

A second criticism of the Uniform Act has been its failure to specify a penalty for failure to comply with the registration and reporting provisions. The following is the method adopted in Oregon to meet the need. It is similar to legislation in force in California.

(1) No tax exemption under ORS 317.080 shall be allowed to any charitable corporation or trustee subject to ORS 61.972 and 128.610 to 128.750 for any year or years for which it fails to file with the Attorney General, on or before the due date, any registration or periodic report required by ORS 61.972 and 128.610 to 128.750.

(2) The exemption shall be disallowed under this action only after the Attorney General has notified the State Tax Commission in writing that the charitable corporation or trustee subject to the provisions of ORS 61.972 and 128.610 to 128.750 has failed to file any such registration or periodic report on or before the due date thereof.

(3) If an exemption is disallowed under this section, such exemption may be reinstated when the registration or periodic reports are filed. However, any such charitable corporation or trustee shall pay the minimum tax imposed by ORS chapter 317 for any year or years for which its exemption was disallowed under this section.

(4) No exemption shall be disallowed under this section for income years commencing before January 1, 1964.

---

[1] Ore. Rev. Stat., sec. 128.740.

5. ILLINOIS RULES AND REGULATIONS FOR THE ADMINISTRATION OF CHARITABLE TRUSTS

The rules and regulations promulgated by the Attorney General of Illinois are presented as an example of the type of implementation which is desirable for the administration of the Uniform Act.

By virtue of the authority vested in the Attorney General under the provisions of the Charitable Trust Act, approved July 31, 1961, as amended, the Attorney General of the State of Illinois hereby promulgates the following rules and regulations to provide for the creation of the Division of Charitable Trusts in the Office of the Attorney General of the State of Illinois, to provide a Register for the registration of all charitable trusts which are subject to the Charitable Trust Act, as amended, of Illinois and to provide for the administration of that Act.

CREATION OF CHARITABLE TRUST DIVISION—REGISTER OF TRUSTEES—1. There is established in the Office of the Attorney General of the State of Illinois, a Division of Charitable Trusts. The Division of Charitable Trusts shall establish and maintain in the Offices of the Attorney General, Charitable Trust Division, Springfield, Illinois, a Register of Charitable Trusts which shall contain a listing of all Trustees subject to the provisions of the Charitable Trust Act, as amended, and of the particular trust or other relationship under which they hold property for charitable purposes. A subregister of Charitable Trusts shall be maintained in the Chicago Office of the Attorney General with respect to all charitable trusts maintained in the Counties of Cook, Lake, McHenry and DuPage.

To WHOM RULES APPLY—2. Any Trustee, as defined in Section 3 of the Charitable Trust Act, as amended, and interpreted in paragraph 3 and 4 of these Rules and Regulations, not otherwise exempted under the provisions of Section 4 of the Charitable Trust Act, as amended, holding property of any kind whatsoever, having a value in excess of $4,000, is subject to and must comply with the Charitable Trust Act, as amended, and with these Rules and Regulations.

Definition of Charitable Trust—(a) The Term "Charitable Trust" in the Act and in these Rules and Regulations is deemed to mean any relationship whereby real or personal property is held for a charitable purpose or purposes.

Limitation of Term "Holding Property."—(b) The term "holding property" excludes any persons or legal entities who are mere title holders or cus-

500

todians or depositories of property which is held for charitable purposes and over which they have no powers or duties relative to the administration of such property.

Determination Whether Trust Covered by Act, As to Value—(c) Any charitable trust, the assets of which have a fair cash market value in excess of $4,000, is subject to the Charitable Trust Act, as amended, and to these Rules and Regulations. A charitable trust, the assets of which fluctuate under and over a fair cash market value of $4,000, is subject to the Charitable Trust Act, as amended, and these Rules and Regulations, if the assets of the trust have a fair cash market value in excess of $4,000, on any day of the fiscal or calendar year of the trust or if the receipts and/or disbursements of the trust exceed $4,000, during said calendar or fiscal year.

DEFINITION OF TRUSTEE—3. The Term "Trustee" as defined in Section 3 of said Act includes any legal entity, irrespective of its character, which presently holds a vested interest in real or personal property for any charitable purpose.

EXEMPT TRUSTEES—4. The Charitable Trust Act, as amended, does not apply to the following entities, each of which is exempt from the Charitable Trust Act, as amended:

Governmental Bodies—(a) The United States, any State, Territory or possession of the United States, the District of Columbia, the Commonwealth of Puerto Rico, or any of their agencies or governmental subdivisions:

Religious Bodies—(b) Corporations sole, or other religious corporation, religious trusts or religious organization, holding property for religious, charitable, hospital or educational purposes, or for the purpose of operating a cemetery or a home or homes for the aged. Any agency or agencies however formed, affiliated with and directly supervised by such a religious corporation, trust or organization is also exempt. An officer, director or trustee of any religious corporation, religious trust or religious organization who holds property in his official capacity for like purposes is likewise exempt;

Other Exempt Trustees—(c) All Charitable organizations, foundations, trusts, corporations or other legal entities formed, established, organized and operated for the purpose of and engaged in the operation of schools or hospitals or for the purpose of operating cemeteries or homes for the aged. This is construed to be limited only to such entities which are both organized and operated as institutions for any one of the exempted purposes. Any of the entities mentioned in this subsection which is engaged in both exempt and nonexempt purposes is subject to the provisions of the Charitable Trust Act, as amended, and of these Rules and Regulations to the extent of its activities in nonexempt purposes.

DUTY TO REGISTER AND REPORT—5. *Trust Existing on July 31, 1961*—(a) When any part of the income or principal of a charitable trust, which is subject to the provisions of the Charitable Trust Act, as amended, was received for application for charitable purposes on or prior to July 31, 1961, the Trustee thereof shall file with the Division of Charitable Trusts, Office of the Attorney General, Springfield, Illinois, on or before January 31, 1962, a Registration Statement and a copy of the written instrument under which the trustee holds property for charitable purposes.

Trusts Established Subsequent to July 31, 1961—(*b*) A trustee of a charitable trust subject to the Charitable Trust Act, as amended, which was created, formed, organized or established after July 31, 1961, shall file a Registration Statement and a copy of the written instrument under which said trustee holds property for charitable purposes within six (6) months after property is received for application for a charitable purpose.

When Trust Becomes Subject to Act—Vested Remainders—(*c*) Property is received for application to charitable purposes whenever property is held for charitable purposes or whenever there is a vested remainder for charitable purposes. Where there is a vested charitable remainder preceded by a life estate, a Registration Statement, a copy of the written instrument and annual Periodic Report shall be filed by the trustee, if there is an express trust, or by the life tenant, if there is not an express trust. Banks and trust companies or individuals acting as co-fiduciary or co-fiduciaries with banks or trust companies are not required to file annual periodic reports under this sub-section. Subsequent annual reports may be waived from time to time by the Attorney General. The written instrument filed in those situations where there is a vested charitable remainder will, upon written request, be marked and held confidentially and will not be open for public inspection until such time as the charitable remainder vests in possession.

Provision for Nondisclosure—Gifts to Noncharitable Purposes—(*d*) Every trustee of a charitable trust subject to the provisions of the Charitable Trust Act, as amended, who is required to file a copy of the written instrument under which he holds property for charitable purposes, may in those instances in which the trusts for charitable purposes are combined in the written instrument with bequests or devises, in trust or otherwise, for other than charitable purposes, furnish an additional copy of the written instrument with the bequests or devises, in trust or otherwise, for other than charitable purposes omitted from the additional copy. Whenever an additional copy of the written instrument is filed as herein authorized, it shall be open for public inspection and the copy of the written instrument wherein property is held for both charitable and private purposes shall not be available for inspection by the public.

Filing of Amendments to Trust Instrument—(*e*) Whenever any written instrument under which property is held for charitable purposes has been filed with the Attorney General as required herein and that instrument is subsequently altered or amended, the trustee shall file a copy of the amendment or alteration within thirty (30) days after the alteration or amendment is made.

DUTIES OF BANKS AND TRUST COMPANIES—6. Banks and Trust Companies, authorized to accept and execute trusts in Illinois, and any individual or individuals acting as co-fiduciary with any such bank or trust company is required to file a Registration Statement and a copy of the written instrument under which they hold property for charitable purposes in the manner and within the time specified in Rule 5 of these Rules and Regulations but they are not required to complete paragraph 5 of the Registration Statement.

FILING OF PERIODIC REPORTS—7. *Who Shall File and Where.* (a) Every person or persons, corporation or other legal entity subject to this Act, with the exception of Banks and Trust Companies and individual or individuals acting as co-fiduciary or co-fiduciaries with a Bank or Trust Company, shall in addition to filing a Registration Statement and a copy of the written instrument under which they hold property for charitable purposes file an annual Periodic Report under oath. The annual Periodic Report shall be filed in the Office of the Attorney General, Division of Charitable Trusts, Springfield, Illinois. Annual Periodic Reports shall be in accordance with the form required by the Attorney General.

Period of Grace—(b) The first Periodic Report shall cover the first calendar or fiscal year of the trust ending after the trust becomes subject to the Act. The first Periodic Report shall be due on or before the expiration of six (6) months after the close of said first calendar or fiscal year of the trust ending after the trust becomes subject to the Act.

Filing of Annual Reports—(c) Every Trustee of a charitable trust subject to the reporting provision of the Charitable Trust Act, as amended, shall, subsequent to the filing of his first Report, file an annual Periodic Report for each subsequent year during the existence of the charitable trust except as herein provided. Annual Reports shall cover the twelve (12) month period ending with the calendar or fiscal year of the Trust and they shall be due on or before the expiration of six (6) months after the close of said calendar or fiscal year of the Trust. A Trust which commences reporting on either a calendar or fiscal year basis shall continue such method of reporting unless the Attorney General permits a different method of reporting as provided in paragraph (e) of this Rule.

Effect of Adversary Proceedings—(d) In the case of proceedings now pending, or upon the commencement of adversary proceedings, the Trustee shall file a report with the Attorney General informing him of that fact, together with the title and number of the cause and the name of the Court. The Trustee shall, upon entry of final decree in the cause, report that fact to the Attorney General and shall furnish the Attorney General with a certified copy of the final decree.

Application to Change Date for Filing Reports—(e) The Trustee of a charitable trust subject to this Act may make written application to the Attorney General requesting that the due date of filing the annual Periodic Report as specified above, be changed so as to correspond with the calendar or fiscal year of the trust. The Attorney General may suspend the filing of reports as to a particular charitable trust or relationship for a reasonable, specifically designated time upon written application of the trustee filed with the Attorney General and after the Attorney General has filed in the register of charitable trusts a written statement that the interests of the beneficiaries will not be prejudiced thereby and that Periodic Reports are not required for proper supervision by his Office.

Report under Solicitation Act as Periodic Report—(*f*) Every person or persons, corporation or other legal entity registered under "An Act to Regulate Solicitation and Collection of Funds for Charitable Purposes" and required to file Periodic Reports under that Act on the long Annual Report form (CS 2) shall not be required to file a Periodic Report under the Illinois Charitable Trust Act, as amended, for any year in which it has filed an affidavit stating it has filed a report under "An Act to Regulate Solicitation and Collection of Funds for Charitable Purposes" for that year on the long annual Report form (CS 2).

Account Filed with Court as Periodic Report—(*g*) A copy of an account filed by the trustee in any court having jurisdiction of the trust or other relationship, if the account has been approved by the court in which it was filed, may be filed as a Periodic Report required by this section.

Audit by Certified Public Accountant as Periodic Report—(*h*) An audit of any charitable trust subject to the Charitable Trust Act, as amended, certified as being true and correct and in accordance with generally accepted accounting principles by any Certified Public Accountant and containing substantially the information required on the Periodic Report Form of the Attorney General may be filed as a part of the Periodic Report filed by trustees as required by this Section.

Annual Statement by Bank or Trust Company as Periodic Report—(*i*) An annual statement prepared by any bank or Trust Company authorized to accept and execute trusts in Illinois, for any charitable trust which is subject to the Charitable Trust Act and for which charitable trust the Bank or Trust Company is acting under an agency account may be filed by the Trustee as a part of the Periodic Report required by this Section provided that the annual statement contains substantially the information required in the Periodic Report Form of the Attorney General.

FILING OF APPLICATIONS FOR TAX EXEMPTION—8. The Trustee or Trustees of a charitable trust subject to the Illinois Charitable Trust Act of 1961, as amended, except Banks or Trust Companies and an individual or individuals acting as co-fiduciary or co-fiduciaries with a Bank or Trust Company, shall file with the Attorney General a copy of any application for Federal income tax exemption and also a copy of any application for exemption for real or personal property taxes in the State of Illinois.

INSPECTION OF REGISTER AND RECORDS BY THE GENERAL PUBLIC—9. The Register and records of any Charitable Trust registered in the Office of the Attorney General may be inspected at reasonable times by any member of the general public who can show to the satisfaction of the Attorney General or his Authorized Assistant Attorney General, that the interest of the inquirer may be directly or indirectly affected by the administration of said Trust.

DISCRETION OF ATTORNEY GENERAL REGARDING DISCLOSURE OF IN-
FORMATION—10. Information disclosed to the Attorney General as to the
names and addresses of recipients of benefits of a charitable trust shall be
available to the general public only at the discretion of the Attorney General or his authorized assistant attorney general.

AMENDMENT OF RULES AND REGULATIONS—11. These Rules and Regulations may be amended at any time and from time to time by the Attorney
General.

Approved and Promulgated by
me this 13th day of March, 1964.

WILLIAM G. CLARK
Attorney General

6. MASSACHUSETTS REGULATIONS—INVESTIGATORY PROCEEDINGS[1]

The Massachusetts registration and reporting statute, although it does not follow the language of the Uniform Act, is similar in nature. The section of the Regulations promulgated by the Director of Public Charities in that state is presented as an example of procedural rules that have been adopted to provide certain safeguards for charities under investigation.

3.1 Proceedings under this regulation shall be undertaken for the purpose of investigation and are not adjudicative hearings within the meaning of General Laws Chapter 30A, sections 10 and 11. The aim is to secure the facts in as direct and simple a manner as possible.

3.2 All investigative proceedings shall be held in private unless in the Director's discretion, it is in the public benefit to have a public investigation.

3.3 Proceedings may be formal or informal in the discretion of the Director. Such hearings will be scheduled to meet at the convenience of the Director.

3.4 The Director, or an Assistant Attorney General appointed by the Director, shall conduct the proceedings. He shall not be bound by common law, or statutory rules of evidence, or technical or formal rules of procedure, but shall conduct the hearing in such manner as best calculated to conform to the provisions of the act and a spirit of justice. He may exclude unduly repetitive evidence, whether offered on direct examination or cross-examination of witnesses. He may, within his discretion, order that a transcript of the proceedings be made.

3.5 All parties notified shall appear at the time and place set for the proceeding with such books, records and other papers as may be relevant to an investigation of the proper administration of said public charity.

3.6 In the discretion of the Director or his representative, the proceeding may be continued from day to day, or be set to be continued at another date within 30 days of the date of the first hearing without a new notification of the proceeding.

3.7 Every party shall have the right to call and examine as witnesses any person whose testimony is relevant to the matter at hand, to introduce

---

[1] Commonwealth of Massachusetts, Department of the Attorney General, *Regulations of the Director of Public Charities,* Boston, effective July 26, 1962, art. 3 (mimeographed).

exhibits, to cross-examine witnesses who testify and to submit rebuttal evidence.

3.8 Affidavits and supporting statements under oath shall be subject to review and investigation by the Division of Public Charities of the Department of the Attorney General.

3.9 At the request of any of the parties under investigation, and with the approval of the Director, a transcript of the proceedings may be made available to any party, provided that the costs be paid by the party so requesting it.

3.10 If after an investigatory proceeding it is felt by the charity under investigation that additional evidence has come into its possession which would materially affect a decision by the Director as to the administration of that charity, such evidence should be submitted in writing to the Director forthwith, who may, if, in his discretion it is desirable, hold an additional proceeding, or do whatever is otherwise necessary to examine the evidence.

3.11 The Director may, after reviewing the evidence, prepare a finding as to whether such public charity has complied with the law in administration of such charitable funds as have been entrusted with it.

7. MASSACHUSETTS STATUTE—DISSOLUTION OF CHARITABLE CORPORATIONS[1]

One of the areas in need of legislative attention in almost every state is the procedure for dissolution of corporations formed for charitable purposes. The following legislation, adopted in Massachusetts in 1963, represents one method for assuring that upon dissolution the funds of a charitable corporation will be applied cy pres *for charitable purposes similar to those for which they were originally donated.*

SECTION 11A. A charitable corporation constituting a public charity, organized under the provisions of general or special law, which desires to close its affairs may, by vote of a majority of its board of directors or other governing body, authorize a petition for its dissolution to be filed in the supreme judicial court setting forth in substance the grounds of the application for dissolution and requesting the court to authorize the administration of its funds for such similar public charitable purposes as the court may determine. The provisions of this section shall constitute the sole method for the voluntary dissolution of any such charitable corporation.

SECTION 11B. If any charitable corporation described in section eleven A fails to comply for two consecutive years with the provisions of section eight F of chapter twelve requiring the filing of annual financial reports with the office of the attorney general, or if the attorney general is satisfied that such corporation has become inactive and that its dissolution would be in the public interest, the attorney general may petition the supreme judicial court for the dissolution of such corporation, requesting the court to authorize the administration of its funds for such similar public charitable purposes as the court may determine, and the court, after notice by mail or otherwise as it may order, may dissolve such corporation. The attorney general may include as many corporations in a single application as he deems fit, and the court may include in its decree any or all of said corporations. The clerk of the supreme judicial court shall submit to the commissioner of corporations and taxation a list of corporations so dissolved.

---

[1] Mass. Gen. Laws Ann., ch. 180, secs. 11A and 11B.

APPENDIX C. REPORTING FORMS

1. Internal Revenue Service, Form 990–A
2. California Form for Initial Registration of Charitable Trust
3. California Charitable Trust Analysis
4. California Registry Record Card
5. Illinois Periodic Report Form
6. Illinois Schedule of Securities
7. Massachusetts Annual Report Form
8. English Statement of Account

RETURN OF ORGANIZATION EXEMPT FROM INCOME TAX
Section 501(c)(3) of the Internal Revenue Code

GENERAL INSTRUCTIONS

A. Who must file Form 990–A.—An annual statement of gross income, receipts, disbursements, etc., is required by law of every organization which is exempt from tax as described in section 501(c)(3) of the Code, excepting only (1) a religious organization; (2) an educational organization if it normally maintains a regular faculty and curriculum and normally has a regularly organized body of pupils or students in attendance at the place where its educational activities are regularly carried on; (3) a charitable organization, or an organization for the prevention of cruelty to children or animals, if supported in whole or in part by funds contributed by the United States or any State or political subdivision thereof, or primarily supported by contributions of the general public; (4) an organization operated, supervised, or controlled by or in connection with a religious organization described in section 501(c)(3). This return must be filed on or before the 15th day of the fifth month following the close of the annual accounting period. Return must be filed with the District Director of Internal Revenue for the district in which is located the principal place of business or principal office of the organization. An organization having no place of business or principal office in any internal revenue district in the United States must file with the Director of International Operations, Internal Revenue Service, Washington, D.C., 20225. The law provides penalties for failure to furnish the information required by this form.

B. Group returns.—A group return on this form may be filed by a central, parent, or like organization for two or more local organizations which (a) are chartered by, or affiliated or associated with, the central organization at the close of the central organization's annual accounting period, (b) are subject to the general supervision and examination of the central organization, and (c) are exempt from tax under a group ruling. Each local organization annually must authorize the central organization to include it in the group return and must also annually file statements verified under oath or affirmation with the central organization of the information required to be included in the group return. The group return shall be in addition to the separate return of the central office organization but in lieu of separate returns by the local organizations included in the group return. There shall be attached to such group return schedules showing separately (a) the total number, names, addresses, and employer identification numbers of the local organizations included, and (b) the same information for those not included therein. Prior to, or simultaneous with, the filing of a group return, the central organization must notify each district director for the district in which is located the principal place of business or principal office of each local organization included in the group return that the local organization has or has not been, or will or will not be, included in such group return. The filing with each district director concerned of a copy of the schedules listing the organizations included in and excluded from the group return constitutes notice as required by the preceding sentence.

C. Public inspection of Form 990–A.—In addition to Part I, organizations described in A above are also required by law to file certain information on Part II of this form which is made available to the public. In connection with Part II of this form all required information must be submitted except that the organization may omit any information relating to a trade secret, patent, process, style of work, or apparatus which would adversely affect the organization, or any information which would adversely affect the national defense. In such cases, the organization must submit this type of information only with Part I, together with a statement identifying which items are being withheld from Part II and the reasons for doing so. Schedules supporting specific entries or other information limited to Part I must be attached only to Part I of the return. These schedules must not be included on the same sheet with those applicable to Part II since this information is open to public inspection.

D. Signature and verification.—The return must be signed either by the president, vice president, treasurer, assistant treasurer or chief accounting officer, or other corporate officer (such as tax officer) who is authorized to sign. A receiver, trustee, or assignee must sign any return which he is required to file on behalf of a corporation. If the return is filed on behalf of a trust, it must be signed by the duly authorized trustee or trustees. The return must also be signed by any person, firm, or corporation who prepared the return. If the return is prepared by a firm or corporation, it should be signed in the name of the firm or corporation. The verification is not required if the return is prepared by a regular full-time employee of the organization.

E. Form 990–T.—Section 511 of the Code imposes a tax in the case of certain organizations described in sections 401(a) and 501(c) (2), (3), (5), (6), and (17), on income derived (a) from operation of a business enterprise which is unrelated to the purpose for which such organization received an exemption or (b) from certain rentals from property leased to others on a long-term basis. (Use Form 990–T.)

F. Form 1099.—Every organization engaged in a trade or business (which includes for this purpose all exempt functions) shall make information returns on Forms 1099 and 1096 with respect to payments made during the calendar year in the course of such trade or business of fixed or determinable salaries, wages, commissions, fees, and other forms of compensation for services rendered aggregating $600 or more (to the extent not reported on Form W–2), and rents, royalties, annuities, pensions, and other gains, profits, and income aggregating $600 or more. (See Section 1.6041–1, Income Tax Regulations.) Where the aggregate compensation of an employee is $600 or more and a portion thereof is required to be reported on Form W–2, the remainder must be reported on Form 1099, regardless of amount. Forms 1099 and 1096 are required to be submitted for payments of certain interest aggregating $10 or more.

G. Attachments.—The schedules contained on the official form should be used unless the entry spaces provided are not sufficient for your needs. Attachments must contain the name and address of the organization as well as the required information and must follow the format of the schedules and must be presented in the same sequence as the lines of the form. See General Instruction C relating to information subject to public inspection.

H. Organizations organized or created in a foreign country or United States possession.—Amounts must be reported in United States currency (state conversion rate used) and information must be furnished in the English language. All items must be reported in aggregate including amounts from both within and without the United States.

I. Officers, directors, trustees, etc.—Attach a schedule to pages 2, 4, and 6 indicating (1) the name and position of each official (officer, director, trustee, etc.) of your organization (whether or not compensated); (2) the time each devoted to his position; and (3) the compensation (including salary and expense account allowance), if any, paid to each. In addition, the schedule attached to page 2, but not to pages 4 and 6, shall indicate (by placing the appropriate letter next to the name of each official) whether the official was:

    (a) the creator or a substantial contributor,

    (b) a brother or sister, spouse, ancestor, or lineal descendent of the creator or substantial contributor,

    (c) an employee of the creator or substantial contributor or of a business venture owned (50 percent or more of voting stock or 50 percent or more of value of all stock of a corporation, or a 50 percent or larger interest in the capital or profits of an unincorporated business venture), directly or indirectly, by the creator and/or substantial contributor,

    (d) an attorney or accountant of the creator or substantial contributor or of a business venture owned (50 percent or more of voting stock or 50 percent or more of the value of all stock of a corporation, or a 50 percent or larger interest in the capital or profits of an unincorporated business venture), directly or indirectly, by the creator and/or substantial contributor, or

    (e) none of the above.

J. Market value of assets.—Attach a statement to pages 2, 4, and 6 showing as of the end of the year: (a) the total market value of your investments in governmental bonds, etc., nongovernmental bonds and corporate stocks which are regularly traded in an over-the-counter market or on a stock exchange; (b) your estimate of the total fair market value of your other assets (including, but not limited to, governmental bonds, etc., nongovernmental bonds and corporate stocks which are not regularly traded in an over-the-counter market or on a stock exchange); and (c) the total of (a) and (b).

8. Attach a schedule to pages 1, 3, and 5 showing with respect to each asset (whether or not depreciable) sold or exchanged: (a) date acquired, manner of acquisition, date sold, and to whom sold: (b) gross sales price; (c) cost, other basis, or value at time of acquisition if donated (state which); (d) expense of sale and cost of improvements subsequent to acquisition; (e) if depreciable property, depreciation since acquisition; and (f) gain or loss—(b) plus (e) minus the sum of (c) and (d).

13. Attach a schedule to pages 1, 3, and 5 in support of contributions, gifts, grants, scholarships, etc., showing: (a) each class of activity; (b) separate total for each activity; (c) name and address of donee and amount of distribution to donee; and (d) relationship of donee, if related by blood, marriage, adoption, or employment (including children of employees) to any person or corporation having an interest in the organization such as creator, donor, director, trustee, officer, etc. Activities should be classified according to purpose in greater detail than merely charitable, educational, religious, or scientific. For example, payments for nursing service, for laboratory construction, for fellowships, or for assistance to indigent families should be so identified.

Although the actual distribution of cash, securities or other property is to be entered on this line the expenses in connection with the distributions and those expenses incurred for philanthropic programs operated by the organization itself are not to be included on this line but should be entered on line 12 and in column 4 of Schedule A.

Where the fair market value of the property at the time of disbursement is the measure of the contribution and is used in arriving at the amount to be entered on this line the schedule must also show: (1) description of the contributed property; (2) book value of the contributed property; (3) the method used to determine the book value; and (4) the date of the gift. In such case the difference between fair market value and book value should be reflected in the books of account.

17. In all cases where money, securities or other property aggregating $100 or more is received directly or indirectly from one person in one or more transactions during the year attach an itemized schedule to page 1 (not to pages 3 and 5) showing the name, address, date received, and the total amount received from each such person. If the contribution is in the form of property the description and the fair market value of such property shall also be furnished. (The term "person" includes individuals, fiduciaries, partnerships, corporations, associations, and other organizations.)

21. Attach a schedule to pages 1, 3, and 5 for contributions, gifts, grants, scholarships, etc., which were paid out within the year, showing the same information required in Instruction 13. For those disbursements made in prior years only the total need be shown.

Schedule A.—See General Instruction J for schedule required to be submitted concerning the officers, directors, and trustees of your organization.

For depreciation attach a schedule to pages 1, 3, and 5 showing: (a) kind of property; (b) date acquired; (c) cost or other basis (exclude land); (d) depreciation taken in prior years; (e) method of computation; (f) rate (%) or life (years); and (g) depreciation this year (total additional first-year depreciation claimed must be shown on a separate line of the depreciation schedule).

Expenses to be entered in column 2 of Schedule A should be extended to columns 3 through 6 on the basis of accounting records. If such records do not provide for this division, expenses may be divided on any reasonable basis, such as an approximation of the use of a facility or the time spent by an individual.

Schedule B.—The balance sheet should agree with the books of account or any differences should be reconciled.

(1) In all cases where investments in corporate stocks at the close of the taxable year include 5 percent or more of any class of stock of any corporation, attach a schedule to pages 2, 4, and 6 showing: (a) name of corporation, class of stock and whether the stock is voting or nonvoting; (b) number of shares owned of each class at beginning and end of the taxable year; (c) total number of shares outstanding of each class; (d) value of stock as recorded in the books and included in line 7; (e) estimate of fair market value of stock; (f) date acquired; (g) manner of acquisition; and (h) dividends received on each class of such stock.

(2) In any case in which you do hold 5 percent or more of any class of stock of any corporation, indicate those in which your holdings plus the sum of the holdings of the following:

  (a) the creator of your organization,
  (b) a substantial contributor to your organization,
  (c) a brother or sister, spouse, ancestor or lineal descendent of such creator or substantial contributor, and
  (d) a business venture owned (50 percent or more of voting stock or a 50 percent or more of value of all stock of a corporation, or a 50 percent or larger interest in the capital or profits of an unincorporated business venture), directly or indirectly, by any of the above,

constitute 50 percent or more of the voting stock or 50 percent or more of all stock of the corporation. Attach to page 2, but not to pages 4 and 6, a schedule showing the class of stock and number of shares owned (if known) in such corporation at the beginning and end of the year by the parties described in (a) through (d) of this instruction.

(3) If your total accounts and notes receivable exceed $5,000, attach a schedule to pages 2, 4, and 6 indicating the total amount of accounts receivable and/or notes receivable as of the end of the year which are attributable to each of the following categories: (a) receivables arising in connection with your organization's exempt activities, for example, scholarship loans; (b) receivables arising out of related or unrelated business activities; (c) receivables arising out of transactions in an account with a securities broker-dealer; and (d) other receivables. With respect to receivables described in (d), indicate for each receivable of $1,000 or more: (1) name of debtor; (2) amount of debt; (3) rate of interest, if any; and (4) circumstances out of which such debt arose including, in the case of funds lent by your organization, the use, if known, to which the borrower intended to put the borrowed funds.

(4) If your total accounts, bonds and notes payable exceed $5,000, attach a schedule to pages 2, 4, and 6 indicating the total amount of accounts payable and/or bonds and notes payable as of the end of the year which are attributable to each of the following categories: (a) the purchase of supplies and services used in connection with your organization's exempt activities; (b) debts arising out of related or unrelated business activities; (c) the purchase of securities from a securities broker-dealer; and (d) other debts. With respect to debts described in (d), indicate for each debt of $1,000 or more: (1) name of creditor; (2) amount of debt; (3) rate of interest, if any; and (4) circumstances out of which such debt arose including, in the case of funds borrowed by your organization, the use to which you put the borrowed funds.

Instructions 990-A (1964)

511

FORM **990–A**
U.S. Treasury Department
Internal Revenue Service

RETURN OF ORGANIZATION EXEMPT FROM INCOME TAX—1964

Section 501(c)(3)
of the Code

or other taxable year beginning ...., 1964, and ending ...., 19......

Legal name of organization	Address (number, street, city or town, State and Postal ZIP code)	Employer Identification No.
Please type or print		

PART I Part I (pages 1 and 2) information required pursuant to Sections 6033, 6001 and other applicable sections of the Internal Revenue Code. **NOTE: One copy of Part I and two copies of Part II must be filed.**

Line No.
1. Gross sales or receipts from business activities.....................
2.   Less: Cost of goods sold or of operations (attach schedule).....................
3. Gross profit from business activities.....................
4. Interest.....................
5. Dividends.....................
6. Rents.....................
7. Royalties.....................
8. Gain (or loss) from sale of assets, excluding inventory items (See Instruction 8).....................
9. Other income (attach schedule.—Do not include contributions, gifts, grants, etc.   (See line 17.)).....................
10.   Total gross income (lines 3 to 9, inclusive).....................
11. Expenses of earning gross income from column 3, Schedule A.....................

DISBURSEMENTS MADE WITHIN THE YEAR OUT OF CURRENT OR ACCUMULATED INCOME FOR PURPOSES FOR WHICH EXEMPT, AND ACCUMULATION OF INCOME

12. Expenses of distributing current or accumulated income from column 4, Schedule A.....................
13. Contributions, gifts, grants; scholarships, etc. (See Instruction 13).....................
14. Accumulation of income within the year (line 10 less the sum of lines 11, 12, and 13).....................
15. Aggregate accumulation of income at beginning of the year.....................(.....................)
16. Aggregate accumulation of income at end of the year.....................(.....................)

RECEIPTS NOT REPORTED ELSEWHERE

17. Contributions, gifts, grants, etc., received (See Instruction 17).....................
18.   Less: Expenses of raising and collecting amount on line 17, from column 5, Schedule A.....................
19. Net contributions, gifts, grants, etc., received.....................

DISBURSEMENTS MADE OUT OF PRINCIPAL FOR PURPOSES FOR WHICH EXEMPT

20. Expenses of distributing principal from column 6, Schedule A.....................
21. Contributions, gifts, grants, scholarships, etc.:   (a) Paid out in prior years (.....................)
                                                       (b) Paid out within the year (See Instruction 21).....................

Schedule A—Allocation of Expenses (See Instructions for Attachments Required)

1. Item	2. Total	3. Expenses of earning gross income	4. Expenses of distributing income	5. Expenses of raising and collecting principal	6. Expenses of distributing principal
(a) Compensation of officers, etc.					
(b) Other salaries and wages..........					
(c) Interest					
(d) Taxes......................					
(e) Rent					
(f) Depreciation (and depletion)........					
(g) Miscellaneous expenses (attach sch.)					
(h) Totals....................					
		Enter on line 11	Enter on line 12	Enter on line 18	Enter on line 20

Under penalties of perjury, I declare that I have examined this return, including accompanying schedules and statements, and to the best of my knowledge and belief it is true, correct, and complete.   If prepared by a person other than taxpayer, his declaration is based on all information of which he has any knowledge.

CORPORATE SEAL			
Date	Signature of officer		Title
Date	Individual or firm signature of preparer		Address

	Beginning of Year		End of Year	
ASSETS	Amount	Total	Amount	Total
1. Cash..				
2. Accounts receivable (See instructions)...............				
Less: Reserve for bad debts....................				
3. Notes receivable (See instructions)..................				
Less: Reserve for bad debts....................				
4. Inventories..				
5. Investments in governmental obligations..............				
6. Investments in nongovernmental bonds, etc...........				
7. Investments in corporate stocks (See instructions)......				
8. Mortgage loans (Number of loans _____).........				
9. Other investments (attach schedule).................				
10. Depreciable (and depletable) assets (attach schedule)...				
Less: Reserve for depreciation (and depletion)...				
11. Land				
12. Other assets (attach schedule).....................				
13. Total assets.................................				
LIABILITIES AND NET WORTH				
14. Accounts payable (See instructions).................				
15. Contributions, gifts, grants, etc., payable.............				
16. (a) Bonds and notes payable (See instructions).......				
(b) Mortgages payable........................				
17. Other liabilities (attach schedule)				
18. Capital stock: (a) Preferred stock				
(b) Common stock.....................				
19. Membership certificates............................				
20. Principal or other capital				
21. Reserves (attach schedule).........................				
22. Accumulated income or earned surplus:				
(a) Attributable to ordinary income................				
(b) Attributable to gains from sale of assets.........				
23. Total liabilities and net worth.................				

1. Date of current exemption letter _____

2. Attach a detailed statement of the nature of your business, charitable, and all other activities.

3. Have you attached the information required by:
(a) Instruction I?...................... ☐ Yes ☐ No
(b) Instruction J? .... ☐ Yes ☐ No

4. Have you filed a tax return on Form 990-T for this year?... ☐ Yes ☐ No
If "Yes," where filed? _____

5. In what year was your organization formed? _____
In what State or country? _____

6. If successor to previously existing organization(s), give name(s) and address(es) of the predecessor organization(s) _____
_____

7. If you have capital stock issued and outstanding, state with respect to each class of stock—
(a) The number of shares outstanding............... _____
(b) The number of shares held by individuals........ _____
(c) The number of shares held by organizations...... _____
(d) The number of shareholders at end of year....... _____
(e) Whether any dividends may be paid........... ☐ Yes ☐ No

8. If you acquired capital assets out of income, attach itemized list and amount thereof.

9. Have any changes not previously reported to the Internal Revenue Service been made in your articles of incorporation or bylaws or other instruments of similar import?.... ☐ Yes ☐ No
If "Yes," attach a copy of the amendments.

10. Have you had any sources of income or engaged in any activities not previously reported to the Internal Revenue Service?.................................. ☐ Yes ☐ No
If "Yes," attach detailed statement.

11. Did you hold any real property for rental purposes with respect to which there is an indebtedness incurred in acquiring the property or in making improvements thereto or which was acquired subject to a mortgage or similar lien?........ ☐ Yes ☐ No
If "Yes," attach detailed statement.

12. Have you during the year either advocated or opposed (including the publishing or distributing of statements) any legislation, national, State, or local?.............. ☐ Yes ☐ No
If "Yes," attach a detailed description of such activities and copies of any such statements.

13. Have you during the year participated in, or intervened in (including the publishing or distributing of statements) any political campaign on behalf of or in opposition to any candidate for public office?.................... ☐ Yes ☐ No
If "Yes," attach a detailed description of such activities and copies of any such statements.

14. After July 1, 1950, did—
The creator of your organization, or
A contributor to your organization, or
A brother or sister (whole or half blood), spouse, ancestor, or lineal descendent of such creator or contributor, or
A corporation owned (50 percent or more of value of all stock) directly or indirectly by such creator or contributor—
(a) Borrow any part of your income or corpus?........ ☐ Yes ☐ No
(b) Receive any compensation for personal services from you?................................ ☐ Yes ☐ No
(c) Have any part of your services or assets made available to him? .... ☐ Yes ☐ No
(d) Purchase any securities or other property from you?.. ☐ Yes ☐ No
(e) Sell any securities or other property to you?........ ☐ Yes ☐ No
(f) Receive any of your income or corpus in other transactions? .... ☐ Yes ☐ No
If answer to any question is "Yes," attach detailed statement unless previously reported. If previously reported, give year(s).

15. Do you hold 5 percent or more of any class of stock in any corporation?................................... ☐ Yes ☐ No
If "Yes," you must submit the information required by the instructions for Schedule B.

☆ U.S. GOVERNMENT PRINTING OFFICE : 1965—O—737-705   o59—16—78519-1

513

REGISTRATION OF CHARITABLE TRUST

Date:_____

1. Name of   Charitable Trust
            or
            Charitable Corporation

    Address of headquarters:

2. Charitable Trust under:

    A. Estate of

        Will probated County of   Probate No.

        Last account rendered on

    B. Inter vivos trust of

        Date of instrument

    C. Charitable Corporation or corporation formed for the administration of a Charitable Trust

        Name of corporation: Address:

3. Names and addresses of trustees or directors and officers of corporation:

4. Attached hereto are the following documents:

5. Description and value of Trust assets:

6. Purpose of the Trust:

7. Name and address of recipients of benefits under the Charitable Trust:

Registration No. CT_____

Date of Registration_____

For use of the Registrar's office only

Executed by

_____
Name   Title

_____
Address

SEE OTHER SIDE FOR INSTRUCTIONS

[California Form for Initial Registration of Charitable Trust]

514

INSTRUCTIONS FOR PREPARING AND FILING
REGISTRATION FORM OF CHARITABLE TRUST

WHO MUST FILE

Pursuant to Sec. 12581 of the Gov. Code and Sec. 300 of the Calif. Adm. Code, Title 11, all Trustees holding property for charitable purposes in the State of California must register with the Registrar of Charitable Trusts except those parties exempt by Sec. 12583 of the Government Code.

WHEN TO FILE

Pursuant to Sec. 12585 of the Gov. Code and Sec. 300, Calif. Adm. Code, Title 11, every Trustee subject to the Uniform Supervision of Trustees for Charitable Purposes Act shall file with the Attorney General within six months after any part of the income or principal is authorized or required to be applied to charitable purposes.

NAMES AND ADDRESSES OF TRUSTEES OR CORPORATE OFFICERS (Item 3)

In the case of a testamentary or inter vivos trust, please submit the names and addresses of all individual and corporate trustees.

In the case of a Charitable Corporation or corporation created for the administration of a Charitable Trust, please submit names, titles, and addresses of all corporate directors and officers.

DOCUMENTS REQUIRED TO BE ATTACHED (Item 4)

Testamentary Trust: A certified copy of Will and Decree of Distribution
Inter Vivos Trust: A certified copy of instrument creating Trust
Corporate Trust: A certified copy of the Articles of Incorporation and amendments thereof and By-Laws.

FINANCIAL STATEMENT (Item 5)

Please present a detailed description of all assets and liabilities, including cash on hand and in banks, name and number of investment securities at cost or book value, personal and real property, etc. Attach separate sheets when necessary, to supply all information.

EXECUTION OF REGISTRATION FORM

Where there is a single trustee, the form is to be executed by that individual.

Where there is a group of individuals or corporation holding as trustees, any one of the trustees may execute the form. In the case of a charitable corporation the form should be executed by an authorized officer.

WHERE TO FILE

Please forward (1) copy of completed form to the Registrar of Charitable Trusts, Room 306, 923 12th Street, Sacramento.

If additional information is required, please refer to the Uniform Supervision of Trustees for Charitable Purposes Act (Secs. 12580-12595, Gov. Code) and the Administrative Rules and Regulations pursuant to the aforesaid Act (Secs. 300-310, Title 11, Calif. Adm. Code).

[California Form for Initial Registration of Charitable Trust, page 2]

CHARITABLE TRUST ANALYSIS

Name of   Charitable Trust
            or
            Charitable Foundation

Address: County:

Charitable Trust under:

A. Estate of

   Will probated County of

   Last account rendered:

B. Inter vivos trust of

   Date of instrument:

C. Charitable Corporation:

Trust purpose:_____

_____

_____

_____

_____

Description and value of trust assets: Date_____

   Cash_____

   Other current_____

   Investments_____

   Property-Equipment_____

   Other-describe_____

   Total_____

Date created:_____

Date registered:_____

Reporting period_____

Audited by_____Date_____

TRUST CLASSIFICATION	
Testamentary	Intervivos
Corporation	Bank
Co-Trustee	Individual
Other	

JUS 625 (5-62)

[*California Charitable Trust Analysis*]

516

Provisions for use of income, type of investments, powers of trustees, beneficiaries, etc. _____
_____
_____
_____
_____

Trustee: _____ Address: _____ Bond

Trustee: _____ Address: _____ Bond

FINANCIAL DATA

	CAPITAL ACCOUNT—SURPLUS			DISTRIBUTION OF FUNDS					
Date	Year End Balance	Income or Donated Capital	Expended	Religious	Education	Medical Scientific Research	Charitable	Adm'n or Operations	Accumulated Income

Remarks:_____
_____
_____
_____
_____

[*California Charitable Trust Analysis, page 2*]

517

[California Registry Record Card]

518

PERIODIC REPORT OF CHARITABLE TRUST

REGISTRATION NO. CT_____

Charitable Trust
1. Name of   or
     Charitable Corp.

2. Covering period of   , 19____ to   , 19____

3. Summary of Assets-Liabilities

4. Income:

5. Expenditures:

6. Names and addresses of recipients of benefits under the Charitable Trust:

7. If during the period of this report there have been any changes in the provisions of the Trust, please explain.

I swear under oath that this report (including any accompanying schedules and statements) has been examined by me and to the best of my knowledge and belief is a true, correct and complete report.

	Trustee	Place of Execution

Subscribed and sworn to before me this _____

day of _____, A.D. 19____.	Trustee	Place of Execution

(Notarial Seal) Notary Public	Trustee	Place of Execution

Form AGCT2   Please prepare this form in duplicate.

[Illinois Periodic Report Form]

519

WHERE TO FILE

Please forward completed forms to WILLIAM G. CLARK, ATTORNEY GENERAL, State of Illinois, Springfield, Illinois.

If additional information is required, please refer to the Charitable Trust Act (Sections 51 to 64 of Chapter 14 of the Illinois Revised Statutes, 1961).

WHO MUST FILE

Pursuant to Sec. 57, paragraph (a) of Chapter 14 of the Illinois Revised Statutes, 1961, every Trustee except those exempt under Secs. 54 and 56 of Chapter 14 of the Illinois Revised Statutes, 1961, must file with the Attorney General a periodic written report under oath.

WHEN TO FILE

The first periodic report shall be filed as required by paragraph (d) of Section 57 of Chapter 14 of the Illinois Revised Statutes, 1961.

ALTERNATIVE METHOD OF FILING

Section 57, paragraph (c) of Chapter 14 of Illinois Revised Statutes, 1961, provides for an alternative method of filing report.

ITEMS 3, 4 and 5

Please submit detailed financial statements (in duplicate) showing:

(a) A list of all assets and money on hand at the beginning and ending of such year. Securities in an investment portfolio with a total valuation in excess of $100,000.00 shall be scheduled on a form provided by the Attorney General.

(b) A list of all gains or losses from assets sold and investments made during the year, including statement of moneys derived from any sale and money placed in each investment.

(c) A statement of all receipts and income during the year, contributions, gifts or grants giving amount and source.

(d) A detailed statement of all disbursements and expenses during the year.

(e) A statement of the purposes for which the distributions, donations or payments have been made giving the name, address and amount disbursed to each recipient of benefits under the Charitable Trust.

(f) Other pertinent information concerning the Trust and its administration. When requested by the Attorney General any periodic report shall be supplemented to include such additional information as the Attorney General deems necessary to enable him to ascertain whether the corporation, trust or other relationship is being properly administered.

MODIFICATION IN TRUST STRUCTURE (Item 7)

Please submit a detailed report of any changes in trust indenture or any change of Trustee. In the case of a corporation formed for the administration of a charitable purpose, please submit any amendments to the Articles of Incorporation or changes in. By-Laws; and any changes in officers or directors of the corporation.

CERTIFICATION

Each Trustee must certify to the correctness of the periodic report in the manner provided on the form before a notary public or other officer authorized to administer oaths. In the case of a corporate Trustee certification shall be made by an authorized officer.

REGISTRATION NUMBER

Please enter in the space provided the permanent CT number assigned to this Charitable Trust. This number will be found on the copy of the Registration Statement returned to you.

Form AGCT2

355

[Illinois Periodic Report Form, page 2]

SCHEDULE OF SECURITIES

REGISTRATION NO. CT_____

Name of Organization		Period

SUMMARY OF INVESTMENTS

	Principal_____		Income_____	
Liquid Reserve — Cash . . .	$	%	$	%
Bonds				
Preferred Stocks				
Common Stocks				
Total Investment Account .		100%		100%

DIVERSIFICATION OF COMMON STOCKS

	PRINCIPAL			INCOME	
Industrial	Amount	%		Amount	%
Automobile and Accessories .	$			$	
Aviation					
Business Machines					
Chemicals					
Drugs					
Electrical Equipment					
Farm & Ind. Equipment . . .					
Food Products					
Machinery					
Merchandising					
Metal (non-ferrous)					
Miscellaneous					
Oil					
Railroad Equipment					
Steel					
Tobacco			PRINCIPAL		
			Amount	%	
TOTAL INDUSTRIALS			$		
Public Utilities					
Railroads					
Bank and Finance					
Insurance					
Others					
TOTAL COMMON STOCKS . . .			$	100	100

Form AGCT4   (49246—10M—12-61)

[Illinois Schedule of Securities]

DATE ACQUIRED	TYPE AND NAME OF SECURITY	INVENTORY BEGINNING PERIOD		PURCHASES		
		Shares or Principal	Cost	Number Shares	Cost Share	Gross Cost

[*Illinois Schedule of Securities, page 2*]

522

SALES			AMOUNT GAIN OR LOSS	INVENTORY END OF PERIOD			PERCENT-AGE OF TOTAL	ANNUAL INCOME	CURRENT % RETURN ON MARKET VALUE
Number Shares	Price Share	Gross Selling Price		Number Shares or Principal	Cost Value	Market Value			

[*Illinois Schedule of Securities, page 3*]

523

DIVISION OF PUBLIC CHARITIES
DEPARTMENT OF THE ATTORNEY GENERAL

REPORT TO BE FILED BY TRUSTEES OR GOVERNING BOARDS OF PUBLIC CHARITIES SUBJECT TO THE PROVISIONS OF G. L. c. 12, ss. 8B to 8J, INCLUSIVE (AS AMENDED)

This report shall be filed with the Division of Public Charities, Office of the Attorney General, State House, Boston, Mass., on or before June first in each year or on or before the sixtieth day following the end of a fiscal year ending in April or May. This report shall be for the last preceding fiscal year or last preceding calendar year, if no fiscal year.

FOR CALENDAR YEAR   Or other taxable year beginning   , 19   , and ending   , 19

Please type or print plainly

Legal name of organization   Address (number, street, city or town, postal zone, and State)

Telephone:

Names of Trustees, or President, Secretary and Treasurer   **Address**

....
....
....
....

State nature of activities (Attach detailed statement) ....

....

State the legal form of your organization. Corporation .... Statute under which incorporated .... Trust: intervivos ....
testamentary .... Unincorporated association .... Other .... Date organized ....

SCHEDULE A — RECEIPTS, EXPENSES AND ACCUMULATIONS AND DISTRIBUTIONS

Line No.	RECEIPTS	Principal Account	Income Account
1.	Gross sales or receipts		
2.	Less: Cost of goods sold or of operations (attach schedule)		
3.	Gross profit		
4.	Interest		
5.	Dividends		
6.	Rents and royalties		
7.	Gain (or loss) from sale of assets		
8.	Fees or dues from or on behalf of beneficiaries		
9.	Subscriptions and donations		
10.	Legacies received during year		
11.	Other income (attach itemized statement)		
12.	Total gross income (total lines 3 to 11)		
	(a) Total principal and income receipts		

	EXPENSES	Attributable to Fund Raising	Attributable to Program
13.	Compensation of officers, directors, trustees		
	(Number............)		
14.	Salaries and wages of employees		
	(Number: Full time............Part time............)		
15.	Interest		
16.	Taxes		
17.	Rent		
18.	Depreciation and depletion		
19.	Commissions paid for soliciting funds		. . . .
20.	Miscellaneous expenses (attach itemized statement)		
21.	Administrative and operating expenses (not included above)		
	(attach itemized statement)		
22.	Total expenses (lines 13 to 21 inclusive)		
	(a) Total expenses, fund raising and program		

ACCUMULATIONS AND DISBURSEMENTS

23.	Total net principal and income receipts. [line 12 (a) less line 22 (a)]	
24.	Disbursements:	
	(a) Funds transferred to affiliated organizations out of state (attach statement designating recipient and purpose)	
	(b) Contributions, gifts, grants, etc., paid during year	
25.	Net accumulation of principal and income within the year [line 23 less line 24 (a) and (b)]	
26.	Aggregate accumulation of principal or income at beginning of year	
27.	Accumulation of principal and income at end of year (line 25 plus line 26)	

THERE SHALL BE A FEE OF THREE DOLLARS FOR FILING THIS REPORT, TO BE PAID TO THE DIVISION OF PUBLIC CHARITIES AT TIME OF FILING. **PLEASE MAKE CHECKS PAYABLE TO THE COMMONWEALTH OF MASSACHUSETTS.**

A public charity which annually furnishes or publishes a financial report containing information as to endowment and other funds, real estate or tangible personal property, income and expenditures may file a copy of such report for any year with the Division as its report for such year as to the matters covered by said report. A public charity required by law to file accounts in the Probate Court may file a copy of such account for any year with the Division as its report for such year as to the matters covered by said account. This report shall not apply to property held for any religious purpose by any public charity. Failure for two successive years to file a report as required by chapter 12, section 8F, as amended, authorizes appropriate action to compel compliance.

(OVER)

[Massachusetts Annual Report Form]

SCHEDULE B — BALANCE SHEETS

ASSETS	Beginning of Year		End of Year	
	Amount	Total	Amount	Total
1. a. Checking accounts				
b. Savings accounts				
2. Notes and accounts receivable				
Less: Reserve for bad debts				
3. Inventories				
4. Investments in governmental obligations				
5. Investments in nongovernmental bonds, etc.				
6. Investments in corporate stocks				
7. Other investments (itemize)				
8. Capital assets:				
(a) Depreciable (and depletable) assets				
Less: Reserve for depreciation (and depletion)				
(b) Land				
9. Other assets (itemize)				
10. Total assets				
LIABILITIES				
11. Accounts payable				
12. Bonds and notes payable:				
(a) With original maturity of less than 1 year				
(b) With original maturity of 1 year or more				
13. Mortgages payable				
14. Other liabilities (itemize)				
15. Total liabilities				
NET WORTH				
16. Total net worth				

1. State the costs of programs designed to educate or inform the public which also include an appeal for contributions (see instruction 2).

2. Has your organization ever been enjoined by any court from soliciting contributions?_____If "yes," attach detailed statement.

3. Are your accounts audited?_____ By whom_____

Address_____

4. Does audit include an examination of securities?_____

5. Do you have federal tax exemption letter?_____Date_____

CERTIFICATION BY OFFICERS

UNDER PENALTY OF PERJURY, I/WE CERTIFY THAT THE INFORMATION FURNISHED IN THIS STATEMENT AND ALL CONTINUATION SHEETS IS TRUE AND CORRECT TO THE BEST OF MY/OUR KNOWLEDGE.

_____
Signature of President or other authorized officer

_____   _____
Title   Date signed

_____   _____   _____
Signature of Chief Fiscal Officer   Title   Date signed

CERTIFICATION BY INDEPENDENT PUBLIC ACCOUNTANT

I/WE CERTIFY THAT I/WE HAVE EXAMINED THE FINANCIAL RECORDS OF THE PUBLIC CHARITY AND FIND THIS FINANCIAL STATEMENT CORRECT.

_____
Signature of independent public accountant

_____
Address

A certification by an independent public accountant is required if the public charity has gross receipts or five thousand dollars or more or investment income of one thousand dollars or more. General Laws, chapter 12, section 8F, as amended.

GENERAL INSTRUCTIONS

1. The receipts portion of Schedule A contains both a principal account and an income account. The principal account is provided so that grants and contributions which are intended by the donor or contributor to be applied to a permanent endowment fund or principal account may be reported without giving the impression that income is being unreasonably accumulated. Receipts which are to be applied to current expenses and disbursements should be reported in the income column and not in the principal column.

2. Chapter 12, section 8F, provides that the costs of programs designed to educate or to inform the public which include a solicitation of funds shall be separately reported and clearly distinguished from the costs of such programs which do not include such a solicitation. Some agencies which solicit from the public distribute printed literature, finance radio and television broadcasts and utilize other media for educational and informational purposes. When such communications include a solicitation of funds, a problem arises as to a valid apportionment between educational (charitable) and fund-raising costs. No effort has been made to interfere with the independent judgment of the officers of such agencies; however, such expenditures must be specially noted on the annual report.

10M-8-64-938669

[Massachusetts Annual Report Form, page 2]

Name of CHARITY	CHARITY COMMISSION REFERENCE NUMBER :
PLACE.................................... COUNTY.......................... (note 3)	

STATEMENT of ACCOUNT for year ending...19
(note 4)

Particulars of Trustees (*note 5*)

Name	Address	Occupation or description

(433) Wt56993·2719 10/61 10,000 JC&SLtd Gp952

[English Statement of Account]

526

LAND AND

OCCUPIED FOR PURPOSES OF THE CHARITY *(note 6)*		
Description	Acreage (if known)	Description
Land and Buildings not representing permanent endowment *(note 9)*		Land and Buildings not representing permanent endowment *(note 9)*
Land and Buildings representing permanent endowment *(note 9)*		Land and Buildings representing permanent endowment *(note 9)*

INVESTMENTS (STOCKS, SHARES,

Description *(note 10)*

Expendable *(note 12)*

Non-Expendable *(note 13)*

RENTCHARGES OR SIMILAR FIXED PAYMENTS

Description of property charged	Amount		
	£	s.	d.

(2)

[English Statement of Account, page 2]

527

OF ASSETS

BUILDINGS

INCOME PRODUCING *(note 7)*

Acreage (if known)	Tenant	Term or Tenancy *(note 8)*	Rent £	s.	d.

MORTGAGES ETC.)

Names of Stockholders *(Note 11)*

TO THE CHARITY *(note 14)*

Names and addresses of	
Owner	Person from whom payment is received

(3)

[English Statement of Account, page 3]

528

A. Producing Income	£	s.	d.
RECEIPTS FROM LAND AND BUILDINGS			
Aggregate rents received			
Easements and wayleaves			
Income tax repayments			
Grants from local authorities towards improvements and rebuilding			
Money borrowed for improvement or rebuilding			
Other receipts			
Total Receipts			

LESS PAYMENTS (*note* 15)	£	s.	d.
Repairs			
Insurance			
Agent's Fees			
Surveyor's Fees			
Legal Costs			
Rates			
Sinking Fund or Extraordinary Repair Fund contributions			
Other outgoings (*note* 16)			
Total Payments			
Net Income (carried to p. 6)			

(4)

[English Statement of Account, page 4]

529

	B. Occupied for purposes of the Charity (*note* 17)	£	s.	d.

PAYMENTS

  Repairs

  Insurance

  General rates

  Water rate

  Electricity

  Gas

  Sinking Fund or Extraordinary Repair Fund contributions

  Repayment (and interest) of loans for improvement and rebuilding

  Other outgoings (*note* 16)

Total Payments

	£	s.	d.

LESS RECEIPTS

  Rents from occasional lettings

  Easements and Wayleaves

  Exchequer subsidies and grants from local
    authorities towards improvement or rebuilding

  Money borrowed for improvement or rebuilding

  Contributions from almspersons or other beneficiaries

Total Receipts

Net Expenditure (carried to p. 7)

(5)

[English Statement of Account, page 5]

530

	Moneys expendable		
	£	s.	d.
BALANCE brought forward from last account			
NET INCOME FROM LAND AND BUILDINGS (brought forward from p. 4)			
INCOME FROM OTHER INVESTMENTS (*note* 18)			
RENTCHARGES ETC.			
FIXED ANNUAL PAYMENTS TO THE CHARITY NOT ATTACHED TO LAND (*note* 19)			
SUBSCRIPTIONS (*note* 20)			
OTHER INCOME RECEIVED (*note* 21)			
INCOME TAX REPAYMENTS (*note* 22)			
SALE OF LAND OR OTHER INVESTMENTS (*note* 23)			
TOTAL			

	Moneys not expendable		
	£	s.	d.
BALANCE brought forward from last account			
BEQUESTS OR GIFTS (*note* 27)			
SALE OF LAND OR OTHER INVESTMENTS (*note* 28)			
TOTAL			

(6)

[English Statement of Account, page 6]

531

as income

	£	s.	d.

ADMINISTRATION

    Stationery, postage and telephone

    Salary of clerk or other paid officer

    Audit fee

    Rent

    Travelling expenses

    Appeals for funds

    Other expenses

EXPENDITURE ON OBJECTS OF THE CHARITY (*note* 24)

Net expenditure on land and buildings occupied for purposes of the charity
(brought forward from p. 5)

PURCHASE OF LAND OR OTHER INVESTMENTS (*note* 25)

BALANCE (*note* 26)

TOTAL

as income

	£	s.	d.

PURCHASE OF LAND OR OTHER INVESTMENTS (*note* 29)

OTHER EXPENDITURE (*note* 30)

BALANCE (*note* 31)

TOTAL

(7)

[English Statement of Account, page 7]

532

STATEMENT OF ALL MONEYS OWING TO THE CHARITY (*note* 32)	£	s.	d.
INCOME TAX REFUND DUE FOR YEARS................................			
MONEYS OWING FROM OTHER SOURCES			
TOTAL			

STATEMENT OF ALL MONEYS OWING BY THE CHARITY (*note* 32)	£	s.	d.
TOTAL			

TRUSTEES' CERTIFICATE (*note* 33)	AUDIT CERTIFICATE (If auditor has been appointed) (*note* 34)
I/We certify that the foregoing Statement of Account is correct.	*Signature of Auditor* .... *Occupation or qualification* ....

This statement of account is forwarded by:—

Name ....

Address ....

....

....

(8)

[*English Statement of Account, page 8*]

533

APPENDIX D. LIST OF CASES

535

INDEX

Index

543

and Patman investigation, 365–373; in a pluralistic society, 49–53, 72, 192, 358; "private," 190–191; prohibited transactions, 179–181; and Reece Committee, 360–365; statutes permitting incorporation as, 120–122; survey of, in Texas, 249; survey of, in Washington, 255; and tax laws, 64–72, 158–193, 356, 407; Texas, definition of, 251; Treasury Department Report on, 374–380; as trusts, 82–111; in United States, 43–48, 375

Frankalmoign. See Tenure

Franklin, Benjamin, 43–44, 302–303; and Franklin Foundation, Inc., 88–89, 129

Franklin Foundation. *See* Franklin, Benjamin

Fratcher, William F., 105*n*

Fraud, 439; and statute of limitations, 218

Freund, Ernst, 35*n*

Fulmer, David R., 387*n*

Fund-raising organizations, 12. *See also* Solicitation

GENERAL charitable intent, 74

General Corporation Law. *See* New York

General incorporation statutes, 62, 64, 113. *See also* Incorporation; Charitable corporations

Georgia, 76, 239; law of trusts in, 220; legal requirements: charitable corporations, 481, charitable trusts, 466

Gibb, H. A. R., 16*n*

Gifts, 141; and estate taxes, 368; tax on, 71

Girard, Stephen, 38

Gilbert's Act (1786), 27

Giles, D. P. F., 422*n*

Goodwin, Angier L., 361*n*

Government spending, 11, 49. *See also* Philanthropy; United States

Gray, John Chipman, 80*n;* defines charitable trust, 56; on vesting of trust, 87

Greeks, 11; and "living legal heir," 14

Gross national product, 48

Guardian ad litem, 213

Guilds, 11, 22, 23

HALDANE, Lord, 60

Hamlin, Robert H., 229*n*

Harvard College, 77, 201

Harvard Law Review, Notes, 90*n*, 126*n*, 127*n*, 130*n*, 136*n*, 143*n*, 217*n*

Harvard Law School, 9

Harvard Legislative Research Bureau, 232

Hawaii, 241; attorney general, role of, 253–254; *cy pres* in, 253; legal requirements: charitable corporations, 481, charitable trusts, 466

Hays, Brooks, 358

Hays, Wayne L., 363

Health and welfare organizations, 345

Henry VIII, 17, 20, 23

Henry V, 20

Henry II, 17

Henry VI, 22

Hobhouse, Arthur, 88*n*

Holdsworth, H. V., 19*n*

Hollis, Ernest V., 14*n*, 15*n*

Holmes, Oliver Wendell, 219

Hornstein, George D., 138*n*, 142*n*, 143*n*, 156*n*

Houghteling, James L., 19*n*, 220*n*

House of Lords, 60–61

House of Representatives, United States. *See* Congress, United States

Howard, Lawrence C., 303*n*

Hudson Bay Company, 34

Hurst, J. Willard, 220*n*

IDAHO, 199; legal requirements: charitable corporations, 481, charitable trusts, 466

Illegality of purpose, 58. *See also* Charitable purposes

Illinois: abuses uncovered in, 333–338; administration of supervisory program, 335–336, 338–339; adoption of Uniform Act in, 332–333; attorney general, duties of, 211, 332–337; coverage of Uniform Act, 266–267, 332–333; investigation of charities in, 337–338; legal requirements: charitable corporations, 481, charitable trusts, 467; legislation proposed in, 333; number of charities registered, 336; operation of Uniform Act in, 332–339; regulations, 333–334, text, 500–505; report forms, 336, 519–523; reporting requirements, 333, 334; supervision of solicitation, 333

Immunity, from tort actions: of charitable corporations, 153; of charitable trusts, 110–111

Imperfect provisions. *See* Charitable trusts, imperfect provisions for

Impossibility, 73, 75–78. See also *Cy pres*

Impracticability, 73, 75–78. See also *Cy pres*

Income, 48, 90, 128, 160, 188, 383, 408; accumulation of, 90, 171–178;

destination of, and tax exemption, 159, 171; and Internal Revenue Code, 285, 362, 403; and Internal Revenue Service, 171–176; and Patman investigation, 367–368; and prohibited transactions, 179–183; and Treasury Department Report, 377–378; unreasonable accumulations and misuse of, 171–179, 186, 187–188, 246, 329, 401, 402; and *Vaqf,* 16

Income Tax Acts (1913–1918), 65

Income tax law. *See* Tax laws

Incorporation, 62–64, 122, 129, 191; California laws on, 120; chartering provisions, 225, 435, 479–490 *passim;* contractual nature of charter, 113; and *fundatio incipiens,* 206; in Indiana, 122; and legislation, 225; in Massachusetts, 117–119, 227; in Michigan, 120–121; in New York, 114–116; in Pennsylvania, 116–117; in South Carolina, 119–120, 227; by special acts of legislature, 41, 62–64, 113–114; of trustees of charitable trusts, 129. *See also* Charitable corporations; Corporations; Nonprofit corporations

Incorporators, 133

Indefinite existence, privilege of, 17

Indefiniteness of beneficiaries. *See* Beneficiary

Indiana, 213, 223; attorney general, role of, 235, 239, 240; introduction of Uniform Act in, 260; laws concerning incorporation in, 122; legal requirements: charitable corporations, 482, charitable trusts, 467; supervision of bank and trust companies in, 229

Inexpediency of trust, 76. See also *Cy pres*

Influence, donor-related, 47, 377–378

Inheritance tax, 71

Insolvency, 128

Instructions, petition for, 108, 195–196

Intention, general charitable. See *Cy pres*

Interest, exempt from tax on unrelated business income, 167, 186

Interested parties, to suits to enforce charities, 202–206

Inter vivos trusts, 83; duty to account, Appendix A, Table 1, 464–478

Internal Revenue Bulletin, 382, 408; and Revenue Procedures, 382; and Rulings, 382–386

Internal Revenue Code, 52, 158–193, 276, 285, 357, 364, 402, 436, 437,

441; accumulations provisions, 171–176, 362; definition of charitable purpose, 64–70; and exemption from taxation, 65–66, 158–193, 374, 383–395; and Internal Revenue Service Rulings, 382; and private inurement, 59, 180; proposed amendments to, 186, 354–356; and record-keeping, 386–387; sanctions for violation of, 401. *See also* Treasury regulations

Internal Revenue Service, United States, 44, 50, 52, 68, 92, 158–193, 355, 362, 367, 371, 381–398, 407–408, 436, 437; on accumulation of income, 171–176; Alcohol and Tobacco Tax Division, 438; Appellate Division of, 397–398; attitude of, toward section 504, 177; audits, 395–398, 406; and *cy pres,* 72, 119; definition of "charitable," 67; information reporting forms, 387–395, 401, 404, 510–513; and litigation, 383, 397, 398–401; Massachusetts office, 304–305, 312; National Registry of Tax-exempt Organizations, 406, 447, 454–455; operational and organizational tests, 162–166, 381, 384, 396, 401; Oregon office, 350; organization of, 381–382; and Patman report, 369–370; record-keeping requirements, 386–387; Rulings, 382–386, 402; technical advice by, 398; Texas office, 249, 251; and "tracking the statute," 66, 431; and Treasury Department, 374–375, 380

Inurement, 59, 63, 86, 168, 180

Investigation: power of, 450: and attorney general, 233–241; in California, 327–329; in England, 415–417; in Illinois, 337–338; in Iowa, 316; and legislature, 220; in Massachusetts, 300, 307, 309; in Michigan, 343–345; in New Hampshire, 258, 278; in Ohio, 288–289; in Oregon, 349–350; regulations for conduct of, Massachusetts, 506–507; in Rhode Island, 258; in Texas, 251–252; by Treasury Department, 374–381; by United States Congress, 356–373

Investment of funds, 15, 78, 98–100, 195, 215, 435; by charitable corporations, 140, 144–146; diversification of, 100–101, 102, 144–145; in England, 420–423; regulation of, by legislature, 220; state laws governing; Appendix A, Table 1, 464–478; speculation, 99–100, 175–